Sourcebook on
VIOLENCE AGAINST WOMEN

Second Edition

Sourcebook on
VIOLENCE AGAINST WOMEN

Second Edition

Claire M. Renzetti
University of Kentucky

Jeffrey L. Edleson
University of Minnesota

Raquel Kennedy Bergen
Saint Joseph's University

⑤SAGE

Los Angeles | London | New Delhi
Singapore | Washington DC

For information:

SAGE Publications, Inc.
2455 Teller Road
Thousand Oaks, California 91320
E-mail: order@sagepub.com

SAGE Publications India Pvt. Ltd.
B 1/I 1 Mohan Cooperative Industrial Area
Mathura Road, New Delhi 110 044
India

SAGE Publications Ltd.
1 Oliver's Yard
55 City Road
London EC1Y 1SP
United Kingdom

SAGE Publications Asia-Pacific Pte. Ltd.
33 Pekin Street #02-01
Far East Square
Singapore 048763

Printed in the United States of America

Library of Congress Cataloging-in-Publication Data

Sourcebook on violence against women / editors, Claire M. Renzetti, Jeffrey L. Edleson, Raquel Kennedy Bergen. — 2nd ed.
   p. cm.
Includes bibliographical references and index.
ISBN 978-1-4129-7166-9 (pbk. : acid-free paper)
  1. Women—Crimes against. 2. Abused women. 3. Family violence. 4. Sex discrimination against women. I. Renzetti, Claire M. II. Edleson, Jeffrey L. III. Bergen, Raquel Kennedy.

HV6250.4.W65S68 2011
362.82′92—dc22   2010004941

This book is printed on acid-free paper.

10 11 12 13 14   10 9 8 7 6 5 4 3 2 1

Acquisitions Editor:	Kassie Graves
Editorial Assistant:	Veronica Novak
Production Editor:	Catherine M. Chilton
Copy Editor:	Diana Breti
Typesetter:	C&M Digitals (P) Ltd.
Proofreader:	Ellen Brink
Indexer:	Hyde Park Publishing Services LLC
Cover Designer:	Candice Harman
Marketing Manager:	Stephanie Adams

Contents

Foreword to the Second Edition

It is with heavy hearts that we remember the two passionate, tireless advocates who authored the first foreword for this *Sourcebook on Violence Against Women*. When we lost Paul and Sheila Wellstone on October 25, 2002, Minnesotans were deprived of a critical voice in Congress and "the conscience of the Senate," and women everywhere lost *two* powerful voices on domestic violence issues. Paul and Sheila fervently believed that domestic violence wasn't just a law enforcement issue—it was an issue about civil rights, about justice and human dignity.

We honor their memory, however, by carrying on their work today.

In the past several decades, thanks to the work of many individuals and organizations, there has been a sea change in the way our society looks at violence in the home. Police, the courts, and the public used to consider domestic violence a private family matter. It is not surprising that domestic violence was the most underreported crime in the country. Too many women, for too long, silently fought what some advocates have called "the war at home."

There is more awareness today, and in the last two decades, we've passed critical legislation to help combat domestic violence. In fact, last year was the 15th anniversary of the Violence Against Women Act (VAWA), a groundbreaking Act that constituted federal recognition of the harm that domestic violence causes women, families, and society at large. VAWA has already been reauthorized twice and will need to be reauthorized again in 2011—an effort we will support enthusiastically.

Despite this remarkable progress, there is still more to be done.

Last year, a survey done by the National Network to End Domestic Violence found that in one single day, more than 60,000 people received help from domestic violence programs—and *nearly 9,000 requests for help went unanswered* because the resources weren't there. And, despite years of effort to combat this problem, the statistics on domestic violence are still staggering:

- Currently, almost one in four women will experience abuse in her lifetime.
- Women make up 70% of victims killed by an intimate partner—a proportion that has changed very little since 1993.
- One in six children of all ages have reportedly witnessed domestic violence, and more than one in three older children—14 to 17 years of age—reported they have witnessed domestic violence in their lifetime.

We must recognize that it doesn't take a bruise or a broken bone for a child to be a victim of domestic violence. Witnessing violence between adults in the home—especially when it is ongoing—inflicts a very real trauma on kids that can have damaging effects for years to come. In fact, boys who witness domestic violence are statistically far more likely to repeat the cycle of violence by becoming abusers themselves. Thus, preventing violence against women is critical for more than one generation of victims.

This second edition of the *Sourcebook on Violence Against Women* continues the important work that the first edition began. It will be an invaluable resource for policy makers, advocates, researchers, and students who want to understand the constellation of issues surrounding violence against women so that we can better *assist* women who are harmed and

so that we can *prevent* these acts of violence in the future.

As Paul and Sheila Wellstone wrote in the foreword to the first edition, violence against women "is startlingly common, and our efforts to stop it must be relentless to be effective." We vow to be relentless—on behalf of Paul and Sheila, and for domestic violence survivors everywhere. Together, we can fight—and win—the war at home.

Amy Klobuchar, United States Senator

Al Franken, United States Senator

Minnesota

Foreword to the First Edition

Ten years ago, we began a journey. With the guidance of researchers, educators, and advocates, we set out to learn everything we could about the violence against women that affects so many. We traveled around the country to hear the stories of battered women and their children, to see firsthand the operation of shelters and crisis centers, and, ultimately, to gather the tools needed to create effective public policy. We were fueled by a collective passion not only to pass legislation that would affect the lives of women living with violence but also to concurrently create a heightened awareness of this epidemic.

The grassroots efforts of women's organizations, college students, advocates, educators, policy makers, and courageous women who have survived this violence have caused a paradigm shift. In 1994, Congress passed the most comprehensive antiviolence legislation to date. The Violence Against Women Act (VAWA) of 1994 put a legislative frame around the whole of our efforts. Our work now continues in the spirit of expanding this law and its enforcement, increasing women's access to services, and providing tools for those community-based organizations to expand their research, collaborations, and services.

As we consulted the enormous amount of information available, we felt the lack of a comprehensive resource that would augment our experiences. We recognized that such a resource would serve as a valuable educational tool for the general public. We have now found a compilation of all of these resources in the *Sourcebook on Violence Against Women*.

In the *Sourcebook*, we find a uniquely comprehensive resource on violence against women issues. Topics include types of violence, prevention and direct intervention strategies, and an informative essay on VAWA. Drs. Renzetti, Edleson, and Bergen have brought policy makers, advocates, and researchers together to address these issues in striking form, and the *Sourcebook* will serve as a comprehensive tool for students and consumers across lines of gender, age, and profession.

For the first time in one book, great minds from three domains address the issue of violence against women in a more effective and thus lifesaving form. For too long, researchers, advocates, and policy makers have engaged in separate efforts, and thus, their outcomes have lacked full efficacy. Only when all three entities work together can these issues be addressed authentically to truly help those who experience this violence. This shared work of a concerted group of experts promises to affect all of us by saving the lives of women.

The *Sourcebook* encompasses multiple aspects of violence against women, including rape, female genital mutilation, sexual assault, and domestic violence. It addresses prevention and direct intervention by providing information on services, shelters, and other intervention strategies that will improve the way that violence against women is addressed, prosecuted, and prevented through education. In this book, we find ideas that will be catalysts to awareness, prevention, and intervention. The book will serve as a resource to people of any class, gender, age, and profession and will help to instill in our society the values that will alleviate violence against women.

Violence against women happens to the women we love, the women with whom we work and worship, our neighbors, and our friends. Violence knows no boundaries, not economic status, sexual identity, rural or urban residence, race or religious affiliation, age or gender. It is startlingly common, and our efforts to stop it must be relentless to be effective.

The *Sourcebook* will facilitate these efforts. It will affect our communities and ourselves by providing ideas and awareness, which will lead to stronger prevention and intervention.

Drs. Renzetti, Edleson, and Bergen have combined communities of thinkers in a concerted effort to challenge this convention of behavior and to change the lives of women by alleviating fear and ending the cycle of violence. It is a controversial and forward-thinking piece of work, which addresses topics that warrant attention and have often been taboo. This unfiltered look at the violence that permeates women's lives will no doubt enrich our understanding and expand our capacity to effect social and legislative change. *Sourcebook on Violence Against Women* is a landmark in this journey.

Paul D. Wellstone, United States Senator

Sheila Wellstone, National Domestic Violence Advocate

August, 2000

St. Paul, Minnesota

Preface

Welcome to the second edition of the *Sourcebook on Violence Against Women*. When Kassie Graves, editor at Sage, contacted us about revising the *Sourcebook,* the three of us had already discussed the possibility. The first edition had been widely used by faculty, students, researchers, practitioners, and librarians, and we received much helpful feedback. But much more material had been written in the nearly 10 years since the first edition was published, so the need for an update was critical. Not only had the literature on violence against women grown and matured, but it had also branched into new areas, both substantive and geographic. We felt the time was right for a second edition and we were pleased that Kassie thought so, too.

This edition of the *Sourcebook* is composed of 18 chapters, organized into three Parts: theoretical and methodological issues in researching violence against women (Chapters 1–3), types of violence against women (Chapters 4–9), and prevention and direct intervention (Chapters 10–18). Each Part opens with a brief introduction that previews the forthcoming chapters. Each chapter is original and was written specifically for this volume. As in the first edition, one of our goals was to be thorough in coverage, but it is nearly impossible to include all the topics worthy of discussion in this ever-growing field and still keep the book to a manageable size. We asked contributors to be cognizant of diversity issues and cultural contexts. We asked that, whenever possible, contributors discuss the intersecting effects of inequalities of race and ethnicity, social class, physical ability and disability, age, sexual orientation, and geographic location. Some topics that appeared in the first edition are covered here, of course, but we also include new topics in this second edition, such as assessment, pornography, economic issues, legislative initiatives to address violence against women, primary prevention, faith-based programs and initiatives, and school-based programs. Once again, our objective is less to provide exhaustive coverage and more to encourage discussion and debate about critically important topics.

Also new to this edition are the personal reflections that follow each chapter. We asked prominent researchers and practitioners in the field of violence against women to tell us what sparked their interest in their particular specialty, where they see the field headed in relation to their specialty, and what they consider to be their major contributions or the major contributions of others to their specialized domain. These brief autobiographies provide insight into the individual motivations and accomplishments of professionals working in the area of violence against women. We hope they, along with the chapters, will inspire students especially to seriously consider a career in this challenging, but highly rewarding, field.

As in the first edition, the ordering of the editorship for this book is arbitrary; the labor was shared equally among the editors, and the end product is the result of the genuine teamwork that characterized the entire editing process. Of course, we have incurred many debts over the past

16 months, so words of gratitude are in order. First, we thank Charles (Terry) Hendrix, retired editor extraordinaire of books on interpersonal violence for Sage. It was Terry who planted the idea for the first edition of the *Sourcebook* in our heads 10 years ago and encouraged us to pursue this project and many others. We also thank Kassie Graves, the current editor at Sage, who supported publication of the second edition; production editor Catherine Chilton; and copy editor Diana Breti. The book is better for your attention and care. We are indebted most of all to the chapter and personal reflection authors for their contributions to the *Sourcebook* and for their unflagging commitment to ending violence against women. We remember the late Senator Paul Wellstone and Sheila Wellstone, who wrote the foreword to the first edition and who worked tirelessly to address the problem of violence against women. And we thank Senator Amy Klobuchar (D-MN) and Senator Al Franken (D-MN) for writing the foreword to this edition and for their advocacy in Congress on behalf of women victims of violence.

Claire Renzetti wishes to acknowledge her sons, Sean and Aidan Curran, because she is proud of the young men they have grown to be: gentle men who respect others, appreciate difference, and seek nonviolent solutions to disagreements and conflict. Jeffrey Edleson wishes to acknowledge his partner, Sudha Shetty, who has shown him how a passionate advocate for battered women and their children can make a difference both in their day-to-day lives and in the systems worldwide that affect them. He also acknowledges his four sons, Daniel, Eli, Nevin, and Neil, who have all become young men and from whom he has learned so much. Raquel Kennedy Bergen wishes to acknowledge her children, Michael Ryan and Devon, who teach her the importance of loving, supportive relationships every day. She is also grateful to her Rape Education Prevention Program (REPP) students at Saint Joseph's University, who exemplify commitment and passion for ending violence against women. Finally, we're grateful to each other for hard work, collegiality, good humor, and most of all for our friendship over many years. With every project on which we have collaborated, our energy and support have sustained one another through even the most difficult and frustrating times, both personal and professional.

Acknowledgments

SAGE Publications would like to thank the following reviewers:

Stephanie Riger
University of Illinois at Chicago

Justin Holcomb
University of Virginia

Lu Zhang
The Ohio State University

Daniel Saunders
University of Michigan

Nancy Berns
Drake University

PART I

Theoretical and Methodological Issues in Researching Violence Against Women

One of the questions frequently raised with regard to violence against women is why does it happen? Why are women violently victimized, particularly by people—usually men—whom they know, trust, and often love and who claim to love them? In the first chapter of the *Sourcebook*, Walter DeKeseredy and Martin Schwartz discuss some of the answers that have been developed in response to these questions. DeKeseredy and Schwartz review some of the major theoretical perspectives that are used to explain violence against women. These include psychological, evolutionary, social learning, and feminist theories. But as DeKeseredy and Schwartz point out, despite the large number of theories that have been developed, no single theory fully accounts for all types of violence against women. Moreover, they discuss the (often heated) debate among violence against women theorists and researchers about how to define violence against women and what labels to apply to certain types

of behavior. These disagreements are not mere academic exercises; as DeKeseredy and Schwartz emphasize, how violence against women is defined and what behaviors get "counted" as abusive or violent may affect the extent to which policy makers see the problem as important and, therefore, worthy of funded services. And these definitions and labels may also impact, for better or for worse, the self-concepts and help-seeking behaviors of women who have been victimized.

The significance of definitions is also taken up in Chapter 2 by Jaquier, Johnson, and Fisher, who address the question, How do we know what we know about violence against women? Jaquier and her colleagues offer an overview of several critical methodological issues in the study of violence against women, including how we operationalize the phenomenon; that is, how we translate abstract concepts such as abuse and harm into more concrete entities that can be *measured*. The authors consider different ways researchers may identify perpetrators, relationships, and study participants; cross-cultural differences in definitions and translational problems; variations in counting methods and reference periods; and differences in research designs, sampling strategies, and data collection methods. As they show, all of these issues present decisions to be made by researchers undertaking a violence against women study—decisions that have consequences for how much violence against women is uncovered by the study, its frequency, and its severity. This point is particularly important because, as Jaquier and her colleagues note, researchers have an ethical responsibility to minimize underreporting of violence. The authors discuss a number of other ethical issues, some of which will be familiar to readers (e.g., protecting research participants' confidentiality and ensuring their informed consent). But Jaquier, Johnson, and Fisher also emphasize our ethical responsibilities to protect the safety of the research participants

and the research team, to make study participation accessible to women with disabilities or who are deaf, and to maximize the cultural competence of the research team and inclusivity of the research for women from diverse cultural backgrounds and religious traditions.

Chapter 3, by Hamby and Cook, moves the discussion of data collection from the research setting to various practice settings, such as health care, criminal justice, and social service agencies. They review various tools that practitioners use to screen for violent victimization, assess the dangerousness of an abusive situation or the risk for future violence or lethality, develop and implement a safety plan for victims, and assess children who have been exposed to violence in the home. Hamby and Cook remind us that data are not collected simply for the purposes of testing theories or counting behaviors. Data are also used daily by practitioners to inform potentially life-saving decisions.

CHAPTER 1

Theoretical and Definitional Issues in Violence Against Women

Walter S. DeKeseredy and Martin D. Schwartz

In the first edition of this book, we stated what was obvious to experts in the field: The number of studies on violence against women has increased dramatically in recent years (DeKeseredy & Schwartz, 2001). Nearly 10 years later, we can easily repeat this observation. Certainly, it is a major challenge to keep up with the empirical and theoretical work on one of the world's most compelling social problems. That the field's leading periodical, *Violence Against Women: An International and Interdisciplinary Journal,* is able to publish monthly is an important statement on the amount of time, money, and effort devoted around the world to enhancing a social scientific understanding of the myriad ways in which women are harmed by intimate partners and strangers in private and public places.

Although new studies are being conducted daily and new theories are being constructed and tested, one thing we do not have is an agreed-upon firm definition of violence against women. As Kilpatrick (2004) correctly points out, the debate about whether to define violence against women narrowly or broadly is "old, fierce, and unlikely to be resolved in the near future" (p. 1218). Similarly, what the authors of this chapter observed more than 15 years ago still holds true: "Right now, there is an important battle being waged over the nature of women's behavior and its role in woman abuse" (Schwartz & DeKeseredy, 1993, p. 249). One location for this battle is that many people use language that specifically names women as the objects of abuse or names men as the abusers: They use terms such as "woman abuse," "violence against women," and "male-to-female violence." Others fervently oppose these specific labels and instead use gender-neutral terms such as "family violence" or "intimate partner violence" (IPV),

Authors' Note: The authors would like to thank Claire M. Renzetti, Jeffrey L. Edleson, and Raquel Kennedy Bergen for their helpful comments and criticisms.

often claiming that women are as violent as men in marriage, common-law relationships, dating, and other intimate relationships. One important objective of this chapter is to describe and evaluate narrow, broad, gender-neutral, and gender-specific definitions. The second objective is to review some of the most widely read and cited theories of violence against women.

Broad Versus Narrow Definitions

Definitions of violence in intimate relationships are important and warrant considerable scrutiny because of the power conveyed by "scientific" and "political authority" (Muehlenhard, Powch, Phelps, & Giusti, 1992). Indeed, the ways acts are defined have major effects on research techniques, policies, and ultimately, the lives of many people. Further, definitions are used politically as tools in social struggles. Together with poverty, unemployment, terrorism, and other social problems, violence against women is a highly politicized topic of social scientific inquiry, and definitions of this harm reflect this reality (Ellis, 1987).

Narrow Definitions

Many researchers, policy makers, journalists, and members of the general public focus only on physical abuse or sexual assaults involving penetration. Psychological, verbal, spiritual, and economic abuse are absent from their formulations for several reasons, including the claim that grouping these harms with physically injurious behaviors muddies "the water so much that it might be impossible to determine what causes abuse" (Gelles & Cornell, 1985, p. 23). Many other proponents of narrow legalistic definitions are political conservatives, who argue that violence-against-women studies are often ideologically driven and are designed to artificially inflate the rates of woman abuse to make

political points (Dutton, 2006; Fekete, 1994; Gilbert, 1994). Similar attacks also come from some feminist quarters. For example, Fox (1993) states that "by combining what is debatably abusive with what everyone agrees to be seriously abusive," the latter becomes trivialized (p. 322). In fact, Fox views psychological or emotional victimization as "soft-core abuse." Similarly, some researchers (e.g., Archer, 2000), right-wing fathers' rights groups, and other antifeminists who claim that women are as violent as men do not include homicide, stalking, sexual assault, separation/divorce assault, strangulation, and a host of other harms that thousands of women experience daily in their definitions (DeKeseredy & Dragiewicz, 2007).

There are some major problems with narrow legalistic definitions. For example, the U.S. National Violence Against Women Survey (NVAWS) was introduced as a crime and personal safety survey, one that excluded a broad range of hurtful behaviors exempt from the purview of the law (DeKeseredy, Rogness, & Schwartz, 2004; Straus, 2005). Not surprisingly, then, the NVAWS uncovered a very low incidence (1.8% in the previous 12 months) of women victimized by one more of these acts committed by an intimate partner: rape, physical assault, rape and/or physical assault, and stalking (Tjaden & Thoennes, 2000). The problem is it seems that unless women clearly label hurtful behaviors as "criminal" in their minds, they tend not to report them on a survey of criminal behavior (Koss, 1996; Schwartz, 2000). In fact, many women who experience what the law defines as rape do not label their assaults as such or even as a form of victimization (Littleton & Henderson, 2009; Schwartz & Leggett, 1999). By comparison, when surveys are not operated in the context of criminal assault and victimization, there are major reporting differences (Fisher, 2009). Mihalic and Elliot (1997) found that up to 83% of the marital violence incidents reported in surveys of family behavior are not reported in contexts where the emphasis is on criminal assault and victimization.

Thus, most large-scale representative sample surveys that are not contextualized as crime surveys elicit much higher figures. These often use modified versions of popular measures such as the Conflict Tactics Scale (CTS) originally developed by Straus (1979) or a rendition of Koss, Gidycz, and Wisniewski's (1987) Sexual Experiences Survey. As a general statement, these studies show that at least 11% of North American women in marital/cohabiting relationships are physically abused by their male partners in any 12-month period, and each year at least 24% of North American female undergraduates experience some variety of sexual assault (DeKeseredy, 2009a; DeKeseredy & Flack, 2007).

In other words, if we limit our operational definitions of intimate male-to-female violence to the limited realm of the criminal law and acts that people perceive to be covered there, then we will uncover relatively less intimate violence against women. If we use broader definitions of conflict and violence, the amount of violence uncovered is many times higher.

There are a number of reasons why many researchers, advocates, and practitioners worry about low rates uncovered by government studies such as the NVAWS. Perhaps one of the most important is that policy makers tend to listen only to large numbers (Bart, Miller, Moran, & Stanko, 1989; DeKeseredy, 2000). When narrow definitions are used, some government officials offer these findings as a rationale for withholding funding to deal with the problem (Jiwani, 2000; Smith, 1994). Narrow definitions not only exacerbate the problem of underreporting, they trivialize women's real-life feelings and experiences. For example, in 30 American states, men who rape their wives are exempt from prosecution in some situations, such as when the victims are physically or mentally impaired (Bergen, 2006), even though marital rape causes much pain and suffering.

Another common worry is that narrow definitions discourage abused women from seeking social support. If a survivor's male partner's brutal conduct does not coincide with what

researchers, criminal justice officials, politicians, or the general public refer to as abuse or violence, she may be left in a "twilight zone" where she knows that she has been abused but cannot define it or categorize it in a way that would help her or cause her to seek help (DeKeseredy, 2009b; Duffy & Momirov, 1997). As stated by a rural Ohio woman harmed by separation/divorce sexual assault, "I don't sit around and share. I keep it to myself. . . . I'm not one to sit around and talk about what's happened" (cited in DeKeseredy & Schwartz, 2009, p. 49). In a study of rape survivors by Pitts and Schwartz (1993), all of the women who were encouraged by their "most helpful" person to self-blame denied that they had been raped, while all of the women who were encouraged to believe that they were not at fault claimed that they had been raped. As Pitts and Schwartz point out, not only do women who deny their rape fail to seek social support, but too often society "takes away their right to feel angry about it" (p. 396).

Finally, despite great methodological advancements in the field, there is an issue that should be of great worry to quantitative methodologists. We have now seen that narrow legalistic questions elicit fewer responses (Walby & Myhill, 2001). Are the women who do respond in fact representative of all women in the sample, or has the scientific credibility of the entire study been compromised (Smith, 1994)?

Broad Definitions

A central argument of this chapter is that how one defines violence is one of the most important research decisions that a methodologist will make (Ellis, 1987). This has been particularly debated in the areas of psychological and emotional abuse. Psychological abuse can be just as injurious as physical violence, if not more so (Adams, Sullivan, Bybee, & Greeson, 2008). For example, Follingstad, Rutledge, Berg, Hause, and Polek (1990) found that 72% of their abused female interviewees reported that psychological abuse had a more severe effect on them than did physical abuse. Some, like this rural Ohio woman interviewed by DeKeseredy and Schwartz (2009), say that most physical wounds heal, but the damage to their self-respect and ability to relate to others caused by emotional, verbal, and spiritual violence affects every aspect of their lives:

> I couldn't care less if I ever have sex again in my life. I could care less if I ever had another relationship with a man again in my life. Oh, it's scarred me for life. I think it's physically, mentally, well maybe not so much physically, but emotionally has scarred me for life. You know, and that's the reason why I don't socialize myself with people. I isolate myself from people because if I don't, I get panic attacks. And the dreams they, they're never gone. They're never gone. I mean, I don't care how much you try to put it out of your head; the dreams always bring it back, always. I've been in a sleep clinic where they would videotape me sleeping, being in and out of bed, crawling into a corner screaming, "Please don't hurt me, don't shoot me, don't whatever." (p. 83)

Similarly, many women are harmed in immeasurable ways by sexual assaults that do not involve forced penetration, such as unwanted acts when they were drunk or high or when they were unable to give consent (Bahar & Koss, 2001; DeKeseredy & Schwartz, 2009). Then there are married and cohabiting women who are "blackmailed" into having sex with their partners. For example, one of Russell's (1990) pregnant respondents went into labor and desperately needed medical attention. However, her husband did not take her to the hospital until she had sex with him. Research also shows that many women have unwanted sex "out of a sense of obligation" (Bergen, 1996) because of ex-partners' threats of fighting for sole custody of children, or they are coerced into having sex for other reasons that do not involve the use of or threats of force.

Regardless of whether they find psychological abuse to be more damaging than physical harms,

women who are the targets of intimate interpersonal violence are rarely only victimized by one type of assault. Rather, they typically suffer from a variety of injurious male behaviors that include physical violence, psychological abuse, economic blackmail, or abuse such as denying the woman money even if she earns a wage, harm to animals or possessions to which she has an attachment, or stalking behavior. For example, 80% of the 43 rural Ohio women interviewed by DeKeseredy, Schwartz, Fagen, and Hall (2006) stated that they were victimized by two or more of these forms of abuse.

Of central concern to a growing number of scholars and practitioners is the problem of coercive control, which frequently involves psychologically and emotionally abusive behaviors that are often subtle, hard to detect and prove, and seem to be more forgivable to people unfamiliar with the abuse of women and its consequences. Two prime examples are threatening looks and criticism (Kernsmith, 2008). Many men also use other tactics of coercive control to suppress their intimate female partner's personal freedom, including what Evan Stark (2007) refers to as "microregulating a partner's behavior" (p. 229). This, then, is another key reason why many feminist scholars assert that we should develop and operationalize broad definitions similar to the one offered below by DeKeseredy and MacLeod (1997):

> Woman abuse is the misuse of power by a husband, intimate partner (whether male or female), ex-husband, or ex-partner against a woman, resulting in a loss of dignity, control, and safety as well as a feeling of powerlessness and entrapment experienced by the woman who is the direct victim of ongoing or repeated physical, psychological, economic, sexual, verbal, and/or spiritual abuse. Woman abuse also includes persistent threats or forcing women to witness violence against their children, other relatives, friends, pets, and/or cherished possessions by their husbands, partners, ex-husbands, or ex-partners. (p. 5)

Definitions such as this one are often criticized for including "everything but the kitchen sink." Of course, including too many behaviors under the rubric of violence may result in a breakdown of social exchanges between people as they label each other's behaviors as abusive or violent (Duffy & Momirov, 1997). Moreover, it is much more difficult to study 50 behaviors at once than to study one or two. Nevertheless, a growing literature shows that large numbers of abused women reject the notion that "sticks and stones may break my bones but words will never hurt me." For reasons offered here and elsewhere (e.g., DeKeseredy, 2000), many nonviolent, highly injurious behaviors are just as worthy of in-depth empirical, theoretical, and political attention as those that cause physical harm. Furthermore, physical abuse, sexual abuse, economic abuse, and psychological abuse are not mutually exclusive.

Despite an ongoing antifeminist backlash against broad definitions of violence, a growing number of researchers recognize the merits of these formulations. Consider the U.S. NVAWS (Tjaden & Thoennes, 2000). Despite the problems with this study identified previously, it included measures of stalking, physical violence, sexual assault, and emotionally abusive or controlling behaviors. However, a major problem still remains. Despite the trend toward using broad definitions, we still see variance in incidence and prevalence rates across studies, even when they use similar measures. This problem is due to sampling differences, different data-gathering techniques (e.g., telephone interviews vs. computer surveys), and other methodological factors (DeKeseredy & Schwartz, 2001).

Gender-Neutral Versus Gender-Specific Definitions

The title of this book clearly identifies women as the primary targets of violence in intimate relationships. Many readers obviously support this gender-specific position. Still, since the mid-1990s, the naming of violence against women once again has shifted toward gender-neutral terms (DeKeseredy & Dragiewicz, 2009). Some government agencies, researchers, and community groups have reclaimed or reasserted the terms "domestic violence" or "intimate partner violence" as a way of speaking about woman abuse as well as other forms of violence, such as those that occur in same-sex relationships. There are also antifeminist organizations (e.g., fathers' rights groups), politicians, journalists, and researchers that push for the use of gender-neutral language; they repeatedly claim that women are as violent as men. They do not just advocate more attention to male victims (they usually ignore same-sex victims after claiming that abuse in lesbian couples proves women are just as violent as men). Rather, they demand the renunciation of feminism and the research, laws, and programs they deem feminist (Dutton, 2006; Girard, 2009).

Gender symmetrical CTS data are typically used to support conservatives' calls for gender-neutral language. For example, in Canada, Statistics Canada's 2004 General Social Survey (GSS) found that 7% of the women and 6% of the men interviewed for this national study reported at least one incident of violence committed by a current or former spouse between 1999 and 2004 (Mihorean, 2005). These results and similar ones uncovered by studies done in the U.S. and elsewhere (e.g., Moffitt, Caspi, Rutter, & Silva, 2001; Straus, Gelles, & Steinmetz, 1981; Straus & Gelles, 1986) have been seized upon to support the argument that there is resurgence of what Steinmetz (1977–78) referred to as "the battered husband syndrome" (Jiwani, 2000). According to psychologist Donald Dutton (2006), "in Canada and the United States, women use violence in intimate relationships to the same extent as men, for the same reasons, with largely the same results" (p. ix).

Do bidirectional or gender symmetrical CTS data really show that men and women are equally violent? First, the CTS only provides raw counts of violent acts and thus misses the fact that much male and female violence is used for different reasons (Jiwani, 2000). As demonstrated by studies that added context, meaning, and motive measures to the CTS (e.g., DeKeseredy, Saunders, Schwartz, & Alvi, 1997), a common cause of women's violence in intimate relationships is self-defense, while men typically use violence to control their partners (DeKeseredy & Dragiewicz, 2007). As Ellis asserts, "ignoring context, meaning, and motive is misinforming . . . and not separating different types of violence is misleading" (cited in Foss, 2002, p. A8). In other words, unless we know exactly why people use violence, it is, to say the least, highly problematic to draw conclusions about the causes of such behavior based solely on crude counts of hits, slaps, kicks, and the like.

That some women strike some men, sometimes with the intent to injure, should not be the subject of debate. Still, relying on simple counts of behaviors does not mitigate and change the meaning of the conclusion that women are the overwhelmingly predominant victims of intimate adult violence for several reasons. For example, in addition to ignoring important contextual issues, the CTS or other crude counts of behavior alone cannot accurately determine gender variations in intimate violence because of the following:

- Males are more likely to underreport violence perpetration (Edleson & Brygger, 1986; Heckert & Gondolf, 2000; Hilton, Harris, & Rice, 2000; Szinovacz & Egley, 1995).
- Females are more likely to overreport violence perpetration (Hilton et al., 2000; Szinovacz, 1983; Szinovacz & Egley, 1995).
- Abusers regularly minimize, deny, and justify their violence and abuse (Anderson & Umberson, 2001; Buchbinder & Eisikovits, 2004; Heckert & Gondolf, 2000; Henning & Holdford, 2006; Ptacek, 1999; Totten, 2003).
- The CTS measures only conflict-instigated violence and ignores male violence used to control women or violence that may not stem from any single identifiable cause (e.g., dispute, difference, or spat; DeKeseredy & Schwartz, 1998).

- The CTS excludes several types of abusive behavior, such as forced isolation, separation assault, stalking, and threats to take the children (Jiwani, 2000).
- Surveys based on self-reports of victimization necessarily omit homicide, familicide, and homicide-suicide (DeKeseredy & Dragiewicz, 2009).
- The CTS does not take into account fear, dependency, and female devaluation (Barnett, Miller-Perrin, & Perrin, 2005; Koss, Goodman, Browne, Fitzgerald, Puryear-Keita, & Russo, 1994).

In addition to using Canadian GSS data and similar findings to support the claim of the bidirectionality of violence, proponents of gender symmetry artificially narrow the definition of violence between intimates to obscure injurious behaviors that display marked gender asymmetry (e.g., Archer, 2000; Dutton, 2006), such as sexual assault, strangulation, separation/divorce assault, stalking, and homicide. Not at all an unacceptable or hysterical broadening of the definition of violence, these behaviors are commonly part of abused women's experiences (DeKeseredy & Dragiewicz, 2007; DeKeseredy & Schwartz, 2009).

Typologies of Intimate Partner Violence and Abuse

Some scholars attempt to explain the gap between gendered and gender-neutral definitions of violence by offering typologies (Johnson, 2008; Johnson & Ferraro, 2000, Pence & Dasgupta, 2006). Within these typologies, the form of violence labeled as coercive control, woman abuse, battering, or as intimate terrorism is qualitatively different than infrequent, noninjurious acts that invoke no fear or coercion. However, studies based on the CTS or other decontextualized measures provide no information that can be used to characterize incidents as representative of one type of violence or another. It is impossible, then, to make accurate claims about the motives of violence based on numbers of acts (DeKeseredy & Dragiewicz, 2009). Certainly, motivations for violent and controlling behavior vary, and even Johnson, who developed the most popular typology, readily admitted that "qualitative research and rich interview data would be necessary to thoroughly understand the meaning and social context" (cited in National Institute of Justice, 2000).

Another problem with Johnson's (2008) typology is that he claims to identify a very small number of cases that, to him, exemplify "mutual coercive control." In such cases, he contends that

> both members of the couple are violent and controlling, each behaving in a manner that would identify him or her as an intimate terrorist if it weren't for the fact that their partner also seems to be engaged in the same sort of violent attempt to control the relationship. (p. 12)

The main problem with this assertion is that, as Evan Stark (2006) observes, while there is evidence that some women often use force to control their male partners, "they typically lack the social facility to impose the comprehensive levels of deprivation, exploitation, and dominance found in coercive control. I have never encountered a case of coercive control with a female perpetrator and male victim" (p. 1024).

As of yet, typologies are speculative and their application is therefore premature (DeKeseredy & Dragiewicz, 2009). Moreover, some critics, like Pence and Dasgupta (2006), caution that typologies are likely to be misused. They further note that it is easy for abusers and their allies to paint individual incidents as "situational" or aberrant violence even when they are not, and that this can have life and death consequences. Although shelter staff and scholars recognize that not all violence is the same and not all violence that takes place in the home is necessarily battering (Dasgupta, 2002; Osthoff, 2002), there is no tool that can discern whether an individual act is part of a broader pattern of coercive control. Accordingly,

antiviolence advocates continue to call for assessments that place violence and abuse in the context of the relationship, family, community, culture, and history (Bonisteel & Green, 2005).

Theories of Violence Against Women in Intimate Relationships

In one of the most comprehensive reviews of the theoretical literature on violence against women, Lewis Okun (1986) pointed out at least 20 distinct theories of either family violence, woman abuse, or other types of violence in conjugal relationships. Almost 25 years have passed since the publication of his book, and during this time, many more perspectives on violence against women have been developed and tested. Even so, no single theory can fully explain violence against women (Brownridge, 2009). Certainly, we will not review all of the relevant theories here. Instead, we will present the major arguments of some of the most widely used and cited contemporary theoretical perspectives. We begin by turning to psychological approaches.

Psychological Approaches

Why do men assault the women they love? One of the most common answers to this question is that these men must be "sick" or mentally disturbed. How could a "normal" person punch, kick, stab, rape, or shoot someone he deeply loves and depends on? The media contribute to the widespread belief that men who assault or kill female intimates are "sick." For example, the media's use of quotations such as, "We don't know what happened" typically "makes the cause of death appear inexplicable or the result of a man's suddenly having 'snapped'" (Myers, 1997, p. 110). There is also much discussion about the contribution of male personality disorders.

Personality Disorders

Psychological accounts of violence against women are not as popular today as they were in the early 1970s, but several researchers still contend that many men beat women because they are mentally ill, suffer from personality disorders, or consume large quantities of drugs or alcohol. For example, one of Dutton's (2006) key assertions is that most perpetrators of intimate partner violence have personality disorders and that "this reality has been concealed by misleading theories that wife assault is normatively acceptable, an absurd assertion without empirical support" (p. xi). Dutton further argues that psychoeducational groups, such as the common batterer intervention programs, are highly problematic and therefore, "public policy must be driven by recognition of attachment-based personality disorder as central to therapeutic change" (p. xi).

Certainly, it is difficult sometimes to see men like this one who abused his rural Ohio partner as anything other than sick:

> He ended up bringing someone into the relationship, which I didn't want, but he told me that if I didn't do it he would leave me. And I ended up staying with him. He was more into group sex and, uh, trying to be the big man. He wanted sex in a group thing or with his buddies or made me have sex with a friend of his. See one time he made me have sex with a friend of his for him to watch, and then he got mad and hit me afterwards. I mean he tied me up so I could watch him have sex with a 13-year-old girl. And then he ended up going to prison for it. So, I mean it was nasty. (cited in DeKeseredy & Schwartz, 2009, p. 70)

Does this man suffer from a personality disorder? Perhaps he does, but most abusers do not (Jasinski, 2001). If only a handful of men abused their current or former partners, it would be easy to accept arguments such as Dutton's. Unfortunately,

data presented throughout this book show that a substantial number of women are abused by men in North America and elsewhere. And, it is estimated that only about 10% of male-to-female violence incidents are spawned by mental illness; thus, psychological perspectives cannot explain the other 90% (Brownridge, 2009; Gelles & Straus, 1988). Moreover, widely read and cited data derived from 840 male batterers in four cities who participated in intake sessions prior to program counseling show that less than half of these men showed signs of personality disorders and only 25% showed signs of severe mental disorder (Gondolf, 2003). The author of the study correctly concluded that "there is little evidence for a prevailing 'abusive personality' typified by borderline personality tendencies" (Gondolf, 1999, p. 13).

As Katz (2006) notes in his analysis of men who abuse women:

> Most men who assault women are not so much disturbed as they are disturbingly normal. Like all of us, they are products of familial and social systems. They are our sons, brothers, friends, and coworkers. As such, they are influenced not only by individual factors, but also by broader cultural attitudes and beliefs about manhood that shape their psyches and identities. And *ours*. (p. 28)

There are some other problems with explanations that emphasize personality disorders or psychopathy. For example, if violent husbands, cohabiting and estranged partners, and boyfriends are in fact suffering from some disorder, then why do so many of them only beat their wives and not their bosses, friends, or neighbors? Admittedly, many men do attack these others, but men who beat or rape women in intimate relationships generally do not have convictions for violence outside the home. If we are dealing with men who have terrible problems with self-control, how do they manage to keep from hitting people until they are at home alone with their loved ones? How do they manage to exercise self-control until they are in a situation where they can generally get away with beating someone up? If they are "out of control," then why do they only beat their partners instead of killing them (DeKeseredy & Schwartz, 1996)? These questions cannot be answered by theories such as Dutton's (2006) that ignore the unequal distribution of power between men and women in North American society and in intimate or domestic contexts (Bograd, 1988; Jasinski, 2001).

Evolutionary Perspectives

Some evolutionary psychologists (e.g., Daly & Wilson, 1988) argue that male violence against women is the result of competition for sexual access to women. The concept of male proprietariness is emphasized in evolutionary thought, and it is defined as "the tendency [of men] to think of women as sexual and reproductive 'property' they can own and exchange" (Wilson & Daly, 1992, p. 85). Proprietariness refers to "not just the emotional force of [the male's] own feelings of entitlement but to a more pervasive attitude [of ownership and control] toward social relationships [with intimate female partners]" (p. 85).

Men kill not only men, but also women. Why, then, do so many men beat, rape, or kill female intimates? As Kimmel (2000) notes, "to murder or assault the person you are trying to inseminate is a particularly unwise reproductive strategy" (p. 244). Another challenge to evolutionary theory is that many societies have much lower rates of male violence than those of the United States and Canada. So if "boys will be boys," they "will do so differently" (Kimmel, 2000), depending on where they live, their peer groups, social class position and race, and a host of other factors (DeKeseredy & Schwartz, 2005; Messerschmidt, 1993).

Because violence against female intimates is an ongoing, ever-changing problem, numerous scholars, practitioners, and activists contend that we must constantly reflect on our past contributions to the field and develop new ways of understanding and preventing the myriad highly injurious and sometimes lethal behaviors that typically occur in private places. Thus, despite the criticisms of the above two perspectives, many sociologists, including those who are feminists, are integrating some psychological accounts into their analyses of how gender and other sociocultural forces influence rape, beatings, stalking, psychological abuse, and the like.

Social Psychological Perspectives

Frequently referred to as either process theories (Malley-Morrison & Hines, 2004), micro-oriented perspectives (Jasinski, 2001), or as individual-level explanations (Johnson, 1996), social psychological theories focus on the subjective experiences of individuals in large- and small-scale social settings (Ellis, 1987). Social psychology is defined here as "an attempt to understand and explain how the thought, feeling, and behavior of individuals are influenced by the actual, imagined, or implied presence of others" (Allport, 1968, p. 1).

Social Learning Theory

There are various types of social learning theories, but all of them share one common argument: Violence and aggression are not inherent properties of the individual; rather, they are learned behaviors. The social learning theory that is most often used to explain woman abuse in intimate relationships is the intergenerational transmission theory (Levinson, 1989). Briefly, proponents of this theory maintain that male children are more likely to grow up to assault female intimates if their parents abused them or if they observed their fathers assaulting their spouses (Hines & Malley-Morrison, 2005).

The intergenerational transmission theory has some empirical support and is accepted across the political spectrum. However, as Straus et al. (1981) correctly points out, it is wrong to "put the whole burden of violence on what is learned in the family" (p. 122). For example, many people who were raised in relatively nonviolent homes abuse their female partners and children. On the other hand, there are many people who have directly experienced child abuse or have watched their fathers beat their mothers but who have never beaten their marital/cohabiting partners or children (Barnett et al., 2005). While many children's violent fathers may be directly or indirectly teaching them to become wife beaters, their mothers may spend a substantial amount of time and effort teaching them that wife beating is wrong and that their future wives/cohabiting partners deserve to be treated much better than they are being treated (Dobash & Dobash, 1979). Children are not "hollow beings" who emulate whatever they see. Most of them have a sense of justice and fairness, and many are likely to regard wife beating as "bad" or "evil" (DeKeseredy & MacLeod, 1997; Dobash & Dobash, 1979).

This is not to say that the family is not a key "training ground" for woman abuse and child abuse (Straus et al., 1981). However, people also learn violence and other forms of intimate abuse from external sources such as the media and male peers.

Feminist Theories

Unlike the theories reviewed thus far, feminist perspectives focus on how broader social forces such as patriarchy contribute to violence against women. There are different definitions of patriarchy, but it is referred to here as "a sexual system of power in which the male possesses superior power and economic privilege" (Eisenstein, 1980, p. 16). In addition to paying much attention to the ways in which patriarchy is related to myriad male assaults on women, feminist theorists reject narrow, legalistic definitions of violence and favor the broader ones described earlier in this chapter (Renzetti, 2008). It is difficult to review feminist accounts in a few pages because there

are competing definitions of feminism and there are many different types of feminism (Maidment, 2006). However, for the purpose of this chapter, we offer Daly and Chesney-Lind's (1988) definition of feminism as "a set of theories about women's oppression and a set of strategies for change" (p. 502).

While there are a variety of feminist theories of woman abuse in adult heterosexual relationships, most of them share the view that men abuse women to maintain power and control over them (DeKeseredy & MacLeod, 1997; Saunders, 1988). Most feminist accounts also assert the following:

- Gender, power, and patriarchy are key explanatory factors.
- Intimate relationships change over time and must be understood in that context.
- It is essential to listen to women's experiences to develop a theory of woman abuse.
- Scholarship and research should be used to support women (Bograd, 1988; Dobash & Dobash, 1979; Jasinski, 2001).

Feminists are also united by a deep desire to eliminate all forms of gender inequality and their injurious consequences, such as violence against women. Moreover, the goal of feminist scholars is "not to push men out so as to pull women in, but rather to gender the study of crime and criminal justice" (Renzetti, 1993, p. 232), as well as other social problems (e.g., poverty, unemployment, health care). Gender refers to "the sociocultural and psychological shaping, patterning, and evaluating of female and male behavior" (Schur, 1984, p. 10).

Even today, most experts would agree with Okun's (1986) assertion that feminism is "the most important theoretical approach to conjugal violence/woman abuse" (p. 100). However, of all the variants of feminist thought scattered throughout the literature, it is radical feminism that has had the greatest impact on the sociological study of woman abuse (DeKeseredy, Ellis, & Alvi, 2005). Radical feminists contend that the most important set of social relations in any society is found in patriarchy. All other social relations, such as class, are secondary and originate from male-female relations (Beirne & Messerschmidt, 1991). Applied to violence against women, radical feminist theory argues that men engage in this behavior because they need or desire to control women (Daly & Chesney-Lind, 1988). This statement made by British feminist Jill Radford (1987) exemplifies this perspective: "It is clear that men's violence is used to control women, not just in their own individual interests, but also in the interests of men as a sex class in the reproduction of heterosexuality and male supremacy" (p. 43).

Radical feminists have played a vital role in "breaking the silence" on the multidimensional nature of male-to-female victimization (Kelly, 1988), and they have successfully demonstrated that this problem is "widespread" and "omnipresent" in advanced Western societies and elsewhere (Liddle, 1989). Nevertheless, other feminists have criticized radical feminists on several grounds, including that they ignore the influence of social class and tend to see all men as being equally likely to victimize female intimates (Messerschmidt, 1993). Although woman abuse certainly occurs in all classes and occupations, a large literature shows that some groups are more likely than others to produce batterers, rapists, and other types of woman abusers (Schwartz, 1988).

An interesting methodological debate between radical feminist theorists and other feminists concerns the proper subjects for research on abuse. Most work in this tradition has consisted of in-depth interviews with women who have first-hand experience with violence. An important argument that is a central component of feminist research is the validation of women's experiences. Some critics feel that by not listening to men, but rather to women talking about their experiences with men, radical feminist researchers do not take into account the accuracy of information about men's motives for violence (LaFlame, 2009; Liddle, 1989). Attacks on patriarchy, according to some feminist critics, would

be better conducted by studying the social construction of male offenders (Scully, 1990).

Radical feminism has also been criticized from the right. For example, Dutton (2006), among others (e.g., Gelles, 1993), refers to radical feminist theories of woman abuse as single-factor accounts that have little explanatory value in social science. Radical feminist theories such as Radford's (1987) are also seen by some conservative social scientists as political agendas and as difficult to verify (Fekete, 1994; Levinson, 1989). However, most feminists have no problem being labeled political, and they hope that their work will help reduce much pain and suffering. There is now a large feminist theoretical literature combining both macro- and micro-level forces, such as unemployment, globalization, deindustrialization, life events stress, intimate relationship status, familial and societal patriarchy, substance abuse, male peer support, and other factors (DeKeseredy & Dragiewicz, 2007). Today, many feminist scholars strongly agree with what Claire Renzetti (1997) argued more than a decade ago:

> Of course, while the causes of and solutions to the problems are not individualistic, but rather structural, we cannot lose sight of individuals. The challenge we confront is to disentangle the complex relationships between individuals and society, including our own roles in this dialectic. A tall order, no doubt, but the only one with any chance of real success. (p. vii)

Integrated Theories

Although there are some prominent scholars who strongly oppose theoretical integration (e.g., Hirschi, 1989) or the creation of what Jasinski (2001) refers to as multidimensional theories, such work is increasingly being done today and here we offer two main examples: DeKeseredy and Schwartz's (2002) economic exclusion/male peer support model and the ecological framework, which has roots in the pioneering scholarship of Bronfenbrenner (1977).

Economic Exclusion/Male Peer Support Model

Feminists point out that some women are more vulnerable than others to violence, including women living in poverty (DeKeseredy, Schwartz, & Alvi, 2008; Holzman & Piper, 1998). For example, in DeKeseredy, Alvi, Schwartz, and Perry's (1999) survey of six public housing estates, 19.3% of the 216 women surveyed stated that they were harmed by one or more of the listed forms of physical violence. This is much higher than what is found in surveys of the general population. Even so, the possibility exists that this figure for public housing women is still too low, as Renzetti and Maier (2002) discovered in a qualitative study that 33% reported victimization.

Why is victimization so high in public housing? DeKeseredy and Schwartz (2002) do not blame physical conditions. Instead, they offer a theory heavily informed by Sernau's (2001, p. 24) web of exclusion model, DeKeseredy and Schwartz's (1993) expanded male peer support model, and Young's (1999) work on social exclusion.

Briefly, in their attempt to show how macro-level forces shape male interpersonal dynamics and woman abuse, DeKeseredy and Schwartz (2002) argue that recent economic transformations in North America (e.g., the shift from a manufacturing to a service-based economy) displace working class men and women who often end up in urban public housing or other "clusters of poverty" (Sernau, 2001). Unable to economically support their families and live up to their culturally defined role as bread winner, socially and economically excluded men experience high levels of stress because "their normal paths for personal power and prestige have been cut off" (Raphael, 2001). Such stress prompts them to

seek social support from male peers with similar problems.

Such support may help men resolve intimate relationship problems or facilitate the management of their stress, "but there are no guarantees that such a resolution is free of cost" (Vaux, 1985, p. 102). As demonstrated by studies of woman abuse in dating (e.g., DeKeseredy, 1988a; Schwartz & DeKeseredy, 1997), male peer support may alleviate dating life events stress, but it can also have negative consequences for the health and safety of women. For example, DeKeseredy (1988b) found that for men with high levels of such stress, social ties with abusive peers were strongly related to woman abuse in Canadian university dating. Similarly, patriarchal male peer support in public housing promotes sexual assault and other highly injurious "macho activities" (Raphael, 2001).

The economic exclusion/male peer support model fills several gaps in the theoretical literature on violence against women, but it is not a predictive model. Further, like any social scientific perspective, it can be improved. For example, consistent with integrated male peer support theories of woman abuse on campus and in rural communities (e.g., Godenzi, Schwartz, & DeKeseredy, 2001; DeKeseredy, Donnermeyer, Schwartz, Tunnell, & Hall, 2007), DeKeseredy and Schwartz's (2002) theory of public housing woman abuse does not specifically address whether members of patriarchal male peer groups are intentionally recruited into these alliances or whether they gravitate to such groups as a way of selectively attempting to sustain or receive support for their earlier acquired values and behaviors. The model also does not specify that men may interact with and be influenced by peers who live away from public housing. Another point to consider is that like every male peer support model, racial/ethnic variations in male peer support dynamics remain to be examined.

DeKeseredy and Schwartz's (2002) model responds to the call for moving the experiences of socially and economically marginalized women to the center of empirical and theoretical work on woman abuse (Ptacek, 1999).

Ecological Models

Ecological models address multiple levels of influence and maintain that violence against women should be examined within a nested set of environmental contexts or systems (Brownridge, 2009; Graham-Bermann & Gross, 2008; Hines & Malley-Morrison, 2005). Ecological models include the following levels:

- Macrosystem—This refers to broader cultural factors, such as patriarchal attitudes and beliefs about gender relations in intimate relationships.
- Exosystem—This concept refers to informal and formal social networks that connect intimate relationships to the broader culture.
- Microsystem—This refers to the relationship in which violence takes place.
- Ontogenic—This level refers to a person's individual development and what such development brings to the above three levels. (Brownridge, 2009; Dutton, 2006)

In sum, then, according to ecological theorists, to obtain a rich understanding of why men assault women,

> we need to understand the genetic endowments of those individuals, the microsystem in which they grew up, the microsystem in which they are currently embedded, characteristics of the neighborhood within which their family functions (including the availability of social support and social services, and relationships between the community and criminal justice system), and the larger society that embraces all the separate neighborhoods. (Hines & Malley-Morrison, 2005)

Ecological models are appealing to many researchers because they direct attention to different levels of analysis and to a broad range of factors that contribute to violence against women (Dasgupta, 2002; Dutton, 2006). Moreover, these models are flexible and can be modified to fit the topic being studied and the scholar's personal style (Brownridge, 2009; Heise, 1998). However, any ecological model is extremely difficult, if not impossible, to test in its entirety. Conducting a study that effectively addresses all four levels identified here would be "prohibitively expensive" and involve doing sophisticated longitudinal research with a very large sample (Graham-Bermann & Gross, 2008). Furthermore, to the best of our knowledge, there has never been an attempt to conduct a study that addresses each of the above levels of the ecological model.

Conclusion

There is sharp disagreement over what constitutes violence against women. There is also a growing number of attempts to explain why women are assaulted by male intimates, some of which were briefly reviewed here. Whatever theory resonates for readers, it is undeniable that the long-term attention given to the issue of violence against women has created profound opportunities for social transformation. At the core of this social change was the act of naming violence as an issue in itself, rather than as a reaction or inevitable outcome of another problem. Naming violence against women by their male partners as a separate problem symbolically transformed women from invisible appendages of male intimate partners to separate individuals (DeKeseredy & MacLeod, 1997).

If defining violence against women is the subject of much debate, the same can be said about theorizing this gendered problem. For example, at the time of writing this chapter, there were heated exchanges between some psychologists (e.g., Dutton, 2006) and feminist scholars (e.g., DeKeseredy & Dragiewicz, 2007; Gondolf, 2003) about what they respectively assert to be the primary determinants of violence against women. Still, despite the widespread nature of male-to-female abuse, many people find psychological perspectives to be the most appealing because they still believe that violence against women is a function of mental illness and that it can be easily solved through individual therapy or counseling. On the other hand, sociological accounts are not popular among the general population because they call for transforming our social, political, economic, and cultural order (Loseke, Gelles, & Cavanaugh, 2005), which is a more difficult task and challenges those who gain from maintaining the status quo.

For many women, especially those who are battered, psychologically abused, or sexually assaulted, a key point to consider here is whether researchers' definitions and theories are sensitive to their subjective experiences. The experiences of women who live with abuse or its memories are touchstones for people working to end all forms of violence against women. These touchstones are vital sources of commonality across the varied perspectives that scholars bring to violence against women and its prevention, some of which have been summarized in this chapter (DeKeseredy & MacLeod, 1997).

References

Adams, A. E., Sullivan, C. M., Bybee, D., & Greeson, M. R. (2008). Development of the scale of economic abuse. *Violence Against Women, 15,* 563–588.

Allport, G. W. (1968). The historical background of modern social psychology. In G. Lindzey & E. Aronson (Eds.), *The handbook of social psychology* (pp. 1–80). Reading, MA: Addison-Wesley.

Anderson, K. L., & Umberson, D. (2001). Gendering violence: Masculinity and power in men's accounts of domestic violence. *Gender & Society, 15,* 358–380.

Archer, J. (2000). Sex differences in aggression between heterosexual partners: A meta-analytic review. *Psychological Bulletin, 126,* 651–680.

Bahar, K., & Koss, M. P. (2001). From prevalence to prevention: Closing the gap between what we know about rape and what we do. In C. M. Renzetti, J. L. Edleson, & R. K. Bergen (Eds.), *Sourcebook on violence against women* (pp. 117–142). Thousand Oaks, CA: Sage.

Barnett, O. W., Miller-Perrin, C. L., & Perrin, R. D. (2005). *Family violence across the lifespan: An introduction* (2nd ed.). Thousand Oaks, CA: Sage.

Bart, P. B., Miller, P. Y., Moran, E., & Stanko, E. A. (1989). Guest editors' introduction. *Gender & Society, 3,* 431–436.

Beirne, P., & Messerschmidt, J. W. (1991). *Criminology.* New York: Harcourt Brace.

Bergen, R. K. (1996). *Wife rape: Understanding the response of survivors and service providers.* Thousand Oaks, CA: Sage.

Bergen, R. K. (2006, February). Marital rape: New research and directions. *VAWnet,* 1–13.

Bograd, M. (1988). Feminist perspectives on wife abuse: An introduction. In K. Yllo & M. Bograd (Eds.), *Feminist perspectives on wife abuse* (pp. 11–26). Newbury Park, CA: Sage.

Bonisteel, M., & Green, L. (2005). *Implications of the shrinking space for feminist anti-violence advocacy.* Retrieved from http://www.crvawc.ca/documents/ShrinkingFeministSpace_AntiViolenceAdvocacy_OCT2005.pdf.

Bronfenbrenner, U. (1977). Toward an experimental ecology of human development. *American Psychologist, 32,* 513–531.

Brownridge, D. A. (2009). *Violence against women: Vulnerable populations.* New York: Routledge.

Buchbinder, E., & Eisikovits, Z. (2004). Between normality and deviance: The breakdown of batterers' identity following police intervention. *Journal of Interpersonal Violence, 19,* 443–467.

Daly, K., & Chesney-Lind, M. (1988). Feminism and criminology. *Justice Quarterly, 5,* 497–538.

Daly, M., & Wilson, M. (1988). *Homicide.* New York: Aldine deGruyter.

Dasgupta, S. D. (2002). A framework for understanding women's use of nonlethal violence in intimate relationships. *Violence Against Women, 8,* 1364–1389.

DeKeseredy, W. S. (1988a). Woman abuse in dating relationships: The relevance of social support theory. *Journal of Family Violence, 3,* 1–13.

DeKeseredy, W. S. (1988b). *Woman abuse in dating relationships: The role of male peer support.* Toronto: Canadian Scholars' Press.

DeKeseredy, W. S. (2000). Current controversies in defining nonlethal violence against women in intimate heterosexual relationships: Empirical implications. *Violence Against Women, 6,* 728–746.

DeKeseredy, W. S. (2009a). Girls and women as victims of crime. In J. Barker (Ed.), *Women and the criminal justice system: A Canadian perspective* (pp. 313–345). Toronto: Emond Montgomery.

DeKeseredy, W. S. (2009b). Patterns of violence in the family. In M. Baker (Ed.), *Families: Changing trends in Canada* (pp. 179–205). Whitby, ON: McGraw-Hill Ryerson.

DeKeseredy, W. S., Alvi, S., Schwartz, M. D., & Perry, B. (1999). Violence against and the harassment of women in Canadian public housing. *Canadian Review of Sociology and Anthropology, 36,* 499–516.

DeKeseredy, W. S., Donnermeyer, J. F., Schwartz, M. D., Tunnell, K. D., & Hall, M. (2007). Thinking critically about rural gender relations: Toward a rural masculinity crisis/male peer support model of separation/divorce sexual assault. *Critical Criminology, 15,* 295–311.

DeKeseredy, W. S., & Dragiewicz, M. (2007). Understanding the complexities of feminist perspectives on woman abuse: A commentary on Donald G. Dutton's *Rethinking domestic violence. Violence Against Women, 13,* 874–884.

DeKeseredy, W. S., & Dragiewicz, M. (2009). *Shifting public policy direction: Gender-focused versus bidirectional intimate partner violence.* Report prepared for the Ontario Women's Directorate. Toronto: Ontario Women's Directorate.

DeKeseredy, W. S., Ellis, D., & Alvi, S. (2005). *Deviance and crime: Theory, research and policy.* Cincinnati: LexisNexis.

DeKeseredy, W. S., & Flack, W. F. (2007). Sexual assault in colleges and universities. In G. Barak (Ed.), *Battleground criminal justice* (pp. 693–697). Westport, CT: Greenwood.

DeKeseredy, W. S., & MacLeod, L. (1997). *Woman abuse: A sociological story.* Toronto: Harcourt Brace.

DeKeseredy, W. S., Rogness, M., & Schwartz, M. D. (2004). Separation/divorce sexual assault: The current state of social scientific knowledge. *Aggression and Violent Behavior, 9,* 675–691.

DeKeseredy, W. S., Saunders, D. G., Schwartz, M. D., & Alvi, S. (1997). The meanings and motives for women's use of violence in Canadian college dating relationships: Results from a national survey. *Sociological Spectrum, 17,* 199–222.

DeKeseredy, W. S., & Schwartz, M. D. (1993). Male peer support and woman abuse: An expansion of DeKeseredy's model. *Sociological Spectrum, 13,* 394–414.

DeKeseredy, W. S., & Schwartz, M. D. (1996). *Contemporary criminology.* Belmont, CA: Wadsworth.

DeKeseredy, W. S., & Schwartz, M. D. (1998). Measuring the extent of woman abuse in intimate heterosexual relationships: A critique of the Conflict Tactics Scales. Harrisburg, PA: VAWnet, the National Online Resource Center on Violence Against Women. Retrieved April 2, 2001, from http://www.vawnet.org.

DeKeseredy, W. S., & Schwartz, M. D. (2001). Definitional issues. In C. M. Renzetti, J. L. Edleson, & R. K. Bergen (Eds.), *Sourcebook on violence against women* (pp. 23–34). Thousand Oaks, CA: Sage.

DeKeseredy, W. S., & Schwartz, M. D. (2002). Theorizing public housing woman abuse as a function of economic exclusion and male peer support. *Women's Health and Urban Life, 1,* 26–45.

DeKeseredy, W. S., & Schwartz, M. D. (2005). Masculinities and interpersonal violence. In M. S. Kimmel, J. Hearn, & R. W. Connell (Eds.), *Handbook of studies on men & masculinities* (pp. 353–366). Thousand Oaks, CA: Sage.

DeKeseredy, W. S., & Schwartz, M. D. (2009). *Dangerous exits: Escaping abusive relationships in rural America.* New Brunswick, NJ: Rutgers University Press.

DeKeseredy, W. S., Schwartz, M. D., & Alvi, S. (2008). Which women are more likely to be abused? Public housing, cohabitation and separated/divorced women. *Criminal Justice Studies: A Critical Journal of Crime, Law, and Society, 21,* 283–293.

DeKeseredy, W. S., Schwartz, M. D., Fagen, D., & Hall, M. (2006). Separation/divorce sexual assault: The contribution of male peer support. *Feminist Criminology, 1,* 228–250.

Dobash, R. E., & Dobash, R. (1979). *Violence against wives: A case against the patriarchy.* New York: Free Press.

Duffy, A., & Momirov, J. (1997). *Family violence: A Canadian introduction.* Toronto: Lorimer.

Dutton, D. G. (2006). *Rethinking domestic violence.* Vancouver: University of British Columbia Press.

Edleson, J., & Brygger, M. (1986). Gender differences in reporting of battering incidences. *Family Relations, 35,* 377–382.

Eisenstein, Z. (1980). *Capitalist patriarchy and the case for socialist feminism.* New York: Monthly Review Press.

Ellis, D. (1987). *The wrong stuff: An introduction to the sociological study of deviance.* Toronto: Collier Macmillan.

Fekete, J. (1994). *Moral panic: Biopolitics rising.* Montreal: Robert Davies.

Fisher, B. (2009). The effects of survey question wording on rape estimates: Evidence from a quasi-experimental design. *Violence Against Women, 15,* 133–147.

Follingstad, D. R., Rutledge, L. L., Berg, B. J., Hause, E. S., & Polek, D. S. (1990). The role of emotional abuse in physically abusive relationships. *Journal of Family Violence, 5,* 107–120.

Foss, K. (2002, June 27). Men as likely to face abuse from partner, StatsCan says. *The Globe and Mail,* p. A8.

Fox, B. J. (1993). On violent men and female victims: A comment on DeKeseredy and Kelly. *Canadian Journal of Sociology, 18,* 320–324.

Gelles, R. J. (1993). Through a sociological lens: Social structure and family violence. In R. J. Gelles & D. R. Loseke (Eds.), *Current controversies in family violence* (pp. 31–46). Newbury Park, CA: Sage.

Gelles, R. J., & Cornell, C. P. (1985). *Intimate violence in families.* Beverly Hills, CA: Sage.

Gelles, R. J., & Straus, M. A. (1988). *Intimate violence: The causes and consequences of abuse in the American family.* New York: Simon & Schuster.

Gilbert, N. (1994). Miscounting social ills. *Society, 31,* 18–36.

Girard, A. (2009). Backlash or equality? The influence of men's and women's rights discourses on domestic violence legislation in Ontario. *Violence Against Women, 15,* 5–23.

Godenzi, A., Schwartz, M. D., & DeKeseredy, W. S. (2001). Toward a gendered social bond/male peer support theory of university woman abuse. *Critical Criminology, 10,* 1–16.

Gondolf, E. W. (1999). MCMI results for batterer program participants in four cities: Less "pathological" than expected. *Journal of Family Violence, 14,* 1–17.

Gondolf, E. W. (2003). MCMI results for batterers: Gondolf replies to Dutton's response. *Journal of Family Violence, 18,* 387–389.

Graham-Bermann, S., & Gross, M. (2008). Ecological models of violence. In C. M. Renzetti & J. L. Edleson (Eds.), *Encyclopedia of interpersonal violence* (pp. 212–215). Thousand Oaks, CA: Sage.

Heckert, D. A., & Gondolf, E. (2000). Assessing assault self-reports by batterer program participants and their partners. *Journal of Family Violence, 15,* 181–197.

Heise, L. L. (1998). Violence against women: An integrated, ecological framework. *Violence Against Women, 4,* 262–290.

Henning, K., & Holdford, R. (2006). Minimization, denial, and victim blaming by batterers: How much does the truth matter? *Criminal Justice and Behavior, 33,* 110–130.

Hilton, N. Z., Harris, G. T., & Rice, M. E. (2000). The functions of aggression by male teenagers. *Journal of Personality and Social Psychology, 79,* 988–994.

Hines, D., & Malley-Morrison, K. (2005). *Family violence in the United States: Defining, understanding, and combating abuse.* Thousand Oaks, CA: Sage.

Hirschi, T. (1989). Exploring alternatives to integrated theory. In S. F. Messner, M. D. Krohn, & A. E. Liska (Eds.), *Theoretical integration in the study of deviance and crime* (pp. 37–49). Albany: SUNY Press.

Holzman, H. R., & Piper, L. (1998). Measuring crime in public housing: Methodological issues and research strategies. *Journal of Quantitative Criminology, 14,* 331–351.

Jasinski, J. L. (2001). Theoretical explanations for violence against women. In C. M Renzetti, J. L. Edleson, & R. K. Bergen (Eds.), *Sourcebook on violence against women* (pp. 5–22). Thousand Oaks, CA: Sage.

Jiwani, J. (2000). *The 1999 general social survey on spousal violence: An analysis.* Retrieved May 1, 2002, from http://www.casac.ca/survey99.htm.

Johnson, H. (1996). *Dangerous domains: Violence against women in Canada.* Scarborough, ON: Nelson Canada.

Johnson, M. P. (2008). *A typology of domestic violence: Intimate terrorism, violent resistance, and situational couple violence.* Boston: Northeastern University Press.

Johnson, M. P., & Ferraro, K. (2000). Research on domestic violence in the 1990s: Making distinctions. *Journal of Marriage and the Family, 62,* 948–963.

Katz, J. (2006). *The macho paradox: Why some men hurt women and how all men can help.* Naperville, IL: Sourcebooks.

Kelly, L. (1988). *Surviving sexual violence.* Minneapolis: University of Minnesota Press.

Kernsmith, P. (2008). Coercive control. In C. M. Renzetti & J. L. Edleson (Eds.), *Encyclopedia of interpersonal violence* (pp. 133–134). Thousand Oaks, CA: Sage.

Kilpatrick, D. G. (2004). What is violence against women? Defining and measuring the problem. *Journal of Interpersonal Violence, 19,* 1209–1234.

Kimmel, M. S. (2000). *The gendered society.* New York: Oxford University Press.

Koss, M. P. (1996). The measurement of rape victimization in crime surveys. *Criminal Justice and Behavior, 23,* 55–69.

Koss, M. P., Gidycz, C. A., & Wisniewski, W. (1987). The scope of rape: Incidence and prevalence of sexual aggression and victimization in a national sample of higher education students. *Journal of Consulting and Clinical Psychology, 50,* 455–457.

Koss, M. P., Goodman, L. A., Browne, A., Fitzgerald, L. F., Puryear-Keita, G. K., & Russo, N. F. (1994). *No safe haven.* Washington, DC: American Psychological Association.

LaFlame, M. (2009, August 14). Book review: Dangerous exits: Escaping abusive relationships in rural America. *Online Journal of Rural Research and Policy,* 1–3.

Levinson, D. (1989). *Family violence in cross-cultural perspective.* Newbury Park, CA: Sage.

Liddle, A. (1989). Feminist contributions to an understanding of violence against women—three steps forward, two steps back. *Canadian Review of Sociology and Anthropology, 26,* 759–775.

Littleton, C., & Henderson, C. E. (2009). Evaluation of predictors of PTSD symptomology among college rape victims. *Violence Against Women, 15,* 148–167.

Loseke, D. R., Gelles, R. J., & Cavanaugh, M. M. (2005). Controversies in conceptualization. In D. R. Loseke, R. J. Gelles, & M. M. Cavanaugh (Eds.), *Current controversies on family violence* (2nd ed., pp. 1–4). Thousand Oaks, CA: Sage.

Maidment, M. R. (2006). Transgressing boundaries: Feminist perspectives in criminology. In W. S. DeKeseredy & B. Perry (Eds.), *Advancing critical criminology: Theory and application* (pp. 43–62). Lanham, MD: Lexington.

Malley-Morrison, K., & Hines, D. A. (2004). *Family violence in a cultural perspective: Defining, understanding, and combating abuse.* Thousand Oaks, CA: Sage.

Messerschmidt, J. W. (1993). *Masculinities and crime: Critique and reconceptualization.* Lanham, MD: Roman & Littlefield.

Mihalic, S. W., & Elliot, D. (1997). If violence is domestic, does it really count? *Journal of Family Violence, 12,* 293–311.

Mihorean, K. (2005). Trends in self-reported spousal violence. In K. AuCoin (Ed.), *Family violence in Canada: A statistical profile 2005* (pp. 13–32). Ottawa: Statistics Canada.

Moffitt, T. E., Caspi, A., Rutter, M., & Silva, P. A. (2001). *Sex differences in antisocial behavior.* Cambridge: Cambridge University Press.

Muehlenhard, C. L., Powch, I. G., Phelps, J. L., & Giusti, L. M. (1992). Definitions of rape: Scientific and political implications. *Journal of Social Issues, 48,* 23–44.

Myers, M. (1997). *News coverage of violence against women: Engendering blame.* Thousand Oaks, CA: Sage.

National Institute of Justice. (2000). *Workshop on gender symmetry.* Retrieved March 2, 2008, from http://www.ojp.usdoj.gov/nij/topics/crime/violence-against-women/workshops/gender symmetry.htm.

Okun, L. (1986). *Woman abuse: Facts replacing myths.* Albany: State University of New York Press.

Osthoff, S. (2002). But, Gertrude, I beg to differ, a hit is not a hit is not a hit: When battered women are arrested for assaulting their partners. *Violence Against Women, 8,* 1521–1544.

Pence, E., & Dasgupta, S. D. (2006). *Re-examining battering: Are all acts of violence against intimate partners the same?* Duluth: Praxis International. Retrieved April 17, 2007, from http://www.praxisinternational.org/pages/library/files/pdf/ReexaminingBattering.pdf.

Pitts, V. L., & Schwartz, M. D. (1993). Promoting self-blame among hidden rape survivors. *Humanity & Society, 17,* 383–398.

Ptacek, J. (1999). *Battered women in the courtroom: The power of judicial response.* Boston: Northeastern University Press.

Radford, J. (1987). Policing male violence—policing women. In J. Hanmer & M. Maynard (Eds.), *Women, violence and social control* (pp. 30–45). Atlantic Highlands, NJ: Humanities Press International.

Raphael, J. (2001). Public housing and domestic violence. *Violence Against Women, 7,* 699–706.

Renzetti, C. M. (1993). On the margins of the malestream (Or, they still don't get it, do they?): Feminist analyses in criminal justice education. *Journal of Criminal Justice Education, 4,* 219–234.

Renzetti, C. M. (1997). Foreword. In W. S. DeKeseredy & L. MacLeod (Eds.), *Woman abuse: A sociological story* (pp. v–vii). Toronto: Harcourt Brace.

Renzetti, C. M. (2008). Feminist theories of interpersonal violence. In C. M. Renzetti & J. L. Edleson (Eds.), *Encyclopedia of interpersonal violence* (pp. 271–272). Thousand Oaks, CA: Sage.

Renzetti, C. M., & Maier, S. L. (2002). Private crime in public housing: Fear of crime and violent victimization among women public housing residents. *Women's Health and Urban Life, 1,* 46–65.

Russell, D. E. H. (1990). *Rape in marriage: Expanded and revised edition.* New York: Macmillan Press.

Saunders, D. G. (1988). Wife abuse, husband abuse, or mutual combat? A feminist perspective on the empirical findings. In K. Yllo & M. Bograd (Eds.), *Feminist perspectives on wife abuse* (pp. 90–113). Newbury Park, CA: Sage.

Schur, E. M. (1984). *Labeling women deviant: Gender, stigma, and social control.* Philadelphia: Temple University Press.

Schwartz, M. D. (1988). Ain't got no class: Universal risk theories of battering. *Contemporary Crises: Law, Crime and Social Policy, 12,* 373–392.

Schwartz, M. D. (2000). Methodological issues in the use of survey data for measuring and characterizing violence against women. *Violence Against Women, 8,* 815–838.

Schwartz, M. D., & DeKeseredy, W. S. (1993). The return of the "battered husband syndrome" through the typification of women as violent. *Crime, Law and Social Change, 20,* 249–265.

Schwartz, M. D., & DeKeseredy, W. S. (1997). *Sexual assault on the college campus: The role of male peer support.* Thousand Oaks, CA: Sage.

Schwartz, M. D., & Leggett, M. S. (1999). Bad dates or emotional trauma? The aftermath of campus sexual assault. *Violence Against Women, 5,* 251–271.

Scully, D. (1990). *Understanding sexual violence.* Boston: Unwin Hyman.

Sernau, S. (2001). *Worlds apart: Social inequalities in a new century.* Thousand Oaks, CA: Pine Forge Press.

Smith, M. D. (1994). Enhancing the quality of survey data on violence against women: A feminist approach. *Gender and Society, 8,* 109–127.

Stark, E. (2006). Commentary on Johnson's conflict and control: Gender symmetry and asymmetry in domestic violence. *Violence Against Women, 12,* 1019–1025.

Stark, E. (2007). *Coercive control: How men entrap women in personal life.* New York: Oxford University Press.

Steinmetz, S. (1977–78). The battered husband syndrome. *Victimology, 3–4,* 499–509.

Straus, M. A. (1979). Measuring intrafamily conflict and violence: The Conflict Tactics (CT) Scales. *Journal of Marriage and the Family, 41,* 75–88.

Straus, M. A. (2005). Women's violence toward men is a serious social problem. In D. R. Loseke, R. J. Gelles, & M. Cavanaugh (Eds.), *Current controversies on family violence* (pp. 55–78). Thousand Oaks, CA: Sage.

Straus, M. A., & Gelles, R. J. (1986). Societal change and change in family violence from 1975 to 1985 as revealed by two national surveys. *Journal of Marriage and the Family, 48,* 465–479.

Straus, M. A., Gelles, R. J., & Steinmetz, S. K. (1981). *Behind closed doors: Violence in the American family.* New York: Anchor.

Szinovacz, M. E. (1983). Using couple data as a methodological tool: The case of marital violence. *Journal of Marriage and the Family, 45,* 633–644.

Szinovacz, M. E., & Egley, L. C. (1995). Comparing one-partner and couple data on sensitive marital behaviors: The case of marital violence. *Journal of Marriage and the Family, 57,* 995–1010.

Tjaden, P., & Thoennes, N. (2000). *Extent, nature, and consequences of intimate partner violence: Findings from the National Violence Against Women Survey.* Washington, DC: U.S. Department of Justice.

Totten, M. (2003). Girlfriend abuse as a form of masculinity construction. *Men and Masculinities, 6,* 70–92.

Vaux, A. (1985). Variations in social support associated with gender, ethnicity, and age. *Journal of Social Issues, 41,* 89–110.

Walby, S., & Myhill, A. (2001). New survey methodologies in researching violence against women. *British Journal of Criminology, 41,* 502–522.

Wilson, M., & Daly, M. (1992). Til death do us part. In J. Radford & D. E. H. Russell (Eds.), *Femicide: The politics of woman killing* (pp. 83–98). New York: Twayne.

Young, J. (1999). *The exclusive society.* London: Sage.

Chapter Authors

Walter S. DeKeseredy is Professor of Criminology, Justice, and Policy Studies at the University of Ontario Institute of Technology (UOIT). He has published 14 books and close to 70 scientific journal articles on a variety of topics, including woman abuse in intimate relationships, criminological theory, and crime in public housing. In 2008, the Institute on Violence, Abuse, and Trauma gave him the Linda Saltzman Memorial Intimate Partner Violence Researcher Award. He also jointly received (with Martin D. Schwartz) the 2004 Distinguished Scholar Award from the ASC's Division on Women and Crime and the 2007 inaugural UOIT Research Excellence Award. In 1995, he received the Critical Criminologist of the Year Award from the ASC's Division on Critical Criminology, and in 2008, the Division on Critical Criminology gave him the Lifetime Achievement Award.

Martin D. Schwartz is Professor of Sociology Emeritus at Ohio University. He is a 2008 Fellow of the Academy of Criminal Justice Sciences and has received distinguished scholar awards from two different divisions of the American Society of Criminology: Women and Crime and Critical Criminology. At Ohio University, he has been named Graduate Professor of the Year and Best Arts and Sciences Professor. In addition, he was named Presidential Research Scholar, an honor that recognizes achievement in research. He has written or edited (often with Walter S. DeKeseredy) 21 editions of 12 books, 70 journal articles, and 65 book chapters, government reports, and essays. Most recently, he coauthored *Dangerous Exits: Escaping Abusive Relationships in Rural America* (Rutgers University Press, 2009).

Personal Reflection

Evan Stark

Anne Flitcraft and I were introduced to the battered women's movement in the summer of 1975, when our friend Sharon Vaughan welcomed us to Women's Advocates in St. Paul, Minnesota, the first shelter for battered women in the U.S. Over the next few years, we hid victimized women and their children in our home and helped open a shelter in New Haven, Connecticut. Starting with Anne's thesis at Yale medical school, we also conducted a series of NIMH-funded studies that showed that domestic violence was the leading cause of injury for which women sought medical attention and that, after the onset of abuse, battered women were at greatly elevated risk for a range of health, behavioral, and psychosocial problems. We equated abuse with injurious violence and assumed the secondary problems experienced by battered women were the byproduct of this "trauma" as well as of medicine's failure to identify abuse or intervene appropriately. This understanding guided our thinking through the 1980s, as it did most in the field, and when we fought successfully to reform the institutional response in health, law, criminal justice, and public policy. Most interventions remain predicated on the equation of abuse with episodic violent acts.

Fatal and the most injurious partner violence declined over the next two decades, a major achievement. But overall, levels of partner violence did not decline. Millions of perpetrators were arrested, but almost none went to jail. Shelters and court orders provided short-term protection but few long-term improvements in women's safety. The domestic violence revolution was stalled. A huge gap remained between the strategies men used to oppress women in personal life and the prevailing definition of abuse.

Like so much research since, our work at Yale showed that the hallmark of women's physical abuse is frequent, even routine, but relatively minor assaults extending over a considerable period, rather than the episodic and severe violence targeted by most interventions. But if traumatic violence didn't explain why abused women became "entrapped" and developed a problem profile found among no other class of assault victims, what did? The answer lay in what the women we had sheltered told us: "The violence wasn't the worst part."

Because I was repeatedly challenged to explain why women had killed abusive partners whose physical violence had not been life threatening, I gradually came to ask about and then to appreciate the full spectrum of oppressive tactics men deploy in 60% to 80% of the cases we see in the justice and helping system. Drawing on the prevailing sentiment among advocates, which had remained marginal to research and theory, I mapped the technology of "coercive control" and sketched an alternative theory of abuse that applied a feminist critique of male domination to the anomalous evidence that had accumulated in the violence paradigm. Coercive control, not violence, explained the unique health profile we had identified among battered women. Abuse was not "gendered" by men's greater propensity for violence (surveys consistently show sexual differences in partner violence to be minor) but because persistent sexual inequalities enabled men to set violence in the context of an ongoing course of intimidation, isolation, exploitation, sexual degradation, and control. Coercive control was also gendered by its substantive target. If control tactics extended to necessities such as money, mobility, communication, and speech, their principal means were the micromanagement of how women enacted their default roles as wives, mothers, and homemakers, a key element of their inequality. The main harms here were not physical but sociopolitical; they involved what men kept women from doing for themselves by harming their liberty, autonomy, and dignity as well as their physical security. These harms are "invisible in plain sight" because women lack full personhood. Because coercive control crosses social space—explaining why women who are single, separated, or divorced are at the highest risk—and encompasses the range of activities and sites where women live, this is where resistance and reconstruction must begin, in rejoining the struggle for "safety" to the fight for women's liberation.

CHAPTER 2

Research Methods, Measures, and Ethics

Véronique Jaquier, Holly Johnson, and Bonnie S. Fisher

Over the last several decades, measuring the scope and nature of violence against women has evolved into a global issue. Violence against women has captured the interest of researchers, advocates, clinicians, and service providers in a variety of disciplines including anthropology, criminology, epidemiology, medicine, psychology, sociology, and women's studies.

Obtaining accurate estimates of violence against women and advancing the understanding of its correlates and consequences are among the goals of these fields despite their different epistemological and theoretical perspectives, which vary considerably from "traditional" positivist to feminist to family conflict. These different frameworks have shaped choices about the methods, measures, and ethical considerations of those engaged in violence against women research. These three topics—methods, measures, and ethical issues—have been, and continue to be, central to the discussions that influence the measurement, design, and implementation of research and the interpretation of study results.

Academic interest in research methods, measures, and ethics surrounding the study of violence against women coincided with the international momentum for change to address gender inequalities in all aspects of social and family life (e.g., pay, reproduction, maternity leave) and to raise awareness of sexual and domestic violence that the Women's Movement generated in the 1970s. Throughout that decade, feminists in the United States sparked interest in the definition of rape by successfully lobbying for rape statute reforms that included addressing legal definitional issues such as the inclusion of marital rape and forms of penetration other than vaginal or anal. By the late 1970s and early 1980s, interest in violence against women research spread among sociologists and psychologists who began to address issues related to the quality of measurement and sampling. During this time, several pioneering studies were carried out. Lenore Walker (1979) listened to battered women describe the intimate details of their lives and defined the battered woman syndrome, Murray Straus (1979) developed the Conflict Tactics Scales (CTS) to measure physical aggression among couples, and Diana Russell (1982) included questions on marital rape in her community study. At that time, both scholars and policy makers had overlooked these forms of violence against women, in part due to the cultural norms of respect for privacy and family life, but these studies opened avenues for further inquiry. In the early 1980s, the *Ms. Magazine* Campus Project on Sexual Assault, directed by Mary Koss and her colleagues, advanced measurement with the development of the Sexual Experiences Survey (SES), which used explicit, behaviorally specific items to measure rape and other forms of sexual coercion and victimization typically hidden from legal and social scrutiny (Koss & Gidycz, 1985; Koss & Oros, 1982). Further advancing the measurement of forcible rape, Dean Kilpatrick and his colleagues undertook the National Women's Study to estimate the scope of forcible rape among women in the U.S. They developed explicitly worded questions to measure its extent, which "provide clear answers for the first time to the critical elements of forcible rape: use of force or threat of force, lack of consent, and sexual penetration" (Kilpatrick, Edmunds, & Seymour, 1992, p. 15).

Collectively, these early contributions sparked debate on two methodological issues that centered on the measurement quality of violence against women. First, Koss's, Kilpatrick's, and their colleagues' studies called into question the validity (i.e., the indicator measures the phenomenon it is intended to measure) and reliability (i.e., the indicator consistently produces the same value each time the phenomenon is measured) of the two "official" national estimates of rape produced by the National Crime Survey (NCS) and the FBI's Uniform Crime Reports (UCR). Second, in contrast to prior studies with small and unrepresentative samples, research directed by Koss and Kilpatrick addressed sampling design issues that would help produce generalizable results on different forms of violence against women.

The findings of both Koss's college students study and Kilpatrick's adult women study were influential for both government and academic researchers. New survey items were developed, including a redesign of the NCS (renamed the National Crime Victimization Survey [NCVS]) in 1992 to more accurately measure incidents of

rape, sexual assault, and domestic violence (Bachman & Saltzman, 1995). The passage of the Violence Against Women Act in 1994—and its continued Congressional support—also funded multidisciplinary collaborations to develop and apply a variety of quantitative and qualitative methods and measures that have advanced the understanding of the extent and nature of violence against women and the effectiveness of prevention and treatment interventions (Jordan, 2009). During the mid-1990s, the U.S. government's commitment to multidisciplinary approaches to studying violence against women became clear when the National Institute of Justice (NIJ) and Centers for Disease Control and Prevention (CDC) jointly funded the National Violence Against Women survey (NVAWS; Tjaden & Thoennes, 2000). The NVAWS not only incorporated the CTS and Kilpatrick and colleagues' operationalization of forcible rape, but it also included measures of the newly criminalized behavior of stalking. Continuing into the late 1990s and early 2000s, Linda Saltzman, Kathleen Basile, and their colleagues at the CDC made recommendations for uniformity in the use of terminology, definitions, and data collection for the behaviors that encompassed intimate partner violence (e.g., physical violence, psychological or emotional abuse; Saltzman, Fanslow, McMahon, & Shelley, 2002) and the components of sexual violence (Basile & Saltzman, 2002).

Collectively, these methodologically focused efforts in the U.S., coupled with international and comparative studies, have continued to improve the quality of research methods and measures used in the study of violence against women. With the goal of assessing the true extent of violence against women, researchers have put tremendous effort into developing, revising, and assessing screening instruments. Yet, no single method or measure has been established as a "gold standard." Rather, methods and measures that are considered most appropriate to answer specific research or evaluation questions must be selected, explained, and ultimately justified and defended by the investigators. The complexity of research questions continues to spark researchers' methodological creativity in their attempts to more fully understand the scope and nature of violence against women while minimizing and responding to possible risks to the safety and well-being of the participants and the research team. There is now widespread agreement at the international level about the importance of ethical and methodological rigor in the collection of violence against women data (Department of Economic and Social Affairs, 2006; Koss & White, 2008).

In this chapter, we provide a discussion of the methods, measures, and ethical issues that comprise this field of research. We begin with a brief overview of quantitative and qualitative sources of violence against women data, identify critical methodological issues that underlie the measurement of violence against women, and describe research and sampling designs and data collection strategies commonly used to measure women's experiences of male violence. We review a sample of widely used self-report victimization surveys and consider ethical issues surrounding women's personal safety and well-being that researchers and service providers face at the onset, during, and at the completion of these studies.

Quantitative and Qualitative Sources of Violence Against Women Data

Statistics such as police or court records offer an interesting, yet limited, perspective on women's experiences of violence. Official crime statistics represent offenses known to the police, yet research has consistently shown that both sexual violence and intimate partner violence are among the most underreported of all crimes (Fisher, Daigle, Cullen, & Turner, 2003; Johnson, Ollus, & Nevala, 2008; Tjaden & Thoennes, 2000). Other sources of criminal justice data, such as offenses formally brought to court, are even more limited, especially for cases of sexual and domestic violence against women, which are often

dropped by police and prosecutors (Garner & Maxwell, 2009).

Public health and medical sources (e.g., hospital records, trauma registry, patient records, and death certificates) provide data on the number and nature of incidents that are brought to health agencies, the type of injuries sustained, and, sometimes, partial information on the circumstances of these incidents. Most hospital records do not provide information regarding perpetrators and prior victimization. One interesting exception is the development, in some countries, of special medico-legal units that offer consultation to victims of violent crime, including victims of intimate partner violence, and collect data in the course of their work (e.g., Hofner, Burquier, Huissoud, Romain-Glassey, Graz, & Mangin, 2009).

It is not uncommon for researchers to recruit participants through convenience sampling in hospitals, emergency departments, crisis centers, or shelters (e.g., Boyle & Hassett-Walker, 2008). These collection strategies provide valuable information, yet the generalizability of the findings is compromised to the extent that the results cannot be said to represent the population at large (e.g., the fact that a large proportion of victims surveyed in shelters have a low socioeconomic status does not mean that all victims will have the same characteristics). In addition, establishing ongoing surveillance systems is a complicated enterprise because researchers need to provide staff with adequate training in, for example, incident screening, case definitions, and data collection (Moracco, Runyan, & Dull, 2003).

Qualitative data are very important for obtaining information on the circumstances of an assault or the cyclical nature of domestic violence; yet, given the intensity of collecting these types of data (e.g., face-to-face interviews that last an hour or more), the richest qualitative data often comes from small convenience samples. In her work *Getting Played*, Jody Miller (2008) explores the gendered practices of violence and aggression in disadvantaged urban communities. She combines the administration of the CTS and qualitative interviews to juxtapose survey data with interviews with African American young women and men and highlights that young men's and women's narrative accounts differ markedly.

An interesting inclusion of qualitative data in a large-scale statistical survey is seen in the NCVS. Although the survey items are essentially quantitative (i.e., closed-ended questions with structured responses), it contains qualitative information in the form of incident summaries provided by respondents. Narratives are not victims' verbatim responses but statements transcribed by interviewers; however, they can provide valuable information regarding victims' perception of the incident. For example, in analyzing 944 accounts of women who experienced at least one sexual victimization incident, Karen Weiss (2009, p. 817) distinguishes between victims' statements that excuse offenders' responsibility (e.g., "He didn't mean to hurt me"; "He didn't know what he was doing") and justifications that either deny injury (e.g., "No harm done"; "Nothing really happened") or blame the victim for the assault (e.g., "I deserved it"; "I didn't try hard enough to stop it").

It is generally agreed that population surveys, in which random samples of women are interviewed about their experiences of violence using detailed, behaviorally specific questions, yield more valid and reliable estimates of the prevalence of these phenomena in the population (Fisher, 2009). We turn now to the methodological issues confronting researchers in their quest to produce reliable and valid estimates of the prevalence of male violence against women.

Methodological Issues

Each decision researchers make concerning methodological approaches and the measures they use to estimate the scope and nature of violence against women will have an effect on the obtained estimates and will affect comparability across studies. Some of the critical differences in

estimates of violence against women are due to the way in which these experiences are measured, eligibility criteria used for identifying perpetrators and respondents, methods of counting victims, and reference period.

Differences Due to the Operationalization of Violence Against Women. The process of operationalization refers to the translation of an abstract concept (e.g., victimization, domestic violence, stalking) into survey questions intended to measure attributes of the concept (e.g., hitting, choking, threatening with a gun). Disciplines ranging from public health to traditional social sciences approach the topic from a particular perspective due to differing research agendas and orientations. Understanding the nature of human behavior, especially the types of deviant behavior, is the central tenet of social sciences such as criminology, sociology, and psychology. Researchers in these disciplines tend to focus on identifying factors that put women at risk of victimization and the consequences of violence, so as to inform the prevention of violence and treatment of victims and perpetrators. On the other hand, measuring the impact of violence on an individual's health and well-being is the focus of the public health and medical fields. It involves identifying risk factors associated with morbidity (injuries such as bruises, broken bones, and the severity of these injuries) and including specific links to reproductive health and mortality (deaths). These fields rely heavily on identifying those at high risk of victimization and injury to reduce risk and prevent injuries and death due to violence.

A number of researchers have described and documented the methodological challenges of conceptually and operationally defining violence against women (DeKeseredy, 2000; Fisher & Cullen, 2000; Kilpatrick, 2004; Saltzman, 2004; Tjaden, 2004). These challenges aside, most researchers agree that there are four major forms of non-lethal violence against women: verbal, emotional, physical, and sexual violence. The forms and the types of behaviors included in each form differ across disciplinary fields as well as among researchers within specific disciplines. Including all four forms and multiple behaviors within forms will result in a different victimization estimate than if only one or two forms, or one or two behaviors, are included. For example, whether sexual violence includes penile-vaginal, anal, oral, and/or digital penetration will affect victimization estimates; similarly, including threats of physical harm when measuring the extent of physical violence results in higher estimates than including physical assaults alone (Jaquier & Fisher, 2009). Thus, measurement of violence against women can differ due to the forms and behaviors included in the definition. Generally, narrow definitions produce lower estimates than broader ones that include a wide range of behaviors (DeKeseredy, 2000; see also Chapter 1, this volume).

Even if two studies use the same definition, they might produce different estimates based on how violence against women is operationalized. In a study of sexual violence, for example, one study might use behaviorally specific terms that graphically describe the acts in question, such as "inserting his penis into your vagina or anus." Another study might use more colloquial terms in its questions, such as "rape" or "sexual assault," and assume the respondent defines the behavior in the same way the researcher has defined it. The usefulness of behaviorally specific questions cannot be overemphasized, not necessarily because they produce larger estimates of rape, but because they use words and phrases that describe to the respondent exactly what behavior is being measured. Using behaviorally specific screening questions appears to cue more women to recall their experiences (Fisher, 2009; Fisher & Cullen, 2000).

Another issue that affects the operationalization and measurement of violence against women is whether single or multiple items are used to measure a form of violence. For example, Koss and Oros's (1982) original 13-item SES was revised into a 10-item scale: Questions were reworded to increase their clarity, and three separate questions were used to measure rape (Koss, Gidycz, & Wisniewski, 1987). If a respondent answered "yes" to any of the three rape items, she was categorized and counted as having experienced rape. The SES was recently revised again and developed into four different versions: two forms (i.e., a short and a long form) intended to measure sexual victimization and two forms intended to measure perpetration of sexual violence (Koss et al., 2007). In this new version, three items are used to operationalize attempted rape and three items are used to operationalize forcible rape. This revised SES also introduced subquestions to distinguish between forms of sexual coercion (e.g., lies, verbal pressure) and rape (e.g., use of threats, force, or while intoxicated). This is considered a single-stage measurement process because measurement is based on the responses to questions at a single point in time. Others have operationalized violence against women using a two-stage measurement process, similar to the process used in the NCVS or the British Crime Survey (see also the National College Women Sexual Victimization Study by Fisher, Cullen, & Turner, 1999). The first stage consists of a series of behaviorally specific screeners embedded within short descriptive cues that are intended to prompt respondents' recall. If a respondent answers "yes" to any question, she is then routed to an incident or victim form in which detailed questions are asked about the experience. Responses to these questions are then used to categorize and count the type of violence that occurred.

Differences Due to Criteria Used for Identifying Types of Perpetrators, Relationships, and Respondents. The sex of the perpetrator is relevant when producing estimates of violence against women. Some research considers any violent behavior directed at a female by anyone—male or female—as violence (e.g., NCVS, NVAWS). Others only take into account acts committed by a male perpetrator against a female, like the Canadian Violence Against Women Survey (Johnson, 1996) or the International Violence Against Women Survey

(Johnson et al., 2008). Inevitably, such a decision affects victimization estimates.

Intimate partner violence research has grown exponentially and has developed a variety of definitions of intimate partners. Early efforts to quantify intimate partners restricted the definition to current and former spouses and cohabiting partners. Recently, the definition has been broadened to include boyfriends and dating partners, to reflect the similarities in the dynamics of violence in all intimate relationships. Researchers often confront challenges in applying this definition internationally because, in some cultural contexts, relationships outside marriage are taboo or specific terminology does not exist for them (Goodwin, 1999). For example, the term "boyfriend" was translated into the French word *ami* in the Swiss component of the International Violence Against Women Survey mentioned in the previous paragraph. Intimate partner violence could not be operationalized for comparative purposes to the U.S. definition because of the ambiguous meaning of the word *ami,* which can refer either to an intimate relationship or to a platonic friendship (Jaquier, Fisher, & Killias, 2006). Similarly, violence between same-sex partners has been the topic of specific publications and has been considered within some partner violence studies.

Even though the CDC provides guidelines as to what types of relationships are considered intimate relationships, there is no standardization of who is included in these relationships nor how detailed the classification should be (Saltzman et al., 2002). In the NVAWS, Patricia Tjaden and Nancy Thoennes (2000) adopted a very detailed construction of the victim-offender relationship, including 27 different types of intimate partners such as current spouse, first ex-husband, third male partner, up to the eighth male or female partner. For most surveys, this classification is considered overly complex and categories of relationship type are limited to a few.

Prevalence estimates of violence against women are also affected by the age of eligible participants. The International Violence Against Women Survey restricted participation to women 18 to 69 years of age, and the British Crime Survey to women and men aged 16 to 59. This is in contrast to the Canadian and the U.S. surveys on violence against women, which included participants 18 years of age and older. Samples that exclude subgroups of the population who are generally at lower risk of violence, such as older women, are not comparable to those with no age-related exclusions.

Differences Due to Methods of Counting. Across studies, researchers have used different criteria to count the number of victims; each criterion has an effect on victimization estimates. When multiple types of violence are measured, one method is to count which individuals have experienced each type of violence in order to distinguish victims from nonvictims. How to count those who have experienced more than one type of victimization requires another decision. One option is to calculate a total based on those who have experienced at least one of these types of violence; another option is a hierarchical scoring algorithm based on a criterion, say, the most "serious" type of violence experienced. For example, most researchers who use Koss's SES categorize victims based on the most serious type of victimization the respondent reported. If the respondent reported having experienced sexual coercion and a completed rape, she would be categorized as a complete rape victim (see McMullin, Wirth, & White, 2007). Incidents in the U.S. victimization survey, the NCVS, are classified according to the most severe type of sexual victimization that occurred during an incident. For example, if the victim indicated she had experienced a completed rape and a sexual assault during the same incident, the incident was classified as a completed rape. Using the most serious or severe criterion leads to underestimating the scope of less serious types of violence, but each victim is counted once.

Counting those who have experienced more than one violent incident poses challenges, too, especially since there is not a consensus among researchers as to the counting criteria or the naming of such phenomena. Those who have experienced the same type of violence more than once have been referred to as *repeat victims*. *Revictimization* is a term that is used to describe those who experienced childhood or adolescent physical or sexual abuse and then experienced a subsequent physical or sexual victimization as an adult (Daigle, Fisher, & Guthrie, 2007). Recently, the terms *polyvictimization* and *multivictimization* appeared in the criminological literature to describe the fact that some victims experience multiple forms or types of violence (see Sabina & Straus, 2008).

Differences Due to Reference Period. Many crime victimization surveys focus on a 12-month reference period, in contrast to violence against women surveys, such as the National Women's Study, the NVAWS, and the future National Intimate Partner and Sexual Violence Surveillance System, which use a lifetime reference period. The Canadian Violence Against Women Survey refers to adult "lifetime prevalence," which incorporates incidents that happened after the respondent's 16th birthday. Researchers administering the SES typically use "since the age of 14" as the reference period, whereas the WHO Multi-Country Study on Women's Health and Domestic Violence Against Women asked respondents about incidents that occurred since the age of 15 (Garcia-Moreno, Jansen, Ellsberg, Heise, & Watts, 2005). Different studies present estimates that are labeled as adult lifetime prevalence but vary in their precise definition of this reference period.

Research Designs

Depending on the objectives and goals of the study and specific research questions, researchers make decisions that will structure data collection as well as the types of data analyses that can be performed. The most common research designs are summarized in Table 2.1.

A large number of violence against women studies employ a cross-sectional research design. For example, the U.S. and Canadian violence against women surveys used a cross-sectional design to collect data from respondents during their one-time field period (Johnson, 1996; Tjaden & Thoennes, 2000).

Longitudinal designs that collect data from a particular sample at more than one point in time have been used less frequently than cross-sectional designs. Trend, panel, and cohort designs are examples of longitudinal research designs. Trend designs typically track rates from independent samples—for example, rates of intimate partner violence—to examine patterns over time. Panel and cohort designs collect data from sampling units over some time period, such as weekly for six months or every three months for a year. Two distinctions can be made between panel and cohort design. First, the sample units in a cohort design are selected based on characteristics they have in common, such as being born in the same year or graduating in the same year from high school. Panel sampling units are typically randomly selected and are not selected based on a common characteristic. Second, cohort studies, especially in the medical fields, typically have a comparison group in which the sampling units do not have the characteristic that defined the original sample (Paterson & Bechhofer, 2000).

The British Crime Survey and the Victimization modules of the Canadian General Social Survey annually interview a cross-section of the population to estimate the proportion of victims at that point in time (i.e., a cross-sectional design) and use these estimates to calculate an annual victimization rate. Annual victimization rates over several years provide an indication of trends over time. An example of a panel design is the work directed by Maria Testa and her colleagues that examined women's vulnerability to sexual victimization by intimate and nonintimate male

Table 2.1	Types of Research Design: Description and Examples	

Type of Research Design	Description	Example
Cross-sectional	Data are collected from sample units at one point in time.	A sample of women is interviewed in 2001.
Longitudinal	Data are collected from sample units over time.	
Trend	Data are collected from a sample and studied at different points in time. Samples are composed of different sample units but represent the same population.	A sample of women is interviewed in 2000. Another sample of women, drawn from the same general population, is interviewed in 2001.
Panel	Data are collected from the same sample units at different points in time.	A sample of women is interviewed annually over the course of five years, beginning in 2001.
Cohort	Data are collected at different points in time from sample units comprising the cohort. A cohort shares a common characteristic(s) (e.g., birth year). The comparison group may be another cohort or selected from the same population from which the cohort was drawn. Alternatively, subcohorts within the cohort also can be compared with each other.	A birth cohort of a sample of women born in 1980 is interviewed at age 16, 20, 24, and 28. Two groups are identified within the birth cohort based on the respondents' victimization status and then group comparisons are made on different variables of interest.

perpetrators (Testa, VanZile-Tamsen, & Livingston, 2007). The authors used a 3-year panel design consisting of three waves of data collection, 12 months apart. Similarly, Kilpatrick and his colleagues conducted a three-wave panel study in which a national probability sample was followed for 2 years to assess the association between physical/sexual abuse and substance use (Kilpatrick, Acierno, Resnick, Saunders, & Best, 1997). The NCVS also employs a complex panel design in which each month a sample of housing units are part of the panel; household members aged 12 and older are interviewed about their victimization experiences every 6 months for a total of 3½ years before being rotated out. Cohort studies include research by Miriam Ehrensaft and colleagues that followed a birth cohort of male and female adolescents prospectively at three different time points to identify the relationship between psychiatric disorders and intimate partner violence (Ehrensaft, Moffitt, & Caspi, 2006). The researchers used mental disorder diagnostics recorded at age 18 to distinguish two groups: adolescents with mental disorders and adolescents without (i.e., the comparison group). When the original birth cohort was between 24 and 26 years old, the researchers measured intimate partner violence in each group. When the cohort was 26 years old, mental disorders were diagnosed again for the two groups. The objective was to assess whether mental disorders raised the risk of involvement in abusive relationships and abuse increased the risk of further mental disorders, controlling for prior psychiatric episodes.

Each study design has its strengths and weaknesses in terms of testing relationships among the measures of interest. For example, panel and cohort designs are preferred for examining causal and reciprocal relationships, something that is more difficult in other designs, especially cross-sectional design, even when such studies include retrospective questions (e.g., child and/or adolescent abuse items in a survey administered to adults). However, longitudinal studies are costly to implement because they require multiple time points of data collection. Also, in panel and cohort designs, sample units are subject to attrition (which occurs when respondents drop out, die, or cannot be traced) and other threats (e.g., historical event, a change in the measuring instrument) that, if not addressed statistically, could compromise the validity of the results.

Sampling Designs

The choice of sampling design is critical because it can influence the generalizability of findings. The most commonly used techniques in violence against women studies are described here, starting with simple random sampling, which is the basic technique used by researchers to ensure that results can be generalized to the population at large. The random digit dialing technique used in large telephone surveys, like the NVAWS in the U.S., relies on the principles of simple random sampling. Stratification techniques are used when the researcher wants to make comparisons between groups in the population and some groups vastly outnumber others. Rather than select a random sample from the total population, the researchers divide the population into strata, then elements are randomly drawn from each stratum, such as geographic areas. One example is the Canadian General Social Survey, in which each province is divided into Census Metropolitan Areas (CMAs; i.e., large urban areas) and non-CMAs for a total of 27 strata. Sometimes social science research requires the selection of samples from populations that cannot be easily listed for sampling purposes, forcing researchers to rely on more complex sample designs. For example, multistage cluster sampling requires random sampling of clusters within clusters. An initial sample of groups of elements (i.e., clusters), such as cities, is selected, then clusters within each cluster are sampled (e.g., neighborhoods, then city blocks, then residences). This method can be used in developing countries where census data or other listings of populations are not available. A drawback is that multistage cluster sampling is subject to sampling errors at each stage when different elements are selected; sampling weights must be used to address the sampling design effects inherent in multistage sampling (see Lohr, 1999).

Various violence against women studies have relied on cluster sampling. Koss's original SES questionnaire was administered to female students selected into a sample that began with the identification of clusters of universities (Koss & Oros, 1982). Studying the sexual victimization of college women, Bonnie Fisher and colleagues used a complex two-stage sample process (Fisher et al., 1999). First, schools were stratified by the size of the total student enrollment and the location of the school and then were selected into the sample using a probability proportionate to the total size of the female student enrollment. Second, female students currently enrolled in the selected schools were randomly selected into the sample.

Nonprobability methods are sometimes used for a variety of reasons, including convenience for the researcher (e.g., women residing in a local women's shelter) or because no sampling frame exists. Among the limitations of nonprobability sampling is that there is no way to guarantee that the sample is representative of the population from which it was drawn, hence generalizability of the results is compromised. The use of inferential statistics is also questionable with nonprobability samples, yet these types of statistics are widely used with nonprobability samples. Many studies in violence against women research are interested in specific subgroups of women and so rely on convenience samples derived from universities, shelters, community centers, or criminal justice settings. For example, Jennifer Cole and colleagues recruited women from court where they came to obtain a protection order against a violent partner and interviewed these women after 12 months to see whether they had been abused by a new partner (Cole, Logan, & Shannon, 2008). Catalina Arata (2000) used a convenience sample of undergraduate female students to select victims of childhood sexual abuse to test a model for predicting adult/adolescent sexual revictimization and post-assault functioning.

Data Collection Strategies

Violence against women studies have relied on various data collection processes that mirror the variety of strategies that exist in the field of behavioral (e.g., anthropology, criminology/victimology, epidemiology, psychology, sociology, women's studies, gender studies) and medical sciences (e.g., medicine, nursing, public health). Interviews and surveys are the most common approaches used to collect violence against women data and can take multiple forms, including face-to-face interviews, self-administered surveys in person or via mail or e-mail, Web-based, computer-assisted (e.g., Audio/Computer-Assisted Personal Interviewing [A/CAPI] or Computer-Assisted Self-Interviewing [CASI]), or telephone-assisted (e.g., Computer-Assisted Telephone Interviewing [CATI]). Observational data on women's experiences of violence are obviously scarce, as many incidents occur in private settings. However, data have sometimes been collected in studies exploring attitudes or responses to violence against women, like in the work directed by Christina DeJong to study police intervention in intimate partner violence cases (DeJong, Burgess-Procter, & Elis, 2008). Case study data are more common and can be used in exploratory research, or in textbooks and training material, to provide readers with illustrations of typical situations. Finally, physical examination has also been used, in the form of sexual assault exams or autopsy reports, to collect forensic evidence (see Du Mont & White, 2007).

No single data collection strategy can address all the various dimensions relevant to the understanding of the scope and nature of violence against women. The choice of data collection strategy stems from the type of data that is needed to answer the research question, balanced by the strengths and weaknesses of the strategy. For example, there are numerous strengths to survey research. Surveys are a relatively cost-effective means of collecting a wide range of information from a large sample of women and can be administered in different languages, which is important for cross-national research. Despite these strengths, there are limitations to survey research as well, such as recall bias, social desirability bias, or survey item wording effects that influence the reliability of the estimates (Fisher, 2009; Fisher & Cullen, 2000; Tourangeau & McNeeley, 2002). Balancing weaknesses of a specific data collection strategy may require researchers to use more than one strategy. This is known as triangulation and is used to guard against the findings being influenced by the means by which the data were collected.

Characteristics of Victimization Surveys

Researchers in many disciplines have administered surveys using a variety of modes to collect information about victimization experiences and related issues from large samples of women. Table 2.2 provides examples of some of the most widely known surveys that have been used in the U.S. and internationally to measure violence against women. A summary of each survey's measures, including forms of violence considered, measurement processes, and reference frame, are highlighted along with research and sampling design, mode of data collection, and data availability.

General Victimization Surveys That Include Measures of Violence Against Women. Table 2.2 describes three national-level studies and one multi-country study that measure violence against women in the context of a general victimization survey. Empirical evidence suggests that general victimization surveys do not accurately measure violence against women, especially gendered violence, because questions consist of a few rather broad screeners that are not behaviorally specific and are often gender neutral. As a result, these types of surveys generally underestimate the scope of violence against women. Commonly introduced as "crime surveys," they do not encompass specific introductory questions to cue respondents to think specifically about victimizations in private settings or those involving male intimate partners, nor do they train interviewers to respond to issues of safety or emotional trauma. Similarly, the International Crime Victims Survey, first administered in 1989 to allow cross-national comparisons of victimization estimates, remains poorly designed to measure violence against women. There is only one gender-neutral question to measure threats or assault and another question to measure sexual offenses in general.

Many crime surveys, for example in the U.S., Canada, or United Kingdom, were redesigned in the beginning of the 1990s to improve the reporting of sexual victimization and violence by intimate partners. Revisions included adding new questions to broaden the spectrum of incidents, improving existing question wording, and introducing new methods of cueing. As a result, the NCVS rates of intimate partner violence almost doubled after the redesign. Another addition was the development of topical supplements administered from time to time (e.g., the Workplace Risk Supplement and the Stalking Victimization Supplement of the NCVS in the U.S. or the British Crime Survey Interpersonal Violence Module). Changes in methods of interviewing that provide respondents greater privacy have also improved disclosure rates. Offering respondents to the British Crime Survey a laptop computer so that they could complete a module of questions in privacy resulted in a tenfold increase in disclosures of sexual assault (Percy & Mayhew, 1997) and doubled disclosures of partner violence (Walby & Myhill, 2001).

Dedicated Violence Against Women Surveys. Specialized surveys on violence against women have grown rapidly in number since the early 1990s. Statistics Canada's Violence Against Women Survey 1993 was the first national survey dedicated to the topic of violence against women. Relying on the combined use of a social science methodology and feminist knowledge of the nature and context of violence against women, it used multiple specific and sensitive questions and relied on behaviorally specific descriptions of acts, rather than single screening questions. In addition, researchers paid particular attention to diverse ethical issues: Female interviewers were specially selected and trained to respond to respondent safety and emotional trauma and were offered emotional support themselves. The survey produced rates of sexual assault and spousal violence twice as high as the generic crime victimization survey (Johnson, 1996). Following the Canadian model, many national surveys on violence against women were conducted in the 1990s (e.g., in the U.S., Australia, New Zealand, Finland, and Sweden).

The latest development in the U.S. is the National Intimate Partner and Sexual Violence

(Text continues on p. 40)

Table 2.2 Examples of Victimization Surveys and Their Measures and Methods

Name of Survey / Sponsor	Forms of Violence Measured[a]	Measurement Process (Reference frame)	Research Design	Sampling Design	Data Collection and Its Administration	Data Availability (URL)
General Victimization Surveys That Include Measures of Violence Against Women						
National Crime Survey/National Crime Victimization Survey U.S. Department of Justice, Bureau of Justice Statistics	Rape Sexual assault Simple assault Aggravated assault	Single screeners using short cues, followed up with an incident report for each occurrence to classify which type of victimization, if any, occurred (within last 6 months)	Panel (3.5-year rotation)	Multistage cluster sample Household members aged 12 and older in all selected housing units ~76,00 households comprising nearly 135,000 persons	Face-to-face interviews (1st and 5th) and telephone interview using CATI Conducted annually since 1973; redesigned in 1992	National Archive of Criminal Justice Data, Interuniversity Consortium for Political and Social Research (www.icpsr.umich.edu)
British Crime Survey British Home Office	Domestic physical violence Sexual violence (i.e., rape, indecent exposure, sexual threats, sexual touching) Stalking	Individual screeners combining multiple acts of violence in their possible answers, followed up with a victim report for each occurrence to classify which type of victimization, if any, occurred (within last 12 months)	Cross-sectional	Stratified multi-stage random sample applied to the Small Users Postcode Address File ~46,000 adults aged 16 and older (with a boost sample of 2,000 16- to 24-year-olds)	Face-to-face interviews; self-completion for the interpersonal violence module First carried out in 1982; annually since 2001. Specific DV/IPV modules not conducted annually	UK Data Archive, University of Essex (www.dataarchive.ac.uk)

Name of Survey Sponsor	Forms of Violence Measured[a]	Measurement Process (Reference frame)	Research Design	Sampling Design	Data Collection and Its Administration	Data Availability (URL)
Canada's General Social Survey on Victimization Statistics Canada	Physical assault Sexual assault Physical and sexual violence, emotional abuse and controlling behavior by spouses Stalking	Screeners for sexual and physical assault by perpetrators other than spouses, followed by an incident report to determine type of victimization (within last 12 months) Spousal violence measured through modified CTS; screener questions only (within last 5 years) Stalking measured through detailed screener questions (within last 5 years)	Cross-sectional	Stratified multi-stage random sample using random digit dialing (RDD) Approximately 25,000 persons aged 15 and older	Telephone interviews using CATI Victimization module administered approximately every 5 years, 1988–2009	Statistics Canada (www.statcan.gc.ca)
International Crime Victims Survey and European Survey on Crime and Safety	Sexual offenses (i.e., grab, touch, assault for sexual reasons) Assaults or threats	Single screeners not behaviorally specific (within past 5 years)	Cross-sectional	RDD to landline telephone numbers or random sample of numbers based on official or telephone	Telephone interview using CATI in 24 countries; face-to-face interviews	Tilburg University (rechten.uvt.nl/icvs)

(Continued)

Table 2.2 (Continued)

Name of Survey Sponsor	Forms of Violence Measured[a]	Measurement Process (Reference frame)	Research Design	Sampling Design	Data Collection and Its Administration	Data Availability (URL)
National agencies for ICVS; consortium led by Gallup Europe, co-financed by the European Commission for EU-ICS				registries in 30 countries and 33 capital or main cities Target sample size: 2,000 interviews in each country	Periodically administered with no fixed timetable. First administration 1989	
Dedicated Violence Against Women Surveys						
The National Violence Against Women Survey National Institute of Justice and Centers for Disease Control and Prevention	Physical violence and threats Sexual violence Emotional abuse and controlling behavior by current/former spouse/live-in partner Stalking Both heterosexual and same-sex violence	Multiple behaviorally specific gate questions leading to perpetrator-specific follow-up questions (lifetime and within last 12 months)	Cross-sectional	RDD to landline telephone numbers within U.S. Census regions 8,000 English- or Spanish-speaking women 18 and older	Telephone interview using CATI One-time administration, 1995–1996	National Archive of Criminal Justice Data, Interuniversity Consortium for Political and Social Research (www.icpsr.umich .edu)

Name of Survey Sponsor	Forms of Violence Measured[a]	Measurement Process (Reference frame)	Research Design	Sampling Design	Data Collection and Its Administration	Data Availability (URL)
The National Intimate Partner and Sexual Violence Surveillance System Centers for Disease Control and Prevention, National Institute of Justice, and Department of Defense	Intimate partner physical aggression, psychological aggression, and sexual violence Sexual assault Stalking Both heterosexual and same-sex violence	Multiple behaviorally specific gate questions leading to perpetrator-specific follow-up questions (lifetime prevalence and within last 12 months)	Cross-sectional	RDD telephone survey of English- and Spanish-speaking persons, aged 18 years and older, living in the United States	Telephone interview using CATI Conducted annually. Funding secured for the first 4 years.	From the Centers for Disease Control and Prevention Field period fall 2009; first full year of data collection 2010
Canada's National Violence Against Women Survey Statistics Canada	Male-only physical violence and threats, sexual assault, and sexual harassment Physical and sexual violence, emotional abuse, and controlling behaviors by current/former male spouse or live-in partner	Behaviorally specific screening questions Modified CTS for intimate partner violence (lifetime since age 16 and within last 12 months)	Cross-sectional	Stratified probability sample of 12,300 women 18 and older	Telephone interview using CATI One-time administration, 1993	Statistics Canada (www.statcan.gc.ca)

(Continued)

Table 2.2 (Continued)

Name of Survey Sponsor	Forms of Violence Measured[a]	Measurement Process (Reference frame)	Research Design	Sampling Design	Data Collection and Its Administration	Data Availability (URL)
The International Violence Against Women Survey *European Institute for Crime Prevention and Control*	Physical violence and threats by intimate partners and other men Sexual violence by intimate partners and other men Emotional abuse and controlling behaviors by current and former intimate partners Childhood physical and sexual victimization	Multiple behaviorally specific screening questions (lifetime since age 16 and within last 12 months)	Comparative cross-sectional	National representative sample of women aged 18 to 69 Country samples ranged from 900 to 25,000	Telephone interviews using CATI or face-to-face interviews One-time administration, 2002–2006	Forthcoming HEUNI (www.heuni.fi)
The WHO Multi-Country Study on Women's Health and Domestic Violence Against Women *World Health Organization*	Male-only intimate partner physical violence, emotional abuse and controlling behaviors Sexual violence Male-only non-partner physical and sexual violence	Multiple behaviorally specific screening questions (lifetime and within last 12 months)	Cross-sectional	Two-stage cluster sampling design of women aged 15 and older One or two sites in each country (i.e., one large city and one province); target sample size: 1,500 women	Face-to-face interviews One-time administration	Data are not publicly available

Name of Survey Sponsor	Forms of Violence Measured[a]	Measurement Process (Reference frame)	Research Design	Sampling Design	Data Collection and Its Administration	Data Availability (URL)
Domestic Violence/Family Conflict Surveys						
National Family Violence Surveys (1975 and 1985) *Family Research Laboratory at University of New Hampshire*	Physical violence and verbal aggression between family members	CTS: 18 items, 8 items involving the use of force and violence (within last 12 months and over the course of the current relationship)	Cross-sectional	National probability sample of 2,143 households in which at least one couple resided (i.e., married or cohabiting couples; January–April, 1976) Repeated in 1985 with 6,002 adult respondents	Face-to-face interviews	1975 dataset: Sociometrics Corporation (www.socio.com) 1985 dataset: UCLA Institute for Social Science Research Data Archives (www.sscnet.ucla.edu/issr/da/)
International Dating Violence Study *International consortium*	Dating partner physical assault, psychological aggression, and sexual coercion	Revised CTS: 12 items, 5-item minor physical violence and 7-item severe physical violence (within last 12 months)	Cross-sectional	Convenience samples of university students, 18 or older, who had been in a dating relationship for at least a month	Self-completion questionnaires distributed in class One-time administration in 16 countries	Available to consortium members (pubpages.unh.edu/~mas2/ID.htm)

a. The exact term used to label the form of violence in the respective survey is noted in this column.

Surveillance System mentioned previously, developed by the CDC in collaboration with the NIJ and the Department of Defense. Since 2009, data on intimate partner, sexual violence, and stalking victimization have been collected annually, using a random-digit-dialing telephone survey of English- and Spanish-speaking persons aged 18 years and older. As sample sizes increase, it is anticipated that stable state-level lifetime prevalence data will be available for both women and men in most states (Centers for Disease Control and Prevention, 2008; Daneshvar, 2009).

The latest development in cross-cultural research on violence against women is international comparative studies. Two examples are the International Violence Against Women Survey (Johnson et al., 2008) and the WHO Multi-Country Study (Garcia-Moreno et al., 2005), which were developed to facilitate comparisons of the prevalence of violence against women across a number of countries. Relying on a standard methodology—identical core questionnaire and similar sampling and administrative procedures—the International Violence Against Women Survey was conducted in 11 countries, of which 9 are included in the comparative publication, while the WHO Multi-Country Study was conducted in 10 countries representing different geographical, cultural, and rural/urban settings.

Domestic Violence/Family Conflict Surveys. Surveys measuring domestic violence have been dominated by the CTS methodology developed by Straus and his colleagues at the University of New Hampshire (Straus, 1979). Under the CTS perspective, domestic violence is seen as a form of family conflict, similar in its circumstances and origins to other forms of family violence. Assaults by husbands on wives are considered the same as assaults by wives on husbands, each episode representing a means of handling interpersonal conflict. The CTS has also been used in studies on dating violence, including the International Dating Violence Study, in which university students in 16 countries were interviewed to compare the extent of violent conflict

resolution strategies among heterosexual couples (Straus, 2004).

The CTS approach has been criticized by many researchers for ignoring the gendered dimension of violence against women, as well as the gendered imbalance of power within intimate relationships (DeKeseredy & Dragiewicz, 2007; Dobash & Dobash, 2004). Because it does not include data on the motives and consequences of violent episodes, studies employing the CTS give rise to the idea of gender symmetry in partner violence. The CTS was revised in 1996 to include sexual coercion and physical injury scales, both of which produce marked gender differences (Straus, Hamby, Boney-McCoy, & Sugarman, 1996).

When looking across surveys in Table 2.2, it is evident that there is much variation across their measures and methods. The effects of the methodological characteristics, along with the definitions of forms of violence, must be taken into account in any cross-survey comparisons of estimates of prevalence, severity, and impacts of violence. Without such consideration, invalid comparisons might be made, resulting in erroneous conclusions about differences or similarities across samples from different surveys.

Ethical Considerations in Studying Violence Against Women

Standard ethical guidelines in social science research require researchers to minimize risks and maximize benefits of participation, ensure anonymity and confidentiality, ensure free and informed consent to participate, and ensure that the benefits of research are fairly distributed (Palys & Atchison, 2008). These requirements take on special meaning when researchers interview women about violence.

There is now agreement among violence against women researchers that the following principles should be built into the research design at the outset, to ensure that any study involving interviewing women about violence is conducted in a safe and ethical manner (see Ellsberg & Heise, 2005, p. 36):

- safety considerations for respondents both during and following the interview;
- safety considerations for the research team when studies are conducted in face-to-face settings;
- protecting confidentiality of information and anonymity of respondents;
- ensuring informed consent;
- minimizing and responding to emotional distress of respondents and interviewers;
- accessibility of data collection efforts for women with disabilities and deaf women, as well as language, cultural, and religious minorities;
- data storage and accessibility; and
- minimizing underreporting of violence.

These guidelines apply to all interview situations, whether the study involves a specialized survey dedicated to violence against women, a module added to a crime victimization survey, or any other type of data collection instrument.

Safety Considerations

Violent partners are often very controlling about women's contacts with others, so they may react with violence if they know a woman has been talking to outsiders about their actions, or has participated in a research study, especially one focused on violent victimization. Guidelines produced by the WHO to minimize risk to respondents recommend interviewing only one woman per household, to reduce the number of people who are aware of the nature of the study; not broadcasting the nature of the study to the wider community; and not conducting research on violence with men in the same areas where women have been interviewed (Ellsberg & Heise, 2005, p. 38).

Most specialized studies on violence against women that use probability samples take the approach of introducing the survey in the initial stages as a survey on a more general topic, such as women's personal safety (e.g., the NVAWS in the U.S. and the International Violence Against Women Survey) or women's health and life experiences (e.g., WHO Multi-Country Study) so as not to alert abusive family members to the nature of the questions to follow. Any letters or telephone messages inviting participation in the survey must be framed in language that will not jeopardize the safety of participants (Fontes, 2004). Interviewers also must be trained to ensure that they are attuned to safety issues, place a priority on conducting interviews in private, and are skilled at adjusting the timing and location of interviews in response to participants' concerns about their safety. In telephone surveys, interviewers can provide participants with a toll-free telephone number so that they can call back if they have to interrupt the interview for any reason (Johnson, 1996). In face-to-face settings, interviewers can quickly switch to a fake questionnaire if they are interrupted by family or community members, or can undertake to interview other family members simultaneously with a less sensitive questionnaire to guard the privacy and safety of the women responding (Andersson et al., 2009).

The safety of interviewers comes into play when studies are conducted in face-to-face settings and interviewers must travel to unsafe locations. It is common practice to provide interviewers with escorts as they conduct their work.

Confidentiality, Anonymity, and Informed Consent

Free and informed consent means ensuring that respondents have sufficient knowledge early in the research process about the purpose of the research, what their participation will involve, and possible risks or costs entailed in their participation. In order for participants' consent to be given freely, researchers must not use their authority to coerce abused women into participating, as might be the case when the interviews take place in a shelter or other service setting. Researchers must be particularly aware of religious, cultural, and racial hierarchies that might make some women feel obligated to provide the interviewer with the information she requests (Fontes, 2004). If incentives are provided, it must be made clear that the incentive will not be revoked if respondents discontinue the interview or refuse to answer any questions (Fontes, 2004).

Researchers grapple with the implications of advising respondents in the initial stages about the sensitive topics that will be addressed because it is feared that such explicit information may serve to deter participation and put abused women in danger. Most state the focus of the survey in general terms at the outset, then describe the nature of the questions more explicitly immediately prior to sections containing questions about violence and remind respondents of the voluntary nature of their participation (Ellsberg & Heise, 2005).

Access to and control of all personal information must be rigorously protected against breaches of confidentiality. All data must be presented in a format that is sufficiently aggregated so that no individual can be identified. Case study information should be presented anonymously, with critical details changed so that the information cannot be traced back to a specific individual or setting.

Minimizing and Reacting to Emotional Distress

Emotional distress is a natural reaction to traumatic experiences, and it is likely that, for some women, reliving experiences of violence through participation in a research project can be upsetting. The need to guard against emotional distress must inform the design of survey questions and the training of interviewers. Since intimate partner violence and sexual violence are stigmatizing experiences, and recalling these experiences may be traumatic or humiliating, researchers must ensure that questions are framed in nonjudgmental language and that interviewers approach these questions with sensitivity. Interviewers must be trained to be aware of the potential effects of these questions and to be empathetic in their responses.

The research team has an ethical obligation to provide information to respondents about sources of support in the local community who are available to respond to emotional distress. Depending on the community, this support might include crisis centers, crisis hotlines, shelters for abused women and their children, religious groups, women's groups, and other community-based support. In face-to-face settings, interviewers must provide this information in a format that is easy to conceal (e.g., a small card that includes contact numbers).

Emotional trauma is not uncommon among interviewers after hearing about women's experiences over the course of the research study, particularly if interviews trigger memories of their own experiences of abuse. Research directors have an ethical obligation to provide regular opportunities for interviewers to debrief with supervisors and with one another, and to stimulate discussion about stress-reducing activities throughout the course of the study, in order to prevent burnout and attrition (Campbell, 2001).

In addition to physical and emotional harm, other harms that might accompany participation in a research study include economic harm (if the woman separates from the abuser), social harm (damage to the reputation of the woman or her family), or political harm (if participation is seen as a betrayal of one's cultural community); these risks can be minimized by planning and consulting with the local community (Fontes, 2004).

Selection and Training of Interviewers

Many ethical considerations, such as those related to the safety of respondents, minimizing distress, and maximizing disclosures, cannot be assured without the careful selection and training of interviewers. As most violence against women is perpetrated by males, priority should be given to selecting female interviewers who are knowledgeable and comfortable discussing these issues, who are empathetic and nonjudgmental, and who have good interviewing skills. In-depth training should cover the following issues (Johnson et al., 2008):

- gender-based violence;
- how violence affects women;
- societal myths concerning women or violence and how these myths might lead women to make certain decisions (such as not reporting to police or seeking help);
- ways to ensure safety for respondents and for the interviewers themselves;
- responses to emotional trauma, techniques of stress management and self-care; and
- ways to encourage honest disclosures of violence.

Accessibility of Data and Presentation of Research Results

The final set of ethical considerations relates to the accurate interpretation of research results and the maximization of the benefits. As a general ethical principle, researchers must ensure that the benefits to be realized from the research study are fairly distributed across society. This requires that groups are equally represented or that underinclusion does not deny them access to the benefits of the research. This becomes particularly important in diverse societies where participation may be restricted for certain groups on the basis of language, disability, or lack of sensitivity to cultural or religious norms. Certain groups may not receive the benefits of the research if their perspectives and concerns are not adequately represented.

Related to this is the principle that researchers must strive to minimize underreporting of violence. This means building on and drawing from the growing body of experience and the scientific literature in the field. Experiences of sexual and intimate partner violence are likely to be underreported unless special attempts are made to build rapport with respondents, incorporate behaviorally specific and sensitive question wording, and ensure privacy and safety. It is unethical to implement poorly designed studies that underestimate levels of violence because of the harm this may do to service agencies working to prevent violence and provide support to victims. Experts agree that more accurate results will be obtained by avoiding emotionally laden and unreliable terms such as "violence," "abuse," "assault," or "rape" and employing behaviorally specific terms that provide many opportunities for disclosure and by cueing respondents to include various victim-offender relationships (Fisher & Cullen, 2000).

Maximizing the benefits of the research also means reporting results accurately, disseminating results widely to advocates and policy makers, providing access to the data to other researchers, and making the shortcomings of the research known (Ellsberg & Heise, 2005).

Conclusion

Researchers from a variety of disciplines have developed a range of quantitative and qualitative measures and methods that they employ to obtain valid and reliable estimates of violence against women, to better inform the study of its nature, and to rigorously evaluate prevention and treatment interventions. There is no single measure or method that can answer all research questions, no agreed-upon best measure of providing the most accurate estimates or one-size-fits-all evaluation method. Rather, a creative combination of measures and methods coupled with ethical considerations is needed not only in the research planning stages, but also throughout the data collection and post-data collection phases, as well as the interpretation, presentation, and publication of the findings.

References

Andersson, N., Cockcroft, A., Ansari, N., Omer, K., Chaudhry, U. U., Khan, A., et al. (2009). Collecting reliable information about violence against women safely in household interviews: Experience from a large-scale national survey in South Asia. *Violence Against Women, 15,* 482–496.

Arata, C. M. (2000). From child victim to adult victim: A model for predicting sexual revictimization. *Child Maltreatment, 5,* 28–38.

Bachman, R., & Saltzman, L. E. (1995). *National Crime and Victimization Survey. Violence Against Women Survey: Estimates from the redesigned survey.* Washington, DC: U.S. Department of Justice, Bureau of Justice Statistics.

Basile, K. C., & Saltzman, L. E. (2002). *Sexual violence surveillance: Uniform definitions and recommended data elements.* Atlanta, GA: Centers for Disease Control and Prevention.

Boyle, D. J., & Hassett-Walker, C. (2008). Individual-level and socio-structural characteristics of violence: An emergency department study. *Journal of Interpersonal Violence, 23,* 1011–1026.

Campbell, R. (2001). *Emotionally involved: The impact of researching rape.* New York: Routledge.

Centers for Disease Control and Prevention. (2008). Intimate partner violence: Data sources. Retrieved October 14, 2009, from http://www.cdc.gov/violenceprevention/intimatepartnerviolence/datasources.html.

Cole, J., Logan, T. K., & Shannon, L. (2008). Women's risk for revictimization by a new abusive partner: For what should we be looking? *Violence and Victims, 23*(3), 315–330.

Daigle, L. E., Fisher, B. S., & Guthrie, P. (2007). The reoccurrence of victimization: What researchers know about its terminology, characteristics, causes, and prevention. In R. C. Davis, A. J. Lurigo, & W. G. Skogan (Eds.), *Victims of crime* (3rd ed., pp. 211–232). Thousand Oaks, CA: Sage.

Daneshvar, M. I. (2009). Proposed data collections submitted for public comment and recommendations. *Federal Register, 74,* 7695–7696.

DeJong, C., Burgess-Procter, A., & Elis, L. (2008). Police officer perceptions of intimate partner violence: An analysis of observational data. *Violence and Victims, 23,* 683–696.

DeKeseredy, W. S. (2000). Current controversies on defining nonlethal violence against women in intimate heterosexual relationships: Empirical implications. *Violence Against Women, 6,* 728–746.

DeKeseredy, W. S., & Dragiewicz, M. (2007). Understanding the complexities of feminist perspectives on woman abuse: A commentary on Donald G. Dutton's *Rethinking domestic violence. Violence Against Women, 13,* 874–884.

Department of Economic and Social Affairs, Statistics Division. (2006). *The world's women 2005: Progress in statistics.* New York: United Nations.

Dobash, R. P., & Dobash, R. E. (2004). Women's violence to men in intimate relationships: Working on a puzzle. *British Journal of Criminology, 44,* 324–349.

Du Mont, J., & White, D. (2007). *The uses and impacts of medico-legal evidence in sexual assault cases: A global review.* Geneva, Switzerland: World Health Organization.

Ehrensaft, M. K., Moffitt, T. E., & Caspi, A. (2006). Is domestic violence followed by an increased risk of psychiatric disorders among women but not among men? A longitudinal cohort study. *American Journal of Psychiatry, 163,* 885–892.

Ellsberg, M., & Heise, L. (2005). *Researching violence against women. A practical guide for researchers and activists.* Geneva, Switzerland: World Health Organization.

Fisher, B. S. (2009). The effects of survey question wording on rape estimates: Evidence from a quasi-experimental design. *Violence Against Women, 15,* 133–147.

Fisher, B. S., & Cullen, F. J. (2000). Measuring the sexual victimization of women: Evolution, current controversies, and future research. In D. Duffee (Ed.), *Criminal justice 2000. Measurement and analysis of crime and justice* (pp. 317–390). Washington, DC: U.S. Department of Justice, National Institute of Justice.

Fisher, B. S., Cullen, F. J., & Turner, M. G. (1999). *Extent and nature of sexual victimization of college women: A national-level analysis.* Washington,

DC: U.S. Department of Justice, National Institute of Justice.

Fisher, B. S., Daigle, L. E., Cullen, F. J., & Turner, M. G. (2003). Reporting sexual victimization to the police and others: Results from a national-level study of college women. *Criminal Justice and Behavior, 30*, 6–38.

Fontes, L. A. (2004). Ethics in violence against women research: The sensitive, the dangerous, and the overlooked. *Ethics and Behavior, 14*, 131–174.

Garcia-Moreno, C., Jansen, H. A. F. M., Ellsberg, M., Heise, L., & Watts, C. (2005). *WHO multi-country study on women's health and domestic violence against women: Initial results on prevalence, health outcomes, and women's responses.* Geneva, Switzerland: World Health Organization.

Garner, J. H., & Maxwell, C. D. (2009). Prosecution and conviction rates for intimate partner violence. *Criminal Justice Review, 34*, 44–79.

Goodwin, R. (1999). *Personal relationships across cultures.* London: Routledge.

Hofner, M.-C., Burquier, R., Huissoud, T., Romain-Glassey, N., Graz, B., & Mangin, P. (2009). Characteristics of victims of violence admitted to a specialized medico-legal unit in Switzerland. *Journal of Forensic and Legal Medicine, 16*, 269–272.

Jaquier, V., & Fisher, B. S. (2009). Establishing the content validity of threats, physical violence and rape against women across two national surveys. *International Journal of Comparative and Applied Criminal Justice, 33*, 249–271.

Jaquier, V., Fisher, B. S., & Killias, M. (2006). Cross-national survey designs: Equating the National Violence Against Women Survey and the Swiss International Violence Against Women Survey. *Journal of Contemporary Criminal Justice, 22*, 90–112.

Johnson, H. (1996). *Dangerous domains: Violence against women in Canada.* Toronto: Nelson.

Johnson, H., Ollus, N., & Nevala, S. (2008). *Violence against women: An international perspective.* New York: Springer.

Jordan, C. E. (2009). Advancing the study of violence against women: Evolving research agendas into science. *Violence Against Women, 15*, 393–419.

Kilpatrick, D. G. (2004). What is violence against women? Defining and measuring the problem. *Journal of Interpersonal Violence, 19*, 1209–1234.

Kilpatrick, D. G., Acierno, R., Resnick, H. S., Saunders, B. E., & Best, C. L. (1997). A 2-year longitudinal analysis of the relationships between violent assault and substance use in women. *Journal of Consulting & Clinical Psychology, 65*, 834–847.

Kilpatrick, D. G., Edmunds, C. N., & Seymour, A. K. (Eds.). (1992). *Rape in America: A report to the nation.* Arlington, VA: National Victim Center.

Koss, M. P., Abbey, A., Campbell, R., Cook, S., Norris, J., Testa, M., et al. (2007). Revising the SES: A collaborative process to improve assessment of sexual aggression and victimization. *Psychology of Women Quarterly, 31*, 357–370.

Koss, M. P., & Gidycz, C. A. (1985). The Sexual Experiences Survey: Reliability and validity. *Journal of Consulting and Clinical Psychology, 53*, 442–443.

Koss, M. P., Gidycz, C. A., & Wisniewski, N. (1987). The scope of rape: Incidence and prevalence of sexual aggression and victimization in a national sample of higher education students. *Journal of Consulting and Clinical Psychology, 55*, 162–170.

Koss, M. P., & Oros, C. (1982). Sexual Experiences Survey: A research instrument investigating sexual aggression and victimization. *Journal of Consulting and Clinical Psychology, 50*, 455–457.

Koss, M. P., & White, J. W. (2008). National and global agendas on violence against women: Historical perspective and consensus. *American Journal of Orthopsychiatry, 78*, 386–393.

Lohr, S. L. (1999). *Sampling: Design and analysis.* Pacific Grove, CA: Duxbury.

McMullin, D., Wirth, R., & White, J. (2007). The impact of sexual victimization on personality: A longitudinal study of gendered attributes. *Sex Roles, 56*, 403–414.

Miller, J. (2008). *Getting played: African American girls, urban inequality, and gendered violence.* New York: New York University Press.

Moracco, K. E., Runyan, C. W., & Dull, L. (2003). *Violence against women: Synthesis of research for public health policymakers.* Washington, DC: National Institute of Justice.

Palys, T., & Atchison, C. (2008). *Research decisions: Qualitative and quantitative perspectives* (4th ed.). Toronto: Thompson Nelson.

Paterson, L., & Bechhofer, F. (2000). *Principles of research design in the social sciences.* New York: Routledge.

Percy, A., & Mayhew, P. (1997). Estimating sexual victimization in a national crime survey: A new approach. *Studies on Crime and Crime Prevention, 6,* 125–150.

Russell, D. E. H. (1982). *Rape in marriage.* New York: MacMillan.

Sabina, C., & Straus, M. A. (2008). Polyvictimization by dating partners and mental health among U.S. college students. *Violence and Victims, 23,* 667–682.

Saltzman, L. E. (2004). Issues related to defining and measuring violence against women. Response to Kilpatrick. *Journal of Interpersonal Violence, 19,* 1235–1243.

Saltzman, L. E., Fanslow, J. L., McMahon, P. M., & Shelley, G. A. (2002). *Intimate partner violence surveillance: Uniform definitions and recommended data elements.* Atlanta, GA: Centers for Disease Control and Prevention.

Straus, M. A. (1979). Measuring intrafamily conflict and violence: The Conflict Tactics Scales. *Journal of Marriage and the Family, 41,* 75–88.

Straus, M. A. (2004). Prevalence of violence against dating partners by male and female university students worldwide. *Violence Against Women, 10,* 790–811.

Straus, M. A., Hamby, S. L., Boney-McCoy, S., & Sugarman, D. B. (1996). The Revised Conflict Tactics Scales: Development and preliminary psychometric data. *Journal of Family Issues, 17,* 283–316.

Testa, M., VanZile-Tamsen, C., & Livingston, J. A. (2007). Prospective prediction of women's sexual victimization by intimate and nonintimate male perpetrators. *Journal of Consulting & Clinical Psychology, 75,* 52–60.

Tjaden, P. (2004). What is violence against women? Defining and measuring the problem. A response to Kilpatrick. *Journal of Interpersonal Violence, 19,* 1244–1251.

Tjaden, P., & Thoennes, N. (2000). *Full report of the prevalence, incidence, and consequences of violence against women: Findings from the National Violence Against Women Survey.* Washington, DC and Atlanta, GA: U.S. Department of Justice, National Institute of Justice, and U.S. Department of Mental and Human Services, Centers for Disease Control and Prevention.

Tourangeau, R., & McNeeley, M. E. (2002). Measuring crime and crime victimization: Methodological issues. In J. V. Pepper & C. V. Petrie (Eds.), *Measurement problems in criminal justice research [Workshop summary]* (pp. 10–42). Washington, DC: National Academies Press.

Walby, S., & Myhill, A. (2001). New survey methodologies in researching violence against women. *British Journal of Criminology, 41,* 502–522.

Walker, L. E. (1979). *The battered woman syndrome.* New York: Harper & Row.

Weiss, K. G. (2009). "Boys will be boys" and other gendered accounts: An exploration of victims' excuses and justifications for unwanted sexual contact and coercion. *Violence Against Women, 15,* 810–834.

Chapter Authors

 **Véronique Jaquier**, Ph.D., is a Lecturer and a senior researcher at the University of Lausanne, Ecole des sciences criminelles. Trained in social psychology and criminology in Switzerland and the United States, she has taught classes in victimology, violence against women, victims' rights, and counseling. Her latest publications include a coauthored book questioning stereotypes of women's violence and violence against women, and her dissertation focused on the relevance and validity of a cross-cultural approach to violence against women. Using her multidisciplinary perspective, Dr. Jaquier's current research includes violence against women, in particular methodological issues arising in the measurement of victimization and comparative research, and issues surrounding the policing and sentencing of domestic violence cases and the relevance of international experiences for the Swiss context.

Holly Johnson is an Associate Professor of Criminology at the University of Ottawa, Canada. Her interest and involvement in research on violence against women spans two decades. She was principal investigator of Statistics Canada's first national survey on violence against women, which pioneered a methodology for interviewing women about their experiences of sexual assault and intimate partner violence, and is a collaborator on the International Violence Against Women Survey. She has authored numerous peer-reviewed journal articles, books, and statistical reports on this topic. She is coauthor of *Violence Against Women in Canada: Research and Policy Perspectives* with Professor Myrna Dawson and *Violence Against Women: An International Perspective* with Natalia Ollus and Sami Nevala. She served as expert advisor to the Secretary-General's report on violence against women and the World Health Organization panel on primary prevention of sexual violence and intimate partner violence. She is a member of the UNECE Task Force on Violence Against Women Surveys and the UN Expert Group on Indicators of Violence Against Women. She is also co-investigator of the Canadian Observatory on the Justice System's Response to Intimate Partner Violence.

Bonnie S. Fisher is a Professor in the Division of Criminal Justice at the University of Cincinnati and a senior research fellow at the Criminal Justice Research Center. She coedited the *Encyclopedia of Victimology and Crime Prevention* (Sage, 2010) with Professor Steven Lab and coauthored *Unsafe in the Ivory Tower: The Sexual Victimization of College Women* (Sage, 2010) with Professors Francis Cullen and Leah Daigle. She also coedited *Campus Crime: Legal, Social, and Political Perspectives* (2nd ed.) and *Violence at Work: Causes, Patterns, and Prevention.* Her latest research includes examining the extent and nature of sexual victimization and alcohol- and drug-enabled sexual assault among college women, explaining the nature of recurrent sexual victimization, and advancing the measurement of violence against women from a cross-national perspective. Among her current projects is finishing a book-length manuscript with Professor John Sloan, titled *The Dark Side of the Ivory Tower: Campus Crime as a Social Problem* (2011).

Personal Reflection

Ronet Bachman

Conducting research on measurement issues was inevitable for me because I went to graduate school at the University of New Hampshire and was part of the Family Research Laboratory (FRL), which at the time was the stage for the extremely contentious controversy over the gender symmetry results found by the Conflict Tactics Scale (CTS) in the Family Violence Surveys (Straus, Gelles, & Steinmetz, 1980). Every summer when the FRL hosted a conference on family violence, researchers and practitioners would converge on Durham, NH, and sessions more often than not reached crescendos, with raw emotion pouring through the seams of the conference center. The graduate students working at the conferences, including myself, would often need debriefing therapy sessions for weeks afterward—and I am totally serious about this! Of course, everyone in attendance was personally committed to abolishing violence in general and violence in the family in particular. The problem arose between the parties in agreeing on how best to measure it.

As I was finishing a post-doctoral fellowship at the FRL, the Bureau of Justice Statistics was in the process of redesigning its National Crime Victimization Survey (NCVS) to better measure incidents of victimization, including rape and violence perpetrated by family members. What a challenge! It was all I needed to pack my bags and accept a position at the Bureau of Justice Statistics. At that time, however, the government wouldn't approve the use of words like penis, anus, and vagina, so the questions retained global references to "rape," instead of being behavior specific, which we knew was more likely to result in disclosure by respondents. Fortunately, with the passage of the Violence Against Women Act in 1994, Congress mandated the federal government to more accurately measure this violence. Enter the Violence Against Women and Men Surveys that were conducted by Patricia Tjaden and Nancy Thoennes. I was fortunate to have the opportunity to be a part of the negotiations that occurred while this survey instrument was being designed. And for this survey, Congress also wanted stalking victimization to be added, which provided an additional challenge. What is the best way to measure stalking? Should you count as stalking notes that are left on a car at night or only count incidents that involve some direct verbal or physical contact? Should a respondent be classified as a stalking victim if she is only somewhat fearful of harm by the perpetrator or count her only if she is very fearful? The estimates obtained, of course, are significantly affected by these decisions. As you can see, measurement is extremely important.

Since my time as an undergraduate, I have also realized that teaching students about the ethical dimensions of the research process is also extremely important because, despite the presence of Institutional Review Boards (IRB) at all universities and federal agencies, conducting ethical research ultimately resides with individual researchers. When I was a psychology major nearly 30 years ago, we conducted experiments using so-called volunteer students who had to participate in at least two experiments a semester to pass their Introduction to Psychology course. Is this truly volunteering? My main interest back then was to determine the effects of alcohol on certain behaviors, and I had no problem getting students drunk to do this; in fact, I don't recall ever having to provide justification for any of my experiments.

Of course, times have changed a bit, but there is still a great deal of variability in the extent to which researchers protect their human subjects. For example, imagine interviewing a 12-year-old girl who tells you that she was raped by her uncle in the last 6 months. Do you have the responsibility to report this to someone? According to most state guidelines and the federal government, researchers are typically not covered under the category of "mandatory reporters," so what do you do? If she becomes distraught and emotional recalling the event, do you have the responsibility to provide her with a rape crisis hotline number? You may be surprised to learn that the National Crime Victimization Survey still does not provide such information, but the National Violence Against Women and Men Surveys did. Both are federally funded surveys. The main point is that despite all of the legal protections provided to research participants, there is still a great deal of variability in how similar projects are conducted.

Reference

Straus, M. A., Gelles, R. J., & Steinmetz, S. K. (1980). *Behind closed doors: Violence in the American family.* New York: Doubleday/Anchor.

CHAPTER 3

Assessing Violence Against Women in Practice Settings

Processes and Tools Practitioners Can Use

Sherry Hamby and Sarah L. Cook

Important, potentially life-saving decisions must be made about violence against women every day. Victims, and the professionals who help them, face many difficult questions. Does this trauma victim in the emergency department need assistance beyond attending to her physical injuries? Should this perpetrator be put on probation or sentenced to jail? How can this victim become safer? Are the children in this family being exposed to and traumatized by the abuse of their parent? As even these few examples demonstrate, a variety of providers will interact with victims, perpetrators, and others exposed to violence. These include victim advocates, health care providers, law enforcement and judicial personnel, batterers' group facilitators, child protective workers, and teachers.

A variety of tools have been developed to aid these professionals, to promote community safety, and to better meet the needs of victims, perpetrators, and their family members. In this chapter, the tools are organized into five categories.

The first category is screening tools, which are designed to help professionals identify women who have been victimized but may not be recognized as victims without some initiative on the part of providers. Logically, identification of victims and perpetrators must occur first, through screening, victim help seeking, or reports to law enforcement. The second category is dangerousness assessments. These can be used with either perpetrators or victims to help identify the highest-risk cases and provide some guidance on the likely severity of future violence. Third, there are safety planning tools, which are primarily for victims seeking help. Although safety planning tools are often used independently of other instruments, they should be used after the dangerousness assessment has taken place (either formally or informally). The level of risk helps determine the best safety planning actions. The final two categories cover newer instruments that are designed to meet additional needs: tools to measure children's exposure to intimate partner violence, and integrated approaches that help victims of violence against women incorporate other life issues into safety planning.

Screening Tools: Identifying Victims and Perpetrators

Screening: What Is It and Who Does It?

Professionals in a variety of settings use universal screening protocols to detect potential problems, provide immediate intervention or treatment if necessary, and refer clients or patients for further assessment or treatment. The term *universal* means that the protocol is used with all individuals who come into a service setting, regardless of presumed risk. Theoretically, screening is an efficient method for identifying violence against women that, if left undetected, could cause significant harm. Screening protocols are usually brief, inexpensive, and designed to be acceptable and inoffensive to patients and clients. For example, pediatricians universally screen children entering kindergarten for vision problems. The examination is brief, does not require elaborate or expensive equipment, and parents rarely object. Vision screens have a low threshold for referral because the consequences of a false positive (i.e., making a referral when none is actually needed) are not harmful, particularly in comparison to the consequences of making a false negative (i.e., missing a child truly in need of further evaluation). Pediatricians are an excellent point of contact for universal screening because school systems require a physician's exam for all children entering school.

In the late 1980s and early 1990s, the American Medical Association and related organizations, such as the American College of Obstetricians and Gynecologists, responded to calls by advocates and violence against women experts to implement universal screening protocols for sexual assault and domestic violence (Stevens, 2007). In 1992, the Joint Commission on the Accreditation of Healthcare Organizations mandated that all hospitals must develop and implement policies and procedures to identify and refer victims of abuse (Daugherty & Houry, 2008). The military services also encourage routine screening (Gielen et al., 2006).

Yet, approximately 20 years later, few women today are ever screened for violence against women. In a nationally representative sample of women aged 18 and older, only 7% reported they have ever been asked about domestic or family violence by a health care professional (Klap, Tang, Wells, Starks, & Rodriguez, 2007). One study documents a 32% rate of screening for sexual assault in a convenience sample (Littleton, Berenson, & Radecki Breitkopf, 2007).

Low screening rates for violence against women may not be surprising. Due to several barriers, universal screening programs for adults are difficult to implement for many health conditions. For example, although health care providers urge adults to schedule annual physical exams, many adults do not, for a variety of reasons (e.g., lack of health insurance, lack of time, and perception of invulnerability). In contrast to children, adults are not generally excluded from any particular benefit due to the lack of an annual physical exam. Health care providers have surmounted some of these challenges to screening for some health conditions. In lieu of waiting for individuals to come into offices and clinics for annual examinations, health professionals take screening protocols to public settings frequented by large numbers of people. For example, blood pressure cuffs to screen for hypertension are now available at most pharmacies, grocery stores, and fire stations.

Challenges and Benefits of Implementing Screening

In the case of violence against women, some of the same general barriers exist, and additional barriers exacerbate the challenges of universally implementing screening. These factors conspire to make screening protocols difficult to implement and to maintain. For example, annual gynecological examinations are one opportunity for violence against women screening. Not all women get these exams, however, and those who do may receive the exam from a general practitioner, an internist, or an obstetrician-gynecologist who is not trained to screen for violence or who views screening as less important than other goals. Second, patients who have experienced physical or sexual assault may be apprehensive of a gynecological exam, which can be highly personal and invasive. The physical and psychological demands of the examination may trigger disturbing memories and heighten feelings of vulnerability (e.g., Halligan, Michael, Wilhelm, Clark, & Ehlers, 2006).

Third, sexual and physical victimization carry significant social stigma. Feeling shame, and perhaps blame, women may be reluctant to discuss their experiences (Tjaden & Thoennes, 2000). Revealing abuse may trigger secondary victimization, if a professional minimizes or denies a woman's experience, violates confidentiality, or if medical documentation of abuse results in the loss of health insurance. Women who are mothers may fear disclosure could lead to loss of custody of their children or legal complications for their abusers, who are fathers and sole providers in many families (Cook, Woolard, & McCollum, 2004).

Fourth, physicians may be uncomfortable asking necessary questions due to lack of training and evidence-based guidelines, personal unease, as well as personal or family history of victimization, particularly in the case of sexual victimization (Daugherty & Houry, 2008; Stevens, 2007). Plus, physicians may be unsure of the most helpful ways to respond should a woman disclose abuse experiences. They may fear that women will go "underground," particularly if states have mandatory reporting laws. Contrary to these fears, evidence indicates few patients report they would not be likely to seek care in an emergency department. In fact, more women reported they would be *more* likely to seek care because of these laws (Daugherty & Houry, 2008).

Goals of Screening

Despite these obstacles, primary health care fields such as family practice and internal medicine and many specialties such as pediatrics, emergency medicine, and oncology continue to encourage physicians to screen for violence against women. The Family Violence Prevention Fund published *National Consensus Guidelines* (2004) on identifying and responding to domestic violence victimization in health care settings to help establish protocols in a range of settings and professional disciplines. More recently, the Centers for Disease Control and Prevention (CDC) issued a compendium, *Intimate Partner Violence and Sexual Violence Victimization Assessment Instruments for Use in Healthcare Settings* (Basile, Hertz, & Back, 2007). This compendium lists and compares numerous screening instruments and provides the text of the instruments. We describe how advocates and practitioners can use this compendium later in the chapter.

The most obvious reason to screen for violence against women in health care settings is to detect it, provide necessary treatment, and make appropriate referrals. A second, less obvious, goal of screening is to inform the evaluation of the patient's presenting problems and treatment outcomes. For example, sexual violence is associated with a host of physical, reproductive health, and mental health problems including chronic pain, unintended pregnancy, risky sexual behavior, substance use, anxiety, depression, and sleep disturbances (Stevens, 2007). Understanding the potential role of sexual violence in these problems is critical for a comprehensive understanding of a patient's presenting problems. In relation to understanding treatment outcomes, consider the case of a woman who appears to be unable to adhere to a treatment regimen. Understanding that her inability to adhere is due to a batterer withholding or blocking access to ongoing medical care will lead to a different strategy for improving adherence than if her inability is due to lack of health insurance.

Screening protocols are not limited to health care settings. Currently, it is possible to find discussions or evaluations of screening protocols for domestic violence in employee assistance programs (Falk, Shepard, & Elliott, 2002), community mediation centers (Clemants & Gross, 2007), oral health (Love, Gerbert, Caspers, Bronstone, Perry, & Bird, 2001), mental health (Samuelson & Campbell, 2005), public health partner notification systems (Klein, 2001), the military (Gielen et al., 2006), and child and adult welfare systems (Rivers, Maze, Hannah, & Lederman, 2007). Stevens (2007) recommends additional venues in which to screen for sexual violence, including primary health care and family planning service settings, substance abuse treatment programs, and Veterans Administration facilities.

As in health care settings, screening in some of these settings has (or would have) purposes beyond detection, intervention, and referral for domestic violence. For example, in community mediation centers, one purpose of screening is to identify and understand the potential impact of domestic violence on the outcome of mediation. In partner notification systems, the goal is to ensure an STD/HIV-positive patient's safety after abusive sexual partners are notified of possible infection. In child welfare systems, a goal is to detect threats to a child's well-being due to domestic violence against a caregiving parent, usually a mother.

Screening for violence against women may not seem controversial; however, not all professionals embrace the practice. For example, despite widespread policies encouraging universal screening, not all health care experts support it. The U.S. Preventive Services Task Force (USPSTF) is an independent panel organized by the U.S. Department of Health and Human Services' Agency for Healthcare Research and Quality. It consists of experts in primary care and prevention who systematically review evidence of effectiveness for clinical preventive services and develop recommendations. In 2004, the USPSTF found "insufficient evidence to recommend for or against specific screening instruments to detect family or intimate partner violence"

(Nelson, Nygren, McInerney, & Klein, 2004, p. 388). Specifically, the panel found limited or conflicting evidence to support universal screening as a method for identifying risk for current or future abuse. In addition, the panel found no evidence that screening reduces harm to women and no evidence that it increases risk to women. As a result, they could not determine the balance of benefits and harms of the practice.

Regardless, some assert that screening in health care settings should be done because "it is the right thing to do" (Chapin & Mackie, 2007; Thompson et al., 2000). Others cite the potential harm that could result from not screening (Stevens, 2007). Failing to detect the direct and indirect health, mental health, behavioral, and interpersonal effects of violence against women could result in the continuation of abuse, more frequent emergency room visits, and even death (Daugherty & Houry, 2008). For example, in one inner-city emergency department, women who screened positive for domestic violence were 11 times more likely to experience physical violence four months later than women who screened negative (Houry et al., 2004). The debate about the effectiveness of screening raises an important question: How should screening be evaluated? Is accuracy of detecting current or future abuse the only outcome of interest? Is the absence of negative outcomes or increase in help seeking important? Moreover, is it the screening instrument itself or the complete protocol that should be evaluated? These questions need further systematic evaluation.

To date, only one study has attempted to examine whether screening hurts or helps victims of domestic violence (Houry et al., 2008). In a methodologically rigorous study of male and female emergency department patients, no adverse events, such as a partner's interference with the screening, occurred for any of the 26% of patients who disclosed abuse. The protocol in this study used a computer kiosk. Some patients in this study also participated in follow-up interviews, either in person or by telephone. Again, no patients reported any injuries or increase in abuse resulting from their participation in the study. Among those patients who lived in the local police district, there was no increase in the number of 911 calls for domestic violence in the six months following the emergency department visit. Thus, across three different methods (i.e., computer, interview, and public records) to assess harm due to screening, none was detected.

Screening Protocols and Screening Instruments: What Is the Distinction?

A screening protocol is a *system* of identifying, intervening with or treating, and referring patients or clients. Protocols increase the likelihood that a certain practice is implemented consistently in any particular setting. For example, the AVDR protocol includes *asking* about abuse, providing *validating* messages, *documenting* presenting signs, and *referring* victims to services (Love, 2000). This rather straightforward protocol might be appropriate for settings such as dental offices where patients interact with a small number of professionals. In settings where patients encounter many professionals, protocols may consist of multiple components. For example, after carefully evaluating needs in an emergency department, Waller, Hohenhaus, Shah, and Stern (1996) developed a seven-step protocol with two screening points. The needs assessment showed that a protocol would require close coordination among emergency room staff, hospital police, the hospital social work department, and the domestic violence agency. More recently, computer-assisted protocols have been developed and evaluated (Houry et al., 2008; Rhodes, Drum, Anliker, Frankel, Howes, & Levinson, 2006). Patients are asked to complete a computer-assisted screening installed in kiosks in waiting rooms. If victimization is indicated, the computer issues a report to flag the patient's file, telling the physician to conduct further assessment. Model protocols (e.g., Ambuel, Hamberger, & Lahti, 1996) and guidance (Family Violence Prevention Fund, 2004) are available, but protocols need to be adapted for the constraints, needs, and logistics of specific settings.

Few studies examine systemic factors that influence the adoption and consistent use of screening protocols (Thurston & Eisener, 2006).

Provider characteristics, such as the sense that one has the skills to screen a patient, fear of offending patients, and safety concerns, can also influence screening behavior. Existing survey data are strengthened by findings from an experimentally evaluated, intensive intervention to improve domestic violence identification and management in primary care clinics. The intervention consisted of training, frequent newsletters, clinic educational rounds, and environmental support and cues such as posters in examination areas, cue cards, and the routine use of health questionnaires containing questions about domestic violence. Compared to control clinics, the intervention increased intervention clinics' provider self-efficacy and decreased fear of offending and safety concerns at 9 and 21 months later (Thompson et al., 2000). At nine months, documentation in charts of providers asking about domestic violence was 3.9 times more likely in intervention clinics than in control clinics.

A screening instrument is a *tool* used in one component of a protocol. Screening instruments are usually one of the first components of most protocols. Screening instruments contain scientifically evaluated and field-tested questions. In contrast to protocols, which may need to be adjusted for specific settings, available screening instruments can often be used as published. As noted above, a number of screening instruments are available for professional use (Basile et al., 2007). We excerpted from the CDC compendium those instruments with published data on accuracy and present these in Table 3.1. Note that most of these instruments have been developed in health care settings. Although some include questions about sexual assault, none of the instruments are specific to sexual assault. Below, we discuss the features of these instruments that may guide practitioners' selections.

Screening Instruments: Evaluating Available Choices

Selection of an instrument should be guided by its accuracy. Other characteristics to consider

Table 3.1

Screening Instrument	Characteristics	Administration Method	Populations Studied	Sensitivity/ Specificity
Abuse Assessment Screen (AAS; (McFarlane, Parker, Soeken, & Bullock, 1992)	5 items assess frequency and perpetrator of physical, sexual, and emotional abuse. Body map to document area of injury.	Clinician administered	Abused pregnant and nonpregnant African American, Hispanic, and white women in health and prenatal clinics and emergency departments	Using the ISA as the standard: sensitivity = 93%; specificity = 55%
HITS Tool for Intimate Partner Violence Screening (Sherin, Li, Zitter, & Shakil, 1998)	4 items assess the frequency of IPV	Self-report or clinician administered	Female patients in family practice settings; male patients in health care settings	Using CTS or ISA as standard: English version, sensitivity = 86%– 96%; specificity = 91%–99%. Using WAST as standard: Spanish version, sensitivity = 100%; specificity = 86%. Using CTS as standard: English version (men only), sensitivity = 88%; specificity = 97%.
Ongoing Violence Assessment Tool (Ernst, Weiss, Cham, Hall, & Nick, 2004)	4 items assess ongoing physical and emotional IPV	Self-report	Women and men in emergency departments; Tested on African Americans, Hispanics, and whites	Using ISA as standard: sensitivity = 86%–93%; specificity = 83%–86%
Partner Violence Screen (PVS; (Feldhaus et al., 1997)	3 items assess physical IPV in the last year and current safety	Clinician administered	Women and men in emergency room settings in the United States and Canada	Using the ISA and CTS as standard (respectively): sensitivity = 64.5%/71%; specificity = 90.3%/84.4%

Screening Instrument	Characteristics	Administration Method	Populations Studied	Sensitivity/ Specificity
Women Abuse Screening Tool– Short (WAST; Brown, Lent, Brett, Sas, & Pederson, 1996)	2 items assess tension in relationship and how respondent and partner work out arguments	Self-report	Abused and nonabused English speaking women in clinical health care settings and women's shelters	Using criterion cut-off score of 1: sensitivity = 91.7%; specificity = 100%
WAST–Spanish version (Fogarty & Brown, 2002)	8 items assess physical, sexual, and emotional IPV	Self-report	Abused and nonabused Spanish-speaking women in clinical health care settings and women's shelters	Using items 5 & 7 and comparing to WAST: sensitivity = 89%; specificity = 94%
Women's Experience of Battering (Smith, Tessaro, & Earp, 1995)	10 items assess emotional IPV or battering	Self-report	African American and white women in family practice settings	Using ISA as standard: sensitivity = 89%; specificity = 91%

Source: Adapted from Basile et al. (2007).

Note: No instruments with the sole purpose of screening for sexual violence have been published; CTS = Conflict Tactics Scales; IPV = intimate partner violence; ISA = Index of Spouse Abuse; WAST = Woman Abuse Screening Tool.

are acceptability to potential patients and clients, feasibility, and cultural sensitivity. All of these characteristics are important. The most accurate and valid instrument is useless if it is long, expensive, and not culturally sensitive. If instruments and protocols are to be used consistently in environments with great demands on resources, the screening instruments need to be brief, inoffensive, and inexpensive.

Accuracy is measured in terms of *sensitivity* and *specificity*. Sensitivity refers to the extent that an instrument correctly identifies true cases (in this instance, a woman with a victimization history). Specificity refers to an instrument's ability to exclude non-cases (i.e., women without victimization histories). Sensitivity and specificity are expressed in terms of percentages. For example, a screening tool with 95% sensitivity means

that the instrument correctly identified 95% of women who had, indeed, experienced domestic violence but missed 5% of women who should have been detected. A tool with 90% specificity means that the instrument correctly classified 90% of women with no history as nonvictims but incorrectly classified 10% of women with no history as victims.

To determine sensitivity and specificity, a second measurement of "caseness" is needed against which the screening instrument is compared. In the medical and mental health fields, the gold standard for comparisons is a clinical diagnosis. In the absence of a gold standard in the violence against women field, many of the screening instruments are assessed relative to a lengthier and more specific instrument such as the Conflict Tactics Scale (Straus, Hamby, Boney-McCoy, &

Sugarman, 1996) or the Index of Spouse Abuse (Hudson & McIntosh, 1981). For example, the HITS and the Abuse Assessment Screen (AAS) for Use in Pregnancy were both compared to the CTS and ISA for detecting women who had experienced abuse (see Table 3.1). For women, the HITS had sensitivity rates from 86% to 96% and specificity from 91% to 99%. For men, sensitivity using the CTS was 88% and specificity was 97%. Instruments with high sensitivity and specificity are desirable because they effectively target resources to those in need.

Screening instruments also need to be feasible. By definition, they should be *brief.* Brevity is hard to achieve when accuracy is also important. Nevertheless, the majority of screening instruments in the compendium contain fewer than 10 questions (see Table 3.1). Questions in these instruments are often structured and direct. For example, the HITS asks four specific questions: How often does your partner (1) physically hurt you, (2) insult or talk down to you, (3) threaten you with harm, and (4) scream or curse at you? The HITS focuses solely on the frequency of victimization. In contrast, the WAST combines direct questions (e.g., the frequency of being hit, kicked, or pushed) with two questions about relationship quality (the level of tension in the relationship and how arguments are worked out). The WAST also includes a question known as a "safety" item: Do you ever feel frightened by what your partner says or does?

A second dimension of feasibility is cost. Screening methods can be self-administered in pencil and paper format at little to no cost or administered verbally by a nurse during a triage or clinical interview with minor costs to staff time. Computerized methods have up-front equipment and ongoing maintenance costs, but evidence supporting use of computer kiosks makes a compelling case for the use of technology despite its costs. Computer screening increases the odds of patient-physician communication about domestic violence by 75% (Rhodes et al., 2006). If discussion leads to informed treatment and referral to effective services that reduce the costs resulting from unaddressed trauma, the cost of a few computer terminals is a worthwhile investment.

Some advocates have encouraged the sole use of "safety" questions such as "Do you feel safe at home?" "Do you ever feel afraid of your partner?" or "How are things at home?" instead of direct questions, as a way to ensure acceptability to patients. The rationale is that mothers may be reluctant to answer direct questions, especially when children are present, or that direct questions are too sensitive and may offend some (Zink, Levin, Putnam, & Beckstrom, 2007). Although these are valid concerns, comparisons between safety questions and structured screening instruments illustrate that safety items are less accurate (Feldhaus, Koziol-McLain, Amsbury, Norton, Lowenstein, & Abbott, 1997; Peralta & Fleming, 2003; Zink et al., 2007). Similarly, routine social service interviews covering domestic violence, health behaviors, and psychological risks failed to detect many cases of remote and recent domestic violence that the Abuse Assessment Screen (AAS) detected in a sample of women seeking prenatal care (Norton, Peipert, Zierler, Lima, & Hume, 1995). Recent data show women have higher rates of satisfaction with visits to emergency rooms when they are asked about domestic violence (Rhodes et al., 2006) and are comfortable with being screened for sexual victimization history (Littleton et al., 2007).

Cultural sensitivity is a final, but critical, dimension to consider (Betancourt, Green, Carrillo, & Ananeh-Firempong, 2003). In the best circumstances, culturally sensitive screening instruments should be developed by those with expertise in measurement development *and* diverse populations, although it may be difficult to surmise this information from research reports. A second issue is whether an instrument has been used *successfully* in diverse populations defined by race, ethnicity, geographic location, age, gender, or socioeconomic status. Just over one third of the instruments in the compendium have been used with women and men with minority racial or ethnic status in the U.S. Not all screening instruments that have been used with racial or ethnic minority populations have been evaluated with respect to accuracy, but the few that have been appear to work similarly in majority and minority groups. Unfortunately, few studies evaluate the accuracy of instruments according to dimensions of diversity other than race or ethnicity.

The cultural sensitivity of those who conduct or respond to information from screening instruments is also relevant. Optimally, screening would not be based on women's obvious individual characteristics, such as socioeconomic class, race, ethnicity, age, or sexual orientation. Evidence for biases in screening practices is mixed, and the interpretation of it is difficult due to noncomparable study methods. For example, convenience samples of medical residents show no bias in the prevalence of screening with respect to the race of the patient (white vs. African American women) or socioeconomic status (Baig, Shadigian, & Heisler, 2006). Medical chart reviews in an inner-city hospital showed that women presenting with medical and trauma-related illnesses and those who came to the emergency department in daylight hours were more likely to be screened than those with psychiatric illness or those who presented during the night shift. No differences were found with respect to race, employment status, or gender of health care provider (usually a nurse; Larkin, Hyman, Mathias, D'Amico, & MacLeod, 1999). In the Rhodes et al. (2006) study mentioned above, the equal risk of domestic violence at both urban and suburban hospitals, coupled with the low rates of physician-patient communication about intimate partner violence at the suburban hospital, raise a red flag signaling a bias against addressing intimate partner violence with affluent white women. In fact, physicians were 70% less likely to ask women in a suburban emergency department about experience with abuse than women in the urban setting. Weeks, Ellis, Lichstein, and Bonds (2008) documented that health care practices serving predominantly African American and lower-income women screened patients at higher rates, but that the differential rates were due to practice-related factors rather than patient characteristics. In Littleton and colleagues' (2007) study of sexual assault screening, women with less education and Latina women, particularly those who were Spanish speaking, were less likely to report having been screened. Clearly, culturally sensitive screening is a topic ripe for additional study and research.

Dangerousness Assessment and Recidivism Risk: Identifying the Most Threatening Cases

Dangerousness Assessment of Batterers

Few batterers serve long jail sentences. Many perpetrators of intimate partner violence who are identified by law enforcement are either not prosecuted at all; are punished with probation, fines, or diversion to batterers programs; or are released early on parole (Hilton & Harris, 2009a). State and federal governments do not have the resources to incarcerate batterers indefinitely or even keep them under prolonged supervision through probation or parole. Even if they did, these would be excessive punishments for some who perpetrate intimate partner violence. Although there is considerable debate about the appropriateness of various judicial responses to partner violence (Hilton & Harris, 2009a), current practices have spawned an interest in discriminating between more and less dangerous offenders, with the aim of keying interventions to the level of risk.

This is one of the main impetuses behind the development of dangerousness assessments. The dangerousness assessments can help a victim to recognize the extent of the danger her partner poses to her so she can make plans that take into account this estimated risk. They can also help identify the risk of future offending by perpetrators and the appropriateness of various interventions and punishments.

Can Dangerousness Assessment Predict the Lethality of Perpetrators?

There has been keen interest in reducing the greatest danger, intimate partner homicide. Although not all intimate partner murderers have prior law enforcement contact, many do. It would be ideal if those offenders could be identified and kept off the streets and if victims could know with some precision whether their lives are in danger.

Unfortunately, predicting lethality turns out to be extraordinarily difficult. The two main reasons for this are (1) the rarity of intimate partner homicide and (2) the commonness of most lethality predictors.

The Rarity of Intimate Partner Homicide. Of course, in some senses, intimate partner homicide is not rare at all—even one homicide is one too many. Further, the United States has by far the highest homicide rate, including intimate partner homicide, of any industrial democracy (Hemenway, Shinoda-Tagawa, & Miller, 2002). Nonetheless, from a statistical point of view, even in the U.S., intimate partner homicide has a very low base rate in the total population, with about 1,500 such murders annually (Fox & Zawitz, 2007), or about 1.15 per 100,000 people (age-adjusted rate; Paulozzi, Saltzman, Thompson, & Holmgreen, 2001).

Intimate partner homicide also has a low base rate even in comparison to the portion of the population who perpetrate domestic violence. Although precise estimates are hard to obtain, the best data indicate that each year, approximately 2 million people perpetrate partner violence in the U.S. alone (Straus & Gelles, 1990; Tjaden & Thoennes, 2000). Intimate partner murderers even make up a small proportion of people arrested for physical or sexual assault each year, which in the U.S. is about 1.8 million (U.S. Department of Justice, 2008). Further, some of these murderers have no prior record of police contact. Trying to identify a few hundred murderers among the millions who perpetrate intimate partner violence or the millions arrested

for assault is like trying to find the proverbial needle in a haystack.

High Frequency of Risk Factors for Intimate Partner Homicide. How can the most dangerous perpetrators be identified? Researchers have tried to answer this question by finding characteristics that are common among intimate partner murderers or, to put it even more precisely, more common among intimate partner murderers than among perpetrators of nonlethal intimate partner violence (Campbell et al., 2003). It turns out that there are many such characteristics. Those most commonly mentioned on dangerousness assessments include prior victimization, batterer's drug and alcohol problems, batterer's obsessiveness and jealousy, batterer's threats to kill the victim or her children, batterer's access to (AAS) and familiarity with weapons, batterer's violence outside the home, stalking, batterer's suicidal ideation and behavior, partners are separated, or victim is fleeing (Laing, 2004; Websdale, 2000).

Although it is useful that there are so many characteristics, the predictability of lethality remains poor. This is because few, if any, intimate partner murderers have *all* of these characteristics, and some may have *none*. Further, and even more problematic for the goal of predicting lethality, *many* nonhomicidal people have these characteristics, too. Substance abuse, violence against acquaintances and strangers, and mental health issues are common in the general population and even more common in the population of people who have been arrested for intimate partner violence or are seeking treatment for violence. Yet, the vast majority of these people, despite their many difficulties, will never murder.

Statistically, this issue is known as the problem of false positives. Most people who possess many, or even all, of the characteristics listed on dangerousness assessments will never become murderers. They will be falsely labeled as "positive" for lethality risk. To the extent that lethality risk is the reason they are being punished more severely—by long jail sentences, for example—these harsher punishments are undeserved.

On the other hand, some murderers may appear to be low risk on dangerousness assessments. These are false negatives; they are incorrectly being labeled as not lethal when they are. Because lethal behavior is rare and the personal and behavioral characteristics of murderers are also commonly found in the general population, lethality assessments have, in statistical parlance, both low sensitivity (they are not good at detecting the problem of lethality) and low specificity (they are not good at making sure that whatever they detect is the specific feature one is trying to assess, in this case, lethality).

A Switch From Lethality Prediction to Dangerousness Assessment

Because of the tremendous, and probably insurmountable, problems in predicting lethality, some authors of dangerousness assessment measures now focus on dangerousness, that is, the future likelihood of perpetrating severe, injurious violence. This can be done with much higher accuracy, largely because severe violence has a much higher base rate. Some estimates of severe intimate partner violence are as high as 4% of the U.S. population, versus the 0.001% for intimate partner homicide (Straus & Gelles, 1990).

This makes severe intimate partner violence roughly 4,000 times more common than intimate partner homicide, which means that false positives can be greatly reduced because the phenomenon is not so rare. Dangerousness assessment measures can be acceptably accurate as predictors of severe intimate partner violence risk to use in real-life decision making. It should be noted, however, that it is statistically impossible for any measure to achieve 100% accuracy. There is always error. A careful reader may also have noted that another way to increase the accuracy of dangerousness assessment measures would be to identify a personality, behavioral, or perhaps even genetic characteristic that is almost always associated with dangerous (or even lethal) batterers, but seldom

found among the rest of the population and even rare among the most dysfunctional segments of the population. That has not yet been done but is theoretically possible. Unfortunately, one still does sometimes see authors make inappropriate claims regarding lethality assessment (e.g., McCloskey & Grigsby, 2005), referring to very common individual characteristics as "red flags."

It is important to remember that, unless there is the identification of a rare and highly correlated trait, assessments of lethality are not sufficiently accurate for use with individual perpetrators or victims.

Dangerousness Assessment: Some Choices

Assessing Whether Batterers Will Kill. Barbara Hart (1990) developed one of the first checklists of risk factors to consider when evaluating the homicide potential of an offender. She does emphasize that "assessment is tricky and never fool-proof," although her emphasis is, nonetheless, on identifying increased homicide risk and the need for emergency intervention following a domestic violence incident. The factors she developed have not been empirically tested (Laing, 2004). Some of them, such as threats of more serious violence, are common to many risk assessments, while others are unique, such as "centrality of the partner." A brief description is provided for each item, such as this definition of centrality of the partner:

> A man who idolizes his female partner, or who depends heavily on her to organize and sustain his life, or who has isolated himself from all other community, may retaliate against a partner who decides to end the relationship. He rationalizes that her "betrayal" justifies his lethal retaliation.

Although used less often today than more formally developed instruments, the Hart checklist is important as one of the first widely known efforts to identify the riskiest perpetrators.

Danger Assessment Scale and Danger Assessment Scale 2. Campbell's (1986) Danger Assessment Scale (DAS) is probably the best-known and most widely used of all dangerousness assessment instruments. Unlike many of the dangerousness assessment instruments described in this chapter, which are designed for working with perpetrators, the DAS is designed to be completed by the victim to assist in her safety planning. It was based on existing literature and consultation with advocates and other experts on battering. The first portion of the instrument measures the frequency and severity of battering by having a victim complete a calendar of the past year. In the revised version (DAS2), the second part contains 20 items that ask about various risk factors (e.g., Does he own a gun? Has he ever threatened or tried to commit suicide? Campbell, 2005).

The DAS has been used in a number of empirical studies and was generally found to distinguish between higher and lower risk groups (Laing, 2004). It is even statistically correlated with lethality risk (Campbell et al., 2003). Like all scales, however, it does not have perfect predictive validity and so must be used in individual cases with caution.

Spousal Assault Risk Assessment. The Spousal Assault Risk Assessment (SARA) is intended to facilitate structured information gathering to enhance clinical judgments (Kropp, Hart, Webster, & Eaves, 1995). This approach avoids purely statistical approaches to risk prediction because of the problems described in the sections above, while also making professional analyses more systematic. It contains 20 items that are scored for their presence or absence in three general areas: criminal history, social functioning, and mental health. One positive feature of these items is that none are general demographic characteristics that apply to many nonviolent individuals. Completing the SARA requires an ability to make specific judgments regarding psychological disorders, and it is therefore most appropriately used by trained clinicians (Kropp & Hart, 2004).

The SARA items have been shown to discriminate between batterers versus other types of offenders and between repeat and nonrepeat offenders (Kropp & Hart, 2000). As with other dangerousness assessments, however, despite these significant associations, many batterers may be classified incorrectly. For example, 32% of nonrepeat offenders were labeled as high risk, while 40% of repeat offenders were labeled as moderate or low risk in this same study.

Brief Spousal Assault Form for the Evaluation of Risk. Like the SARA, this tool is also designed to facilitate structured professional judgment. Kropp and Hart (2004) developed the Brief Spousal Assault Form for the Evaluation of Risk (B-SAFER) to meet the need for a shorter instrument that can be used by those without extensive mental health training. It has been validated in several samples, including ones based in Canada, Sweden, and Hong Kong (Au, Cheung, Kropp, Yuk-Chung, Lam, & Sung, 2008; Kropp & Hart, 2004). The B-SAFER victim interview contains 10 sections. The sections are evenly split between those pertaining to the known history of spousal assault (Has your partner ever threatened to hurt or kill you?) and general psychosocial adjustment (Has the use of drugs or alcohol caused problems in your partner's social functioning?). Preliminary studies found that police using B-SAFER recommended more management strategies for higher-risk offenders and that the B-SAFER discriminated batterers from other counseling patients (Au et al., 2008; Kropp & Hart, 2004).

Ontario Domestic Assault Risk Assessment. The Ontario Domestic Assault Risk Assessment (ODARA) is designed to estimate the risk of wife assault recidivism. It was developed primarily to aid law enforcement decisions about the appropriate level of custody following arrest (Hilton & Harris, 2009b; Hilton, Harris, Rice, Lang, Cormier, & Lines, 2004). The ODARA contains 13 items using information that will usually be available to law enforcement, such as "Has a prior sentence to a term of 30 days or more" (Hilton et al., 2004). The ODARA has been shown in multiple samples to help distinguish recidivists from nonrecidivists (Hilton & Harris, 2009b; Hilton et al., 2004). It is about as accurate as other scales that have been similarly validated.

Severe Intimate Violence Partner Risk Prediction Scale. The Severe Intimate Violence Partner Risk Prediction Scale (SIVIPAS), developed in Spain, is one of the few (along with B-SAFER) to be validated on a European sample (Echeburúa, Fernández-Montalvo, de Corral, & López-Goñi, 2009). It is designed to be completed by a law enforcement or service provider, and it contains a checklist of factors, such as "Existence of physical violence that can cause injuries," which can be scored as present or absent. Its stated goals are to predict both femicide and severe violence, although it has only been validated on its ability to distinguish severe violence from less severe violence. Echeburúa et al.'s validity study presents a good example of the challenges of prediction. At their recommended cutoff of 10 or more positives out of 20 items, only 48% of "severe" batterers are correctly identified and almost 1 in 5 perpetrators of minor violence are wrongly identified as severe abusers.

Given this fairly low accuracy, one troubling aspect of this scale is its emphasis on immigrant status as a primary risk factor (Echeburúa et al., 2009). This is a good example of the potential harm of using very common characteristics as indicators of risk. Spain, like other industrialized countries, has a very large immigrant population. The use of demographic characteristics as risk markers could lead to the institutionalization of patently discriminatory practices and lead to thousands of perpetrators being treated more harshly than they deserve.

Other Measures to Assess Offenders. A number of relatively informal and clinically oriented guides have been developed over the years. Although few of these are standardized and most are not widely used, they do address some important issues and thus perhaps deserve a brief mention. McCloskey and Grigsby (2005) have synthesized several sources to develop a checklist to help identify the "primary victim"

and "primary batterer" in a relationship. These can be useful in cases of same-sex relationships or when both parties have used violence and are claiming to be the primary victim. Identifying the primary victim is important because the batterer may be exaggerating his victimization or minimizing his violence in an attempt to get out of trouble. Many domestic violence agencies, state attorney's offices, and other organizations have developed a variety of guidelines, sometimes based on the above measures, to help assess offenders (for a review, see Websdale, 2000).

Risk of Recidivism Among Rapists

Risk assessment is also performed with sexual assault offenders. The focus here is primarily on the risk of criminal recidivism, that is, the likelihood that the offender will rape again. Rates of sexual reoffending are as high as 30% to 60% in some studies, especially those with longer follow-up periods (Långström, 2002). This means both that identifying likely reoffenders is an important public safety issue and that such identification is statistically possible. Current research indicates that the use of formal assessment instruments improves identification over clinical judgment alone (Hanson & Thornton, 2000). As with tools designed for intimate partner violence perpetrators, rape recidivism instruments are far from perfectly accurate and will assign some perpetrators to a higher risk category than they apparently deserve (based on best available information about reoffending). Similarly, all of these scales also have the potential to miss individuals at risk for serious reoffending. Recidivism prediction remains an inexact science. On the positive side, there has been some important progress made in this area in the last 10 to 15 years.

Assessing Rape Recidivism Risk: Available Choices

There are several instruments designed to identify higher-risk sex offenders. Most of them emphasize demographic, and sometimes personality, characteristics associated with recidivism. Some of the better validated instruments are described briefly below. Most of these have fair to good predictive ability. Although frequently used instruments such as the Static-99 have more validity information than some, existing evidence suggests they are all similarly and moderately effective in predicting sexual recidivism (Langton, Barbaree, Seto, Peacock, Harkins, & Hansen, 2007). Most important, they also generally outperform unstructured professional judgments (Hanson & Morton-Bougon, 2009).

Static-99 and Static 2002. The Static-99 and its revision, the Static 2002, are the most commonly used measures of sexual recidivism. The Static-99 is a 10-item actuarial instrument designed for use with adult males. The Static 2002 is a revision that led to the removal of two items and the addition of six others. They include items such as whether the perpetrator has ever assaulted "any unrelated victims" or "any male victims." It is moderately associated with recidivism and commonly used in much of the English-speaking world (Hanson & Thornton, 1999; Langton et al., 2007).

Rapid Risk Assessment for Sexual Offense Recidivism. The Rapid Risk Assessment for Sexual Offense Recidivism (RRASOR) is one commonly used tool, popular perhaps because it is a very simple scale composed of only four items. The items were selected from a literature review of risk factors and chosen because they are easily scored from official records: prior sexual offenses, age less than 25, extrafamilial victims, and male victims (Hanson, 1997). In a direct comparison of the predictive accuracy of four different measures using a Swedish sample of sex offenders, only the RRASOR performed better than chance in the identification of sexual recidivists (Sjöstedt & Långström, 2002). Nonetheless, the association with recidivism is modest, with an average correlation of only .27 across several samples (Hanson, 1997). Hanson recommends that it be used with other relevant information, particularly deviant sexual preferences.

Violence Risk Scale-Sexual Offender Version. The Violence Risk Scale-Sexual Offender Version (VRS-SO) assesses recidivism risk and helps identify treatment goals. It includes 24 items, 7 that measure "static" variables, which are demographic variables such as age at release, and 17 that measure "dynamic" items, which are primarily personality characteristics and behaviors, such as a sexually deviant lifestyle and poor insight, but also includes a rating of community support. Preliminary data suggest at least some of these dynamic items, such as cognitive distortions, can be changed with a subsequent reduction in recidivism risk (Olver, Wong, Nicholaichuk, & Gordon, 2007).

General Crime Recidivism Measures Used With Sex Offenders. There are also a number of instruments that were not developed specifically for sex offenders that are nonetheless sometimes used with them, for example, the Violence Risk Appraisal Guide (Webster, Harris, Rice, Cormier, & Quinsey, 1994) and the Psychopathy Checklist–Revised (Hare, 1991). In general, however, these instruments (1) do not predict sexual recidivism as well as general criminal recidivism, (2) do not always predict sexual recidivism better than chance, and (3) do not predict sexual recidivism as well as specific sex offender measures (Hanson, 1997; Hanson & Thornton, 2000; Sjöstedt & Långström, 2002). With more instruments available that are specifically designed to assess sexual, not just criminal, recidivism, it is probably preferable to use the more specific instruments when possible.

Summary: Assessing Dangerousness and Recidivism Risk

Although existing validity studies show that risk assessments for violence against women are correlated with future criminal behavior, it is equally true that existing studies also show that many individuals are mislabeled as high or low risk. Some validity studies have set rather easy criteria to establish validity. For example, simply discriminating between batterers and nonbatterers is not particularly difficult and is far from the goal of identifying the most dangerous batterers. Despite the huge life-saving potential of accurate lethality prediction, it is unlikely that this is an attainable goal. Intimate partner homicide is just too rare, and many of the characteristics that are most closely associated with homicide risk, such as unemployment, simply describe far too many low-risk perpetrators.

The following should be remembered regarding risk assessment (Laing, 2004). First, it should never be relied upon exclusively. Second, it is important not to privilege "scientific" questionnaire findings over women's own assessments of the risk of reassault or escalation. Third, often full information on all risk factors is not available. Finally, many research findings may be based on incomplete knowledge of reoffending (Hilton & Harris, 2009b). For example, if only arrest data are used to represent recidivism, then assaults not known to the police will not be included.

Safety Planning: Helping Victims Avoid Battering and Batterers

Safety plans are the most popular tools to help victims. They serve the goal of risk management, which is a common coping response to all kinds of bad events, not just violence against women. The goal is to help victims minimize the risk of future violence, especially severe and injurious violence. In this respect, safety plans are counterparts to dangerousness assessment measures, which are a type of risk assessment.

Most existing safety plans vary from dangerousness assessments in important respects, however. First, safety plans focus much more on the environment of the victim and specific steps she can take. These typically include strategies that can be used during assaults, such as avoiding the kitchen and its knives or other rooms with weapons. Safety plans often include strategies to implement at other times, such as placing copies of important documents in a safe place so it will be easier to establish a new residence.

Second, dangerousness assessments were developed almost exclusively by researchers who sought to identify quantitative correlates of homicidal and other severe violent behavior. Safety plans, on the other hand, largely emerged from a qualitative approach and are based on the experiences of advocates working with victims. The earliest safety plans were developed about 20 years ago (Hart & Stuehling, 1992), but there have been few quantitative evaluations of them, although victim advocacy itself has been found to be helpful. Many dangerousness assessments are copyrighted instruments that cost money to use, but many safety plans are available for free on the Internet and elsewhere to maximize their use by victims in need.

Safety Plans: Some Available Choices

Personalized Safety Plan. Although adapted from a plan developed by the San Diego Attorney's office in 1990, this plan and its many variants have been disseminated widely because of Barbara Hart's personal activism as legal director for the Pennsylvania Coalition Against Domestic Violence (Hart & Stuehling, 1992). The plan is organized into several sections that have influenced many other safety plans: safety during a violent incident, safety when preparing to leave, safety in my own residence, safety with a protection order, safety on the job and in public, safety and drug or alcohol use, safety and my emotional health, and items to take when leaving.

Safety during a violent incident includes practicing which doors or windows to use during an escape and teaching children how to call the police. Preparing to leave can involve leaving extra clothes with a friend and keeping a small amount of money on hand at all times. Safety in a victim's residence, with a protection order, on the job and in public all involve steps to keep the batterer away and unaware of the victim's whereabouts, such as changing locks and providing employers with copies of restraining orders. Safety as it relates to drug use and mental health involves attending to one's personal needs and identifying sources of social support and help. Each of these sections has a place where a victim can write in her own strategies. The plan is phrased in the first person, for example, "I can use a different bank and take care of my banking at hours different from those I used when residing with my battering partner."

National Coalition Against Domestic Violence Safety Plan. The National Coalition Against Domestic Violence Safety Plan (NCADV, 2009) is an important source of information and resources for women and advocates all over the country. Their relatively brief safety plan has two main sections, "If you are still in the relationship" and "If you have left the relationship." Recommendations for those still in an abusive relationship include widely accepted suggestions such as avoiding rooms with weapons during arguments and developing a code word or sign to use to let family, coworkers, and others know when to call for help. The NCADV recommends that women who have left the relationship change their phone number and vary their routine, among other suggestions. Making copies of important papers and documenting any contact with the batterer are also emphasized.

National Center for Victims of Crime Safety Plan. The National Center for Victims of Crime Safety Plan (1998) is widely available because it is the one used by the National Domestic Violence Hotline. It includes the following sections: Personal Safety with an Abuser, Getting Ready to Leave, General Guidelines for Leaving an Abusive Relationship, and After Leaving the Abusive Relationship. The section on personal safety, like the similar section in the NCADV, emphasizes what to do during an attack and includes more specific suggestions on avoiding injuries and practicing escape with children. Other sections contain suggestions on getting important papers, minimizing the abuser's access to information on the victim's whereabouts, getting a restraining order, and other steps. This plan also suggests acquiring job skills and setting aside money.

Web-Based Materials. Today, one of the first places that many victims look for help is the Internet. Several prominent nonprofit organizations, as well as hundreds of shelters, state domestic violence coalitions, government or law enforcement agencies, and other organizations and individuals, have posted safety plans and other content for victims online. One advantage of this emerging phenomenon is that access to information is much improved: It is available anywhere there is an Internet connection, 24 hours a day, for free. Disadvantages include the challenges of navigating all of this information and evaluating the relative quality of different materials.

Examples of Web-based resources are those provided by the American Bar Association and a group known as AARDVARC (an acronym of "An Abuse, Rape, and Domestic Violence Aid and Resource Collection"). The American Bar Association materials are noteworthy for the details on the legal aspects of victimization, with three sections: Using the Law to Help You, Criminal Proceedings, and Be Safe at the Courthouse. Their plan not only suggests getting a restraining order, as many other plans do, but also makes concrete suggestions about what a victim can ask the judge to do, such as give her possession of the car, and other steps she can take, such as request notification when the batterer is released from jail. The AARDVARC plan has a few notable features. For example, it is one of the very few that has any detailed recommendations on financial safety and independence or issues related to children.

Summary: Safety Plans

There are literally thousands of safety plans available, most of which include very similar content. Almost all safety plans emphasize ways to avoid serious injury during an attack and steps that can be taken to make it easier and safer to leave, especially regarding documentation and avoiding future contact with the batterer.

It is surprising that there has been very little formal evaluation of the effectiveness of safety plans. They have received much less formal validation than have most dangerousness assessment or rape recidivism tools, perhaps in part because court fees and judicial mandates have supported the development of more formal assessments for perpetrators. Unfortunately, this lack of information leaves the usefulness of safety plans an open question. They remain, however, a staple of victim advocacy.

Children's Exposure: Identifying Children's Involvement in Parents' Intimate Partner Violence

Nationally representative survey data suggest that as many as 1 in 6 children will witness physical assault between their parents (Hamby, Finkelhor, Turner, & Ormrod, 2010). Children who are exposed to intimate partner violence suffer adverse psychological consequences (Kitzmann, Gaylord, Holt, & Kenny, 2003; Lang & Stover, 2008; Wolfe, Crooks, Lee, McIntyre-Smith, & Jaffe, 2003) and are increasingly becoming the focus of interventions themselves. Not all children are equally affected by exposure to intimate partner violence, however, and there is a need to identify not only whether or not children have been exposed, but also details of the extent of the exposure (Edleson, Ellerton, Seagren, Kirchberg, Schmidt, & Ambrose, 2007). Most tools to measure children's exposure to intimate partner violence are simply adaptations of questionnaires that assess for the presence of intimate partner violence or questionnaires that assess children's exposure to violence more generally, and they may include questions that capture reports of violence between parents as well (see Edleson et al., 2007 for a review).

Child Exposure to Domestic Violence Scale. The Child Exposure to Domestic Violence Scale (CEDV) is one of the few scales developed explicitly to assess child exposure to intimate partner violence. It has also been explicitly developed for use in clinical and other applied settings. In 45 items, the CEDV assesses exposure to various forms of intimate partner violence and also assesses how the youth were exposed (e.g., hearing the violence while it was happening). Subsequent items ask about the child's responses to the incident, such as calling for help. Although this is a relatively new scale, early psychometric results are promising (Edleson, Shin, & Armendariz, 2008). Rates of exposure were high in a clinical sample; more than half of the children knew their mother was sometimes hurt by her partner. A variety of responses were also very commonly reported, including trying to physically stop fights (42%) and calling for help (48%). Three CEDV response items were adapted for a nationally representative survey and were also commonly reported in that community sample, ranging from 24% (calling for help) to 50% (yelling at parents) of exposed youth (Hamby et al., 2010; see http://www.mincava.umn.edu/cedv/ for the most recent version of the questionnaire, a user's manual, and other supporting materials).

Integrated Approaches: Incorporating Multiple Life Issues Into Safety Planning

The CEDV provides a good example of the recent increased focus on issues other than the victim's physical danger (Edleson et al., 2008). The unfortunate reality is that batterers not only threaten victims' personal physical safety, they also often threaten other family members and friends, make it difficult to work or establish financial independence, and can threaten legal problems, such as reporting the victim to law enforcement or trying to take full custody of their children. These types of constraints have a substantial impact on the decision making of intimate partner violence victims (Hamby & Gray-Little, 2007). Integrated approaches to coping with violence against women explicitly incorporate other considerations. These approaches can be used alone or in conjunction with tools that focus on a particular area.

Woman-Defined Advocacy. Jill Davies and her colleagues were some of the first to advocate explicitly for linking a comprehensive risk assessment to safety planning and to incorporate other risks, besides the risk of life-threatening violence, into safety planning (Davies, 2009; Davies, Lyon, & Monti-Catania, 1998). For example, this approach includes an assessment of risk to children. Woman-defined advocacy also emphasizes the assessment of resources and options much more than do most other safety plans, another integrative feature of this approach. Davies and colleagues identify three sources of options: the advocate, the battered woman, or another agency or system. Unlike most tools reviewed in this chapter, the woman-defined advocacy approach does not use a closed-ended checklist, but rather an interview guide that takes an advocate and a client through a discussion of risks and options.

Probably the most distinctive feature of the woman-defined advocacy approach is the explicit emphasis on options and priorities that would lead to a woman remaining in contact with her partner (Davies, 2009; Davies et al., 1998). Depending on a woman's individual circumstances, including "life-generated risks" such as poverty or court-ordered visitation with the couple's joint children, staying or remaining in contact with her partner may be the best available option. Davies emphasizes the need to make plans that incorporate all of the circumstances a woman faces.

Victim Inventory of Goals, Options, and Risks. The Victim Inventory of Goals, Options, and Risks (VIGOR) shares some elements with woman-defined advocacy, such as an inclusion of risks besides physical danger and a recognition that contact with the partner may be inevitable or even the best option for some women (Hamby,

2008, 2009). It differs from woman-defined advocacy primarily in its explicit adoption of the multiple criteria decision-making process (MCDM). MCDM is a well-established method that is frequently used in environmental sciences, engineering, and related fields (Hajkowicz, 2008), but also offers considerable promise as a method for helping intimate partner violence victims (Hamby, 2008). In MCDM, the existence of numerous important and potentially conflicting objectives is explicitly recognized. For example, a recent article using MCDM discussed the problem of finding a route to transport nuclear waste (Chen, Wang, & Lin, 2008). The objectives of that task could include picking a route that is (a) as short as possible, (b) avoids high-risk roads, (c) is near emergency assistance, and (d) avoids major population centers. MCDM offers a weighted decision-making procedure to select the best route, given that some objectives (such as c and d) might lead to opposing recommendations.

An even more important advantage of MCDM is that, unlike other approaches such as cost-benefit analysis, MCDM allows for the inclusion of objectives that are not easily assigned a quantitative value. For example, it is popular in environmental science because it can include objectives such as maintaining a pristine natural environment. This latter feature makes it particularly well-suited to addressing the situations of many intimate partner violence victims because the value of intangibles such as custody of one's children can be included in the risk assessment and risk management process.

The VIGOR involves a four-step process. In the first step, risks are identified, including the risk of physical danger and the physical risks posed to others, financial risks, legal risks, and social risks. In MCDM terms, these latter risks are known as "derivative losses," which cascade from the initial bad event (Jiang & Haimes, 2004). These risks are then prioritized and the top five to six risks are identified. The second step is the identification of strengths and resources. The third step involves the identification of as many options as possible. These would include "traditional" advocacy options such as going to a shelter or getting a restraining order and also other options such as couples counseling, job training, or other possibilities suggested by the resources inventory. In the fourth step, a grid is created, and each option is evaluated in terms of how well it would address each high-priority risk. An option has "strict dominance" if it is better than others at addressing some risks and at least as good as other options for all risks. Although no option may have strict dominance, the best available option or options can be put into action. Rather than a generic checklist of safety precautions, the VIGOR produces a personalized plan that links coping responses to specific risks.

Conclusion

Violence against women remains a sensitive and often stigmatized topic, and many cases will remain unidentified if victims and perpetrators must initiate self-identification. The good news is that fairly simple screening tools will greatly increase the number of people who are identified. Similarly, formalized dangerousness assessment and safety planning greatly increase the comprehensiveness of the issues that are addressed when planning interventions and coping strategies. At least with regard to dangerousness or recidivism assessment, evidence indicates these tools and processes are an improvement over informal, unstructured judgments.

Although such tools have extremely important uses, it is equally important to bear in mind their limitations. Screening tools will not identify all victims; they will only identify those who are willing to disclose when asked. Although this does turn out to be many more victims than the number who will initiate a conversation about victimization without being asked, it still may miss some cases, especially those who are most fearful of seeking help or who may have had bad experiences with providers or law enforcement in

the past. Although risk assessments are correlated with the perpetration of severe physical and sexual violence, they are mathematically incapable of reliably determining who is at risk to commit homicide. Similarly, although safety planning can provide several concrete strategies for working toward safety, these steps are no guarantee of safety in and of themselves. Despite these caveats, formal tools can greatly enhance all stages of assessment and intervention for both victims and perpetrators.

References

Ambuel, B., Hamberger, L. K., & Lahti, J. (1996). Partner violence: A systematic approach to identification and intervention in outpatient health care. *Wisconsin Medical Journal, 95,* 292–297.

Au, A., Cheung, G., Kropp, P. R., Yuk-Chung, C., Lam, G., & Sung, P. (2008). A preliminary validation of the Brief Spousal Assault Form for the Evaluation of Risk (B-SAFER) in Hong Kong. *Journal of Family Violence, 23,* 727–735.

Baig, A., Shadigian, E., & Heisler, M. (2006). Hidden from plain sight: Residents' domestic violence screening attitudes and reported practices. *Journal of General Internal Medicine, 21,* 949–954.

Basile, K. C., Hertz, M. F., & Back, S. E. (2007). *Intimate partner violence and sexual violence victimization assessment instruments for use in healthcare settings: Version 1.* Atlanta, GA: Centers for Disease Control and Prevention.

Betancourt, J. R., Green, A. R., Carrillo, J. E., & Ananeh-Firempong, O. (2003). Defining cultural competence: A practical framework for addressing racial/ethnic disparities in health and health care. *Public Health Reports, 118,* 293–302.

Brown, J. B., Lent, B., Brett, P. J., Sas, G., & Pederson, L. L. (1996). Development of the Woman Abuse Screening Tool for use in family practice. *Family Medicine, 28,* 422–428.

Campbell, J. C. (1986). Nursing assessment for risk of homicide with battered women. *Advances in Nursing Science, 8,* 36–51.

Campbell, J. C. (2005). *Danger assessment.* Retrieved May 13, 2009, from http://www.dangerassessment.org/WebApplication1/pages/da/.

Campbell, J. C., Webster, D., Koziol-McLain, J., Block, C. R., Campbell, D., Curry, M. A., et al. (2003). Assessing risk factors for intimate partner homicide. *NIJ Journal, 250,* 14–19.

Chapin, M. G., & Mackie, C. F. (2007). Research evidence to update practice guidelines for domestic violence screening in military settings. *Military Medicine, 172*(7), ii–iv.

Chen, Y., Wang, C., & Lin, S. (2008). A multi-objective geographic information system for route selection of nuclear waste transport. *Omega: The International Journal of Management Science, 36,* 363–372.

Clemants, E., & Gross, A. (2007). "Why aren't we screening?" A survey examining domestic violence screening procedures and training protocol in community mediation centers. *Conflict Resolution Quarterly, 24,* 413–431.

Cook, S. L., Woolard, J. L., & McCollum, H. C. (2004). The strengths, competence, and resilience of women facing domestic violence: How can research and policy support them? In K. Maton, C. Schellenbach, B. Leadbeater, & A. Solarz (Eds.), *Investing in children, youth, families, and communities* (pp. 97–115). Washington, DC: American Psychological Association.

Daugherty, J. D., & Houry, D. E. (2008). Intimate partner violence screening in the emergency department. *Journal of Postgraduate Medicine, 54,* 301–305.

Davies, J. (2009). *Advocacy beyond leaving: Helping battered women in contact with current or former partners.* San Francisco, CA: Family Violence Prevention Fund.

Davies, J., Lyon, E., & Monti-Catania, D. (1998). *Safety planning with battered women: Complex lives/difficult choices.* Thousand Oaks, CA: Sage.

Echeburúa, E., Fernández-Montalvo, J., de Corral, P., & López-Goñi, J. (2009). Assessing risk markers in intimate partner femicide and severe violence. *Journal of Interpersonal Violence, 24,* 925–939.

Edleson, J. L., Ellerton, A. L., Seagren, E. A., Kirchberg, S. L., Schmidt, S. O., & Ambrose, A. T. (2007). Assessing child exposure to adult domestic violence. *Children and Youth Services Review, 29,* 961–971.

Edleson, J. L., Shin, N., & Armendariz, K. (2008). Measuring children's exposure to domestic violence: The development and testing of the Child Exposure to Domestic Violence (CEDV) Scale. *Children and Youth Services Review, 30,* 502–521.

Ernst, A. A., Weiss, S. J., Cham, E., Hall, L., & Nick, T. G. (2004). Development of a screen for ongoing intimate partner violence. *Violence and Victims, 18,* 131–141.

Falk, D. R., Shepard, M. F., & Elliott, B. A. (2002). Evaluation of a domestic violence assessment protocol used by employee assistance counselors. *Employee Assistance Quarterly, 17*(3), 1–15.

Family Violence Prevention Fund. (2004). *National consensus guidelines on identifying and responding to domestic violence victimization in health care settings.* San Francisco: Family Violence Prevention Fund.

Feldhaus, K. M., Koziol-McLain, J., Amsbury, H. L., Norton, I. M., Lowenstein, S. R., & Abbott, J. T. (1997). Accuracy of 3 brief screening questions for detecting partner violence in the emergency department. *Journal of the American Medical Association, 277,* 1357–1361.

Fogarty, C. T., & Brown, J. B. (2002). Screening for abuse in Spanish-speaking women. *Journal of the American Board of Family Practitioners, 15,* 101–111.

Fox, J. A., & Zawitz, M. W. (2007). Homicide trends in the United States. *Bureau of Justice Statistics.* Retrieved May 14, 2009, from http://www.ojp.usdoj.gov/bjs/homicide/homtrnd.htm#contents.

Gielen, A. C., Campbell, J., Garza, M. A., O'Campo, P., Dienemann, J., Ku, J., et al. (2006). Domestic violence in the military: Women's policy preferences and beliefs concerning routine screening and mandatory reporting. *Military Medicine, 171,* 729–735.

Hajkowicz, S. (2008). Rethinking the economist's evaluation toolkit in light of sustainability policy. *Sustainability: Science, Practice, & Policy, 4*(1), 17–24.

Halligan, S. L., Michael, T., Wilhelm, F. H., Clark, D. M, & Ehlers, A. (2006). Reduced heart rate responding to trauma reliving in trauma survivors with PTSD: Correlates and consequences. *Journal of Traumatic Stress, 19,* 721–734.

Hamby, S. (2008, September). *A holistic approach to understanding the coping strategies of victims.* Paper presented at the 13th International Conference on Violence, Abuse, & Trauma, San Diego, CA.

Hamby, S. (2009, October). *Multiple criteria decision making: A new approach to risk assessment and management.* Paper presented at the 5th National Conference on Health and Domestic Violence, New Orleans, LA.

Hamby, S., Finkelhor, D., Turner, H., & Ormrod, R. (2010). *Exposure to intimate partner violence and other forms of family violence: Nationally representative rates among U.S. youth.* Washington, DC: Office of Juvenile Justice and Delinquency Prevention.

Hamby, S. L., & Gray-Little, B. (2007). Can battered women cope? A critical analysis of research on women's responses to violence. In K. Kendall-Tackett & S. Giacomoni (Eds.), *Intimate partner violence* (pp. 28-1–28-19). Kingston, NJ: Civic Research Institute.

Hanson, R. K. (1997). *The development of a brief actuarial risk scale for sexual offense recidivism* (Report no. 1997-04). Ottawa, ON: Department of the Solicitor General of Canada.

Hanson, R. K., & Morton-Bougon, K. E. (2009). The accuracy of recidivism risk assessments for sexual offenders: A meta-analysis of 118 prediction studies. *Psychological Assessment, 21,* 1–21.

Hanson, R. K., & Thornton, D. (1999). *Static 99: Improving actuarial risk assessments for sex offenders* (Report 99-02). Ottawa, ON: Department of the Solicitor General of Canada.

Hanson, R. K., & Thornton, D. (2000). Improving risk assessments for sex offenders: A comparison of three actuarial scales. *Law and Human Behavior, 24,* 119–136.

Hare, R. D. (1991). *Manual for the Hare Psychopathy Checklist, Revised.* Toronto, Canada: Multi-Health Systems.

Hart, B. J. (1990). Assessing whether batterers will kill. *Barbara J. Hart's collected writings.* Retrieved May 13, 2009, from http://www.mincava.umn.edu/documents/hart/hart.html#id2376223.

Hart, B. J., & Stuehling, J. (1992). Personalized safety plan. *Barbara J. Hart's collected writings.* Retrieved May 11, 2009, from http://www.mincava.umn.edu/documents/hart/hart.html#id2375465.

Hemenway, D., Shinoda-Tagawa, T., & Miller, M. (2002). Firearm availability and female homicide victimization rates among 25 populous high-income countries. *Journal of the American Medical Women's Association, 57,* 100–104.

Hilton, N. Z., & Harris, G. T. (2009a). Criminal justice responses to partner violence: History, evaluation, and lessons learned. In D. W. J. Lutzker (Ed.), *Preventing partner violence: Research and evidence-based intervention strategies* (pp. 219–243). Washington, DC: American Psychological Association.

Hilton, N. Z., & Harris, G. T. (2009b). How nonrecidivism affects predictive accuracy: Evidence from a cross-validation of the Ontario Domestic Assault Risk Assessment (ODARA). *Journal of Interpersonal Violence, 24,* 326–337.

Hilton, N. Z., Harris, G. T., Rice, M. E., Lang, C., Cormier, C. A., & Lines, K. J. (2004). A brief actuarial assessment for the prediction of wife assault recidivism: The Ontario Domestic Assault Risk Assessment. *Psychological Assessment, 16,* 267–275.

Houry, D., Feldhaus, K., Peery, B., Abbott, J., Lowenstein, S. R., al-Bataa-de-Montero, S., et al. (2004). A positive domestic violence screen predicts future domestic violence. *Journal of Interpersonal Violence, 19,* 955–966.

Houry, D., Kaslow, N. J., Kemball, R. S., McNutt, L., Cerulli, C., Straus, H., et al. (2008). Does screening in the emergency department hurt or help victims of intimate partner violence? *Annals of Emergency Medicine, 51,* 433–442.

Hudson, W. W., & McIntosh, S. R. (1981). The assessment of spouse abuse: Two quantifiable dimensions. *Journal of Marriage and the Family, 43,* 873–888.

Jiang, P., & Haimes, Y. Y. (2004). Risk management for Leontief-based interdependent systems. *Risk Analysis, 24,* 1215–1229.

Kitzmann, K. M., Gaylord, N., Holt, A., & Kenny, E. (2003). Child witnesses to domestic violence: A meta-analytic review. *Journal of Consulting and Clinical Psychology, 71,* 339–352.

Klap, R., Tang, L., Wells, K., Starks, S. L., & Rodriguez, M. (2007). Screening for domestic violence among adult women in the United States. *Journal of General Internal Medicine, 22,* 579–584.

Klein, S. J. (2001). Screening for risk of domestic violence within HIV partner notification: Evolving practice and emerging issues. *Journal of Public Health Management & Practice, 7*(5), 46–49.

Kropp, P. R., & Hart, S. D. (2000). The Spousal Assault Risk Assessment (SARA) guide: Reliability and validity in adult male offenders. *Law and Human Behavior, 24,* 101–118.

Kropp, P. R., & Hart, S. D. (2004). *The development of the Brief Spousal Assault Form for the Evaluation of Risk (B-SAFER): A tool for criminal justice professionals.* Ottawa, ON: Department of Justice Canada.

Kropp, P. R., Hart, S. D., Webster, C. D., & Eaves, D. (1995). *Manual for the Spousal Assault Risk*

Assessment Guide (2nd ed.). Vancouver: British Columbia Institute on Family Violence.

Laing, L. (2004). *Risk assessment in domestic violence.* Sydney: Australian Domestic and Family Violence Clearinghouse.

Lang, J. M., & Stover, C. S. (2008). Symptom patterns of youth exposed to intimate partner violence. *Journal of Family Violence, 23,* 619–629.

Långström, N. (2002). Long-term follow-up of criminal recidivism in young sex offenders: Temporal patterns and risk factors. *Psychology, Crime, & Law, 8,* 41–58.

Langton, C. M., Barbaree, H. E., Seto, M. C., Peacock, E. J., Harkins, L., & Hansen, K. T. (2007). Actuarial assessment of risk for reoffense among adult sex offenders. *Criminal Justice and Behavior, 34,* 37–59.

Larkin, G. L., Hyman, K. B., Mathias, S. R., D'Amico, F., & MacLeod, B. A. (1999). Universal screening for intimate partner violence in the emergency department: Importance of patient and provider factors. *Annals of Emergency Medicine, 33,* 669–675.

Littleton, H. L., Berenson, A. B., & Radecki Breitkopf, C. (2007). An evaluation of health care providers' sexual violence screening practices. *American Journal of Obstetrics & Gynecology, 196,* 564.e1–564.e7.

Love, C. V. (2000). Oral health care professionals' attitudes and behaviors regarding domestic violence: The need for an effective and compassionate response. *Dissertation Abstracts International, 60*(12-B), 6373. (UMI No. 9954078)

Love, C., Gerbert, B., Caspers, N., Bronstone, A., Perry, D., & Bird, W. (2001). Dentists' attitudes and behaviors regarding domestic violence. *Journal of the American Dental Association, 132,* 85–93.

McCloskey, K., & Grigsby, N. (2005). The ubiquitous clinical problem of adult intimate partner violence: The need for routine assessment. *Professional Psychology: Research and Practice, 36,* 264–275.

McFarlane, J., Parker, B., Soeken, K., & Bullock, L. (1992). Assessing for abuse during pregnancy: Severity and frequency of injuries and associated entry into prenatal care. *Journal of the American Medical Association, 267,* 3176–3178.

National Center for Victims of Crime. (1998). *Safety plan guidelines.* Retrieved May 11, 2009, from http://www.ndvh.org/get-help/safety planning/#1.

National Coalition Against Domestic Violence. (2009). *Safety plan.* Retrieved September 9, 2009, from http://www.ncadv.org/protectyourself/SafetyPlan .php.

Nelson, H., Nygren, P., McInerney, Y., & Klein, J. (2004). Screening women and elderly adults for family and intimate partner violence: A review of the evidence for the U.S. Preventive Services Task Force. *Annals of Internal Medicine, 140,* 387–396.

Norton, L. B., Peipert, J. F., Zierler, S., Lima, B., & Hume, L. (1995). Battering in pregnancy: An assessment of two screening methods. *Obstetrics and Gynecology, 85,* 321–325.

Olver, M. E., Wong, S., Nicholaichuk, T., & Gordon, A. (2007). The validity and reliability of the Violence Risk Scale-Sexual Offender Version: Assessing sex offender risk and evaluating therapeutic change. *Psychological Assessment, 19,* 318–329.

Paulozzi, L. J., Saltzman, L. E., Thompson, M. P., & Holmgreen, P. (2001). Surveillance for homicide among intimate partners–United States, 1981–1998. *Morbidity & Mortality Weekly Report, 50*(SS03), 1–16.

Peralta, R., & Fleming, M. (2003). Screening for intimate partner violence in a primary care setting: The validity of "Feeling Safe at Home" and prevalence results. *Journal of the American Board of Family Medicine, 16,* 525–532.

Rhodes, K. V., Drum, M., Anliker, E., Frankel, R. M., Howes, D. S., & Levinson, W. (2006). Lowering the threshold for discussions of domestic violence: A randomized controlled trial of computer screening. *Archives of Internal Medicine, 166,* 1107–1114.

Rivers, J. E., Maze, C. L., Hannah, S. A., & Lederman, C. S. (2007). Domestic violence screening and service acceptance among adult victims in a dependency court setting. *Child Welfare, 86,* 123–144.

Samuelson, S. L., & Campbell, C. D. (2005). Screening for domestic violence: Recommendations based on a practice survey. *Professional Psychology: Research and Practice, 36,* 276–282.

Sherin, K. M., Li, X. Q., Zitter, R. E., & Shakil, A. (1998). HITS: A short domestic violence screening tool for use in a family practice setting. *Family Medicine, 30,* 508–512.

Sjöstedt, G., & Långström, N. (2002). Assessment of risk for criminal recidivism among rapists: A comparison of four different measures. *Psychology, Crime, & Law, 8,* 25–40.

Smith, P. H., Tessaro, I., & Earp, J. L. (1995). Women's experiences with battering: A conceptualization from qualitative research. *Women's Health Issues, 5*(4), 173–182.

Stevens, L. (2007). *Screening for sexual violence: Gaps in research and recommendations for change.* Retrieved October 12, 2009, from http://www.vawnet.org.

Straus, M. A., & Gelles, R. J. (1990). *Physical violence in American families: Risk factors and adaptations to violence in 8,145 families.* New Brunswick, NJ: Transaction.

Straus, M. A., Hamby, S. L., Boney-McCoy, S., & Sugarman, D. B. (1996). The Revised Conflict Tactics Scales (CTS2): Development and preliminary psychometric data. *Journal of Family Issues, 17*(3), 283–316.

Thompson, R. S., Rivara, F. P., Thompson, D. C., Barlow, W. E., Sugg, N. K., Maiuro, R. D., et al. (2000). Identification and management of domestic violence: A randomized trial. *American Journal of Preventive Medicine, 19,* 253–263.

Thurston, W. E., & Eisener, A. (2006). Successful integration and maintenance of screening for domestic violence in the health care sector. *Trauma, Violence, & Abuse, 7,* 83–92.

Tjaden, P., & Thoennes, N. (2000). *Extent, nature, and consequences of intimate partner violence: Findings from the National Violence Against Women Survey.* Washington, DC: National Institute of Justice.

U.S. Department of Justice. (2008). *Crime in the United States 2007.* Retrieved May 14, 2009, from http://www.fbi.gov/ucr/cius2007/data/table_29.html.

Waller, A. E., Hohenhaus, S. M., Shah, P. J., & Stern, E. A. (1996). Development and validation of an emergency department screening and referral protocol for victims of domestic violence. *Annals of Emergency Medicine, 27,* 754–760.

Websdale, N. (2000). *Lethality assessment tools: A critical analysis.* Retrieved May 14, 2009, from http://www.vawnet.org/Assoc_Files_VAWnet/AR_lethality.pdf.

Webster, C. D., Harris, G., Rice, M., Cormier, C., & Quinsey, V. (1994). *The violence predictions scheme: Assessing dangerousness in high risk men.* Toronto, ON: University of Toronto, Centre for Criminology.

Weeks, E. K., Ellis, S. D., Lichstein, P. R., & Bonds, D. E. (2008). Does health care provider screening for domestic violence vary by race and income? *Violence Against Women, 14,* 844–855.

Wolfe, D. A., Crooks, C. V., Lee, V., McIntyre-Smith, A., & Jaffe, P. G. (2003). The effects of children's exposure to domestic violence: A meta-analysis and critique. *Clinical Child and Family Psychology Review, 6*(3), 171–187.

Zink, T., Levin, L., Putnam, F., & Beckstrom, A. (2007). Accuracy of five domestic violence screening questions with nongraphic language. *Clinical Pediatrics, 46,* 127–134.

Chapter Authors

Sherry Hamby, Ph.D., is a Research Associate Professor of Psychology at Sewanee, the University of the South, studying the methodological challenges of violence research. She also holds appointments at the University of North Carolina at Chapel Hill and the Université de Lausanne. She is author or coauthor of more than 50 publications on family violence and youth victimization, including *The Conflict Tactics Scales Handbook* (Western Psychological Services, 2003) and *Sortir Ensemble et Se Respecter* (IES Editions, 2009), the first Swiss dating violence prevention program. She has also been appointed editor of a new APA journal, *Psychology of Violence.* A licensed clinical psychologist, she has received awards from the National Register for Health Service Providers in Psychology and the American Professional Society on the Abuse of Children.

Sarah L. Cook, Ph.D., is Professor of Psychology at Georgia State University. Her research focuses on how social scientists measure aggression against women, prevention interventions, and ethical issues in violence and trauma research. She has confronted the problem of aggression against women as a peer educator, rape crisis advocate, child protection social worker, and consultant to local and state advocacy organizations. Currently, she serves as chair of the board of directors for the Georgia Network to End Sexual Assault and is a member of the Sexual Violence Applied Research Advisory Group of the National Online Resource Center on Violence Against Women.

Personal Reflection

Mary Ann Dutton

 My clinical, forensic, and research efforts have combined to sharpen my attention to assessment in the field of violence against women. My interest in battered women and assessment began in the late 1970s when I was completing my dissertation research, which examined the role that intimacy and conflict played in couples' verbal communication. From the beginning of my academic career, I focused my research on domestic violence. I began an applied clinical research and training program by developing a specialized clinic, the Family Violence Program (FVP), for the assessment of and intervention for both victims and offenders, which was staffed by doctoral psychology students. For the next 12 years, in addition to providing intervention, the FVP routinely assessed clients' violence and victimization experiences, mental health, drug and alcohol use, social support, coping strategies, attributions about the violence, and more.

Forensic cases involving violence against women increasingly focused my attention on assessment issues. In 1984, I accepted my first forensic case involving a battered woman who had been charged with murdering her abusive husband. This and several hundred additional forensic cases highlighted the need for an assessment protocol, to enable me to write an informative report for the retaining attorney and to respond knowledgeably to both direct examination and cross-examination.

In my view, the assessment of violence against women is expanding across the spectrum of the ecological framework and is incorporating diverse assessment methods to do so. On one end of the spectrum, assessment of physiological stress (e.g., cortisol, immune panel, catecholamines, NPY), neurological response (e.g., fMRI), and genetic markers offer the possibility of understanding the complexities of the effects of violence against women in relation to the body and the brain. At the opposite end of the ecological continuum, assessment of the social network and the institutional responses within which violence against women occurs provides a perspective that advances our understanding of its sociopolitical aspects.

Assessment of violence against women is also beginning to include longitudinal perspectives that elucidate the development of violence against women and the interrelationships between violence/abuse, strategic coping responses, institutional responses to violence against women, and the short- and long-term emotional and socioeconomic impacts of violence against women.

In my work, I have tried to provide the field of assessment of violence against women with a framework for understanding battered women's response to violence, both the ways in which women respond to violence and abuse through their coping strategies and the ways in which exposure to violence and abuse results in traumatic effects. My colleagues and I have also offered to the field a method for measuring violence-related threat appraisal. Finally, through generous funding from the National Institute of Justice, a national team of experts and I have developed a method for assessing coercion (demands, coercive threats, surveillance) in intimate relationships, which can add to our understanding of violence against women beyond the assessment of physical, sexual, and psychological abuse.

PART II

Types of Violence Against Women

The past 40 years has seen an explosion of research and knowledge about the pervasiveness and serious consequences of the many forms of violence against women. The goal of this section of the book is to provide a greater understanding of how women experience violence in their lives. The chapters in this section cover a variety of types of violence, including sexual harassment, intimate partner violence, and sexual violence. However, this section also contributes to our understanding of the complexity of women's experiences of violence by focusing on cultural variations, economic issues, and the connection between pornography and violence against women. As in previous chapters, the authors included in this section draw on their expertise to provide readers with a look at cutting-edge research of the causes, consequences, and types of violence against women.

In Chapter 4, Phoebe Morgan and James Gruber explore the problem of sexual harassment of women and girls. For the past 35 years, researchers in the U.S. have documented the serious problem of sexual harassment of women in the workplace, and there is growing interest in this problem globally. As Morgan and Gruber indicate, women who work in male-dominated

occupations (such as the military) and sexualized workplaces are particularly vulnerable to sexual harassment. Morgan and Gruber also examine women's experiences of sexual harassment in educational institutions with a focus on the experiences of college women and high school girls. In this chapter, they explore the harmful consequences, professionally and personally, of sexual harassment.

Chapter 5, by Rebecca Campbell and Stephanie Townsend, complements Chapter 4 with a focus on women's experiences of sexual violence. In this chapter, the authors discuss the prevalence and impact of women's experiences of sexual violence. Most important, they address the extant research and discuss how differing definitions shape our understanding of the prevalence and nature of women's experiences. They also provide a thoughtful discussion of the myriad effects of sexual violence on the lives and health of women. Lastly, they consider women's disclosure experiences and the too-frequent experience of secondary victimization that occurs when women choose to disclose their experiences of sexual violence to others.

As Kathleen Basile and Michele Black argue in Chapter 6, intimate partner violence is a serious social and public health problem. They argue that violence by intimates is experienced by approximately one out of four women during their lifetimes. This chapter provides a broad overview of the many forms of violence against women that are perpetrated by intimate partners and the unique complexities that accompany women's experiences when their abuser is an intimate partner. Basile and Black address the diversity of women's experiences of intimate partner violence, with an emphasis on certain populations that have historically received little scholarly attention, including older women, immigrant women, women in same-sex relationships, and rural women.

In Chapter 7, Ana J. Bridges and Robert Jensen explore the relationship between violence against women and pornography. The authors ask important questions, including how normalizing pornography affects the culture and influences women's experiences of violence. Bridges and Jensen provide an overview of the history of the pornography industry, highlight important cases of pornography and the law, and review some of the major debates surrounding pornography. In a detailed and thought-provoking way, they address the controversial question, What are the effects of pornography? In exploring the answers to this question, Bridges and Jensen discuss the ways in which pornography may be implicated in sexual violence and consider the negative consequences of pornography consumption in the United States and globally.

Lisa Fontes and Kathy McClosky expand the global perspective of this book in Chapter 8 by focusing on violence against women in a cultural context. The authors argue that violence against women is a global problem; however, certain forms of violence manifest under certain cultural conditions. Fontes and McClosky discuss a multitude of forms of violence against women and girls that are not often addressed in the U.S., including missing girls, honor killings, dowry violence, and female genital cutting. They also highlight two areas of research that remain particularly understudied: violence against lesbian women and rape as a weapon of terror and war. They conclude with the important argument that "culture stands prominently as a factor in *all* situations where women are subjected to violence, not solely in cases where women come from visible minority groups."

In the final chapter of this section, Claire Renzetti considers the important topic of economic issues and violence against women. We often hear that the problem of violence against women is not limited to any social class, and while research indicates that this is certainly true, we also know that poor women have an elevated risk of experiencing intimate partner violence. As Renzetti's chapter indicates, there are three primary factors—financial strain, unemployment, and living in an economically disadvantaged neighborhood—that must be considered with regard to violence against women. Other factors that Renzetti considers include social support networks and social service systems. Renzetti makes the important point that employment can be both a protection against violence against women and a risk factor, and she offers thought-provoking suggestions for working to break the relationship of intimate partner violence and economic distress.

CHAPTER 4

Sexual Harassment

Violence Against Women at Work and in Schools

Phoebe Morgan and James E. Gruber

Around the globe, the unwanted sexual attention of men is a common condition of employment and education for women and girls. The experience is universal—transcending all levels of socioeconomic and educational status and cutting across most national and cultural identities. The type and severity of the harm done is subject to interpretation, which is mediated by such things as gender ideology, sexual orientation, nationality, and race relations. Despite these variations, the two most common complaints are the loss of employment and the loss of educational opportunity.

Nearly 35 years ago, U.S. feminists coined the term *sexual harassment* to describe this multifaceted ubiquity among women (Farley, 1978; MacKinnon, 1979; Wehrli, 1976). Since that time, the issue of sexual harassment has been a potent focal point of the struggle for women's rights throughout the entire world. As a result, answers to such fundamental and practical questions as what behaviors constitute sexual harassment, what are the risk factors, what is the harm done,

who should be held accountable, and how to best prevent it have too often become fodder for political theater. For at the core of these queries lie the larger questions of who has the right—or more accurately, the power—to define what constitutes violence against women, what is the role of government in defining it, and to what extent should an employer or school be held accountable when its members commit it.

An exhaustive exploration of all points of contention is too great a task for this book chapter. We offer, instead, a highlighting of the trends most pertinent to those committed to ending violence against women. Before we do so, three caveats further explicate our choices:

- A significant body of scholarship and government statistics consistently substantiates a need for more attention to the sexual harassment of men and boys. The number of male survey respondents who experience sexual harassment has consistently increased, as have their complaints to the Equal Employment Opportunity Commission (see, e.g., Stockdale, 2008). Their harassers are overwhelmingly male, but their harassment and complaint experiences are different from those of their female counterparts in a number of important ways. In other publications, we have joined the chorus calling for greater attention to the sexual harassment of men (Gruber & Morgan, 2005; Morgan & Gruber, 2008). But, in keeping with the scope of this collection, the analysis we present in this chapter is limited to the experiences of women and girls.

- Recent efforts to make sexual harassment laws more politically acceptable and palatable to the business community have led to a reinvention of sexual harassment as a form of general workplace/classroom incivility rather than a form of discriminatory violence. We remain wary of this approach and conceptualize sexual harassment as a form of sexual violence—committed primarily by men, primarily against women—and place it on a continuum that ranges from the smallest gestures of sexism that women encounter every day through the all-too-frequent murder of women and girls by men. As such, it is the most widespread form of violence against women in the world today (Merkin, 2008).

- Despite the fact that the practice of sexual harassment has been sufficiently documented across history and around the globe, the scholarly literature remains skewed toward the American experience (Willness, Steele, & Lee, 2007). As charter members of the International Consortium Against Sexual Harassment, we see this chapter as an opportunity to continue our efforts to correct that bias. Thus, in researching this chapter, we made a special effort to take a global approach to the problem and highlight implications of globalization for this pernicious form of violence against women.

With these caveats in mind, the following pages present an overview of contemporary trends in the sexual harassment literature in two parts. While the first part focuses on the sexual harassment of working women, the second part addresses the literature regarding the sexual harassment of women and girls at all levels of education. Within each part, we will draw upon government policy, legal cases, and research findings to address these common questions: What is sexual harassment? How prevalent is it? What are the risk factors? What is the harm? In addition, we also address the challenges posed by the globalized workplace and multicultural classroom.

Sexual Harassment Against Women at Work

The United States Equal Employment Opportunity Commission (EEOC) defines sexual harassment as follows:

> Unwelcome sexual advances, requests for sexual favors, and other verbal or physical conduct of a sexual nature constitute sexual harassment when this conduct explicitly or implicitly affects an individual's employment, unreasonably interferes with an individual's work performance, or creates an intimidating, hostile, or offensive work environment. (EEOC, 2009)

In addition to the definition, the EEOC publishes compliance guidelines for employers. The guidelines support efforts to encourage the reporting of unwelcome sexual attention, hold employers responsible for preventing sexual harassment, and make retaliation against victims and their witnesses legally actionable.

Today a substantial body of case law establishes the constitutionality of the EEOC's definitions and guidelines under U.S. law. Since 1985, 14 U.S. Supreme Court rulings have further clarified the types of behaviors that constitute sexual harassment, who is liable for it, and the limits of that liability. In two cases, the Court made clear that although sexual harassment is defined as an inherently harmful condition of employment, one does not have to lose employment, wages, or psychological well-being to qualify for compensation (*Harris v. Forklift Systems,* 1993; *Meritor Savings Bank v. Mechelle Vinson,* 1986). In 1998, the Court ruled that although sexual harassment is a form of sex discrimination, same-sex sexual harassment is actionable (*Oncale v. Sundowner Offshore Services,* 1998) and that employers are vicariously and strictly liable for harassment by supervisors (*Burlington Industries, Inc. v. Ellerth,* 1998; *Faragher v. City of Boca Raton,* 1998). In 2001, the Court further clarified the scope of employer liability by concluding that employers are liable for sexual harassment that could have been prevented, regardless of the supervisory relationship—or lack thereof—between the harassed and harasser(s) (*Pollard v. Dupont,* 2001). More recently, the U.S. Supreme Court decided that all forms of retaliation—including retaliation against those who participate in an investigation as witnesses or investigators—are legally actionable (*Crawford v. Nashville and Davidson County, TN,* 2009).

In 1992, the U.S. Congress passed legislation allowing sexual harassment cases access to jury trials and plaintiffs the right to sue for punitive awards of up to $500,000 (see Civil Rights Act of 1991). Doing so significantly increased the financial risks to employers and therefore added more "teeth" to the existing law. In 2007, U.S. employers paid $50 million to EEOC claimants alone. The prospect of seven- and eight-figure jury awards like those against the Los Angeles Police Department ($3.1 million), Vons Supermarket ($18 million), Baker and McKenzie ($6.9 million), and Wal-Mart ($50 million) has caused employers to take their potential liability more seriously (see Goodwin, 2003; Grimsley, 1996; Harris, 2009; Kim, 2008).

The Globalization of Anti-Sexual Harassment Policy

The United States may be "ground zero" in the anti-sexual harassment movement, but the transformation of unwanted sexual attention from simply the price women pay for employment into a socially unacceptable and illegal behavior is decidedly a global phenomenon. Although approaches vary, prohibitions against the sexual harassment of working women can be found on all continents. In legal and cultural environments most like the United States (e.g., Canada, the United Kingdom, Australia, South Africa, and Israel), the American model (as codified by the EEOC and legitimized by the U.S. Congress and the courts) has been adopted almost whole cloth and with similar results (Lee, 2001; Zalesne, 2002). But across Europe, Africa, and Asia, the American approach is culturally and legally incongruent. As such, American anti-sexual harassment policy has at times been criticized as another manifestation of the "McDonaldization" of the world—a model, therefore, to both follow and to avoid (Cahill, 2001; Zippel, 2004).

Although the European Union (EU) addressed the issue of sexual harassment as early as 1976, it was not until 2002 that membership in the European Union required the adoption of a declaration that sexual harassment violates the "equal treatment for men and women as regards access to employment, vocational training and promotion, and working conditions." This EU directive declares sexual harassment to be "contrary to the principle of equal treatment between women and men" and employers are encouraged to "take preventive measures against sexual harassment in the workplace, in accordance with national legislation and practice" (EU, 2002). In short, it obligates all members to outlaw sexual harassment and establish agencies similar to the U.S. EEOC and presents 27 nations with the daunting task of creating meaningful congruence between the EU directive and local legal systems and cultural norms (Moline, 2002). Compliance for some members required more effort than for others. In socialist-led countries, for example, coworker sexual harassment has not been explicitly covered (Cahill, 2001). So, France was forced to broaden its limited definition of sexual harassment as an abuse of power by someone in an official capacity to include unwanted sexual attention by coworkers, subordinates, and vocational trainers

(Dobbin, 2006). Among members with strong commitments to universal rights codified by the United Nations, compliance with the 2002 directive has cast sexual harassment as a violation of the human right to dignity (Samuels, 2003). As a result, in Greece, where compliance with the EU's directive has yet to be achieved, a judge applied the United Nations dictate on workplace dignity to justify his ruling in a sexual harassment case (Zippel, 2004).

The farther east sexual harassment policies travel, the less Westernized they become. Although most governments in the Middle and Far East have joined the ranks of those who believe sexual harassment should be banned, without a history of civil or worker rights, legislatures have reformed criminal law. For example, on March 22, 2009, members of the Saudi Arabian parliament began a heated debate of a bill that, if passed, would criminalize sexual harassment and hold managers of companies and other institutions responsible for preventing it (Ghafour, 2009). Those found guilty could serve up to a year in jail and pay significant fines.

Until recently, Sharia law was deemed, at least by lawmakers, a sufficient deterrent against the sexual harassment of women in the workplace. But, increasingly, competitive participation in a globalized economy has demanded a legal environment conducive to the success of multinational organizations and, relatedly, the expectations of a cross-cultural workforce. More than 7 million expatriates are employed in Saudi Arabia alone. Transnational corporations like Time Warner, Mitsubishi, Siemens, and Exxon Mobil employ about 50% of the world's paid laborers (Steger, 2003). Consequently, Saudi Arabia joins a growing list of Muslim countries like Malaysia, Indonesia, Tunisia, and Egypt that have turned to criminal law as a way to adapt Western sexual harassment prohibitions to a religion-based legal system.

In the communist nation of the People's Republic of China, a Sichuan office manager had the unfortunate opportunity to be the first person convicted under a law similar to the one pondered by the Saudi Arabian parliament (Branigan, 2008). *The Guardian* reported Mr. Liu served six months in jail for "holding [a female colleague] by the neck and kissing her against her will" (Branigan, 2008).

Prevalence

A substantial body of survey research consistently finds the problem of employment-related sexual harassment to be both endemic and global. A stratified random survey of all U.S. government employees found that 44% of all female government employees had experienced sexual harassment within two years of the survey (United States Merit Systems Protection Board [USMSPB], 1994). A replication of the USMSPB survey conducted with Japanese civil servants found 26% of females had experienced sexual harassment within two years of the survey (Huen, 2007), and another with Canadian workers found 50% of the female respondents and 18% of the men had experienced sexual harassment within two years (Canadian Human Rights Commission, 1983). When simply asked whether they had been exposed to sexual harassment at their current place of employment, 3.2% of Danish women, 18% of Finnish, and 20% of Spanish women said "yes" (European Foundation for the Improvement of Living and Working Conditions, 2007).

Differences in rates may be due, at least in part, to the extent to which questionnaires rely upon objective or subjective labeling. For example, in a 1982 randomized telephone survey of Los Angeles workers, 50% of the female respondents had experienced at least one of the behaviors labeled by the EEOC guidelines as sexual harassment, but only 20% of them said they considered their experiences to be sexual harassment (Gutek, 1985). Despite definitional and methodological variation, the European Commission (1999) conservatively estimates the incidence rate among European women to be 30–50%.

Risk Factors

Without doubt, gender is the most significant predictor of sexual harassment. Although the number of men who experience sexual harassment and who file complaints with government agencies is increasing, women are overwhelmingly the targets of it and men are most often the perpetrators. Among U.S. government workers, for example, 93% of the women who experienced sexual harassment were targeted by men; similarly, 94% of all sexual harassment complaints filed with Israeli organizations were made by women against men (Bior, 2008). A United Nations report published a similar (95%) rate among Danish organizations (see European Union, 2004).

Additionally, research consistently points to the degree of male dominance as a significant risk factor. Both men and women who work in domains (i.e., organizations, workgroups, industries, or occupations) overpopulated by men are at a higher risk of being sexually harassed than are those who do not (Morgan & Gruber, 2008; Willness et al., 2007). Thus, despite the fact that the U.S. Department of Defense has had a zero tolerance policy since 1991, the rates of overall victimization among U.S. military and reservists are significantly higher (61%) and the types of harassment reported more severe than among nonmilitary workers (Street, Stafford, Mahan, & Hendricks, 2008; Vijayasiri, 2008).

In addition to numerical dominance, normative dominance also plays a role. The risk of sexual harassment is higher in domains in which one's ability to conform to masculine norms is a tacit measure of work performance. Thus, women who do "men's" work—policing, firefighting, coal mining, and architectural design, for example—are more likely to be sexually harassed than those whose jobs do not depend upon the ability to "work like a man" (Gruber & Morgan, 2005).

Another salient risk factor is the extent to which the work environment is sexualized (Parker, 2008). Such environments foster beliefs that sexual attraction between workers is natural and unavoidable. A survey of human resource professionals found that in nearly one-quarter of the sexual harassment claims they handle, the relationship began as a workplace romance (Pierce, Broberg, McClure, & Aguinis, 2004). As in the now-iconic complaint filed by Mechelle Vinson against her former boyfriend and supervisor, in a sexualized environment, harassment is too often the response when one member of the couple attempts to change the terms of a previously consensual relationship. In the service sector, managing the unwanted sexual attention of customers and clients is an occupational hazard for those expected to wear sexy uniforms or use their sexual charms to sell products (Deadrick, 2001). Similarly, those whose work requires interaction with men in an intimate setting are at a higher risk of sexual harassment than those who work in more bureaucratic or professional venues. Nurses, for example, are more often harassed "bedside" than in other, less intimate settings, and the incidence rate of sexual harassment of registered nurses by patients is close to that of military women (Hesketh et al., 2003; Kane-Urrabazo, 2007). The sexual harassment of domestic workers is similarly problematic. DeSouza and Cerqueria's (2009) survey of 360 Brazilian workers found sexual harassment among live-in domestics was significantly more frequent, and the consequences more severe, than among day workers, and the place harassment most often occurred was their own bedroom. In fact, the sexual harassment of migrant domestic workers has become so problematic that learning how to fend off sexual advances has become a standard part of their orientation training (Bencomo, 2005).

Finally, a meta-analysis of the findings from 41 studies finds evidence that an overall environmental tolerance for mistreatment, discrimination, and incivility of various kinds provides fertile ground for the normalization of sexual harassment as acceptable behavior (Willness et al., 2007). While occasional acts of unwanted sexual attention can occur in any workplace, sexual harassment becomes endemic in settings in which putting up with abuse, or even violence, is a tacit occupational requirement. In correctional and mental health institutions, for example, workers are expected to tolerate, rather than report to their superiors, all but the most extreme forms of sexual violence (Hesketh et al., 2003). A City of Los Angeles personnel survey found, for example, that while women in the protective services had the highest rate of sexual harassment, they also filed the smallest proportion of formal complaints (Texeira, 2002).

Harm

The negative impacts of sexual harassment on the mental and physical health of women workers have been well documented. A study of military reservists found a significant correlation between having been sexually harassed and a range of medical conditions (Street et al., 2008). But more important, almost a decade after service, the reservists who had been sexually harassed while serving their country reported significantly poorer health than those who had not been harassed. When mental resiliency has been compromised, sexual harassment can precipitate depression, eating disorders, and instances of Post-Traumatic Stress Disorder (PTSD). Among female Gulf War veterans, sexual stress (i.e., stress due to sexual harassment and sexual assault while on duty) was found to be nearly four times as influential in the development of PTSD as other duty-related stressors (O'Donohue et al., 2006).

In addition, sexually harassed workers tend to report lower job and life satisfaction scores than their counterparts (Fineran & Gruber, 2008). Somewhat related is an erosion of trust. Even when the source of harassment is someone other than a supervisor, targets of sexual harassment often attribute the experience to their organization's leadership (Murray, Sivasubramaniam, &

Jacques, 2001). And sexually harassed women report not only lowered confidence in leadership, but also a distrust of men as a group (Van Roosmalen & McDaniel, 1998). Although differences in the number of adverse outcomes can be found between Danish and Finnish women and between Scandinavian and American women (Kauppinen & Gruber, 1993), a meta-analysis of the research findings from 41 studies found evidence of severe negative effects in all socioeconomic groups, at all educational levels, and across all cultures, countries, age groups, and vocations (Willness et al., 2007).

Sexual Harassment in the Globalized Workplace

The forces of globalization have played a significant part in transforming the world's opinion about the problem of sexual harassment and in facilitating an international effort to prohibit it. Although approaches may vary, the majority of governments, NGOs, and multinational companies have policies prohibiting sexual harassment as well as procedures for prevention and sanction. But to those seeking to meaningfully address the problem, globalization also presents formidable challenges. In the globalized workplace, workers are increasingly mobile, a growing number of the organizations that employ them are multinational in scope, and the cultural context in which they interact with others is increasingly complex.

In 2008, a UK court awarded Christina Rich £2 million in her lawsuit against PricewaterhouseCoopers (Alleyne, 2008). The world's largest award to a sexual harassment plaintiff was the result of claims of unwanted sexualized attention experienced in the firm's Australian office where, unlike in the UK or the U.S., awards are limited to damages only. The Australian firm operates under an American umbrella company that coordinates the work of 146,000 employees in 150 countries. In today's globalized world, where the top 200 multinational companies account for almost half the world's economy, Rich's case is more typical than aberrant.

In 2008, Nike Incorporated, an Oregon-based company, employed 30,000 worldwide. But 100% of its products are made by Asian workers, the majority of whom are women (Steger, 2003). The sexual abuse and assault of Asian sweatshop workers is both endemic and egregious, and because sexual harassment laws in many Asian countries are either nonexistent or not enforced, Western companies like Nike that have clear prohibitions and that provide sensitivity training become magnets for the most talented and skilled Asian workers (Chhabra, 2008).

Even more vulnerable to sexual harassment than sweatshop workers are migrant workers. The transitory nature of migrant work has precluded documentation of its prevalence. But, journalist and activist reports suggest the problem is significant. In Guntur, India, in 2007, the harvest of chilis and cotton was delayed due to a shortage of labor that local agencies attributed to the district's notoriety for sexual harassment (Pradesh, 2007). According to the Taipei Foreign Workers Consulting Center, the sexual harassment of foreigners working in that city—particularly of domestic assistants—has become acute (Lui, 2003).

Undocumented workers are perhaps the most vulnerable of all because they are excluded from local justice mechanisms. As a result, undocumented Latinas reported to the EEOC that they were forced to exchange sex for employment in the hotel industry and for protection from deportation (Vellos, 1997). In countries without government agencies to hold employers accountable, foreign workers turn to their embassies and consulates for assistance. Human Rights Watch claims embassies in the Middle East are flooded with workers complaining of sexual abuse, assault, and forced labor (Turner, 2007). Interviews with 100 domestic workers seeking assistance found that 13 of them had been repeatedly raped by their employers, and the others had routinely been fondled, had received demands for sex, and were offered money to perform sexual favors.

Sexual Harassment of Women and Girls in Schools

The transformation of sexual harassment from a personal problem to a social one and from a socially accepted practice to an illegal one began in the workplace. But since the early 1970s, awareness has grown that sexual harassment is equally problematic in educational settings. In 1982, the definition of sexual harassment codified by the EEOC was adopted, almost entirely, by the U.S. Office of Civil Rights to conceptualize sexual harassment as a form of educational discrimination and therefore a violation of the U.S. Civil Rights Act of 1964. As was the case with workplace harassment, initially policy development and research studies were often piecemeal. Although scholarly writing on sexual harassment of college women began in the early 1980s, the victimization of high school girls did not become a focus until the early 1990s.

Sexual Harassment on College Campuses

The first insights into the problem of sexual harassment on campuses came from interviews with women students who provided narratives of their experiences with male staff, particularly faculty. Hall and Sandler (1982) chronicled the routine nature of sexist comments, sexual overtures, and general disregard of women's concerns. This "chilly climate" impacted the lives of thousands of women students across the country. About the same time, Dzeich and Werner (1984) focused on the predatory behavior of male professors who groped, fondled, and sexually bribed their students, often without sanctioning of any sort from peers or administrators. Both works provided a national wake-up call about a pervasive problem that had received scant attention. As was true with studies of workplace harassment, the discovery of sexual harassment on college campuses began with case studies of women who provided sordid details about their experiences and later resulted in surveys and interviews of large numbers of women. In this regard, Michele Paludi's book, *Ivory Power: The Sexual Harassment of Women on Campus* (1991), was a landmark publication that presented a comprehensive overview of theory, research problems, and substantive findings on sexual harassment. The chapters covered legal issues, profiles of victims and perpetrators, descriptions of women's coping responses, and training and prevention strategies.

A contributor to Paludi's book, Louise Fitzgerald, conducted one of the first large-scale surveys of women students and staff. She and her colleagues found high levels of harassment—over 50%—on two campuses (Fitzgerald et al., 1988). This publication introduced their measure of harassment, the Sexual Experiences Questionnaire (SEQ). For two decades, Fitzgerald and her colleagues have continued to develop the SEQ and to expand the populations on which it is used. The SEQ focuses on three forms of sexual harassment: gender harassment, unwanted sexual attention, and sexual coercion. *Gender harassment* refers to behaviors that convey sexist and degrading attitudes toward women. Crude sexual remarks, stereotypic comments about women's competence or abilities, or obscene gestures are examples. *Unwanted sexual attention* includes offensive touching, stroking, or fondling; asking personal questions of a sexual nature; or repeated requests for dates or sex. *Sexual coercion* includes sexual bribery (offering a reward or threatening punishment as a means of obtaining sexual favors) and sexual assault. Along with the SEQ, survey items developed by the American Association of University Women Educational Foundation (AAUW) present most of the information we have about sexual harassment on college campuses and in U.S. secondary schools (AAUW, 1993, 2001, 2005).

More recent SEQ-based studies reveal that sexual harassment is a widespread problem for women on college campuses. Cortina, Swan, Fitzgerald, and Waldo (1998) found that half the women on a large campus—49% of undergraduates and 53% of graduate students—had been harassed by a college professor. They also found

an alarmingly high percentage of sexual assault (11%) among women in their sample. A more recent survey found that 56% of women students had experienced harassment from faculty, staff, or peers over a 12-month period (Huerta, Cortina, Pang, Torges, & Magley, 2006). Gender harassment impacted nearly all the women (92%), unwanted sexual attention was experienced by more than half (53%), and 5% were victims of sexual coercion. A large national sample of college students sponsored by the AAUW found that 62% of women students had experienced harassment during their college careers, especially during their first year (Hill & Silva, 2005). More than half (57%) were the targets of sexual jokes or comments, and more than one in four (28%) had experienced physical contact of a sexual nature. Approximately 5% were victims of sexual bribery. These results parallel those of Gross, Winslett, Roberts, and Gohm (2006), who found that 28% of women students had experienced unwanted sexual contact of a physical nature.

Similar to the research on workplace harassment, studies of women on college campuses showed that some women are more likely to be victims of harassment than others. Sexual orientation is a significant predictive factor in this regard. Lesbian and bisexual women report rates of harassment that are significantly higher than their heterosexual peers. Cortina et al. (1998) revealed that 81% of such women had been sexually harassed; Hill and Silva (2005) found 73%. Race and ethnicity are also predictive factors, but the research results are conflicting. In an SEQ-based study, African American and Hispanic women had somewhat higher harassment rates than white women (62% and 60%, respectively, versus 56%), though these differences were not significant. The AAUW survey, however, found significantly higher rates among whites (64%) than among either African Americans or Hispanics (54%). However, there were no differences in physical contact sexual harassment between the groups. Finally, field of study is a predictor of sexual harassment. Specifically, women in male-dominated fields are more likely to experience discrimination and harassment than women in fields with balanced gender ratios. Perhaps the most well-known "wake-up call" in this regard began with a series of complaints in the early 1990s by Professor Nancy Gibson, a biologist at M.I.T., about a lack of laboratory space and research support (see Miller & Wilson, 1999, for a comprehensive summary). After she read M.I.T's sexual harassment policy statement that said "sexual harassment was to be in a place where the atmosphere is so threatening that you couldn't do your work," she thought, "This is my entire life." She filed suit against the university and caught the attention of other women faculty at M.I.T. who had suffered for years in silence—and then the attention of women scientists across the country, who began studies of discrimination and harassment on their own campuses. Like Gibson, Carla Corroto (2005) presented an insider's perspective on the mistreatment and abuse of women in the male-dominated discipline of architecture. She provided details about the complex meanings of male power and privilege by describing the far reaches of normative dominance during a three-year stint as a faculty member in a school of architecture. In addition to the frequent sexualized comments that women students received from male faculty and peers about their dress and physical attributes, the landscape of graduate school—in particular, architectural studios—was claimed as male space. For example, a number of male students listened to sex-talk call-in shows and hung pornographic images of women on studio walls. The complaints of women students to faculty and administrators about the discriminatory and harassing behavior of their peers fell on deaf ears.

Perhaps the clearest examples of the impact of "double dominance" in education are from surveys of military academies. In 2003, the exposure of sexual harassment and assault at the Air Force Academy—where, among other findings, 12% of senior women cadets testified that they had been victims of rape or attempted rape during their academic careers—led to a federally sponsored investigation of all three military academies. Compared to studies of university students,

studies of women in military academies revealed they experienced higher levels of sexual harassment (59–62%) and sexual assault (4–6%) *during a 12-month period* (Cook, Jones, Lipari, & Lancaster, 2005). In contrast, Hill and Silva's (2005) national survey of college women found that 62% had been sexually harassed over the course of their *entire academic career.* Perhaps a silver lining to these dismal statistics is that both male and female cadets perceived that problems with harassment and assault had improved during the course of their training.

In academic settings, the frequency of harassment is significantly associated with adverse psychological outcomes. Schneider, Swan, and Fitzgerald (1997) tabulated how often respondents had been harassed, regardless of the type of harassment, and found that higher frequencies, as measured by the SEQ, significantly predicted life satisfaction, mental health, and PTSD symptoms. But targets of low-frequency harassment experienced adverse outcomes too, though not to the degree that victims of more frequent harassment did. Women who were "doubly victimized" by sexual harassment *and* sexual assault had significantly poorer evaluations of women's treatment on campus, felt less accepted and respected by faculty and peers, and indicated a lower likelihood of returning to school to continue their studies (Cortina et al., 1998). The short-term effects of harassment include psychological distress, low academic satisfaction, and physical illness; the cumulative impact reveals disengagement from the academic environment and poorer academic performance. These results were especially striking when the perpetrator was a faculty member or administrator. A strong relationship between harassment severity and PTSD was found among college students as well (McDermut, Haaga, & Kirk, 2000). Rather than using a simple frequency measure, McDermut and colleagues divided the SEQ categories into "severe" and "mild" forms and found that victims of the former had higher scores on all three PTSD subscales (re-experiencing the harassment, avoidance and numbing, and hypervigilance). A majority of women in a recent national' survey reacted with embarrassment and/or anger to their sexual harassment experiences (Hill & Silva, 2005). A smaller percentage (5–8%) of the respondents had serious concerns about whether or not they could be successful in their chosen field, complete their undergraduate coursework, or attend post-graduate education (pp. 28–29).

Are women on U.S. campuses harassed more frequently (or differently) than their peers on other campuses around the globe? The answer to such a straightforward question is complicated because of differing research techniques and surveys that have been used to collect data, varying focal time periods (e.g., harassed in the last 12 months versus ever harassed while a student), and crucially, different cultural understanding about "sexual harassment." A review of SEQ-based studies from countries outside the United States reveals the complexity (DeSouza & Solberg, 2003).

According to international indicators of gender equality, such as the United Nations' GEM (Gender Empowerment Measure), Scandinavian countries have some of the highest levels of gender parity in the world. But does this translate into less sexual harassment on college and high school campuses? Two comparative studies—one of college students and a second of high school students (see Witkowska & Menckel, 2005)—provide evidence in this regard. Undergraduates at a major Finnish university were compared to American students who completed similar SEQ-based surveys (Gruber, Husu, & Kauppinen, 2007). In contrast to American students, Finns experienced significantly less sexual harassment from instructors. Also, both Finnish male and female undergraduates were more sensitized to the problem of sexual harassment and, more generally, gender discrimination. That is, a larger proportion of Finns of both sexes labeled a wider range of sexually based behaviors as constituting "sexual harassment." For more than half a century, the Finnish government has aggressively pursued policies and initiatives aimed at addressing gender inequality. Consequently, for decades

Finns have had much greater exposure to the problems of gender imbalance in a variety of contexts—marriage and parenting, job discrimination, wage/salary inequity, and access to higher education (Gruber et al., 2007).

Sexual Harassment in Secondary Schools

Sexual harassment in secondary schools differs from that found on college campuses in at least two ways. First, secondary schools seem to have significantly higher rates of victimization (see AAUW, 1993, 2001), and in contrast to college campuses and workplaces, there are no significant gender differences in victimization (AAUW, 1993, 2001; Gruber & Fineran, 2008). In all three types of settings, however, males are perpetrators to a much larger extent than females.

Sexual harassment in secondary schools is primarily peer to peer, although the AAUW (2001) estimated that one in four girls has been harassed by school personnel (teacher, coach, school bus driver, etc.). The most comprehensive reports on sexual harassment were conducted by the AAUW in 1993, with a follow-up in 2001. Their recent report, *Hostile Hallways* (2001), found that 81% of students in U.S. schools reported sexual harassment from their peers during their school years (83% of girls and 79% of boys). These and other studies of secondary schools find that peer sexual harassment is widespread, with incidence rates between 50% and 88% (AAUW, 1993; Fineran & Bennett, 1999; Permanent Commission on the Status of Women [PCSW], 1995; Roscoe, Strouse, & Goodwin, 1994; Stratton & Backes, 1997; Trigg & Wittenstrom, 1996). These studies provided descriptive analyses of harassment—type of behavior, when and where it occurred, or student responses to it—but did not explore the effects of context, as many studies of workplace harassment have done. A few recent studies have addressed this problem. The Organizational Tolerance of Sexual Harassment Scale, which has been used widely in workplace studies, was adapted for a survey of high school students. The results found that school environments that are perceived as tolerant of sexual harassment of girls not only have higher rates of harassment, especially severe harassment, but are associated with poorer health and school outcomes (self-esteem, body image, sense of safety at school) for girls (Ormerod, Collinsworth, & Perry, 2008). The findings from a study of sexual minorities in high school parallel those from women workers. Chesir-Teran and Hughes (2009) explored the impact of programs and policies that were developed to create more tolerant and safer school environments for lesbian, gay, bisexual, and transgender students. Similar to Gruber's (1998) study of working women, their study showed proactive programs were more effective in creating tolerance and reducing victimization than was the mere promulgation of policy statements (e.g., postings of statements in public settings).

The AAUW (1993, 2001) reports indicated that more than 50% of male and female students experienced sexual comments, jokes, gestures, or looks. More than 30% of boys and girls experienced being touched, grabbed, pinched, or brushed up against in a sexual manner by schoolmates. In a study by Fineran and Bennett (1999), unwanted sexual attention, including pressure for dates and sex, was reported by approximately 43% of girls and 30% of boys, while in the PCSW (1995) studies, 25% of girls and 5% of boys reported unwanted sexual attention. Though gender differences in victimization are small, differences in *perpetration* are large and significant: Boys perpetrate sexual harassment more frequently than girls (AAUW, 1993, 2001; DeSouza & Ribeiro, 2005; Fineran & Bennett, 1999; PCSW, 1995; Stratton & Backes, 1997; Trigg & Wittenstrom, 1996). Compared to workplaces or college campuses, secondary schools seem to present unique sexual harassment challenges for young women. The amount of sexualized physical contact is significant—being grabbed or brushed up against, being forced to kiss a boy, or having their clothes pulled, for example. Also, one in five girls report being the targets of sexual rumors. With the

widespread use of text messaging and the Internet, it is likely that this figure will only increase. In a recent survey, more than three-quarters of secondary school girls who had been victims of sexual rumors labeled the experience as "very upsetting" (Gruber & Fineran, 2008).

Research of military women has consistently identified homophobia as a significant factor affecting both the severity and frequency of sexual harassment (see Embers-Herbert, 2005). Emerging research of girls suggests the problem is not limited to the military. Lesbian and bisexual girls experience much higher levels of sexual harassment than do heterosexual girls. The Massachusetts Youth Risk Behavior Survey found that gay, lesbian, and bisexual students were more likely than their peers to have been threatened with or injured by a weapon at school or to have experienced dating violence and nonconsensual sex (Massachusetts Department of Education, 2007). These results parallel those of Fineran (2002) and Williams, Connolly, Pepler, and Craig (2005), who found that sexual minority students were physically assaulted and sexually harassed more frequently than were heterosexual students. A recent report by the Gay, Lesbian, and Straight Education Network (2005) on Michigan schools revealed that two-thirds of students in their sample were sexually harassed because they were, or appeared to be, gay or lesbian. More than 80% of these students reported hearing derogatory homophobic comments.

Compared to the research on sexual orientation, which finds substantial differences in rates of sexual harassment victimization between sexual minorities and heterosexuals, studies of racial differences reveal few real differences. American research on sexual harassment (AAUW, 2001; Fineran & Gruber, 2004) as well as on bullying reports insignificant differences between racial groups (Nansel, Overpeck, Pilla, Ruan, Scheidt, and Simons-Morton, 2001; Peskin, Tortolero, & Markham, 2006). However, an Israeli survey that found that Arab boys were at significantly greater risk of sexualized intimidation than any other group may provide insight into some of the reasons for the conflicting results for race and ethnicity (Zeira, Aster, & Benbenishty, 2002). They explained the difference between the two groups as resulting largely from a significant socioeconomic gap. Arab students attended poorer schools that were located in low-income, unstable communities with higher levels of crime and violence. The socioeconomic factor may be the missing piece in understanding race differences in school sexual harassment in the United States because public schools are highly race segregated.

There is some evidence that a national climate that promotes gender equality may affect sexual harassment in high school. By adapting the survey items from the AAUW's *Hostile Hallways* study (2001) to a national survey of Swedish students, Witkowska and Menckel (2005) found substantial differences between the experiences of Swedish and American girls on *all* the comparable survey items. Most notably, Swedish girls experienced significantly fewer instances of both verbal (e.g., sexual jokes or comments, sexual rumors, sexual name-calling) and physical contact (grabbing or groping, pulling clothes down) harassment from their peers than their American counterparts. They also experienced substantially less harassment from their teachers. Also, in contrast to American students, who typically perceived sexual harassment as horseplay, Swedish adolescents were more likely to label specific incidents of harassment as problematic. Sweden, similar to Finland, has perennially had one of the highest GEM scores in the world. These results may be due to decades-long government mandates and programs that have focused on gender inequality in all facets of Swedish life (see Eliasson & Lundy, 1999).

The research on sexual harassment in secondary schools is clear on two points: Harassment causes significant harm to students' physical and mental health as well as school attachment and satisfaction and academic achievement, and the harm is greater for girls, who find harassment to be more threatening and upsetting. Compared to other students, victims of harassment report a considerable number of adverse outcomes,

including loss of appetite, loss of interest in non-school activities, nightmares or disturbed sleep, feelings of isolation from friends and family, and feeling afraid (AAUW, 1993, 2001; Chiodo, Wolfe, Crooks, Hughes, & Jaffe, 2009; PCSW, 1995; Stratton & Backes, 1997). Two recent studies by Gruber and Fineran (2007, 2008) provide specific details on the health impacts of harassment. In the first, middle school and high school girls were compared on six outcomes (self-esteem, mental and physical health, trauma symptoms, life satisfaction, and substance abuse). They found significant relationships between sexual harassment victimization and adverse outcomes on all six outcomes for both grade levels. Girls in high school experienced more sexual harassment, but middle school girls reported more *harm* from harassment. The authors argued that middle school girls are more vulnerable to the impact of sexual harassment because they are dealing with a number of issues during a critical developmental stage (e.g., dating, body image, social relationships) that challenge their emotional reserves. The second study compared the same health outcomes for boys and girls (disregarding grade level). It found that girls not only experienced a greater number of adverse health outcomes because of sexual harassment, but that the impact on each was greater. The results parallel those of a study of adolescents in the Netherlands (Timmerman, 2004). Students were asked how often they had experienced one or more of 19 types of "unwanted sexual behaviors" adapted from the AAUW surveys. In both the U.S. and Netherlands studies, girls had more psychosomatic complaints (e.g., headaches, sleep problems) and poorer self-esteem than boys as a result of sexual harassment. Perhaps most troubling of all is the fact that harassment is not an isolated event in a particular grade, but is instead a predictable, ongoing series of incidents. Chiodo and her colleagues (2009) found that victimization in ninth grade predicted harassment victimization and dating violence, as well as substance abuse and delinquency, by the eleventh grade. The long-term effects of peer victimization begin early in life. Kochenderfer and Ladd (1996) found that harassment affected both loneliness and school avoidance among *kindergartners.*

Sexual minority students experience greater harm as a result of harassment, along with higher victimization rates. An annual school survey, the Massachusetts Youth Risk Behavior Survey, found that when compared to their heterosexual peers, gays, lesbians, and bisexuals had higher suicide rates and were more likely to skip school because they felt unsafe (Massachusetts Department of Education, 2007). Supporting this very negative picture, Gruber and Fineran (2007, 2008) found in a study of eighth graders that gay, lesbian, and bisexual victims of harassment had poorer mental health, more trauma (PTSD) symptoms, and felt more fearful than their heterosexual peers.

The New Focus on Bullying (and the Decline of Sexual Harassment)

In the wake of highly publicized school shootings during the past decade, many educators and public officials have embraced zero tolerance policies to stem school violence (Stein, 2003). The focus of these prevention programs has been bullying. The surge of interest in bullying can be seen easily in a perusal of the online literature, where the volume of studies, papers, and prevention programs that address bullying far exceeds those on sexual harassment. Moreover, sexual harassment is currently viewed by some researchers as a subset or variation of bullying, rather than as a distinct phenomenon. The drift from sexual harassment to bullying is unfortunate because it "degenders harassment . . . and [places] it into a more psychological, pathologizing realm" (Brown, Chesney-Lind, & Stein, 2007, p. 1257). As a result, sexual harassment as a theoretical and legal construct is more directly and clearly related to hegemonic masculinity and subsequently taps more potently into structural and culturally sanctioned roles and meanings

(masculine-feminine, male-female, heterosexual-homosexual) that are core components of social stratification. In contrast, research and theory on bullying tends to focus on the personal or psychological characteristics of bullies, situational factors that prompt bullying, or the reciprocity of bullying behaviors (a significant number of adolescents are characterized as "bully/victim"). One of the strengths of sexual harassment theory is that it prioritizes the fact that gender- and sexually based experiences are primarily unidirectional and power based. Specifically, some people (females and sexual minorities) experience more harm (physical, psychological, and emotional) than others because of the onerous weight of gender and sexual categorizations. The term "sexual bullying" has surfaced recently and has muddled the definition of both sexual harassment and bullying. Some researchers view school sexual harassment as an adolescent form of bullying (McMaster, Connolly, Pepler, & Craig, 2002; Pellegrini, 2001). This increasing appeal of bullying prevention over sexual harassment is problematic for three reasons (Brown et al., 2007). First, antibullying efforts are not reinforced by the law as sexual harassment is, thereby shifting the responsibility of bullying from school administrators to victims. Also, anti-bullying programs are broad and arbitrary, making it difficult to systematically police unacceptable behaviors. Finally, anti-bullying efforts sometimes mislabel serious, illegal behavior in a way that deflates both the gravity of the behavior and the effect on its victims. A bullying paradigm loses sight of the fact that most bullies are male, that girls experience more harm than boys from sexual harassment, and that homophobic comments are used routinely (mostly by boys) to humiliate and control others—primarily other boys (AAUW, 2001; Kimmel & Mahler, 2003; McGuffey & Rich, 1999). Two studies by Jessie Klein (2006a, 2006b) have highlighted the role of gender and sexual stratification in school shootings—a fact that escaped public scrutiny because of a focus on "bullying": Most of the school shooters targeted girls primarily, and the shooters, who fell well outside the range of acceptable masculine body types, had weathered attacks on their masculinity, including homophobic taunts, for months and, in some cases, years. In contrast, the bullying paradigm creates "a tyranny of sameness" (Brown et al., 2007, p. 1263) in which gender, race, social class, and ethnicity differences are blurred, if not ignored entirely.

Conclusion

The research reported in this chapter makes it clear that sexual harassment is one of the most endemic forms of violence against women and girls today. Despite widespread prohibition around the world, unwanted sexual attention is an unavoidable condition of work and education for a significant number of women and girls. The types of behaviors that constitute it and the type and severity of harm that result from it vary by region, occupation, and discipline. How seriously complaints are taken and the amount of protection and remediation offered vary by nationality and organization. Globalization has been a dual-edged sword in the campaign to protect women. Transnationalism has facilitated a global dissemination of American sexual harassment policy and research. Adoption of U.S. policy has standardized expectations and practices for multinational corporations and international educational programs. Recent replications of American survey methodology and the application of measurements like the SEQ among non-U.S. populations have begun to yield a rich harvest of cross-comparative research. And while these advances promise to improve the lives of many women workers and students, the most vulnerable among us—sweatshop workers, migrant workers, undocumented workers, military cadets, foreign exchange students, and young girls—continue to endure the most pernicious forms of sexual harassment.

As the world struggles to survive the most significant economic recession since the Great Depression, the global hemorrhaging of employment and educational opportunities will only increase the number of women and girls vulnerable to sexual harassment. To balance their meager budgets, governments, employers, universities, and schools have already begun to reduce or cut completely vital resources for prevention and protection. So, while lawmakers were exceptionally prolific in their efforts to prohibit sexual harassment during an era of unprecedented economic expansion, the question remains whether their efforts will be sufficient in this time of extreme economic contraction.

References

Alleyne, R. (2008, April). Christina Rich in £2 million settlement. *Telegraph.co.uk*. Retrieved April 25, 2009, from http://www.telegraph.co.uk/finance/markets/2787246/Christina-Rich-in-2-million-settlement.html.

American Association of University Women Educational Foundation. (1993). *Hostile hallways: The AAUW survey on sexual harassment in the American schools.* Washington, DC: Author.

American Association of University Women Educational Foundation. (2001). *Hostile hallways: Bullying, teasing and sexual harassment in school.* Washington, DC: Author.

American Association of University Women Educational Foundation. (2005). *Drawing the line: Sexual harassment on campus.* Retrieved March 11, 2010, from http://www.aauwmo.org/Drawing_the_Line.htm.

Bencomo, C. (2005, December). Physical and verbal abuse, and sexual harassment and exploitation. *Inside the home, outside the law: Abuse of child domestic workers in Morocco.* Human Rights Watch, *17*(12), 16–20. Retrieved January 17, 2009, from http://www.hrw.org/en/node/11491/section/6.

Bior, H. (2008, February 16). Sexual harassment filed in 80% of orgs. *Haaretz.com.* Retrieved April 13, 2009, from https://www.haaretz.co.il/hasen/spages/954483.html.

Branigan, T. (2008, July 16). Manager becomes first man jailed under Chinese harassment laws. *The Guardian.CO.UK.* Retrieved April 4, 2009, from http://www.guardian.co.uk/world/2008/jul/16/china.gender?gusrc=rss&feed=networkfront.

Brown, L., Chesney-Lind, M., & Stein, N. (2007). Patriarchy matters: Toward a gendered theory of teen violence and victimization. *Violence Against Women, 33,* 1249–1273.

Burlington Industries, Inc. v. Ellerth, 524 U.S. 742 (1998).

Cahill, M. (2001). *Social construction of sexual harassment law: The role of national, organizational and individual context.* Surrey, UK: Ashgate.

Canadian Human Rights Commission. (1983). *Unwanted sexual attention and sexual harassment: Results of a survey of Canadians.* Ottawa: Minister of Supply and Services, Canada.

Chesir-Teran, D., & Hughes, D. (2009). Heterosexism in high school and victimization among lesbian, gay, bisexual, and questioning students. *Journal of Youth and Adolescence, 38,* 963–975.

Chhabra R. (2008, October 22). Workplace equality— Putting harassment on notice. *Ethical Corporation.* Retrieved April 25, 2009, from http://www.ethical corp.com/content.asp?ContentID=6140.

Chiodo, D., Wolfe, D., Crooks, C., Hughes, R., & Jaffe, P. (2009). The impact of sexual harassment victimization by peers on subsequent adolescent victimization and adjustment: A longitudinal study. *Journal of Adolescent Health, 45,* 246–252.

Civil Rights Act of 1991, Pub. L. No. 102-166, 105 Stat. 1071 (1991).

Cook, P., Jones, A., Lipari, R., & Lancaster, A. (2005, December) *Service academy 2005 sexual harassment and assault survey.* DMDC Report No. 2005–018. Arlington, VA: DMDC.

Corroto, C. (2005). The architecture of sexual harassment. In J. E. Gruber & P. Morgan (Eds.), *In the company of men: Male dominance and sexual harassment* (pp. 271–293). Boston: Northeastern University Press.

Cortina, L., Swan, S., Fitzgerald, L., & Waldo, C. (1998). Sexual harassment and assault: Chilling the climate for women in academia. *Psychology of Women Quarterly, 22,* 419–441.

Crawford v. Nashville and Davidson County, TN, 555 U.S. 061595, U.S. (2009).

Deadrick, D. (2001). Service with a smile: Legal and emotional issues. *Journal of Quality Management, 6,* 99–110.

DeSouza, E., & Cerqueria, E. (2009). From the kitchen to the bedroom: Frequency rates and consequences of sexual harassment among female domestic workers in Brazil. *Journal of Interpersonal Violence, 24,* 1264–1284.

DeSouza, E., & Ribeiro, J. (2005). Bullying and sexual harassment among Brazilian high school students. *Journal of Interpersonal Violence, 20,* 1018–1038.

DeSouza, E. R., & Solberg, J. (2003). Incidence and dimensions of sexual harassment across cultures. In M. Paludi & C. Paludi (Eds.), *Academic and workplace sexual harassment: A handbook of cultural, social science, management, and legal perspectives* (pp. 3–30). Westport, CT: Praeger.

Dobbin, F. (2006). Sexual harassment: The global and the local. *Sociological Forum, 21,* 709–713.

Dzeich, B., & Weiner, L. (1984). *The lecherous professor: Sexual harassment on campus.* Boston: Beacon Press.

Eliasson, M., & Lundy, C. (1999). Organizing to stop violence against women in Canada and Sweden. In L. Briskin & M. Eliasson (Eds.), *Women's organizing and public policy in Canada and Sweden* (pp. 276–314). Montreal: McGill-Queen's Press.

Embers-Herbert, M. S. (2005). A missing link: Institutional homophobia and sexual harassment in the military. In J. E. Gruber & P. Morgan (Eds.), *In the company of men: Male dominance and sexual harassment* (pp. 215–242). Boston: Northeastern University Press.

European Commission. (1999). *Sexual harassment in the European Union.* Retrieved April 13, 2009, from http://www.un.org/womenwatch/osagi/pdf/shwor kpl.pdf.

European Foundation for the Improvement of Living and Working Conditions. (2007). *Violence, bullying and sexual harassment in the workplace.* Retrieved April 13, 2009, from http://www.euro found.europa.eu/ewco/reports/TN0406TR01/TN 0406TR01.pdf.

European Union. (2002). Directive/73/EC of the European Parliament and of the Council of 23 September 2002. *Official Journal of the European Communities.* Retrieved April 13, 2009, from http://eur-lex.europa.eu/LexUriServ/LexUriServ.do? uri=OJ:L:2002:269:0015:0020:EN:PDF.

European Union. (2004, June). Report on sexual harassment in the workplace in EU member states. Retrieved April 13, 2009, from http://www.unece .org/stats/gender/publications/Multi-Country/ SexualHarassmentReport.pdf

Faragher v. City of Boca Raton, 524 U.S. 775 (1998).

Farley, L. (1978). *Sexual shakedown.* New York: McGraw Hill.

Fineran, S. (2002). Sexual minority students and peer sexual harassment in high school. *Journal of School Social Work, 11,* 50–69.

Fineran, S., & Bennett, L. (1999). Gender and power issues of peer sexual harassment among teenagers. *Journal of Interpersonal Violence, 14,* 626–641.

Fineran, S., & Gruber, J. E. (2004, January). *Impact of sexual harassment victimization on the mental and physical health and coping responses of 8th-grade students.* Paper presented at the Annual Conference of the Society for Social Work Research, New Orleans, LA.

Fineran, S., & Gruber, J. E. (2008). Mental health impact of sexual harassment. In M. A. Paludi (Ed.), *The psychology of women at work: Challenges and solutions for our female workforce* (pp. 89–107). Westport, CT: Praeger.

Fitzgerald, L., Shullman, S., Bailey, N., Richards, M., Swecker, J., Gold, Y., et al. (1988). The incidence and dimensions of sexual harassment in academia and the workplace. *Journal of Vocational Behavior, 32,* 152–175.

The Gay, Lesbian, and Straight Education Network. (2005). *Social climate study: The experiences of gay, lesbian, bisexual, and transgendered youth in our nation's schools.* Retrieved March 11, 2010, from http://www.glsen.org/binary-data/GLSEN_ATTACHMENTS/file/585-1.pdf.

Ghafour, A. (2009, March 22). Bill to curb workplace harassment triggers heated debate. *Arab News.* Retrieved April 4, 2009, from http://www.arabnews.com/?page=1&section=0&article=120585.

Goodwin, J. (2003). Walmart named in Columbia, Mo. sexual harassment lawsuit. *Columbia Daily Tribune.* Retrieved March 11, 2010, from http://www.accessmylibrary.com/coms2/summary_0286 6954517_ITM

Grimsley, K. (1996, December 22). Sexual harasser can often prey on many victims. *Washington Post.* Retrieved April 9, 2009, from http://www.washingtonpost.com/wp-adv/classifieds/careerpost/library/harrass1.htm

Gross, A., Winslett, A., Roberts, M., & Gohm, C. (2006). An examination of sexual violence against college women. *Violence Against Women, 12,* 288–305.

Gruber, J. (1998). The impact of male work environments and organizational policies on women's experiences of sexual harassment. *Gender & Society, 12,* 301–320.

Gruber, J., & Fineran, S. (2007). The impact of bullying and sexual harassment on middle and high school girls. *Violence Against Women, 13,* 627–643.

Gruber, J., & Fineran, S. (2008). Comparing the impact of bullying and sexual harassment victimization on the mental and physical health of adolescents. *Sex Roles, 59,* 1–13.

Gruber, J., Husu, L., & Kauppinen, K. (2007, August). *From G.E.M. to the classroom: Exploring links between gender equality and sexual harassment of university students in two nations.* Paper presented at the annual meeting of the American Psychological Association, San Francisco, CA.

Gruber, J. E., & Morgan. P. (Eds.). (2005). *In the company of men: Male dominance and sexual harassment.* Boston: Northeastern University Press.

Gutek, B. (1985). *Sex and the workplace.* San Francisco: Jossey-Bass.

Hall, R., & Sandler, B. (1982). *The classroom climate: A chilly one for women?* Washington, DC: Association of American Colleges, Project on the Status and Education of Women.

Harris, M. (2009, January 23). Appeals court upholds sexual harassment award. *The Ventura County Star.* Retrieved April 9, 2009, from http://www.venturacountystar.com/news/2009/jan/23/appeals-court-upholds-sexual-harassment-award

Harris v. Forklift Systems, 510 U.S. 17 (1993).

Hesketh, K., Duncan S., Estabrooks, C., Reimer, M., Giovanetti, P., Hyndman, K., et al. (2003). Workplace violence in Alberta and British Columbia hospitals. *Health Policy, 63,* 311–321.

Hill, C., & Silva, E. (2005). *Drawing the line: Sexual harassment on campus.* Washington, DC: American Association of University Women Educational Foundation.

Huen, Y. (2007). Workplace sexual harassment in Japan. *Asian Survey, 47,* 811–827.

Huerta, M., Cortina, L., Pang, J., Torges, C., & Magley, V. (2006). Sex and power in the academy: Modeling sexual harassment in the lives of college women. *Personality and Social Psychology Bulletin, 32,* 616–628.

Kane-Urrabazo, C. (2007). Sexual harassment in the workplace: It is your problem. *Journal of Nursing Management, 15,* 608–613.

Kauppinen, K., & Gruber, J. (1993). The antecedents and outcomes of women-unfriendly behavior. *Psychology of Women Quarterly, 17,* 431–456.

Kim, V. (2008, November 13). LAPD officer awarded $3.6 in retaliation suit. *Los Angeles Times.*

Retrieved April 9, 2009, from http://articles
.latimes.com/2008/nov/13/local/me-lapd13

Kimmel, M., & Mahler, M. (2003). Adolescent masculinity, homophobia, and violence: Random school shootings, 1982–2000. *American Behavioral Scientist, 46,* 1439–1458.

Klein, J. (2006a). An invisible problem: Everyday violence against girls in schools. *Theoretical Criminology, 10,* 147–177.

Klein, J. (2006b). Sexuality and school shootings: What role does teasing play in school massacres? *Journal of Homosexuality, 51,* 39–62.

Kochenderfer, B., & Ladd, G. (1996). Peer victimization: Cause or consequence of school maladjustment? *Child Development, 67,* 1305–1317.

Lee, D. (2001). He didn't sexually harass me, as in harassed for sex . . .he was just horrible": Women's definitions of unwanted male sexual conduct at work. *Women's Studies International Forum, 24,* 25–38.

Lui, R. (2003, August 31). Foreign workers' woes increase. *Taipei Times.* Retrieved April 25, 2009, from http://www.taipeitimes.com/news/taiwan/archives/2003/08/31/2003065934

MacKinnon, C. (1979). *Sexual harassment of working women.* New Haven, CT: Yale.

Massachusetts Department of Education. (2007). *2005 Youth Risk Behavior Survey.* Malden, MA: Author.

McDermut, J., Haaga, D., & Kirk, L. (2000). An evaluation of stress symptoms associated with academic sexual harassment. *Journal of Traumatic Stress, 13,* 397–411.

McGuffey, C., & Rich, M. (1999). Playing in the gender transgression zone: Race, class, and hegemonic masculinity in middle school. *Gender & Society, 13,* 608–627.

McMaster, L., Connolly, J., Pepler, D., & Craig, W. (2002). Peer to peer sexual harassment in early adolescence: A developmental perspective. *Development and Psychopathology, 14,* 91–105.

Meritor Savings Bank v. Mechelle Vinson, 477 U.S. 57 (1986).

Merkin, R. S. (2008). Cross-cultural differences in perceiving sexual harassment: Demographic incidence rates of sexual harassment in Latin America. *Journal of Psychology, 10*(02), 277–290.

Miller, D., & Wilson, R. (1999, April 2). MIT acknowledges bias against female faculty members. *Chronicle of Higher Education,* p. A18.

Moline, A. (2002, July 22). European Union tells members to bar sex harassment. *Women's E-News* Retrieved April 4, 2009 from http://www.womensenews.org/article.cfm/dyn/aid/980/context/archive

Morgan, P., & Gruber, J. E. (2008). Sexual harassment and male dominance: Toward an ecological approach. In M. A. Paludi (Ed.), *The psychology of women at work: Obstacles and the identity jungle* (pp. 85–108). Westport, CT: Praeger.

Murray, W., Sivasubramaniam, N., & Jacques, P. (2001). Supervisory support, social exchange relationships and sexual harassment consequences. *Leadership Quarterly, 12,* 1–29.

Nansel, T., Overpeck, R., Pilla, W., Ruan, P., Scheidt, K., & Simons-Morton, B. (2001). Bullying behaviors among U.S. youth: Prevalence and association with psychological adjustment. *Journal of the American Medical Association, 285,* 2094–2100.

O'Donohue, W., et al. (2006, January). Sexual harassment as diagnosable PTSD trauma. *Psychiatric Times, 23,* 50–54, 59–62.

Oncale v. Sundowner Offshore Services, 523 U.S. 75 (1998).

Ormerod, A., Collinsworth, L., & Perry, L. (2008). Critical climate: Relations among sexual harassment, climate, and outcomes for high school girls and boys. *Psychology of Women Quarterly, 32,* 113–125.

Paludi, M. (Ed.). (1991). *Ivory power: Sexual harassment on campus.* Albany, NY: SUNY Press.

Parker, K. (2008). Ambient harassment under Title VII: Reconsidering workplace environment. *Northeastern University Law Review, 102,* 945–986.

Pellegrini, A. (2001). A longitudinal study of heterosexual relationships, aggression, and sexual harassment during transition from primary school through middle school. *Applied Developmental Psychology, 22,* 119–133.

Permanent Commission (CT) on the Status of Women. (1995). *In our own backyard: Sexual harassment in Connecticut's public high schools.* Hartford, CT: Author.

Peskin, M., Tortolero, S., & Markham, C. (2006). Bullying and victimization among black and Hispanic adolescents. *Adolescence, 41,* 467–484.

Pierce, C., Broberg, B. J., McClure, J. R., & Aguinis, H. (2004). Responding to sexual harassment complaints: Effects of a dissolved workplace romance on decision-making standards. *Organizational Behavior & Human Decision Processes, 95,* 66–82.

Pollard v. Dupont, 532 U.S. 843 (2001).

Pradesh, A. (2007, March 22). Sexual harassment deters migration to Guntur. *The Hindu.* Retrieved April 25, 2009, from http:/www.hindunet.com

Roscoe, B., Strouse, J. S., & Goodwin, M. P. (1994). Sexual harassment: Early adolescents' self-reports of experiences and acceptance. *Adolescence, 29,* 515–523.

Samuels, H. (2003). Sexual harassment in the workplace: A feminist analysis of recent developments in the UK. *Women's Studies International Forum, 26,* 467–482.

Schneider, K., Swan, S., & Fitzgerald, L. (1997). Job-related and psychological effects of sexual harassment in the workplace. *Journal of Applied Psychology, 82,* 401–415.

Steger, M. (2003). *Globalization, a very short introduction.* Oxford: Oxford University Press.

Stein, N. (2003). Bullying or sexual harassment? The missing discourse of rights in an era of zero tolerance. *Arizona Law Review, 45,* 783–799.

Stockdale, M. (2008). The sexual harassment of men: Articulating the approach-rejection theory of sexual harassment. In J. E. Gruber & P. Morgan (Eds.), *In the company of men: Male dominance and sexual harassment* (pp. 117–142). Boston: Northeastern University Press.

Stratton, S., & Backes, J. (1997, February/March). Sexual harassment in North Dakota public schools: A study of eight high schools. *High School Journal, 80,* 163–172.

Street, A. E., Stafford, J., Mahan, C. M., & Hendricks, A. (2008). Sexual harassment and assault experienced by reservists during military service. *Journal of Rehabilitation Research and Development, 45,* 409–420.

Texeira, M. (2002). Who protects and serves me? *Gender & Society, 16,* 524–545.

Timmerman, G. (2004). Adolescents' psychological health and experiences with unwanted sexual behavior. *Adolescence, 39,* 817–825.

Trigg, M., & Wittenstrom, K. (1996). That's the way the world goes: Sexual harassment and New Jersey teenagers. *Initiatives, Special Issue: Sexual Harassment, 57*(2), 55–65.

Turner, J. (2007, November). *Exported and exposed: Abuse against Sri Lankan domestic workers in Saudi Arabia, Kuwait, Lebanon, and the United Arab Emirates.* Human Rights Watch, *19*(16C), 1–130. Retrieved January 17, 2009, from http://www.hrw.org/en/node/10592/section/2

United States Equal Employment Opportunity Commission. (2009). *Sexual harassment.* Retrieved April 9, 2009, from http://www.eeoc.gov/types/sexual_harassment.html

United States Merit Systems Protection Board. (1994). *Sexual harassment in the federal workplace: Trends, progress and continuing challenges.* Retrieved April 13, 2009, from http://www.mspb.gov/netsearch/viewdocs.aspx?docnumber=253661&version=253948&application=ACROBAT

Van Roosmalen, E., & McDaniel, S. (1998) Sexual harassment in academia: A hazard to women's health. *Women & Health, 28*(2), 33–55.

Vellos, D. (1997, Spring). Immigrant Latina domestic workers and sexual harassment. *American University Journal of Gender and the Law,* 407–432.

Vijayasiri, G. (2008). Reporting sexual harassment: The importance of organizational culture and trust. *Gender Issues, 25,* 43–61.

Wehrli, L. (1976). *Sexual harassment in the workplace: A feminist analysis for social change.* Unpublished master's thesis, Massachusetts Institute of Technology.

Williams, T., Connolly, J., Pepler, D., & Craig, W. (2005). Peer victimization, social support, and psychosocial adjustment of sexual minority adolescents. *Journal of Youth and Adolescence, 34,* 471–482.

Willness, C., Steele, P., & Lee, K. (2007). A meta-analysis of antecedents of workplace sexual harassment. *Personnel Psychology, 60,* 127–162.

Witkowska, E., & Menckel, E. (2005). Perceptions of sexual harassment in Swedish high schools: Experiences and school-environment problems. *European Journal of Public Health, 15,* 78–85.

Zalesne, D. (2002). Sexual harassment law in the United States and South Africa: Facilitating the transition from legal standards to social norms. *Harvard Women's Law Review, 25,* 143–220.

Zippel, K. (2004). Transnational advocacy networks and policy cycles in the European Union: The case of sexual harassment. *Social Politics: International Studies in Gender, State and Society, 11,* 57–85.

Zeira, A., Aster, R., & Benbenishty, R. (2002). Sexual harassment in Jewish and Arab public schools in Israel. *Child Abuse and Neglect, 26,* 146–166.

Chapter Authors

Phoebe Morgan is a Professor of Criminology and coordinates the Faculty Ombuds Program at Northern Arizona University. She holds an M.S. and a Ph.D. in Justice Studies (ASU) and certificates in Women's Studies (ASU) and organizational mediation (UArk). She teaches courses about women and justice, security, and dispute resolution. With James Gruber, she edited *In The Company of Men: Male Dominance and Sexual Harassment* (Northeastern University Press, 2005). Her work appears in *Psychology of Women & Work, Law & Society Review, PS, Law, Culture & the Humanities, Criminal Justice Education, WSA Journal, Affilia, Classic Papers on VAW, Everyday Sexism in the Third Millennium,* and *Investigating Difference.* She regularly facilitates harassment sensitivity trainings and dispute resolution workshops. She is currently researching globalization and sexual harassment policy.

James E. Gruber, Ph.D., Professor of Sociology at the University of Michigan-Dearborn, has published research on sexual harassment for more than 25 years. He was among the first researchers to conduct studies of workplace sexual harassment in the early 1980s and cross-national studies in the early 1990s. His work on the experiences of women in male-dominated occupations resulted in a recent book, *In The Company of Men: Male Dominance and Sexual Harassment* (Northeastern University Press, 2005), coedited with Dr. Phoebe Morgan. Since 2002, Dr. Gruber and Dr. Susan Fineran have presented conference papers and published journal articles on bullying and sexual harassment among adolescents. Two recent publications with Dr. Fineran studied the effects of bullying and sexual harassment at school: "The Impact of Bullying and Sexual Harassment on Health Outcomes of Middle and High School Girls," published in *Violence Against Women* (2007), and "Comparing the Impact of Bullying and Sexual Harassment Victimization on the Mental and Physical Health of Adolescents" (*Sex Roles,* 2008). He has also coauthored an article in *Child Abuse & Neglect* (September, 2009) that examines the effects of workplace sexual harassment on adolescent girls.

Personal Reflection

Nan Stein

In 1979, while I was a graduate student in education at Harvard University, I started to work for the Massachusetts Department of Education as an educational specialist in the Bureau of Student Services. This was a time of student activism, with a wave of new laws at the state and federal levels that extended the rights of students—Title IX of the Federal Education Amendments (1972) and Chapter 622 of the Massachusetts General Laws (1971). Our unit had our own dedicated lawyer, separate from the office of the general counsel, to ensure and publicize student rights and to guarantee their participation in educational matters as mandated by law.

Besides our activist adult staff, we also employed six high school students in our Boston office who served in our "student service center." In this capacity, they answered calls and questions from other Massachusetts students who called a toll-free number. Their questions ranged from how to find scholarships for college to matters about student rights in schools, especially their rights to protest and speak out against their school administrators. These six students were trained by our staff, particularly by the lawyer and by their (male) supervisor.

Though I was not the supervisor of these students who worked in the student service center, it got to me, fourth hand, that there was one boy among the student workers (four were girls) who was behaving in a way that was sexually offensive to the girls and whose behavior was making it hard for them to concentrate on their work. It sounded to me like "sexual harassment in the workplace," but this boy had no authority over the girls—he could not hire or fire them, give them a raise or demote them, or give them a poor evaluation or a glowing one. Sexual harassment had already begun to emerge as an issue for women in the workplace; surveys had been conducted, but in 1979, the EEOC had yet to issue its guidelines. But my political/feminist activism included knowing some leaders in the workplace sexual harassment movement, and I was aware of their efforts to both push the law and make a loud fuss through activism and protests. I was inspired by their efforts and started on a quest to extend the realm of sexual harassment protections to young people in schools.

At the Department of Education, we formed a committee and called ourselves "the sexual harassment task force," and we started to write a manual that we titled "Who's Hurt and Who's Liable: Sexual Harassment in Massachusetts Schools." We deliberately put the word "liability" in the title, even though we knew that we were inventing the application of liability, but we knew it would capture the attention of school administrators. The first edition, which I still have in my possession, came out in 1979, and subsequent editions were published by the Department of Education in 1982, 1983, and 1986. Each edition had a legal update from our office of the general counsel (thereby imprinting the official seal of approval of the Department of Education), but generally, the point of the manual was to serve as a guide for personnel in school districts to teach them about this "new" problem of peer-to-peer sexual harassment and engage them in prevention activities.

Our task force included personnel from outside agencies as well as local schools and high school students. Members developed a variety of activities for use in schools, testing and improving them through in-service presentations to school personnel around the state and at national conferences and at workshops for students around the state.

In addition, in 1981, we conducted a survey of 200 Massachusetts students from rural, urban, and suburban schools, which demonstrated that we had hit upon a ubiquitous problem that all the students knew about and were experiencing or witnessing. We also conducted qualitative interviews with 60 female students who were enrolled in nontraditional shop courses at vocational high schools, to understand their experience as a minority in those courses (e.g., girls who were taking auto mechanics or electricity). These students taught us about the daily assaults that they suffered from boys and classmates, the strategies that they invented to warn and protect each other, and the indifference of their instructors. When these students dropped out of the nontraditional courses, we had a set of questions for their guidance counselors to ask them in order to learn whether sexual harassment was behind their withdrawal from these courses. Without a doubt, these girls were being denied their rights as guaranteed under Title IX—their right to an equal educational opportunity.

Girls who were enrolled in comprehensive schools also insisted that I come to their schools to learn about how sexual harassment manifested in a school environment that had equal enrollment of boys and girls. All throughout my now-30-year journey into learning about and researching sexual harassment among students, I have tried to listen to students and to let them lead me to the problems as they experienced them. I have always been inspired by young people who have made public their experiences of sexual harassment, whether as targets, witnesses, or bystanders. Some of these students I have known personally, others only by the name of their lawsuits, and thousands more merely as respondents to my surveys. I am indebted to them all, justice makers and seekers.

CHAPTER 5

Defining the Scope of Sexual Violence Against Women

Rebecca Campbell and Stephanie M. Townsend

Introduction

Sexual violence is perpetrated against women at an alarming rate in the United States. The purpose of this chapter is to provide an overview of the *scope* of this problem, by which we mean both the prevalence of sexual violence and the impact of surviving and disclosing sexual violence on women's well-being. We will begin by tracing the historical evolution of the terms "rape," "sexual assault," and "sexual violence" and how these differing definitions have been used in research. We will present a concise review of the prevalence literature and then explore the impact of sexual violence on women's psychological, physical, and sexual health. Finally, we will examine the nature of survivors' disclosures of their experiences and the reactions they receive from others.

Although much of the information presented in this chapter refers to survivors as individuals, it is important to keep in mind that sexual violence is primarily a social phenomenon. The social nature of the violence is perhaps illustrated best by examining theories about the causes of sexual violence that have been developed in a variety of disciplines. These theories can be divided into three categories (see Jasinski, 2001). Micro-oriented theories emphasize intra-individual and social psychological explanations. These include social learning theories, theories of personality and psychopathy, biological and physiological causes, the role of alcohol, social exchange theory, and social resource theory. Macro-oriented theories emphasize socio-cultural explanations such as feminist theories, family violence perspectives, and subcultures of violence. Multidimensional theories attempt to integrate individual and social factors. Although each of these theoretical orientations contains important perspectives, they are each weakened by the tendency to emphasize a single factor or a small constellation of factors, which oversimplifies the issues (Heise, 1998; O'Neil & Harway, 1997; see also Chapter 1, this volume).

An ecological framework allows for a comprehensive, integrated picture of sexual violence to emerge (Bronfenbrenner, 1979). At the center of an ecological framework are individual factors. In regard to the etiology of sexual violence, these include aggression in the family of origin and abuse in childhood (Heise, 1998), early and frequent dating and sex that reinforced a false sense of entitlement to sex (Abbey, McAuslan, Zawacki, Clinton, & Buck, 2001), and hormonal and neuroanatomical factors that increase the tendency toward violence (O'Neil & Harway, 1997). However, individual factors are not sufficient to explain sexual violence in our society. In order to account for the role of social structures, extra-individual factors must also be considered.

Thus, the second level of the ecological framework is the microsystem, or relationships between individuals and their immediate settings. These may include characteristics of the immediate settings in which assaults occur. From this perspective, the relationship between alcohol use and sexual violence may be considered (Mohler-Kuo, Dowdall, Koss, & Wechsler, 2004; Testa, Livingston, VanZile-Tamsen, & Frone, 2004; Ullman, 2003), as well as the intimacy of the relationship between the perpetrator and survivor, physical isolation, misperception of women's cues (Abbey et al., 2001), and a pattern of impersonal sex (Malamuth, Linz, Heavey, Barnes, & Acker, 1995).

The third level to consider is the exosystem, or the formal and informal social structures that may influence or determine what happens in the microsystem. Most often-studied factors at this level are rape myths, those "attitudes and generally false beliefs about rape that are widely and persistently held, and that serve to deny and justify male sexual aggression against women" (Lonsway & Fitzgerald, 1994, p. 133). These may work together with other factors, such as willingness to commit sexual assault if there was a guarantee not to be punished (Abbey, McAuslan, & Ross, 1998). Additionally, other social structures and community norms may also play a role, such as sex magazine circulation (Baron & Straus, 1989).

Finally, the macrosystem level focuses on institutional and historical patterns of the culture. These may be explicit or implicit and have the effect of instilling meaning and motivation at the other levels. For example, identity development in a culture that links masculinity and dominance has been theorized to produce the need to risk danger for excitement and to reinforce a lack of empathy; because sexual violence includes attributes associated with dominant masculinity, it is seen as validating the perpetrator's masculinity (Heise, 1998). Similarly, when rigid gender roles that reinforce male success and power are challenged, men may respond to defend their masculine self-esteem by targeting the perceived source of conflict, that is, women (O'Neil & Harway, 1997). Furthermore, correlational data have demonstrated a relationship between gender inequality and social disorganization; in turn, social disorganization is correlated with higher rates of sexual violence (Baron & Straus, 1989).

An ecological framework of sexual violence is outlined here as a backdrop for understanding the current research on the scope of sexual violence. Although sexual violence is most often perpetrated by individual men against individual women, it is important not to lose sight of the fact that those individuals behave, think, and feel within a social context. Of particular importance is that the impact of sexual violence on women and their healing from the trauma are not individual experiences, as will be discussed in the second half of this chapter. Rather, they are integrally connected to the people and communities around them.

Defining Rape, Sexual Assault, and Sexual Violence

In the relatively short history of research on sexual violence against women, substantial effort has gone into naming and defining this problem (see Kilpatrick, 2004, for a historical review). Early research in the field was guided by legal terminology and definitions, and as such, "rape" was the common nomenclature in the literature. Rape statutes vary across federal, state, and tribal jurisdictions, but most laws typically define it as an act of penile/vaginal penetration committed by some degree of force or the threat of force (Berger, Searles, & Neuman, 1988; Estrich, 1987). In the 1980s, most rape laws were overhauled because they were woefully incomplete in their specification of sexually violating acts and the tactics perpetrators use to commit these acts (Fischer, 1989). Many states replaced the offense of rape with a gender neutral offense, "sexual assault," which was often defined as an act of unwanted sexual penetration or touch committed by the use of force, threat of force, or when the victim was incapacitated or otherwise unable to provide consent (Berger et al., 1988). As a new criminal classification, "sexual assault" represented a broader spectrum of sexually violating acts, up to and including rape (Koss & Achilles, 2008).

The difficulties of translating legal conceptualizations into social science research became readily apparent in the 1980s. Groundbreaking work by Mary Koss and colleagues established that many survivors do not label their experiences as "rape," particularly if the assault was committed by someone they know (Koss, 1985; Koss, Gidycz, & Wisniewski, 1987). As a result, early research based on the legal definition of "rape" was drastically underestimating the problem of sexual victimization. In other words, many women had experienced an event that met the legal classification of rape, but they did not self-identify as rape victims. Even more had experienced an event that qualified as criminal sexual assault (which, again, includes a wider variety of sexually violating acts), but there was no readily understood label for these experiences. Koss (1985) referred to these survivors as "hidden victims"—those hurt by an illegal act, but unrecognized as such by society and by themselves. Koss and colleagues discovered that a more accurate way to assess sexual victimization was to use behaviorally specific questions, which do not require self-identification or self-labeling. The academic discourse also shifted to favor the term "sexual

assault," and researchers began studying a broader spectrum of sexually violating acts and tactics used to commit them.

The next shift in terminology came about because of growing dissatisfaction with the strong *legal* emphasis on defining sexual violence against women (Kilpatrick, 2004). Research in the 1980s and 1990s revealed the detrimental impact of sexual victimization on survivors' psychological and physical health. Some sexually violating events are criminal, but others may not be and nevertheless are still quite harmful to individuals' well-being. Therefore, from a *public health* perspective, it is important to capture sexual violations that have costly ill-effects for survivors and for society. In 2002, two major public health entities, the Centers for Disease Control and Prevention (CDC) and the World Health Organization (WHO), introduced the term "sexual violence" into research and policy discussions.

The CDC definition is rooted in public health surveillance models and seeks to codify, as specifically as possible, a set of behaviors that encompass both contact and noncontact sexually violating acts:

Nonconsensual completed or attempted contact between the penis and the vulva or between the penis and the anus involving penetration, however slight; nonconsensual contact between the mouth and the penis, vulva, or anus; nonconsensual penetration of the anal or genital opening of another person by a hand, finger, or other object; nonconsensual intentional touching, either directly or through the clothing, of the genitalia, anus, groin, breast, inner thigh, or buttocks; or nonconsensual non-contact acts of a sexual nature such as voyeurism and verbal or behavioral sexual harassment. All of the above acts also qualify as sexual violence if they are committed against someone who is unable to consent or refuse. (Basile & Saltzman, 2002, p. 9)

The WHO's definition was not designed for public health surveillance, so its definition places less emphasis on articulating comprehensive behaviors, and instead draws upon another disciplinary focus in public health, namely the social context of health problems:

> Any sexual act, attempt to obtain a sexual act, unwanted sexual comments or advances, or acts to traffic, or otherwise directed, against a person's sexuality using coercion, by any person regardless of their relationship to the victim, in any setting, including but not limited to home and work. (Jewkes, Sen, & Garcia-Moreno, 2002, p. 149)

The CDC and WHO definitions of "sexual violence" are more expansive and inclusive of the multitude of ways (and settings) in which people can be sexually violated. "Rape" is one form of "sexual assault" and "sexual violence," but many manifestations of "sexual violence" would not be consistent with most legal definitions of "rape" or "sexual assault." Legal and public health conceptualizations are intended to serve different purposes.

Throughout these definitional evolutions, the tension between how women label their experiences and the terms researchers and legal personnel have created, however painstakingly, to describe those events remains unresolved. Koss's original findings from the mid-1980s that some women do not define their experiences as rape, even though what they encountered would in fact meet the legal criteria, have been replicated by multiple independent research teams (see Kahn, 2004, for a review). These results pose quite a challenge for researchers and victim advocates alike because as Gavey (1999) noted, "when women's voices don't always tell 'our story,' it can be troubling how to proceed" (p. 68). Delving into this issue, Hamby and Koss (2003) conducted qualitative focus groups with diverse groups of women to understand the "everyday vocabulary of coercion and sexuality" (p. 254). They found that the terms *unwanted*,

nonvoluntary, and *forced against your will*, which have been used in a variety of national sexual violence prevalence projects, are not interchangeable in their meaning and indeed are hard for less educated women to understand. To some extent, this problem of differential meaning will always be a challenge for quantitative survey methods, but the qualitative work by Hamby and Koss highlights how critical it is that the language researchers use actually connects to women's lived experiences. Building on this work, Koss and colleagues (2007) recently revised the Sexual Experiences Survey (SES), the most widely used instrument to assess sexual victimization and perpetration, to bring more congruence in terminology.

Given that it is quite difficult to find the right language for experiences that do meet the legal definition of rape or sexual assault, how should we characterize other sexually violating experiences that do not meet the legal threshold? Hamby and Koss (2003) noted, "There is a continuum of degrees of coercion. On one end is physically forced compelling and on the other end are fully consensual acts. Between these two ends are many shades of gray" (p. 252). As Hamby and Koss found in their series of focus groups that represented participants who have historically had little input into the legal definitions of sexual violence or how it is studied, coercion

> is a complicated construct that is not well captured by all-or-none conceptualizations of forced versus not forced. . . . At some point along the continuum, the degree of coercion falls below current legal standards for meeting the definition of a crime but still includes unwantedness. (p. 252)

The phrase "gray rape" has been used in the media to suggest that it is hard to tell what is really rape (see Stepp, 2007). This portrayal of rape is problematic because it can serve to discredit survivors and to justify why perpetrators should not be held accountable for their crimes. What constitutes rape *is* clear; what *is not* clear are the varying degrees of sexual coercion that women encounter throughout their lives. Gavey (2005) argued that the reason why it is so difficult to find language to describe these experiences is heterosexual norms create a "cultural scaffold" for rape—what is "just sex" gets closer and closer to sexual violation depending on the extent to which "power is allowed to infuse sex in different ways for women and men—ways that consistently foreground men's rather than women's rights and desires" (p. 75). In other words, it is likely that women do experience multiple instances of sexual coercion in their sexual lives, and there is no common nomenclature to express these events and their meaning. Although some sexual violence assessment instruments, such as the revised SES, attempt to capture various forms of sexual coercion, there remains a pressing need for research (likely qualitative) to bring voice to the language women use to describe sexual coercion.

The Prevalence of Sexual Violence Against Women

Given the difficulties of defining experiences of sexual violence, it is not surprising that establishing prevalence rates is a formidable challenge. In addition to differences between studies in how sexual violence is defined, evidence suggests that respondents are more or less likely to disclose their experiences depending on the research methodology being used (Testa, Livingston, & VanZile-Tamsen, 2005). Even within the same methodology, the phrasing used, number of questions, ordering of questions, and presence or absence of other questions can all affect the likelihood that someone who has experienced sexual violence will reveal that information when participating in research (Abbey, Parkhill, & Koss, 2005). Most notably, surveys that ask a series of questions about specific behaviors, for example, "Someone had oral sex with me or made me have oral sex with them without my consent by threatening to physically harm me or someone close to me" (item from the

Sexual Experiences Survey Short Form Victimization; Koss et al., 2007) yield higher disclosure rates than surveys that rely on general questions, for example, "During your life, have you ever been forced to have sexual intercourse against your will?" (item from the National College Health Risk Behavior Survey; Brener, McMahon, Warren, & Douglas, 1999). Therefore, some of the differences found across studies may be explained by differences in research methodology.

In general, national studies based on samples that adequately represent the population are preferred over local studies due to concerns that the limited size and geographic coverage of local studies may bias the findings (Schwartz & DeKeseredy, 2000). National studies in the United States that are heavily relied upon include the National Women's Study (Kilpatrick, Edmunds, & Seymour, 1992), National Violence Against Women Survey (Tjaden & Thoennes, 1998), the Youth Risk Behavior Surveillance (Grunbaum et al., 2002), and the *Ms.* Project on Campus Sexual Assault (Koss et al., 1987; Warshaw, 1988). Crime statistics reported in the Uniform Crime Reports are often used to document incidents of sexual violence that are reported to law enforcement (Federal Bureau of Investigation, 2007).

An earlier review of large-scale, national community-based and college-based studies found that women's reports of *lifetime* prevalence ranged from 14.8% to 36.1% (Bachar & Koss, 2001). Younger women and girls appear to be at greater risk of victimization than older women. For example, the National Women's Study found that among the women who reported having been raped, 32.3% were between the ages of 11 and 17, 29.3% were less than 11 years old, and 22.2% were between 18 and 24 years old. Only 13.2% of women who reported their age at the rape were older than 24 years (Kilpatrick et al., 1992).

Whereas sexual violence is prevalent throughout all communities in the United States, some subgroups of women face unique risks. For example, there is growing concern for women in the military because emerging evidence indicates that military personnel (both women and men)

may experience higher rates of sexual trauma than the general population (Suris & Lind, 2008). In a comprehensive review of studies reporting prevalence rates of sexual violence in the military, Suris and Lind (2008) found most studies reported that 20–43% of women in the military had experienced some form of sexual violence (recall that 14–36% of civilian women have lifetime prevalence of sexual violence). Although differences in methodology yield some differences between studies, their review revealed that women who are younger, enlisted women (vs. officers), and women with little or no college education are at higher risk for sexual victimization. These risk factors are particularly important in light of the hierarchical structure of the military system in which these factors often intersect. Consequently, a military woman with one risk factor is likely to have other risk factors as well (e.g., enlisted women are less likely to have completed college degrees). Interestingly, these risk factors parallel findings from a study of predictors of tolerance of sexual harassment among men in the U.S. Army (Rosen & Martin, 1998). That study found that rank and age were negatively correlated with tolerance of sexual harassment, hostility toward women, and negative masculinity, but were positively correlated with acceptance of women.

While Suris and Lind's (2008) study focused on veterans of active duty service, the rates of sexual violence are also apparently high among reservists who have not also served in the active duty forces. A survey that included all seven reserve branches found that 60% of female reservists reported a history of sexual harassment, including workplace-based sexual assault during their military service (Street, Stafford, Mahan, & Hendricks, 2008). This project also found that younger women were at higher risk, and those who first served before 1990 and had

served five years or more were also at higher risk. This study did find notable differences in prevalence rates between the seven reserve branches for all forms of sexual harassment as well as for sexual assault. This may indicate that different military systems and social contexts have responded differently to the integration of women in the reserves and to the specific issues of sexual violence.

Debates over differences in prevalence findings and the methodologies used to arrive at prevalence rates are valuable for improving the specificity of findings. However, it is important not to lose sight of the consistent finding across more than two decades of research on violence against women: Sexual violence in all its forms is perpetrated against women at an alarming rate. It is a "pervasive fact of American life" (Buchwald, Fletcher, & Roth, 1993, p. 9) and one that has profound consequences for survivors, their families, and our communities.

The Impact of Sexual Violence on Women's Health

Psychological Health Impact. Sexual violence has a devastating impact on victims' emotional and physical health.[1] Immediately post assault, many victims experience shock, fear, agitation, confusion, and social withdrawal (Herman, 1992). Some may also endure flashbacks, sleeping problems, and emotional detachment, which are symptoms consistent with post-traumatic stress disorder (PTSD; Koss, Bailey, Yuan, Herrera, & Lichter, 2003). Indeed, PTSD is perhaps the most common mental health sequelae of sexual violence. A recent comprehensive review of the literature on psychological impact by Campbell, Dworkin, and Cabral (2009) found that 7–65% of women with a lifetime history of sexual assault

---

[1]As noted previously, there are important definitional distinctions between "rape," "sexual assault," and "sexual violence"; however, the extant research on impact (psychological, physical, and/or sexual) rarely differentiates (or clarifies) the exact nature of the sexual violation. Given the definitional evolution in this field, it is likely that most research on impact has captured the aftermath of rape or attempted rape.

develop PTSD. Women who have experienced military sexual trauma may be at higher risk for developing PTSD because of their other exposures to traumatic events (e.g., combat; Street et al., 2008; Suris & Lind, 2008). Many sexual victimization survivors (13–51%) meet diagnostic criteria for depression in addition to PTSD. Most sexual assault victims develop fear and/or anxiety (73–82%) and 12% to 40% experience generalized anxiety. Approximately 13% to 49% of survivors become dependent on alcohol, while 28% to 61% may use other illicit substances. It is not uncommon for victims to experience suicidal ideation (23–44%), and 2% to 19% may attempt suicide. For most sexual assault survivors, these psychological distress symptoms decline within the first few months post assault, but it is not uncommon for women to continue to experience emotional distress for up to two years post assault (Koss & Figueredo, 2004). Not all survivors experience these negative psychological health effects to the same extent. Sociodemographic variables and characteristics of the assault itself impact victims' post-assault psychological distress (see Campbell et al., 2009, for a review; Macy, Ermentrout, & Johns, this volume).

Physical Health Impact. As described by Macy and Ermentrout (this volume), sexual violence also negatively affects women's physical health. Survivors of sexual violence are more likely than nonvictims to report gastrointestinal symptoms (e.g., nausea, diarrhea, indigestion, constipation, abdominal pain), muscular/skeletal problems (e.g., back pain, headaches, and muscle soreness), cardiopulmonary symptoms (e.g., rapid heart rate, pain in heart or chest, shortness of breath), neurological symptoms (e.g., fainting, dizziness, sleep problems, numbness/tingling in the body), and gynecological problems (e.g., pelvic pain, pain during intercourse, menstrual symptoms; Eby, Campbell, Sullivan, & Davidson, 1995; Golding, 1994, 1996; Kimerling & Calhoun, 1994; Martin et al., 2008; Street et al., 2008; Wenzel, Leake, & Gelberg, 2000). The number and frequency of these symptoms are considerably higher than national averages for women (National

Center for Health Statistics, 1999) and are not related to differences in previous chronic diseases, injuries, or differences in family history of disease (Waigandt, Wallace, Phelps, & Miller, 1990). As with psychological impact, there are variations in the degree of physical health distress victims experience as a function of sociodemographic and assault characteristics.

Sexual Health Impact. Recent studies have revealed that sexual victimization may also compromise women's sexual and reproductive health. Women with histories of childhood sexual abuse and/or adult sexual assault have been found to have more sexual partners, to be more likely to engage in high-risk practices (e.g., unprotected anal sex), to be less likely to use condoms (or be assertive about condom use), and to be more likely to have multiple STD infections in their lifetimes compared to women who have not been sexually victimized (Gidycz, Orchowski, King, & Rich, 2008; He, McCoy, Stevens, & Stark, 1998; Wingood & DiClemente, 1997; Wyatt, Gutherie, & Notgrass, 1992; see Stoner et al., 2008 for replication in experimental laboratory research). Yet, the relationship between victimization and sexual health risk may be more complex because not all survivors exhibit increased risk behavior post assault. In fact, several studies suggest that childhood sexual abuse and adult sexual victimization are associated with marked decreases in sexual activity. Sexual indifference (including abstinence) has been reported in 29–65% of samples of childhood sexual abuse and adult rape survivors (Chapman, 1989; Mackey, Hacker, Weissfield, Ambrose, Fisher, & Zobel, 1991; Walker et al., 1992). For example, Burgess and Holmstrom's (1979) longitudinal study of rape survivors found that most women (71%) had substantially decreased their sexual activity post rape and 38% reported abstaining from sex.

Indeed, Campbell, Sefl, and Ahrens (2004) found three distinct patterns of post-assault sexual health behaviors among a sample of urban rape survivors. Using cluster analysis methodology, they identified a high-risk group (34% of their sample) who reported substantial increases from pre to post rape in their frequency of sexual activity, number of sexual partners, (in)frequency of condom use, and frequency of using alcohol or drugs during sex. The second cluster comprised 18% of the sample and showed increases in frequency of sexual activity and number of partners, but mitigated that risk with increased condom use. But nearly half of their sample (48%) were low risk and indicated that their sexual health behaviors became much less risky post rape. The survivors in the high-risk cluster were significantly younger than the women in the other two groups and also had higher levels of psychological and physical health distress. These women were also more likely to have been assaulted by someone they knew (e.g., acquaintance, friend, dating partner).

Causal Linkages Between Psychological and Physical Health. Sexual violence negatively affects women's mental and physical health, and emerging data suggest that these effects are causally interrelated. As Dutton, Green, Kaltman, Roesch, Zeffiro, and Krause (2006) summarized: "PTSD is not the only mental health reaction following trauma, yet it appears to be a linchpin in the relationship between exposure to violence and negative health outcomes" (p. 959). Emerging data suggest that PTSD functions as a mediator, such that abuse compromises women's physical health through its impact on their psychological well-being (Friedman & Schnurr, 1995; Green & Kimerling, 2004; Kendall-Tackett, 2009; Schnurr & Green, 2004; Schnurr & Jankowski, 1999). For example, in a study of college women, Eadie, Runtz, and Spencer-Rodgers (2008) found that PTSD symptom severity partially mediated the relationship between sexual assault experiences and physical health outcomes. Similar, but slightly different results emerged from Campbell, Greeson, Bybee, and Raja's (2008) study of female veterans, most of whom were African American. In that sample, PTSD fully mediated the relationship between the kinds and amount of lifetime violence women experienced and

their physical health symptomatology. Post-hoc exploratory analyses suggested that the amount of sexualized violence experienced predicted additional variance in physical health outcomes above and beyond that explained by patterns of violence co-occurrence. In other words, the amount of sexual violence women had endured throughout their lifespan was particularly detrimental to women's mental and physical health. Both the Eadie et al. and Campbell et al. studies used cross-sectional designs, so causality cannot be inferred, but the findings may be useful for guiding future prospective longitudinal research.

Understanding the biopsychological mechanisms by which PTSD affects health is a growing focus in this field, and preliminary evidence points to the importance of the hypothalamic-pituitary-adrenal [HPA] axis. The stress of violence triggers both an acute and a chronic stress response, which increases the sensitivity of the negative feedback system in the HPA axis, resulting in lowered cortisol levels. This shift in cortisol levels creates an autoimmune/inflammatory response, and if cellular immunity is depressed or inflammation is unchecked, chronic inflammatory disorders, chronic pain syndromes, and recurrent pain symptoms may result (Abbas & Lichtman, 2001). Studies of childhood sexual abuse survivors have found hormonal disruption and dysregulation of the HPA axis (DeBellis et al., 1994; King, Mandansky, King, Fletcher, & Brewer, 2001). In a study of adult sexual assault victims obtaining medical forensic exams, Groer, Thomas, Evans, Helton, and Weldon (2006) found that victims had significantly different immune/inflammatory functioning compared to non-assaulted controls.

In one of the most comprehensive studies on this topic to date, Woods, Page, O'Campo, Pugh, Ford, and Campbell (2005) developed a bio-psych-immunologic theoretical model to explain how intimate partner violence (which included assessment of sexual assault within the relationship) affects women's physical health. This model was empirically validated in a predominantly African American sample of 62 intimate partner violence victims (about half also experienced sexual assault in the relationship) and 39 non-abused women. Their results demonstrated that PTSD mediated the relationship between IPV and interferon-γ (a measure of Th1 cell response), suggesting that the stress of violence compromises immune system functioning. Manifest physical health problems, particularly pain symptoms, typical among abused women may be due, in part, to alterations in their immune system. Campbell and colleagues (2008) examined whether the PTSD mediation effect would be different for pain- vs. non–pain-related health symptoms, and found that the relationship was indeed significantly stronger to pain symptoms. As noted previously, prospective longitudinal research is sorely needed to evaluate these implied causal hypotheses.

Disclosures and Social Reactions to Sexual Violence

In the ideal situation, the negative psychological, physical, and sexual health impacts would be ameliorated when survivors reach out to others for support. Tragically, this is often not the case. Many survivors wait for years before telling anyone about their experiences, and some remain silent throughout their lives. Others speak out but receive negative reactions that can exacerbate the trauma. These negative reactions can be victimizing in and of themselves. This "secondary victimization" can include victim-blaming attitudes, behaviors, and practices that cause additional trauma (Campbell & Raja, 1999). Understanding the scope of sexual violence necessitates exploration of two key issues: the decision to disclose sexual violence and the social reactions that survivors receive when they do choose to disclose.

Disclosure Experiences. Prior to disclosing an experience of sexual violence, the survivor must first identify her experience as warranting disclosure. Additionally, whether or not she labels the

experience as sexual violence may impact how she describes the experience when telling another person about it. A review of almost two decades of research found that older women and women who have been victimized previously are more likely to label their experiences as rape (Fisher, Daigle, Cullen, & Turner, 2003). This review also found that certain characteristics of the experience are associated with labeling it as rape, including assaults by strangers, being threatened with force, having arms twisted or being held down, being hit or slapped, use of a weapon, the survivor resisting physically or verbally, and physical injury. In other words, assaults that adhere more to the stereotype of rape are more likely to be labeled as such. However, these stereotypical assaults are not the most common. Therefore, substantial numbers of women may fail to define their experiences as a form of sexual violence because they do not adhere to a narrow expectation of what constitutes rape. The review additionally found that regardless of what occurred during the assault, women are more likely to label their experience as rape if at least six months has passed since the assault. This may account for why many survivors delay disclosure. It has been found that among those women who disclose the assault, one-third tell someone immediately after the attack, one-third disclose days or weeks afterwards, and one-third delay a year or more post assault (Ullman & Filipas, 2001).

Researchers have consistently found that most female survivors will disclose the assault at some time, with estimates ranging from 65% to 95% of women disclosing to at least one person (Ahrens, Cabral, & Abeling, 2009; Ahrens, Campbell, Ternier-Thames, Wasco, & Sefl, 2007; Starzynski, Ullman, Filipas, & Townsend, 2005; Ullman & Filipas, 2001). On average, survivors tell three to four different people (Ahrens et al., 2009; Filipas & Ullman, 2001; Ullman, Townsend, Filipas, & Starzynski, 2007) and they are most likely to tell friends or family (Filipas & Ullman, 2001; Starzynski, Ullman, Townsend, Long, & Long, 2007). However, when it comes to disclosures to other support providers, studies have found varying rates depending on the type of provider. The difficulty of synthesizing findings across studies is exacerbated by different approaches to combining categories (e.g., separating mental health, rape crisis, and clergy disclosures vs. combining those same three categories into a single category). It does appear that in general survivors are more likely to disclose to mental health support providers than to medical or legal personnel (Ahrens et al., 2009; Golding, Siegel, Sorenson, & Burnam, 1989). However, not all groups of survivors have the same patterns of disclosure. It appears that white women are far more likely than women of color to turn to mental health professionals and that this difference is even greater for rape crisis centers (Campbell, Wasco, Ahrens, Sefl, & Barnes, 2001; Starzynski et al., 2007). Additionally, survivors who suffer from PTSD symptoms, those who told more people about the assault, and lesbian and bisexual women are more likely to turn to mental health professionals, including rape crisis centers (Starzynski et al., 2007).

Social Reactions. Once a survivor discloses her experience to another person, her recovery is influenced not only by her own thoughts and feelings but also by the ways people respond to her. Although a survivor may have a high level of social support when coping with life issues generally, her support system may fail her when it comes to providing support to recover from sexual violence. One of the most comprehensive attempts to capture assault-specific reactions is the Social Reactions Questionnaire (SRQ; Ullman, 2000). In addition to assessing several aspects of supportive behavior, such as emotional support, instrumental support, and information support, the measure also assesses five aspects of negative social reactions: treating the survivor differently, distracting the survivor, taking control of the situation, blaming the survivor, and focusing on the responder's own feelings rather than the survivor's feelings. It has been consistently found that negative responses are related to higher levels of PTSD

symptoms; surprisingly, positive responses do not seem to be related to lower levels of post-traumatic stress (Campbell, Sefl, Barnes, Ahrens, Wasco, & Zaragoza-Diesfeld, 1999; Ullman & Filipas, 2001; Ullman et al., 2007). However, positive responses may have other important effects that aid in the survivor's recovery.

While the experiences of women in the armed services likely share many characteristics with the civilian population, there is reason to believe that the social and organizational context of the military, specifically the emphasis on the importance of the unit over the individual, may give rise to a higher frequency of negative social reactions (Campbell & Raja, 2005). In a study of female veterans and reservists who had experienced sexual assault either within or outside their military service, it was found that most survivors who sought help from legal or medical systems reported that the contact made them feel guilty, depressed, anxious, distrustful of others, and reluctant to seek further help (Campbell & Raja, 2005). Although the number of negative social reactions did not significantly differ between the military and civilian contexts, certain types of behaviors were more common among military personnel. Consistent with the valuing of the unit over the individual, in military cases the survivor was more likely to be discouraged from reporting. In many cases, military officials refused to take a report or directly told the survivor that the incident was not serious enough to pursue. Survivors who sought military medical help for the assault also reported more distress from those disclosure experiences than those who sought medical treatment in civilian settings.

Conclusion

In the 25 years since academic researchers began sustained study of sexual violence against women, the devastating scope of this problem has become clearer. Definitions and assessments have become more refined over time, which has helped reveal the staggering prevalence of these crimes in our society. Although the 1-in-4 prevalence rates from the 1980s were at first shocking (and later hotly debated, but nevertheless replicated), it appears those figures may in fact underestimate the prevalence among high-risk groups of women, such as those serving in the military. This means that there are millions of women who struggle with the after-effects of sexual victimization, including PTSD, depression, and suicidal ideation. Emerging research suggests that these psychological sequelae may play a causal role in the development of physical health problems, which are also extremely common and burdensome to survivors. And yet, when survivors reach out to their friends, family, and social systems for help and support after the assault, they often do not receive the help they need. These negative social reactions exacerbate victims' psychological and physical health trauma. These empirical findings are consistent with ecological theoretical models, which emphasize that the trauma of sexual victimization is not an individual-level problem. Reducing the scope of sexual violence—or better yet, ending it—requires multi-level intervention.

References

Abbas, A. K., & Lichtman, A. H. (2001). *Basic immunology*. Philadelphia: W.B. Saunders.

Abbey, A., McAuslan, P., & Ross, L. T. (1998). Sexual assault perpetration by college men: The role of alcohol, misperception of sexual intent, and sexual beliefs and experiences. *Journal of Social and Clinical Psychology, 17*, 167–195.

Abbey, A., McAuslan, P., Zawacki, T., Clinton, A. M., & Buck, P. O. (2001). Attitudinal, experiential, and situational predictors of sexual assault perpetration. *Journal of Interpersonal Violence, 16*, 784–807.

Abbey, A., Parkhill, M. R., & Koss, M. P. (2005). The effects of frame of reference on responses to questions about sexual assault victimization and perpetration. *Psychology of Women Quarterly, 29*, 364–373.

Ahrens, C. E., Cabral, G., & Abeling, S. (2009). Healing or hurtful: Sexual assault survivors' interpretations of social reactions from support providers. *Psychology of Women Quarterly, 33*, 81–94.

Ahrens, C. E., Campbell, R., Ternier-Thames, K., Wasco, S., & Sefl, T. (2007). Deciding whom to tell: Expectations and outcomes of sexual assault survivors' first disclosures. *Psychology of Women Quarterly, 31*, 38–49.

Bachar, K., & Koss, M. P. (2001). From prevalence to prevention: Closing the gap between what we know about rape and what we do. In C. M. Renzetti, J. L. Edleson, & R. K. Bergen (Eds.), *Sourcebook on violence against women* (pp. 117–142). Thousand Oaks, CA: Sage.

Baron, L, & Straus, M. A. (1989). *Four theories of rape in American society: A state-level analysis*. New Haven: Yale University Press.

Basile, K. C., & Saltzman, L. E. (2002). *Sexual violence surveillance: Uniform definitions and recommended data elements*. Atlanta: CDC.

Berger, R. J., Searles, P., & Neuman, W. L. (1988). The dimensions of rape reform legislation. *Law and Society Review, 22*, 329–357.

Brener, N. D., McMahon, P. M., Warren, C. W., & Douglas, K. A. (1999). Forced sexual intercourse and associated health risk behaviors among female college students in the United States. *Journal of Consulting and Clinical Psychology, 67*, 252–259.

Bronfenbrenner, U. (1979). *The ecology of human development: Experiments by nature and design*. Cambridge, MA: Harvard University Press.

Buchwald, E., Fletcher, P. R., & Roth, M. (1993). Are we really living in a rape culture? In E. Buchwald, P. R. Fletcher, & M. Roth (Eds.), *Transforming a rape culture* (pp. 7–10). Minneapolis: Milkweed Editions.

Burgess, A. W., & Holmstrom, L. L. (1979). Rape: Sexual disruption and recovery. *American Journal of Orthopsychiatry, 49*, 648–657.

Campbell, R., Dworkin, E., & Cabral, G. (2009). An ecological model of the impact of sexual assault on women's mental health. *Trauma, Violence, & Abuse, 10*, 225–246.

Campbell, R., Greeson, M. R., Bybee, D., & Raja, S. (2008). The co-occurrence of childhood sexual abuse, adult sexual assault, intimate partner violence, and sexual harassment: A mediational model of PTSD and physical health outcomes. *Journal of Consulting and Clinical Psychology, 76*, 194–207.

Campbell, R., & Raja, S. (1999). The secondary victimization of rape victims: Insight from mental health professionals who treat survivors of violence. *Violence and Victims, 14,* 261–275.

Campbell, R., & Raja, S. (2005). The sexual assault and secondary victimization of female veterans: Help-seeking experiences with military and civilian social systems. *Psychology of Women Quarterly, 29,* 97–106.

Campbell, R., Sefl, T., & Ahrens, C. E. (2004). The impact of rape on women's sexual health risk behaviors. *Health Psychology, 23,* 67–74.

Campbell, R., Sefl, T., Barnes, H. E., Ahrens, C. E., Wasco, S. M., & Zaragoza-Diesfeld, Y. (1999). Community services for rape survivors: Enhancing psychological well-being or increasing trauma? *Journal of Consulting and Clinical Psychology, 67,* 847–858.

Campbell, R., Wasco, S. M., Ahrens, C. E., Sefl, T., & Barnes, H. E. (2001). Preventing the "second rape": Rape survivors' experiences with community service providers. *Journal of Interpersonal Violence, 16,* 1239–1259.

Chapman, J. D. (1989). A longitudinal study of sexuality and gynecologic health in abused women. *Journal of the American Osteopathic Association, 89,* 619–624.

DeBellis, M. D., Chrousos, G. P., Dorn, L. D., Burke, L., Helmers, K., Kling, M. A., et al. (1994). Hypothalamic-pituitary-adrenal axis dysregulation in sexually abused girls. *Journal of Clinical Endocrinology and Metabolism, 78,* 249–255.

Dutton, M. A., Green, B. L., Kaltman, S. I., Roesch, D. M., Zeffiro, T. A., & Krause, E. D. (2006). Intimate partner violence, PTSD, and adverse health outcomes. *Journal of Interpersonal Violence, 21,* 955–968.

Eadie, E. M., Runtz, M. G., & Spencer-Rodgers, J. (2008). Posttraumatic stress symptoms as a mediator between sexual assault and adverse health outcomes in undergraduate women. *Journal of Traumatic Stress, 21,* 540–547.

Eby, K. K., Campbell, J. C., Sullivan, C. M., & Davidson, W. S. (1995). Health effects of experiences of sexual violence for women with abusive partners. *Health Care for Women International, 16,* 563–576.

Estrich, S. (1987). *Real rape: How the legal system victimizes women who say no.* Cambridge, MA: Harvard University Press.

Federal Bureau of Investigation. (2007). *Crime in the United States.* Washington, DC: Department of Justice. Retrieved May 19, 2009, from http://www.fbi.gov/ucr/cius2007/index.html.

Filipas, H. H., & Ullman, S. E. (2001). Social reactions to sexual assault victims from various support sources. *Violence and Victims, 16,* 673–692.

Fischer, K. (1989). Defining the boundaries of admissible expert testimony on rape trauma syndrome. *University of Illinois Law Review, 3,* 691–734.

Fisher, B. S., Daigle, L. E., Cullen, F. T., & Turner, M. G. (2003). Acknowledging sexual victimization as rape: Results from a national-level study. *Justice Quarterly, 20,* 535–574.

Friedman, M. J., & Schnurr, P. P. (1995). The relationship between trauma, post-traumatic stress disorder, and physical health. In M. J. Friedman, D. S. Charney, & A. Y. Deutch (Eds.), *Neurobiological and clinical consequences of stress: From normal adaptation to post-traumatic stress disorder* (pp. 507–524). Philadelphia, PA: Raven.

Gavey, N. (1999). "I wasn't raped, but . . ." In S. Lamb (Ed.), *New versions of victims: Feminists struggle with the concept* (pp. 57–81). New York: New York University Press.

Gavey, N. (2005). *Just sex? The cultural scaffolding of rape.* London: Routledge.

Gidycz, C. A., Orchowski, L. M., King, C. R., & Rich, C. L. (2008). Sexual victimization and health-risk behaviors: A prospective analysis of college women. *Journal of Interpersonal Violence, 23,* 744–763.

Golding, J. (1994). Sexual assault history and physical health in randomly selected Los Angeles women. *Health Psychology, 13,* 130–138.

Golding, J. (1996). Sexual assault history and women's reproductive and sexual health. *Psychology of Women Quarterly, 20,* 101–121.

Golding, J. M., Siegel, J. M., Sorenson, M. A., & Burnam, J. A. (1989). Social support sources following sexual assault. *Journal of Community Psychology, 177,* 92–107.

Green, B. L., & Kimerling, R. (2004). Trauma, post-traumatic stress disorder, and health status. In P. P. Schnurr & B. L. Green (Eds.), *Trauma and health: Physical health consequences of exposure to extreme stress* (pp. 13–42). Washington, DC: American Psychological Association.

Groer, M. W., Thomas, S. P., Evans, G. W., Helton, S., & Weldon, A. (2006). Inflammatory effects and immune system correlates of rape. *Violence and Victims, 21,* 796–808.

Grunbaum, J. A., Kann, L., Kinchen, S. A., Williams, B., Ross, J. G., Lowry, R., et al. (2002). Youth risk behavior surveillance—United States, 2001. *Morbidity and Mortality Weekly Report, 51,* No. SS-4.

Hamby, S. L., & Koss, M. P. (2003). Shade of gray: A qualitative study of terms used in the measurement of sexual victimization. *Psychology of Women Quarterly, 27,* 243–255.

He, H., McCoy, H. V., Stevens, S. J., & Stark, M. J. (1998). Violence and HIV sexual risk behaviors among female sex partners of male drug users. *Women & Health, 27,* 161–175.

Heise, L. L. (1998). Violence against women: An integrated, ecological framework. *Violence Against Women, 4,* 262–290.

Herman, J. L. (1992). Complex PTSD: A syndrome in survivors of prolonged and repeated trauma. *Journal of Traumatic Stress, 5,* 377–391.

Jasinski, J. L. (2001). Theoretical explanations for violence against women. In C. M. Renzetti, J. L. Edleson, & R. K. Bergen (Eds.), *Sourcebook on violence against women* (pp. 5–22). Thousand Oaks, CA: Sage.

Jewkes, R., Sen, P., & Garcia-Moreno, C. (2002). Sexual violence. In E. Krug, L. Dahlberg, J. A. Mercy, A. B. Zwi, & R. Lozano (Eds.), *World report of violence and health* (pp. 147–182). Geneva, Switzerland: World Health Organization.

Kahn, A. S. (2004). What college women do and do not experience as rape. *Psychology of Women Quarterly, 28,* 9–15.

Kendall-Tackett, K. (2009). Psychological trauma and physical health: A psychoneuroimmunology approach to the etiology of negative health effects and possible interventions. *Psychological Trauma, 1,* 35–48.

Kilpatrick, D. G. (2004). What is violence against women? Defining and measuring the problem. *Journal of Interpersonal Violence, 19,* 1209–1234.

Kilpatrick, D. G., Edmunds, C. N., & Seymour, A. K. (1992). *Rape in America: A report to the nation.* Arlington, VA: National Victim Center.

Kimerling, R., & Calhoun, K. (1994). Somatic symptoms, social support, and treatment seeking among sexual assault victims. *Journal of Consulting and Clinical Psychology, 62,* 333–340.

King, J. A., Mandansky, D., King, S., Fletcher, K., & Brewer, J. (2001). Early sexual abuse and low cortisol. *Psychiatry & Clinical Neurosciences, 55,* 71–74.

Koss, M. P. (1985). The hidden rape victim: Personality, attitudinal, and situational characteristics. *Psychology of Women Quarterly, 9,* 193–212.

Koss, M. P., Abbey, A., Campbell, R., Cook, S., Norris, J., Testa, M., et al. (2007). Revising the SES: A collaborative process to improve assessment of sexual aggression and victimization. *Psychology of Women Quarterly, 31,* 357–370.

Koss, M., & Achilles, M. (2008). *Restorative justice responses to sexual assault.* Retrieved March 3, 2008, from http://www.vawnet.org.

Koss, M. P., Bailey, J. A., Yuan, N. P., Herrera, V. M., & Lichter, E. L. (2003). Depression and PTSD in survivors of male violence: Research and training initiatives to facilitate recovery. *Psychology of Women Quarterly, 27,* 130–142.

Koss, M. P., & Figueredo, A. J. (2004). Cognitive mediation of rape's mental health impact: Constructive replication of a cross-sectional model in longitudinal data. *Psychology of Women Quarterly, 28,* 273–286.

Koss, M. P., Gidycz, C. A., & Wisniewski, N. (1987). The scope of rape: Incidence and prevalence of sexual aggression and victimization in a national sample of higher education students. *Journal of Consulting and Clinical Psychology, 55,* 162–170.

Lonsway, K. A., & Fitzgerald, L. F. (1994). Rape myths: In review. *Psychology of Women Quarterly, 18,* 133–164.

Mackey, T. F., Hacker, S. S., Weissfield, L. A., Ambrose, N. C., Fisher, M. G., & Zobel, D. L. (1991). Comparative effects of sexual assault on sexual functioning of child sexual abuse survivors and others. *Issues in Mental Health Nursing, 12,* 89–112.

Malamuth, N. M., Linz, D., Heavey, C. L., Barnes, G., & Acker, M. (1995). Using the confluence model of sexual aggression to predict men's conflict with women: A 10-year follow-up study. *Journal of Personality and Social Psychology, 69,* 353–369.

Martin, S. L., Rentz, E. D., Chan, R. L., Givens, J., Sanford, C. P., Kupper, L. L., et al. (2008). Physical and sexual violence among North Carolina women: Associations with physical health, mental health, and functional impairment. *Women's Health Issues, 18,* 130–140.

Mohler-Kuo, M., Dowdall, G. W., Koss, M. P., & Wechsler, H. (2004). Correlates of rape while intoxicated in a national sample of college women. *Journal of Studies on Alcohol, 65,* 37–45.

National Center for Health Statistics. (1999). *Vital and health statistics: Current estimates from the National Health Interview Survey, 1996.* Washington, DC: U.S. Department of Health and Human Services.

O'Neil, J. M., & Harway, M. (1997). A multivariate model explaining men's violence toward women: Predisposing and triggering hypotheses. *Violence Against Women, 3,* 187–203.

Rosen, L. N., & Martin, L. (1998). Predictors of tolerance of sexual harassment among male U.S. Army soldiers. *Violence Against Women, 4,* 491–504.

Schnurr, P. P., & Green, B. L. (2004). A context of understanding the physical health consequences of exposure to extreme stress. In P. P. Schnurr & B. L. Green (Eds.), *Trauma and health: Physical health consequences of exposure to extreme stress* (pp. 3–10). Washington, DC: American Psychological Association.

Schnurr, P. P., & Jankowski, M. K. (1999). Physical health and post-traumatic stress disorder: Review and synthesis. *Seminars in Clinical Neuropsychiatry, 4,* 295–304.

Schwartz, M. D., & DeKeseredy, W. S. (2000). Aggregation bias and woman abuse: Variations by male peer support, region, language, and school type. *Journal of Interpersonal Violence, 15,* 555–565.

Starzynski, L. L., Ullman, S. E., Filipas, H. H., & Townsend, S. M. (2005). Correlates of women's sexual assault disclosures to informal and formal support sources. *Violence and Victims, 20,* 417–432.

Starzynski, L. L., Ullman, S. E., Townsend, S. M., Long, L. M., & Long, S. M. (2007). What factors predict women's disclosure of sexual assault to mental health professionals? *Journal of Community Psychology, 35,* 519–638.

Stepp, L. S. (2007, September). A new kind of date rape. *Cosmopolitan Magazine.* Retrieved March 19, 2010, from http://www.cosmopolitan.com/sex-love/tips-moves/new-kind-of-date-rape.

Stoner, S. A., Norris, J., George, W. H., Morrison, D. M., Zawacki, T., Davis, K. C., et al. (2008). Women's condom use, assertiveness, and sexual risk-taking: Effect of alcohol intoxication and adult victimization. *Addictive Behaviors, 33,* 1167–1176.

Street, A. E., Stafford, J., Mahan, C. M., & Hendricks, A. (2008). Sexual harassment and assault experienced by reservists during military service: Prevalence and health correlates. *Journal of Rehabilitation and Development, 45,* 409–419.

Suris, A., & Lind, L. (2008). Military sexual trauma: A review of prevalence and associated health consequences in veterans. *Trauma, Violence, & Abuse, 9,* 250–269.

Testa, M., Livingston, J. A., & VanZile-Tamsen, C. (2005). The impact of questionnaire administration mode on response rate and reporting of consensual and nonconsensual sexual behavior. *Psychology of Women Quarterly, 29,* 345–352.

Testa, M., Livingston, J. A., VanZile-Tamsen, C., & Frone, M. R. (2004). The role of women's substance use in vulnerability to forcible and incapacitated rape. *Journal of Studies on Alcohol, 64,* 756–764.

Tjaden, P., & Thoennes, N. (1998). *Prevalence, incidence, and consequences of violence against women: Findings from the National Violence Against Women Survey.* Washington, DC: U.S. Department of Justice.

Ullman, S. E. (2000). Psychometric characteristics of the Social Reactions Questionnaire. *Psychology of Women Quarterly, 24,* 257–271.

Ullman, S. E. (2003). A critical review of field studies on the link of alcohol and adult sexual assault in women. *Aggression and Violent Behavior, 8,* 471–486.

Ullman, S. E., & Filipas, H. H. (2001). Predictors of PTSD symptom severity and social reactions in sexual assault victims. *Journal of Traumatic Stress, 14,* 369–389.

Ullman, S. E., Townsend, S. M., Filipas, H. H., & Starzynski, L. L. (2007). Structural models of the relations of assault severity, social support, avoidance coping, self-blame, and PTSD among sexual assault survivors. *Psychology of Women Quarterly, 31,* 23–37.

Waigandt, A., Wallace, D., Phelps, L., & Miller, D. (1990). The impact of sexual assault on physical health status. *Journal of Traumatic Stress, 3,* 93–102.

Walker, E. A., Katon, W. J., Hansom, J., Harrop-Griffiths, J., Holm, L., Jones, M. L., et al. (1992). Medical and psychiatric symptoms in women with childhood sexual abuse. *Psychosomatic Medicine, 54,* 658–664.

Warshaw, R. (1988). *I never called it rape: The Ms. Report on recognizing, fighting, and surviving date and acquaintance rape.* New York: Harper & Row.

Wenzel, S., Leake, B., & Gelberg, L. (2000). Health of homeless women with recent experience of rape. *Journal of General Internal Medicine, 15,* 265–268.

Wingood, G. M., & DiClemente, R. J. (1997). Child sexual abuse, HIV sexual risk, and gender relations of African American women. *American Journal of Preventive Medicine, 13,* 380–384.

Woods, A. B., Page, G. G., O'Campo, P., Pugh, L. C., Ford, D., & Campbell, J. C. (2005). The mediation effect of posttraumatic stress disorder symptoms on the relationship of intimate partner violence and IFN levels. *American Journal of Community Psychology, 36,* 159–174.

Wyatt, G. E., Gutherie, D., & Notgrass, C. M. (1992). Differential effects of women's child sexual abuse and subsequent sexual revictimization. *Journal of Consulting and Clinical Psychology, 60,* 1–7.

Chapter Authors

Rebecca Campbell, Ph.D., is a Professor of Psychology at Michigan State University. Her research examines how the legal, medical, and mental health systems respond to the needs of rape survivors. She is currently conducting two NIJ-funded studies on the effectiveness of Sexual Assault Nurse Examiner (SANE) programs in the prosecution of adult and adolescent sexual assault. She is the author of *Emotionally Involved: The Impact of Researching Rape* (2002, Routledge), which won the 2002 Distinguished Publication Award from the Association for Women in Psychology. She received the 2007 Distinguished Contributions to Psychology in the Public Interest Award (Early Career) from the American Psychological Association.

Stephanie M. Townsend, Ph.D., has worked in the movement to end sexual violence for almost two decades. She has been the director of a rape crisis program, served on state and national boards of directors, and conducted research. Her research focuses on community responses to sexual violence with an emphasis on primary prevention and Sexual Assault Nurse Examiner programs. In addition to research, she conducts external evaluations and provides technical assistance to state sexual assault coalitions and community-based rape crisis and prevention programs.

Personal Reflection

Carolyn West

I was 13 years old and armed with an adult library card. The very first book that I checked out was *Scream Quietly or the Neighbors Will Hear*, which was published in 1977 by Erin Pizzey. At that moment, I decided to become a clinical psychologist. Several months after receiving my B.A. in psychology, I was enrolled in a doctoral program. I found an article on dating violence and quickly fell in love with teaching and research.

Two life-altering events led me to work in the area of sexual violence. First, I took an undergraduate Women's Studies course on Female Sexuality and began working as a sex educator. I quickly learned that many people held misconceptions about sexuality, especially sexual violence. Second, while pursuing my doctoral degree I became a victim of academic sexual harassment, which is a very common experience. I found my voice and began giving interviews to the local media. After a successful lawsuit, I became deeply devoted to writing, training, and lecturing on sexual and interpersonal violence.

I hope that my work on sexual violence in the lives of African American women has been a contribution. More recently, I have been investigating the sexualization of black adolescent girls in rap music and hip hop culture. Teaching is another way that I contribute to the field. Over the years, I have developed courses on Family Violence and Sex Crimes and Sexual Violence. With the help of campus security, I have developed a R.A.D. (Rape Aggression Defense) Program for my students and community members. Lecturing internationally, conducting workshops, and giving media interviews are other ways that I contribute to the field. My life's work is to educate, empower, and inspire others to eliminate sexual assault and violence.

CHAPTER 6

Intimate Partner Violence Against Women

Kathleen C. Basile and Michele C. Black

Introduction

Intimate partner violence is a major social and public health problem with significant costs to individuals, families, communities, and society. Intimate partner violence affects women across all ages, cultures, racial and ethnic backgrounds, sexual orientations, and income levels, although not necessarily equally, which we will expand upon in later sections. Overall, about 1 in 4 women experience intimate partner violence at some point in their lifetime (Breiding, Black, & Ryan, 2008b; Tjaden & Thoennes, 2000). National estimates indicate that approximately 1.5 million women each year experience a total of 4.8 million physical assaults or rapes by intimate partners (Tjaden & Thoennes, 2000). Each year there are approximately 2 million injuries to women and nearly 1,200 women are killed by an intimate partner (Bureau of Justice Statistics, 2007; National Center for Injury Prevention and Control,

2003). Beyond the risk of injury and death, intimate partner violence has also been associated with a range of significant short- and long-term negative mental and physical health outcomes. As alarming as these numbers may seem, they are likely to substantially underestimate the true magnitude of the problem. First, much of the violence goes unreported because of the stigma and fear associated with intimate partner violence. Second, an increased understanding of the full impact, cost, and consequences of this violence on mental and physical health, including long-term and indirect consequences (e.g., chronic disease, disability) is now emerging.

Defining Intimate Partner Violence

Intimate partner violence includes threatened or completed physical or sexual violence or

Authors' Note: The findings and conclusions in this report are those of the authors and do not necessarily represent the official position of the Centers for Disease Control and Prevention. The authors wish to acknowledge Patricia Mahoney, Linda M. Williams, and Carolyn M. West, who authored the original chapter on intimate partner violence in the first edition of this volume. Their excellent and comprehensive work served as a helpful blueprint for the development of this updated chapter.

psychological abuse committed by a spouse, ex-spouse, current or former boyfriend or girlfriend, or dating partner (Saltzman, Fanslow, McMahon, & Shelley, 1999). It includes violence committed by cohabiting or noncohabiting partners and both opposite and same-sex partners. An extraordinary growth in research has occurred during the past 20 years with respect to these forms of violence. One challenge in interpreting the existing research and making comparisons between studies has been the lack of a shared definition of intimate partner violence. In 1999, the Centers for Disease Control and Prevention (CDC) published *Intimate Partner Violence Surveillance: Uniform Definitions and Recommended Data Elements* in an effort to improve and standardize data collected on intimate partner violence (Saltzman et al., 1999). Using uniform language and consistent definitions over time enables the field to improve understanding of the problem and identify those at increased risk. The data will help inform public policies and prevention strategies and will help guide and evaluate progress toward reducing the substantial health and social burden associated with all forms of intimate partner violence. Although stalking is not widely included as a form of intimate partner violence, in the years since the publication of the original CDC uniform definitions, a better understanding of the nature and extent of stalking by an intimate partner has demonstrated that it is also an important component of intimate partner violence by both current and former partners (Melton, 2007; Rosenfeld, 2004; Tjaden & Thoennes, 2000).

The use of the term *intimate partner violence* warrants discussion. The terms *domestic violence, woman abuse,* and *violence against women* have been frequently used in the past and are still used by many researchers and service providers, in part because the gendered nature of violence in intimate relationships is central to the understanding and prevention of such violence. The broader, more inclusive term intimate partner violence accommodates (1) the need to include violence that occurs between partners outside of marriage or cohabitation, and (2) the need to describe the violence that both women and men experience in intimate relationships. Although the use of the label intimate partner violence may be considered gender neutral, it in no way implies that women and men experience such violence to the same degree or with the same impact. Women experience more frequent and more severe intimate partner violence compared to men and are much more likely to suffer negative consequences because of the abuse.

Defining what constitutes intimate partner violence continues to be challenging and complex. The majority of the research on intimate partner violence has focused on discrete acts of aggression (usually physical aggression) that cause injury (e.g., the number of times someone has been hit, kicked, or punched by an intimate partner). However, fully understanding and preventing intimate partner violence requires an understanding of the patterns of violence; the overlap of the types of violence; and the meanings, motives, and contexts in which the experiences occur. Some studies have distinguished between "minor" and "severe" abuse based on their potential for injury (e.g., a slap versus a punch with a fist). The severity and frequency of behaviors may or may not be factored in. Further, studies often combine individuals who have experienced one slap by a partner with those who have experienced multiple episodes of a range of physically violent behaviors, without information regarding the emotional or physical impact of the behaviors. More effort is needed to improve the consistency of definitions across studies.

Battering is on the severe end of the continuum of intimate partner violence. Battering is conceptually distinct from discrete acts of violence and refers to an enduring, traumatic, and complex experience of control by an intimate partner that shapes a woman's behavior, her view of self, and beliefs about the controllability of her life (Smith, Tessaro, & Earp, 1995). According to Dobash, Dobash, Wilson, and Daly (1992), battering is experienced in the context of continuous intimidation and coercion. Johnson (1995) introduced the term *intimate terrorism* (formerly *patriarchal terrorism*) to the intimate partner violence lexicon to describe systematic use of violence, economic subordination, threats, isolation, and other control tactics on an intimate partner. Johnson distinguished intimate terrorism from *common couple violence,* which he described as usually minor violence that occurs when conflicts get "out of hand." Although common couple violence, as its name suggests, is perpetrated by both male and female partners, the vast majority of intimate terrorism is perpetrated by men against their female partners. In the same vein as battering, intimate terrorism involves a pattern of dominance and coercive control (e.g., isolation, intimidation, abuse of children, limiting access to resources; Dutton & Goodman, 2005). Most intimate partner violence seen in law enforcement, courts, and social services is severe violence consistent with battering or intimate terrorism (Johnson, 1995).

Prevalence and Incidence of Intimate Partner Violence Against Women

Prevalence of violence is generally defined as the percentage of people in a particular population who have experienced a specific form of violence (e.g., being punched) at least once during a specified period of time (e.g., past 12 months, ever in lifetime; Gail & Benichou, 2000; Kilpatrick, 2000). *Incidence* is generally defined as the percentage of people who experienced a specific form of violence for the first time during a specified time period (usually the past 12 months; Gail & Benichou, 2000). Multiple episodes of violence can be described

through the use of frequency statistics (e.g., the percentage of women who were raped twice during the past 12 months). Prevalence and incidence can also be reported as *rates* (e.g., the number of women per 100,000 women in the population who have experienced a specific form of violence).

Physical Violence

Data from the National Violence Against Women Survey (NVAWS) indicate that 22.1% of women experience some form of physical violence by an intimate partner at some time during their life (Tjaden & Thoennes, 2000). Women who are physically assaulted by an intimate partner experience an average of 3.4 separate assaults per year. More recently, in a 2005 Behavioral Risk Factor Surveillance System (BRFSS) study of 16 U.S. states and 2 territories by Breiding and colleagues (2008b), 26.4% of women reported experiencing some combination of physical violence (threatened, attempted, or completed) and nonconsensual sex by an intimate partner in their lifetime (Breiding et al., 2008b). Although data from NVAWS and BRFSS were collected a decade apart, the prevalence estimates are remarkably similar; the BRFSS estimate is likely higher because it includes nonconsensual sex. In the BRFSS study, the prevalence of nonconsensual sex and/or completed physical violence for women was 1.4% for the last 12 months and 23.6% for the lifetime, while in the NVAWS study, the prevalence for women of physical assault and/or completed or attempted forced penetration by an intimate partner was 1.5% for the last 12 months and 24.8% for the lifetime.

Sexual Violence

Rape has historically been defined as sexual intercourse by a man against a woman *other than his wife* (Herman, 1984; Russell, 1990). Until 1977, it was legally impossible in all states for a wife to be raped by her husband (Whatley, 1993). Given this historical backdrop for sexual violence in the context of marriage, it is not surprising that it is relatively prevalent. Studies of rape in marriage (defined as forced nonconsensual vaginal intercourse) have consistently shown that between 10% and 14% of ever-married or cohabiting women have been raped by their intimate partner at some point in their life (Basile, 2002; Finkelhor & Yllo, 1985; Russell, 1990). In addition, spouses have forced anal or oral sex on one-fourth to one-third of maritally raped women (Bergen, 1996; Campbell & Alford, 1989; Finkelhor & Yllo, 1985; Russell, 1990).

Beyond rape victimization, women experience other forms of sexual victimization by intimate partners, such as coercion to have intercourse, unwanted sexual touch, or sexual harassment. For example, Basile (2002) documented several kinds of coercive sex experiences in a national sample of women, such as having sex because they thought it was their "duty" (43%), having sex after a partner begged and pleaded with them to do so (26%), and having sex after their partner said things to bully them (9%). Some researchers have defined sexual violence in the context of intimate relationships more broadly to include controlling a woman's reproductive rights (e.g., controlling decision making about contraceptive use, forced pregnancy, or abortion; Abraham, 1999; Heise, 1993).

Psychological Abuse

Psychological abuse has been recognized as a part of the experience of intimate partner violence against women from the field's inception, particularly in early accounts of battered women (Walker, 1979). Studies of battered women have shown that psychological abuse can happen in isolation (psychological battering) or with physical and/or sexual violence (Smith, Thornton, DeVellis, Earp, & Coker, 2002). Some studies have shown that psychological abuse precedes other forms of intimate partner violence, such as physical violence (as reviewed in O'Leary, 1999). Previous work has found lifetime rates of psychological abuse victimization of women of 14% and 4% with a current partner (Coker et al., 2002). There have been challenges, though, with how best to define this component of intimate partner violence, which in turn affects our understanding of the extent of the problem. Researchers now distinguish between expressive (verbal) psychological aggression (e.g., yelling, insulting, demeaning a partner) and instrumental psychological aggression, including coercive control and entrapment behaviors (e.g., isolating a partner from family and friends, monitoring, controlling access to money or what to wear; reviewed by O'Leary, 1999). There is limited understanding of when expressive or instrumental aggression should be considered psychologically abusive. An act of psychological aggression, when experienced in isolation, may not be harmful. However, studies have shown that psychological abuse can have severe consequences, even when controlling for other forms of intimate partner violence (Arias & Pape, 1999; Basile, Arias, Desai, & Thompson, 2004; Smith et al., 2002).

Stalking

The recognition of stalking as a component of intimate partner violence is fairly recent. Historically, the behaviors that comprise stalking (e.g., monitoring, harassing) have been studied as part of psychological abuse (e.g., Sackett & Saunders, 1999; Shepard & Campbell, 1992). Since the release of the NVAWS estimates on stalking (Tjaden & Thoennes, 1998), research has recognized the role of stalking as a distinct part of intimate partner violence against women (e.g., Basile et al., 2004). Most research has defined stalking as repetitive, unwanted contact that is perceived by the victim to be threatening or intrusive (Rosenfeld, 2004). Even though the media's coverage of stalking would suggest it is most commonly committed by strangers against celebrities, national estimates from the NVAWS reveal that the majority of stalking incidents experienced by women (59%) are by a current or former intimate partner (Tjaden & Thoennes, 2000). The NVAWS found that 4.8% of women have been stalked by an intimate partner at some point in their lives. In addition, 503,485 women are stalked annually by an intimate partner, which equates to an annual victimization rate of 5 out of every 1,000 women. Because each victim identified in the NVAWS only reported one perpetrator for stalking in the 12 months prior to the survey, incidence rates for stalking are the same as the 12-month prevalence rates. It is important to note that the NVAWS only counted an incident as stalking if the behaviors (e.g., following, vandalizing, loitering) happened on more than one occasion and the woman was very frightened *or* believed that she or someone close to her would be seriously harmed or killed when she was being stalked (Tjaden & Thoennes, 2000). Stalking is more likely than other types of intimate partner violence (e.g., physical or sexual violence) to occur when a relationship ends. A recent review found a prior intimate relationship between victim and stalker to be one of the best predictors of stalking violence, along with explicit threats, a history of substance abuse, and the absence of psychosis (Rosenfeld, 2004). A recent qualitative study of intimate partner violence victims found that women who were not currently in a relationship with their abuser, whose abuser had a drug or alcohol problem, who experienced more controlling behaviors by their abusers, and who had experienced prior stalking by their abusers were at the highest risk of severe stalking (Melton, 2007).

Femicide

Femicide is the killing of women. Women are more likely to be killed by an intimate partner than by all other perpetrator categories combined

(Brown, Williams, & Dutton, 1999), and nearly three out of every four intimate partner violence homicide victims are women (McFarlane, Campbell, & Watson, 2002). Women are nearly four times more likely to be shot by a spouse or ex-spouse than by a stranger (Wiebe, 2003). In one urban fatality review, 94% of intimate partner homicide victims were women, and 43% of these women were killed in their bedrooms (Dick, MacDonald, & Dick, 2006). Another study found that 80% of lethal intimate partner firearm injuries occurred in the home (Finlay-Morreale, Tsuei, Fisher, Davis, & Johannigman, 2009). Many femicide victims experienced severe and chronic sexual, physical, and psychological abuse by the same intimate partner who killed them, and many were stalked (Campbell, Webster et al., 2003; McFarlane et al., 2002). The rate of intimate partner violence homicide among African American women is twice that of white women (Puzone, Saltzman, Kresnow, Thompson, & Mercy, 2000).

Overlap of Types of Violence

Numerous studies have demonstrated the substantial overlap between physical, sexual, psychological, and stalking intimate partner violence victimization (Tjaden & Thoennes, 2000). Data from the NVAWS demonstrated that 81% of women who were stalked by a current or former intimate partner were also physically assaulted by that partner, and 31% were sexually assaulted by that partner (Tjaden & Thoennes, 2000). Using the same NVAWS data, Miller (2006) demonstrated that more than 11% of women physically assaulted by an intimate partner were also raped and stalked by that partner. Researchers examining rape in marriage have reported the co-occurrence of sexual and physical violence (e.g., Basile, 1999; Peacock, 1998). In a meta-analysis of 82 studies, Spitzberg and Cupach (2007) found that 32% of stalking cases involved physical violence and 12% involved sexual violence. Other studies have reported overlap between the types of intimate partner violence (Logan, Cole, & Shannon, 2007; Mechanic, Uhlmansiek, Weaver, & Resick, 2002).

Why Is Intimate Partner Violence Unique?

Violence by an intimate partner is qualitatively different from violence perpetrated by others, for a number of reasons. Some of the most important reasons are described below.

The Intimate and Ongoing Nature of the Relationship

Intimate partner violence, as the name suggests, is defined by the intimate nature of the relationship. As defined above, perpetrators in these cases are husbands, cohabiting partners, boyfriends, and the like. In many cases, the perpetrator and victim share many things in common, such as a residence, a bank account, and, in some cases, children. If they do not share a household, the perpetrator typically has access to the victim's home. Further, an intimate partner violence perpetrator is not just someone the victim knows; he is also someone the victim loves or has loved and has shared romance and intimacy with, which further complicates the experience of violence. Another defining factor of an intimate partner violence relationship is its ongoing nature. Victims have a history with their perpetrators and, in many cases, it is a long and complex history and shared life. As such, victims of intimate partner violence often have no safe haven from the violence.

Repetitive and Changing Nature of Violence

Another aspect that differentiates intimate partner violence from other forms of interpersonal violence is that it changes over the course of the relationship. For some women, particularly women in battering relationships, the violence is serial (repeated numerous times by the same perpetrator over the course of the relationship) and often continues after the relationship ends. The violent acts might always be of the same type (e.g., hitting) or might be a combination of types (e.g., hitting, rape, and psychological abuse), and these patterns might change over time. However, this does not describe everyone's experience with intimate partner violence; some women may not experience chronic or repetitive violence. Because violence in many intimate relationships is repetitive, it may become an interwoven part of the relationship for many women and difficult to distinguish from other aspects of the relationship.

Perceptions of Responsibility (Victim Blaming)

Research has documented several ways in which women are blamed for their victimization by an intimate partner (Grothues & Marmion, 2006). The victim is more likely to be blamed for intimate partner violence than for other types of violence against women because of the existing relationship between the victim and abuser. Some of the most common misconceptions that result in blaming victims of intimate partner violence are the woman is somehow causing or "asking for" the violence; if she wanted the violence to stop she could easily leave the abuser; intimate partner violence perpetrators have serious psychological problems; sexual violence in an intimate relationship is about sex, and if the woman provided adequate sex there would be no abuse; and women must like the abuse because they go back to abusive partners (Grothues & Marmion, 2006). Various rape myths also exist, including women lead men on and therefore deserve to be raped; all women want to be raped; and no woman can be raped against her will (Burt, 1980; Ward, 1995). Misconceptions about intimate partner violence against women stem from the ways in which our culture defines the appropriate roles for women and men—in short, passivity for woman and aggressiveness for men. Contrary to the myths, research has documented several reasons why women do not immediately leave violent relationships and why some leave and come back many times before leaving permanently.

Why Women Cannot Easily Leave

"Why doesn't she leave?" is one of the most common questions asked about intimate partner violence victims and one that often reflects a shift of some blame to her for her own victimization. There are countless reasons why a woman stays with a violent partner. Women and their abusive partners often have an interwoven, complex life together that is not easy to walk away from, financially or emotionally. For example, consider a woman who has small children, a shared bank account, a residence and other assets in both her and her abuser's name, and numerous bills that would be difficult to pay on her own even though she is working full time. Some women are unemployed and must rely financially on their abusive partners. A woman might not leave because her violent partner threatened to kill her, himself, or kidnap their children if she leaves. Many women who have violent partners still have an emotional connection to their partners; they would like the violence to end, but not necessarily the relationship. Again, this may be complicated by the emotional connection that her children may have to the perpetrator or relationships she has with the perpetrator's family. These examples represent only a few of the reasons why it may be difficult to leave a violent partner.

Stages of Relationships

In this section, we discuss different life stages in which intimate partner violence against women

is likely to occur, including adolescent dating relationships, pregnancy, separation or divorce, and old age. But first, we briefly discuss childhood experiences with violence that often "set the stage" for later intimate partner violence.

Early Experiences With Violence

Nationally representative findings from NVAWS on the relationship between childhood maltreatment and later intimate partner violence victimization show that childhood physical and sexual abuse survivors were more likely to be in currently physically violent relationships and to have experienced forced sex by a current intimate partner than women who did not experience child abuse (Desai, Arias, Thompson, & Basile, 2002). In addition, findings from a review by Black, Heyman, and Slep (2001) show that women who experienced prior unwanted sexual experiences by a variety of perpetrators and under certain circumstances (e.g., blood relatives, non-blood relatives, unwanted sexual experience prior to age 14) were more likely to be victims of marital rape. Others have found that adolescents who had parents who were violent to each other were more likely to report higher rates of dating violence victimization (Arriaga & Foshee, 2004).

Adolescent Dating Relationships

Adolescent dating violence may set the stage for later intimate partner violence. Several recent studies have shown that rates of physical, sexual, and psychological victimization of female adolescent dating partners are high. For example, the 2007 National Youth Risk Behavior Survey (YRBS) found that 8.8% of female adolescents reported being a victim of physical violence by a dating partner in the last year (CDC, 2008). Another longitudinal study found that approximately one third of adolescents reported psychological or physical violence by a dating partner

(Halpern, Oslak, Young, Waller, Martin, & Kupper, 2001).

Although researchers have been studying teen dating violence for a few decades, it has only recently been recognized as a public health issue with different risk factors and consequences than adult intimate partner violence. One way that teen dating violence seems to differ from adult intimate partner violence is that several studies have shown similar numbers of girls and boys reporting physical aggression by a dating partner (Capaldi, Kim, & Shortt, 2007; O'Leary, Smith-Slep, Avery-Leaf, & Cascardi, 2008). However, girls are significantly more likely than boys to experience sexual victimization by a dating partner (Molidor, Tolman, & Koeber, 2000; Swahn, Simon, Arias, & Bossarte, 2008). Girls are also more likely than boys to experiences injuries from teen dating violence (Swahn et al., 2008) and to experience long-term health behavior impacts, such as suicide attempts, depression, unprotected sex, and binge drinking (Ackard, Eisenberg, & Neumark-Sztainer, 2007; Black, Eaton, Noonan, & Breiding, 2006; Olshen, McVeigh, Wunsch-Hitzig, & Rickert, 2007). Some suggest that adolescent experiences of intimate partner violence are different from adult experiences (e.g., more reports of mutual physical aggression in adolescent relationships) because of less traditionally defined power imbalances in adolescent relationships, a lack of experience communicating and negotiating in romantic relationships, and the stronger influence of peer attitudes and behaviors in adolescence (Mulford & Giordano, 2009).

Intimate Partner Violence During Pregnancy

Whether pregnant women are at increased risk for physical intimate partner violence compared to women who are not pregnant is still in debate. Available evidence suggests that pregnancy does not significantly increase the risk of violent victimization, nor does it serve as a protector against violence (Jasinski, 2004). Most researchers have found that women who experience intimate partner

violence during pregnancy were also victimized prior to pregnancy (Jasinski, 2004). Depending on the population and study design used, the prevalence of physical intimate partner violence during pregnancy varies greatly. One study found that 5.8% of women delivering live-born infants reported experiencing physical intimate partner violence during pregnancy or in the year prior to their pregnancy (Silverman, Decker, Reed, & Raj, 2006). Other studies have found that more than 20% of women reported experiencing physical intimate partner violence during pregnancy (e.g., Gazmararian, Lazorick, Spitz, Ballard, Saltzman, & Marks, 1996; Jasinski, 2001). Several studies have found that women who experience physical violence, psychological abuse, or forced sex during pregnancy are at greater risk for a range of adverse pregnancy outcomes, including preterm delivery and miscarriage (Brown, McDonald, & Krastev, 2008; Morland, Leskin, Block, Campbell, & Friedman, 2008; Pallitto, Campbell, & O'Campo, 2005). Similarly, the infants of mothers experiencing intimate partner violence are also at increased risk for a range of adverse outcomes, including fetal trauma and increased risk for low birth weight (Jasinski, 2004; Morland et al., 2008). A longitudinal study of 76 pregnant women in North Carolina examined the patterns of physical, psychological, and sexual violence occurring before, during, and after pregnancy (Macy, Martin, Kupper, Casaneuva, & Guo, 2007). Rates of physical violence peaked during the first three months of pregnancy; rates of both psychological and sexual violence were highest during the first month after infant delivery. Larger and more comprehensive studies are needed to improve the understanding of the relationship between pregnancy and intimate partner violence over time.

Separation, Divorce, and Intimate Partner Violence

Violence in the context of ending a relationship is an important aspect of intimate partner violence. Divorce literature indicates that women are more likely than men to end an intimate relationship (Hewitt, Baxter, & Western, 2005); it is well established that the process of relationship dissolution is one of the most dangerous times for women who are trying to escape abusive male partners (Brownridge, 2006b; Dawson, Bunge, & Balde, 2009; Dawson & Gartner, 1998; Wilson & Daly, 1993). Rage, despair, loss of control, and patriarchal expectations of male rights and dominance are common motives behind lethal violence males perpetrate against their estranged female partners (Brownridge, 2006b). Non-lethal intimate partner violence also increases dramatically when women try to leave relationships. For example, nearly half of stalking victims report that the stalking began after the relationship ended (Tjaden & Thoennes, 2000). Studies have also documented an increased risk of sexual violence by a current or former intimate partner just before, during, or after terminating a relationship (DeKeseredy, Rogness, & Schwartz, 2004). Most of the research regarding post-separation violence does not differentiate between violence that happened before and after the dissolution. However, the relatively few studies that do distinguish between pre- and post-separation intimate partner violence demonstrate that separated and divorced women have significantly elevated risk for intimate partner violence compared to currently married women. Some studies estimate a 30-fold increase in risk for non-lethal intimate partner violence for separated women compared to married women and a 9-fold increase in risk for divorced women (Brownridge, 2006b). A large-scale nationally representative study in Canada found that separated women and divorced women had nine times and four times the prevalence of intimate partner violence, respectively, compared to married women (Brownridge et al., 2008).

Intimate Partner Violence Among Older Women

Intimate partner violence against elderly women has traditionally been included under the umbrella of "elder abuse." In addition, the term *domestic violence* is commonly used to describe violence between romantic partners, but for abuse of elders it includes violence by anyone in the home or family. Although most of these studies include violence by any person (partners, family members, acquaintances, care providers), a substantial proportion (between 30% and 71%) of elder abuse of women is perpetrated by intimate partners (Lundy & Grossman, 2004; Mouton, Rovi, Furniss, & Lasser, 1999; Teaster, 2002). Data from the 2005 BRFSS reveal that lifetime prevalence of intimate partner violence (including threatened, attempted, or completed physical violence or unwanted sex) for U.S. women 55 to 64 years old was 26.5% and was 12.9% for those over 65 years old (Breiding et al., 2008b). The prevalence of intimate partner violence against women in the last 12 months decreased with each successive decade (ranging from 3.8% for 18- to 24-year-olds to 0.4% for 55- to 64-year-olds). Although the overall prevalence does decrease substantially with age, the problem in no way disappears; 0.4% translates to nearly 70,000 women aged 55 to 64 experiencing intimate partner violence each year. During the next several decades, the number of older women who experience intimate partner violence will increase dramatically as the population ages and life expectancy increases.

Perpetrators

Understanding the characteristics of perpetrators and factors associated with committing intimate partner violence is critical to preventing intimate partner violence. Given that Chapter 3 covers this topic at length, we limit our discussion here to a brief review of key risk factors for perpetration.

Childhood Experiences With Violence

Numerous studies have linked childhood physical and sexual abuse and witnessing violence between parents or other caregivers to intimate partner violence perpetration. For example, a review of 10 articles published between 1995 and 2004 reported that all studies found a significant relationship between physical intimate partner violence perpetration as an adult and physical abuse in childhood, poor relationship with a mother, or witnessing marital violence (Gil-Gonzalez, Vives-Cases, Ruiz, Carrasco-Portino, & Alvarex-Dardet, 2008). Others have found a relationship between child sexual abuse and intimate partner violence perpetration (Fang & Corso, 2008; Riggs, Caulfield, & Street, 2000). Although the existing research linking childhood experiences with violence in the family to sexual violence perpetration against an intimate (e.g., marital rape) is sparse, inconsistent, and dated, it suggests that perpetrators of marital rape are more likely to have been exposed as a child to violence in the home (Bowker, 1983; Shields & Hanneke, 1988). Other childhood and adolescent experiences with violence have also been linked to later intimate partner violence perpetration. For example, one study found that adolescents who were classified as bullies reported more aggression with their boyfriends/girlfriends than a comparison group of nonbullies, suggesting that youth who are involved in bullying are at risk to develop unhealthy adult intimate relationships (Connolly, Pepler, Craig, & Taradash, 2000).

Alcohol and Drug Use or Abuse

Studies have repeatedly found a relationship between alcohol and drug use or abuse and perpetration of physical and psychological intimate partner violence (see reviews in Parrott, Drobes, Saladin, Coffey, & Dansky, 2003; Riggs et al., 2000; Schumacher, Feldbau-Kohn, Smith-Slep, & Heyman, 2001; Stith, Smith, Penn, Ward, & Tritt, 2004; Testa, 2004). Studies relating alcohol or drug use or abuse with sexual intimate partner violence are less clear but suggest that there is an association (e.g., Finkelhor & Yllo, 1985; Russell, 1990).

Anger, Hostility, and Masculinity

Numerous reviews have connected general anger and hostility to physical intimate partner violence (Norlander & Eckhardt, 2005; Riggs et al., 2000; Schumacher et al., 2001; Stith et al., 2004), and recent work has shown that hostile men who drink alcohol excessively are more likely to commit physical intimate partner violence (Schumacher, Homish, Leonard, Quigley, & Kearns-Bodkin, 2008). Hostile attitudes toward women in particular have also been linked to the perpetration of both physical and sexual intimate partner violence (Holtzworth-Munroe, Meehan, Herron, Rehman, & Stuart, 2000; Malamuth, Linz, Heavey, Barnes, & Acker, 1995). Increasingly, intimate partner violence researchers have focused on masculinity and its relationship to intimate partner violence perpetration. Masculinity is a multidimensional concept that has been measured differently in different studies. In a review, Moore and Stuart (2005) found the strongest relationships between masculinity and intimate partner violence when the following were used to define masculinity: (1) the *gender role stress/conflict approach,* Pleck's (1995) paradigm that gender roles are inconsistent and changing, which leads men to overcompensate by being violent when they violate gender role expectations; and (2) *indirect approaches* of using attitudinal measures, particularly measures of beliefs about wife beating.

Mental Health Conditions

A variety of mental health conditions have been associated with intimate partner violence perpetration. For example, studies have shown that men who are depressed are more likely to perpetrate physical intimate partner violence (Schumacher et al., 2001; Stith et al., 2004), and men who have Post-Traumatic Stress Disorder (PTSD) are more likely to perpetrate both physical and psychological intimate partner violence (Delsol & Margolin, 2004; Parrott et al., 2003; Rosenbaum & Leisring, 2003).

Underserved Populations

Racial and Ethnic Minority Women

For decades, numerous studies have found an association between race and ethnicity and the occurrence of intimate partner violence (Ellison, Trinitapoli, Anderson, & Johnson, 2007; Lockhart, 1987; Tjaden & Thoennes, 2000). Rates of reported intimate partner violence by African Americans, American Indians and Alaska Natives, and mixed races are generally higher compared to other racial and ethnic groups (Breiding et al., 2008b; Ellison et al., 2007; Tjaden & Thoennes, 2000). Intimate partner violence victimization rates for U.S. women (including rape, physical violence, and stalking) were 24.8% among white non-Hispanics, 29.1% among African American non-Hispanics, 15.0% among Asian Pacific Islanders, 37.5% among American Indians and Alaska Natives, 23.4% among Hispanics, and 30.2% among mixed-race participants (Tjaden & Thoennes, 2000).

Findings relating race and ethnicity to the risk of intimate partner violence remain contentious. Because researchers often do not control for socioeconomic status (SES), differences that appear to be racial or ethnic are likely to be, in part, due to socioeconomic differences. Minority populations generally have higher rates of poverty, lower average income, and lower education levels, and studies have shown that SES factors are associated with intimate partner violence (Breiding et al., 2008b; Greenfeld et al., 1998). In one of the largest studies of intimate partner violence conducted in the United States, lifetime prevalence ranged from 24.2% among women with household incomes above $50,000 to 35.5% among those with incomes less than $15,000 (Breiding et al., 2008b). Additionally, African American, Hispanic, and other minority populations may be living in socially disadvantaged and disorganized communities that are likely to have more social stressors. Such stressors include racism, limited and overcrowded housing options, increased exposure to crime and poverty,

unemployment, and other financial strains. The cumulative toll of these issues may increase frustration and increase the likelihood of intimate partner violence. Additionally, some cultural aspects of religion and spirituality may either legitimize or condemn intimate partner violence (Nason-Clark, 2000). Although differences found among racial and ethnic groups are helpful in identifying groups that may benefit from targeted prevention efforts, racial and ethnic groups represent complex, heterogeneous, and diverse groups that are likely to benefit from differing prevention efforts (Breiding, Black, & Ryan, 2008a).

Immigrant Women

Immigrant populations are increasing in many countries. Their unique circumstances and the complex combination of political, economic, and social forces often make them especially vulnerable to intimate partner violence. Yet, information is relatively limited regarding the extent and magnitude of intimate partner violence among immigrant women (Pan, Daley, Rivera, Williams, Lingle, & Reznik, 2006). It is commonly perceived that intimate partner violence among immigrants is higher than levels in their adopted cultures because they import the violence with them. However, evidence suggests the opposite may be true. For example, nearly half of Latinas in one study reported that intimate partner violence against them had increased since their immigration to the U.S. (Dutton, Orloff, & Hass, 2000). Immigrant women may also be more likely to experience increased intimate partner violence because their situations are exacerbated by immigration-related factors (e.g., legal status, language proficiency, increased stress, limited social networks; Menjívar & Salcido, 2002). Another common assumption is that intimate partner violence decreases as time in the adopted country increases. Unfortunately, eliminating stressors related to recent immigration does not necessarily decrease risk for intimate partner violence. As immigrant women adapt to the culture of their adopted country, changes in gender roles and responsibilities may become a significant source of conflict in an already stressful family environment (Pan et al., 2006). As women begin the process of acculturation, and perhaps become less dependent as a result of employment or other financial resources, their male partners may attempt to regain control by using violence. Arranged marriages provide another example of the difficulties immigrant women may face. Those who opt out of such arrangements may increase their own power but also increase their isolation as they lose the support of family and friends. Staying in arranged marriages that are abusive may trap women in violent intimate relationships with few viable options. Given the increasing numbers of immigrants in developed countries, the magnitude of intimate partner violence in these populations should remain under consideration (Ely, 2004; U.S. Census Bureau, 2008).

Same-Sex Relationships

Estimates regarding the extent of violence by female same-sex partners vary substantially. Prevalence rates range from 8%-60% in studies that used varying definitions of violence, time frames, and sampling procedures (Turrell, 2000). A community-based convenience sample of 229 lesbians found that 12.2% reported experiencing at least one incident of intimate partner violence in the past year (Rose, 2003). The NVAWS is the only population-based study to include same-sex partners. Of the 79 women who reported ever having lived with a same-sex intimate partner, 11.4% reported being victimized by a female partner (Tjaden & Thoennes, 2000). Although the prevalence of same-sex intimate partner violence has varied depending on the study, it is generally believed that the experience of intimate partner violence and the rates overall are similar to those found in heterosexual samples (Brown & Groscup, 2009; Wise & Bowman, 1997). Representative prevalence data on same-sex intimate partner violence is

needed to better understand this problem. However, it is difficult to identify representative samples for same-sex intimate partner violence research given the discrimination and homophobic attitudes that are prevalent in society. Also, internalized homophobia of the same-sex victim and/or perpetrator, defined as the personal acceptance and internalization of negative attitudes held by some members of society toward homosexuals (Renzetti, 1992), may serve as a risk factor for lesbian intimate partner violence because it keeps lesbian victims isolated from support networks, social services, and other help-seeking avenues, and it contributes to low self-esteem and a perception of powerlessness.

Women With Disabilities

Women with disabilities are a vulnerable population with specific and unique risks for experiencing violence, depending on the form and severity of their disabilities. A 2001 review, however, found almost no literature on risks of abuse among disabled women (Curry, Hassouneh-Phillips, & Johnston-Silverberg, 2001). Furthermore, very little of the limited research available focused on intimate partner violence—most focused on sexual violence experienced by developmentally disabled women. One explanation for this lack of attention may be the misperception that disabled women are single and/or asexual (Barnett, Miller-Perrin, & Perrin, 2005). Prior to 2007, the two or three studies that provided information on intimate partner violence among disabled women were small convenience samples that were neither representative of women nor of the disabled (Ridington, 1989; Young, Nosek, Howland, Changpong, & Rintala, 1997). Brownridge (2006a) used a large, representative sample of married or cohabiting women to compare intimate partner violence among women with disabilities to women without disabilities. Multivariate analysis showed that women with disabilities were significantly more likely to report experiencing violence by an intimate partner in the past five years; women with disabilities were twice as likely to report being beaten, kicked, bit, or hit and three times more likely to report being forced into sexual activity. Young women with disabilities were the most vulnerable. The study also demonstrated that patriarchal dominance and sexual proprietary behaviors were strongly linked to an increased likelihood of violence for women with and without disabilities.

Rural Women

Approximately 21% of the U.S. population lived in rural areas in 2000. Although there has been little research attention paid to rural intimate partner violence, a recent study by Breiding, Ziembroski, and Lynberg (2009) found that approximately 1 in 4 rural women experienced intimate partner violence at some time during their life, similar to the rate experienced by the U.S. population as a whole. Rural populations, however, may be more vulnerable to the associated risks of intimate partner violence because of the general perception that rural communities are pastoral and peaceful with a better quality of life than urban communities and, therefore, intimate partner violence resources are "not needed." There are fewer domestic violence shelters, physical and mental health professionals, and law enforcement personnel per capita than for those living in nonrural areas (e.g., Lohmann & Lohmann, 2005; Merwin, Snyder, & Katz, 2006).

Isolation, poverty, lack of social support, and related stress are all characteristics of rural communities that may make it especially difficult for those who experience intimate partner violence. In addition, rural residents are more likely to be underinsured than are those in many urban and suburban areas (Mueller & MacKinney, 2006; Patterson, 2006), further limiting victims' abilities to seek either primary or mental health care for physical and mental health problems associated with experiencing intimate partner violence. Other unique challenges affect a rural community's ability to address intimate partner violence. They are often made up of tightly knit social networks in which, paradoxically, individuals depend heavily on one another yet value privacy and self-sufficiency to a great degree (Greenberg Quinlan Rosner Research, 2002; Phillipson & Allan, 2004). In addition, rural populations may display more traditional gender roles than other populations (Oughton, 2007); such norms may create an environment in which intimate partner violence may be viewed as more socially acceptable (Little & Morris, 2005; Midgley, 2006). These dynamics may contribute to decreased reporting of intimate partner violence. Additional research is needed to improve our understanding of intimate partner violence occurring in rural areas.

The Military

Military families experience unique stressors that may increase the risk of intimate partner violence (e.g., frequent relocations, deployment, hypermasculine military culture). Although data on the incidence and prevalence of intimate partner violence in the military are limited, researchers comparing civilian and military populations generally find higher rates of intimate partner violence in the military. For example, the one-year prevalence of intimate partner violence victimization among women was 29.9% in one study (Pan, Neidig, & O'Leary, 1994) and 32% in another study (Rosen, Knudson, Brannen, Fancher, Killgore, & Barasich, 2002). Comparing results between military and nonmilitary samples presents unique methodological challenges. In addition to military populations being younger and lower income (and thus more likely to have increased rates of intimate partner violence compared to older populations), victims of intimate partner violence in the military may be less likely to participate in surveys or report experiencing intimate partner violence if their superiors or their spouses' superiors have access to the survey research records (Campbell, Garza et al., 2003). Because of the increase in number and length of deployments and family stressors that contribute to intimate partner violence, further monitoring and evaluation of intimate partner violence in the military is warranted.

Consequences and Costs

Beyond the risk of death and injury, intimate partner violence has been associated with a range of significant short- and long-term negative mental and physical health outcomes. Psychological and mental health consequences include PTSD, depression, anxiety, substance abuse, and suicidal behaviors and ideation (e.g., Bonomi et al., 2006; Carbone-López, Kruttschnitt, & Macmillan, 2006; Coker et. al, 2002). Victims of rape in marriage have been found to experience particular psychological trauma compared to victims of rape by nonintimates due to the loss of trust in the spouse or partner, fear of continued assault given the likelihood for continued interaction, and overall questioning of the meaning of the relationship and sex within it (Shields & Hanneke, 1992; Temple, Weston, Rodriguez, & Marshall, 2007). Current heavy or binge drinking (a form of self-medication) and other health risk behaviors (including smoking, increased body mass, and risk factors for HIV and other sexually transmitted diseases) have also been associated with experiencing intimate partner violence (Breiding et al., 2008a). Other physical health problems associated with intimate partner violence include poor general health, chronic disease, physical disability, somatic syndromes, chronic pain, arthritis, migraines, hearing loss, angina, functional gastrointestinal disorders, and changes in endocrine and immune functions (e.g., Coker, Smith, & Fadden, 2005; Pico-Alfonso, Garcia-Linares, Celda-Navarro, Herbert, & Martinez, 2004).

Evidence from several studies suggests that one underlying mechanism that might link intimate partner violence and chronic diseases is the biologic response to long-term or ongoing stress. For example, the link between violence, stress, and somatic disorders (e.g., fibromyalgia, chronic fatigue syndrome, irritable bowel syndrome) has been well established; these same stress responses have been linked to various chronic diseases (Crofford, 2007; Pico-Alfonso et al., 2004).

Intimate partner violence is costly because it endangers the health and well-being of women in many different ways. Data from the NVAWS indicated that the cost of intimate partner violence against women in the U.S. was an estimated $5.8 billion in 1995 (95% confidence interval: $3.9 to $7.7 billion). The annual cost of rape alone committed by intimate partners is estimated at $320 million. The annual cost was an estimated $342 million for intimate partner stalking and an estimated $893 million for intimate partner murder. Max, Rice, Finkelstein, Bardwell, and Leadbetter (2004) estimated that the $5.8 billion 1995 cost of intimate partner violence updated to 2003 dollars would total more than $8.3 billion. These cost estimates from the NVAWS are based on medical expenditures and lost productivity. For several reasons, however, they are likely to be substantial underestimates of the overall economic and social burden of intimate partner violence. For example, the NVAWS cost estimates (1) are only for the most recent victimization; (2) include most, but not all, medical expenditures (e.g., HIV testing, indirect medical costs associated with the long-term physical health impact of exposure to chronic stress); (3) do not include the extensive criminal justice or social services costs associated with intimate partner violence; and (4) do not include the significant costs related to pain, suffering, and decreased quality of life for the victim or for secondary victims (e.g., children, other family members; National Center for Injury Prevention and Control, 2003).

In addition to costs associated with victimization, recent research is beginning to make a connection between likelihood of male perpetration of intimate partner violence and work productivity. Rothman and Corso (2008) found that male state agency employees in New England who had a propensity for aggression against their intimate partners were more likely than employees with a low propensity for abuse to (1) report being absent from work or missing portions of the work day, (2) underperform when they are on the job, (3) be feeling ill while on the job, and (4) make mistakes on the job. These findings show that the costs of intimate partner violence result not only from the consequences of victimization but from the impact of the abusive behaviors on the perpetrators themselves.

Next Steps

Great strides have been made in the understanding of intimate partner violence against women since the NVAWS was conducted in the mid-1990s. However, an improved understanding of the context, impact, and consequences of intimate partner violence is still needed, including the patterns of abuse (beyond discrete physical acts) and level of impact beyond physical injuries (e.g., fear, perceived risk of harm, effect on well-being, interference with reproduction and social networks). The ability to distinguish between high impact and low impact intimate partner violence is critically needed to allow us to better describe the populations that are most affected by intimate partner violence and direct limited resources to those who most need them. In addition, more frequent data that measures the full range of intimate partner violence behaviors consistently over time is essential to inform public policies and the development of effective prevention strategies at both the national and state levels.

Another weakness of the intimate partner violence field as a whole is that much of the scholarship focuses on one type of intimate partner violence, physical violence. Many studies include psychological abuse or some combination of types in one measure, but as Black and colleagues (2001) have shown, there are very few studies examining risk factors associated with sexual intimate partner violence perpetration, and there are very few studies that have looked at all types of intimate partner violence (physical, sexual, psychological, and stalking violence) in the same study to determine the overlap of perpetration and the shared and unique risk and protective factors for all components of

intimate partner violence. Future studies would benefit from integrating detailed measures of stalking into the conceptualization of intimate partner violence. The recent work of White, McMullin, Swartout, Sechrist, and Gollehon (2008) reveals that men who "dual perpetrate" physical and sexual intimate partner violence are a unique group with different risk factors than men who perpetrate one or the other type of intimate partner violence. Their work stresses the importance of integrating research on sexual and physical intimate partner violence. Future work integrating all types of intimate partner violence would also greatly benefit the field.

As discussed in other chapters, there is a need for more research to understand the influence of all levels of the social ecology on intimate partner violence (Chapter 5) and to understand the protective factors for intimate partner violence (i.e., factors that prevent someone at risk for perpetration from becoming a perpetrator, as discussed in Chapter 18). Finally, this review chapter has shown that there are certain segments of the population about whom we do not know enough with regard to the experience of intimate partner violence. In particular, further research should focus more on same-sex samples, Native Americans, disabled women, and elderly women. Also, the field would benefit from a better understanding of the global impact of intimate partner violence and how correlates vary by cultural context.

References

Abraham, M. (1999). Sexual abuse in South Asian immigrant marriages. *Violence Against Women, 5,* 591–618.

Ackard, D. M., Eisenberg, M. E., & Neumark-Sztainer, D. (2007). Long-term impact of adolescent dating violence on the behavioral and psychological health of male and female youth. *Journal of Pediatrics, 151,* 476–481.

Arias, I., & Pape, K. T. (1999). Psychological abuse: Implications for adjustment and commitment to leave violent partners. *Violence and Victims, 14*(1), 55–67.

Arriaga, X. B., & Foshee, V. A. (2004). Adolescent dating violence: Do adolescents follow in their friends', or their parents', footsteps? *Journal of Interpersonal Violence, 19*(2), 162–184.

Barnett, O., Miller-Perrin, C. L., & Perrin, R. D. (2005). *Family violence across the lifespan: An introduction* (2nd ed.). Thousand Oaks, CA: Sage.

Basile, K. C. (1999). Rape by acquiescence: The ways in which women "give in" to unwanted sex with their husbands. *Violence Against Women, 5,* 1036–1058.

Basile, K. C. (2002). Prevalence of wife rape and other intimate partner sexual coercion in a nationally representative sample of women. *Violence and Victims, 17,* 511–524.

Basile, K. C., Arias, I., Desai, S., & Thompson, M. P. (2004). The differential association of intimate partner physical, sexual, psychological, and stalking violence and post-traumatic stress symptoms in a nationally representative sample of women. *Journal of Traumatic Stress, 17*(5), 413–421.

Bergen, R. K. (1996). *Wife rape: Understanding the responses of survivors and service providers.* Thousand Oaks, CA: Sage.

Black, D. A., Heyman, R. E., & Slep, A. M. S. (2001). Risk factors for male to female partner sexual abuse. *Aggression and Violent Behavior, 6,* 269–280.

Black, M. C., Eaton, D., Noonan, R., & Breiding, M. (2006). Prevalence and associated health risk behaviors of physical dating violence victimization among high school students—United States, 2003. *Morbidity & Mortality Weekly Report, 55,* 532–535.

Bonomi, A. E., Thompson, R. S., Anderson, M., Reid, R. J., Carrell, D., Dimer, J. A., et al. (2006). Intimate partner violence and women's physical, mental, and social functioning. *American Journal of Preventive Medicine, 30,* 458–466.

Bowker, L. H. (1983). Marital rape: A distinct syndrome? *Social Casework, 64,* 347–352.

Breiding, M. J., Black, M. C., & Ryan, G. W. (2008a). Chronic disease and health risk behaviors associated with intimate partner violence—18 U.S. states/territories, 2005. *Annals of Epidemiology, 18,* 534–544.

Breiding, M. J., Black, M. C., & Ryan, G. W. (2008b). Prevalence and risk factors of intimate partner violence in eighteen U.S. states/territories, 2005. *American Journal of Preventive Medicine, 34*(2), 112–118.

Breiding, M. J., Ziembroski, J. S., & Lynberg, M. C. (2009, Summer). Prevalence of rural intimate partner violence in 16 U.S. states, 2005. *Journal of Rural Health,* 240–246.

Brown, M. J., & Groscup, J. (2009). Perceptions of same-sex domestic violence among crisis center staff. *Journal of Family Violence, 24,* 87–93.

Brown, S. J., McDonald, E. A., & Krastev, A. H. (2008). Fear of an intimate partner and women's health in early pregnancy: Findings from the Maternal Health Study. *Birth, 35*(4), 293–302.

Brown, A., Williams, K. R., & Dutton, D. G. (1999). Homicide between intimate partners. In M. D. Smith & M. A. Zahn (Eds.), *Homicide: A sourcebook of social research* (pp. 149–164). Thousand Oaks: Sage.

Brownridge, D. A. (2006a). Partner violence against women with disabilities: Prevalence, risk, and explanations. *Violence and Victims, 12*(9), 805–822.

Brownridge, D. A. (2006b). Violence against women post-separation. *Aggression and Violent Behavior, 11,* 514–530.

Brownridge, D. A., Chan, K. L., Hiebert-Murphy, D., Ristock, J., Tiwari, A., Leung, W. C., et al. (2008). The elevated risk for non-lethal post-separation violence in Canada: A comparison of separated, divorced, and married women. *Journal of Interpersonal Violence, 23*(1), 117–135.

Bureau of Justice Statistics. (2007). Retrieved September 11, 2009, from http://www.ojp.usdoj.gov

Burt, M. R. (1980). Cultural myths and supports for rape. *Journal of Personality and Social Psychology, 38,* 217–230.

Campbell, J. C., & Alford, P. (1989). The dark consequences of marital rape. *American Journal of Nursing, 89,* 946–949.

Campbell, J. C., Garza, M. A., Gielen, A. C., O'Campo, P., Kub, J., Dienemann, J., et al. (2003). Intimate partner violence and abuse among active duty military women. *Violence Against Women, 9*(9), 1072–1092.

Campbell, J. C., Webster, D. W., Koziol-McClain, J., Block, C., Campbell, D., Curry, M. A., et al. (2003). Risk factors for femicide in abusive relationships: Results from a multisite case control study. *American Journal of Public Health, 93*(7), 1089–1097.

Capaldi, D. M., Kim, H. K., & Shortt, J. W. (2007). Observed initiation and reciprocity of physical aggression in young, at-risk couples. *Journal of Family Violence, 22,* 101–111.

Carbone-López, K., Kruttschnitt, C., & Macmillan, R. (2006). Patterns of intimate partner violence and their associations with physical health, psychological distress, and substance use. *Public Health Rep, 121*, 382–392.

Centers for Disease Control and Prevention. (2008, June 6). Youth Risk Behavior Surveillance: United States, 2007. Surveillance Summaries. *Morbidity & Mortality Weekly Report, 57*(No. SS-4).

Coker, A. L., Davis, K. E., Arias, I., Desai, S., Sanderson, M., Brandt, H. M., et al. (2002). Physical and mental health effects of intimate partner violence for men and women. *American Journal of Preventive Medicine, 23*, 260–268.

Coker, A. L., Smith, P. H., & Fadden, M. K. (2005). Intimate partner violence and disabilities among women attending family practice clinics. *Journal of Women's Health, 14*, 829–838.

Connolly, J., Pepler, D., Craig, W., & Taradash, A. (2000). Dating experiences of bullies in early adolescence. *Child Maltreatment, 5*(4), 299–310.

Crofford, L. J. (2007). Violence, stress, and somatic syndromes. *Trauma, Violence, & Abuse, 8*, 299–313.

Curry, M. A., Hassouneh-Phillips, D., & Johnston-Silverberg, A. (2001). Abuse of women with disabilities: An ecological model and review. *Violence Against Women, 7*, 60–79.

Dawson, M., Bunge, V. P., & Balde, T. (2009). National trends in intimate partner homicides: Explaining declines in Canada, 1976–2001. *Violence Against Women, 15*(3), 276–306.

Dawson, R., & Gartner, R. (1998). Differences in the characteristics of intimate femicides: The role of relationship state and relationship status. *Homicide Studies, 2*, 378–399.

DeKeseredy, W. S., Rogness, M., & Schwartz, M. D. (2004). Separation/divorce sexual assault: The current state of social and scientific knowledge. *Aggression and Violent Behavior, 9*, 675–691.

Delsol, C., & Margolin, G. (2004). The role of family-of-origin violence in men's marital violence perpetration. *Clinical Psychology Review, 24*, 99–122.

Desai, S., Arias, I., Thompson, M. P., & Basile, K. C. (2002). Childhood victimization and subsequent adult revictimization assessed in a nationally representative sample of women and men. *Violence and Victims, 17*(6), 639–653.

Dick, G., MacDonald, A., & Dick, A. (Eds.). (2006). *Hamilton County Violence Review Team. A research report: Intimate partner homicide–Hamilton County, Ohio, 1997–2006.* Cincinnati, OH: University of Cincinnati.

Dobash, R. P., Dobash, R. E., Wilson, M., & Daly, M. (1992). The myth of marital symmetry in marital violence. *Social Problems, 39*, 71–91.

Dutton, M. A., & Goodman, L. A. (2005). Coercion in intimate partner violence: Toward a new conceptualization. *Sex Roles, 52*, 743–756.

Dutton, M., Orloff, L., & Hass, G. A. (2000). Characteristics of help-seeking behaviors, resources and services needs of battered immigrant Latinas: Legal and policy implications. *Georgetown Journal of Poverty, Law, and Policy, 7*(2), 30–49.

Ellison, C. G, Trinitapoli, J. A., Anderson, K. L., & Johnson, B. R. (2007). Race/ethnicity, religious involvement, and domestic violence. *Violence Against Women, 13*(11), 1094–1112.

Ely, G. E. (2004). Domestic violence and immigrant communities in the United States: A review of women's unique needs and recommendations for social work practice and research. *Stress, Trauma, and Crisis, 7*, 223–241.

Fang, X., & Corso, P. (2008). Gender differences in the connections between violence experienced as a child and perpetration of intimate partner violence in young adulthood. *Journal of Family Violence, 23*(5), 303–313.

Finkelhor, D., & Yllo, K. (1985). *License to rape: Sexual abuse of wives.* New York: The Free Press.

Finlay-Morreale, H. E., Tsuei, B. J., Fisher, B. S., Davis, K., & Johannigman, J. A. (2009). Close is dead: Determinants of firearm injury lethality in women. *The Journal of Trauma, Injury, Infection, and Critical Care, 66*, 1207–1211.

Gail, M. H., & Benichou, J. (Eds.). (2000). *Encyclopedia of epidemiologic methods* (pp. 432–437, 728–729). West Sussex, UK: Wiley & Sons.

Gazmararian, J. A., Lazorick, S., Spitz, A., Ballard, T. J., Saltzman, L. E., & Marks, J. A. (1996). Prevalence of violence against pregnant women. *Journal of the American Medical Association, 275*(24), 1915–1920.

Gil-Gonzalez, D., Vives-Cases, C., Ruiz, M. T., Carrasco-Portino, M., Alvarex-Dardet, C. (2008). Childhood experiences of violence in perpetrators as a risk factor of intimate partner violence: A systemic review. *Journal of Public Health, 30*, 14–22.

Greenberg Quinlan Rosner Research. (2002, November). *Perceptions of rural America: National state legislator survey.* Battle Creek, MI: W.K. Kellogg Foundation.

Greenfeld, L. A., Rand, M. R., Craven, D., Klaus, P. A., Perkins, C. A., Ringel, C., et al. (1998). *Violence by intimates: Analysis of data on crimes by current or former spouses, boyfriends, and girlfriends* (NCJ Publication No. 167237). Washington, DC: U. S. Department of Justice, Office of Justice Programs, Bureau of Justice Statistics.

Grothues, C. A., & Marmion, S. L. (2006). Dismantling the myths about intimate violence against women. In P. K. Lundberg-Love & S. L. Marmion (Eds.), *"Intimate" violence against women: When spouses, partners, or lovers attack* (pp. 9–14). Westport, CT: Praeger/Greenwood.

Halpern, C. T., Oslak, S. G., Young, M. L., Waller, M. W., Martin, S. L., & Kupper, L. L. (2001). Partner violence among adolescents in opposite-sex romantic relationships: Findings from the National Longitudinal Study of Adolescent Health. *American Journal of Public Health, 91,* 1679–1685.

Heise, L. L. (1993). Reproductive freedom and violence against women: Where are the intersections? *Journal of Law, Medicine, & Ethics, 21*(2), 206–216.

Herman, D. (1984). The rape culture. In J. Freeman (Ed.), *Women: A feminist perspective* (pp. 20–34). Palo Alto, CA: Mayfield.

Hewitt, B., Baxter, J., & Western, M. (2005). Marriage breakdown in Australia: The social correlates of separation and divorce. *Journal of Sociology, 4*(2), 163–183.

Holzworth-Munroe, A., Meehan, J. C., Herron, K., Rehman, U., & Stuart, G. L. (2000). Testing the Holtzworth-Munroe and Stuart (1994) batterer typology. *Journal of Consulting and Clinical Psychology, 68,* 1000–1019.

Jasinski, J. (2001). Pregnancy and violence against women: An analysis of longitudinal data. *Journal of Interpersonal Violence, 16*(7), 712–733.

Jasinski, J. (2004). Pregnancy and domestic violence: A review of the literature. *Trauma, Violence, & Abuse, 5*(1), 47–64.

Johnson, M. (1995). Patriarchal terrorism versus common couple violence. *Journal of Marriage and the Family, 57,* 283–294.

Kilpatrick, D. G. (2000). *Rape and sexual assault.* Retrieved March 22, 2010, from http://www.musc.edu/vaw prevention/research/sa.shtml.

Little, J., & Morris, C. (2005). *Critical studies in rural gender issues.* Aldershot, UK: Ashgate.

Lockhart, L. L. (1987). A reexamination of the effects of race and social class on the incidence of marital violence: A search for reliable difference. *Journal of Marriage and the Family, 49,* 603–610.

Logan, T. K., Cole, J., & Shannon, L. (2007). A mixed-methods examination of sexual coercion and degradation among women in violence relationships who do and do not report forced sex. *Violence and Victims, 22,* 71–94.

Lohmann, N., & Lohmann, R. A. (2005). *Rural social work practice.* New York: Columbia University Press.

Lundy, M., & Grossman, S. F. (2004). Elder abuse: Spouse/intimate partner abuse and family abuse among elders. *Journal of Elder Abuse & Neglect, 16*(1), 85–102.

Macy, R. J., Martin, S. L., Kupper, L. L., Casaneuva, C., & Guo, S. (2007). Partner violence among women before, during, and after pregnancy—multiple opportunities for intervention. *Women's Health Issues, 17,* 290–299.

Malamuth, N. M., Linz, D., Heavey, C. L., Barnes, G., & Acker, M. (1995). Using the confluence model of sexual aggression to predict men's conflict with women: A 10-year follow-up study. *Journal of Personality and Social Psychology, 69,* 353–369.

Max, W., Rice, D. P., Finkelstein, E., Bardwell, R. A., & Leadbetter, S. (2004). The economic toll of intimate partner violence against women in the United States. *Violence and Victims, 19*(3), 259–272.

McFarlane, J., Campbell, J. C., & Watson, K. (2002). Intimate partner stalking and femicide: Urgent implications for women's safety. *Behavioral Sciences and the Law, 20,* 51–68.

Mechanic, M. B., Uhlmansiek, M. H., Weaver, T. L., & Resick, P. A. (2002). The impact of severe stalking experienced by acutely battered women: An examination of violence, psychological symptoms and strategic responding. In K. E. Davis, I. H. Frieze, & R. D. Maiuro (Eds.), *Stalking: Perspectives on victimization and perpetration* (pp. 89–111). New York: Springer.

Melton, H. C. (2007). Predicting the occurrence of stalking in relationships characterized by domestic violence. *Journal of Interpersonal Violence, 22*(1), 3–25.

Menjívar, C., & Salcido, O. (2002). Immigrant women and domestic violence: Common experiences in different countries. *Gender & Society, 16*(6), 898–920.

Merwin, E., Snyder, A., & Katz, E. (2006). Differential access to quality rural healthcare: Professional and policy challenges. *Family & Community Health, 29*(3), 186–194.

Midgley, J. (2006). Gendered economies: Transferring private gender roles into the public realm through rural community development. *Journal of Rural Studies, 22,* 217–231.

Miller, J. (2006). A specification of the types of intimate partner violence experienced by women in the general population. *Violence Against Women, 12,* 1105–1131.

Molidor, C., Tolman, R. M., & Koeber, J. (2000). Gender and contextual factors in adolescent dating violence. *The Prevention Researcher, 7,* 1–4.

Moore, T. M., & Stuart, G. L. (2005). A review of the literature on masculinity and partner violence. *Psychology of Men & Masculinity, 6*(1), 46–61.

Morland, L. A., Leskin, G. A., Block, R. C., Campbell, J. C., & Friedman, M. J. (2008). Intimate partner violence and miscarriage: Examination of the role of physical and psychological abuse and posttraumatic stress disorder. *Journal of Interpersonal Violence, 23*(5), 652–669.

Mouton, C. P., Rovi, S., Furniss, K., & Lasser, N. L. (1999). The associations between health and domestic violence in older women: Results of a pilot study. *Journal of Women's Health & Gender-Based Medicine, 8*(9), 1173–1179.

Mueller, K. J., & MacKinney, A. C. (2006). Care across the continuum: Access to health care services in rural America. *Journal of Rural Health, 22*(1), 43–49.

Mulford, C., & Giordano, P. C. (2009). Teen dating violence: A closer look at adolescent romantic relationships. *National Institute of Justice Journal, 261,* 34–40.

Nason-Clark, N. (2000). Making the sacred wife: Women abuse and communities of faith: Presidential address. *Sociology of Religion, 61,* 349–368.

National Center for Injury Prevention and Control. (2003). *Costs of intimate partner violence against women in the United States.* Atlanta, GA: Centers for Disease Control and Prevention.

Norlander, B., & Eckhardt, C. I. (2005). Anger, hostility, and male perpetrators of intimate partner violence: A meta-analytic review. *Clinical Psychology Review, 25,* 119–152.

O'Leary, K. D. (1999). Psychological abuse: A variable deserving critical attention in domestic violence. *Violence and Victims, 14*(1), 3–23.

O'Leary, K. D., Smith-Slep, A. M., Avery-Leaf, S., & Cascardi, M. (2008). Gender differences in dating aggression among multiethnic high school students. *Journal of Adolescent Health, 42,* 473–479.

Olshen, E., McVeigh, K. H., Wunsch-Hitzig, R. A., & Rickert, V. I. (2007). Dating violence, sexual assault, and suicide attempts among urban teenagers. *Archives of Pediatrics and Adolescent Medicine, 161,* 539–545.

Oughton, E. (2007). Rural gender relations issues and case studies. *European Review of Agricultural Economics, 34*(2), 290–293.

Pallitto, C. C., Campbell, J. C., & O'Campo, P. (2005). Is intimate partner violence associated with unintended pregnancy? A review of the literature. *Trauma, Violence, & Abuse, 6*(3), 217–235.

Pan, A., Daley, S., Rivera, L. M., Williams, K., Lingle, D., & Reznik, V. (2006). Understanding the role of culture in domestic violence: The Ahimsa project for safe families. *Journal of Immigrant and Minority Health, 8*(1), 35–43.

Pan, H. S., Neidig, P. H., & O'Leary, K. D. (1994). Predicting mild and severe husband-to-wife physical aggression. *Journal of Consulting and Clinical Psychology, 62,* 975–981.

Parrott, D. J., Drobes, D. J., Saladin, M. E., Coffey, S. F., & Dansky, B. S. (2003). Perpetration of partner violence: Effects of cocaine and alcohol dependence and posttraumatic stress disorder. *Addictive Behavior, 28,* 1587–1602.

Patterson, P. D. (2006). Emergency medical services and the federal government's evolving role: What rural and frontier emergency medical services advocates should know. *Journal of Rural Health, 22*(2), 97–101.

Peacock, P. (1998). Marital rape. In R. K. Bergen (Ed.), *Issues in intimate violence* (pp. 225–235). Thousand Oaks, CA: Sage.

Phillipson, C., & Allan, G. A. (2004). *Networks and social exclusion: Sociological and policy perspectives.* United Kingdom: Ashgate.

Pico-Alfonso, M. A., Garcia-Linares, M. I., Celda-Navarro, N., Herbert, J., & Martinez, M. (2004). Changes in cortisol and dehydroepiandrosterone in women victims of physical and psychological intimate partner violence. *Biological Psychiatry, 56,* 233–240.

Pleck, J. H. (1995). The gender role strain paradigm: An update. In R. F. Levant & W. S. Pollack (Eds.), *A new psychology of men* (pp. 11–32). New York: Basic Books.

Puzone, C. A., Saltzman, L., Kresnow, M., Thompson, M., & Mercy, J. (2000). National trends in intimate partner homicide: United States, 1976–1995. *Violence Against Women, 6*(4), 409–426.

Renzetti, C. M. (1992). *Violent betrayal: Partner abuse in lesbian relationships.* Newbury Park, CA: Sage.

Ridington, J. (1989). *Beating the "odds": Violence and women with disabilities* (Position Paper 2). Vancouver, BC: DisAbled Women's Network of Canada.

Riggs, D. S., Caulfield, M. B., & Street, A. E. (2000). Risk for domestic violence: Factors associated with perpetration and victimization. *Journal of Clinical Psychology, 56,* 1289–1316.

Rose, S. (2003). Community interventions concerning homophobic violence and partner abuse against lesbians. *Journal of Lesbian Studies, 7*(4), 125–139.

Rosen, L. H., Knudson, K. H. Brannen, S. J., Fancher, P., Killgore, T. E., & Barasich, G. G. (2002). Intimate partner violence among U.S. Army soldiers in Alaska: A comparison of reported rates and survey results. *Military Medicine, 167,* 688–691.

Rosenbaum, A., & Leisring, P. A. (2003). Beyond power and control: Towards an understanding of partner abusive men. *Journal of Comparative Family Studies, 34,* 7–22.

Rosenfeld, B. (2004). Violence risk factors in stalking and obsessional harassment: A review and preliminary meta-analysis. *Criminal Justice and Behavior, 31*(1), 9–36.

Rothman, E. F., & Corso, P. S. (2008). Propensity for intimate partner abuse and workplace productivity: Why employers should care. *Violence Against Women, 14*(9), 1054–1064.

Russell, D. E. H. (1990). *Rape in marriage.* Bloomington: Indiana University Press.

Sackett, L. A., & Saunders, D. G. (1999). The impact of different forms of psychological abuse on battered women. *Violence and Victims, 14,* 105–177.

Saltzman. L. E., Fanslow, J. L., McMahon, P. M., & Shelley, G. A. (1999). *Intimate Partner Violence Surveillance: Uniform definitions and recommended data elements, version 1.0.* Atlanta, GA: Centers for Disease Control and Prevention, National Center for Injury Prevention and Control.

Schumacher, J. A, Feldbau-Kohn, S., Smith-Slep, A. M., & Heyman, R. E. (2001). Risk factors for male-to-female partner physical abuse. *Aggression and Violent Behavior, 6,* 281–352.

Schumacher, J. A., Homish, G. G., Leonard, K. E., Quigley, B. M., & Kearns-Bodkin, J. N. (2008).

Longitudinal moderators of the relationship between excessive drinking and intimate partner violence in the early years of marriage. *Journal of Family Psychology, 22*(6), 894–904.

Shepard, M. F., & Campbell, J. A. (1992). The Abusive Behavior Inventory: A measure of psychological and physical abuse. *Journal of Interpersonal Violence, 7,* 291–305.

Shields, N., & Hanneke, C. R. (1988). Multiple sexual victimization: The case of incest and marital rape. In G. T. Hotaling, D. Finkelhor, J. T. Kirkpatrick, & M. A. Straus (Eds.), *Family abuse and its consequences: New directions in research* (pp. 255–269). Thousand Oaks, CA: Sage.

Shields, N., & Hanneke, C. R. (1992). Comparing the psychological impact of battering, marital rape, and stranger rape. *Clinical Sociology Review, 10,* 151–169.

Silverman, J. G., Decker, M. R., Reed, E., & Raj, A. (2006). Intimate partner violence victimization prior to and during pregnancy among women residing in 26 U.S. states: Associations with maternal and neonatal health. *Obstetrics & Gynecology, 195,* 140–148.

Smith, P. H., Tessaro, I., & Earp, J. (1995). Women's experiences with battering: A conceptualization from qualitative research. *Women's Health Issues, 5,* 173–182.

Smith, P. H., Thornton, G. E., DeVellis, R., Earp, J., & Coker, A. L. (2002). A population-based study of the prevalence and distinctiveness of battering, physical assault, and sexual assault in intimate relationships. *Violence Against Women, 8*(10), 1208–1232.

Spitzberg, B. H., & Cupach, W. R. (2007). The state of the art of stalking: Taking stock of the emerging literature. *Aggression and Violent Behavior, 12,* 64–86.

Stith, S. M., Smith, D. B., Penn, C. E., Ward, D. B., & Tritt, D. (2004). Intimate partner physical abuse perpetration and victimization risk factors: A meta-analytic review. *Aggression and Violent Behavior, 10,* 65–98.

Swahn, M. H., Simon, T. R., Arias, I., & Bossarte, R. M. (2008). Measuring sex differences in violence victimization and perpetration within date and same-sex peer relationships. *Journal of Interpersonal Violence, 23*(8), 1120–1138.

Teaster, P. A. (2002). *A response to the abuse of vulnerable adults: The 2000 survey of state adult protective services.* Washington, DC: National Center on Elder Abuse.

Temple, J. R., Weston, R., Rodriguez, B. F., & Marshall, L. L. (2007). Differing effects of partner and nonpartner sexual assault on women's mental health. *Violence Against Women, 13*(3), 285–297.

Testa, M. (2004). The role of substance use in male-to-female physical and sexual violence. *Journal of Interpersonal Violence, 19*(12), 1494–1505.

Tjaden, P., & Thoennes, N. (1998). *Stalking in America: Findings from the National Violence Against Women Survey.* Washington, DC: U.S. Department of Justice.

Tjaden, P., & Thoennes, N. (2000). *Extent, nature, and consequences of intimate partner violence* (NCJ 181867). Washington, DC: U.S. Department of Justice, National Institute of Justice.

Turrell, S. A. (2000). A descriptive analysis of same-sex relationship violence for a diverse sample. *Journal of Family Violence, 15,* 281–293.

U.S. Census Bureau. (2008). *United States foreign-born population.* Retrieved October 21, 2009, from http://www.census.gov/population/www/socdemo/foreign/acst2.html

Walker, L. E. (1979). *The battered woman.* New York: Harper & Row.

Ward, C. A. (1995). *Attitudes toward rape: Feminist and social psychological perspectives.* London: Sage.

Whatley, M. (1993). For better or worse: The case of marital rape. *Violence and Victims, 8,* 29–39.

White, J. W., McMullin, D., Swartout, K., Sechrist, S., & Gollehon, A. (2008). Violence in intimate relationships: A conceptual and empirical examination of sexual and physical aggression. *Children and Youth Services Review, 30,* 338–351.

Wiebe, D. J. (2003). Sex differences in the perpetrator-victim relationship among emergency department patients presenting with nonfatal firearm-related injuries. *Annals of Emergency Medicine, 42,* 405–412.

Wilson, M., & Daly, M. (1993). Spousal homicide risk and estrangement. *Violence and Victims, 8,* 3–15.

Wise, A. J., & Bowman, S. L. (1997). Comparison of beginning counselors' responses to lesbian vs. heterosexual partner abuse. *Violence and Victims, 12*(2), 127–135.

Young, M. E., Nosek, M. A., Howland, C. A., Changpong, G., & Rintala, D. H. (1997, December). Prevalence of abuse of women with disabilities. *Archives of Physical Medicine and Rehabilitation, 78,* S34–S38.

Chapter Authors

Kathleen C. Basile, Ph.D., is a lead behavioral scientist in the Division of Violence Prevention at the National Center for Injury Prevention and Control, Centers for Disease Control and Prevention (CDC). Dr. Basile joined CDC in 2000. She received her Ph.D. in Sociology from Georgia State University in 1998. Her work at CDC focuses on etiological research to inform the prevention of violence. Her main research interests are the prevalence, risk factors, and consequences of sexual violence and intimate partner violence against adults and adolescents. She has published numerous journal articles and book chapters on these topics.

Michele C. Black has a Ph.D. in epidemiology and a M.A. in public health. She joined the Centers for Disease Control and Prevention (CDC) as an epidemic intelligence service officer in 1988 and has worked and published across a range of public health disciplines. She joined CDC's Division of Violence Prevention in 2002 and is the lead scientist for the National Intimate Partner Violence and Sexual Violence Surveillance System. Her current work is focused on surveillance methods, ethics regarding survey research on intimate partner violence, and the differences between women's and men's experiences with intimate partner violence.

Personal Reflection

Barbara Hart

I was battered by my partner, Lawrence Baldwin, for almost two years. I withdrew from the people I loved and who loved me because I was ashamed of remaining with him. I withdrew from women in my "consciousness-raising" group, friends in the civil rights and anti-war movements, men with whom I worked, and Lawrence's family, all of whom intervened in his violence to protect me. They offered safe haven and unqualified support, yet I withdrew. I ceased communication with my family.

My father reached out to me and began monthly visits. He asked three questions: What is wrong? What can I do to help? What will restore you to hope? I did not open up to him for many months. But he encouraged me to think about my return from despair to an active, vibrant life of justice making. (He had started mentoring me in hands-on social justice work when I was 7 years old.) I came to understand that by staying, I was compromising not only my safety and well-being, but I was exposing my allies to his violence, which I realized was unconscionable. I concluded that I could find the fortitude to leave and stay gone if I could go to law school and acquire the knowledge and skill necessary to advocate for economic and social justice for the disenfranchised. My parents offered to pay my debt and to pay one semester of law school tuition. I left.

I moved to Washington, DC to attend law school. A dear friend offered me housing. She was a woman I admired above all others. I did not know that she had been severely physically and psychologically battered until I moved in. I was shocked; for the first time I deeply understood that it was not my fault that I had been battered, and I began forgiving myself for staying with Lawrence *and* for leaving him. I supervised visitation of my friend's preschooler by her father. When he abducted her, my law school friends and I persuaded the prosecutor that the father's conduct was felonious. He was charged with felony abduction, and a warrant was issued that was forwarded to the FBI's "wants and warrants" database. Eighteen months later, based on that warrant, the child was found and returned to her mother. My friend asked the prosecutor to drop the criminal charges on condition that her ex-husband waive all custody and access rights during the child's minority. The deal was struck. I learned that both the criminal and civil legal systems offer remedies to battered women and that the more meaningful remedy in this instance was the civil relief—elimination of access to the child for the next 12 years.

My course was charted. For more than 35 years, it has been my privilege to forge safety and justice with and for abused women and people living in poverty—through law, public policy, movement building, establishing shelter and advocacy programs, and engaging constituents and communities. My life has been rich in the work and in the deep friendships birthed in the struggle.

As for the future, I trust that we will expand the safeguards and economic justice that the law and policy and human services can offer, while opening ourselves to the profound cultural work that will end misogyny, racism, and homophobia and create peace and justice for women.

CHAPTER 7

Pornography

Ana J. Bridges and Robert Jensen

In a pornography-saturated culture in which women are routinely targets of sexualized intrusion and violence, it may seem odd to have to defend the claim that the study of sexually explicit material is relevant to the study of violence against women. In a rape culture that is increasingly pornified, such an inquiry might seem obvious, yet people routinely deny that such research is needed or reject its value in public deliberations on the issue. As a result, we begin this chapter at an elementary level.

Human beings are storytelling animals; stories are a primary way we communicate what it means to be a person in the world. When we tell stories we not only report on our experiences in the world but also contribute to a collective understanding of that world, which will influence the experiences and understandings of others. Stories matter. In any culture, the stories that people tell will reveal things about how they collectively make sense of the world, and that sense of the world will shape how people act. Stories shape attitudes, and attitudes affect behavior (Dines, 2010).

The study of stories is valuable in trying to understand both ideology and material conditions—how people in a culture think and feel, and how those thoughts and feelings play out in actions. In the United States, the dominant storytelling is visual and digital—various kinds of movies that come to us on screens. One popular genre uses graphic, sexually explicit images. Inquiry into this genre, commonly called pornography, should not assume a particular relationship between the storytelling and the ideology or material conditions, but should recognize that a relationship of some sort is plausible and deserves study.

One diversionary strategy is to caricature that research agenda as an attempt to answer the question, "Does pornography cause rape?" Such a research question would be absurd, for the relationship between a form of storytelling and behavior is not simple or straightforward. This essay is rooted in more complex and productive questions: How are gender, power, and sexuality constructed in contemporary mass-marketed pornography? Is there a relationship between those constructions and the levels of sexual intrusion and violence in contemporary culture? What are the effects on people's intimate experiences? How does the normalizing of such pornography affect the culture?

While there may never be definitive answers to those questions, research deepens our understanding and can guide education and public policy. So, why would anyone avoid such inquiry? We believe that this avoidance is rooted in a fear of what such inquiry might reveal about the construction of gender/sex and power/violence in a mass-mediated patriarchal society. This fear makes the study all the more important.

Our investigation begins with basic terminology and law and then charts the growth of the contemporary pornography industry in the last half of the 20th century and the resulting debates. We examine the content of pornography and focus on questions about pornography's effects on its consumers, their partners, and the wider society. We conclude with reflections on the social and political implications of this inquiry.

Terminology and Law

People throughout history have represented sexuality in literature and art, but pornography did not emerge as a mass industry until the 1950s, eventually breaking into mainstream distribution outlets and becoming a major entertainment industry by the end of the 20th century. Although still proscribed by law in a variety of ways, pornography is increasingly accepted as a routine part of contemporary culture, especially youth culture.

Pornography is sometimes used to describe all sexually explicit books, magazines, movies, and Internet sites, with a distinction made between softcore (nudity with limited sexual activity not including penetration) and hardcore (graphic images of actual sexual activity including penetration). Pornography is often distinguished from erotica; erotica is material that depicts sexual behavior with mutuality and respect, and pornography is sexual material based on hierarchy. Laboratory studies often construct three categories of pornography: overtly violent; nonviolent but degrading; and sexually explicit but neither violent nor degrading.

The terms *indecency* and *obscenity* have specific legal meanings. Indecency regulations define a category of words and images that can be regulated in broadcasting (over-the-air radio and television)—language or material that, in context, depicts or describes sexual or excretory organs or activities in terms patently offensive as measured by contemporary community standards for the broadcast medium. The Federal Communications Commission administers indecency regulations.

Criminal obscenity prosecutions in the United States were infrequent and uncontroversial until the post–World War II era. In *Miller v. California* (1973), the Supreme Court established a three-part test for obscenity—material that appeals to the prurient interest (an unhealthy interest in sex); portrays sexual conduct in a patently offensive way; and does not have serious literary, artistic, political, or scientific value—and identified contemporary community standards as the measure. A strict application of state and federal obscenity laws could lead to prosecution of much contemporary pornography, but enforcement occurs only when there is political support. The availability first of mail-order and later of computer pornography has ensured that graphic, sexually explicit material can be obtained easily anywhere. The only exception is child pornography—material that is either made using children or in some fashion appears to use children. The former is illegal without question (*New York v. Ferber*, 1982) and available only underground; the legal status of the latter remains uncertain (*Ashcroft v. Free Speech Coalition*, 2002; *United States v. Williams*, 2008), although as of this writing it appears that computer-generated child pornography (in which no actual children are used in the production) and pseudo-child pornography (in which performers 18 and over are presented as children) are legal unless proven to be obscene.

The Pornography Industry

Pornography in the post–World War II era moved from being a profitable underground business with ties to organized crime to a profitable industry that operates openly and includes small producers as well as corporations with substantial assets. Pornography has its own trade magazines (such as *Adult Video News* and *XBIZ),* annual national convention (Adult Entertainment Expo), and awards shows. Heterosexual pornography makes up the bulk of the commercial market, with a significant amount of gay male pornography and a smaller amount of material produced commercially for lesbians. There is pornography dedicated to any imaginable sexual niche or fetish, and sexually explicit material is distributed using all communication technologies: print, photographs, film, telephones, video, DVD, computers, and mobile devices.

Playboy magazine, which debuted in December, 1953, was the first sex magazine to break into mainstream distribution channels. In the 1960s and 1970s, pornographic films moved into public theaters. In the 1980s, video swamped other forms, with the number of new pornographic video/DVD titles released each year increasing from 1,500 in 1986 to 13,000 in 2007. Pornography for the home VCR sparked "probably the most revolutionary change in our business," according to Philip D. Harvey, founder and president of Adam & Eve ("Adult Education," 2006). Computers dramatically changed the landscape, fueled by the so-called "triple-A engine" of accessibility, affordability, and anonymity (Cooper, Putnam, Planchon, & Boies, 1999). Anecdotal evidence suggests the ease of clicking among sites can increase addictive-like behavior, which pornographers seek to exploit to increase profits (Morrison, 2004). In the 2000s, mobile devices—cell phones, iPods, and other digital devices—have been a growth market for pornographers (Caplan, 2008).

The pornography industry has not only used various technologies but has also been central to their development. For example, pornography's profitability drove early innovation in Internet technology, as the pornographers pioneered streaming audio and video, flash and chat, the click-through ad banner, the pop-up window, high-speed Internet connections, security improvements, and a la carte pay services (Coopersmith, 2006).

While there are no reliable statistics on the industry's revenues, annual sales in the United States are commonly estimated at $10 billion or higher (Lane, 2000, p. xiv), a figure that has been challenged (Akman, 2001). For comparative purposes, the Hollywood box office—the amount of money Americans spent to go out to the movies—was $9.79 billion in 2008 (Motion Picture Association of America, 2008). Because there is no reliable way to chart the amount of money generated by pornographic Web sites, and other segments of the industry are almost as difficult to track, any estimates of the industry's revenues are rough and may well be underestimates.

One of the most important things to remember about the pornography industry is that it is an industry; the DVDs and Internet sites are not created by artists struggling to understand the mysteries of sexuality. While easy, low-cost digital technology has led to an increase in amateur pornography posted to the Internet, the majority of pornography is produced for profit, including profits for mainstream media corporations. Through ownership of cable distribution companies and Internet services, the large companies that distribute mainstream media also often distribute pornography. Until Rupert Murdoch's News Corp. sold its stake in 2006 to Liberty Media (another mainstream conglomerate), News Corp. was a major owner of DirecTV, which sells more pornographic films than Larry Flynt. Nearly $200 million a year is spent by the 8.7 million subscribers to DirecTV (Egan, 2000). Among News Corp.'s other holdings are Fox networks, Twentieth Century Fox, *New York Post, TV Guide,* and HarperCollins, which published the best-selling book of the pornography industry's most famous performer, Jenna Jameson (Jameson & Strauss, 2004).

Just as other media enterprises' business models have been disrupted by the Internet, commercial pornographers face challenges. Younger consumers report rarely paying for sexually explicit images online, either because they are using amateur pornography or know how to access commercial pornography without paying. While pornography remains a good business for most producers, profitability is not ensured. Playboy Enterprises—which includes online, television, and mobile products—has been considering reorganization or a possible sale after poor financial performance.

Although there is little systematic research on pornography performers, anecdotal evidence suggests it is a harsh business for women. The industry promotes high-profile performers such as Jenna Jameson and Tera Patrick as examples of successful women, but most female performers do not have influence or accumulate wealth. Producers and directors interviewed agree that the industry "chews up and spits out" women at an increasingly rapid pace. Former pornography performer Sharon Mitchell, now executive director of the Adult Industry Medical Healthcare Foundation, reports that the industry recruits naïve young women and that "the average lifespan of a porn star now is anywhere from six months to three years, tops, and then they've got no money" (Calvert & Richards, 2006, p. 287). Mitchell's organization, which is supported by the pornography industry, provides HIV/STD testing and other health services to performers. In a radio interview, she spoke of mixed feelings about her work:

> We've put a lot of people into rehab, we help a lot of people leave porn and get an education, we have a scholarship program, and with all this, some days, you know, when I see a young girl walk in and I just know that she's just going to get run over by all these producers and agents and types of things that she probably hasn't experienced or even thought of experiencing, I think, "Am I just fattening them up for the kill? What am I doing?" (Simon, 2007)

In abstracted debates about pornography, amid talk about "fantasies" and "sexual expression," it can be easy to forget that what a viewer watches on the screen is not a simulation. A scene featuring the penetration of a woman by three men at the same time is not generated by a computer, nor is it a carefully constructed stunt. It is a record of a sexual act. The scene may start as one man's fantasy and become another's, and it may express someone's idea about what is sexually arousing, but it is made real using the body of a real woman. As Andrea Dworkin (1995) put it, "Pornography happens to women."

Debates on Pornography

Until the 1970s, debates pitted liberal advocates of sexual freedom against conservative proponents of traditional sexual morality. That changed with the feminist critique, which emerged out of the struggle against sexual violence during the second wave of the women's movement in the 1960s and highlighted ways in which pornography eroticizes domination and subordination. Feminist critics argued for a focus not on subjective sexual mores but on the harm to women used in pornography and against whom pornography is used. Other feminists rejected that analysis, leading to what became known as the "porn wars" or the "sex wars" in the early 1980s. From this have emerged three major positions within feminism: (1) antipornography feminists, typically identified as "radical feminists"; (2) anticensorship feminists who are critical of misogynistic pornography but reject the legal approach radical feminists proposed; and (3) a pro-pornography group that valorizes pornography as a discourse that subverts traditional gender norms and has liberatory potential for women's sexuality.

The feminist critique explored the cultural support for men's violence by looking at pornography and popular culture, highlighting misogynistic images in advertising and entertainment, and critiquing the underlying ideology that legitimized or celebrated violence against women. This led to activist groups, such as Women Against Pornography in New York, which used slideshows and tours of pornography districts to educate and protest. There was a flurry of this kind of activism in the late 1970s and early 1980s, but radical feminists didn't face organized opposition from other feminists until a legal strategy was developed by writer/activist Andrea Dworkin and lawyer/law professor Catharine MacKinnon (MacKinnon & Dworkin, 1997). Rejecting criminal obscenity law, they drafted a civil rights ordinance to allow women to pursue damages against producers and consumers. Passed in 1983 by the Minneapolis City Council but vetoed by the mayor, it was then passed and signed into law in Indianapolis in 1984 but rejected on constitutional grounds in the federal courts (*American Booksellers Association v. Hudnut,* 1985). Efforts to pass the law in other jurisdictions continued into the 1990s.

The ordinance proposed a shift away from a moral framework (what kind of sex is consistent with the dominant sexual mores) and toward a political one (resistance to patriarchal power). Rooted in the radical feminist argument that women are oppressed in part through sexual subordination, Dworkin and MacKinnon identified pornography as a means of sexualizing inequality and a practice of sex discrimination. The ordinance created five causes of action: coercion into making pornography; the forcing of pornography on unwilling people; assault resulting from pornography; defamation through pornography; and trafficking in pornography. The trafficking clause, allowing any woman to bring a case against any pornographer, was the hardest to square with contemporary First Amendment interpretation.

Anticensorship feminists (Burstyn, 1985) were skeptical about state intervention in sexual matters, even under the umbrella of civil law that empowered women, and rejected the ordinance as a threat to women's freedom and autonomy (Strossen, 1995). The Feminist Anti-Censorship Task Force (FACT) produced a legal brief that became a focus of debate. Some of the women in FACT also articulated a pro-pornography position that would become more prominent in the 1990s and 2000s, as the liberal rejection of the radical critique increasingly leaned toward the argument that pornography can be a subversive and liberatory text. Many of these concepts have their origins in postmodern theories developed by literary, art, and film scholars, such as Linda Williams (1989).

For radical feminists, the production of pornography in patriarchy exploits women. While not denying the ability of women in the industry to make choices, the feminist anti-pornography movement focuses on the economic, social, and cultural factors that influence women's choices to perform, such as histories of sexual abuse in childhood, the violence of pimps, and the control of boyfriends and other men. Pro-pornography feminists insist that women are making rational choices given the reality of employment opportunities and that some women prosper in the industry.

Content of Pornography

"Is pornography pornographic?" Is sexually explicit material "pornographic" in the critical feminist sense, a site of the social subordination of women? Andrea Dworkin (1988) identified what we call the elements of the pornographic:

1. *Objectification:* when "a human being, through social means, is made less than human, turned into a thing or commodity, bought and sold."

2. *Hierarchy:* "a group on top (men) and a group on the bottom (women)."

3. *Submission:* when acts of obedience and compliance become necessary for survival, members of oppressed groups learn to anticipate the orders and desires of those who have power over them, and their compliance is then used by the dominant group to justify its dominance.

4. *Violence:* "systematic, endemic enough to be unremarkable and normative, usually taken as an implicit right of the one committing the violence." (pp. 266–267)

The two main categories in today's pornographic movie industry (whether distributed on DVD, pay-per-view outlets, or the Internet) are "features" and "wall-to-wall/gonzo." Feature movies most resemble a Hollywood movie, with plot and characters, whether delivered as a complete film on DVD or as increasingly popular separate scenes on a Web site (Richtel, 2009). Although most consumers of any style of pornography are men, the industry markets features as "couples movies" that appeal to women. Wall-to-wall movies are all-sex productions with no pretense of plot or dialogue. Many of these movies are shot gonzo style, in which performers acknowledge the camera and often speak directly to the audience. In addition, there are specialty titles—movies that feature sadomasochism and bondage, fetish material, transsexuals—that fill niche markets.

The majority of hardcore movies include oral, vaginal, and anal sex, almost always ending with ejaculation on the woman. In the wall-to-wall/gonzo movies, double penetration (anal and vaginal penetration by two men at the same time), other multiple penetrations, and aggressive oral penetration of women are increasingly common, as are hair pulling, slapping, and rough treatment. In a study of pornographic heterosexual videotapes, Brosius, Weaver, and Staab (1993) found that the tapes typically presented a world in which women were younger, more sexually active, and more expressive than

men; women were frequently depicted in subordinate positions (e.g., kneeling down in front of a partner); and sexual contact was frequent among strangers while sex between committed partners was rare. A more recent content analysis of 50 best-selling adult videos revealed a similar ideology of inequality and violence. Nearly half of the 304 scenes analyzed contained verbal aggression (e.g., name calling or verbal threats), while more than 88% showed physical aggression (including hair pulling, open-hand slapping or spanking, choking, and whipping). Seventy percent of aggressive acts were perpetrated by men and 87% of acts were committed against women. Fewer than 5% of the aggressive acts provoked a negative response from the target, such as requests to stop. This pornographic "reality" was further highlighted by the relative infrequency of more positive behaviors (verbal compliments, embracing, kissing, or laughter), portrayed in fewer than 10% of the scenes (Wosnitzer & Bridges, 2007).

Combining these kinds of quantitative studies with qualitative analyses using more interpretive methods, the main themes of pornographic films can be summarized as (1) all women always want sex from men, (2) women like all the sexual acts that men perform or demand, and (3) any woman who does not at first realize this can be easily persuaded with a little force (Dworkin, 1979; Jensen, 2007). Such force is rarely necessary, however, for most of the women in pornography are the "nymphomaniacs" of men's fantasies. While both men and women are portrayed as always sexual, men typically are the sexual subjects, controlling the action and dictating the terms of the sex. Women are the sexual objects, whose job it is to fulfill male desire.

As pornography depicting conventional sexual acts has become commonplace, gonzo producers have pushed the limits of social norms and women's bodies with the routine use of DPs (double penetrations: vaginal and anal penetration by two men at the same time), double vag (two men penetrating a woman vaginally), double anal (two men penetrating a woman anally), gagging (forcing the penis down a woman's throat so far that she gags), and ATM (ass to mouth, in which a man removes his penis from a woman's anus and places it directly into her mouth or the mouth of another woman).

Nearly every scene ends with the "cum shot" or "money shot"—male ejaculation into a woman's mouth or on her face or body. As one pornography director put it, "it's like a dog marking its territory" (Sun & Picker, 2008). Another veteran pornographic director and actor put it more bluntly:

> I'd like to really show what I believe the men want to see: violence against women. . . . [but] the most violent we can get is the cum shot in the face. Men get off behind that because they get even with the women they can't have. (Stoller & Levine, 1993, p. 22)

Effects of Pornography

The most common research question has been whether pornography, particularly material that explicitly eroticizes violence and domination, contributes to elevated rates of sexual violence against women, children, and other vulnerable people. Pornography's supporters and some researchers argue there is no conclusive evidence. Other researchers contend the evidence points to some effects with some groups of men.

The experiences of men and women—both those who use pornography and those against whom pornography is used—provide specific examples of how pornography can (1) be an important factor in shaping a male-dominant view of sexuality; (2) contribute to a user's difficulty in separating sexual fantasy and reality; (3) be used to initiate victims and break down resistance to sexual activity;

and (4) provide a training manual for abuse (Jensen, 2007). In her review of the research, Diana Russell (1998) argues that pornography is a causal factor in the way that it can (1) predispose some males to desire rape or intensify this desire; (2) undermine some males' internal inhibitions against acting out rape desires; (3) undermine some males' social inhibitions against acting out rape desires; and (4) undermine some potential victims' abilities to avoid or resist rape (p. 121).

No one argues that pornography is the sole causal factor in rape—obviously, all men who use pornography do not rape, and some men who rape do not use pornography. But it is possible to inquire into the ways in which pornography might be *implicated* in sexual violence. In other words, pornography alone doesn't "make men do it," but pornography is a significant part of a world in which sexualized aggression, aggression through sex, and sexual intrusions along a continuum are common in women's lives.

In the past decade, researchers have tended to shift the focus from pornography and sexual violence to other adverse outcomes, including effects on important relationships in women's lives. After describing theoretical models that suggest mechanisms by which pornography exerts its effects, we provide an overview of findings from research studies that highlight how researchers are attempting to understand the spectrum of pornography's effects on interpersonal relationships.

Theoretical Models for Understanding Pornography's Effects

What are the mechanisms by which pornography affects users' attitudes and behaviors? We describe four theoretical models from the psychological and sociological literature that attempt to answer this question.

Imitation Model

A simple model for media effects is the *imitation model* (Silbert & Pines, 1984), which theorizes that consumers imitate what they see. While there is some indirect support for such a theory, the imitation model cannot account for the complexities of the relationship between media and individual behavior. Critics of antipornography efforts have focused their attacks on this model, stating that consumers are aware of differences between reality and what is supposedly pornographic fantasy (Loftus, 2002).

Social Learning Model

Slightly more complex is the *social learning model,* based on Albert Bandura's (1967) research on how behaviors that are rewarded are more likely to be imitated. If pornography shows a man overpowering a woman and she derives pleasure from the attack (a script for what is called the "rape myth"; Bauserman, 1996), the viewer learns that such behavior leads to rewards (both self and partner sexual gratification) and is more likely to imitate it. Feminists argue that the violent and degrading treatment of women combined with the powerful reinforcer of sexual arousal makes pornography potentially harmful. Studies have demonstrated that the combination of sexual arousal and violence results in more misogynist attitudes and behaviors than depictions of violence against women or sexually explicit media alone (Malamuth, 1984).

Sexual Script Model

Scripts—memory structures that provide rules for behaving—evolve over time and with repeated exposure (Lakshmi-Ratan & Iyer, 1988). Pornography provides information about gender roles and sexuality that rarely includes affection, relationships, expressions of love, or foreplay and afterplay (Mosher & MacIan, 1994; Wosnitzer & Bridges, 2007), and it has become one of the primary sex educators for adolescents (Rideout, 2001). Scripts in pornography emphasize conventional beauty standards, insatiable sexual appetites, excitement of sexual novelty, and sex outside a primary romantic relationship (Brosius et al., 1993).

These scripts for sexual intimacy nearly always fall short of real life because maintaining intimate relationships is not always easy. Learning about gender roles through consistently unrealistic portrayals of sexuality, including pornography and soap operas or romantic novels, has been found to lead to reduced sexual and relational satisfaction (Shapiro & Kroeger, 1991). The importance of the sexual scripts usually seen in pornography may explain why women are more likely than men to respond negatively to pornography. Media that portray women as subordinates, sexually ready and intimate with virtual strangers, and objects of aggression—coupled with a lack of emphasis on intimate relationships and more positive behaviors—likely spark negative reactions from most female consumers. Mosher and MacIan's (1994) study, in which men and women watched either "conventional" or "femme" videos, suggests that conventional pornography is a turn-off to most women because it does not fit their sexual scripts.

Other Cognitive Models

Cognitive models focus on internal thoughts and beliefs or interpretations of stimuli that then drive behavior. They may explain why the same event can have different meanings for different people, why one woman may be indifferent or even encouraging of her partner's pornography use while another is devastated (Bridges, Bergner,

& Hesson-McInnis, 2003). The first of these models, *permission-giving beliefs,* refers to any thoughts the user may have that serve to rationalize behavior, such as "everyone is doing it." For pornography users in particular, numerous permission-giving thoughts (such as "women in pornography clearly enjoy it") justify behavior (Layden, 2008; Loftus, 2002). Many women report thinking that their partner's behavior is preferable to his having a real-life affair, that all men view pornography, and that it is a relief at times that her partner does not turn to her to fulfill his frequent sexual demands (Bridges et al., 2003). The *perceptions of social norms* model describes how heavy users of pornography are unable to recognize how uncommon their behavior may be; heavy use results in an overestimation of how frequently certain sexual activities are practiced. For example, adolescent boys with higher pornography consumption are more likely to engage in anal sex and group sex and to report "hook-ups" (Häggström-Nordin, Hanson, & Tydén, 2005).

Cognitive models place the problem and solution firmly inside the individual. Although changing social norms may involve community-wide education campaigns, the proposed mechanism of change remains at the level of the individual's thoughts (Perkins, 2002; Schultz, Nolan, Cialdini, Goldstein, & Griskevicius, 2007).

Cognitive and behavioral models also assume rational choices by consumers: The viewer chooses to behave in a way that has been modeled and reinforced by media, or permission-giving thoughts serve to neutralize other thoughts that may turn him away from pornography (e.g., "I could get fired for this"). Behavioral economists challenge this model, noting that "cold" rational choices are different from those made while in a "hot" or aroused state (Ariely & Loewenstein, 2006). That study asked college men to answer a series of questions about sexual interests and behaviors while in a "cold" state of mind (simply reading the items) or in a "hot" state of mind (while masturbating to pornographic pictures).

Questions included items related to risky sexual behavior, such as condom use; sexual arousal, such as finding elderly women, young girls, or shoes sexually arousing; sexual behavior, such as interest in slapping someone during sex, bondage, or anal sex or bestiality; and sexual violence, such as willingness to coerce someone in order to have sex. During the aroused state, all but two questions were significantly more likely to be endorsed.

Cultural Climate Model

The cultural climate theory considers larger contextual and societal factors, positing that pornography contributes to an environment in which violence against women becomes acceptable (Krafka, Linz, Donnerstein, & Penrod, 1997). These effects are seen in men's perceptions of women and in women's perceptions of themselves. Exposure to pornography might be expected to result in reduced self-esteem and body image satisfaction, increased sense of vulnerability to violence, and an increased sense of defenselessness in women. Similarly, this climate rewards displays of hypermasculinity and trivializes or excuses violence against women. Partial support for this has been found (Krafka et al., 1997), though obviously pornography is not the only medium that portrays women as victims, vulnerable, sexually available, and degraded; pornographic norms for gender relationships and sexuality infuse other forms of media, such as music videos, reality television shows, and even children's toys. It is difficult to determine how pornography's specific or unique effects can be differentiated from a general climate of gender inequality in a pornified culture (American Psychological Association, 2007; Paul, 2005). Studies show that exposure to sexualized imagery and pornography relate to earlier initiation of sexual activity, increased sexual risk-taking behavior, and tolerant attitudes toward sexual promiscuity (Wingood, DiClemente, Harrington, Davies, Hook, & Oh, 2001).

Third-Person Effects

People typically perceive others as being susceptible to media influences but believe that they are immune. Although a majority of people believe that others' behavior is influenced by pornography, only a small minority report their own behavior as being similarly influenced (Häggström-Nordin et al., 2005). Public education must include information about both pornography's effects and this perceptual bias.

The cultural climate hypothesis suggests the need for a widespread cultural change in how sexuality is constructed. A ban on certain materials would be insufficient because pornography norms are infused throughout the culture. Along with specific policy proposals, we need new models of healthy sex and gender that do not view sex appeal as defined by physical appearance or value people only for certain sexual behavior, and in which sexuality is expressed between consenting beings with real freedom to choose.

Pornography's Effects on Interpersonal Relationships

Pornography tells a particular story about sexual behavior. Although sex is not required for intimacy (or emotional closeness), people often use sex to increase or express intimacy (Rasmussen & Kilborne, 2007). Therefore, does pornography use impact intimate relationships and, if so, how?

Pornography Increases Negative Attitudes Toward Women

Given the relationship between attitudes and behaviors, changes in attitudes connected to pornography use have implications for changes in behavior toward women. Garcia (1986) found that use of erotic material (nonviolent, nondegrading, sexually explicit materials) did not have

any impact on male college students' attitudes toward women but that use of pornographic materials (sexually explicit materials that included elements of coercion or violence) was positively correlated with beliefs that women should occupy more gender-defined, traditional roles.

Material that perpetuates the myth that women secretly desire to be forced into sex and enjoy such encounters could be expected to lead to decreased empathy for rape victims and milder punishments for alleged perpetrators. Linz, Donnerstein, and Penrod (1988) exposed college men to graphically violent sexual films, degrading but nonviolent pornographic films, or degrading but nonviolent and nonsexual films and found that participants in the violent, sexual film group showed significantly less sympathy for the rape victims. Participants in the nonsexual but degrading film group generally did not differ significantly from control subjects in ratings of sympathy for the rape victim. Krafka et al. (1997) had college women view sexually explicit but nonviolent films, sexually explicit and violent films, mildly explicit but graphically violent films, or no film (control group). Women in the graphically violent condition showed reduced empathy for a rape victim and a decreased sense of personal vulnerability to crimes.

In a review of studies examining attitudes toward rape, Linz (1989) found that of the seven studies reviewed with a brief (<1 hour) exposure to pornography, six found significant negative effects of violent pornography exposure (reduced sympathy for victims, increased sense of the woman's responsibility for the rape, and decreased punishments for the perpetrator). Of the seven longer exposure studies (>1 hour), five showed negative effects such as more lenient sentences for the rapist, less empathy for the victim, less support for women's equality, and greater endorsement of their own likelihood of raping were they assured they would not be caught. The two studies showing no effects showed only nonviolent erotica compared to a control group.

Pornography Leads to Blunted Affect

Anxiety-provoking stimuli lose their ability to evoke strong affective reactions with repeated exposure (Marks & Dar, 2000). Researchers have argued that similar processes can occur with violent and degrading pornography (Russell, 1998), though such affective blunting in response to degradation and violence against women is dangerous, not beneficial. A study of college men demonstrated that repeated exposure to violent, sexually suggestive material leads to declines in reported negative emotions (such as reported anxiety and depression) associated with viewing such disturbing material (Linz et al., 1988). Krafka et al. (1997) found that emotional blunting occurred in women who had watched sexually explicit violent films and mildly explicit "slasher" films, leading to significant declines in measures of hostility, anxiety, and depression.

Pornography Increases Dominating Behaviors

Mulac, Jansma, and Linz (2002) attempted to measure behavior, rather than attitudes, toward women to determine whether exposure to pornography resulted in more dominating, degrading, and sexualizing behaviors. Male participants were randomly assigned to one of three films (erotica, nonsexual news coverage of war, or pornography) and then paired with a female participant in a problem-solving task. Men who endorsed more masculine traits and who also viewed the sexually explicit films (both erotica and pornography) showed more dominant behaviors, touched their female partners for longer periods of time, and ignored their partner's contributions more often than males who viewed the news clips. Men in the pornography condition interrupted their partners more and showed more anxious behaviors than those in the other groups. Women whose partners had

viewed sexually explicit materials showed similar levels of anxiety, physical proximity, partner touch, and gazing at their partners, suggesting that women are affected by a partner's use of sexually explicit material even when they are unaware of that use.

Pornography's Effects on Romantic Relationships

Sexually explicit materials are sometimes incorporated into romantic relationships by couples who view such materials together and report it enhances their sex lives (Bridges et al., 2003). Sexually explicit materials may be acceptable alternatives when a partner is gone or too tired for sexual relations and the use is usually perceived as benign by both partners (Clark & Wiederman, 2000; Moll & Bridges, 2009). Sexually explicit materials have been used successfully by some marital and sex therapists (Robinson, Manthei, Scheltema, Rich, & Koznar, 1999), although we should question whether apparent short-term "success" through introducing external stimuli to deal with sexual issues in a relationship impedes real progress in deepening intimacy.

However, more often than not pornographic materials are used outside the dyad, in private, and often without the knowledge of the romantic partner (Cooper, Scherer, Boies, & Gordon, 1999). The combination of secrecy, extra-dyadic sexual activity, and perceptions of the alternative "reality" portrayed in pornography lead many women to find such use by their partners to be disturbing (Bridges et al., 2003).

Pornography Use Can Be Addictive

Researchers have described pornography addiction and identified several risk factors for compulsive use (Carnes, 1992; Cooper, Delmonico, & Burg, 2000; Levert, 2007; Maltz & Maltz, 2008). Researchers have found that depression and stress were risk factors for compulsive pornography use that occurred despite negative consequences to the person's occupational or relationship functioning (Coombes, 2002; Cooper, Putnam, et al., 1999; Kafka, 2000; Schneider, 2000).

Partners of Pornography Users Are Affected

One study showed that a partner's pornography use nearly doubled the odds that a battered woman reported being sexually assaulted (Shope, 2004). Partners of identified "sexual addicts" reported feelings of hurt, betrayal, lowered self-esteem, mistrust, anger, feelings of being unattractive and objectified, feeling their partners had less interest in sexual contact, pressure from the partner to enact things from the online fantasy, and a feeling that they could not measure up to the women online (Schneider, 2000).

Senn (1993) found that women who had had frequent, repeated exposure to pornography and found it difficult to avoid in their daily lives were the most negative about such materials and tended to identify with the women in pornography (29% of the sample). Women who generally held neutral to mildly positive views on pornography (7% of the sample) were conflicted when considering its impact on their personal romantic relationships, feeling that it created unrealistic standards of attractiveness and sexual prowess and had lowered their self-esteem. They viewed themselves as very distinct from the women in the pornography.

Crucial to evaluating all this research is a recognition that it is affected by the distribution and shape of power in a society at a given time. The more recent studies cited have been conducted in a society in which pornography is normalized. How might women's responses today, in a porn-saturated world, differ from women's responses at the height of the feminist antipornography movement, when there was more social support for a critical analysis? When behaviors such as men's pornography use are seen as simply "the way things are," do women adjust their expectations to adapt?

Cross-Cultural Research

Studies of pornography's effects have found relationships between pornography use and many variables to be similar across cultures. Positive associations between pornography consumption, permissive attitudes toward sexuality, and increased sexual risk taking have been replicated in Asia and Europe. A study of adolescents in Taiwan found a significant association between pornography use and attitudes and behaviors, such as greater permissiveness regarding extramarital sexual encounters and greater likelihood of having engaged in sex (Lo & Wei, 2005). A study of Chinese young men found a strong positive association between Internet pornography use and sexually permissive attitudes (Lam & Chan, 2007). In a study of unmarried women in rural China, many attributed their earlier engagement in sexual behavior and engaging in unprotected or risky sex to having viewed pornographic materials, particularly with boyfriends (Wang & Davidson, 2006). Swedish teens who had watched pornographic films were significantly more likely to have engaged in oral and anal sex than teens who had not (Johansson & Hammarén, 2007).

Cross-cultural research has pointed to the relationship between pornography consumption, increased sexual aggression, and decreased sexual and body satisfaction. A study of Italian high school students found strong associations between pornography use and having sexually harassed or raped a peer (Bonino, Ciairano, Rabaglietti, & Cattelino, 2006). Canadian male college students who used pornography gave more negative evaluations of their genitals and sexual abilities (Morrison, Ellis, Morrison, Bearden, & Harriman, 2006). A Croatian study found that men who viewed paraphilic materials (sadomasochism, bondage, bestiality, and violence or coercive sexual acts) reported decreased intimacy with sexual partners and decreased sexual satisfaction compared to men who viewed nonparaphilic materials (Štulhofer, Buŝko, & Landripet, 2008).

Studies in Denmark found that men viewed pornographic materials more often and at an earlier age and preferred more hardcore materials than did women (Hald, 2006). Danish participants perceived their pornography use to have neutral or positive, rather than negative, effects across a variety of domains (Hald & Malamuth, 2008). Swedish junior and high school girls were more likely to consider pornographic materials degrading and to hold negative attitudes toward such materials than were their male counterparts (Johansson & Hammarén, 2007).

Conclusion

The radical feminist critique of pornography has been marginalized in the dominant culture's discussion. The movement's civil rights ordinance has been defeated in legislative and judicial arenas. In public discourse, the only antipornography position that gets serious attention in the mainstream media is antifeminist, usually grounded in conservative religious objections that include not only objections to pornography but attacks on lesbian/gay rights and rejection of sex outside heterosexual marriage. But no determination of the success of a political project that is barely three decades old is final. In our experience, while the feminist critique does not resonate with everyone, a significant percentage of women who learn about it find it helpful in understanding pornography use by men in their lives and also the larger sexual system. Increasingly, men who are conflicted about their own pornography use are open to the critique. While the pornography industry has been successful, success is not necessarily permanent or stable.

On the social front, as pornographers have expanded the sexual script to increasingly cruel and degrading sexual acts, the obvious question is, "What's next?" What kind of sexual activity might pornographers explore as they exhaust the current sexual scripts? Directors and producers concede that they do not know (Jensen, 2007). Will the industry push toward evermore brutal depictions? Is the future of American porn more explicit violence? Will the industry at some point cross a line that the general public will reject, leading to political support for more effective regulation?

On the economic front, the digital revolution has undermined traditional business models for music, mainstream movies, and television, and pornography is no different. Porn producers are concerned about routine copyright violations and the ready availability of short teasers that pornography producers post to advertise their films. Ironically, the pornography industry's success at normalizing its products has contributed to the increase in homemade pornography posted on the Internet for free.

Finally, these developments and questions should be considered as part of larger questions about the commodified and mass-mediated nature of modern life in the First World. Apart from the specific issues raised by sexually explicit media, should we be concerned that more aspects of our life are turned into market transactions, that more of our understanding of the world is mediated? Do these trends erode some aspects of human interaction that are necessary for a just and sustainable human society? These questions may defy definitive answers but are crucial to investigate.

References

Adult education. (2006, August). *Adult Video News, 58.*

Akman, D. (2001, May 25). How big is porn? *Forbes.com.* Retrieved July 23, 2009, from http://www.forbes.com/2001/05/25/0524porn.html

American Booksellers Association v. Hudnut, 771 F.2d 323 (7th Cir. 1985).

American Psychological Association. (2007). *Report of the APA Task Force on the Sexualization of Girls.* Washington, DC: Author. Retrieved July 23, 2009, from www.apa.org/pi/wpo/sexualization.html

Ariely, D., & Loewenstein, G. (2006). The heat of the moment: The effect of sexual arousal on sexual decision making. *Journal of Behavioral Decision Making, 19,* 87–98.

Ashcroft v. Free Speech Coalition, 535 U.S. 234 (2002).

Bandura, A. (1967). Behavioral psychotherapy. *Scientific American, 216,* 78–86.

Bauserman, R. (1996). Sexual aggression and pornography: A review of correlational research. *Basic and Applied Social Psychology, 18,* 405–427.

Bonino, S., Ciairano, S., Rabaglietti, E., & Cattelino, E. (2006). Use of pornography and self-reported engagement in sexual violence among adolescents. *European Journal of Developmental Psychology, 3,* 265–288.

Bridges, A. J., Bergner, R. M., & Hesson-McInnis, M. (2003). Romantic partner's use of pornography: Its significance for women. *Journal of Sex and Marital Therapy, 29,* 1–14.

Brosius, H. B., Weaver, J. B., III, & Staab, J. F. (1993). Exploring the social and sexual "reality" of contemporary pornography. *Journal of Sex Research, 30,* 161–170.

Burstyn, V. (Ed.). (1985). *Women against censorship.* Vancouver, BC: Douglas & McIntyre.

Calvert, C., & Richards, R. D. (2006). Porn in their words: Female leaders in the adult entertainment industry address free speech, censorship, feminism, culture and the mainstreaming of adult content. *Vanderbilt Journal of Entertainment and Technology Law, 9,* 255–299.

Caplan, J. (2008, June 18). The iPhone's next frontier: Porn. *Time.* Retrieved July 23, 2009, from http://www.time.com/time/business/article/0,8599,1815933,00.html

Carnes, P. (1992). *Out of the shadows: Understanding sexual addiction.* Center City, MN: Hazelden.

Clark, C. A., & Wiederman, M. W. (2000). Gender and reactions to a hypothetical relationship partner's masturbation and use of sexually explicit media. *Journal of Sex Research, 37,* 133–141.

Coombes, A. (2002). Computer infidelity: Online chat, porn increasing factors in divorce. *CBS Marketwatch.* Retrieved July 23, 2009, from http://www.marketwatch.com/story/online-chat-porn-contributing-to-divorce-lawyers-say

Cooper, A., Delmonico, D. L., & Burg, R. (2000). Cybersex users, abusers, and compulsives: New findings and implications. *Sexual Addiction & Compulsivity, 7,* 4–29.

Cooper, A., Putnam, D. E., Planchon, L. A., & Boies, S. C. (1999). Online sexual compulsivity: Getting tangled in the net. *Sexual Addiction and Compulsivity, 6,* 79–104.

Cooper, A., Scherer, C. R., Boies, S. C., & Gordon, B. L. (1999). Sexuality on the internet: From sexual exploration to pathological expression. *Professional Psychology: Research and Practice, 30,* 154–164.

Coopersmith, J. (2006). Does your mother know what you really do? The changing nature and image of computer-based pornography. *History and Technology, 22,* 1–25.

Dines, G. (2010). *Pornland: How porn hijacked our sexuality.* Boston: Beacon.

Dworkin, A. (1979). *Pornography: Men possessing women.* New York: Perigee. (Reprint edition, 1989, Dutton)

Dworkin, A. (1988). *Letters from a war zone.* London: Secker & Warburg. (Reprint edition, 1989, Dutton)

Dworkin, A. (1995). Pornography happens to women. In L. Lederer & R. Delgado (Eds.), *The price we pay: The case against racist speech, hate propaganda, and pornography* (pp. 181–190). New York: Hill and Wang.

Egan, T. (2000, October 23). Wall Street meets pornography. *New York Times,* p. 1.

Garcia, L. T. (1986). Exposure to pornography and attitudes about women and rape: A correlational study. *Journal of Sex Research, 22,* 378–385.

Häggström-Nordin, E., Hanson, U., & Tydén, T. (2005). Associations between pornography consumption and sexual practices among adolescents in Sweden. *International Journal of STD and AIDS, 16,* 102–107.

Hald, G. M. (2006). Gender differences in pornography consumption among young heterosexual Danish adults. *Archives of Sexual Behavior, 35,* 577–585.

Hald, G. M., & Malamuth, N. M. (2008). Self-perceived effects of pornography consumption. *Archives of Sexual Behavior, 37,* 614–625.

Jameson, J., & Strauss, N. (2004). *How to make love like a porn star: A cautionary tale.* New York: Regan Books.

Jensen, R. (2007). *Getting off: Pornography and the end of masculinity.* Cambridge, MA: South End Press.

Johansson, T., & Hammarén, N. (2007). Hegemonic masculinity and pornography: Young people's attitudes toward and relations to pornography. *Journal of Men's Studies, 15,* 57–70.

Kafka, M. P. (2000). The paraphilia-related disorders: Nonparaphilic hypersexuality and sexual compulsivity/addiction. In S. R. Leiblum & R. C. Rosen (Eds.), *Principles and practice of sex therapy* (3rd ed., pp. 471–503). New York: Guilford Press.

Krafka, C., Linz, D., Donnerstein, E., & Penrod, S. (1997). Women's reactions to sexually aggressive mass media depictions. *Violence Against Women, 3,* 149–181.

Lakshmi-Ratan, R. A., & Iyer, E. (1988). Similarity analysis of cognitive scripts. *Journal of the Academy of Marketing Science, 16,* 36–42.

Lam, C. B., & Chan, D. K. S. (2007). The use of cyberpornography by young men in Hong Kong: Some psychosocial correlates. *Archives of Sexual Behavior, 36,* 588–598.

Lane, F. S. (2000). *Obscene profits: The entrepreneurs of pornography in the cyber age.* New York: Routledge.

Layden, M. (2008, November). *Use of pornography, including Internet pornography, nonconsensual sex, use of prostitutes, acceptance of the rape myth and permission-giving beliefs.* Paper presented at the 42nd Annual Meeting of the Association for Behavioral and Cognitive Therapies, Orlando, FL.

Levert, N. P. (2007). A comparison of Christian and non-Christian males, authoritarianism, and their relationship to Internet pornography addiction/compulsion. *Sexual Addiction and Compulsivity, 14,* 145–166.

Linz, D. (1989). Exposure to sexually explicit materials and attitudes toward rape: A comparison of study results. *Journal of Sex Research, 26,* 50–84.

Linz, D. G., Donnerstein, E., & Penrod, S. (1988). Effects of long-term exposure to violent and sexually degrading depictions of women. *Journal of Personality and Social Psychology, 55,* 758–768.

Lo, V., & Wei, R. (2005). Exposure to internet pornography and Taiwanese adolescents' sexual attitudes and behaviors. *Journal of Broadcasting and Electronic Media, 49,* 221–237.

Loftus, D. (2002). *Watching sex: How men really respond to pornography.* New York: Thunder's Mouth Press.

MacKinnon, C. A., & Dworkin, A. (Eds.). (1997). *In harm's way: The pornography civil rights hearings.* Cambridge, MA: Harvard University Press.

Malamuth, N. M. (1984). Aggression against women: Cultural and individual causes. In N. Malamuth & E. Donnerstein (Eds.), *Pornography and sexual aggression* (pp. 19–52). New York: Academic Press.

Maltz, W., & Maltz, L. (2008). *The porn trap: The essential guide to overcoming problems caused by pornography.* New York: HarperCollins.

Marks, I., & Dar, R. (2000). Fear reduction by psychotherapies: Recent findings, future directions. *British Journal of Psychiatry, 176,* 507–511.

Miller v. California, 413 U.S. 15 (1973).

Moll, C., & Bridges, A. J. (2009). *Women's perceptions of how partner pornography use affects self-esteem: Empirical test of three variables.* Manuscript in preparation.

Morrison, J. (2004, June 1). The distracted porn consumer: You never knew your online customers so well. *AVN Online.* Retrieved July 23, 2009, from http://business.avn.com/articles/16315.html

Morrison, T. G., Ellis, S. R., Morrison, M. A., Bearden, A., & Harriman, R. L. (2006). Exposure to sexually explicit material and variations in body esteem, genital attitudes, and sexual esteem among a sample of Canadian men. *Journal of Men's Studies, 14,* 209–222.

Mosher, D. L., & MacIan, P. (1994). College men and women respond to X-rated videos intended for male or female audiences: Gender and sexual scripts. *Journal of Sex Research, 31,* 99–113.

Motion Picture Association of America. (2008). *Research & statistics.* Retrieved July 23, 2009, from http://www.mpaa.org/researchStatistics.asp

Mulac, A., Jansma, L. L., & Linz, D. G. (2002). Men's behavior toward women after viewing sexually-explicit films: Degradation makes a difference. *Communication Monographs, 69,* 311–328.

New York v. Ferber, 458 U.S. 747 (1982).

Paul, P. (2005). *Pornified: How pornography is damaging our lives, our relationships, and our families.* New York: Times Books.

Perkins, H. W. (2002). Social norms and the prevention of alcohol misuse in collegiate contexts. *Journal of Studies on Alcohol, 14,* 164–172.

Rasmussen, P. R., & Kilborne, K. J. (2007). Sex in intimate relationships: Variations and challenges. In P. R. Peluso (Ed.), *Infidelity: A practitioner's guide to working with couples in crisis* (pp. 11–30). New York: Routledge.

Richtel, M. (2009, July 7). Lights, camera, lots of action, forget the script. *New York Times,* p. 1.

Rideout, V. (2001). *Generation Rx: How young people use the internet for health information.* Retrieved

December 5, 2008, from http://www.kff.org/entmedia/20011211a-index.cfm

Robinson, B. E., Manthei, R., Scheltema, K., Rich, R., & Koznar, J. (1999). Therapeutic uses of sexually explicit materials in the United States and the Czech and Slovak Republics: A qualitative study. *Journal of Sex and Marital Therapy, 25,* 103–119.

Russell, D. E. H. (1998). *Dangerous relationships: Pornography, misogyny, and rape.* Thousand Oaks, CA: Sage.

Schneider, J. P. (2000). Effects of cybersex addiction on the family: Results of a survey. *Sexual Addiction and Compulsivity, 7,* 31–58.

Schultz, P. W., Nolan, J. M., Cialdini, R. B., Goldstein, N. J., & Griskevicius, V. (2007). The constructive, destructive, and reconstructive power of social norms. *Psychological Science, 18,* 429–434.

Senn, C. Y. (1993). Women's multiple perspectives and experiences with pornography. *Psychology of Women Quarterly, 17,* 319–341.

Shapiro, J., & Kroeger, L. (1991). Is life just a romantic novel? The relationship between attitudes about intimate relationships and the popular media. *The American Journal of Family Therapy, 19,* 226–236.

Shope, J. H. (2004). When words are not enough: The search for the effect of pornography on abused women. *Violence Against Women, 10,* 56–72.

Silbert, M. H., & Pines, A. M. (1984). Pornography and sexual abuse of women. *Sex Roles, 10,* 857–868.

Simon, S. (2007, December 8). Promoting healthcare for the porn industry. *NPR News Weekend Edition.* Retrieved July 23, 2009, from http://www.npr.org/templates/story/story.php?storyId=17044239

Stoller, R. J., & Levine, I. S. (1993). *Coming attractions: The making of an X-rated video.* New Haven, CT: Yale University Press.

Strossen, N. (1995). *Defending pornography: Free speech, sex, and the fight for women's rights.* New York: Scribner.

Štulhofer, A., Buško, V., & Landripet, I. (2008). Pornography, sexual socialization, and satisfaction among young men. *Archives of Sexual Behavior.* Retrieved August 25, 2009, from http://www.springerlink.com/content/c1k7r32gj9q72248/fulltext.pdf

Sun, C., & Picker, M. (2008). *The price of pleasure: Pornography, sexuality, and relationships.* Northampton, MA: Media Education Foundation.

United States v. Williams, 553 U.S. 285 (2008).

Wang, B., & Davidson, P. (2006). Sex, lies, and videos in rural China: A qualitative study of women's sexual debut and risky sexual behavior. *Journal of Sex Research, 43,* 227–235.

Williams, L. (1989). *Hard core: Power, pleasure and the "frenzy of the visible."* Berkeley: University of California Press.

Wingood, G. M., DiClemente, R. J., Harrington, K., Davies, S., Hook, E. W., III, & Oh, M. K. (2001). Exposure to X-rated movies and adolescents' sexual and contraceptive-related attitudes and behaviors. *Pediatrics, 107,* 1116–1119.

Wosnitzer, R. J., & Bridges, A. J. (2007). *Aggression and sexual behavior in best-selling pornography: A content analysis update.* Paper presented at the 57th Annual Meeting of the International Communication Association, San Francisco, CA.

Chapter Authors

Ana J. Bridges is Assistant Professor of Clinical Psychology at the University of Arkansas, Fayetteville. Since 1999, she has been investigating the effects of explicit sexual media on women and couples. Her research has been featured in both academic and popular press, including *Psychology Today.*

Robert Jensen is a Professor of Journalism at the University of Texas at Austin and a board member of the Third Coast Activist Resource Center in Austin. He is the author of *All My Bones Shake: Seeking a Progressive Path to the Prophetic Voice* (2009); *Getting Off: Pornography and the End of Masculinity* (2007); *The Heart of Whiteness: Confronting Race, Racism and White Privilege* (2005); *Citizens of the Empire: The Struggle to Claim Our Humanity* (2004); and *Writing Dissent: Taking Radical Ideas from the Margins to the Mainstream* (2002). He is also coproducer of the documentary film *Abe Osheroff: One Foot in the Grave, the Other Still Dancing.*

Personal Reflection

Gail Dines

 I was a 22-year-old grad student and a committed feminist who knew nothing about pornography when a friend dragged me to a feminist antiporn slide show. That night my life changed. I had never seen such images of violence against women and I couldn't understand how some men found them arousing. I started to read all the feminist works on the topic—this didn't take very long because it was the early 1980s and only a handful of books had been written on pornography. The more I read, the more I became convinced that porn is a powerful ideological weapon against women. The images produce and solidify a world view that sees women as "fuck" objects and men as life support systems for erect penises. It dehumanizes and debases both women and men and undermines women's fight for social, economic, and legal equality.

My academic and activist life has been dedicated to fighting the porn industry. I research, write, and lecture on pornography, often traveling from one end of the country to the other giving presentations on the harms of porn. In my travels, I meet a lot of women who have partners who are heavy users of porn. They feel diminished and demeaned by their partners' use and, for many, it feels as if he is having an affair. I also meet many men who want to stop using porn but can't, and this scares them because they feel they have lost control of their lives. Often after a lecture I feel drained because I have heard so many stories that are filled with pain and anguish. While the porn industry and their pals in the media insist that porn is just harmless fun, I get to see the real havoc that this industry wreaks on people's lives.

As a way to jumpstart the feminist antiporn movement, I recently co-founded the group Stop Porn Culture. Our first major project was the creation of a new antiporn slide show that examines the nature and effects of contemporary porn. We give this show away for free, and it is now being used across the country in classrooms, community groups, and antiviolence organizations. We don't expect to close the industry down soon, especially given its ever-growing power, but what we have done is to develop some consciousness about the reality of the porn industry—a consciousness that we hope will form the bedrock of a dynamic and energized antiporn movement.

CHAPTER 8

Cultural Issues in Violence Against Women

Lisa Aronson Fontes and Kathy A. McCloskey

Introduction

Violence against women is undeniably a cross-cultural phenomenon. Violence against women appears in a remarkable variety of forms internationally, from sordid to sanitized; from secretive to sacred; in bedrooms and battlegrounds; censured as well as supported by courts, clergy, and communities throughout the world (Watts & Zimmerman, 2002). At the same time, certain forms of violence against women are deeply embedded in specific cultural contexts; that is, harm is inflicted in certain ways and supported by structures and ideologies that permit a specific form of violence to continue in its own precise context (Heise, 1998; Heise, Ellsberg, & Gottermoeller, 1999; Sokoloff, 2005). While we might say, then, that the phenomenon of violence against women is global and general, we must add that its manifestations are also shaped by the values and circumstances of particular cultures. Violence against women does not look the same across cultures.

Due to this variability, prevention and recovery programs must attend to cultural issues if they are to be relevant to the real lives of women across the globe (Heise, 1998; University of Melbourne, 2000). If we avoid considering culture, we commit the grave error of assuming that everyone is "the same," which usually means applying unquestioningly to all women certain ideas that have been generated by and for those from the dominant cultural groups in industrialized nations. Nevertheless, discussing a stigmatized topic like violence against women from a cultural perspective feels risky. When we discuss any particular kind of violence against women within a particular culture, we risk contributing to overgeneralization and stereotypes. If we offer suggestions for preventing violence against women or ameliorating its effects in varying cultural contexts, we risk advocating models for contexts where they won't fit. As we embark on this chapter, we are held back by our desire to avoid stereotyping and exoticizing violence against women, yet simultaneously propelled forward by our commitment to end violence against women and girls everywhere.

Surveying violence against women worldwide feels like standing at the edge of a terrible abyss where millions of women and girls, near and far away, both resist and submit to torture. As people who are academically trained, we think that if we could just make sense of the disordered chaos before us, perhaps we could help. But as we contemplate such a task, it proves hard to know how to group such a survey of anguish and horror into categories that help us—as we say colloquially—wrap our minds around the problem. As a potentially helpful way to do this, this chapter concentrates mostly on cultural issues in the manifestations of violence against women and then briefly discusses prevention and research.

Culturally Based Violence Against Women: Manifestations

First, we must avoid stereotyping. Only rare forms of violence are inflicted against every woman in a culture, and there are few forms of violence against women that belong exclusively to any particular culture. Instead, most forms of violence against women are familiar and hardly raise an eyebrow; that is, the everyday slapping, beating, and sexual assault of females of all ages around the world that have largely become commonplace and unremarkable (Watts & Zimmerman, 2002).

Furthermore, when we discuss a form of violence against women that appears in a given culture, we risk "essentializing" that culture. In other words, we risk underestimating differences among people in that culture and supporting racist discourses that construct members of minority cultural groups, or non-Western nations, as a homogenous "other." In this chapter, we try mightily to avoid this perspective, recognizing that appalling levels of violence against women are present in the dominant culture

in the United States and other Western industrialized nations. We also know that there are people from all cultures who work diligently to end violence against women throughout the world. We see violence against women in all societies—including our own—as both cultural and criminal; that is, although violence against women has different cultural explanations and takes different forms based on location and time, all violence against women still merits legal and criminal justice responses. Violence against women is never "just cultural" and therefore acceptable, any more than assaults on any other particular group of people would be considered tolerable because they are "cultural."[1]

When categorizing various types of violence against women, reports from the United Nations (UN, 2006) show that physical abuse alone (without other forms of abuse) is reported at high rates across the globe. In their most recent multicountry study, the World Health Organization (WHO, 2005) also found that women reported high rates of physical violence at the hands of a partner, ranging from 13% in Japan to 61% in rural Peru. Even so, most women reported that the violence was part of an ongoing pattern of verbal, physical, and sexual abuse, and all three types are most likely to occur together. As noted in the WHO report, "Only in the urban settings in Brazil and Thailand, and in Japan and Serbia and Montenegro, was the overlap between physical and sexual abuse less than 30%" (p. 7). The physical abuse of women and girls, therefore, cannot be understood without also taking into consideration the sexualized context of that violence. Because sexual and physical violence against females so commonly occur together, or at least within the same gendered cultural scripts, the discussion below incorporates and integrates both types of violence across the lifespan.

---

[1]The desire to preserve cultural autonomy has been used as an excuse for failing to eliminate certain harmful practices that curtail women's right to live without violence—perhaps the most basic human right. We reject these cultural arguments. The United Nations Secretary General's *Report on Violence Against Women* (2006) wryly notes that the same (male) leaders who advocate the use of modern technologies to advance the interests of their people often resist measures to assure the physical safety or advancement of women in the name of "tradition." This almost seems to imply that women alone do and should serve as the repositories of traditional cultural identity and therefore must be sacrificed in the name of culture.

Missing Girls

Females are subject to violence even before birth. In many cultures, girl children are seen as less valuable than boy children, in part because when they grow up, girls are expected to marry young and then live with and care for their husband's families, whereas a boy and his future bride will care for *his* parents. Additionally, inheritance and the family name are typically transmitted through male children. Women's participation in the household and family in which they were born is seen, therefore, as transitory. Furthermore, a woman's place in her new (husband's) family is often not secured until she produces a male heir (Das Gupta, 1987). All too often, the dowry extracted for girls in many cultures means that the birth of a girl is greeted with sorrow and a sense of loss, rather than celebration. In India, the birth of a second daughter is sometimes seen as punishment for a sin committed in a past life (McGivering, 2003).

The selective abortion of girl fetuses, the infanticide of girl newborns, and the underfeeding and death by malnutrition of girl children has resulted in the widespread reduction in female children worldwide each year (a phenomenon known as *missing girls*). Despite legislation prohibiting selective abortion for sex determination, in 2003 there were 119 boys born for every 100 girls in China and 115 boys born for every 100 girls in India (Hsu, 2008), even though the natural birth ratio is 103–106 boys for every 100 girls (Yoon, 2006). In some regions of India, the sex ratio is far more skewed. One study of births in India reported that girl children conceived to families that have already given birth to girls are particularly at risk of being aborted because of their sex (Jha, Kumar, Vasa, Dhingra, Thiruchelvam, & Moineddin, 2006). Girls conceived in families in which the mothers had higher levels of education were more likely to be "missing" than girls in families in which the mother had lower levels of education, presumably reflecting greater access to prenatal sex detection and abortion services. Half a million girls are "missing" annually in India (Jha et al., 2006); in other words, half a million female fetuses are aborted annually in India because of their sex. The only positive side of this problem, if it may be called that, is that the option of prenatal sex-selective abortion appears to have resulted in a decrease in the starving to death of unwanted girl children in India (Levinson et al., 2003). The problem of missing girls is not restricted to India and China, however; it has also been found in Taiwan, South Korea, Pakistan, Vietnam, and some sub-Saharan African countries (Watts & Zimmerman, 2002). This problem is apt to worsen as sex-determination technology continues to proliferate and decrease in cost in countries where women and girls are undervalued.

The correlate to the lowered sex ratios in the births of girls is a shortage of young women of marriageable age a couple of decades later.[2] One would think that the relative scarcity of women in some regions would raise their status. Unfortunately, this does not appear to be the case. In China, each year tens of thousands of women from rural families are abducted and sold as brides to men from other impoverished rural provinces (Rosenthal, 2001). Some of these women were married and raising families of their own when they were abducted. In India, in some cases girls are obligated to serve as wives or producers of heirs to more than one man, often brothers, and then essentially discarded. Their function as producers of the next generation of males is seen as more important than their value as wives and mothers. Additionally, in countries where there is a gender imbalance leading to a

---

[2]In China, unmarried men with few prospective brides are called *bare branches* (Hsu, 2008). In the Punjab countryside, such men are called *bechara*, which means "one without food or resources," because they lack the support and labor of a wife (Kaur, 2008). These unmarried men are also likely to be denied a family inheritance. A bachelor brother essentially has the status of a family servant in his siblings' homes and may be forced to sleep in a shed or move from home to home of his various siblings.

shortage of brides, women from even lower-income regions or countries are sometimes "imported" to serve as brides. These young women are extremely vulnerable to violence and exploitation of every kind, especially if they have arrived against their will in a new land where they do not speak the language and do not have friends, family, or a social network (Kaur, 2008). For example, Korean men are responding to the shortage of women by traveling to Vietnam, where they can essentially purchase from poor families a young attractive bride, who will then be isolated and relatively powerless when she returns to Korea with her groom (Onishi, 2007). It appears we should not pin our hopes on the possibility that a shortage of wives will raise women's status.

Incest and the Sexual Abuse of Girls

The sexual abuse of girls within and outside their families is both an effect of the subjugation of women and a way to ensure its continuation; girls who are forced to submit to boys and men in this way learn a deep lesson about their relative powerlessness. Globally, up to 1 in 5 women and 1 in 10 men report being sexually abused as children (WHO, 2005). While appalling numbers of boys are abused sexually within and outside the home, girls are still far more likely to be victimized in most cultures that have been studied. For instance, the WHO (2002) reports:

> Studies conducted mostly in developed countries indicate that 5–10% of men report a history of childhood sexual abuse . . . with adolescents in developing countries, the percentage of males reporting ever having been the victims of sexual assault ranges from 3.6% in Namibia and 13.4% in the United Republic of Tanzania to 20% in Peru. (p. 154)

The WHO (2005) reports even higher numbers of girls are sexually abused both within their

families (incest, forced sexual initiation, child brides, etc.) and outside the home (at religious institutions, schools, camps, residential facilities, the workplace, on sports teams, etc.). Indeed, sexual and physical violence against girls is rampant across the globe. Many women worldwide report that their first sexual experience at a young age was not consensual (24% of women in rural Peru, 28% in Tanzania, 30% in rural Bangladesh, and 40% in South Africa).

Often, the closer the relationship between the abuser and the victim, the more the victim blames herself for the assault (Hershkowitz, Horowitz, & Lamb, 2007). In studies conducted in Western countries, it has also been shown that sexual abuse contributes to a broad range of negative outcomes for victims, including greater likelihood of physical and psychological problems, teen pregnancy, substance abuse, and homelessness (Goodkind, Ng, & Sarri, 2006; McMahon & Puettl, 1999). Girls who have been victimized sexually in their childhood are also at elevated risk of further victimization in their childhood and adult years (Grauerholz, 2000; Tjaden & Thoennes, 2000). Girls of all social strata throughout the world are victimized sexually. However, girls who live in extreme poverty and girls whose families have been disrupted appear to be especially vulnerable (Robin, Chester, Rasmussen, Jaranson, & Goldman, 1997; WHO, 2002, 2005).

Cultural issues can make girls especially vulnerable in particular ways. For instance, a cultural emphasis on shame may make it difficult for girls to resist or disclose sexual assaults (Fontes, 2007). Cultures that do not allow access to family planning may have an increased number of unwanted and underprotected girls who are then vulnerable to abuse. Some theorists suggest that a lack of involvement by fathers in girls' upbringing may make them more likely to abuse their own daughters (Rohner & Rohner, 1980). Other factors that may place girls from a given culture at risk for sexual abuse include the sexualization of all girls or certain groups of girls within a culture, tolerance of adult sexual practices with girls, authoritarian attitudes that require girls to obey adults unquestioningly, socialization of boys and men toward aggressive sexuality, and the lack of formal or informal resources that would offer girls safety. For example, children who live in remote communities, such as on Indian reservations in the United States or in small, isolated ethnic enclaves, may have particular difficulty protecting themselves from abuse by family or clan members or members of their ethnic group because of feelings of group loyalty (Fontes, 1993, Robin et al., 1997).

Cultures have practices and beliefs that protect against sexual abuse, as well as other practices and beliefs that place children at risk (Fontes, 1995; Plummer & Njuguna, 2009). Factors that might protect girls from a given culture from sexual abuse include intolerance of adult sexual practices with children, a high value placed on girls and women, extended family supervision of children, close relationships between mothers and their children, strong social sanctions against abuse, views of children as nonsexual beings, support for children to speak up and make their needs known, socialization toward cooperative mutually agreeable sexual activity, open discussions of sexuality, and both formal and informal resources that protect children. However, without further research in this area, these ideas are speculative.

Violence Against Young Women Prior to Cohabitation or Marriage

In this section, we examine three forms of violence related to women in what may be called a "premarried" state. That is, in cultures in which heterosexual marriage is the expected norm, the period when girls are seen to be of marriageable age but are not yet "taken" poses special risks. Here we will discuss dating violence, violence inflicted on women who refuse a man's advances, and "honor" killings.

Dating Violence. The social concept of dating is characteristic of modern societies in Europe, the Americas, Australia, and New Zealand, but relatively new in many other countries where marriages are arranged and young women's contact with men outside the family is closely monitored prior to marriage. The Western idea that young women can become intimate with men before marriage creates a situation in which gender role imperatives are acted out mostly in private. This privacy sets the stage for "invisible" violence against women because it provides maximum deniability for abusers and shames victims; young women may be seen as somehow culpable for the violence because they have consented to be in an intimate setting with a male. Throughout the world, both young women victims and men who have perpetrated violence report a great deal of physical and sexual violence in dating relationships (Gavey, 2005).

Most cultures traditionally see sexual interaction as a male/female struggle in which men are always ready for sex while women should try to avoid it, at least outside marriage. Cáceres (2005) describes how these ideas present themselves in Peru: "All 'normal' men but no 'decent' women willingly engage in heterosexual activity" (p. 127). This gender struggle model of sexuality can make it seem acceptable and unremarkable for males to prey upon females. If a young woman is assaulted, she or her caretakers may be blamed for having let their guard down. The boy or man in question is seen as having done what boys or men will do. Thus, dating violence usually becomes decontextualized in societies in which premarital romances happen.

Furthermore, young women are often both physically and socially unable to defend themselves when they find themselves alone with men in dating situations. Men's sexual socialization often includes the rape imperative script: No doesn't mean no; it means try harder (Gavey, 2005). Additionally, males (but not females) commonly learn how to fight physically and use force to get what they want. The common dating self-selection strategies—men should always be physically larger, stronger, and more socially powerful than their dates—also make it more difficult for women to either resist or report assaults.

Violence Upon Refusing a Man's Propositions. In countries where marriages are not arranged by families, presumably women have the option to choose their dating, sexual, and marriage partners, as well as the option to refuse potential partners. However, women's supposed autonomy in sexual decision making may run counter to men's sexual scripts and pride. If men feel they have a right to choose a sexual/marriage partner with or without the woman's consent, and if they feel their pride has been hurt by a refusal, they may exact revenge in violent ways. For instance, in a practice known as "streamlining," groups of young South African men have been sexually assaulting young women who refuse to date or have a sexual relationship with a member of their group (Jewkes, 2005), while spurned suitors in Bangladesh and India sometimes throw acid at women who have refused their advances, resulting in permanent disfigurement and sometimes blindness (UN, 2006).

Another aspect of sexual scripts that works against women's sexual autonomy is the assumption that once men are aroused, they cannot control their sexual impulses. This sort of discourse is used in many parts of the world to justify sexual assault. For instance, Cambodian young men explained their group sexual assaults of girls, called *bauk,* by referring to themselves as being "blindly stricken with passion" (Wilkinson, Bearup, & Soprach, 2005, p. 164). It is not hard to understand, then, that when girls are sexually assaulted they might feel they are in some way responsible for the abuse because they provoked such a response in men. One South African girl described concealing her body even from family members: "When my father, my uncle, or my brother is there I don't wear [tight trousers] because if they rape me, I can't blame them" (Jewkes, Penn-Kekanna, & Rose-Junius, 2005). Whether the cultural norm governing the display of women's bodies is one that is highly sexualized and permits revealing clothing (American Psychological Association, 2007) or one that requires covering the body from head to toe (Hussain, 2001), women are held responsible for male sexual aggression.

Honor Killings and Assaults. In many developing countries, arranged marriages place a high price on a young woman's virginity upon marriage, which will partially determine her value as a bride. Until a woman passes from the hands of her father into the hands of her husband, her sexual "purity" is closely monitored by members of her family, and her movements may be narrowly restricted. In some societies, she may be prohibited from going to school, all ostensibly in the interest of ensuring her purity.

Honor killings are the extreme, but logical, conclusion to efforts to maintain a family's honor by means of a girl or woman's chastity. The category of honor killings covers a broad range of murderous acts against women for supposed affronts to a family's honor, such as wedding without parental permission, having sex outside marriage, or allegedly showing sexual interest or impropriety of any kind (Borka, 2009). Sometimes women are murdered by family members when they are victims of rape; the victimization is considered a disgrace to the woman's family because the woman was not married to the rapist. The UN (2006) estimates that 5,000 people, mostly women, are killed annually in the name of honor, mostly in South Asia and the Middle East as well as in South Asian and Middle Eastern communities in Australia, Europe, and the United States.

In addition to those who are murdered, countless others are maimed by "honor" assaults of various kinds. Honor assaults are usually perpetrated by a male member of the woman's family and are most often conducted in public, thus influencing the conduct of other women (UN, 2006). These crimes are, in essence, a way for male family members to try to save face or regain social status among their peers by eliminating the alleged source of sexual misconduct—the woman (Vahdati, 2009). Religious states sometimes grant impunity to perpetrators of honor crimes, in effect supporting the claim that a woman's alleged sexual impropriety merits a violent assault or death sentence. These attacks are often conducted in particularly brutal ways in public and are sometimes sanctioned by tribal or national laws (Sidahmed, 2001). In essence, such attacks are similar to domestic violence incidents in Western industrialized nations where women are maimed and murdered by their boyfriends and husbands for allegedly showing sexual impropriety or disrespect.

In some communities that practice forms of traditional Islamic law, women and girls may also be sexually assaulted, forced to marry, beaten, or killed as a form of vengeance in response to an alleged wrongdoing on the part of one of the female's male family members. In this case, the woman's body is seen as a valid target for attacking the family. This practice came to the world's attention with the case of Mukhtar Mai of Pakistan. After suffering a brutal gang rape that was mandated by elders in her community in response to a false allegation of an impropriety by her 12-year-old brother, Mukhtar Mai refused to commit suicide as was expected of her and instead brought her assailants to trial (Karkera, 2006).

From these Western and non-Western examples alike, it is clear that prior to cohabitation or marriage, young women are held responsible for the violence of boyfriends, potential suitors, and family members who seek to impose cultural sanctions for perceived failure to follow local female gender norms. These cultural norms obviously vary from location to location and serve to justify violence against women both before and after marriage.

Violence Against Women During Cohabitation or Marriage

Forced Marriages. Forced marriages differ from arranged marriages. In an arranged marriage, a matchmaker or members of the bride and groom's family choose the prospective partners for their offspring, but the prospective bride and groom may reject the choice. In forced marriage, which is practiced in parts of the Middle East, Africa, and Asia, minor girls are forced into marriages, usually with much older male partners. The United Nations Human Rights Council (UNHCR, 2010) identified five kinds of forced marriages: child marriages, compensation marriages, incestual marriages, kidnapping marriages, and trafficking marriages. Child marriages are quite common in Saudi Arabia, for example, where it is not unusual for 10- and 12-year-old girls to be married to men in their sixties (Admon, 2009). The United Nations International Children's Emergency Fund (UNICEF, 2009) documents high rates of girls forced into early marriages in the following countries: Niger (75%), Chad (72%), Mali (71%), Bangladesh (64%), Guinea (63%), Central African Republic (61%), Mozambique (56%), and Nepal (51%). In Afghanistan, a staggering 60% of marriages involve brides under the age of 16; many of these forced marriages involve girls under the age of 14 who are given to a groom in order to resolve a father's debt or to resolve family or tribal conflict, a practice called *swara*, which is a form of compensation marriage (UNICEF, 2009). In other compensation marriages, a family may give a young daughter in marriage in exchange for food for the rest of the family. The receiving family or tribe may choose to keep the young woman as a bride or as a slave for labor or sex (UN, 2002; UNHCR, 2010). Kidnapping marriages occur in Kyrgyzstan and Uzbekistan and among the Hmong of Thailand and Laos, where a bride may be kidnapped and forced to marry her kidnapper to preserve her family's honor. Trafficking marriages involve women who are kidnapped for the financial benefit of the trafficker and forced into marriages. These kinds of marriages are becoming more common in societies where gender imbalance has led to a shortage of women of marriageable age.

Women whose first sexual experiences occurred in forced marriages report that these experiences are often violent precursors to a lifetime of sexual assault, beatings, subjugation, and unwanted pregnancies (Santhya & Jejeebhoy, 2005). Additionally, women who give birth before the age of 15 are five times as likely to die in childbirth as women who give birth in their twenties (UNICEF, 2009). Thus, just as women are subjected to violence before marriage or cohabitation, so are they subjected to violence within marriage, and similarly, such violence usually goes unreported and undetected by outsiders (Abrahams, Jewkes, Hoffman, & Laubsher, 2004). Violence may exist whether the marriage partners are self-selected, matched, or forced.

For instance, in industrialized countries, if a husband beats or rapes his wife or ultimately kills her, a common response in the community might be one of surprise ("He seemed like such a nice guy," "There was no sign this was coming," etc.). Even if friends and family do know about his violence beforehand, the cultural imperative in Western industrialized nations is often to stay out of a family's "private business" (Zorza & Pines, 2007). Thus, in Western cultures, violence against women during marriage is heavily influenced by the nuclear family arrangement of the male/female heterosexual dyad in one relatively isolated household. Furthermore, violence in the nuclear family arrangement becomes visible only when it spills out into the wider family or community. In the developed world, a wealthy family is likely to have greater privacy. It is no accident that violence against women comes to the attention of the authorities at a greater rate in communities of lower socioeconomic status than those with higher status; wealth buys privacy.

Violence in marriage and cohabitation is highly prevalent in the developing world as well. A recent study of the WHO found that prevalence rates of physical violence experienced by women at the hands of a male partner varied from 13% in Japan to 61% in Peru, and the rates of both physical and sexual violence by a partner were consistently found to be higher in rural than urban settings throughout the world (WHO, 2005).

Dowry Violence. Dowry violence refers to violence concerning marriage-related payments given by the bride's family at the time of the wedding and also to violence threatened or inflicted after the wedding as a way of pressing the bride's family to provide the groom's family with a larger payment. In South Asia, violence in marriage is often used as a form of pressure to extract the transfer of wealth from the bride's family to the groom's (Bloch & Rao, 2000). Brides in rural India have typically been matched by their parents with a selected groom and typically have no real police protection from violence or recourse to divorce. Bloch and Rao (2000) write, "Once the wedding is celebrated and the newly married bride has moved to her husband's home, she is not only a bride but also a potential hostage" (p. 7).

This particular form of violence against women is most common in South Asian countries such as India, Pakistan, and Bangladesh, but it is also found in enclaves of people from these nations in the United States, Great Britain, and elsewhere. Dowry violence can take various forms, including beating, starvation, burning, assaults with acid that blind and/or disfigure the woman, and murder. The violence is most often inflicted by the groom, but it may also be inflicted by other members of his family.

A strange legal tangle has recently occurred in India, where domestic violence is difficult to prosecute unless it occurs in the context of dowry violence. This has resulted in some attorneys pressing women who are seeking protection from domestic violence to claim falsely that the assaults were related to a dowry, leading to a widespread discrediting of genuine claims of dowry-related violence (Ahmed-Ghosh, 2004). One source estimated that a young married woman is being beaten, burnt to death, or pushed to commit suicide every six hours in India (Ahmed-Ghosh, 2004). Young women between the ages of 15 and 34 are more than three times as likely as young men to be killed by fire in India, and many of these burnings are thought to be due to dowry- or domestic violence-related assaults in which the women are doused with gasoline and then set ablaze; these killings are often reported officially as kitchen fires (Sanghavi, Bhalla, & Das, 2009).

Violence Against Widows

For cultural reasons, in many parts of the world a woman's worth is tied to her husband's. Unmarried women, including widows, may have no clear place in society and have limited or no legal rights as enfranchised adults. In developed countries, the abuse of widows appears more subtle and usually takes the form of poverty and isolation, as well as elder abuse that occurs privately, while in developing countries, violence may take more overt forms (UN, 2001).

Widows may be directly subjected to violence or encouraged to commit suicide because they are seen as a drain on a family's or community's resources. For instance, many elderly, impoverished, widowed women in Ghana are accused of witchcraft and may either be murdered by family or community members or may be subjected to a range of physical, sexual, and economic abuses (Adinkrah, 2004). In Nigeria, a divorced or widowed woman is referred to as *bazarawa,* meaning "a thing that has been used" (UN, 2002, p. 21).

India is estimated to have 40 million widows (McGivering, 2002), some of whom were promised in marriage while they were children to a much older man, who then died before the marriage was consummated (UN, 2001). Because Hinduism frowns on widows remarrying, widows often live the remainder of their lives as outcasts and may be forced to beg for survival. In some parts of Africa, including Zambia, Kenya, Malawi, Uganda, Tanzania, Ghana, Senegal, Angola, Ivory Coast, Congo, and Nigeria, a widow is considered "unclean" and is required to have sexual intercourse with a relative of her late husband or with a community member who is considered the village cleanser before she can be reintegrated into her community. It is believed that the entire village will be subject to bad luck if she refuses, and any misfortune in the village would be blamed on her. Of course, this coerced sexual activity may

not only be psychologically traumatic; it may also expose the widow, the ritual cleanser, and the cleanser's wives to HIV/AIDS (LaFraniere, 2005).

Other Forms of Violence Against Women

Violence Against Lesbians. Women who are attracted to other women and are in relationships with them violate the standard global norms of compulsory heterosexuality. Thus, lesbians worldwide are subjected to both gender-related and homophobic violence. For instance, according to a report from the Human Rights Watch (2001), young lesbians in the United States "do not experience sexism and homophobia as separate events; instead, the two forms of harassment are mutually reinforcing. It is simply impermissible, according to rigid rules of social behavior, for girls to reject boys" (p. 12). Because lesbian girls and women are subjected to the double whammy of being both female and nonconforming in their sexual orientation, they are discriminated against severely, including being subject to peer and family rejection, harassment, job and housing discrimination, and physical assault, rape, and murder. The true extent of hate crimes against lesbians is currently unknown, but the information available suggests that such crimes are all too common in the Western world. For instance, in a study from Australia, many lesbians reported that they were sexually assaulted because of their sexual orientation by gang members, strangers, and acquaintances; 70% reported physical abuse, threats of violence, or verbal abuse in a public place because of their sexual orientation (Mason, 1993).

Lesbianism is officially denied as a well-kept secret in much of the developing world, especially in those countries where women must submit to marriage to survive (Human Rights Watch, 2008; Mason, 1993). In Kyrgyzstan, family members control lesbians by "creating financial dependency, enforcing curfews, dictating their movement within and outside the home, and isolating them from sympathetic family and friends. In some cases, families capture women who escape and force them to return" to marriages to men (Human Rights Watch, 2008, p. 11). In addition, punitive and "curative" rape of lesbians is widespread. A 22-year-old victim of such violence reported the following:

> In 2002 I had a girlfriend from a very strict family. We were hiding our relationship from everyone, but someone still told her brothers . . . once we were going for a walk. Her brothers approached us, told her to go home, and took me behind the corner to "talk." And there . . . the two of them raped me. They told me, "This is your punishment for being this way" . . . I told my girlfriend about what happened to me . . . they beat her too. (Human Rights Watch, 2008, pp. 15–16)

It shouldn't be surprising, given the amount of societal discrimination and violence against lesbians, that many lesbians internalize the message that they are not normal and do not deserve basic human rights, or that they turn on each other in relationships. Intimate partner violence does occur in lesbian relationships (Renzetti & Miley, 1996), and similar to heterosexual battering, it cuts across class, race, and ethnic lines (Kanuha, 2005).[3]

Unique structural barriers may impede lesbian victims from seeking relief from partner violence (Elliott, 1996). Often, services are not geared to lesbian victims, and the same homophobia found in the larger society is also found in the social service arena. Indeed, because of the need for self-protective secrecy, manipulation by the violent partner can take the form of threats to "out" the victim at work or to family members, as well as psychological abuse that reminds the victim she will not receive the same response from police or shelters as would a heterosexual woman

(Elliott, 1996; Kanuha, 2005). Unfortunately, little is known about lesbian relationship violence in developing countries.

Sexual Assault in War. Rape continues to be an all-too-common tool of terror in combat zones. Rape of women and children has been used as a tool of war by all countries throughout history, most recently in Bosnia-Herzegovina, Serbia, Liberia, Sierra Leone, Democratic Republic of the Congo, Burundi, Colombia, Sudan, Somalia, and Burma, just to name a few. Rape is used both as a weapon of war by individual soldiers and a strategy of war by groups determined to destroy communities and drive people from their land. Across the world, women and children are increasingly being targeted for sexual atrocities during war, and the level of violence seems to have increased (Ward & Marsh, 2006). The widespread use of rape during the wars in Rwanda and Sierra Leone led to thousands of women being turned out of their homes, shunned by their families and communities, infected with sexually transmitted diseases (especially HIV), and forced to bear the children of their rapists (WHO, 2005). Thus, civilian populations are increasingly victimized as a result of civil wars that pit communities against each other along religious and ethnic or racial lines.

In the Democratic Republic of the Congo, these assaults have reached new levels of brutality as gangs of soldiers rape women and children and then tear apart their organs with knives or sticks or shoot bullets into their vaginas and anuses, ensuring a lifetime of infection, incontinence, and suffering if they survive the assaults. The assaults are often conducted in front of the victims' families and communities, ensuring maximum trauma and humiliation for all involved. A Congolese gynecologist, Denis Mukwege, treats dozens of these assault victims

---

[3]In large population surveys using different methods, it has been shown that the greatest risk for intimate partner violence results from residing with a male, regardless of sexual orientation. That is, women living with men were at highest risk for relationship violence, followed by men living with men, men living with women, and women living with women (Tjaden & Thoennes, 2000).

each day. He describes the public nature of these assaults as especially damaging:

> The whole family and the entire neighborhood is traumatized by what they have seen. The ordinary sense of family and community is lost after a man has been forced to watch his wife being raped, or parents are forced to watch the rape of their daughters, or children see their mothers raped. Neighbors are witnesses to this. Many flee. Families are dislocated. Social relationships are lost. There is no more social network, village network. Not only the victims have been destroyed; the whole village is destroyed. (Hebert, 2009, p. A21)

Rape as a weapon of war can be used to "reward" soldiers or motivate male troops, as a means to torture or humiliate a conquered population, or to create mass exodus from a geographic location (Médicins Sans Frontières/Doctors Without Borders [MSF], 2009). The aftermath of such sexual violence perpetrated during war is far reaching. During post-war transition periods, the number of sexual assaults perpetrated by civilian men against women and children increases exponentially, with most aggressors known to the victims (MSF, 2009). Furthermore, after war large numbers of women and children are displaced and forced into sexual slavery or forced into prostitution to survive; sadly, post-war reconstruction and recovery efforts rarely acknowledge this problem, seldom taking into consideration the needs of victims or the moral requirement of holding perpetrators accountable (Ward & Marsh, 2006).

Female Genital Cutting. Female genital cutting (or FGC, also called female genital mutilation) is a traditional practice thought to have begun about 2,000 years ago in Egypt (UN, 2002). According to the UN, approximately 135 million women have been mutilated, and an additional 2 million are thought to be at risk of mutilation each year in Northern Africa, some Middle Eastern countries, and in some Muslim countries and communities in Asia, including Malaysia, Indonesia, Sri Lanka, Bangladesh, and India. Throughout the world, some immigrants from these countries also engage in cutting the genitals of female infants and children. FGC refers to several types of traditional cutting procedures performed on women and girls, often as part of coming-of-age rituals. The mildest of these procedures involves removing the clitoral hood. The most severe procedure involves cutting off the clitoris, the labia menora, and most of the external labia, and sewing a girl or woman's genitals closed with a thread or thorns, with just a minute opening remaining for the passage or urine and menstrual blood. A girl's legs may then be bound together for up to 40 days from hips to ankle, to ensure the formation of scar tissue (UN, 2002).

According to the United Nations Population Fund (UNFPA, 2007), FGC is usually carried out in extremely unhygienic circumstances, often with a dirty, unsterilized instrument such as a scissors, a razor blade, or a sharp piece of glass. Short- and long-term health hazards result. In the short term, girls suffer from local and systemic infections, abscesses, ulcers, delayed healing, septicemia, tetanus, gangrene, severe pain and hemorrhage that can lead to shock, and damage to the bladder, rectum, and other organs. Long-term complications include urine retention resulting in repeated urinary infections, obstruction of menstrual flow leading to frequent reproductive tract infections and infertility, prolonged and obstructed labor leading to the formation of fistulas, severe pain during intercourse, extremely painful menstruation, and psychological problems such as chronic anxiety and depression (UNFPA, 2007). The pain is intensified when women are cut and re-stitched to allow sexual intimacy and childbirth. Girls and women sometimes die immediately from the procedure or during subsequent years from infection, bleeding, or other complications. Women who bleed upon intercourse because of the small vaginal open caused by FGC are, of course, at greater risk for HIV and other sexually transmitted diseases.

FGC is sometimes justified as a way to ensure the chastity and genital "purity" of girls and women by diminishing their capacity for sexual pleasure. Unmutilated women may also be seen as unclean or "masculine" because of the presence of a clitoris. Practices such as FGC that involve "severe pain and suffering" are considered forms of torture and human rights violations (UN, 2002).[4]

Conclusions

This survey of forms of violence against women in various cultures is far from complete. We have not discussed forced pregnancies or forced abortions, or sex trafficking and other forms of prostitution. We have barely touched on sexual harassment in schools and workplaces, including the military.[5] We have not mentioned entire populations of vulnerable women, such as women who are elderly or incarcerated or who have physical or mental disabilities. A number of these topics are discussed in other chapters in this book, although the cultural bases of these practices are not always addressed.

Culture in Violence Against Women Prevention and Research

As long as cultural norms allow perpetrators of violence to assault women with impunity, such violence will continue. Only cultural and structural changes that both raise the cost of perpetrating violence for abusers and lower the costs of reporting violence for victims will create safety for girls and women. In this section, we focus on changing cultural norms in multicultural societies, where issues of cultural conflict; power differentials; and intersecting gender, ethnic, religious, and social class identities figure most prominently. Unfortunately, we raise many more questions than we can answer.

Creating programs to prevent violence against women is especially challenging in multicultural contexts. Ideas that seem basic, understood by all, and appear "common sense" may become contentious when we examine possible cultural variations in their context and interpretation. For instance, what constitutes violence? What do we do about cultural situations where consent may be forfeited, such as in marriage? How might prevention programming be received in societies where the majority of the population is nonliterate or where people are at war? Is sex traded for

---

[4]Although commentators in Western industrialized countries express consistent outrage and repulsion toward forms of female genital cutting as described above, "cosmetic" genital surgery, including labiaplasty, clitoral unhooding, G-spot augmentation, tightening of the vaginal walls, and hymen reconstruction has become a growth industry in the United States and Europe (Fitzpatrick, 2008). We don't mean to equate the risks entailed in undergoing these various procedures, but we simply note that Western cosmetic procedures might also meet the criteria for female genital mutilation established by the WHO as procedures that intentionally alter or injure female genital organs for non-medical reasons. It is interesting that unnecessary female genital surgery in the West is not perceived as "violent," perhaps because such surgeries are usually performed in medical settings and performed on adult women who consent to the procedures. The American College of Obstetricians and Gynecologists (2007) has critiqued these unnecessary genital surgeries and warned that potential complications include infection, altered sensation, dyspareunia (pain upon intercourse), adhesions, and scarring.

[5]Women who serve in the United States military suffer from a culture that allows them to be routinely subject to sexual assault by their comrades. For instance, nearly a third of United States military women are raped, some 71% are sexually assaulted, and 90% are sexually harassed by the men who serve beside them (Benedict, 2009). Isolated in their combat units and often harassed by their superior officers, military women often find themselves with no protection from repeated harassment, rape, physical assault, or even murder. Less data are available on women who serve in the military in other nations.

money necessarily violent? How about sex for safety? Can women ever opt to accept violence, and should society be protecting them from these "choices"? What are the implications of a professional from one culture imposing ideas of "acceptable" nonviolent relationships or sexuality on someone from another culture? Is this necessarily empowering or disempowering? Is there a right or a wrong way to do prevention programming in a particular culture? Should advocates, health-care providers, mental health professionals, attorneys, and others handle these issues differently depending on the culture of the target group? Whose job is it to prevent violence against women among cultural minority groups? While these topics are hotly debated by those who work on cultural issues in violence against women, the answers are not yet clear.

Prevention remains a relatively impoverished area within the field of violence against women, claiming but a miniscule amount of public funds as compared to criminal investigation and prosecutions and victim treatment. This sad state of affairs seems even sadder when we consider the communities whose members are most likely to be victims of violence against women: the poor and, in the United States, disproportionate numbers of African American, Native American, and Latina women (Amnesty International, 2008; Sokoloff, 2005). Although committed activists throughout the world are working to reduce violence in their communities, a recent survey of the literature reveals a glaring lack of information on how to achieve cultural competence in the prevention of violence against women.

Violence against women is often divided into subcategories such as sexual violence, sexual harassment, and domestic violence. Although in each of these areas there is some discussion of cultural competence, we have not seen writings that pull these threads together into a larger whole to address the serious question, "How can we prevent violence against women from diverse cultures in diverse societies?" The answer undoubtedly involves many strategies aimed at all the levels where change can happen—in individual hearts

and minds; in ethnic, geographic, and religious communities; in local, state, national, and international law; and in the media that both normalize and glorify violence against women.

Members of communities are likely to be best prepared to address violence in their communities. However, people working to end violence against women in their ethnic minority communities may be stymied in their efforts by a lack of resources and by prejudices in the wider society that tolerate violence against women by accepting the defense of culture and tradition. In some cases, assaults are seen as characteristic deficiencies of the assailant's and victim's culture, with an attitude of, "They can't help it and it's okay. That's how those people treat their women." In Australia, police officers were described watching a drunken aboriginal man kicking and stomping on his wife as she lay on the ground, absorbing blows to her ribs and head (Kimm, 2004). The two officers declined to intervene, saying that the beating was aboriginal law. An aboriginal woman bystander protested that it was not aboriginal law for a drunken man in boots to brutally kick and assault a woman. In this case, aboriginal culture was seen as fixed and unchangeable, and therefore the cultural explanation of violent behavior was accepted at face value. Such cultural defenses have even been used successfully in homicide defenses in the United States, Australia, and elsewhere (Kimm, 2004; Levesque, 2001; Yang, 2004). Such cultural defenses make mockery of all women's right to safety.

Prevention and intervention programs can be culturally competent in two ways: they can be multicultural or culture specific. Multicultural programs are culturally *open* and meant to reach *diverse* groups, for example, a public service announcement that is delivered in a way that addresses the needs of various ethnic communities (multicultural), or a school-based sexual abuse prevention program that uses examples relevant to a variety of cultures. Other programs are *culture specific*, targeted to the needs of specific ethnic groups. For instance, a violence prevention announcement on a Spanish-language television station is likely to be culture specific and targeted to Latino viewers; a violence pre-vention program that takes place in a Korean church is clearly targeted to Korean participants.

We recommend both approaches to cultural competence in prevention programs. That is, prevention programs that aim to reach a broad population should work to improve their ability to respond to all populations regardless of cul-tural background—in other words, to demon-strate cultural openness. Additionally, targeted programs established by and in close partner-ship with members of specific cultural commu-nities will succeed in reaching members of those communities who might not be reached by the more general programs.

For girls and women to be safe throughout their lives in all the spheres in which they con-duct their lives, enormous changes in women's status will have to occur in individual, commu-nity, cultural, national, and international con-texts. Attitudes cannot be legislated, but they can be changed by deliberate campaigns designed to reach the general public and members of specific communities. These campaigns can be con-ducted in schools, the media, religious institu-tions, and in cultural communities. Prevention campaigns need to be targeted to men and women, boys and girls, to change the attitudes that allow violence against women to continue unabated across generations.

Unlike attitudes, however, behaviors *can* be legislated. Well-prepared and coordinated crimi-nal justice responses to violence against women do make a difference (Hanmer & Griffiths, 2001; O'Dell, 2009). These responses must include training that will enable officers and prosecutors to work effectively in all cultural communities in partnership with community organizations.

Researching violence against women in cul-turally diverse populations raises numerous methodological, political, and ethical challenges. Methodological challenges include the need to ask questions in conditions that improve the likelihood that respondents will speak truthfully, ensure the accuracy of translated instruments, and ensure that the instruments selected are valid with the populations that are studied.

Political challenges include knowing whom to enlist as collaborators in order to gain access to the population and understanding the risks to individuals and communities of cooperating with a researcher. Ethical challenges abound, including understanding cultural influences on informed consent, providing benefits to individ-ual participants and their community, and the imperative to ensure confidentiality in research conducted in small ethnic communities. We believe that many of the methodological and political issues involved in research on culturally diverse populations are ultimately also ethical issues. Research that is inaccurate, poorly designed, or irresponsibly conducted actually inflicts harm on ethnic minority individuals and their com-munities and therefore is a breach of the most basic ethical mandate to not do harm (non-maleficence; Fontes, 2004). Regrettably, an extensive discussion of such ethical issues is beyond the scope of this chapter. We refer read-ers to resources that have been published else-where (Ellsberg & Heise, 2002; Fontes, 2004).

Conclusion

Although we have discussed a wide range of cul-tural issues that shape violence against women across the globe, this discussion is far from complete. We have omitted discussion of the way broader social issues such as poverty, racism, social class, and immigration impact violence against women in general and in spe-cific populations. We have not critiqued all of the many institutions that seem to promulgate or tolerate women's vulnerability to violence, including international and national economic policies, the media, health-care systems, or the legal and criminal justice system. We have not analyzed the special impact of these systems on women in particular cultural contexts. We have not discussed the sexual harassment of women in school and in public places, although we know these assaults are common and interfere with the rights of women and girls to get an education, support themselves and their fami-lies, and move freely. Similarly, although we feel so grateful to them and admiring of them, we have not praised the individuals and organizations from all cultures who work tirelessly to end violence against women worldwide. We are unable to address all these areas because of space constraints. The topic of cultural issues in violence against women clearly deserves multiple books of its own.

Research about cultural influences on violence against women is relatively new and limited. However, our research, activism, and clinical work lead us to the conclusion that culture stands prominently as a factor in *all* situations where women are subjected to violence, not solely in cases where women come from visible minority groups. No article, checklist, or set of principles can adequately address the range of women's experiences of violence and the multiple cultural milieus that allow the violence to continue both pervasively and invisibly. Cultures are always evolving. Learning about culture will forever challenge both activists and scholars to remain flexible, so they can serve the diverse girls and women who are victims of violence and reduce violence in the future.

References

Abrahams, N., Jewkes, R., Hoffman, M., & Laubsher, R. (2004). Sexual violence against intimate partners in Cape Town: Prevalence and risk factors reported by men. *Bulletin of the World Health Organization, 82*(5), 330–337.

Adinkrah, M. (2004). Witchcraft accusation and female homicide victimization in contemporary Ghana. *Violence Against Women, 10,* 325–356.

Admon, Y. (2009, March 8). Rising criticism of child bride marriage in Saudi Arabia. *The Middle East Media Research Institute.* Retrieved September 8, 2009, from http://www.memri.org/bin/articles.cgi?Page=archives&Area=ia&ID=IA50209

Ahmed-Ghosh, H. (2004). Chattels of society: Domestic violence in India. *Violence Against Women, 10,* 94–118.

American College of Obstetricians and Gynecologists. (2007). Vaginal "rejuvenation" and cosmetic vaginal procedures: ACOG Committee Opinion 378. *Obstetrics and Gynecology, 110,* 737–738.

American Psychological Association. (2007). *Report of the APA task force on the sexualization of girls.* Washington, DC: Author. Retrieved October 15, 2009, from http://www.apa.org/pi/wpo/sexualization.html

Amnesty International. (2008, Spring). *Maze of injustice: Failure to protect indigenous women from sexual violence in the USA—1 year update.* New York: Author.

Benedict, H. (2009). *The lonely soldier.* Boston: Beacon Press.

Bloch, F., & Rao, V. (2000). *Terror as a bargaining instrument: A case study of dowry violence in rural India.* World Bank Policy Research Working Paper No. 2347. Washington, DC: The World Bank.

Borka, A. (2009, January 23). *Pakistani newlyweds live in fear of honour killing.* Retrieved August 20, 2009, from http://www.reuters.com/article/worldNews/idUSTRE50M0FI20090123

Cáceres, C. F. (2005). Assessing young people's non-consensual sexual experiences: Lessons from Peru. In S. J. Jejeebhoy, I. Shah, & S. Thapa (Eds.), *Sex without consent: Young people in developing countries* (pp. 127–138). New York: Zed Books.

Das Gupta, M. (1987). Selective discrimination against female children in rural Punjab, India. *Population and Development Review, 13*(1), 90–95.

Elliott, P. (1996). Shattering illusions: Same-sex domestic violence. In C. M. Renzetti & C. H. Miley (Eds.), *Violence in gay and lesbian domestic partnerships* (pp. 1–8). New York: Haworth Press.

Ellsberg, M., & Heise, L. (2002). Bearing witness: Ethics in domestic violence research. *The Lancet, 359,* 1599–1604.

Fitzpatrick, L. (2008, November 19). Plastic surgery below the belt. *Time Magazine.* Retrieved September 1, 2009, from http://www.time.com/time/health/article/0,8599,1859937,00.html

Fontes, L. A. (1993). Disclosures of sexual abuse by Puerto Rican children: Oppression and cultural barriers. *Journal of Child Sexual Abuse, 2,* 21–35.

Fontes, L. A. (1995). *Sexual abuse in nine North American cultures: Treatment and prevention.* Newbury Park, CA: Sage.

Fontes, L. A. (2004). Ethics in violence against women research: The sensitive, the dangerous, and the overlooked. *Ethics & Behavior, 14,* 141–174.

Fontes, L. A. (2007). Sin vergüenza: Addressing shame with Latino victims of child sexual abuse and their families. *Journal of Child Sexual Abuse, 16,* 61–82.

Gavey, N. (2005). *Just sex? The cultural scaffolding of rape.* New York: Routledge.

Goodkind, S., Ng, I., & Sarri, R. C. (2006). The impact of sexual abuse in the lives of young women involved or at risk of involvement with the juvenile justice system. *Violence Against Women, 12,* 456–477.

Grauerholz, L. (2002). An ecological approach to understanding sexual revictimization: Linking personal, interpersonal, and sociocultural factors. *Child Maltreatment, 5,* 5–17.

Hanmer, J., & Griffiths, S. (2001). Effective policing. In J. Taylor-Browne (Ed.), *What works in reducing domestic violence: A comprehensive guide for professionals* (pp. 123–150). London: Whiting and Birch.

Hebert, B. (2009, February 21). The invisible war. *The New York Times,* p. A21. Retrieved February 21, 2009, from http://www.nytimes.com/2009/02/21/opinion/21herbert.html

Heise, L. (1998). *Violence against women: An integrated ecological framework.* New York: St. Martin's Press.

Heise, L., Ellsberg, M., & Gottermoeller, M. (1999). Ending violence against women. *Population Reports, 27*(11), 8–38.

Hershkowitz, I., Horowitz, D., & Lamb, M. E. (2007). Individual and family variables associated with disclosure and nondisclosure of child abuse in Israel. In M. Pipe, M. E. Lamb, Y. Orbach, & A. Cederborg (Eds.), *Child sexual abuse: Disclosure, delay and denial* (pp. 65–75). New York: Routledge.

Hsu, J. (2008, August 4). There are more boys than girls in China and India. *Scientific American.* Retrieved September 9, 2009, from http://www.scientificamerican.com/article.cfm?id=there-are-more-boys-than-girls

Human Rights Watch. (2001). *Hatred in the hallways: Violence and discrimination against lesbian, gay, bisexual, and transgender students in U.S. schools.* New York: Author. Retrieved September 6, 2009, from http://www.hrw.org/legacy/reports/2001/uslgbt/toc.htm

Human Rights Watch. (2008). *These everyday humiliations: Violence against lesbians, bisexual women, and transgender men in Kyrgyzstan.* New York: Author. Retrieved September 1, 2009, from http://www.hrw.org/reports/2008/kyrgyzstan1008/

Hussain, A. (2001, August 10). Kashmir women face acid attacks. *BBC News.* Retrieved September 2, 2009, from http://news.bbc.co.uk/2/hi/south_asia/1484145.stm

Jewkes, R. (2005). Non-consensual sex among South African youth: Prevalence of coerced sex and discourses of control and desire. In S. J. Jejeebhoy, I. Shah, & S. Thapa, (Eds.), *Sex without consent: Young people in developing countries* (pp. 86–95). New York: Zed Books.

Jewkes, R., Penn-Kekanna, L., & Rose-Junius, H. (2005). "If they rape me, I can't blame them": Reflections on gender in the social context of child rape in South Africa and Namibia. *Social Science & Medicine, 61,* 1809–1820.

Jha, P., Kumar, R., Vasa, P., Dhingra, N., Thiruchelvam, D., & Moineddin, R. (2006). Low male-to-female sex ratio of children born in India: National survey of 1.1 million households. *The Lancet, 367,* 675–762.

Kanuha, V. K. (2005). Compounding the triple jeopardy: Battering in lesbian of color relationships. In N. J. Sokoloff (Ed.), *Domestic violence at the margins: Readings on race, class, gender, and culture* (pp. 71–82). Piscataway, NJ: Rutgers University Press.

Karkera, T. R. (2006). The gang rape of Mukhtar Mai and Pakistan's opportunity to regain its lost honor. *Journal of Gender, Social Policy and the Law, 14,* 163–176.

Kaur, R. (2008, July 26). Dispensable daughters and bachelor sons: Sex discrimination in northern India. *Economic & Political Weekly,* pp. 109–114. Retrieved September 1, 2009, from http://www.scribd.com/doc/4435246

Kimm, J. (2004). *A fatal conjunction: Two laws, two cultures.* Sydney, AU: Federation Press.

LaFraniere, S. (2005, May 11). AIDS now compels Africa to challenge widows' "cleansing." *New York Times.* Retrieved August 25, 2009, from http://www.nytimes.com/2005/05/11/international/africa/11malawi.html

Levesque, R. J. R. (2001). *Culture and family violence: Fostering change through human rights law.* Washington, DC: American Psychological Association.

Levinson, F. J., Mehra, S., Levinson, D., Chauhan, A. K., Koppe, G., Bence, B., et al. (2003). *Morinda revisited: Change in nutritional well-being and gender differences after 30 years of rapid economic growth in rural Punjab, India.* Discussion Paper #24. Medford, MA: Tufts University Food Policy and Applied Nutrition Program.

Mason, G. (1993, November). Violence against lesbians and gay men. *Violence Prevention Today, No. 2.* Canberra, Australia: Australian Government Institute of Criminology. Retrieved September 1, 2009, from http://www.aic.gov.au/publications/vpt/vpt2.html

McGivering, J. (2002, February 2). India's neglected widows. *BBC News.* Retrieved September 1, 2009, from http://news.bbc.co.uk/2/hi/south_asia/1795564.stm

McGivering, J. (2003, February 4). India's lost girls. *BBC News.* Retrieved September 1, 2009, from http://news.bbc.co.uk/2/hi/south_asia/2723513.stm

McMahon, P. M., & Puettl, R. C. (1999). Child sexual abuse as a public health issue: Recommendations from an expert panel. *Sexual Abuse, 11*(4), 257–266.

Médicins Sans Frontières/Doctors Without Borders (2009). *Shattered lives: Immediate medical care vital for sexual violence victims.* Brussels, Belgium: Author.

O'Dell, A. (2009). Why do police arrest victims of domestic violence? The need for comprehensive training and investigative protocols. In K. A. McCloskey & M. H. Sitaker (Eds.), *Backs against the wall: Battered women's resistance strategies* (pp. 49–68). New York: Routledge.

Onishi, N. (2007, February 22). Betrothed at first sight: A Korean-Vietnamese courtship. *New York Times.* Retrieved February 22, 2007, from http://www.nytimes.com

Plummer, C. A., & Njuguna, W. (2009). Cultural protective and risk factors: Professional perspectives about child sexual abuse in Kenya. *Child Abuse and Neglect, 33*(8), 524–532.

Renzetti, C. M., & Miley, C. H. (Eds.). (1996). *Violence in gay and lesbian domestic partnerships.* New York: Haworth Press.

Robin, R. W., Chester, B., Rasmussen, J. K, Jaranson, J. M. & Goldman, D. (1997). Prevalence, characteristics, and impact of childhood sexual abuse in a southwestern American Indian tribe. *Child Abuse & Neglect, 21,* 769–787.

Rohner, R. R, & Rohner, E. (1980). Antecedents and consequences of parental rejection: A theory of emotional abuse. *Child Abuse and Neglect, 4,* 189–198.

Rosenthal, E. (2001, June 25). Harsh Chinese realities feed market in women. *New York Times.* Retrieved September 5, 2009, from http://www.nytimes.com

Sanghavi, P., Bhalla, K., & Das, V. (2009). Fire-related deaths in India in 2001: A retrospective analysis of data. *The Lancet, 373,* 1282–1288.

Santhya, K. G., & Jejeebhoy, S. J. (2005). Young women's experiences of forced sex within marriage: Evidence from India. In S. J. Jejeebhoy, I. Shah, & S. Thapa (Eds.), *Sex without consent: Young people in developing countries* (pp. 59–73). New York: Zed Books.

Sidahmed, A. S. (2001). Problems in contemporary applications of Islamic criminal sanctions: The penalty for adultery in relation to women. *British Journal of Middle Eastern Studies, 28,* 187–204.

Sokoloff, N. J. (Ed.). (2005). *Domestic violence at the margins: Readings on race, class, gender, and culture.* Piscataway, NJ: Rutgers University Press.

Tjaden, P., & Thoennes, N. (2000). *Extent, nature, and consequences of intimate partner violence: Findings from the National Violence Against Women Survey (NCJ-181867).* Washington, DC: United States Department of Justice.

UNICEF. (2009). *Mali: Child marriage is a death sentence for many young girls.* New York: Author. Retrieved September 1, 2009, from http://www.unicef.org/sowc09/docs/SOWC09-Country Example-Mali.pdf

United Nations. (2001). *Widowhood: Invisible women, secluded or excluded.* New York: Author. Retrieved September 1, 2009, from http://www.un.org/women watch/daw/public/wom_Dec%2001%20single%20pg.pdf

United Nations. (2002). *Integration of the human rights of women and the gender perspective: Cultural practices in the family that are violent toward women.* New York: Author.

United Nations. (2006). *In-depth study on all forms of violence against women.* New York: Author.

United Nations Human Rights Council. (2010). *Marriage without consent: Girls' and women's human rights.* Geneva, Switzerland: Author. Retrieved March 16, 2010, from http://www.wunrn.com/powerpoint/forced_marriage.pps

United Nations Population Fund. (2007). *A holistic approach to the abandonment of female genital mutilation/cutting.* New York: Author. Retrieved September 9, 2009, from http://www.unfpa.org/public/global/pid/407

United Nations Secretary General. (2006). *Report on violence against women, Secretary General.* New York: Author.

University of Melbourne. (2000). *Eliminating sexual violence against women: Towards a global initiative—Report of the Consultation on Sexual Violence Against Women.* Melbourne, Australia: Author.

Vahdati, S. (2009, February 26). U.S. beheading is a crime, not an honor killing. *Women's eNews.* Retrieved February 26, 2009, from http://www.womensenews.org/article.cfm?aid=3932

Ward, J., & Marsh, M. (2006). *Sexual violence against women and girls in war and its aftermath: Realities, responses, and required resources—A briefing paper.* Brussels, Belgium: United Nations Population Fund.

Watts, C., & Zimmerman, C. (2002). Violence against women: Global scope and magnitude. *Lancet, 359,* 1232–1237.

Wilkinson, D. J., Bearup, L. S., & Soprach, T. (2005). Youth gang rape in Phnom Penh. In S. J. Jejeebhoy, I. Shah, & S. Thapa (Eds.), *Sex without consent: Young people in developing countries* (pp. 158–168). New York: Zed Books.

World Health Organization. (2002). *World report on violence and health.* Geneva, Switzerland: Author.

World Health Organization. (2005). *WHO multi-country study on women's health and domestic violence against women: Summary report of initial results on prevalence, health outcomes, and women's responses.* Geneva, Switzerland: Author.

Yang, J. A. (2004). Marriage by capture in the Hmong culture: The legal issue of cultural rights versus women's rights. *Law and Society Review at University of California, Santa Barbara, 3,* 38–49.

Yoon, Y. J. (2006). Gender imbalance: The male/female sex ratio determination. *Journal of Bioeconomics, 8,* 253–268.

Zorza, J., & Pines, S. (2007). *What a nice guy: Perfect relationship, secret abuse.* Indianapolis, IN: JIST.

Chapter Authors

Lisa Aronson Fontes, Ph.D., has dedicated 20 years to making mental health and social services more responsive to culturally diverse people. Her two most recent books are *Interviewing Clients Across Cultures* (Guilford Press, 2008) and *Child Abuse and Culture: Working with Diverse Families* (Guilford Press, 2008). She has written widely on cultural issues in child maltreatment and violence against women, cross-cultural research, and ethics. She has worked as a psychotherapist and conducted research in Santiago, Chile and with Puerto Ricans, African Americans, and European Americans in the U.S. She completed a Fulbright Foundation fellowship in Buenos Aires, Argentina. She is on the faculty at the University of Massachusetts, Amherst and at Union Institute & University's Psy.D. program.

Kathy A. McCloskey, Ph.D. (Columbia Pacific), Psy.D. (Wright State University), Diplomate of the American Board of Professional Psychology in Clinical Psychology, is an Associate Professor at the University of Hartford Graduate Institute of Professional Psychology in Hartford, CT. She coedited the book *Backs Against the Wall: Battered Women's Resistance Strategies* (Routledge, 2009). Her specialties include domestic violence, trauma, forensic populations, and the training of doctoral-level clinical psychologists.

Personal Reflection

Anita Raj

I am a second-generation Indian immigrant born in Mississippi in 1970. As the first person in my family to be born in the United States, I grew up with my parents saying that I was the only one of us who could be president. By the age of 10, I knew that as a non-white, non-Christian female, I could never be a U.S. president. By that young age, it was already clear to me that there were disparities in treatment and opportunity based on skin color, national origin, religion, language, and sex, and I was of a "lesser" group across most of these dimensions. Such recognition only increased over time, which led me to work in public health, HIV, and gender-based violence research in particular, where I could document how social disparities increased health risks and how social change was needed to reduce these risks. My work was focused in black and Latino communities, where I could bring recognition of how racism and classism combine with sexism to hurt the health of women, men, and communities.

Then, one day a colleague asked me why I did not do work in my own South Asian immigrant community. In that moment, I realized that I did not feel that I had the right to focus on my own community, as it was more privileged in education and wealth than the general population. I also knew that I was not supposed to bring recognition of our "dirty laundry," as there were already enough negative assumptions made about us. However, I recognized (and continue to recognize) that my community was not immune to the issues of racism, classism, xenophobia, and sexism I had seen in the other communities in which I worked. So I wrote a small grant proposal to look at issues of HIV and spousal violence in my own community; I partnered with a local South Asian community-based organization (SAHELI). I got the grant and helped bring recognition of the heightened vulnerabilities to spousal violence South Asian women are experiencing. That work started me on a path toward understanding spousal violence with a cultural connectedness I had not before experienced; it also led me to understand that I could not just study gender-based violence against women but must actively work against it, with respect for the cultural values that prevent it and with a recognition of the cultural values that maintain it. I found I could support women and my community, even if I was still unable to be a U.S. president.

Over the decade since that first study, I have sought to focus my work on the social vulnerabilities that increase the likelihood of women's victimization from and men's perpetration of gender-based violence, with guidance from my social activist partners in the South Asian community as well as other socially vulnerable communities. This approach provides me with the opportunity to use science in a way that can bring recognition and validation to what activists and advocates see every day; my work has particularly emphasized both unique cultural and contextual variations of gender-based violence (e.g., child marriage, abuse from in-laws) as well as causes of male perpetration of such violence (e.g., the effect of mass incarceration of black men on black women's value in heterosexual relationships). In this way, I am able to be part of the activism to (a) halt gender-based violence and (b) dismantle the social structures that reinforce it and marginalize populations.

As our field grows, I see movement toward research that does not simply identify social disparities that increase risk for gender-based violence but involves development of structural and social change interventions with the potential to eliminate these disparities and, with it, women's vulnerability to victimization. As a U.S. researcher, I no longer go to other nations to teach them about intimate partner violence interventions, but rather I learn from the developing world how to move beyond criminal justice approaches and address gender-based violence via the improvement of women's status. As a global health researcher, I am now part of a cross-national collaboration of researchers, activists, and advocates who do not tell women what their lives and relationships should be but rather support women to make their lives what they wish. Nonetheless, tasks remain: There are still too few gender-based violence interventions with demonstrated effectiveness and even fewer that are culturally tailored for socially vulnerable populations. Next steps for future research in this field will require rigorous evaluation of structural gender-based violence intervention efforts, as well as responses for women unable to leave abusive life contexts. Meeting this challenge will, without question, require consideration of culture, context, and social vulnerabilities; it will also involve researchers who are not ashamed to be activists who support social change for women. At this phase in my career, my goal is to be an activist researcher working in a movement against gender-based violence globally.

CHAPTER 9

Economic Issues and Intimate Partner Violence

Claire M. Renzetti

Introduction

The headlines are by now familiar. News of increases in unemployment, the number of families living in poverty, home foreclosures, and people living in overcrowded conditions became commonplace following the economic recession that began in the United States at the close of 2007 (see, e.g., Eckholm, 2009; Roberts, 2009). At the same time, the media reported increasing rates of domestic violence, both intimate partner violence and child abuse, including cases of familicide (the murder of all family members by another family member who then takes his or her own life), with the perpetrator usually being a husband or father depressed over a recent job loss or severe financial problems (see, e.g., Dethy, 2009; Reimer, 2009; Smith, 2009; Sullivan, 2009). It was not surprising that such reports led many observers to draw the conclusion that economic distress *causes* domestic violence. Although the data I will examine in this chapter do point to a strong association between economic hardship and domestic violence, available research also indicates that the relationship is a complex one.[1]

Three factors, in particular, appear to be directly associated with elevated rates of domestic violence: financial strain, unemployment, and living in economically disadvantaged neighborhoods (U.S. Department of Justice, National Institute of Justice, 2009b). This chapter, therefore, will concentrate on these factors but also take into account how a number of other variables—physical and psychological health issues, social support networks, and social service systems such as Temporary Assistance to Needy Families (TANF, typically referred to as welfare)—may affect, or be affected by, the economic distress-domestic violence relationship. Before turning to the research, however, several qualifying statements are in order.

---

[1]As the U.S. Department of Justice (2009b) points out, the very small number of familicides makes it difficult for researchers to pinpoint how economic distress may contribute to these crimes. They point out that although economic distress appears to be a precipitating factor in some incidents, it is often the case that the couple had a history of conflict over various issues and that economic distress should be considered in conjunction with other risk factors, such as previous domestic violence and access to a gun.

First, this chapter focuses primarily on research conducted in the United States. Although research from other countries could be instructive, there are few international studies available that similarly examine the economic issues I will address here. The association between economic distress and intimate partner violence is discussed in international reports on the problem. For example, the World Health Organization (2002) cites low income as a significant risk factor for intimate partner violence, indicating that conflicts over money and other resources between intimate partners could precipitate violence, as could the sense of hopelessness that derives from living in poverty. However, differences in countries' economic infrastructures as well as their social welfare programs and how they measure various economic indicators make comparisons between the U.S. and other countries in terms of the economic distress–domestic violence relationship difficult, at best.

Second, terms such as *social class*, *socioeconomic status*, and *financial status* are used interchangeably in this chapter to refer to individuals' financial standing as determined by their income and other assets (i.e., their wealth). Sociologists, though, often distinguish between class and status, using *class* strictly as an economic or financial indicator and *status* as an indicator of prestige or how others perceive an individual or group in terms of respect and deference.

Third, the chapter focuses almost exclusively on the relationship between economic distress and intimate partner violence, to a large extent because most of the research on sexual assault and other forms of violence against women has not examined economic issues as extensively as the intimate partner violence research has (for an exception, see Miller, 2008). Many studies of sexual assault, for example, use college samples in which white and middle-class women and men are overrepresented.

Finally, it is important to consider the intersecting variables of race and ethnicity when examining economic distress and domestic violence.

Many studies published since the 1980s have reported higher rates of intimate partner violence among African American couples than white couples (Greenfeld et al., 1998; Hampton & Gelles, 1994; Sorenson, Upchurch, & Shen, 1996; Straus, Gelles, & Steinmetz, 1980; Tjaden & Thoennes, 1998). However, because African Americans are disproportionately represented among the financially disadvantaged and people living in poverty, it may be that social class has a greater effect on intimate partner violence risk than race does. Studies that compare the intimate partner violence rates of African Americans and whites with similar incomes have produced inconsistent findings. In one study, for instance, African Americans and whites with high incomes had similar rates of intimate partner violence, but African Americans with moderate and low incomes had rates of intimate partner violence that were significantly higher than whites in the same income categories (Benson & Fox, 2004). Rennison and Planty (2003), however, found that the effect of race on intimate partner violence rates disappears when annual household income is held constant.

Similar inconsistencies emerge in studies that include Hispanic and Asian American couples (Field & Caetano, 2003; Grossman & Lundy, 2007). The inconsistencies in the research are the result of differences in samples and methods across studies, but they also likely reflect the diversity among Hispanic and Asian American groups. One group for which consistent findings have been obtained is Native Americans. Studies of Native American women show that they have the highest rates of intimate partner violence and sexual assault victimization of any racial or ethnic group of women (Luna-Firebaugh, 2006).

Intimate partner violence among interracial couples is also understudied to date. Hattery (2009) explores the issue in a secondary analysis of data from the National Violence Against Women Survey (NVAWS). She reports low rates of intimate partner violence among heterosexual couples in which the male partner is white and the female partner is black, but relatively high rates of intimate partner violence among couples in which the male partner is black and the female partner is white. Unfortunately, she does not control for the potential intervening effects of social class. Considerably more research is needed, therefore, that disentangles the effects of social class from those of race and ethnicity on intimate partner violence perpetration and victimization.

Financial Strain and Intimate Partner Violence

It is often said that intimate partner violence knows no class boundaries; that is, women in all social classes may be victimized. It is also the case that couples with adequate or substantial financial resources may be better able than those with low income or who are poor to hide their problems from friends, relatives, and neighbors as well as public agencies. Nevertheless, a large body of research documents that intimate partner violence rates are higher among women with fewer economic resources. For example, analyses of data from the redesigned National Crime Victimization Survey (NCVS) found that households in the lowest annual income category had an intimate partner violence rate five times greater than that of households in the highest income category (Greenfeld et al., 1998). And although women who are poor have an elevated risk of intimate partner violence victimization, the data also indicate that it is the poorest among women living in poverty who experience the highest rate of intimate partner violence victimization.

For instance, Lloyd (1997) surveyed 824 economically disadvantaged women living in a single neighborhood in Chicago. She divided the sample into groups, from lowest to highest annual income. She found that although women in all the income categories had high rates of intimate partner violence victimization, women in the lowest annual income group had a rate of severe intimate partner violence victimization three times greater than women in the higher annual income groups. Lloyd's findings are further supported by studies of women receiving welfare benefits. It is estimated that between 8.5% and 41.4% of women receiving welfare are victimized by intimate partner violence in a given year (Tolman, 1999). To put these estimates into perspective, consider that data from the NVAWS indicate that in the general U.S. population, about 1.5% of women experience physical intimate partner violence each year (Tjaden & Thoennes, 1998).

Other studies of women living in poverty have found even higher *lifetime* rates of intimate partner violence victimization. The Worcester Family Research Project (WFRP), a longitudinal study of 216 low-income–housed single mothers and 220 homeless single mothers conducted from 1992 to 1996, found that nearly 33% of the women had experienced severe physical violence by a current or most recent partner, including death threats (about 20%). However, 60% reported physical violence inflicted by at least one male intimate partner during adulthood (Browne, Salomon, & Bassuk, 1999).[2]

Some researchers argue that intimate partner violence perpetrated by low-income men is an expression of the stress and frustration induced by financial strain. Benson and Fox (2004) found, for instance, that among couples who report subjective feelings of strong financial strain, the intimate

[2]The women participating in the WFRP also reported high rates of violent victimization during childhood: 63% had experienced severe physical violence by a parent or caregiver during childhood and 40% had been sexually molested as children. Only 16% of the women, in fact, had not been physically or sexually assaulted during their lifetime. Given that the average age of the study sample—which included non-Hispanic white, African American, and Hispanic women—was only 27, the victimization rates reported are alarming. According to the researchers who conducted the study, most of the women, regardless of their housing circumstances, had enjoyed only brief periods of safety during their life (Browne et al., 1999; see also Miller, 2008).

partner violence rate is 9.5%, whereas it is 2.7% among couples who report subjective feelings of weak or low financial strain. Additional research, however, indicates that the relationship between economic hardship and intimate partner violence may be less direct and is mediated by other factors, including gender ideologies and ecological contexts. In addition, there is evidence that the relationship between economic hardship and intimate partner violence may be *reciprocal;* that is, although economic stress and hardship may increase the risk of intimate partner violence, victimization may lead women into and entrap them in poverty as well as the abusive intimate relationship. In fact, researchers have coined the term *economic abuse* to capture the various abuse tactics some men use to weaken or destroy their partners' financial solvency and sometimes lead to their impoverishment. Examples of economic abuse include purposely ruining the woman's credit rating; incurring large debts without her knowledge, but for which she may be held responsible; and taking money, credit cards, or other property without her knowledge (Allstate Foundation, 2009).

Despite the serious financial consequences of economic abuse for victims, there is little awareness of the problem among the general public. For instance, a national telephone survey of 708 American households conducted by the Allstate Foundation (2009) revealed that 8 out of 10 respondents associated the term *economic abuse* with negative Wall Street financial forecasts or irresponsible spending, rather than domestic violence.

Economic abuse also occurs when a batterer forces an employed woman to turn over her paychecks to him. This raises the issue of the relationship between employment and intimate partner violence, a topic to which I turn next.

What Roles Do Employment and Unemployment Play?

In considering the relationship between employment status and intimate partner violence, it is necessary not only to examine the potential effect of one partner's employment status individually, but also each partner's employment status in relation to the other. To understand this better, I'll begin by discussing the research on women's employment status and then examine studies that have analyzed women's employment status relative to the employment status of their male partners.

Studies on the relationship between women's employment status and intimate partner violence victimization indicate that women with a history of intimate partner violence victimization are as likely as women without such a history to want to work and to be currently employed (Lloyd & Taluc, 1999; Riger & Staggs, 2004). However, intimate partner violence victimization appears to negatively affect women's employment in a number of significant ways. Specifically, compared to women who have not experienced intimate partner violence, women who have experienced intimate partner violence report more days arriving late for work, more absenteeism, more psychological and physical health problems that may reduce their productivity, and greater difficulty sustaining employment over time (Leone, Johnson, Cohan, & Lloyd, 2004; Logan, Shannon, Cole, & Swanberg, 2007; Meisel, Chandler, & Rienzi, 2003; Reeves & O'Leary-Kelly, 2007).[3] The presence and intensity of these difficulties depend, to some extent, on the recency and severity of the intimate partner violence experiences (Lyon, 2002).

Intimate partner violence, then, may disrupt women's employment. At the same time, batterers

---

[3]Several researchers have noted that these employment difficulties are even worse for women with disabilities who have experienced intimate partner violence. For instance, women with disabilities and a history of intimate partner violence victimization are less likely to be employed than both women with disabilities who have no history of intimate partner violence victimization and women without disabilities who do have a history of intimate partner violence victimization (Powers, Hughes, & Lund, 2009; Smith & Hilton, 2008; Smith & Strauser, 2008).

often deliberately try to sabotage their partners' efforts to obtain and maintain paid employment. For example, researchers have documented a variety of disruptive tactics that batterers use, including damaging or destroying women's work clothes or books and other items needed for job training, inflicting visible cuts and bruises to keep women from going to work, promising to babysit but suddenly becoming unavailable to do so, and calling the women repeatedly while they are at work or showing up at the workplace and creating disturbances (Brush, 2003; Logan et al., 2007; Moe & Bell, 2004; Raphael, 2000). Similarly, employed women with disabilities may find the battery removed from an electric wheelchair or their telecommunication device missing or broken, or their abusers may refuse to help them with their daily routines and grooming so they can get ready for work (Smith & Hilton, 2008). Employed women who experience intimate partner violence, especially stalking at work, may lose their jobs as a result, or they may give them up in order to feel safer. In each case, however, the job loss will likely decrease their financial stability and could result in impoverishment for some women (Moe & Bell, 2004; Staggs, Long, Mason, Krishnan, & Riger, 2007).

Unfortunately, most studies of batterers' interference in their partners' employment have used samples of low-income women. As Kwesiga, Bell, Pattie, and Moe (2007) point out, however, research is needed that examines how intimate partner violence victimization affects middle-income women as well as those who hold prestigious or high-paying jobs. On one hand, such jobs afford employees more benefits, such as medical leave, paid vacation, and greater autonomy on the job, which could be helpful when coping with or leaving an abusive relationship. On the other hand, Kwesiga et al. hypothesize that the pressures of such jobs, along with the organizational culture of many professional workplaces (e.g., the expectation that a committed professional does not take time off work for personal problems), may inhibit women experiencing intimate partner violence from using

these benefits. This is certainly a topic worthy of further study.

Recent research points to interesting racial differences in the way abusive men try to control their partners' employment. Hattery (2009) reports that although both white and African American men in her study attempted to control their female partners' employment, white men did so to keep their partners out of the labor force altogether, whereas African American men sought to control where their partners worked, their interactions and relationships with coworkers, and how their earnings were spent. Hattery explains these differences in terms of the intersection of racial and gender inequality in the United States. A measure of a white man's masculinity is how well he can provide for his family, and an indication of his success as a breadwinner is a stay-at-home wife. In contrast, racial discrimination that has resulted in a disproportionate percentage of African Americans living in poverty and suffering higher rates of unemployment regardless of the economic health of the country has meant that many African American women have had to work out of financial necessity. Racial discrimination in the job market has resulted in a concentration of African American men and women in low-wage jobs, forcing them to pool their income for their families' financial survival. And the "war on crime," which has resulted in an unprecedented incarceration rate for African American men, has made many African American women the sole breadwinners for their families, even after men are released from prison, because a criminal record makes stable and adequately paying employment difficult to come by.

Hattery's (2009) analysis raises the possibility that it is not women's employment status per se that may precipitate or aggravate intimate partner violence, but rather their employment status relative to that of their male partners. A considerable body of research indicates that *status incompatibility* between the partners—more specifically, the woman is employed and her male partner is not, or her job has higher income or prestige than his—significantly increases the likelihood of intimate partner violence (Benson & Fox, 2004; Kaukinen, 2004; Lambert & Firestone, 2000). An important intervening variable is the gender ideology to which men adhere. Men who subscribe to traditional gender norms (e.g., masculine men are the family breadwinners and are dominant and superior to women; feminine women are dependent on men) are more likely to feel threatened by women's employment, especially if they are unemployed or underemployed themselves and, therefore, may be more likely to use violence and coercive control to assert dominance in the relationship (Anderson, 2009; Atkinson, Greenstein, & Lang, 2005; MacMillan & Gartner, 1999).

In one study of a sample of low-income African American women, for instance, the researchers found that the greater the women's economic power relative to the men, the more likely the men were to abuse them (Raj, Silverman, Wingood, & DiClemente, 1999). Similarly, in their study of 20 immigrant Mexican women and men thought to be involved in abusive relationships, Grzywacz, Rao, Gentry, Marin, and Arcury (2009) learned that women's employment increased conflict in intimate relationships because it usurped traditional gender norms that prescribe the division of household labor, financial decision making, and women's and men's interactions with one another.[4]

Women's employment, then, may shift the balance of power in the intimate relationship, which to some men is a zero-sum game (i.e., her gain is his loss), thereby precipitating intimate partner violence. The issue is even more salient during the current recession because although the percentage of women in the labor force has not changed significantly, more men than women have lost their jobs. More than 80% of the jobs lost have been lost by men, and economists predict that if this trend continues, women will surpass men in the labor force for the first time in history (Rempell, 2009). This shift will likely alter traditional gender roles in families— a change that some may applaud but that may also generate conflict and increase the risk of intimate partner violence.

Employment, though, may also have a protective effect for some women, not least because it may increase their independence. Employment may raise a woman's self-esteem and provide her not only with financial resources but with psychological resources to cope with or end an abusive relationship (Brush, 2003). Employment may also provide women with an alternative social network. Studies indicate that abused women who are employed and who receive social and tangible support from coworkers and supervisors feel less socially isolated, report improved health, and experience fewer negative employment outcomes (Staggs et al., 2007). These findings point to the importance of social networks, which I will consider shortly along with community and neighborhood context. First, however, I will briefly discuss physical and mental health issues, which affect and are affected by both financial stability and intimate partner violence experiences.

Physical and Mental Health Issues

Several contributors to this book discuss the physical and mental health consequences of

---

[4]Though not about intimate partner violence, Cha and Thebaud's (2009) analysis of how economic conditions and labor market characteristics influence men's gender ideologies also has relevance to this discussion. Cha and Thebaud found that in countries with flexible labor markets, men have less difficulty if they find themselves financially dependent on their female partners because they see the situation as temporary. They can afford, therefore, to be more egalitarian. In contrast, in rigid labor markets, men experience less fluctuation in their employment status, and they tend to be less egalitarian with regard to their views of the breadwinner role.

intimate partner violence and sexual assault for women who are victimized (see Chapters 5, 6, and 15). Other researchers have demonstrated a link between economic disadvantage and health problems (Dunn & Hayes, 2000; Stonks, Van de Mheen, & Mackenbach, 1998). Women who are poor face a number of factors that elevate their risk of illness, including living in substandard housing, greater exposure to communicable diseases, higher exposure to environmental toxins, and various stressors caused by poverty (Sutherland, Sullivan, & Bybee, 2001). Women who live in poverty also do not have the financial resources or insurance that would enable them to obtain health care, or they are forced to postpone treatment until their condition becomes severe. And ill health itself interferes with employment, presenting an additional barrier to financial stability and jobs that offer health insurance benefits.

One question that arises, however, is the extent to which intimate partner violence relative to poverty contributes to women's health problems. Sutherland et al. (2001) found in their research that regardless of income, abused women report more physical health symptoms than nonabused women. Women's experiences of intimate partner violence significantly affect their health, independent of income. In other words, when they held income constant, Sutherland et al. still found significant differences in physical health between abused and nonabused women. Nevertheless, abuse appears to compound the health problems of women who are poor, given that in the Sutherland et al. study, abused women with lower incomes had significantly more health problems than abused women with higher incomes (see also Romero, Chavkin, Wise, & Smith, 2003). Unfortunately, although there is a sizable literature linking mental health symptoms, such as depression, to both violent victimization and poverty (e.g., Afifi, MacMillan, Cox, Asmundson, Stein, & Sareen, 2009; Plichta, 1996; Stonks et al., 1998; Williams & Mickelson, 2004), more research is needed to tease out the relative contributions of each of these contributing factors for abused women across social classes.

Ecological Context: The Importance of Neighborhoods and Social Networks

As I noted at the outset of this chapter, living in an economically disadvantaged neighborhood is a major risk factor for violent victimization (U.S. Department of Justice, National Institute of Justice, 2009a). Studies show that neighborhoods with a high concentration of poverty and high male unemployment rates have higher rates of intimate partner violence, sexual assault, and other violent crime than more affluent neighborhoods (Benson, Fox, DeMaris, & Van Wyk, 2003; DeKeseredy, Alvi, Schwartz, & Tomaszewski, 2003; Miles-Doan, 1998; Raghavan, Mennerich, Sexton, & James, 2006). Researchers have examined several factors associated with economically disadvantaged neighborhoods that might contribute to this elevated risk. For instance, Sampson, Raudenbush, and Earls (1997) argue that economically distressed neighborhoods are characterized by high social disorder and low collective efficacy. By social disorder they mean various social incivilities, such as public intoxication, drug dealing, and street prostitution, that frequently occur in public in the neighborhood. Social disorder tends to be accompanied by other types of crime, including violence (e.g., muggings, gang fights, assaults, homicides). They maintain that although social disorder may occur in any neighborhood, it is more likely to occur in impoverished neighborhoods because residents lack institutional, political, and economic resources. Consequently, residents feel socially isolated from and mistrust their neighbors; they lack collective efficacy (i.e., mutual trust and a willingness to intervene on behalf of the common good).

Other research, however, calls into question the effect of collective efficacy on women's violent victimization by intimates and peers. For example, in interviews with female residents of Philadelphia public housing developments, Renzetti (2003) found that although collective efficacy was relatively strong, it was unrelated to intimate partner violence. Most of the women in this study said they could count on their neighbors to look after their children or to call the police if a suspicious person was hanging around the building or rowdy teenagers were causing trouble—all standard indicators of collective efficacy. Nevertheless, few women thought residents would call the police if a neighbor was being abused by her husband or boyfriend. Thus, intimate partner violence, unlike rowdy teenagers or a suspicious loiterer, may still be viewed as a "private" problem and intervention as "nosing into other people's business."

Browning's (2002) research supports this hypothesis. He found that high collective efficacy reduces intimate partner violence if it occurs in the context of community norms that support intervention into intimate relationships (see also Fox, Benson, Van Wyk, & DeMaris, 1999). Similarly, Miller (2008) found in her study of an impoverished neighborhood in St. Louis that residents were reluctant to intervene in incidents of intimate partner violence even when they occurred in public. In fact, she describes instances in which bystanders appeared to find the abuse entertaining and amusing. And other researchers have identified a downside to high collective efficacy when it comes to intervening in incidents of violence against women. Specifically, some people intervene on behalf of perpetrators who are their friends, thereby protecting the abuser rather than the abused woman (Ames & Dunham, 2002; Renzetti & Maier, 2002; Websdale, 1998).

Miller's (2008) research in St. Louis also indicates that residents' experiences of their neighborhood and its effects on their behavior are gendered. Miller reports that public space in the community was typically "male space." Even though the young men in her study were aware of potential dangers in their neighborhoods and

were sometimes victimized, they were nevertheless active in neighborhood activities and social networks. The young women Miller talked to, on the other hand, regulated their outdoor neighborhood activities, remaining indoors more, especially at night. When they went out, they did so in groups or accompanied by young men. This was their primary strategy for staying safe in their neighborhoods, but Miller's research indicates that it was often unsuccessful because they were typically victimized, especially sexually victimized, by men they knew (see also Renzetti & Maier, 2002).

Miller's (2008) findings lend support to other studies that have examined the intersection of community context and gender norms in explaining the high incidence of intimate partner violence and sexual violence in economically distressed neighborhoods. This body of work is grounded in the assumption that the social structural—including the neighborhood—context in which people live helps shape their values and norms, including gender norms. Echoing Hattery's (2009) research that I discussed earlier, these researchers maintain that economically disenfranchised men—men who are unemployed or underemployed—"may experience high levels of stress because they are unable to attain the status typically associated with masculine success validated by the patriarchal system" through the traditional breadwinner role (Raghavan et al., 2006, p. 1135). But they can assert dominance through violence—against one another, against those who disrespect or cross them, *and against women*. With a great deal of free time on their hands, these men spend time together in male peer support networks that collectively devalue women and regard them as legitimate victims who deserve physical and sexual abuse (Anderson, 1990; Benson, Wooldredge, Thistlethwaite, & Fox, 2004; Bourgois, 1999; DeKeseredy et al., 2003; see also Chapter 1).

Thus, sexual conquest and asserting social and physical control over women is a source of power and a measure of success for powerless men who are unsuccessful by the traditional measures of white, middle-class culture. One problem with this argument, however, is that there is also considerable research showing that similar attitudes and behaviors are common among some more privileged groups of men, including members of college fraternities and athletic teams (see, e.g., Sanday, 2007). Such findings call into question the notion that male peer support networks that endorse or encourage violence against women are restricted to financially disadvantaged men and economically distressed neighborhoods.

In addition to the role men's social support networks may play in the perpetration of violence against women, researchers have also examined how women's social support networks may influence their likelihood of violent victimization as well as their options or coping strategies if they are victimized. I have already noted that support from coworkers and employers may have a protective effect for abused women. For most women, though, social support networks are made up of family members and friends. Researchers have found that if these social supports are tenuous, women may be more likely to enter into or remain in insecure, unsafe, or harmful situations, including abusive intimate relationships. Studies of women living in poverty, in particular, have shown that when their social support networks are weak, or members of those networks are themselves involved in harmful behaviors or relationships, the women are more likely to be—and remain in—an abusive relationship (James, Johnson, & Raghavan, 2004; Rosen, 2004). Raghavan and her colleagues (2006) emphasize the importance of women's "cognitive landscapes" in this regard. In their research with women living in poverty, Raghavan et al. found that intimate partner violence victimization *among members of the women's social networks* was widespread and that this factor increased the women's own likelihood of being intimate partner violence victims. The researchers hypothesize that when intimate partner violence is a common feature of friends' and relatives' lives, it becomes

incorporated into the women's cognitive landscape and is normalized. In other words, intimate partner violence becomes viewed as a normal part of male-female relationships, even as an expression of love or caring and, as a result, women who are victimized may excuse their abusers, see their own behavior as a cause of the abuse, and try to preserve their relationship with the abuser.

Additional research has considered how women's social networks interact with the level of collective efficacy in their immediate environments to promote or restrict help seeking when abuse occurs. Recall from my earlier discussion that collective efficacy refers to one's trust in others in one's environment and one's confidence that these others will intervene or help in a crisis. For instance, in a study of the violent victimization experiences of women living in public housing developments in Camden, NJ, Renzetti and Maier (2002) found the women's social networks to be weak and the level of collective efficacy low. Most women mistrusted those in their immediate environment and said they could not count on them for help for various reasons, including the fact that they perceived these people to be a *source* of problems for them, or they didn't think their neighbors would want to get involved, or they didn't want their neighbors in their "business." Some women reported that in an emergency they could turn to a relative, a clergyperson, or a caseworker, but many women simply said they had no one to rely on but themselves. Still, as I noted previously, even when collective efficacy is high, intervention may not be forthcoming if the problem is intimate partner violence. Moreover, there is no reason to believe that intervention into an intimate partner violence incident would be more forthcoming in more affluent communities, where such behavior is easier to hide, neighbors are often anonymous, and individuals would be risking their reputations were the problem to become known, even among relatives and close friends.

Financial constraints on social support network members, however, may play a role in entrapping women in abusive relationships or worsening their financial circumstances, even when members of these networks want to intervene or are concerned about the women's safety. The majority of intimate partner violence victims state that although they appreciate emotional support from friends and relatives, what they need most is tangible assistance, such as money, housing, food, and transportation (Postmus, Severson, Berry, & Yoo, 2009). The downturn in the economy in recent years has thrown many people, including the relatives and friends of intimate partner violence victims, into financial distress, thereby limiting their ability to provide tangible assistance when it is needed.

Consider housing, for example. Between 25% and 50% of intimate partner violence victims experience housing-related problems when trying to end an abusive relationship (Baker, Cook, & Norris, 2003). Women who must leave their homes to separate from an abuser usually move in with family or friends, at least initially. If their relatives and friends cannot take them in, they may go instead to a battered women's shelter or a homeless shelter. Nearly 20% of intimate partner violence victims, in fact, use a combination of informal (family/friends) and formal (battered women's/homeless shelters) sources of housing assistance when separating from an abuser (Baker et al., 2003). Nevertheless, more than one-third of intimate partner violence victims become homeless as a result of leaving an abusive partner (Baker et al., 2003). With the upsurge in home foreclosures and the growth in unemployment and financial distress, this percentage could increase because fewer intimate partner violence victims can afford housing on their own, and fewer of their relatives and friends can afford to offer them housing assistance. At the same time, battered women's shelters, homeless shelters, and other service providers for intimate partner violence victims are experiencing budget cuts, even though the need for these services appears to be growing.[5]

Can Public Assistance Help?

Most women living in poverty, whether they have experienced intimate partner violence or not, recognize the potential benefits of employment, and it is not surprising that most want to work. It bears repeating that although employment may have a protective effect for some abused women, it may spark an escalation in abuse for others. It is also important to keep in mind that employment is no panacea for women's impoverishment if the jobs they obtain pay minimum or low wages and offer few or no benefits, such as health insurance, while the women incur expenses for transportation to and from their jobs and risk earning just enough money to lose Medicaid and child care benefits.

If women cannot find work, or they are unable to maintain a steady job, they may apply for public financial assistance, commonly called welfare. In 1996, President Bill Clinton signed into law the Personal Responsibility and Work Opportunity Reconciliation Act (PRWORA), which became known as "welfare reform." The former means-tested federal entitlement program, Aid to Families with Dependent Children (AFDC), was replaced with Temporary Assistance to Needy Families (TANF). Certainly few would claim that the AFDC program was generous, but the enactment of TANF imposed more stringent eligibility requirements and benefit restrictions. For instance, TANF established time limits on aid receipt and reduced the cap on the total amount

---

[5]In July, 2009, Governor Arnold Schwarzenegger, in an attempt to reduce California's large budget deficit, eliminated *all* financing for the state's domestic violence program, which forced the closure of several battered women's shelters there. More California shelters are expected to close, given that state financing for most accounted for over 40% of their total budgets. Other states, though not choosing to balance their budgets by totally withdrawing funds for services to battered women and their children, have nonetheless had to reduce their level of funding (McKinley, 2009).

of assistance a family may receive. Lifetime receipt of aid is limited to five years, although states may reduce this time period further or, conversely, extend it under special circumstances. TANF also has employment requirements for nearly all beneficiaries, although states are permitted to establish their own employment expectations. This has resulted in some states requiring even new mothers to participate in work-related activities as soon as their child is three months old (Cancian & Danziger, 2009). States must also try to establish the paternity of dependent children and enforce child support orders because child support is viewed as an important additional source of income for TANF beneficiaries. TANF applicants who are single parents are required to cooperate with child support agencies by helping them establish paternity, locate an absent parent, and obtain a child support order. But women in abusive intimate relationships may be endangered by such requirements because they necessarily alert abusers to the women's location and also risk angering abusers with child support orders (Casey, Fata, Orloff, & Raghu, 2009; Pearson, Griswold, & Thoennes, 2001).

Some observers argue that the true objective of the PRWORA was to reduce the number of people receiving public cash assistance and not to reduce the number of people living in poverty (Riger & Staggs, 2004). However, the federal government has maintained that the primary goal of the law was to move people from welfare dependency to financial self-sufficiency through employment. And available data do show that following enactment of the PRWORA, state welfare rolls declined dramatically, while more women living in poverty, most of whom were single mothers, went to work (Riger & Staggs, 2004). Still, it is also the case, as I have already discussed, that women in abusive relationships face particular barriers to employment, and in recognition of this fact, Congress included the Family Violence Option (FVO) in the PRWORA. The FVO is intended to safeguard against women being unfairly denied public financial assistance because intimate

partner violence victimization prevents them from being able to meet all the TANF requirements. If a state chooses to adopt the FVO—and most states have adopted it—then it may temporarily waive or exempt TANF requirements for women who disclose intimate partner violence, and it may also refer these women to battered women's services.

The FVO appears to have met with limited success. Few women, it appears, disclose intimate partner violence to their TANF caseworkers, request an FVO waiver or exemption, or use the intimate partner violence services. Of the estimated 20%–30% of TANF applicants who are eligible for the FVO, only about 0.5%–3% utilize it (Lindhorst, Meyers, & Casey, 2008; Pearson et al., 2001). This underutilization is due, at least in part, to the failure of TANF caseworkers to adequately and sensitively screen applicants for intimate partner violence (Busch & Wolfer, 2002; Lein, Jacquet, Lewis, Cole, & Williams, 2001; Lindhorst et al., 2008). However, the underutilization also reflects, to some extent, the sentiments of many abused women, who do not see the waivers as the best way to meet their most urgent needs (Lein et al., 2001; Renzetti, 2003; Riger & Staggs, 2004). Certainly, the waivers are appreciated by the women who have received them; they report that the FVO "met a vital safety need," gave them extra time to reconstruct their lives following abuse, and prevented them from losing essential TANF benefits if their abusers interfered with job training or work (Lein et al., 2001; Riger & Staggs, 2004). However, abused women living in poverty often say that the abuse is not the most serious problem with which they have to contend. Their overriding concerns stem from the daily challenges of poverty, including finding work that pays a wage adequate to support themselves and their children; access to safe, reliable, and affordable child care; safe and reliable transportation; and safe and affordable housing (Renzetti, 2003). To conclude this chapter, then, let's consider possible strategies for better addressing the needs of battered women who are poor and of women who experience financial hardship as a result of abuse.

Breaking the Relationship Between Intimate Partner Violence and Economic Distress

While economists debate the prospects for a national financial recovery in the United States, individuals continue to experience unemployment, home foreclosure, and other forms of economic distress. Poverty rates and rates of violence against women appear to be rising. As I have discussed in this chapter, there appears to be a reciprocal relationship between financial hardship and violence against women, and although both problems stubbornly persist, we do have the means to address them. The policies and programs I will examine here are certainly not the only solutions, but research suggests that they can help address both poverty and violence against women.

Some policy analysts and criminologists argue that no program will be effective if it does not address community or neighborhood context because, as I have discussed, the environments in which people live produce behavioral norms or "cognitive landscapes" that influence social interaction. Consequently, an influx of resources for programs to reverse the deterioration of disadvantaged communities and neighborhoods, both urban and rural, is necessary. Studies show that making communities and neighborhoods more livable and stable for residents by, for example, improving municipal services, enforcing building codes, renovating housing, and investing in businesses that provide jobs as well as products and services lowers crime and raises collective efficacy (Sampson & Lauritsen, 1994). As noted earlier, the assumption here is that if residents trust each other and are willing to look out for one another's welfare, then communities become safer places for residents. However, given the research I have reviewed indicating that intimate partner violence and other forms of violence

against women perpetrated by men they know may be seen as "personal" or "private" affairs, educational efforts must also be undertaken to promote norms for intervention when violent incidents occur.

Even if collective efficacy is high, community members cannot—and should not—be expected to handle violent incidents on their own. In addition to trusting one another, residents must also be able to trust authority figures, such as the police. In economically distressed neighborhoods and communities, in particular, trust and confidence in the police as well as social service agencies are typically weak, with "authorities" being seen as unresponsive, and worse, as overly responsive, harassing and sometimes brutalizing residents. Yet, most residents of disadvantaged neighborhoods report that they would like to see better law enforcement and greater police protection (Carr, Keating, & Napolitano, 2005; Miller, 2008; Renzetti & Maier, 2002). Thus, in order to reduce all forms of crime, including violent crimes against women, community policing and police-community relations must be improved to the point that residents perceive that they are treated fairly and respectfully and that the police are a protective presence in their community.

In addition to improving ecological contexts, policies and programs are needed to reduce poverty. Welfare reform was enacted when the economy was robust and jobs were growing, not shrinking as they are today. Few observers expect the government to relinquish its commitment to addressing poverty through employment and reinstate means-tested financial assistance (Cancian & Danziger, 2009; Casey et al., 2009; DeParle, 2009; Riger & Staggs, 2004). Consequently, policy analysts argue that if work is to be a requirement for assistance, then the government must "make work pay." That is, the government must ensure that work opportunities are available for those who have difficulty obtaining and maintaining work (e.g., those with physical and mental health problems, which would include some battered women), enact regulations that provide adequate minimum wages to support a family, and provide benefits for low-wage workers (e.g., subsidized child care) that help them sustain employment (Cancian & Danziger, 2009).

Programs specifically designed to help women become financially stable and independent would benefit all women living in poverty, with or without a history of abuse. But such programs would also help abused women avoid falling into poverty. Christy-McMullin (2000) suggests, for example, that the federal Assets for Independence Act of 1998 (AFIA) should be amended so that it specifically includes abused women. She correctly points out that economic security and independence derive not only from income, which for the vast majority of people living in poverty is depleted completely every month, but also from asset accumulation. The AFIA funds Individual Development Accounts (IDAs) for individuals and families, using money they deposit matched with government contributions. The AFIA, then, provides low-income individuals and families with structured assistance to accumulate savings, similar to the savings incentives that middle-class and wealthier individuals and families enjoy (e.g., tax deferments, Keogh plans). IDA savings may be used for first-time home purchases, small business capitalization, and post-secondary education, but it may also be transferred to eligible family members, such as spouses and children. This transferability could pose a problem for abused women, and Christy-McMullin (2000) recognizes that in its current form, the AFIA is not ideal for women in abusive relationships. Nevertheless, she maintains that the law could be amended to explicitly respond to battered women's financial needs, and she proposes that Congress "mandate states to direct a significant portion of the funds that are being 'saved' from the decreased number of TANF recipients back to abused women via matched government contributions into Individual Development Accounts (IDAs)" (p. 1068).

An amended AFIA would no doubt be beneficial to at least some battered women, but, as I have noted, employment is likely to remain the primary source of income for most women. A number of programs already exist to assist women, including women who have been abused, in improving their employability and achieving self-sufficiency. Most are offered by nonprofit organizations, such as Wider Opportunities for Women (WOW), which provides job training, career development, assistance with the welfare-to-work transition, and advice on retirement security (see http://www.wowonline.org). Similarly, the Allstate Foundation, in collaboration with the National Network to End Domestic Violence, offers the Economic Empowerment Curriculum to help women evaluate their present financial situation and develop short- and long-term financial planning skills (see http://www.Click ToEmpower.org).

The workplace itself must be made safe for women. Employment, we have seen, can be both a risk for and a protection against violence for women. Abusers may stalk and harass their victims at work, and some abusers have assaulted and killed their victims in the workplace. Despite the threat posed to all workers' safety as well as the significant financial costs incurred by intimate partner violence,[6] employers have been slow to recognize the seriousness of the problem and respond accordingly. In fact, some male intimate partner violence perpetrators have told researchers that they have received support from their employers who, for instance, have posted bond for them or testified for them in court (Rothman & Corso, 2008). Consequently, education of employers is critical; they must be made aware of the dangers of supporting abusers and also the steps they can take to increase their female employees' safety while simultaneously helping them maintain their jobs and preserve their financial stability.

---

[6]Researchers estimate that intimate partner violence-related injuries to women cost about $5 billion annually in terms of medical expenses and lost productivity, and about 50% of this cost is incurred by the private sector in the form of health insurance and sick leave benefits (Reeves & O'Leary-Kelly, 2007; Rothman & Corso, 2008).

Employers may be surprised to know that there are several relatively easy things they can do to make their workplaces safer and, therefore, more productive. For example, at the very least, when employers learn that an employee has been arrested for abuse, they should reprimand that employee and encourage or even require completion of a batterer intervention program. Employers who learn that an employee is being victimized should offer emotional support, but they may also offer that employee paid leave or a job transfer to another worksite, perhaps in a different state, if necessary. Moe and Bell (2004) cite as an example the case of a female employee whose abusive partner took her computer, which was necessary for her work. Had her employer simply provided her with another computer, she could have retained her job. Formal and informal outreach by employers helps victimized employees by maintaining a primary source of their income and increasing their safety and security. At the same time, such efforts benefit employers because they retain knowledgeable employees and also generate loyalty and raise morale among employees generally (Moe & Bell, 2004).

Services for women who have been victimized by violence are discussed in detail in other chapters of this book (see Chapters 12 to 16). However, it is important to reiterate here that the current economic downturn is severely impacting already reduced municipal, state, and federal budgets for social programs while the need for funding and services is simultaneously increasing. Therefore, service providers who specialize in various areas (e.g., domestic violence, sexual assault, welfare, health care, housing, legal advocacy) must overcome the commonly held notion that they are in competition with one another for scarce resources to remedy discrete social problems and instead develop truly collaborative partnerships to address the interconnections among these problems. As I have learned from years of listening to women who have been victimized by violence, interventions must not only offer emotional support but also assist women to identify and secure the *tangible* services they most need and want. In the final analysis, it is the wishes of survivors that must be paramount.

References

Afifi, T. O., MacMillan, H., Cox, B. J., Asmundson, G. J. G., Stein, M. B., & Sareen, J. (2009). Mental health correlates of intimate partner violence in marital relationships in a nationally representative sample of males and females. *Journal of Interpersonal Violence, 24*, 1398–1417.

Allstate Foundation. (2009). *Crisis: Economic and domestic violence.* Retrieved July 1, 2009, from http://www.ClickToEmpower.org.

Ames, A. J., & Dunham, K. T. (2002). Asymptotic justice: Probation as a criminal justice response to intimate partner violence. *Violence Against Women, 8*, 6–34.

Anderson, E. (1990). *Streetwise: Race, class, and change in an urban community.* Chicago: University of Chicago Press.

Atkinson, M. P., Greenstein, T. N., & Lang, M. M. (2005). For women, breadwinning can be dangerous: Gendered resource theory and wife abuse. *Journal of Marriage and Family, 67*, 1137–1148.

Baker, C. K., Cook, S. L., & Norris, F. H. (2003). Domestic violence and housing problems: A contextual analysis of women's help-seeking, received informal support, and formal system response. *Violence Against Women, 9*, 754–783.

Benson, M. L., & Fox, G. L. (2004). *When violence hits home: How economics and neighborhood play a role.* Washington, DC: U.S. Department of Justice, National Institute of Justice.

Benson, M. L., Fox, G. L., DeMaris, A., & Van Wyk, J. (2003). Neighborhood disadvantage, individual economic distress and violence against women in intimate relationships. *Journal of Quantitative Criminology, 19*, 207–235.

Benson, M. L., Wooldredge, J., Thistlethwaite, A. B., & Fox, G. L. (2004). The correlation between race and domestic violence is confounded with community context. *Social Problems, 51*, 326–342.

Bourgois, P. (1999). *In search of respect: Selling crack in El Barrio.* New York: Cambridge University Press.

Browne, A., Salomon, A., & Bassuk, S. S. (1999). The impact of recent partner violence on poor women's capacity to maintain work. *Violence Against Women, 5,* 393–426.

Browning, C. R. (2002). The span of collective efficacy: Extending social disorganization theory to partner violence. *Journal of Marriage and Family, 64,* 833–850.

Brush, L. D. (2003). Effects of work on hitting and hurting. *Violence Against Women, 9,* 1213–1230.

Busch, N. B., & Wolfer, T. A. (2002). Battered women speak out: Welfare reform and their decision to disclose. *Violence Against Women, 8,* 566–584.

Cancian, M., & Danziger, S. (2009, Fall). Changing poverty and changing antipoverty policies. *Focus, 26,* 1–5.

Carr, P. J., Keating, J., & Napolitano, L. (2005, November). *We never call the cops and here's why: A qualitative examination of legal cynicism in three Philadelphia neighborhoods.* Paper presented at the Annual Meeting of the American Society of Criminology, Toronto, Canada.

Casey, T., Fata, S., Orloff, L., & Raghu, M. (2009). TANF reauthorization round II: An opportunity to improve the safety net for women and children. *Domestic Violence Report, 6,* 65–66, 71–74, 80.

Cha, Y., & Thebaud, S. (2009). Labor markets, breadwinning, and beliefs: How economic context shapes men's gender ideology. *Gender & Society, 23,* 215–243.

Christy-McMullin, K. (2000). An analysis of the Assets for Independence Act of 1998 for abused women. *Violence Against Women, 6,* 1066–1084.

DeKeseredy, W. S., Alvi, S., Schwartz, M. D., & Tomaszewski, E. A. (2003). *Under siege: Poverty and crime in a public housing community.* Lanham, MD: Lexington Books.

DeParle, J. (2009, February 2). Welfare system failing to grow as economy lags. *New York Times,* pp. A1, A13.

Dethy, F. (2009, June 24). Recession brings rise in domestic abuse cases, need for services goes up as funds fall. *Toledo Blade,* Retrieved June 25, 2009, from http://www.toledoblade.com/apps/pbcs.dll/article?AID=/20090624/NEWS24/906240322

Dunn, J. R., & Hayes, M. V. (2000). Social inequality, population health, and housing: A study of two Vancouver neighborhoods. *Social Science and Medicine, 51,* 563–587.

Eckholm, E. (2009, September 11). Last year's poverty rate was highest in 12 years. *New York Times,* p. A12.

Field, C. A., & Caetano, R. (2003). Longitudinal model predicting partner violence among white, black, and Hispanic couples in the United States. *Alcoholism: Clinical and Experimental Research, 27,* 1451–1458.

Fox, G. L., Benson, M. L., Van Wyk, J., & DeMaris, A. (1999, November). *Economic distress, community context and trajectories of violence against women in intimate relationships.* Paper presented at the Annual Meeting of the American Society of Criminology, Toronto, Canada.

Greenfeld, L. A., Rand, M. R., Craven, D., Klaus, P. A., Perkins, C., & Warchol, G., et al. (1998). *Violence by intimates: Analysis of data on crimes by current or former spouses, boyfriends, and girlfriends.* Washington, DC: U.S. Department of Justice.

Grossman, S. F., & Lundy, M. (2007). Domestic violence across race and ethnicity: Implications for social work practice and policy. *Violence Against Women, 13,* 1029–1053.

Grzywacz, J. G., Rao, P., Gentry, A., Marin, A., & Arcury, T. A. (2009). Acculturation and conflict in Mexican immigrants' intimate partnerships: The role of women's labor force participation. *Violence Against Women, 15,* 1213–1226.

Hampton, R. L., & Gelles, R. J. (1994). Violence toward African American women in a nationally representative sample of African American families. *Journal of Comparative Family Studies, 25,* 105–119.

Hattery, A. J. (2009). *Intimate partner violence.* Lanham, MD: Rowman and Littlefield.

James, S., Johnson, J., & Raghavan, C. (2004). "I couldn't go anywhere": Contextualizing violence and drug abuse: A social network study. *Violence Against Women, 10,* 991–1014.

Kaukinen, C. (2004). Status compatibility, physical violence, and emotional abuse in intimate relationships. *Journal of Marriage and Family, 66,* 452–471.

Kwesiga, E., Bell, M. P., Pattie, M., & Moe, A. M. (2007). Exploring the literature on relationships between gender roles, intimate partner violence, occupational status, and organizational benefits. *Journal of Interpersonal Violence, 22,* 312–326.

Lambert, L. C., & Firestone, J. M. (2000). Economic context and multiple abuse techniques. *Violence Against Women, 6,* 49–67.

Lein, L., Jacquet, S. E., Lewis, C. M., Cole, P., & Williams, B. B. (2001). With the best intentions:

The Family Violence Option and abused women's needs. *Violence Against Women, 7,* 193–210.

Leone, J., Johnson, M., Cohan, C., & Lloyd, S. (2004). Consequences of male partner violence on low-income minority women. *Journal of Marriage and Family, 66,* 472–490.

Lindhorst, T., Meyers, M., & Casey, E. (2008). Screening for domestic violence in public welfare offices: An analysis of case manager and client interactions. *Violence Against Women, 14,* 5–28.

Lloyd, S. (1997). The effects of domestic violence on women's employment. *Law & Policy, 19,* 139–167.

Lloyd, S., & Taluc, N. (1999). The effects of male violence on female employment. *Violence Against Women, 5,* 370–392.

Logan, T. K., Shannon, L. Cole, J., & Swanberg, J. (2007). Partner stalking and implications for women's employment. *Journal of Interpersonal Violence, 22,* 268–291.

Luna-Firebaugh, E. N. (2006). Violence against American Indian women and the Services-Training-Officers-Prosecutors Violence Against Indian Women (STOP VAIW) Program. *Violence Against Women, 12,* 125–136.

Lyon, E. (2002). *Welfare and domestic violence against women: Lessons from research.* Retrieved August 23, 2009, from http://www.vawnet.org

MacMillan, R., & Gartner, R. (1999). When she brings home the bacon: Labor force participation and risk of spousal violence against women. *Journal of Marriage and the Family, 61,* 947–958.

McKinley, J. (2009, September 26). Cuts ravage California domestic abuse program. *New York Times.* Retrieved October 1, 2009, from http://www.nytimes.com/2009/09/26/us/26domestic.html

Meisel, J., Chandler, D., & Rienzi, B. M. (2003). Domestic violence prevalence and effects on employment in two California TANF populations. *Violence Against Women, 9,* 1191–1212.

Miles-Doan, R. (1998). Violence between spouses and intimates: Does neighborhood context matter? *Social Forces, 77,* 623–645.

Miller, J. (2008). *Getting played: African American girls, urban inequality, and gendered violence.* New York: New York University Press.

Moe, A. M., & Bell, M. P. (2004). Abject economics: The effects of battering and violence on women's work and employability. *Violence Against Women, 10,* 29–35.

Pearson, J., Griswold, E. A., & Thoennes, N. (2001). Balancing safety and self-sufficiency: Lessons from serving victims of domestic violence for child support and public assistance agencies. *Violence Against Women, 7,* 176–192.

Plichta, S. B. (1996). Violence and abuse: Implications for women's health. In M. M. Falk (Ed.), *Women's health: The Commonwealth Fund Survey* (pp. 237–270). Baltimore, MD: Johns Hopkins University Press.

Postmus, J. L., Severson, M., Berry, M., & Yoo, J. A. (2009). Women's experiences of violence and seeking help. *Violence Against Women, 15,* 852–868.

Powers, L. E., Hughes, R. B., & Lund, E. M. (2009). *Interpersonal violence and women with disabilities: A research update.* Retrieved October 23, 2009, from: http://www.vawnet.org

Raghavan, C., Mennerich, A., Sexton, E., & James, S. E. (2006). Community violence and its direct, indirect, and mediating effects on intimate partner violence. *Violence Against Women, 12,* 1132–1149.

Raj, A., Silverman, J. G., Wingood, G. M., & DiClemente, R. J. (1999). Prevalence and correlates of relationship abuse among a community-based sample of low-income African American women. *Violence Against Women, 5,* 272–291.

Raphael, J. (2000). *Saving Bernice: Battered women, welfare, and poverty.* Boston: Northeastern University Press.

Reeves, C., & O'Leary-Kelly, A. M. (2007). The effects and costs of intimate partner violence for work organizations. *Journal of Interpersonal Violence, 22,* 327–344.

Reimer, S. (2009, April 27). In families' tragic deaths, a hint of paternalism. *Baltimore Sun.* Retrieved May 3, 2009, from http://www.baltimoresun.com

Rempell, C. (2009, February 6). U.S. women set to surpass men in the labor force. *New York Times.* Retrieved February 23, 2009, from http://www.nytimes.com/2009/02/06/business/worldbusiness/06iht-06women.19978672.html

Rennison, C., & Planty, M. (2003). Nonlethal intimate partner violence: Examining race, gender, and income patterns. *Violence and Victims, 18,* 433–443.

Renzetti, C. M. (2003, September). *Does high collective efficacy help reduce violence against women? Findings from a study of four Philadelphia public housing developments.* Paper presented at the

4th National Trapped by Poverty/Trapped by Abuse Conference, Austin, TX.

Renzetti, C. M., & Maier, S. L. (2002). "Private" crime in public housing: Violent victimization, fear of crime, and social isolation among women public housing residents. *Women's Health and Urban Life, 1*, 46–65.

Riger, S., & Staggs, S. L. (2004). Welfare reform, domestic violence, and employment: What do we know and what do we need to know? *Violence Against Women, 10*, 961–990.

Roberts, S. (2009, September 22). Census data offer a snapshot tinted by recession. *New York Times*, p. A13.

Romero, D., Chavkin, W., Wise, P. H., & Smith, L. A. (2003). Low-income mothers' experience with poor health, hardship, work, and violence. *Violence Against Women, 9*, 1231–1244.

Rosen, D. (2004). "I just let him have his way": Partner violence in the lives of low-income, teenage mothers. *Violence Against Women, 10*, 6–28.

Rothman, E. F., & Corso, P. S. (2008). Propensity for intimate partner abuse and workplace productivity: Why employers should care. *Violence Against Women, 14*, 1054–1064.

Sampson, R. J., & Lauritsen, J. L. (1994). Violent victimization and offending: Individual-, situational-, and community-level risk factors. In A. J. Reiss & J. A. Roth (Eds.), *Understanding and preventing violence* (Vol. 3, pp. 1–114). Washington, DC: National Academy Press.

Sampson, R. J., Raudenbush, S. W., & Earls, F. (1997). Neighborhoods and violent crime: A multilevel study of collective efficacy. *Science, 277*, 918–924.

Sanday, P. R. (2007). *Fraternity gang rape: Sex, brotherhood, and privilege on campus* (2nd ed.). New York: New York University Press.

Smith, D. L., & Hilton, C. L. (2008). An occupational justice perspective of domestic violence against women with disabilities. *Journal of Occupational Science, 15*, 166–172.

Smith, D. L., & Strauser, D. R. (2008). Examining the impact of physical and sexual abuse on the employment of women with disabilities in the United States: An exploratory analysis. *Disability and Rehabilitation, 30*, 1039–1046.

Smith, J. H. (2009, March 2). Domestic violence increases as economic stresses build. *Dayton Daily News*. Retrieved March 14, 2009, from http://www.daytondailynews.com/n/content/oh/ story/news/local/2009/03/02/ddn030209domestic .html

Sorenson, S. B., Upchurch, D. M., & Shen, H. (1996). Violence and injury in marital arguments: Risk patterns and gender differences. *American Journal of Public Health, 86*, 35–40.

Staggs, S. L., Long, S. M., Mason, G. E., Krishnan, S., & Riger, S. (2007). Intimate partner violence, social support, and employment in the post-welfare reform era. *Journal of Interpersonal Violence, 22*, 345–367.

Stonks, K., Van de Mheen, H. D., & Mackenbach, J. P. (1998). A higher prevalence of health problems in low-income groups: Does it reflect relative deprivation? *Journal of Epidemiology and Community Health, 52*, 548–557.

Straus, M. A., Gelles, R. J., & Steinmetz, S. K. (1980). *Behind closed doors: Violence in the American family*. Garden City, NY: Doubleday.

Sullivan, L. (2009, October 4). Experts: Abuse of kids now brutality. *Dayton Daily News*, p. A1.

Sutherland, C. A., Sullivan, C. M., & Bybee, D. I. (2001). Effects of partner violence versus poverty on women's health. *Violence Against Women, 7*, 1122–1143.

Tjaden, P., & Thoennes, N. (1998). *Prevalence, incidence, and consequences of violence against women: Findings from the National Violence against Women Survey*. Washington, DC: U.S. Department of Justice.

Tolman, R. M. (1999). Guest editor's introduction. *Violence Against Women, 5*, 355–369.

U.S. Department of Justice, National Institute of Justice. (2009a). *Economic distress and intimate partner violence*. Retrieved September 23, 2009, from http://www.ojp.usdoj.gov/nij/topics/crime/intimate-partner-violence/economic-distress.htm

U.S. Department of Justice, National Institute of Justice. (2009b). *Murder-suicide in families*. Retrieved September 23, 2009, from http://www .ojp.usdoj.gov/nij/topics/crime/intimate-partner-violence/murder-suicide.htm

Websdale, N. (1998). *Rural woman battering and the justice system: An ethnography*. Thousand Oaks, CA: Sage.

Williams, S. L., & Mickelson, K. D. (2004). The nexus of domestic violence and poverty: Resilience in women's anxiety. *Violence Against Women, 10*, 283–293.

World Health Organization. (2002). *World report on violence and health*. Geneva, Switzerland: Author.

Chapter Author

Claire M. Renzetti received her Ph.D. from the University of Delaware in 1982. She is currently an Endowed Chair in the Center for Research on Violence Against Women and Professor of Sociology at the University of Kentucky, Lexington. She is also editor of the international, interdisciplinary journal, *Violence Against Women;* coeditor with Jeffrey Edleson of the *Interpersonal Violence* book series for Oxford University Press; and editor of the *Gender, Crime, and Law* book series for Northeastern University Press. She has authored or edited 16 books as well as numerous book chapters and articles in professional journals. Much of her research has focused on the violent victimization experiences of economically marginalized women living in public housing developments. She is currently conducting an ethnography of faith-based organizations involved in anti-trafficking work. Dr. Renzetti has held elected and appointed positions on the governing bodies of several national professional organizations, including the Society for the Study of Social Problems, the Eastern Sociological Society, and Alpha Kappa Delta, the sociological honors society.

Personal Reflection

Jill Davies

As a legal aid lawyer representing battered women living in poverty, I had the opportunity to see firsthand the pressing financial and safety needs of my clients. They had complex and difficult decisions to make, almost always involving financial considerations. In addition to dealing with the violence and the effects on their children, they also had to figure out how to pay the rent, put food on the table, and keep the heat on over the winter.

I learned from battered women that safety requires not only freedom from the power and control of an abusive partner, but also the ability to meet basic human needs.

I understood an advocate's role in safety planning was to work in partnership with battered women and to offer advocacy that was defined by their decisions, culture, resources, physical safety, and financial needs.

Advocates and others working to end violence against women continue to expand their awareness of and impact on financial issues. For example, it is now understood that violence makes it harder to find a way out of poverty and that poverty makes it more difficult to escape violence or deal with its effects. These intersecting issues are increasingly being integrated into the analysis and advocacy of both the antiviolence and antipoverty fields.

Yet, there are still many victims living in poverty and still too few responses for victims who need financial resources and protections to be safe. The work ahead requires us to listen to victims, understand how the changing economic conditions affect their safety strategies, and continue to expand their options. Among those efforts must be more meaningful interventions to protect victims' financial resources, as well as increased housing options, access to health care and government benefits, and employment supports that lead to living-wage jobs.

A strength of this field is placing the work to end violence against women in the larger context of society. Advocates know that the experience of victims affects all women. Similarly, the economic status of all women will be a factor in efforts to end violence against them.

PART III

Prevention and Direct Intervention

This part of the book moves from understanding violence against women to taking action to stop it. Half the chapters in this new edition of the *Sourcebook on Violence Against Women* appear in this section, and rightfully so. So much has changed in the 35 years since the first battered women's safe homes and shelters were established in the UK and North America. In each chapter that follows, we continue pairing brief reflections composed by key leaders in the field who have made a major impact in the area upon which the chapter focuses.

Perhaps one of the greatest changes over these decades has been in the area of the law and international treaties. In Chapter 10, Leigh Goodmark examines the first and second generations of change in state and national laws as well as in international treaties. The law has expanded to include regulations that protect battered women from discrimination in their housing and unfair treatment when disclosing their prior victimization to potential employers or health insurers. Legislative changes have also focused on emergent areas of abuse, such as harassment and stalking via new technologies and trafficking for labor and sexual exploitation.

Chapter 11 tackles the often-overlooked area of prevention. Corinne Graffunder, Karen G. Lane, and Rebecca Cline from the U.S. Centers for Disease Control and Prevention describe the key approaches to prevention and how these strategies can be applied to preventing violence against women. They offer numerous concrete examples of how this work is being done and the barriers and challenges that communities face when trying to prevent violence.

In Chapter 12, Raquel Kennedy Bergen and Shauna Maier review the evolution of social intervention in response to sexual assault in the U.S. They provide a brief history of the response to sexual assault in the U.S. and then discuss the specific locations, such as university campuses, where sexual assault services are provided. They conclude with a lengthy discussion of emerging responses targeted to specific groups in the U.S. that are often marginalized.

Complementing the previous chapter, Chapter 13 by Nicole Allen, Sadie Larsen, and Angela Walden reviews the growth of community-based services for battered women and their children. These authors discuss a number of critical issues that services must resolve to successfully serve battered women and their children.

They then look at barriers to successful service delivery, especially to specific women with multiple needs, women in unique settings such as college campuses and rural communities, and women who are members of marginalized communities.

The next four chapters address violence against women and the response of the criminal justice (Chapter 14), health care (Chapter 15), faith-based (Chapter 16), and education (Chapter 17) systems. In each of these domains, major new efforts are evident since the publication of the first edition of this text. In Chapter 14, Susan Miller and her colleagues show the many changes that law enforcement and the courts have made in order to better respond to both domestic violence and sexual assault. They also discuss innovations such as restorative justice and its uses in this system. Rebecca Macy and her colleagues focus on six major aspects of health and violence against women in Chapter 15. They start by examining the physical and mental health impacts of violence and then critically review the variety of health care system responses to violence, ranging from best practices in assessment and care, to specific populations such as pregnant women, and to specific innovations such as trauma-informed health care. In Chapter 16, Tameka Gillum and Shondrah Tarrezz Nash examine both the response of organized religions to victims of violence and how individuals use religion and spirituality as a means to draw strength and heal. They conclude their chapter with a review the many new efforts to address violence against women in faith-based communities and programs. Finally, in Chapter 17, Claire Crooks and her Canadian colleagues describe efforts in education systems to prevent adolescent dating violence. The work of these authors has drawn worldwide attention, and they make a strong argument for intervening early with adolescents in order to prevent violence in teen as well as adult relationships. Their chapter includes a review of the emerging, evidence-based approaches to preventing violence among adolescents and teens.

The book concludes with Chapter 18 by Richard Tolman and Jeffrey Edleson, in which they examine how men are engaged to prevent future violence. This chapter begins with a brief history of how intervention with male batterers evolved in North America and then reviews the controversies and lessons learned about the impact of small-group interventions with men. The second half of their chapter is devoted to more recent innovations that focus on engaging men in early prevention of violence, such as with coaches, opinion leaders, and expectant and new fathers. This is a hopeful note upon which to end this book, a look toward a future in which men and women both actively engage in preventing violence against women and children.

CHAPTER 10

State, National, and International Legal Initiatives to Address Violence Against Women

A Survey

Leigh Goodmark

Women's movements throughout the world have prioritized the development of a legal response to violence against women when setting their agendas for change. Advocates have struggled to enact and enforce laws against intimate partner violence, rape, honor killings, and the trafficking of women, and to train police, prosecutors, lawyers, and judges in using these laws to protect women from the violence that has traditionally been so pervasive and gone unacknowledged by formal institutions. More than 30 years into the legal revolution to combat violence against women, this chapter will discuss a range of current legal initiatives designed to address violence against women and consider some of the pressing questions prompted by the development of this legal response.

First-generation legal solutions to violence against women that focus on using the legal system to protect women from violence and to hold abusers accountable for their actions are now institutionalized in some nations. Rape and intimate partner violence have been criminalized for some time. An elaborate civil law regime exists to address the needs of women leaving violent relationships. This chapter will discuss those first-generation solutions and describe the additional legal framework that has been erected to better protect women from violence as novel intrusions on women's safety, like trafficking and cyberviolence, have become more common. The chapter will briefly evaluate the effectiveness of the legal response to violence against women, focusing on the characterization of victims in the law, the effectiveness of the criminal justice response to violence against women, and the issues around exporting the legal regime to countries just beginning to address violence against women. The chapter will then turn to the question of how international law and human rights norms can be employed to fight violence against women and will consider the interplay of economics and violence against women. The chapter concludes with a brief caution on the limits of the law's ability to redress violence against women.

First-Generation Issues in Responding to Violence Against Women

Immediate victim safety and offender accountability were the predominant concerns in first-generation efforts to use the law to respond to violence against women. Early reform efforts focused on ensuring that police and prosecutors would, in fact, use the power of the law to intervene in violent incidents and to bring offenders to justice. Moving away from a regime in which domestic violence was considered a private, intrafamily issue and rape the fault and private shame of the victim, women's advocates urged police to arrest men who had acted violently and to use the police power of the state both to punish those men and to send a societal message that violence against women would no longer be tolerated.

Reforming rape laws headed the feminist agenda in the early 1970s. Beginning with Michigan's comprehensive rape reforms in 1974 and continuing through the following decade, reformers in the United States and a number of other countries, including Canada, the United Kingdom, Australia, and New Zealand, were successful in removing a number of requirements unique to rape prosecutions that undermined the legal system's ability to hold rapists accountable. These included rescinding laws requiring prompt reporting of rapes, corroboration of the rape victim's testimony, and "resistance to the utmost" throughout the attack; prohibiting

defendants from introducing testimony about the victim's sexual history (rape shield laws); and retiring "Lord Hale's instruction," a caution routinely given to juries about the difficulty of defending oneself against a rape allegation. These changes were expected to increase prosecutors' ability to win rape cases, thereby enhancing both women's safety and offender accountability.

Advocates for women who had been battered argued that police discretion was responsible for the failure to safeguard women and hold their partners accountable. Accordingly, advocates pushed police, using a series of lawsuits charging police with the failure to protect women from violence, to depart from their traditional "take a walk around the block and cool off" response and to make arrests in cases involving domestic violence. In response to those lawsuits, jurisdictions throughout the United States removed procedural barriers that precluded police from making arrests at the scene of a domestic violence incident. Worried that police would still fail to arrest, advocates pushed for mandatory arrest policies, which removed police discretion in arrest decisions and required that police make an arrest whenever probable cause to do so existed. Concerned that prosecutors would fail to act when arrests were made, advocates also pushed for prosecution policies that would ensure that any case that could be tried, would be tried. These no-drop policies compelled prosecutors to bring any triable case before a finder of fact, regardless of the victim's willingness to cooperate.

Recognizing that women who had been battered would need more than the intervention of the criminal justice system to establish long-term safety, advocates developed a civil remedy that would not only require that an abusive husband stay away from his wife, but also provide for a range of other needs: child custody, child support, housing, access to a vehicle, and counseling for her partner. These civil protection orders were unique in that they were a remedy that a woman could access on her own and control— the order would contain only those things that she requested and a judge approved, tailored to her individual situation. The institution of criminal penalties for the violation of a civil protection order enhanced the orders' effectiveness.

Stalking was a primary focus of legal reforms in the 1990s. Recognizing the ineffectiveness of existing harassment, criminal trespass, and threats laws to address stalking, states and countries throughout the world have passed legislation that specifically outlaws a pattern of behavior including pursuing and following, harassment, surveillance, continued approaches, nonconsensual communications, and intimidation (Buzawa & Buzawa, 2003). Newer statutes provide for enhanced penalties for aggravated stalking, add stalking to the list of predicate activities to qualify for civil protection orders, and permit police to make warrantless arrests in stalking cases.

Second-Generation Issues in Responding to Violence Against Women

Having addressed the immediate safety concerns of women experiencing rape, domestic violence, and stalking through criminalization and the development of civil remedies to address the broader needs of victimized women, legislators are now considering laws and policies to address the various legal problems resulting from violence against women. These laws and policies involve areas such as housing, the workplace, and insurance. All are designed to prevent discrimination against and to protect the economic stability of women subjected to violence.

Housing Laws

Violence against women is a leading cause of homelessness among women, not only because women are forced to leave their homes to escape abuse, but also because landlords use violence as a justification for preventing women from entering housing and for ousting women from their homes. Moreover, their inability to break leases without severe financial penalties may keep women tied to unsafe housing, financially precluded from fleeing abusive relationships or concealing their whereabouts from their perpetrators. Legal services providers have documented hundreds of instances of women being denied housing or evicted as a result of violence against them (Ross, 2007). Although the Violence Against Women Act of 2005 contains a number of housing provisions, those provisions apply only to Section 8 and federally subsidized housing. States have led the effort to increase housing protections for women in private housing.

Several states include women who have experienced intimate partner or sexual violence in their comprehensive antidiscrimination housing laws. These laws forbid landlords to refuse to rent to or terminate an existing relationship with a tenant because the tenant or someone in the tenant's household is a victim of intimate partner violence, sexual assault, or stalking or because the police have been called to the home to address violence against women who live there. Wisconsin's law permits discrimination against those whose presence would endanger other occupants or the property itself, but clearly states that a woman's status as a victim of intimate partner violence is not sufficient to justify excluding her from the property. A number of states make intimate partner violence a defense to an action for eviction, precluding landlords from evicting women on the basis of violence in the home, under certain conditions. The laws of the District of Columbia and New Mexico are the strongest, prohibiting a landlord from evicting a tenant with a protective order. Some states require the woman to provide evidence of the violence before she can assert the defense; that proof can include a sworn statement from a law enforcement officer, counselor, or health care professional or a protective order. State laws also protect the woman's right to summon assistance, prohibiting landlords from contractually limiting (in lease documents) a woman's right to call the police to respond to violence or from imposing a penalty for doing so. One state safeguards victims of violence from having their utilities terminated; Massachusetts' protective order statute includes a provision blocking abusers from interfering with a victim's utilities.

States have also made it easier for women who have been victimized to leave their homes for safer surroundings. State laws allow women to terminate leases early when they have been the victims of domestic violence, sexual assault, or stalking. Most laws require some form of documentation and compel the victim to seek the assistance of the legal system, either by securing a protective order or involving law enforcement. Bifurcation of leases is also possible under a number of state laws. Some states allow the victim of violence to terminate her lease, leaving the perpetrator responsible for the balance of the lease. Others empower the landlord to remove the perpetrator from the lease and allow the victim to remain in the home. State laws protect landlords as well, allowing them to seek compensation from perpetrators for unpaid rent and other damages related to domestic violence.

Employment Discrimination

Perhaps nothing is so important for a victim of violence's survival as the ability to find and maintain work. As law professor Deborah Widiss writes, work is "as important for many victims as the availability of a bed in a shelter, prosecution of a batterer, or access to civil legal services" (Widiss, 2008, p. 672). But working can be a challenge for victims of violence. Abusers and stalkers use a variety of tactics to undermine women's attempts to find and keep work: battering incidents on the day of a job interview or the first day of work; failure to provide promised child care; interference with transportation; repeated phone calls and visits to the work site; allegations of improper or illegal activity made to coworkers and supervisors. In 1998, the United States General Accounting Office estimated that abusers harassed between 35% and 56% of employed victims of intimate partner violence at work and that 24% to 52% of those women lost their jobs as a result of abuse. Homicide is the leading cause of work-related death for women; 11% of all rapes occur in the workplace. Dealing with an abuser or stalker is not only perilous for his victim. It can be dangerous at worst, and certainly irritating and distracting at best, for employers and fellow employees as well. It is hardly surprising, then, that many employers terminate employees struggling with violence. Legal scholars have debated whether firing a victim of violence solely because of her status as a victim of violence is a violation of federal law. Court opinions on the point have been mixed. States, however, have stepped into the breach with a number of laws designed to protect victimized employees and help employers maintain safe workplaces.

In several states, an employer is prohibited from terminating an employee based on the belief that the woman is a victim of violence. Although such laws can be beneficial, law professor Nina Tarr (2007) notes that they fail to address the crucial front-end problem of securing a job, given that employers with information about an applicant's history of violence might be leery of making an offer (a prospect that becomes more likely with the ever-increasing electronic access to court records about cases involving violence against women). In a smaller number of states and localities, though, employers are prohibited from making hiring decisions based on their knowledge, belief, or perception that a woman is a victim of violence. Once a victim of violence has found employment, she is protected in a number of states by provisions that enable her to take time off to deal with violence-related issues (like counseling, medical appointments, or court attendance) and that require her employer to make reasonable accommodations in the workplace to address problems created by the violence. Illinois law, for example, suggests that an employer might be required to change an employee's work schedule or telephone number or implement safety procedures if the employer knows that the employee is experiencing violence.

Most states' unemployment insurance laws enable victims of violence who become unemployed as a result of the violence to collect benefits, even if those victims were fired from or voluntarily left their jobs (situations that usually disqualify applicants for unemployment insurance). In most of these states, though, the woman claiming benefits bears the burden of proving that she is a victim of violence. Moreover, some of these laws require "appropriate" victim behavior. In Wisconsin, for example, a woman must show that she was forced to leave her position because an order of protection has been or is likely to be violated (underscoring the assumption that all true victims of violence secure protective orders).

One violence-related employment provision potentially pits victims of violence against their employers and can pose real danger to victims. In a few states, employers can seek restraining orders against individuals who have threatened or perpetrated violence against an employee of the business. In such states, employers can bring court actions against perpetrators of violence without consulting with the victim of that violence, despite the likelihood that retaliation for such action is much more likely to be visited upon the victimized employee than the employer.

Insurance

Until several years ago, insurance companies actively discriminated against victims of violence and vehemently defended their right to do so, arguing that victims of violence used health care services disproportionately. Recognizing that the denial of insurance benefits could cause women to choose not to report violence or seek treatment, states swiftly passed laws prohibiting insurance companies from denying health insurance coverage to victims of violence. State laws vary as to the types of insurance that are covered (health, life, disability, and/or property) and include loopholes that may permit insurers to continue to discriminate against victims of violence. For example, laws that preclude insurers from denying coverage "solely" on the basis of a history of violence may not keep insurers from denying coverage based on the existence of a medical condition caused by that same violence. Only legislation that bars insurers directly or indirectly from using a woman's history of violence to justify underwriting decisions can truly protect victims of violence.

The laws and policies addressed above target the kinds of violence against women that have long been common. But violence against women is evolving because of new technology. In response, federal and state governments are enacting laws and policies targeting these new incursions into women's safety.

Technology and Violence Against Women

When the first domestic violence and stalking laws were passed, no one could have foreseen how technology would facilitate abuse, stalking, and harassment. Today, though, the media is replete with stories about how technology has expanded the potential for violence against women. An angry ex-boyfriend in North Carolina used YouTube videos to threaten the mother of his child, who lives in Connecticut. One-quarter of teenagers report being electronically harassed or threatened by their partners. Young women are pressured to send nude pictures of themselves to their partners via cell phone. The Family Violence Prevention Fund has coined a term for such behaviors: digital dating violence.

Technology has enabled stalkers to employ new means of terrorizing their victims as well. Stalkers use GPS devices to track a victim's whereabouts (Google recently announced a service, Google Latitude, that enables users to track the whereabouts of others from their home computers by installing tracking software on a phone or Wi-Fi device). Stalkers send repeated e-mails or text messages to victims or pose as the victim and disseminate offensive, embarrassing, or harmful information to and about others via e-mail, chat rooms, blogs, or message boards. Stalkers even enlist unwitting third parties to harass their victims. One stalker posted his victim's name, address, and telephone number in an online forum for women with rape fantasies; at least six men came to her home and told her they wanted to rape her. Technology allows the stalker to remain anonymous; to target his victim with greater frequency, at closer range—in her workplace, in her home, and, via cell phone, anywhere else she might go; and to disseminate his threats, defamations, and other messages more widely.

Recognizing that existing domestic violence and stalking laws were inadequate to address cyberviolence, legislatures and courts have expanded the legal protection for women facing such threats. At least six states have passed criminal laws specifically addressing cyberstalking. A number of others amended existing stalking laws to include provisions targeting cyberstalking. These statutes criminalize the kinds of electronic communications described above, although they vary in their reach and in the legal standards they employ. Some require an overt threat. Others provide that a threat must be communicated specifically to the victim; posts on message boards that the victim never sees, then, might not qualify under the statute. Few state statutes cover the unwitting third party scenario.

Similarly, although existing federal laws in the United States address some aspects of cyberstalking, those laws are flawed. They require overt threats of harm, criminalize only anonymous cyberstalking, and apply only to direct communications between perpetrator and victim (again, excluding posts to message boards and blogs and attempts to induce innocent third parties to participate). Even the comprehensive federal statute intended to check cyberstalking, the Interstate Stalking Punishment and Prevention Act, fails to address the innocent third party scenario and situations in which the perpetrator causes harm by posing as the victim. Law professor Naomi Harlin Goodno (2007) has suggested that a comprehensive criminal cyberstalking law would criminalize repeated, intentional conduct by a perpetrator that he knows or should know will cause a victim to fear for her safety. Cyberstalking laws should not require an actual threat of harm, in order to

capture the stalker who literally sends thousands of messages over a short period of time, none of which contains an overt threat but the mass of which could reasonably cause a victim to fear for her safety. Such laws should also explicitly include attempts to engage unwitting third parties in stalking, harassing, or other conduct that could cause the victim to fear for her safety.

A number of states have extended eligibility for civil orders of protection to victims of stalking. Some courts have been willing to interpret their state civil protective orders expansively, enabling them to provide protection to victims of electronic abuse. In the YouTube case mentioned above, for example, Connecticut judge Stephen F. Frazzini found that the state's protective order statute gave him jurisdiction to enter an order against the ex-boyfriend who lived in North Carolina and broadcasted his threats via the Internet, reaching his former girlfriend in Connecticut. Judge Frazzini explained,

> It should have been foreseeable to Fergusan that by placing a video on YouTube threatening Rios in Connecticut he could be hauled into this state to answer an application seeking a restraining order against him. . . . Connecticut has a strong interest in protecting its citizens from domestic abuse. (Malan, 2009)

Judge Frazzini's finding that the Connecticut court had jurisdiction over a nonresident perpetrator by virtue of the threat to a citizen of his state may be the exception rather than the rule. There is some question as to whether the definitions of abuse or stalking used in civil protection orders are sufficiently broad to cover incidents of cyberstalking. In a recent Oregon case, *Osborne v. Fadden* (2009), the court denied a protective order to a woman whose ex-husband and new wife flooded her with over 2,000 e-mails and e-mail solicitations, harassed her and her family and friends by phone, opened credit accounts and subscribed to various services using her name, e-mailed various individuals posing as her, and e-mailed her posing as others. Despite acknowledging that these actions were "troubling," the court found that they failed to cause the woman a reasonable apprehension of bodily harm, as required by the statute. Even the sexual solicitations from third parties that the woman received as a result of the couple's communications were not sufficient to meet the statutory standard. Moreover, protective order laws may not cover electronic communications or may require physical proximity between the victim and perpetrator, rendering them useless to address cyberstalking. With every technological innovation comes the potential for misuse. The law, however, is not particularly well-suited to the kind of quick change required to adapt to new technologies.

Protecting Trafficked Women

In addition to responding to new technology, governments have been looking at old problems that seem to be increasing in magnitude. Trafficking of women is one such problem. Between 14,500 and 17,500 individuals, primarily women and children, are trafficked into the United States each year, according to the United States Department of Justice. Other studies set the figure much higher. Trafficking supports the sex industry and provides cheap or free labor for other employers. Women are lured to the United States by the promise of high-paying jobs, only to find themselves subjected to physical, mental, and emotional abuse. Some trafficked women are threatened that if they report their plight or attempt to escape, the consequences for themselves or their families will be dire. Traffickers have also reintroduced slavery to the United States through "debt bondage," the practice of requiring victims to repay their captors for expenses incurred in bringing them to the United States or beginning their jobs.

To stem the tide of trafficked individuals into the United States and punish traffickers for their brutal treatment of their victims, the United States passed the Trafficking Victims Protection Act in 2000 and supplemented that law in 2003 and 2005. The Act defines and imposes criminal penalties for trafficking; provides civil remedies against traffickers; enables courts to order restitution to victims of trafficking; and provides services, including 5,000 special immigration visas, called T-visas, for victims. Investigation, prosecution, and conviction of traffickers has slowly but steadily increased since the Act's inception.

In the years prior to the passage of the Trafficking Victims Protection Act, seeking assistance or reporting a trafficker carried a real risk of deportation for victims who were in the United States illegally. Their undocumented status discouraged victims from seeking assistance and hampered criminal prosecutions of traffickers. The T-visa, which was designed to safeguard undocumented trafficking victims, purported to address that issue. Some have suggested, however, that the T-visa's main function is less the protection of trafficking victims and more the promotion of criminal prosecution. T-visas are only available to victims who are willing to actively participate in the criminal prosecution of their traffickers. The victim becomes eligible to seek permanent residency after three years of T-visa status only if she cooperates with authorities. The visas can be difficult to obtain. Applicants must show that they will face "extreme hardship" if removed from the United States, and the standard for proving such hardship is high. Moreover, a trafficking victim's T-visa can be revoked if, among other reasons, law enforcement officials inform federal authorities that they deem her participation with prosecution insufficient. The T-visa is an instrumental remedy, designed to coerce victim compliance in criminal investigations and prosecutions. Protection simply because a victim has been trafficked does not exist, regardless of the reasons a victim might be reluctant to participate in a criminal matter. Other federal benefits, too, are conditional upon the application for the T-visa. The requirement that a victim cooperate with the legal system in order to secure legal protection is problematic; the consequences of requiring cooperation will be considered more fully below.

Motherhood and Violence Against Women

Motherhood makes women vulnerable to violence in unique ways. The prospect of becoming pregnant after rape, or having a child with and losing that child to an abuser, is terrifying for many women. In order to protect women from these horrific outcomes, state and federal governments have proposed and enacted a variety of laws designed to ensure that perpetrators of violence against women are prevented from depriving women of their children as well as their safety.

Becoming pregnant as a result of rape is some women's worst nightmare. Worse still is the prospect of having to co-parent that child with, or losing custody of that child to, the rapist. To prevent that scenario, states have enacted laws facilitating the termination of a rapist's parental rights, precluding a rapist from asserting paternity of a child conceived through rape, and denying a rapist the opportunity to seek custody of a child conceived through rape. California law denies the presumption of fatherhood to biological fathers convicted of rape or statutory rape (if the mother was less than 15 years old and the father older than 21 years at the time of conception); a similar law has been proposed, but not enacted, in Maryland. A number of states, including Alaska, Connecticut, Idaho, Missouri, Montana, Oklahoma, Pennsylvania, Texas, Washington, and Wisconsin, permit the termination of a natural father's parental rights if the child is conceived as a result of rape, incest, or another sexual offense. The level of proof of the rape or sexual offense varies. Some states require a conviction prior to permitting termination, while others simply state that the offense must have occurred, resulting in the child's birth. In the latter group of states, arguably, termination could be justified by the mother's testimony or other evidence of the rape or sexual offense,

without a finding in the criminal system that the offense occurred beyond a reasonable doubt. Some termination laws also require the court to find that termination of parental rights is in the child's best interest before severing the rapist's tie with the child.

States have also contemplated denying custody and/or visitation to a parent who has committed specified sexual offenses. The Maryland legislature has considered, but not enacted, a statute that would deny custody and/or visitation to a parent who has committed rape, incest, or sexual assault of a minor under the age of 16 against the other parent, resulting in the conception of the child. The proposed statute does not require a conviction to trigger the custody/visitation ban. The court would be permitted to find that one of the specified crimes has been committed based on a prior statement made by the child's mother to law enforcement, child protective services, or any other third party deemed reliable by the court.

Case law also supports restrictions on a rapist's right to assert his parental status. In *Pena v. Mattox* (1996), the Seventh Circuit Court of Appeals found that a natural father who conceives a child through criminal sexual intercourse has no constitutional right to parent that child. Writing for the Court, Chief Judge Richard Posner explained that in a case involving a sexual crime that society no longer truly abhorred, like adultery, a natural father might be able to make a claim to parent the child. But in cases involving violent sexual offenses like rape, a state is constitutionally permitted to deprive the father of a relationship with the child. A grayer area, under Posner's analysis, involves the rights of fathers who commit sexual offenses like misdemeanor statutory rape. The rights of those fathers may depend on the extent to which the father succeeds in developing a relationship with the child or financially supports the child.

In the face of statistics suggesting that fathers who battered their wives were receiving custody at alarming rates, laws requiring judges to consider domestic violence in the context of child custody decisions were enacted in most states in the United States and in a number of other countries. Such laws generally fall into three categories: laws requiring that evidence of domestic violence be considered in custody determinations; laws that require courts to ascertain the impact of the domestic violence on the child's best interest; and laws that create a presumption against granting custody to a parent who has abused the child's other parent. Visitation laws similarly require courts to factor domestic violence into decisions about a parent's access to a child.

Despite these legislative victories, however, both reported case law and anecdotal evidence are replete with stories of women who have been abused and have lost custody to their partners. Battered Mothers' Testimony Projects in several states in the United States have documented the poor treatment battered mothers receive in the courts, including losing custody of their children to men with documented histories of domestic violence. When custody is granted to an abused mother, courts frequently grant unsafe visitation (requiring the mother to continue to have contact with her abuser) or inadequate child support, denying her the ability to care properly for the child.

International law creates particular challenges for mothers fighting for custody of their children after fleeing domestic violence across international borders. The Hague Convention on the Civil Aspects of International Child Abduction (Hague Convention), a private international treaty currently ratified by 81 countries, governs the return of children wrongfully removed from their states of habitual residence. The Hague Convention was drafted under the assumption that the majority of abductors would be fathers depriving primary caregiver mothers of custody. In such a scenario, the Hague Convention's remedy of returning the child to the place of the child's habitual residence, and to the care of the primary caregiver, for adjudication of custody makes perfect sense. In reality, however, undisputed evidence establishes that the vast majority of child abductors

are mothers and primary caregivers. Many of these mothers claim to have fled with their children to escape domestic violence. At a recent meeting of signatories to the Hague Convention, country after country affirmed the frequency with which domestic violence is raised and expressed concern about the Convention's operation in these cases (Weiner, 2008).

Both in the United States and around the world, the judicial response to these claims has been mixed. Battered mothers have argued that returning to their countries of origin would pose a grave risk of physical or psychological harm to their children or otherwise place their children in intolerable positions, a defense permitted by Article 13(b) of the Convention. Although some courts have indicated a willingness to consider whether a grave risk to a child exists when mothers, but not their children, are battered, many courts, including the courts of Australia, Austria, Quebec, Ireland, Israel, and Scotland, continue to construe the defense narrowly and refuse to connect the battering of mothers with harm to children.

Even when courts have determined that return could cause a grave risk of harm to a child, those courts have looked for ways to ameliorate the risk by guaranteeing the child's safety if return is nonetheless ordered. In cases in Australia and England, for example, courts returned children whose mothers had been threatened with death by their abusers, reasoning that the women and their children could remain in shelters pending the resolution of the custody cases. In some cases, judges impose court-ordered conditions of return called *undertakings*. Undertakings can include such provisions as restraining orders, transportation, and payment of housing expenses for the child and the fleeing parent. Some courts use undertakings to attempt to ensure the safety of women and children in the country from which they fled; other courts have expressed concern about the enforceability of undertakings.

Those concerns are underscored by a 2003 study by the European Network for the Protection of Children, which found that undertakings were generally unenforceable, often not honored, and, in the case of "nonmolestation provisions," always violated. Advocates and scholars argue that confidence in undertakings is misplaced, calling them "illegal, dangerous, unfair, and inefficient" (Hoegger, 2003) and "naïve at best. At worst, they turn a blind eye to injustice" (Bruch, 2004). To address these concerns, some countries are now using "mirror orders," in which judges in both countries enter the same order, attempting to craft orders that comply with the laws and policies of both countries. There is little information on the enforcement of these orders to date, however.

Other defenses to return are available to battered mothers fleeing with their children, but few have been used effectively. One possible defense in cases involving domestic violence, suggests law professor Merle Weiner (2004), is found in Article 20 of the Hague Convention, which allows a court to refuse to return a child if return is not permitted by the signatory's fundamental principles relating to the protection of human rights and fundamental freedoms. Weiner argues that although Article 20 is rarely used, domestic violence is precisely the type of human rights violation that Article 20 should cover. When returning a child would mean re-exposing the child's mother to domestic violence, the Article 20 defense should be employed.

At a 2006 meeting reviewing the operation of the Hague Convention, participants from throughout the world acknowledged that the cases they were seeing were not the cases they expected to see at the Convention's inception. Nations and nongovernmental organizations suggested policy modifications to address the needs of battered mothers fleeing with their children. Among these were proposals to enlarge the grave risk defense under Article 13 and to create a process for formalizing the ordering of undertakings. The United States objected to these promising reforms, however, and attempted to prevent even small changes to the Convention meant to better protect victims of violence fleeing with their children. The United States, instead, continues to assert that the primary goal of the Convention should be to protect parents left behind, regardless of who they are or what they might have done, arguing that abduction is rarely an act of love or protection (Weiner, 2008).

Evaluating the Legal System's Response to Violence Against Women

The legal response to violence against women has been multifaceted and, in some parts of the world, fairly comprehensive. But has the legal response worked—and what does "worked" mean? Advocates, policy makers, and scholars have been asking that question since the inception of criminal justice reforms in the early 1970s. This section will consider three specific aspects of the legal response to violence against women: the characterization of "victims" required by legal reforms, the effectiveness of criminal justice reforms intended to address violence against women, and the appropriateness of exporting legal reforms to countries beginning to address violence against women.

Who Is a Victim?

As discussed earlier, a number of the laws and policies designed to assist victims of violence require women to engage with the legal system in order to establish eligibility. Only "real" victims—victims who act in conformity with stereotypical notions about how women who are battered should act—need apply. To qualify for unemployment benefits in Wisconsin, for example, a woman who has been subjected to domestic violence must show that she was forced to leave her job because her protective order either has been or will be violated—a requirement that presupposes that all "real" victims acquire protective orders. The T-visa for trafficked women is available only to those who actively participate in the criminal prosecutions of their traffickers—participation that must be verified by the investigating officials. Early lease termination in some states is available to victims of domestic violence—but only if they have engaged the legal system in some way, either by cooperating with law enforcement or securing a protective order. In the District of Columbia and New Mexico, landlords are forbidden to evict tenants who are victims of domestic violence—but only when those victims have protective orders.

All of these laws underscore stereotypes and assumptions about who victims of violence are and what society expects them to do to prove their victimization. But many victims never engage formal systems and have strong reasons for deciding against turning to the legal system for assistance. Although the need for proof of victimization may be understandable in some circumstances (e.g., to prevent fraud), the imprimatur of the legal system is far from the only form of proof that a victim can provide. The requirement that a victim obtain a protective order is particularly problematic because it presumes that securing an order is fully within the victim's control. But a victim of violence may be unable to serve her partner with her petition for an order, causing the case to be dismissed. She may be unable to return to court due to fear of retaliation, lack of child care, inadequate transportation, or the threat that she will lose her job if she misses additional work time. She may face a judge who is hostile to claims for protective orders and reluctant to grant them in any circumstance, even if she can present strong evidence to support her claim. In all of these situations, the victim would be no less a victim, but she would be unable to avail herself of the remedy provided by law.

Victims of violence stand to benefit greatly from the protections described in the first section of this chapter. But many more could benefit if those laws did not equate victimization with engagement with the legal system. If proof of one's status as a victim is necessary, the definition of proof should extend beyond showing that the victim has used the legal system. Victims should not be made to earn their protection—as in the case of the T-visa—by requiring them to cooperate with prosecutors.

Reconsidering Criminal Justice Policies

In the 1970s and 1980s, every state in the United States and jurisdictions throughout the world adopted civil and criminal laws and procedures to address violence against women through the legal system. Some of these laws and policies have had their critics, however. Thirty years into the experiment with prioritizing the legal response to violence against women, it seems appropriate to ask whether those widely adopted policies are achieving their stated goals of increasing offender accountability and victim safety and what the unintended consequences of those policies have been.

As discussed earlier, rape law reform was widespread in the 1970s and 1980s. Sociologist Susan Caringella (2009) notes, however, that these successes in changing the law are not translating to better outcomes for victims of rape or sexual assault.

Even the limited research on reforms has shown that results have fallen far short of objectives. For instance, reforms have failed to increase reporting, arrest, and/or conviction rates; they have similarly failed to remove consent and resistance standards and the influential role that past sexual history evidence plays at trials. (p. 2)

Caringella (2009) concludes, "The legal system persists in unfair treatment of women who are raped or sexually assaulted in spite of massive reforms repealing discriminatory standards in legal codes" (p. 3). While Caringella proposes a series of additional reforms intended to address the de facto application of statutes and policies that, on their own, are not working to protect victims, other critics are asking whether the criminal justice system can ever serve the needs of women who have been raped. As law professor Aya Gruber (2009) argues in her recent article, *Rape and the Feminist War on Crime,* rape reforms have failed because they cannot eradicate the stereotypes about women and about how women contribute to their own victimization that pervade the criminal justice system. Moreover, Gruber contends, the criminal law is premised on a notion of an easily vilified stranger rapist; the much more common date rapist does not stir the hatred, disgust, and anger the criminal justice system generally must summon for a successful rape prosecution. Gruber advocates for disengaging from the criminal justice system altogether.

The two major criminal justice reforms in the realm of intimate partner violence, mandatory arrest of perpetrators of domestic violence and victimless prosecution of domestic violence cases, involve removing discretion from system actors—and from victims of violence. The research on the efficacy of mandatory arrest in cases of intimate partner violence is equivocal at best. Although early studies hailed mandatory arrest as a deterrent against further violence, replication studies questioned those first results. One coauthor of the earliest studies, Lawrence Sherman, cautioned against the precipitous adoption of mandatory arrest policies; the other, Richard Berk, argued that states should adopt or maintain mandatory arrest policies until research showed that some other police intervention was more effective (Berk & Newton, 1985; Sherman & Smith, 1992).

Although a majority of jurisdictions in the United States, prompted by funding incentives in the Violence Against Women Act, have adopted some form of preferred or mandatory arrest law or policy, subsequent research has failed to clearly establish the effectiveness of arrest in deterring intimate partner violence.

Similarly, research on the efficacy of no-drop prosecution in securing women's safety and holding offenders accountable has been equivocal. No-drop prosecution has certainly resulted in greater numbers of cases being prosecuted, but not all victimless prosecution jurisdictions report higher numbers of convictions or any impact on overall rates of intimate partner violence. Social science research suggests that no-drop policies may have problematic consequences as well. In a study of Milwaukee's aggressive no-drop policy,

researchers linked the policy to a number of negative outcomes, including longer times for case processing, decreased victim satisfaction, and increases in pretrial crime (Davis, Smith, & Taylor, 2003). What many jurisdictions do report, however, is a rise in the number of victims recanting their previous testimony rather than testifying against their partners at trial, calling into question exactly who no-drop prosecution policies are meant to serve.

At best, the research provides lukewarm support for these criminal justice reforms, and that support must be balanced against their costs. Critics of mandatory arrest and no-drop prosecution have noted the incursions that these policies make into victim autonomy. The decision to recant is a manifestation of the struggle between a victim seeking to protect her right to decide whether to proceed with prosecution and a system determined to use the criminal law to address intimate partner violence. Victim decisions about arrest and prosecution are far more complex than they might seem, involving calculations about the impact of legal system involvement not just on safety, but also on economic stability, divorce, child custody, child support, immigration status, and the relationship itself. Mandatory arrest and no-drop prosecution policies deprive victims of the opportunity to selectively and consciously use arrest and prosecution as a "power resource" (Ford, 1991). The cost of the criminalization of domestic violence has been disempowerment for some battered women.

Few are willing to take Gruber's (2009) extreme position that total disengagement from the criminal law is the appropriate response; much more common are proposals like Caringella's (2009) "middle-ground" strategy to reform law in practice, law as implemented. In the realm of domestic violence law and policy, those proposals include preferred (as opposed to mandatory) arrest policies, which provide police with some discretion to confer with victims of violence before determining whether an arrest is warranted, and "soft" no-drop prosecution policies, which allow prosecutors to move forward with prosecution without the cooperation of the victim but which refrain from coercing victim participation in the process.

Exporting the Law

These critiques of the legal response to violence against women should give pause to those who advocate for the creation of similar legal regimes worldwide. A cottage industry has developed around exporting the United States legal system to countries around the globe. Bar associations, law schools, and nongovernmental organizations regularly send emissaries to help seed American-style legal reforms in less-developed nations, and delegations from those nations visit the United States seeking ideas to take back with them to their home countries. These groups are generally told that the criminalization of violence against women has been an unqualified success and that the development of criminal and civil remedies to address domestic violence is the best way to safeguard victims of violence. Rarely, if ever, do these groups meet with critics of those systems, nor are they provided with the research that calls the efficacy of these policies into question. The unique cultural characteristics and legal frameworks of these countries are lost in an unqualified endorsement of one-size-fits-all policies to respond to violence against women. Moreover, as criminologist Patricia Erwin (2006) notes, the legal framework supporting interventions on behalf of victims of violence in the United States is significantly narrower than that used by other nations, particularly those who have embraced the characterization of violence against women as a human rights issue. The United States' focus on "procedural equality"— that is, using the legal system to address the maltreatment of women—blinds policy makers to the array of subordinating conditions that support women's victimization. Erwin, too, notes that in relying so heavily on the legal system to protect women from violence, women have ceded substantial power to the state—a state that might actively engage in or be complicit in acts of

violence against women. This uncritical promotion of the criminal justice agenda so discomfited noted advocate Ellen Pence that she is no longer willing to conduct international trainings on legal system reform (Erwin, 2006).

The export of American norms on the handling of domestic violence could also stifle policy innovations that are sensitive to the cultural context and local conditions of developing countries. Law professors Raquel Aldana and Leticia Saucedo (2008) describe a domestic violence mediation program in Mulukuku, Nicaragua—a program that would raise the ire of many advocates in the United States, who strongly oppose the use of mediation in cases involving intimate partner violence. But Aldana and Saucedo argue that the criminalization of domestic violence in Nicaragua has been a failure. The state is not seriously committed to enforcement of women's rights, women do not have access to social services, and criminalization addressed neither the rehabilitation of offenders nor reconciliation after violence. In fact, Aldana and Saucedo argue, "The problem of domestic violence in Nicaragua has arguably worsened as a result of the implementation of the adversarial legal system" (p. 1285). Mediation enables the community to address the root causes of domestic violence, including the culture of machismo in Nicaragua—a task for which the criminal justice system is ill-suited.

Using International Law and Human Rights Norms to Combat Violence Against Women

In her celebrated address before the Fourth World Conference on Women in Beijing, China, in September, 1995, then-First Lady Hillary Rodham Clinton declared, "Human rights are women's rights—and women's rights are human rights." Scholars and advocates are exploring the extent to which the laws and treaties that secure human rights on the international level can be used both to address, and more important, prevent, violence against women.

Violence against women violates fundamental human rights: to life, freedom, privacy, safety, economic stability, and family integrity. These rights have been articulated repeatedly in international treaties and charters, including the Universal Declaration of Human Rights, The International Covenant on Civil and Political Rights, the Convention on the Elimination of All Forms of Discrimination Against Women, and the Declaration on the Elimination of Violence Against Women. These rights have been and can be translated into concrete results for victims of violence in a number of different areas.

That rape in the context of war violates international law and human rights norms is now firmly established thanks to decisions from the war crimes tribunals of Rwanda and Yugoslavia. In 1998, Rwanda's war crimes tribunal held that rape and other forms of sexual violence constituted genocide if the crimes were committed with the intent to destroy a targeted group (in this case, the Tutsi population). For the first time in international law, the tribunal held that the purpose of rape could be to annihilate the enemy population. Three years later, the war crimes tribunal in the former Yugoslavia found, for the first time, that rape constituted a war crime under international humanitarian law. These decisions could pave the way for the development of a peremptory norm against rape as a tool of war. Moreover, the International Criminal Court has jurisdiction to hear cases involving rapes committed in wartime. One commentator has suggested that these decisions, as well as provisions in the Geneva Convention, the Genocide Convention, the Torture Convention, and the Hague Convention on the Laws of War, could provide successful grounds for the prosecution of the innumerable rapes committed during the conflict in Darfur (Wagner, 2005).

The international human rights framework is increasingly being applied to violence that has traditionally been deemed a matter of domestic law. Frustrated with court decisions granting custody of and unsafe visitation with their children to their abusers, battered mothers in a number of jurisdictions in the United States are arguing that such decisions violate not only their rights under state and federal law, but also under international treaties and human rights law. The Wellesley Centers for Women's report, *Battered Mothers Speak Out*, documented numerous instances in which the actions of the courts of Massachusetts violated the human rights of battered mothers and their children by giving custody of children to batterers, awarding abusive fathers unsafe visitation, belittling and refusing to consider mother's claims of violence against them and their children, and denying mothers adequate economic support to care for their children properly (Cuthbert, Slote, Driggers, Mesh, Bancroft, & Silverman, 2002). The report gave voice to battered mothers struggling with the Massachusetts court system, in an attempt to spur the system to remedy these violations of state, federal, and international law. Although system actors were resistant to the attempt to apply international laws and human rights norms to the operation of the Massachusetts courts, the report prompted the court system to conduct an internal investigation, which documented many of the same problems.

Jessica Gonzales Lenahan turned to international law remedies after the United States Supreme Court denied her the opportunity to hold police in Castle Rock, Colorado accountable for their failure to protect her three daughters. Lenahan's ex-husband, who was subject to a protective order barring him from seeing the girls except during designated visitations, abducted the girls from their front yard. For 10 hours, police refused to search for the children—then found them after a gun battle with Gonzales in the Castle Rock Police Department (CRPD) parking lot. The girls were dead as a result of gunshot wounds, their bodies found in the back of Gonzales' truck. The Supreme Court held that Lenahan could not pursue a lawsuit against the CRPD in federal court because she did not have a constitutional right to demand to have her protective order enforced. After the Court's ruling in *Town of Castle Rock v. Gonzales* (2005) deprived Lenahan of the opportunity to explore CRPD's responsibility for her daughter's deaths in the courts of the United States, Lenahan turned to the Inter-American Commission on Human Rights (IAHCR) for redress. As Lenahan said in a radio interview, "I was not heard in my own country and I had to go to an outer body to be heard, to help the United States understand where they failed me and my children" (Bettinger-López, 2008). Lenahan asked the IAHCR to find that the CRPD's failure to respond to her calls for help violated her rights to life and freedom from inhumane treatment, equal protection, privacy, family unity, and safety in the home, as well as special protections for women and children found in the American Declaration of the Rights and Duties of Man, and denied her an effective and adequate remedy.

In October, 2007, the Commission ruled that Ms. Lenahan's claim against the United States could go forward, and in March, 2008, the Commission heard the case on its merits. A decision is expected in 2010. Law professor and Lenahan counsel Caroline Bettinger-López (2008) explains why presenting cases like Lenahan's in the context of international human rights law is so important:

> International human rights principles . . . make clear that the government has an affirmative obligation to protect individuals from private acts of violence, to investigate alleged violations and publicly report the results, and to provide an adequate and effective remedy when those duties are breached. . . . By framing domestic violence as a human rights violation, the [Gonzales] case challenges advocates and policymakers to re-think our . . . current approach to domestic violence, and asks whether fundamental rights—to life, security, family, due process, equality, truth, and freedom from torture and cruel, inhuman, and degrading treatment—are being respected and fulfilled. (p. 21)

International law may also provide a way to improve the nonlegal responses to violence against women. International law addresses economic and social rights as well as procedural rights. In her petition to the Commission, Lenahan asked for an investigation into the circumstances surrounding her daughters' deaths and also for reform that would provide remedies for victims of domestic violence consistent with international human rights norms on violence against women and domestic violence. The requested reforms included strengthening services to support victims' economic and social rights; adopting a holistic strategy to address domestic violence; and developing public education campaigns on domestic violence. Although the Commission's decision will not provide Lenahan with a judicially enforceable remedy, Bettinger-López (2008) argues, it will help to define the norms of appropriate handling of cases of domestic violence and provide advocates with a tool to pressure the United States to institutionalize those norms. If Lenahan prevails and intimate partner violence is found to be actionable under international law when the state fails to provide an adequate remedy, surely advocates will continue to explore the potential for addressing other forms of violence against women, like rape and stalking, through international law.

Economics and Violence Against Women

Many of the laws and policies discussed in this chapter are intended to bolster women's economic security because economic insecurity and violence against women are inextricably linked. A recent article about violence against women in Haiti, for example, details the myriad ways in which economic instability contributes to violence against women in that country. Poverty means that many families live in cramped quarters, without doors that lock or adequate lighting. These dangerous conditions in the home are linked to the high rates of sexual abuse, particularly abuse of young girls, in Haiti. Poor girls are sold by their parents to wealthier families, a practice known as *restavék*, where they are routinely raped and exploited. Women identified economic dependence on their partners as the primary cause of their subjugation. Where women are viewed as property, attacks on women are seen as appropriate attempts to control one's most valuable possession. Economic instability in Haiti has contributed to political instability, leading to war-like conditions. Violence against women—rape, sexual slavery, and forced prostitution—has become a tool in Haiti's political war (Faedi, 2008).

Many jurisdictions now recognize economic abuse as a form of violence against women in their domestic violence laws. India's Protection of Women From Domestic Violence Act includes economic abuse in its definition of domestic violence, as do the laws of other countries (e.g., Zimbabwe, Ecuador, and Cambodia) and at least one U.S. state, Michigan. International law may also empower a victim of domestic violence to hold the state responsible for its failure to provide her with the economic wherewithal to access the legal system and escape a violent partner. Expanding the law to include economic abuse is certain to help victims of violence.

But these types of legal responses become available only after women are abused. Addressing the underlying economic instability that contributes to violence against women is a key preventive measure. Alleviating the dire economic conditions in Haiti, for example, could provide women with options beyond abusive relationships, help to stabilize the country, and enable women to escape some of this violence. One major antiviolence initiative in Darfur involves providing stoves to women living in refugee camps. Why stoves? Because scores of women were raped and killed when they left the camps to collect firewood to cook their meals. The stoves require significantly less firewood and, therefore, fewer unsafe trips to gather the wood. These stoves currently provide more protection to women in the camps than the law does and serve as a reminder to expand our vision of how law should be deployed. Creative use of law and policy to improve the economic status of marginalized women must be a central component of future antiviolence strategies. Even the creative use of the law, however, cannot address all of the manifestations of violence against women.

The Limits of the Law

The development of the law to combat violence against women over the last 30 years is astonishing, but there are limits to what the law can do. The United States has perhaps the most comprehensive laws and policies on intimate partner violence in the world, yet the rate of intimate partner violence has not actually declined (when declines in the overall crime rate are taken into account). Although the law serves an expressive function, fundamentally the law is a reactive medium, punishing wrongdoers for harm they have already done. Overreliance on the law, particularly the criminal law, has allowed advocates and policy makers to avoid thinking about preventive responses to violence against women, and that failure does women a grave disservice.

References

Aldana, R., & Saucedo, L. M. (2008). The illusion of transformative conflict resolution: Mediating domestic violence in Nicaragua. *Buffalo Law Review, 55,* 1261–1330.

Berk, R. A., & Newton, P. J. (1985). Does arrest really deter wife battery: An effort to replicate the findings of the Minnesota spouse abuse experiment. *American Sociological Review, 50,* 253–262.

Bettinger-López, C. (2008). Human rights at home: Domestic violence as a human rights violation. *Columbia Human Rights Law Review, 40,* 19–77.

Bruch, C. S. (2004). The unmet needs of domestic violence victims and their children in Hague child abduction convention cases. *Family Law Quarterly, 38,* 529–545.

Buzawa, E. S., & Buzawa, C. G. (2003). *Domestic violence: The criminal justice response.* Thousand Oaks, CA: Sage.

Caringella, S. (2009). *Addressing rape reform in law and practice.* New York: Columbia University Press.

Cuthbert, C., Slote, K., Driggers, M., Mesh, C., Bancroft, L., & Silverman, J. (2002). *Battered mothers speak out: A human rights report on domestic violence and child custody in the Massachusetts family courts.* Wellesley, MA: Wellesley Centers for Women.

Davis, R., Smith, B., & Taylor, B. (2003). Increasing the proportion of domestic violence arrests that are prosecuted: A natural experiment in Milwaukee. *Criminology & Public Policy, 2,* 263–282.

Erwin, P. E. (2006). Exporting U.S. domestic violence reforms: An analysis of human rights frameworks and U.S. "best practices." *Feminist Criminology, 1,* 188–206.

Faedi, B. (2008). The double weakness of girls: Discrimination and sexual violence in Haiti. *Stanford Journal of International Law, 44,* 147–204.

Ford, D. (1991). Prosecution as a victim power resource: A note on empowering women in violent conjugal relationships. *Law and Society Review, 25,* 313–332.

Goodno, N. H. (2007). Cyberstalking, a new crime: Evaluating the effectiveness of current state and federal laws. *Missouri Law Review, 72,* 125–196.

Gruber, A. (2009). Rape, feminism and the war on crime. *Washington Law Review, 84,* 581–660.

Hoegger, R. (2003). What if she leaves? Domestic violence cases under the Hague convention and the insufficiency of the undertakings remedy. *Berkeley Women's Law Journal, 18,* 181–210.

Malan, D. A. (2009, January 6). YouTube threat draws restraining order. *Connecticut Law Tribune.* Retrieved July 30, 2009, from http://www.law.com/jsp/legaltechnology/index.jsp

Osborne v. Fadden, 225 Or. App. 431, 438 (2009).

Pena v. Mattox, 84 F.3d 894, 903 (7th Cir. 1996).

Ross, K. M. (2007). Eviction, discrimination, and domestic violence: Unfair housing practices against domestic violence survivors. *Hasting Women's Law Journal, 18,* 249–268.

Sherman, L., & Smith, D. (1992). Crime, punishment, and stake in conformity: Legal and informal control of domestic violence. *American Sociological Review, 57,* 680–690.

Tarr, N. W. (2007). Employment and economic security for victims of domestic abuse. *Southern California Review of Law and Social Justice, 16,* 371–427.

Town of Castle Rock v. Gonzales, 125 S. Ct. 2796 (2005).

United States General Accounting Office. (1998). *Domestic violence: Prevalence and implications for employment among welfare recipients.* Washington, DC: United States Government Printing Office.

Wagner, J. (2005). The systematic use of rape as a tool of war in Darfur: A blueprint for international war crimes prosecutions. *Georgetown Journal of International Law, 37,* 193–243.

Weiner, M. H. (2004). Strengthening Article 20. *University of San Francisco Law Review, 38,* 701–746.

Weiner, M. H. (2008). Half-truths, mistakes, and embarrassments: The United States goes to the Fifth Meeting of the Special Commission to Review the Operation of the Hague Convention on the Civil Aspects of International Child Abduction. *Utah Law Review,* 221–313.

Widiss, D. A. (2008). Domestic violence and the workplace: The explosion of state legislation and the need for a comprehensive strategy. *Florida State University Law Review, 35,* 669–728.

Chapter Author

Leigh Goodmark teaches family law and supervises students representing clients in the Family Law Clinic at the University of Baltimore School of Law. She previously directed the Children and Domestic Violence Project at the American Bar Association Center on Children and the Law. Before joining the Center on Children and the Law, she represented battered women and children in the District of Columbia in custody, visitation, child support, restraining order, and other civil matters. Her forthcoming book, *A Troubled Marriage: Domestic Violence and the Legal System,* will be published by New York University Press.

Personal Reflection

Kiersten Stewart

My debate coach in high school always said it was my red hair that gave me away. I spent many mornings and much adolescent angst trying to tame the frizzy mane that befuddles me still today. She said it would be wrong to straighten and color these locks; they were too much who I was—all energy and independence, willfulness and determination. A little too sassy, to be sure, but with a forcefulness capable of great things.

I like to think that it is this work, the work to end violence against women and children, that will one day honor her encouraging words. Doing political advocacy on behalf of abused women and children and working to prevent violence is my deepest passion. I believe it is both noble and necessary, though at times the hardest work I could ever do. People often ask why I work in this field. Unlike many who enter it, I wasn't abused. I didn't witness my mother being hurt. Rather, it was the opposite. I had a wonderful childhood, though we certainly didn't fit the traditional mold. I am proud that I was raised by a single mother, barely out of her teens when she had me. I grew up faster than most of my peers, it is true, and there are definitely choices she made that she probably wishes were different. But what I learned from her is what I hear from so many children who grew up in less than perfect and, in some cases, horrific circumstances: that some of the best parts of you, the qualities that best serve you, the experiences that have deeply formed you, are the qualities that come out of challenging circumstances. I do this work because it is so wrong what happens to so many women and children and also because I have a chance to work with some of the most incredibly powerful and resilient people. By doing this work, I bear witness to their pain but also honor their courage.

That's not to say there aren't really hard days. What makes me good at my job is the ability to bring to others—mostly elected legislators and government officials—the deeply personal stories of those who have been hurt and to embolden them to take on this cause with vigor. When, despite my best efforts, they vote the "wrong way" or offer up only a pittance of the money that is necessary, the sense of defeat is enormous. The stories of atrocity and sadness don't just go away at the end of the day. And while the Obama administration creates enormous opportunities—rarely has there been a time when so many people in power share our values and commitment to ending this scourge—we still struggle to get the financial resources necessary to address violence. It will no doubt be better, but the work continues.

The challenge, therefore, both personally and politically, is to find that balance between rage and wisdom. I think this struggle is why I have such a deep and abiding admiration for Paul Wellstone and why I so miss having him in the Senate. He knew how to maintain his clear sense of purpose, his outrage at injustice everywhere, but he also knew how to hold onto the joys in his life, especially his wife and partner, Sheila. I'm sorry I didn't get to know him better, but his energy, too, burst through a wild set of curls. Someday I hope to honor his legacy and the wonderful women who told me to embrace what I had and put it to good use. This is, indeed, the right fight and one I am proud to be part of.

CHAPTER 11

Primary Prevention

Corinne Meltzer Graffunder, Rebecca Cline, and Karen G. Lane

The World Health Organization (WHO), a specialized agency of the United Nations established in 1948 to coordinate international health and public health matters, released the first *World Report on Violence and Health* in 2002 (Krug, Dahlberg, Mercy, Zwi, & Lozano, 2002). The *World Report* documented the health-related burden of violence and defined and described the worldwide impact of violence against women. The purpose of the first *World Report* was to challenge the secrecy, taboos, and feelings of inevitability that surround violent behavior. More important, the report emphasized that violence is preventable. Providing an international platform for public health practitioners to recognize and address violence, the report offers a framework for organizing, developing, and evaluating strategies to *prevent* violence.

This chapter reviews fundamental aspects of a public health approach to prevention, including the application of population-based strategies across a continuum of approaches directed to achieve multidimensional outcomes. We posit in this chapter that commonly the prevention of violence against women is grounded in poorly established, narrowly defined concepts and constructs. This chapter challenges readers to consider a shift in the paradigm for preventing violence against women. Using data to identify populations affected by violence and the social conditions that cause violence, we argue that this shift requires solutions that impact individuals, families, communities, and multiple sectors of society. Offering insight and examples, we conclude this chapter with suggestions and recommendations supporting a philosophical and theoretical framework that expands the understanding and application of prevention science.

Prevention: A Classic Tale

A classic tool used to convey the evolution of prevention is the following story:

> A woman is sitting beside a river when suddenly she hears a shout for help. This shout for help is quickly followed by her observation of a woman struggling, arms and legs

Authors' Note: The findings and conclusions in this submission are those of the authors and do not necessarily represent the views of the Centers for Disease Control and Prevention.

flailing, as she comes down the river. Unable to stand by and watch this woman in crisis, our fisherwoman jumps into the river and pulls the struggling woman to the shore. Just as she is beginning to provide the necessary care to the woman she has just rescued, she is astonished to hear yet another cry for help. Another woman, flailing and in crisis, is coming down the river. She again jumps into the river and pulls this woman out. This happens time and time again until she is no longer surprised to hear the cry for help, at which point the cries multiply. She sees that it is now no longer just one woman in crisis but many women coming down the river, arms and legs flailing. Exhausted and with little incentive to continue these rescue efforts, except her personal motivation and concern for the well-being of these women, she continues to rescue those that she can, realizing sadly that there are many, many more that she is unable to reach, unable to assist. As she grows ever more frustrated with the never-ending stream of women in crisis, she realizes that if she is going to ultimately stop the flow of women coming down the river in crisis, she needs to go upstream and determine what circumstances, conditions, or forces are causing the women to fall into this river.

This parable is salient to those working to prevent violence against women because it acknowledges the importance of providing life-changing, life-saving support, yet recognizes that efforts to address the needs of victims are insufficient to prevent violence. This parable represents "the beginning" of every prevention success celebrated today. Each prevention success story starts with a similar set of questions: Who is impacted by violence against women? What are the circumstances associated with violence against women? What conditions promote, encourage, or facilitate violence against women? Finally, are there forces or actions that deter violence against

women? Answering these questions helps us to understand the relationship between social and cultural norms, institutional practices or policies, and regional (state or national) and global policies and laws, and whether they effectively exacerbate or ameliorate circumstances associated with violence against women. Our fisherwoman is likely to find a *complex set* of interrelated circumstances, conditions, and forces; this complexity must be critically analyzed, and effective, multidimensional strategies must be employed to ensure the reduction or elimination of violence against women.

Prevention Science: Unpacking Complex Problems

A public health approach to prevention navigates complexity by examining multiple factors, and it can reveal characteristics initially not apparent. For example, the National Violence Against Women Survey (Tjaden & Thoennes, 2000) and other research indicate that one in four women experiences intimate partner violence or sexual violence in her lifetime, and within that group, the majority are girls and young women (Basile, Chen, Black, & Saltzman, 2007; Rennison & Welchans, 2000). However, a more complex analysis and the consideration of a broader range of factors are required to understand and begin to address questions such as how female genital mutilation, which is an accepted practice in some countries and has been imported to the U.S., continues to be practiced in some cultural or ethnic subgroups; how cultural norms that condone or promote violence against women are reflected in the media's portrayal of the objectification and abuse of women; and how lack of economic viability creates situations in which women are beholden to or dependent on others, most often men, for family and individual security. Examples such as these begin to build a picture of an intricate interplay of contributing factors.

Data are essential to a more complex analysis and to the subsequent design and implementation of effective strategies. Even when limited, data are useful for "unpacking" complex problems. Unpacking is the breaking down of a concept into orderly and manageable sets or component units (Flaspohler, Duffy, Wandersman, Stillman, & Maras, 2008; Sartori, 1970). Unpacking helps to inform decisions including the following:

- *Who* a particular strategy or tactic will reach;
- *When,* within the trajectory of violent behavior, the strategy or tactic "intervenes";
- *What* the impact of this change will look like, if successful; and
- *Where* we can expect to look to determine our impact or success.

Deliberate consideration helps not only to clarify decision making related to an approach or set of tactics; it allows for clarity regarding the breadth and scope of a strategy and the gaps that may remain.

A Population-Based Approach to Prevention: Answering the Question *Who?*

One of the first questions to consider when working within a prevention framework is, "Who is affected by the problem?" Answering this question requires data that distinguishes among and between various groups or populations of interest. WHO defines three distinct population approaches important in understanding and addressing the prevention of violence: *universal, selected,* and *indicated* (Krug et al., 2002; see Table 11.1).

For example, efforts aimed at preventing high school boys from perpetrating teen dating violence are *universal* if all boys, regardless of the teen dating violence experience, are included. The design of a universal approach is not dependent on whether or not some of the high school boys have already perpetrated teen dating violence, as it is likely that some will have some experience. *Selected approaches* require prevention practitioners to identify specific risk factors, such as hostility toward women or hypermasculinity, and devise strategies that address members of a population who, by virtue of having expressed these particular risk factors, may be at greater risk for perpetrating teen dating violence. Finally, efforts directed to boys who have perpetrated teen dating violence are *indicated approaches* and might include disciplinary action, such as arrest and adjudication in juvenile court or referral to a teen batterer intervention program.

As this example suggests, *selected* and *indicated* population strategies must be informed by an understanding of risk factors (e.g., What puts groups at heightened risk for perpetrating or experiencing violence against women?). Data of interest include factors that are associated with the individuals impacted as well as data related to the conditions, context, or environment that increase or decrease risk. In every case, when considering risk factors there are some factors that

Table 11.1 Population Approaches to Prevention

Universal: Approaches aimed at groups or the general population regardless of individual risk for perpetration or victimization. Groups can be defined geographically (e.g., a school or school district) or by characteristics (e.g., ethnicity, age, gender).

Selected: Approaches aimed at those who are thought to have a *heightened risk* for perpetration or victimization.

Indicated: Approaches aimed at those who have already *perpetrated* or have been *victimized.*

will be and others that will not be modifiable. For instance, when concerned with sexual violence, the data related to rates of victimization clearly indicate heightened risk among women and children. Similarly, the rates associated with perpetration of physical violence, particularly violence resulting in injuries, are disproportionately represented among males. Yet, neither age nor sex are modifiable. Furthermore, the majority of women and children are not victimized, and the majority of men are not perpetrators of violence against women. Thus, effective prevention requires consideration of additional data that define and may help to understand additional factors that underlie or contribute to increased risk for victimization and for perpetration.

Risk reduction strategies focused on factors associated with victimization may be effective in preventing some women from experiencing violence but are likely insufficient to effectively end violence against women. Focusing prevention efforts on the complex interplay of risk factors associated with the perpetration of violence against women may lead to reductions in violence against women.

Important to understanding risk is an understanding of known risk factors for perpetration or victimization that are correlated with violence against women but do not predict or indicate, with certainty, violent behavior. Likewise, no single factor completely explains risk for perpetration of or victimization resulting from violence against women.

The literature related to violence against women identifies a range of risk factors that may contribute to perpetration or victimization (Blum & Ireland, 2004; Loh, Gidycz, Lobo, & Luthra, 2005; Macmillan & Kruttschnitt, 2005; National Institute of Justice, 2004). However, risk factors are not the cause of violence. For instance, data may show that males with dominant attitudes of hypermasculinity, negativity, and superiority toward women are at increased risk of perpetrating acts of violence against women, but that is not the same as the factors that *cause* those attitudes or beliefs. Attitudes, beliefs, and resulting behaviors are learned. In understanding this distinction, it is important to consider whether or not your prevention strategy is directed at changing the societal and cultural norms that form, reinforce, and perhaps, in some instances, even reward these dominant attitudes. Such an approach would be *universal* prevention because the aim is to change the values or norms of the entire group. However, if your prevention strategy is directed to males who already hold dominant attitudes, and you are attempting to decrease the likelihood of their attitudes resulting in violent behavior rather than change their attitudes, then your approach is *selected*.

As the definitions and examples suggest, prevention strategies do not focus exclusively on considering populations affected by violence, but rather emphasize the need to understand risk and the relationship of conditions that contribute to violence within population groups. Defining and refining the population of interest can be an important consideration, given limited prevention resources. In addition, as more and more funding agencies and organizations demand accountability, including the ability to measure or detect impact or change, specificity is needed. However, the population of interest is only one characteristic that needs to be clearly defined within a prevention strategy. The next section addresses the need to define *when*, within a continuum of violence, a prevention strategy is intended to intervene.

The Prevention Continuum: Answering the Question *When?*

Defining *who* a strategy is intended for is one important component of prevention planning. However, if prevention planning were to end at this point, there would remain many ambiguities. For a strategy to be accountable, it must also clarify *when*, within the trajectory or continuum of violence, the prevention effort is designed to intervene. The distinction between types of prevention is specific to when (or whether) violence occurs and is different from the universal, selected, and indicated population categories discussed above. The types of prevention most commonly described are primary, secondary, and tertiary. *Primary* prevention includes activities or approaches that take place before violence has occurred, to prevent initial perpetration or victimization. Primary prevention activities are directed at universal or selected populations, with the goal of preventing the occurrence of violence against women. Activities to decrease or mitigate risk factors and increase protective factors may also be directed at selected audiences for whom risk is greater. These activities are considered primary prevention as long as perpetration or victimization has not yet occurred. *Secondary* prevention includes the immediate response after violence has occurred, to deal with the short-term consequences of violence. *Tertiary* prevention is the long-term response after violence has occurred, dealing with the lasting consequences of the violence.

A common misunderstanding is the substitution of the population concept *universal* (who), with the prevention concept *primary* (when). Efforts to reach a population regardless of risk (universal) are only primary prevention if the outcome of the strategy prevents the initial perpetration of violence or victimization. Therefore, efforts such as educating populations about their rights, available services, or hotlines are universal and secondary or tertiary.

The ability to distinguish primary, secondary, and tertiary strategies and work to ensure they are universally available is important. For instance, as stated, primary prevention includes efforts that result in lower risk for first occurrence of either victimization or perpetration or the elimination of an unwanted behavior. Primary prevention can be focused on reducing or eliminating victimization or perpetration, but these are not one and the same. Often, strategies directed at girls or women provide information, skills, resources, or tools designed to prevent victimization. When the information, skills, resources, or tools are effective, the prevention of abuse for that individual is appropriately labeled as primary. Efforts to prevent perpetration may also include the provision of information, skill building, or resources and tools directed at boys or men and, when effective, they stop that individual from inflicting harm or abuse on any number of potential victims.

Determining *when* is important to ensure that the strategies implemented are appropriate to the context of the problem. Attempts to change conditions may be ineffective if the full context is ignored. For example, teaching healthy relationship concepts to someone in immediate danger from a partner is unlikely to achieve its desired outcome. Comprehensive community-level prevention strategies often combine all three *when* levels of prevention (primary, secondary, and tertiary), adding a dimension to each that recognizes that even within a given level, the range of outcomes is variable.

The Ecology of Prevention: Answering the Questions *What?* and *Where?*

Effective prevention strategies also require deliberate planning and consideration of *what* change is desired and *where* meaningful indicators of the desired change will occur. As has already been stated, preventing violence requires an understanding of the circumstances and factors that influence its occurrence. Many different theoretical models attempt to describe the root causes of violence against women, including biological models; psychological models; cultural models; and grassroots, feminist power-based models (Baron & Strauss, 1989; Sokoloff & Dupont, 2005; Yllo, 1998). Each of these models contributes to a better understanding of violence against women and helps in the development of strategies to sustain protective factors and reduce modifiable risk factors. These models help to answer the question, "*What* change are we trying to realize?"

Ecological models are often used in an effort to recognize, plan, and organize a coordinated approach and answer the question, "*What* change is desired?" While many ecological models exist, the one used here is a four-level model presented in the *World Report on Violence and Health* (Krug et al., 2002). This model offers a framework for understanding the interplay of the individual, relational, social, political, cultural, and environmental factors that influence violence and provides key points for prevention and intervention (Powell, Mercy, Crosby, Dahlberg, & Simon, 1999). Each of the broader ecological niches can have an impact on the niches within it (Stokols, 1992, 1996), allowing psychological models about individual risk factors and feminist models about societal risk factors to be incorporated into a comprehensive strategy. Presented in Figure 11.1, this model includes the following:

- *Individual level:* Biological and personal history factors that increase the likelihood an individual will become a perpetrator or victim of violence are the focus at this level (Krug et al., 2002). Efforts are often designed to target social and cognitive skills and behavior and include approaches such as counseling, therapy, and educational training sessions (Powell et al., 1999).

- *Interpersonal relationship level:* Factors that increase risk as a result of relationships with peers, intimate partners, and family members and shape an individual's behavior and range of experience are the focus at this level (Krug et al., 2002). Efforts include family therapy, bystander intervention skill development, and parenting training (Powell et al., 1999).

- *Community level:* This level focuses on the characteristics of community settings and institutions in which social relationships take place, including schools, workplaces, and neighborhoods. It includes organizational or institutional efforts that influence the norms and values of communities and reinforce beliefs and behaviors (Krug et al., 2002). Community-level efforts are typically designed to impact the climate, systems, and policies in a given setting (Powell et al., 1999).

- *Societal level:* The larger, macro-level factors that influence violence against women, such as gender inequality, religious or cultural belief systems, societal norms, and economic or social policies that create or sustain gaps and tensions between groups of people are the focus at this level (Krug et al., 2002). Societal-level efforts typically involve collaborations by multiple partners to change laws and policies related to violence against women or gender inequality. Efforts to determine societal norms that reinforce, promote, or simply accept violence and the identification of strategies for changing those norms can also be societal and are often influenced by the laws or policies promulgated and enforced (Powell et al., 1999).

Thus, the ecological model supports a comprehensive public health approach that addresses not only an individual's risk factors but also the norms, beliefs, and social and economic systems that create the conditions for violence against women.

Applying the ecological model to prevention planning helps answer the question, "*What?*" However, this model can be mistakenly used to address the question, "*Where?*" One common example of this misperception is a strategy designed to educate students, teachers, and school or university staff that is represented as a community-level strategy because a school is a community institution. However, if a strategy is designed to reach

Figure 11.1 Ecological Model

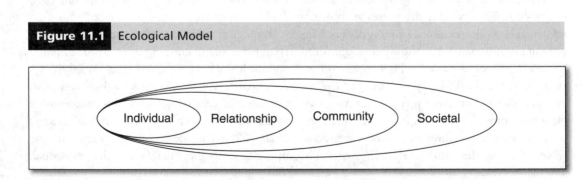

students, faculty, or staff and the outcome is a change in knowledge, attitudes, or behavior, then it is an individual- or group-level strategy. In this case, the community institution (i.e., the school) serves as the stage or platform for the strategy. A community-level strategy is specifically designed to change some aspect or dynamic of the organizational or institutional context. Thus, the focus is specific to a set of conditions or changes in the context or environment believed to support or reinforce unwanted behavior. An example would be the implementation of school policies that prohibit sexual harassment, the extent to which they are enforced, and the resulting increases in students' perceptions of safety or decreases in reported behaviors.

For the purposes of public health planning, and ultimately measuring the impact of any public health intervention, the concept of *where* is related to measurement (e.g., the documentation of the desired change and resulting impact). Thus, the question to be asked and ultimately answered is "*Where* are there markers or indicators that will demonstrate that the desired change is occurring?" For instance, it is important to know where individual or group knowledge, attitudes, or behavior can be measured, monitored, or assessed. Likewise, if a prevention strategy is designed to address community or societal levels of the social ecology, prevention planners need to know where they can find data or information to demonstrate that the desired change(s) has occurred (e.g., community or societal norms, climate, or standards). Measuring individual self-reported perception of safety is one example of "where" the impact of a comprehensive prevention strategy might be measured. Individual self-reports, coupled with school-based incident reports and other sources of data that monitor organizational or community climate, may provide the most complete assessment and relate to more sustainable change.

Developing a Prevention Paradigm: Barriers and Challenges

In working to advance a public health agenda for preventing violence against women, the U.S.

Centers for Disease Control and Prevention (CDC) has engaged in dialogue, consultation, planning, and the development of strategies and recommendations at the international, national, state, and local levels. These efforts have identified significant work occurring across the continuum of prevention, led and coordinated by many stakeholders, and coordinated among partners representing multiple domains. Thus, the growth and advancement of work to prevent violence against women benefits from the experience and experimentation of many who ask the question, "How do we *stop* violence against women from occurring?" However, this collective experience consistently identifies a set of common barriers and challenges to meaningful prevention efforts. Inherent in each of these is a gross oversimplification of the complex analysis required for meaningful and sustainable change. The following highlights each of these barriers briefly:

Prevention as Increasing Awareness, Educating, and Informing

A common prevention paradigm equates prevention with the development and dissemination of effective messages or accurate information. Approaches include curricula designed to provide information or campaigns designed to raise awareness or inform a priority population. At the community level, efforts to educate community members about the extent of the problem often entail the expectation that this information will drive community-level change. Widely accepted theories of change among individuals and within organizations or communities recognize and include a role for accurate information made available in a manner that contributes to heightened awareness, and awareness is one component of early phases of adoption or diffusion (Rogers, 1995, Chapter 1).

Unfortunately, too often what is found within the practice of prevention is that efforts never progress beyond the awareness-raising phase. A disproportionate reliance on awareness-raising or educational approaches suggests a belief that information provided to a potential perpetrator or victim will modify behavior. This is rarely supported theoretically or empirically. The inclusion of accurate and compelling messaging as a component of any prevention approach is necessary, but not sufficient. Effective prevention efforts are multifaceted; they deliberately build upon foundational work that may involve the provision of information or transfer of knowledge, but they necessarily include additional levels of effort directed at a broader range of outcomes. Leaders within the field of prevention of violence against women recognize that it is awareness combined with action that leads to the desired social change.

A tool for thinking about and engaging in primary prevention activities is the Spectrum of Prevention (Davis, Fujie Parks, & Cohen, 2006). Recognizing that norms shape and are shaped by organizational practices and policies, the Spectrum of Prevention provides examples of prevention strategies using an ecological model.

Prevention as Reaching Youth

A second prevention challenge is the common misperception that directs prevention strategies primarily to youth. Prevention strategies based on

Table 11.2	The Spectrum of Prevention

Level	Definition	Sample Strategies
1. Strengthening individual knowledge and skills	Enhancing an individual's capability of preventing injury and violence and promoting safety	Programs that strengthen individuals' communication skills using role-play, peer discussion, etc.
2. Promoting community education	Reaching people with information and resources to prevent violence and promote health and safety	A Peace Walk promotes the message of nonviolence, and the media coverage will reach a broad audience
3. Educating providers	Informing providers who will transmit skills and knowledge to others and model positive norms	Campus health care providers work with fraternities and resident hall directors to promote positive bystander behavior
4. Fostering coalitions and networks	Bringing together groups and individuals for broader goals and greater impact	Officials from state or local departments of health, education, and justice form a network with community representatives and leaders working together to advance prevention efforts
5. Changing organizational practices	Adopting regulations and shaping norms to prevent violence and improve health and safety	State or local school boards integrate gender equity education, including media literacy, within core curriculum
6. Influencing policy and legislation	Enacting laws and policies that support healthy community norms and a violence-free society	School policies against hate crimes, harassment, and bias; work toward establishing a peaceful and respectful climate

Source: Adapted from Davis et al. (2006).

an analysis of individual-level risk factors are likely to identify early life experience with both perpetration and victimization. Thus, if risk factors for violence are present at a young age and violence often occurs to or is perpetrated by youth, then there seems an inherent logic in reaching youth before they become perpetrators or victims. The strategic flaw in focusing exclusively on youth is the known association between violent behavior and the cultural and societal norms that either reinforce or deter behavior (Bandura, 1998; Cohen, Scribner, & Farley, 2000; Emmons, 2000; Smedley & Syme, 2000). Effective public health prevention strategies may include specific strategies directed to youth but should also include strategies directed to factors that influence youth (Schmid, Pratt, & Howze, 1995; Sorenson, Barbeau, Hunt, & Emmons, 2004; Thombs, Wolcott, & Farkash, 1997). Efforts focused on influencers (e.g., parents, teachers, coaches, mentors, bystanders) and changes to community and cultural systems (e.g., media/music; standards and expectations set and reinforced by practice, policy, or regulation) are examples. Even when broadening this construct, it is important to recognize that successful efforts consistently engage and empower youth, increasing their cognitive and emotional intelligence as it relates to a particular area and allowing them to challenge existing norms or standards.

An increasingly popular strategy for prevention is youth leadership and engagement. The following case provides an example of a youth-led prevention effort, highlighting the role and importance of adult and institutional support:

Recognizing the increased influence of peers in the middle school and high school years, a community engages youth in a violence prevention leadership initiative where the students progressively build knowledge and skills in peer-led groups to address gender and social norms regarding relationship violence. They plan and implement an annual teen summit and serve as mentors throughout the year for the younger students. The high school students mentor middle school students, who in turn mentor elementary school students with age-appropriate activities. School personnel, parents, and local businesses, themselves trained as leaders, support these efforts. A teen Web site provides information and a venue for lively discussions about sexual harassment policies and personal and group challenges related to gender roles and violence prevention. The youth are instrumental in the establishment of sexual harassment policies in the schools. The local Men Ending Violence group supports their efforts by advocating with the school district personnel to institute the changes. All of the activities are action oriented, with an eye to making changes at the individual, school, and community levels.

This example places an emphasis on prevention programming that fully engages youth and influencers in a manner that is empirically valid (Blum & Ireland, 2004).

Prevention as Blaming the Victim

In planning violence against women prevention efforts, a concern commonly expressed is the fear that an analysis of risk factors represents a form of victim blaming. Yet, examination of the circumstances and conditions associated with violent victimization is not intended to hold victims responsible or accountable for those conditions. Effective primary prevention requires a thorough analysis of risk factors for victimization and should be linked directly to specific efforts to understand and address the risk and protective factors associated with the perpetration of violence against women.

It is this nexus that is of particular importance for the effective prevention of both initial perpetration and repeat perpetration. Alcohol, as a risk factor, is one example we can use. Research clearly establishes the relationship of alcohol use to increased risk for both victimization and perpetration of violence against women. However, although understanding this relationship is helpful in assessing and possibly even addressing high-risk situations, it does not lead to the conclusions nor the approaches needed to modify the underlying values, beliefs, or norms that are the basis for the violence.

Prevention as Distraction From Intervention

Perhaps most unfortunate is the dichotomy that represents the prevention of violence against women as an "either/or" dynamic between the provision of services for victims and the assurance of accountability for perpetrators. Many prevention efforts are rooted in the experience of survivors or service providers. They recognize the need for effective response but also feel an obligation to prevent violence against women and the resulting physical, emotional, and social consequences. Yet, this obligation makes demands on limited or declining resources. Additionally, an increase in the number of victims can lead to the conclusion that prevention does not work. This belief is likely reinforced by limited prevention experience, focused on inadequate prevention efforts such as one-time education sessions or individual-focused programs. In addition, insufficient funding for community-level prevention research or trials that can adequately saturate, over a sufficient period of time, a community with a diverse set of prevention approaches has led to a poorly established empirical basis for prevention programming.

The necessary and important work of supporting victims and of holding perpetrators accountable must persist, particularly as the prevention challenges described in this chapter contribute to and reinforce a narrowly defined and ineffective prevention paradigm. These barriers, including the inadequate conceptualization of prevention, lead to the implementation of strategies that lack a theoretical or empirical basis and are absent the strategic,

long-term, comprehensive approach necessary to sufficiently address such complex social problems as violence.

Redefining the Prevention Paradigm

The barriers described are some of the challenges that must be overcome if violence against women is to be prevented. Overcoming these challenges requires a shift or expansion of the prevention paradigm. This shift is dependent on at least three key constructs. First is the necessary *leadership,* second is the need to mobilize and engage *communities,* and third is the need to redefine success based on capacity and a commitment to *social change* milestones.

Leadership

Leadership for the prevention of violence against women manifests in formal and informal, direct and indirect forms. The leadership of the women's movement laid the foundation, yet success is likely dependent on the inclusion of leaders, not only among those directly affected, but from the greater proportion of society that believes itself to be unaffected. Efforts to educate the unaffected about how they could become affected, what it is costing them, or why they should be concerned about violence against women provide limited impact. Sustainable prevention efforts involve leaders who support skills building for individuals, commit agency or organizational support, generate alliances across and among sectors, and advance programs and policies that lead to action (Johnson, Hays, & Daley, 2004). Framing issues in terms that express shared values and commonly held beliefs has been shown to be effective in moving social and political will (Dorfman & Wallack, 2007; Dorfman, Wallack, & Woodruff, 2005). Experience suggests that prevention leadership must not focus on who owns the issue, but rather on what the prevention of violence against women looks like when viewed through a multitude of community and societal lenses. Thus, the next generation of leaders working to prevent violence must have the skills to work with partners and in these alliances be prepared to negotiate the common ground necessary to change the underlying norms and conditions that lead to violence against women. Future leaders must be willing to build bridges across a multitude of prevention efforts to maximize scarce resources, both human and financial.

Community Mobilization

Community mobilization approaches help us to understand the relationship between individuals, an organized group process, and social change outcomes (Reppucci, Woolard, & Fried, 1999). Models of community mobilization may reflect community empowerment, defined as a shift toward greater equality in the social relations of power (who has resources, authority, legitimacy, or influence), or may be more specific to advancing particular policy or program objectives (Laverack & Labonte, 2000).

Effective community mobilization can expand the base of community support for the prevention of violence against women. Engaging a community, particularly when using community data, can help a community overcome denial and promote local ownership and decision making. Benefits often include enhanced collaboration between individuals and organizations that may limit competition and redundancy of services and outreach efforts. In addressing violence against women, community mobilization helps to create public pressure to implement laws, policies, and practices that support access to or realignment of funding for organizations and promote long-term, organizational commitment to prevention (Treno & Holder, 1997a, 1997b). The goal of a community mobilization effort is to engage multiple sectors of the population to address a health, social, or environmental issue; to empower individuals and groups to define a standard or criteria the community desires; and to collectively act upon that standard in a meaningful way to facilitate change.

The "active ingredients" of effective community mobilization generally include developing consistent, cohesive messages; conducting assessments and creating action plans; building coalitions and increasing partnerships; influencing and engaging stakeholders and decision makers; developing community leadership; and monitoring the progress being made (CDC, 2008; Goodman et al., 1998).

A case example of community mobilization is the work of the Institute for Community Peace (ICP; http://instituteforcommunitypeace.org/icp/). ICP applies many of these principles when working with communities across the country in collaborative efforts to prevent violence (Bowen, Gwiasda, & Brown, 2004).

ICP commonly responds to communities' concerns after a violent event and presents a case example of how sustainable community prevention efforts evolve. ICP's community mobilization efforts focus initially on crime prevention, acknowledging the impact of violence on the community, addressing criminal behavior, and providing services for those affected. These efforts would be categorized as secondary or tertiary prevention; violence has occurred and the community organizes to begin dealing with its aftermath. Activities may include candlelight vigils or community events that honor victims of violence against women and organizing shelters for battered women or community-level sexual assault response teams.

Following a community response, ICP works to engage the community, seeking clarity about when and where violence occurs and its consequences for the community. This includes forming multi-sector coalitions and seeking participation from those most affected by the violence. Universal awareness is often raised, community resources are assessed, and community-led solutions are identified. Many communities begin to address gaps in health (physical or mental), legal, and other services. Often targeted at selected or indicated populations and focused on secondary or tertiary prevention, this represents a continuation of the community response to violence.

In considering a hierarchy of needs, these early community efforts are likely critical to expand secondary prevention efforts and move toward primary prevention. Yet again, they are not sufficient to create or assure safety. Leadership and civic engagement that develops policies to respond to violence and organize change within community systems and structures supports prevention efforts. The institutional and societal change that supports and reinforces individual- and group-level change emerges.

As concerted efforts shift to promote a culture of equality and nonviolence, the root causes and "isms" that support violence often begin to be addressed. This shift represents community- and societal-level change, as the engaged communities begin to address the interrelationship among forms of violence. Likewise, through this shift communities are more likely to hold residents, institutions, and society accountable for change. Achieved through community support and advocacy that promotes a just and civil society, the desired change is more likely sustained as a result of an effective and participatory citizenry.

Community mobilization is often used outside the United States as a strategy for change. Raising Voices, a Uganda-based nongovernmental organization, uses community education, capacity building, media campaigns, workshops, policy reform, and service delivery as part of a comprehensive strategy to prevent violence against women. Raising Voices' approach to community mobilization includes systematically focusing on primary prevention using a holistic approach. The combination of workshops, community education, and media provides repeated exposure to prevention ideas through varied strategies. The change process used by Raising Voices recognizes community attitudes and

plans for a phased approach to community mobilization that fosters community ownership and is grounded within a human rights framework (Michau, 2007).

Integrating approaches to include human rights, health and well-being, and the prevention of violence in U.S. communities may offer opportunities for expanded, inclusive prevention efforts. Communities mobilized to address domestic and sexual violence, unwanted pregnancy, and alcohol and drug abuse may wish to create collaborative efforts that work toward the mitigation of shared risk factors. Likewise, such collaborative community efforts could work toward increasing shared protective factors such as self-efficacy, family support, or resistance to negative media messages. Understanding that prevention does not exist in a vacuum, and that primary violence prevention compliments appropriate community-based secondary and tertiary prevention (intervention) services, acknowledges that working to reinforce norms to support peaceful relationships, homes, and communities is a long-term process that demands participation from individuals, agencies, organizations, and institutions.

Social Change Movements

Significant to the work of preventing violence against women is that much of the work is rooted in social change and advocacy movements. It is at this nexus that prevention overcomes the challenges described previously. Through a social change or advocacy movement lens, primary prevention is a natural and logical extension of the decades of work and generations of leaders who have guided efforts to address and prevent violence against women.

Sustainable social change movements require a keen awareness of and sensitivity to cultural norms and dynamics. Culture is defined as

the integrated pattern of human knowledge, belief, and behavior that depends upon the capacity for learning and transmitting knowledge to succeeding generations; and the customary beliefs, social forms, and material traits of a group; a shared set of attitudes, values, goals, and practices that characterize an institution or organization; and the set of values, conventions, or social practices associated with a particular field, activity, or societal characteristic. (Merriam-Webster Online, 2009)

Norms are the regularities within communities and societies that shape the behaviors with which people comply and that people disapprove of when deviance occurs (Ullmann-Margalit, 1990).

Understanding, recognizing, and engaging population groups in a culturally appropriate, relevant, and respectful manner is a desired competency for prevention practice. The relevance of a prevention strategy to a particular community or culture is critical to its efficacy. That all communities in a nation, state, region, or county adopt the same prevention strategies is antithetical to the violence prevention paradigm. When members of the dominant culture impose themselves on communities without negotiating differences, prevention efforts often fail and the community may be blamed for lack of will. Prevention practitioners and leaders must be mindful of the power they wield as change agents and, at the same time, have the capacity to negotiate differences in a manner that honors, respects, and values the rich diversity of local communities.

Cultural competence is often represented as a process of developing proficiency in effectively responding in a cross-cultural context. Less commonly emphasized is the importance of applying this proficiency not only to an individual's culture but to understanding and respecting the culture, belief systems, norms, values, practices, and behaviors of groups, organizations, and communities. The multifaceted approach to prevention benefits from efforts that integrate cultural competency as a process by which individuals, agencies, and systems integrate and transform awareness of assumptions, values, biases, and knowledge about themselves and others to respond respectfully and effectively across diverse cultures, language, socioeconomic status, race, ethnic background, religion, gender, sexual orientation, and ability. This process recognizes, affirms, fosters, and values the strengths of individuals, families, and communities and protects and preserves the worth and dignity of each (Wisconsin State Council on Alcohol and Other Drug Abuse, 2008).

This approach to cultural competency considers a range of desired outcomes across the ecological model and considers the competencies required to meaningfully integrate and advance outcomes to prevent violence against women within those cultures. One example is the consideration of culture within a community organization. Schools and other community institutions have distinct cultures and subcultures (teachers, students, administrators, staff, etc.). Thus, whether a school is serving as a point of access to individuals for prevention efforts (e.g., reaching students through a school-based curriculum) or as the target of specific prevention efforts (e.g., developing and enforcing sexual harassment or teen dating violence prevention policies within a school), understanding the characteristics that define the context or "culture" may be important to achieving and sustaining the desired change.

Prevention as a Social Change Paradigm

Throughout this chapter, a more complex paradigm for prevention, one that has been successfully applied in other areas (tobacco control, drunk driving, etc.) has been described. Yet, embracing a more complex model for preventing violence against women may be analogous to swimming upstream. The preponderance of data available that identify behaviors to prevent (e.g., bullying, sexual violence, intimate partner violence, stalking) coupled with a lack of data, research, and consensus on outcomes or standards to promote (e.g., self-esteem or self-respect, community responsibility, supportive adult mentorship, nonviolent role models and messaging) reinforces downstream efforts. Yet, increasingly, communities are going upstream to develop programs that address violence before it occurs and to actively create social change movements that lay the foundation for sustainable, long-term outcomes. Communities are actively electing to promote behaviors, policies, and procedures that reflect gender equity and safety and, as such, emphasize and promote health.

Promoting a desired condition or state is often referred to as a *health promotion effort*. Health promotion is any combination of educational, organizational, economic, and environmental supports for the conditions of living and the behavior of individuals, groups, or communities that are conducive to health (Daniel & Green, 2002). Health promotion assumes that appropriate changes in the social environment will produce changes in individuals and that the support of individuals in the population is essential for implementing environmental changes (McLeroy, Bibeau, Steckler, & Glanz, 1988). An example of a health promotion approach is a strategy to engage men and boys in preventing violence against women. This promotion approach is based on data that supports that the majority of men do not perpetrate violence against women. Promoting positive behaviors such as honesty, respect, and communication and providing role models for young males may aid in developing active allies in preventing violence against women (CDC, 2008). Programs such as Coaching Boys into Men (http://www.endabuse.org/content/features/detail/811/); Mentors in Violence Prevention (http://www.sportinsociety.org/vpd/mvp.php); Boys Will Be Men: Raising Our Sons for Courage, Caring, and Community (http://www.plu.edu/~mav/doc/boys-will.pdf); and Men of Strength Clubs (http://www.mystrength.org) represent efforts to define men's shared leadership role and reinforce

norms to prevent violence against women. These practices, if implemented within the context of a comprehensive approach, contribute to movement upstream.

Encouraging men to take responsibility for promoting respect for women and mentoring boys to adopt attitudes, beliefs, and behaviors that support a culture free of violence is a health promotion perspective. However, challenges remain. Approaches directed to boys and men are primarily individual or group approaches. The important aspects of a health promotion approach, directed to policy, organizational, economic, regulatory, and environmental interventions are largely absent. Efforts to define and promote the shared responsibility of institutions, groups, and individuals remain largely focused on the standard for those institutions working with victims or perpetrators. Men need to define and refine their role and men's work to prevent violence against women, within the broad ecological framework. Women, especially those who have worked in and led the violence against women movement, need to understand and believe that prevention work is being accomplished on their behalf, not at their expense. The need for efforts led by women and men, institutions and communities will not end until violence against women ends. There remains a need for women to advocate on behalf of themselves and others, and there will continue to be a role for women to coach and guide male allies as they work together to develop shared understanding and common outcomes of interest. Getting women and men to work on collective action that moves beyond individual or group strategies to more collective community and societal action is likely the only approach that will yield meaningful and lasting change.

Conclusion

This chapter attempts to make the case for preventing the perpetration of violence against women by recognizing that focusing exclusively on victimization will never lead to the end of violence. In addition, it offers a perspective on prevention that encourages broadening and redefining the paradigm used. However, for prevention practitioners to meaningfully address the perpetration of violence against women, they need data and research that describes behaviors and conditions related to perpetration. Institutions, including CDC, that support prevention efforts must encourage, support, and synthesize this type of research. Researchers must improve empirical methods to quantify and qualify perpetration and conduct robust research addressing individual, organizational, social, and political factors associated with violence against women.

A collective promotion of equity and respect is likely to define the next phase of efforts to prevent violence against women. Applying a positive, health-promoting approach to the prevention of violence against women offers many unknown opportunities and challenges. Yet it is only through the innovative efforts of those working to promote well-being and prevent violence against women that the paradigm of prevention will continue to evolve and strengthen.

References

Bandura, A. (1998). Health promotion from the perspective of social cognitive theory. *Psychology & Health, 13*(4), 623–649.

Baron, L., & Strauss, M. A. (1989). *Four themes of rape in American society: A state-level analysis.* New Haven, CT: Yale University Press.

Basile, K. C., Chen, J., Black, M. C., & Saltzman, L. E. (2007). Prevalence and characteristics of sexual violence victimization among U.S. adults, 2001–2003. *Violence and Victims, 22*(4), 437–448.

Blum, R. W., & Ireland, M. (2004). Reducing risk, increasing protective factors: Findings from the Caribbean Youth Health Survey. *Journal of Adolescent Health, 35*(6), 493–500.

Bowen, L. D., Gwiasda, V., & Brown, M. M. (2004). Engaging community residents to prevent violence. *Journal of Interpersonal Violence, 19*(3), 356–367.

Centers for Disease Control and Prevention. (2008). *Community mobilization guide: A community-based effort to eliminate syphilis in the United States.* Retrieved July 13, 2009, from http://www.cdc.gov/std/see/Community/CommunityGuide.pdf

Cohen, D. A., Scribner, R. A. & Farley, T. A. (2000). A structural model of health behavior: A pragmatic approach to explain and influence health behaviors at the population level. *Preventive Medicine, 30*(2), 146–154.

Daniel, M., & Green, L. W. (2002). Health promotion and education. In L. Breslow & G. Cengage (Eds.), *Encyclopedia of public health.* Retrieved September 21, 2009, from http://www.enotes.com/public-health-encyclopedia/health-promotion-education

Davis, R., Fujie Parks, L., & Cohen, L. (2006). *Sexual violence and the spectrum of prevention: Towards a community solution.* Enola, PA: National Sexual Violence Resource Center.

Dorfman, L., & Wallack, L. (2007, March/April). Moving nutrition upstream: The case for reframing obesity. *Journal of Nutrition Education and Behavior, 39*(2), S45–S50.

Dorfman, L., Wallack, L., & Woodruff, K. (2005). More than a message: Framing public health advocacy to change corporate practices. *Health Education & Behavior, 32*(3), 320–336.

Emmons, K. M. (2000). Health behaviors in a social context. In L. F. Berkman & I. Kawachi (Eds.), *Social epidemiology* (pp. 242–266). New York: Oxford University Press.

Flaspohler, P., Duffy, J., Wandersman, A., Stillman, L., & Maras, M. A. (2008, June). Unpacking prevention capacity: An intersection of research-to-practice models and community-centered models. *American Journal of Community Psychology, 41*(3–4), 182–196.

Goodman, R. M., Speers, M. A., McLeroy, K., Fawcett, S., Kegler, M., Parker, E., et al. (1998). Identifying and defining the dimensions of community capacity to provide a basis for measurement. *Health Education & Behavior, 25*(3), 258–278.

Johnson, K., Hays, C., & Daley, C. (2004). Building capacity and sustainable prevention innovations: A sustainability planning model. *Evaluation and program planning, 27*(2), 135–149.

Krug, E. G., Dahlberg, L. L., Mercy, J. A., Zwi, A. G., & Lozano, R. (Eds.). (2002). *World report on violence and health.* Geneva, Switzerland: World Health Organization.

Laverack, G., & Labonte, R. (2000). A planning framework for community empowerment goals within health promotion. *Health Policy and Planning, 15*(3), 255–262.

Loh, C., Gidycz, C. A., Lobo, T. R., & Luthra, R. (2005). A prospective analysis of sexual assault perpetration: Risk factors related to perpetrator characteristics. *Journal of Interpersonal Violence, 20*(10), 1325–1348.

Macmillan, R., & Kruttschnitt, C. (2005). *Patterns of violence against women: Risk factors and consequences.* Unpublished report, U.S. Department of Justice. Retrieved July 21, 2009, from http://www.ncjrs .gov/pdffiles1/nij/grants/208346.pdf

McLeroy, K. R., Bibeau, D., Steckler, A., & Glanz, K. (1988). An ecological perspective on health promotion programs. *Health Education & Behavior, 15*(4), 351–377.

Merriam-Webster Online. (2009). Retrieved July 13, 2009, from http://www.merriam-webster.com

Michau, L. (2007). Approaching old problems in new ways: Community mobilization as a primary prevention strategy to combat violence against women. *Gender and Development, 15*(1), 95–109.

National Institute of Justice. (2004, November). *Violence against women: Identifying risk factors.* Research in Brief NCJ 197019. Washington, DC: Author.

Powell, K. E., Mercy, J. A., Crosby, A. E., Dahlberg, L. L., & Simon, T. R. (1999). Public health models of violence and violence prevention. In L. R. Kurtz & J. Turpin (Eds.), *Encyclopedia of violence, peace, and conflict* (Vol. 3, pp.1806–1819). San Diego, CA: Academic Press.

Rennison, C. M., & Welchans, S. (2000). *Intimate partner violence.* U.S. Department of Justice, Office of Justice Programs. Retrieved August 4, 2009, from http://www.ojp.usdoj.gov/bjs/pub/pdf/ipv.pdf

Reppucci, N. D., Woolard, J. L., & Fried, C. S. (1999). Social, community, and preventive interventions. *Annual Review of Psychology, 50,* 387–418.

Rogers, E. (1985). *Elements of diffusion in diffusion of innovations* (5th ed.). New York: Free Press.

Rogers, E. M. (1995). *Diffusion of innovations* (4th ed.). New York: Free Press.

Sartori, G. (1970). Concept misformation in comparative politics. *American Political Science Review, 64*(4), 1033–1053.

Schmid, T. L., Pratt, M., & Howze, E. (1995). Policy as intervention: Environmental and policy approaches to the prevention of cardiovascular disease. *American Journal of Public Health, 85*(9), 1207–1211.

Smedley, B. D., & Syme, S. L. (Eds.). (2000). *Promoting health: Intervention strategies from social and behavioral research.* Washington, DC: National Academy of Sciences Press.

Sokoloff, N. J., & Dupont, I. (2005). Domestic violence at the intersections of race, class, and gender. *Violence Against Women, 11*(1), 38–64.

Sorensen, G., Barbeau, E., Hunt, M. K., & Emmons, K. (2004). Reducing social disparities in tobacco use: A social-contextual model for reducing tobacco use among blue-collar workers. *American Journal of Public Health, 94*(2), 230–239.

Stokols, D. (1992). Establishing and maintaining healthy environments. *American Psychologist, 47*(1), 6–22.

Stokols, D. (1996). Translating social ecological theory into guidelines for community health promotion. *American Journal of Health Promotion, 10*(4), 282–298.

Thombs, D. L., Wolcott, B. J. & Farkash, L. G. E. (1997). Social context, perceived norms, and drinking behavior in young people. *Journal of Substance Abuse, 9,* 257–267.

Tjaden, P., & Thoennes, N. (2000). Extent, nature, and consequences of intimate partner violence: Findings from the National Violence Against Women Survey. Washington, DC: Department of Justice.

Treno, A. J., & Holder, H. D. (1997a). Community mobilization: Evaluation of an environmental approach to local action. *Addiction, 92*(Supp. 2), S173–S187.

Treno, A. J., & Holder, H. D. (1997b). Community mobilization, organizing, and media advocacy. *Evaluation Review, 21*(2), 166–190.

Ullmann-Margalit, E. (1990). Revision of norms. *Ethics, 100*(4), 756–767.

Wisconsin State Council on Alcohol and Other Drug Abuse (SCAODA). (2008). Retrieved August 22, 2008, from http://www.scaoda.state.wi.us

Yllo, K. A. (1998). Through a feminist lens: Gender, power, and violence. In K. V. Hansen & A. I. Garey (Eds.), *Families in the U.S.: Kinship and domestic policies.* Philadelphia: Temple University Press.

Chapter Authors

Corinne Meltzer Graffunder, Dr.PH., M.P.H., is the Associate Director for Program Development and Integration, National Center for Injury Prevention and Control, U.S. Centers for Disease Control and Prevention. She has more than 20 years of experience working with national, state and local prevention efforts. As Chief of the Program Implementation and Dissemination Branch within CDC's Division of Violence Prevention, she led numerous efforts to prevent violence against women. Her area of expertise is the application of evidence and research to practice and programs.

Rebecca Cline, LISW-S, ACSW, is Prevention Programs Director for the Ohio Domestic Violence Network (ODVN) and is directly accountable for the DELTA Project, a local, statewide, and national primary prevention initiative funded by the Centers for Disease Control. She worked for 20 years in domestic violence advocacy, health-care training and community education, community organizing, and coalition building. She is past president of the Ohio chapter of the National Association of Social Workers (NASW) and is a former member of the NASW National Board of Directors.

Karen G. Lane, M.Ed., has been the Prevention Program Manager at the Montana Coalition Against Domestic and Sexual Violence since 2003. As the state coordinator for the Montana DELTA Program, she has worked with local, state, and national partners to apply public health principles and community organizing to the prevention of intimate partner and sexual violence. More than 30 years of formal education and experience in building community partnerships, counseling trauma survivors, educating youth and young adults, and consulting with various nonprofit groups gives her a broad perspective.

Personal Reflection

Esta Soler

It was decades ago that I became interested in preventing domestic, sexual, and dating violence. In many ways, it was a natural outgrowth of my longtime civil rights work. I always had a keen interest in helping those whose rights are being violated, trampled, or ignored, and I quickly recognized that a woman who is being battered or raped by a partner—and a child growing up in a home in which that kind of violence occurs—needs champions.

In those days, there weren't a lot of people stepping up to do that work. The ones who did are my heroes to this day. For the most part, the focus then was on the critical work to make services available to victims. We'll never be able to count the lives saved by the domestic violence services we put in place in communities across this country.

In addition to supporting that work, I wanted to focus on advocacy, public policies, and social change. There was a need. At that time, domestic violence was considered a criminal justice issue—a women's issue—and a private problem. And not much else.

We began the Family Violence Prevention Fund with a small federal grant. It was tough in the early days. I remember visiting members of Congress who had never been approached on this issue. The things they said and jokes they made make me angry to this day. I remember approaching media about reshaping their news coverage and not being taken seriously. I remember approaching funders who saw no role for foundations or other donors in addressing this issue and no hope for change.

We've proved them all wrong, I think. A lot of us who dedicated our lives to this work have transformed the way the country understands and perceives this violence. As a nation, we really have come a long way. But there's still much more work to do.

I think what I've brought to this movement is a focus on advocacy, social norms change, public education, and prevention. The Family Violence Prevention Fund was among the first domestic violence organizations to create a role for men who want to be part of the solution. We are proud of that and proud that the field is embracing that work.

But we also know that, at a time when four women are being murdered each day by current or former husbands or boyfriends, when rape and sexual assault plague college campuses, when reproductive coercion is ignored and misunderstood, when battered immigrant women cannot count on culturally appropriate services, when asylum seekers fleeing gender-based violence cannot count on refuge here, and when the funding for vital services is in jeopardy, as much work lies ahead as is behind us. So perhaps my proudest accomplishment, like that of many of my peers, is building a strong, durable organization that will be ready to meet the next round of challenges.

CHAPTER 12

Sexual Assault Services

Raquel Kennedy Bergen and Shana L. Maier

Introduction

Over the past several decades, those who work to prevent violence against women have witnessed an increase in the number of services offered to survivors of sexual assault. More than 1,200 organizations currently provide rape crisis services in the United States, and a variety of other programs have been created to raise awareness and prevent sexual violence (National Sexual Violence Research Center [NSVRC], personal communication, September 11, 2009). In this chapter, we discuss the emergence of rape crisis centers and current challenges faced by these organizations, provide an overview of the many types of services available to address sexual violence, discuss the problem of revictimization, and consider sexual assault service provision to certain marginalized populations in the United States.

History of Rape Crisis Centers

In the early to mid-1970s, the first rape crisis centers in the United States were established by feminists who recognized the unfair plight of rape victims at the hands of a patriarchal society (Gornick & Meyer, 1998). Rape crisis centers began as grassroots organizations that were run collectively and offered a variety of direct services to rape victims, such as hotline counseling and accompaniment to hospitals and police stations. In addition to providing community education, early rape crisis centers had a social change mission (Clemans, 2004; Riger et al., 2002), and their primary focus was to eliminate rape and secure legislative reform that would grant rape victims more rights and protection. The interconnection between direct services and political activism was most pronounced in the early years after rape crisis centers were first established.

Early rape crisis centers were purely volunteer organizations, were collectively run, and did not accept money from state or government agencies. Their budgets consisted of money earned through fundraising efforts (Matthews, 1994), and the centers or programs sometimes were run out of the homes of volunteers (Campbell & Martin, 2002). Volunteers often did *not* collaborate with law enforcement, medical personnel, or the legal system because they were frustrated with their treatment of rape victims and believed such mainstream institutions would interfere with the goals of ending violence against women and improving victims' treatment (Martin, 2005). Instead of working with other institutions to facilitate change, many rape crisis center staff criticized institutions for the mistreatment of rape victims (Martin, DiNitto, Byington, & Maxwell, 1992).

The late 1970s and early 1980s saw an increase in the types of rape crisis centers in the United States. While many retained their feminist roots, some rape crisis centers began to change when many of the original founders grew tired from years of struggle and left the crisis centers (Campbell & Martin, 2002; Gornick, Burt, & Pittman, 1985). Many centers began to accept money from state, government, and law enforcement agencies—sources with which centers may have had adversarial relationships in the past. As a result, the centers became less grassroots oriented and became more professionalized (Bierria, 2007; Matthews, 1994; O'Sullivan & Carlton, 2001). Centers began to hire paid, professional staff and provide training to all staff and volunteers. Centers also developed written policies and procedures for all staff and volunteers, and the division of labor became more formal.

In addition, when centers began to receive public funding, they reduced their level of traditional political activism and increased collaboration with other systems or agencies, such as hospitals and law enforcement, because they were sources of funding. This was challenging given that rape crisis centers had to gain the trust and cooperation of institutions they had criticized in the past (Gornick et al., 1985) and could not as strongly criticize their institutional partners' negative treatment of rape victims (Martin, 2005). Many advocates felt that the state funding relationship caused the rape crisis movement to lose its political stance (Matthews, 1994; Whittier, 1995) and altered the way advocates were able to assist victims (Maier, 2008; Ullman & Townsend, 2007). That is not to say that today's rape crisis centers have completely abandoned activism. Although engaging in political protests and lobbying lawmakers is rare for rape crisis centers, centers now have extensive education and outreach programs. Not only do they provide education in the community, they also train those working with victims in other agencies on the best way to assist them (Schmitt & Martin, 1999).

According to the NSVRC, approximately one quarter of the organizations providing rape crisis services are stand-alone rape crisis centers (personal communication, September 11, 2009). Typically, rape crisis centers today offer direct services to victims including hotline counseling, face-to-face counseling, and accompaniment to police stations, hospitals, and court proceedings (Wasco et al., 2004). Compared to other sexual assault services that are embedded in larger organizational structures, freestanding rape crisis centers tend to be smaller and have smaller budgets. However, these organizations continue to play an important role in meeting the needs of sexual assault survivors. As Riger et al. (2002) write, "The information and support provided by rape crisis hotlines and medical and legal advocates provides a safe, nonjudgmental, and informative way for women, their families, and significant others to talk with people about their experiences and concerns" (p. 9).

Although results vary, most research indicates that the majority of women disclose their experiences of sexual assault at some point (see Campbell & Townsend, Chapter 5, for a discussion of disclosure). After family members and friends, women are most likely to disclose to mental health service providers, which include rape crisis centers (Ahrens, Cabral, & Abeling, 2009; Campbell & Townsend, Chapter 5). Research indicates that, with the exception of hospital-based programs, rape crisis centers reach the largest number of survivors (O'Sullivan & Carlton, 2001; Patterson, 2009). There is also evidence that despite the small budget and staff of many rape crisis centers, they tend to provide the most comprehensive sexual assault services to survivors—particularly to teenagers and women who were raped by strangers—and they also appear to be in a position to most effectively meet the needs of their particular communities (O'Sullivan & Carlton, 2001; Patterson, 2009).

Continuing Challenges Faced by Rape Crisis Centers

Despite their existence for more than 30 years, rape crisis centers face many challenges. First, although rape crisis centers accept and rely on public funding (i.e., federal and state funding, foundation grants), they continue to struggle financially, and budget cuts have exacerbated this problem (Colindres, 2008; Florida Council Against Sexual Violence, 2009; Hutcheson, 2009; Smith, 2008). For some centers, lack of funding is the single most important challenge they face and has resulted in reduction of services to survivors and contributed to problems recruiting and retaining staff (Macy, Giattina, Parish, & Crosby, 2009; Ullman & Townsend, 2007). Because of limited funds, staff members fill multiple roles, which often leads to stress and burnout.

Funding considerations have also led to changes in the nature of the work carried out by rape crisis centers. As indicated above, working in collaboration with other systems or agencies such as law enforcement caused many organizations to alter or reduce their level of political activism so as not to offend their funders. When programs compete for funding, they adapt to the preferences of the funding source (Townsend & Campbell, 2007) or avoid action that alienates them from financial supporters (Riger, 1994). To secure public funding, many centers either abandoned the social change mission that tied them to the activist feminist movement or "de-radicalized" their efforts (Bierria, 2007; Campbell, Baker, & Mazurek, 1998; Lehrner & Allen, 2009; Maier, 2008). Ultimately, this changed the way rape crisis workers are able to advocate for victims (Ullman & Townsend, 2007). This is also true for the domestic violence movement. As a result of interviews with advocates, Lehrner and Allen (2009) concluded that maintaining a social change agenda becomes problematic when organizations are also juggling the demands of funders, collaborating with community agencies, and expanding services to victims.

Another challenge facing rape crisis centers today is that they have increasingly become more professional, with formal recruitment, paid staff and professionally trained counselors, and training for all incoming staff and volunteers (Bierria, 2007; Macy et al., 2009; Ullman & Townsend, 2007). This is also true for nonprofit agencies in general; when nonprofit agencies accept public money, they become more professional and hierarchical and seek to meet the demands of their funding sources (Durazo, 2007; Gilmore, 2007). Although there are certainly benefits to hiring paid, professional staff, one concern is that they may lack the experiences that non-degreed survivors can bring, and they may lack the passion and enthusiasm of the volunteers more evident in the earlier grassroots movements (Macy et al., 2009).

Services to Survivors of Sexual Assault

The passion and commitment of early feminists to provide services to survivors of sexual violence and to work to educate communities about sexual violence is reflected in the work of a variety of programs other than stand-alone rape crisis centers, for example, dual rape crisis/battered women's programs, university-based programs, medical programs such as Sexual Assault Nurse Examiner (SANE) programs, and coordinated community responses such as Sexual Assault Response Teams (SART).

Dual Programs for Rape Survivors and Battered Women

The anti-rape movement and the battered women's movement have distinct histories in the U.S. (see Allen, Larsen, & Walden, Chapter 13 this volume; Brownmiller, 1975; Schechter, 1982). Ideological differences, competition for a limited funding pool, and the ever-expanding cost of service provision have sometimes led to tensions between the two movements. A point of contention has been the relative lack of funding for sexual assault service provision compared to domestic violence services (Burt et al., 2000). Some rape prevention advocates have argued that there is greater stigma surrounding sexual assault than domestic violence in the U.S., and some of the implications of this are greater silence around the issue of sexual assault and the funding issues that have historically plagued many rape crisis programs (Patterson, 2009; Sloan, 2006). There is some evidence that disparities in funding continue, with domestic violence programs receiving more federal funding (such as STOP funds) than rape crisis programs (Patterson, 2009; Zweig & Burt, 2003).

Despite the unique histories and tensions in the past, there are many similarities between services offered by rape crisis centers and battered women's programs. Both generally provide crisis counseling (typically including a 24-hour hotline), medical and legal advocacy, information and referrals, and community education. Additionally, many rape crisis centers and battered women's programs provide ongoing counseling and are involved in working for social change and justice (Riger et al., 2002). Of course, a fundamental difference between the two types of programs is that historically, battered women's programs have provided housing and shelter for women and their children as a primary service, whereas the vast majority of rape crisis centers have not.

Dual programs, sometimes known as joint programs, provide both sexual assault and domestic violence services; there are more than 900 such programs in the United States (NSVRC, personal communication, September 11, 2009). There are some common institutional obstacles faced by survivors of sexual assault and domestic violence when seeking services, such as lack of transportation, lack of available shelter space, income dependency on the abuser, and lack of information about available services (see Allen, Larsen, & Walden, Chapter 13; Campbell & Martin, 2002). However, sexual assault survivors may face additional obstacles in dual programs if the primary focus of the program is domestic violence and volunteers and staff are not well-trained to respond to the needs of sexual assault survivors. Specifically, many sexual assault survivors require comprehensive counseling services (individual as well as group); legal advocacy; and medical advocacy, including the collection of forensic evidence and testing for pregnancy, HIV/AIDS, and sexually transmitted diseases (Campbell & Martin, 2002). If primacy is given to domestic violence, women's experiences of sexual violence may be minimized or not even addressed, given that many women hesitate to disclose their experiences of sexual assault unless they are directly asked (Bergen, 1996; Russell, 1990). Furthermore, some researchers have found that in dual programs, domestic violence services are often given higher priority, both in terms of budgetary dollars and staffing. This may decrease the effectiveness of such organizations in meeting the needs of sexual assault survivors (Macy et al., 2009; Patterson, 2009).

One of the benefits of dual programs may be the provision of services to survivors of intimate partner sexual violence. To date, there has not been a comprehensive study of how organizations (and what types of organizations) can best meet the needs of survivors of intimate partner sexual violence (Patterson, 2009). However, there are some positive indications that dual programs may have the resources to best meet the needs of these survivors. Historically, there have been challenges in providing services to women who are raped by their partners, given that they did not fit the "ideal type" of survivor at battered women's shelters or rape crisis centers. Because sexual assault survivors are frequently in need of safe shelter, housing, medical and legal advocacy, and counseling services from both domestic violence programs and sexual assault programs, many of these survivors have fallen through the cracks with regard to service provision (Bergen, 1996; Russell, 1990).

A national survey of service providers in 2003–2004 found that 65% of organizations include a discussion of rape in intimate partnerships in their outreach efforts, and only 5% of organizations provide support groups specifically for survivors of marital rape. Notably, the most comprehensive services were provided by dual programs—93% of dual programs provide shelter to marital rape survivors and 92% of dual programs include this form of violence in their outreach efforts. Dual programs were the most likely to include intimate partner sexual violence in their mission statements and to routinely ask women about their experiences (Bergen, 2004). Although there is still progress to be made in terms of training staff and volunteers about intimate partner sexual violence (only 56% of dual programs routinely include this in training), there is evidence of collaborative efforts between domestic violence coalitions and rape crisis programs that are working to achieve this end and provide improved services to this population of survivors (Bergen, 2004).

An example of such programming is the Washington Coalition of Sexual Assault Programs (WCSAP). Working in collaboration with law enforcement, prosecutors, domestic violence victim advocates, and other state organizations, WCSAP secured federal funding and created an initiative to better understand and serve the needs of survivors of intimate partner sexual violence. They provide several state-wide training sessions and have worked to implement a state-wide coordinated community response (see WCSAP, 2008). Another coalition that is doing groundbreaking work is the Virginia Sexual and Domestic Violence Action Alliance. This Alliance was formed in 2004 between Virginians Aligned Against Sexual Assault and Virginians Against Domestic Violence, and they now publish a semi-annual journal titled *Revolution* that highlights the strengths and diversity of services for survivors in Virginia.

University-Based Programs

Given the prevalence of sexual violence on college campuses, it is important to consider university-based services. Most typically, college and university mental health centers provide general counseling services for students who have been sexually assaulted (Karjane, Fisher, & Culler, 2005). Increasingly, colleges also provide educational programming to raise general awareness about sexual assault and to direct students to resources. A study by the National Institute of Justice in 2005 found that one-fifth of colleges provided peer education programs on sexual assault, which are generally thought to be the most effective way to reach students. A growing number of universities have student-led groups of advocates who are involved in prevention efforts as well as crisis intervention. These programs can take a variety of forms, but typically they have a volunteer base of students who are trained (sometimes in courses for credit and sometimes by local rape crisis programs) as sexual assault crisis counselors and are thus in a position to provide crisis intervention and advocacy. Peer-based advocacy programs can be very valuable in providing much-needed educational awareness and crisis intervention services as well as helping to foster a sense of community among the volunteers and a commitment to working to end sexual violence.

The most comprehensive college-based programs have moved beyond traditional counseling and peer education efforts to provide primary prevention and a wide range of services and outreach to a diversity of survivors. Culturally competent programs try to avoid the assumption of white heterosexual models of sexual assault and try to reach a diverse population. For example, the Counseling and Mental Health Center at the University of Texas at Austin has instituted a program called *For Men Only: For Male Survivors of Sexual Assault* that offers counseling, educational initiatives, and resources to male survivors (http://www.cmhc.utexas.edu). One of the most innovative programs on college campuses today is *One in Four*. This prevention program, previously called *No More*, was created by John Foubert with an emphasis on men taking an active role in preventing sexual assault by increasing victim empathy and men's aversion to rape. The focus of this rape prevention program is encouraging men to speak directly to other men about sexual violence. There are currently 40 chapters on college campuses across the U.S., in addition to an RV Tour that travels the country to provide prevention programs and workshops to male peer educators (http://www.onein fourusa.org). Both programs indicate the importance of providing outreach and primary prevention to a wide range of survivors, including men who are victimized by sexual violence.

SANE

Due to the negative and inefficient treatment of rape victims by emergency room personnel, the first Sexual Assault Nurse Examiner (SANE) programs began in the late 1970s (see also Macy, Ermentrout, & Johns, Chapter 15). The first SANE program began in Memphis, Tennessee in 1976 (Speck & Aiken, 1995), the second in Minneapolis, Minnesota in 1977 (Ledray, 1999), and the third in Amarillo, Texas in 1979 (Antognoli-Toland, 1985). By March, 2001 there were 403 SANE programs in the United States (Ledray, 2001), and more recent estimates indicate there are more than 500 SANE programs nationwide (International Association of Forensic Nurses, 2009; Ledray, 2005). SANE programs provide immediate, compassionate, culturally sensitive, and comprehensive forensic evaluation and treatment by trained nurses (Houmes, Fagan, & Quintana, 2003; Ledray, 1999; Littel, 2001). In addition to providing general medical treatment and collecting and documenting forensic evidence, SANEs also provide victims with

prophylactic treatment for pregnancy, HIV, and STDs, provide medical referrals when necessary, and may testify in court (Ahrens, Campbell, Wasco, Grubstein, Aponte, & Davidson, 2000; Ciancone, Wilson, Collette, & Gerson, 2000; Ledray, 1995; Littel, 2001; Plichta, Clements, & Houseman, 2007).

SANEs often form a collaborative relationship with other agencies that work with rape victims, including police departments, rape crisis centers, victim services centers, and prosecutors' offices. Most SANE programs are part of a Sexual Assault Response Team (SART). According to Lewis, DiNitto, Nelson, Just, and Campbell-Ruggaard (2003), "The SART approach involves joining law enforcement, medical personnel, and victim advocates in a coordinated effort to provide sexual assault survivors with comprehensive medical attention, emotional support, evidence examinations, and follow-up services" (p. 34). The team approach is essential for various reasons. First, the presence of a SANE and an advocate from a rape crisis center benefits victims. According to Preston (2003),

> The partnership of the SANE and the Rape Crisis Center advocate provides the survivor with trained, medical personnel who have expertise in the rape trauma arena [psychological reactions to rape], while at the same time providing them with a trained advocate who can assist in caring for the emotional needs of the survivor. (p. 244)

SANEs cannot take on the role of advocate because they may be asked to serve as an objective expert during court proceedings. If SANEs appear to be advocates, their credibility and the credibility of the evidence could be questioned at trial (Scalzo, 2006).

Research has indicated that medical treatment of rape victims has improved with the implementation of SANE programs. Victims wait less time for an exam if seen by a SANE, compared to an emergency room doctor (Crandall & Hellitzer, 2003), and SANEs collect more accurate and complete evidence than emergency room doctors and nurses (Ledray & Simmelink, 1997; Littel, 2001; Pennington, Zwemer, & Krebs, 2010). Defendants are more likely to plea bargain once they realize the detail of the forensic evidence (Littel, 2001; Speck & Aiken, 1995), and convictions are more likely due to evidence collected by SANEs and expert testimony provided by them at trial (Crandall & Helitzer, 2003; McGregor, Du Mont, & Myhr, 2002; O'Brien, 1996, cited in Ledray, 1999). Also, treatment by SANEs can be emotionally beneficial to victims. They can provide more compassionate care because they are able to dedicate their time to one patient, unlike emergency room doctors or nurses whose time may be split among multiple patients (Girardin, 2005). Rape victims who receive specialized sexual assault services report feeling more respected, more in control, and more informed (Ericksen, Dudley, McIntosh, Ritch, Shumay, & Simpson, 2002).

SART

As indicated above, most SANE programs function as part of a SART. SARTs typically involve a coordinated effort among community members including victim advocates, law enforcement, the prosecutor's office, and the SANE, with the goal of assisting a survivor of sexual violence through the medical and legal systems (Burgess, Lewis-O'Connor, Nugent-Borakove, & Fanflik, 2006; see also Miller, Iovanni, & Kelley, Chapter 14). These programs began in the early 1990s, in an effort to achieve a "more coordinated and consistent response to sexual assault" (Pennsylvania Coalition Against Rape, 2002). Two important components of SART are to provide better evidence collection and greater support for survivors. A recent research project designed to test the efficacy of SANE and SART interventions found that cases with SANE/SART interventions were 3.5 times more likely than cases without these interventions to end in a conviction of the offender (Burgess et al., 2006). This is likely the result of better forensic evidence collection as well as increased survivor participation in the process. As Burgess et al. argue, the

majority of survivors know their perpetrators, and this can increase the conflicts (including fear of retaliation, physical injury, and divided loyalty) that many survivors experience over the decision to cooperate with law enforcement officials and prosecutors. SARTs can play an important role in recognizing the diverse needs of survivors of sexual assault and increasing communication among team members to minimize trauma, meet the survivor's needs, and increase participation in the legal process (Pennsylvania Coalition Against Rape, 2002).

Revictimization of Rape Victims

Despite the improvement in the treatment of rape victims because of SANEs and SARTs, victims continue to be revictimized by the medical, criminal justice, and legal systems, as well as by members of their community. *Revictimization* refers to the blame and stigmatizing responses to victims by police or others and the trauma that victims experience following the rape itself. More specifically, the term has been used to refer to the distress, alienation, and blame that victims may experience after the assault at the hands of the criminal justice and medical systems (Madigan & Gamble, 1991).

Victims may face revictimization partly because of the persistence of rape myths or false and prejudicial beliefs about rape, rape victims, and rapists. Rape myths have been defined as attitudes and beliefs that are generally false but are widely and persistently held and serve to deny and justify male sexual aggression against women (Lonsway & Fitzgerald, 1994, p. 134). Amir's *Patterns in Forcible Rape* (1971) first introduced the term "victim-precipitated rape." Amir (1971) explains, "Criminology recognizes that it is not always the offender alone who is to be blamed and condemned as responsible for the offense. Sometimes victims can be equally blamed" (p. 229). In other words, if the victim had behaved in a different way or had different characteristics, the crime would not have occurred. The notion that no victim is completely innocent or free from blame persists in current rape myths. To avoid being blamed, women are expected to behave a particular way in order to confirm and reinforce their femininity.

When rape victims turn to the police for assistance and protection, they may be blamed for their victimization, especially if they do not seem to fit the stereotypical image of a "real" victim—someone raped by a stranger wielding a weapon, who sustains obvious physical injuries, who appears to be traumatized, and who reports to the police immediately (Estrich, 1987; Madigan & Gamble, 1991). Victim-blaming questions include questions about a victim's attire at the time of the rape, the use of alcohol or drugs, extent of resistance, prior sexual encounters with the alleged assailant, or decision to be at a certain location at a certain time. Campbell (2006) found that rape survivors reported that police were reluctant to take their report, told them that their cases were not serious enough to pursue further, asked them about prior relationships with perpetrators, and asked them whether they had responded sexually to the rape. Research indicates that most rape victims are dissatisfied with police response (Campbell, 2006; Monroe, Kinney, Weist, Spriggs Dafeamekpor, Dantzler, & Reynolds, 2005).

The medical system can also revictimize rape victims by treating them negatively or not assisting them when they reach out for information and treatment. The experience of victims in the emergency room can seem like a second assault (Campbell, 2006; Campbell, Sefl, Barnes, Ahrens, Wasco, & Zaragoza-Diesfeld, 1999; Campbell, Wasco, Ahrens, Sefl, & Barnes, 2001; Du Mont & Parnis, 2003). Despite greater social awareness of rape, important health concerns that might result from rape (such as unwanted pregnancies, sexually transmitted diseases, and HIV/AIDS) are typically not adequately addressed in emergency rooms (Campbell et al., 2001;

Resnick, Acierno, Holmes, Dammeyer, & Kilpatrick, 2000; Resnick et al., 2002; see also Macy, Ermentrout, & Johns, Chapter 15). Victims may experience long waits in emergency rooms. This is particularly problematic because in order to preserve evidence, victims are unable to eat or drink, use a bathroom, or change clothes before they have been examined. A male emergency room doctor may do the invasive exam, which is particularly traumatizing for victims raped by men. Moreover, emergency room professionals may be resentful of the lengthy time required to conduct an exam and the time commitment if they are asked to testify in court. They may rush the victim through the collection of evidence and exam without proper explanation because they have other patients in the emergency room waiting for their attention (Ahrens et al., 2000; Girardin, 2005, Martin, 2005). Campbell (2005) sampled victims and found that most had negative experiences with emergency room doctors and nurses. Interviews with 81 victims seeking services at two hospitals revealed that 69% of victims from one hospital and 36% from the other hospital said they were treated "impersonally" or "coldly" by emergency room doctors or nurses during the examination (Campbell, 2006, p. 38).

Victims may also have negative experiences with the legal system (Frazier & Haney, 1996; Martin & Powell, 1994). Research has indicated that most victims express concern about achieving justice through the criminal justice system (Konradi & Burger, 2000) and view contact with the legal system as hurtful (Campbell et al., 2001). This is not surprising, given that the vast majority of reported rape cases are not prosecuted (Campbell, 1998, 2005; Campbell et al., 1999; Frazier & Haney, 1996). Victims' negative experiences with the legal and medical systems may be even more pronounced if they are members of marginalized groups and subject to various forms of oppression, discrimination, and unequal access to resources and services in their communities.

Providing Services to Marginalized Groups

During the past several decades, understanding of the variation in women's experiences of sexual violence and the need to respond to a diverse population of survivors has increased. Despite the commitment of those in the anti-rape movement, there is evidence that there are still barriers to overcome in providing services to certain marginalized groups, such as victims of color, victims with disabilities, and victims living in rural communities.

Issues for Women of Color

Research indicates that race and ethnicity can affect victims' responses to rape. When African American women are raped by African American men, they tend not to report to police because they don't want to turn African American men over to the racially biased criminal justice system (Donavan & Williams, 2002; see also Jones, 2009 and Websdale, 2001 for more on African American women's distrust of police). Negative stereotypes about African American women are also detrimental to victims. In particular, the historical stereotype that African American women are promiscuous ("jezebels") contributes to the myth that they are deserving of sexual victimization (Collins, 2000; Donavan & Williams, 2002). Moreover, African American women may not report their victimization to the police because they often fear that the police will not support or believe them (Campbell & Raja, 2005; Thompson Sanders & Smith West, 1992). This fear may be warranted because historically, the police seem to be biased against African American rape victims (Brownmiller, 1975), and prosecution is less likely when rape victims are African American (Campbell et al., 2001; Collins, 2000).

African American victims tend not to seek help from rape crisis workers because the rape crisis movement originated in the white-dominated feminist movement (Ullman & Townsend, 2007; Washington, 2001). Historically, rape crisis centers have been criticized for being dominated by white women who ignore the experiences of women of color (Matthews, 1989; Riger et al., 2002; Washington, 2001; White, 2001). In addition, the perception that African American women are strong and responsible for their family ("matriarchs") contributes to the belief that they should be able to handle their victimization without seeking help or support (Campbell et al., 2001; Collins, 2000; Donavan & Williams, 2002; Neville & Pugh, 1997).

There is much less research on the experiences of other women of color; the unique experiences of Latinas, Asians, and rape victims of other ethnicities have been overlooked. The limited literature indicates that Latinas may be more likely to remain silent about sexual victimization because of the stigma and shame this brings to their families (Low & Organista, 2000). Some Latino families may also have strict, traditional ideas about the roles of men and women. A Latina's sexual purity is essential, according to her culture, and she may be blamed for her sexual victimization because it is her duty to control male sexuality. Men are often portrayed as aggressive and heads of households (*machismo*) while women are required to remain chaste like the Virgin Mary (*marianismo*). Both stereotypes have important implications for sexual assault, women's reporting, and help-seeking behavior.

Issues for Native American Women

A growing body of research indicates the prevalence of violence against women in Native American communities. The National Violence Against Women Study found that compared to other racial and ethnic groups in the United States, Native American women experience the highest rates of sexual victimization (Hamby, 2004; Tjaden & Thoennes, 2000; see also Allen, Larsen, & Walden, Chapter 13). In her review of the extant literature, Hamby (2004) found that

12% to 49% of Native American women experience sexual violence during their lifetimes; frequently they know their assailants, and quite often, their assailants are their intimate partners. However, most Native American women (70% according to a study by Greenfeld & Smith, 1999) hesitate to disclose their experiences to outsiders, fearing stigmatization, victim-blaming, revictimization, and lack of anonymity given the small size of many tribal communities. Not to be minimized given their oppressive treatment in the U.S. is the fact that many distrust "white" organizations affiliated with the federal government and law enforcement (Wahab & Olson, 2004). A further consideration raised by Hamby (2004) is that there is often a conflict between the values of Native American survivors and outsiders, such as rape victim advocates and law enforcement officials. Specifically, the emphasis on prosecution, divorce if the assailant is an intimate partner, and disclosure of the private details of a sexual assault to many individuals in the course of help seeking may sharply clash with the values held in a Native American community (Hamby, 2004). Further cultural clashes may occur if there is a failure to provide culturally sensitive programs and validate healing practices, such as talking circles and naming ceremonies, that are very beneficial for survivors of sexual violence (Wahab & Olson, 2004).

There are many barriers to the provision of services to Native American women, not the least of which are geographic isolation and the great variation in tribal communities (see Allen, Larsen, & Walden, Chapter 13; Wahab & Olson, 2004). Some barriers are deeply entrenched as part of the legacy of oppression of Native Americans by the United States government, such as racism, victim blaming, and ignorance of tribal culture (Hamby, 2004; Wahab & Olson, 2004). Other practical barriers facing service providers are language differences; vast geographic areas to cover; economic constraints; and jurisdictional problems that arise from the complex interaction between tribal, federal, and state laws when there is a sexual assault on tribal lands (Hamby, 2004; Wahab & Olson, 2004).

Despite the barriers, there has been substantial progress in providing culturally specific programs for Native American women at the grassroots level. For example, *Mending the Sacred Hoop*, a project established by Duluth's Domestic Abuse Intervention Program, has been working to end violence against women in Native American communities for almost 20 years. This project works with tribal governments and local communities to develop better sexual assault protocols and coordinated community responses to sexual violence (http://www.theduluthmodel.org/mendingsacredhoop.php). The Minnesota Indian Women's Resource Center is a program that provides resources specifically for victim advocates of Native American women (http://www.miwrc.org; Wahab & Olson, 2004). Another example of a grassroots program is the Native American Women's Health Education Resource Center, which was established in 1985 by members of the Yankton Sioux Reservation in South Dakota. This organization opened a shelter for survivors of domestic violence and sexual assault in 1991, and the Women's Lodge has been very involved in raising awareness about sexual violence in the Native American community through programming and Webcasts. Several years ago, advocates were effective in helping to draw attention to the plight of sexual assault survivors who received poor medical care and forensic examinations in Indian Health Service emergency rooms (http://www.nativeshop.org).

It has been suggested that given the unique history of Native Americans with the U.S. government, programs for Native American women should be grounded in a liberation or oppression framework, with an emphasis on empowerment and self-determination, and many of these grassroots initiatives reflect this focus (see Wahab & Olson, 2004). More research and dialogue is needed to better understand how to overcome the barriers facing survivors of sexual assault and their advocates in Native American communities.

Issues for Women With Disabilities

Research has indicated that having a disability does not provide immunity to sexual violence, and indeed, women with disabilities often experience sexual violence at higher rates than women without disabilities (Elman, 2005; Powers, Hughes, & Lund, 2009). Recent research by Martin et al. (2006) found that compared to women without disabilities, women with disabilities are four times more likely to have been sexually assaulted in the past year. Rape crisis centers have historically been important resources for women with disabilities who have experienced violence. The relative anonymity of rape crisis centers and shelters allows women with disabilities to share their experiences without fear of retribution by their perpetrators, who are often their caregivers. However, lack of information about violence against women with disabilities and specific vulnerabilities may hinder the assistance that programs can provide to this population. As Elman (2005) and other researchers have pointed out, women with disabilities are not a homogenous population (nor are their abusers, as indicated by Powers et al., 2009), but there are a diversity of abilities and conditions, including physical injuries, mental illness, sensory impairment, cognitive impairment, and chronic disease, that must be considered in providing sexual assault services. For example, escape plans that require physical mobility or communication without the assistance of a device or an interpreter may prove to be barriers for some women with disabilities. For a woman who is dependent on her assailant for essential daily care, implementation of an escape plan may be nearly impossible (Elman, 2005; Nosek & Howland, 1998).

There have been a variety of recommendations to improve sexual assault services for women with disabilities (see Elman, 2005; Nosek & Howland, 1998; Powers et al., 2009; VawNet, 2009). At minimum, there is a need for greater education on the provision of sexual assault services for women with disabilities that take into consideration their wide range of abilities and needs. Although many survivors of sexual assault feel stigma, guilt, and isolation, these feelings may be exacerbated in women who have disabilities. To increase reporting of sexual violence, there is a need for TTYs (teletypewriters), 24-hour access to video phones, and skilled interpreters for the hearing impaired (Taylor & Gaskin-Laniyan, 2009). Interpreters should be available to increase reporting to the criminal justice system as well as available for individual and group counseling (Taylor & Gaskin-Laniyan, 2009). Other recommendations include providing services that are architecturally accessible and providing personal assistance to meet the essential daily needs of women with disabilities (Elman, 2005; Nosek & Howland, 1998). There is also a need for primary prevention, such as the innovative audio computer-assisted self-interview program, *Safer and Stronger,* to increase awareness about violence, risk factors, and safety planning among deaf and disabled women (see Oschwald, Renker, Hughes, Arthur, Powers, & Curry, 2009; Powers et al., 2009).

Issues for Women Living in Rural Communities

Over the past decade, there has been an increased focus on violence against women in rural communities. Despite the historic idealistic depiction of rural communities as safe and loving places immune from the social problems of urban life, recent research has indicated high rates of sexual assault and domestic violence in rural communities (DeKeseredy & Schwartz, 2009; Lewis, 2003; Websdale, 1998). Indeed, violence against women in rural communities has been called a "hidden epidemic," given the prevalence of violence and the relative silence surrounding this issue (Lewis, 2003; Royse, 1999). Several research studies have indicated that the rates of violence against women in rural communities are higher than in urban communities (Lewis, 2003; Ruback & Menard, 2001), although sexual assault tends to be highly underreported. Women in rural communities are very likely to either know their assailants or to be involved in a relationship with their assailants, and this frequently poses a barrier to reporting sexual assault (Hamby, 2004; Hunter, Burns-Smith, & Walsh, 1996). Rural communities are also characterized by high acquaintance density and thus high levels of familiarity and a lack of anonymity. Recent research has indicated that many survivors of sexual assault fear retribution by their assailants if they choose to report and believe there is a "good ol' boy network" that will protect their assailant (DeKeseredy & Schwartz, 2009; Websdale, 1998). This has important implications for survivors of sexual violence. In addition to anger, fear, anxiety, shame, depression, and the wide range of responses to sexual violence that many women face, rural women frequently face other barriers that contribute to their inability to recover from sexual violence, including geographic and social isolation, poverty, lack of insurance or underinsurance, and an overall lack of access to community resources (DeKeseredy & Schwartz, 2009).

A need for comprehensive sexual assault services in rural communities has been recently demonstrated (DeKeseredy & Schwartz, 2009; Lewis, 2003). However, there are a variety of challenges for advocates providing sexual assault services in rural communities, including navigating the great geographic distances that must often be traveled to provide medical and legal assistance; isolation; economic constraints, which can limit educational efforts and community outreach; and challenging patriarchal ideology and male privilege, which condones violence against women. The latter requires what DeKeseredy and Schwartz (2009) refer to as "shifting community culture": doing cultural work, such as holding plays and festivals, and staging events that raise awareness about sexual violence against women and confront "rural patriarchy" (p. 116). Shifting culture is also necessary when working with local law enforcement in some rural communities, to challenge the "good ol' boy network" and eliminate the stigma associated with sexual assault. One online organization that is working to raise awareness about

violence against women in rural communities and challenge patriarchal attitudes is RuralWomyn Zone (http://www.ruralwomyn.net). This online community was created by advocates for rural battered and raped women and provides a variety of resources for survivors, advocates, and law enforcement working in rural communities.

Conclusion

Sexual assault services have changed substantially over the past three decades. The original feminist grassroots collectives that served as centers of empowerment and social change have largely evolved into a diverse mix of stand-alone and collaborative programs that provide sexual assault services in a variety of ways. However, while much has changed, the primary commitment to provide support to victims of sexual assault and educate the community and those who work with sexual assault victims to prevent revictimization continues. As this chapter indicates, coordinated responses (such as SANE and SART) are important collaborative approaches to provide services to sexual assault survivors in a more comprehensive way. Some research indicates that given their relative autonomy and flexibility in how they define their service population, free-standing rape crisis centers may be in a better position than other sexual assault service providers to serve their local communities. However, funding issues and budgetary constraints may hinder their efforts. There is a scarcity of research on this question, and more empirical investigation is needed to determine how effective different types of sexual assault service organizations are in responding to survivors' needs.

Some of the challenges facing sexual assault service providers were examined in this chapter, and given the current economic climate, issues such as budgetary constraints will likely continue to hinder this important work. Although there are many challenges and much work to be done in the anti-rape movement, some of the most exciting work is being done at the grassroots level, with communities responding to the needs of marginalized populations. Future research should explore the effectiveness of these programs in meeting the needs of survivors and working for social change.

References

Ahrens, C. E., Cabral, G., & Abeling, S. (2009). Healing or hurtful: Sexual assault survivors' interpretations of social reactions from support providers. *Psychology of Women Quarterly, 33*, 81–94.

Ahrens, C. E., Campbell, R., Wasco, S. M., Grubstein, L., Aponte, G. A., & Davidson, W. S. (2000). Sexual Assault Nurse Examiner programs: Systems for service delivery for sexual assault victims. *Journal of Interpersonal Violence, 15*, 921–943.

Amir, M. (1971). *Patterns of forcible rape.* Chicago: The University of Chicago Press.

Antognoli-Toland, P. (1985). Comprehensive program for examination of sexual assault victims by nurses: A hospital-based project in Texas. *Journal of Emergency Nursing, 11*(3), 132–136.

Bergen, R. K. (1996). *Wife rape: Understanding the response of survivors and service providers.* Thousand Oaks, CA: Sage.

Bergen, R. K. (2004). Studying wife rape: Reflections on the past, present and future. *Violence Against Women, 10*(12), 1407–1416.

Bierria, A. (2007). Pursuing a radical antiviolence agenda inside/outside a non-profit structure. In Incite! Women of Color Against Violence (Eds.), *The revolution will not be funded: Beyond the nonprofit industrial complex* (pp. 151–163). Cambridge, MA: South End Press.

Brownmiller, S. (1975). *Against our will: Men, women and rape.* New York: Simon and Schuster.

Burgess, A., Lewis-O'Connor, A., Nugent-Borakove, M. E., & Fanflik, P. (2006). SANE/SART services for sexual assault victims: Policy implications. *Victims and Offenders, 1*, 205–212.

Burt, M., Zweig, J., Schlichter, K., Kamya, S., Katz, B., Miller, N., et al. (2000). *2000 report: Evaluation of the STOP grants to combat violence against women.* Washington, DC: The Urban Institute.

Campbell, R. (1998). The community response to rape: Victims' experiences with the legal, medical, and mental health systems. *American Journal of Community Psychology, 26*(3), 355–379.

Campbell, R. (2005). What really happened? A validation study of rape survivors' help-seeking experiences with the legal and medical systems. *Violence & Victims, 20*, 55–68.

Campbell, R. (2006). Rape survivors' experiences with the legal and medical systems: Do rape victim advocates make a difference? *Violence Against Women, 12*(1), 30–45.

Campbell, R., Baker, C. K., & Mazurek, T. L. (1998). Remaining radical? Organizational predictors of rape crisis centers' social change initiatives. *American Journal of Community Psychology, 26*(3), 457–483.

Campbell, R., & Martin, P. Y. (2002). Services for sexual assault survivors: The role of rape crisis centers. In R. M. Holmes & S. T. Holmes (Eds.), *Current perspectives on sex crimes* (pp. 227–241). Thousand Oaks, CA: Sage.

Campbell, R., & Raja, S. (1999). Secondary victimization of rape victims: Insights from mental health professionals who treat survivors of violence. *Violence and Victims, 14*(3), 261–275.

Campbell, R., & Raja, S. (2005). The sexual assault and secondary victimization of female veterans: Help-seeking experiences with military and civilian social systems. *Psychology of Women Quarterly, 29*, 97–106.

Campbell, R., Sefl, T., Barnes, H. E., Ahrens, C. E., Wasco, S. M., & Zaragoza-Diesfeld, Y. (1999). Community services for rape survivors: Enhancing psychological well-being or increasing trauma? *Journal of Consulting and Clinical Psychology, 67*(6), 847–858.

Campbell, R., Wasco, S., Ahrens, C., Sefl, T., & Barnes, H. (2001). Preventing the "second rape": Rape survivors' experiences with community service providers. *Journal of Interpersonal Violence, 16*(12), 1239–1259.

Ciancone, A., Wilson, C., Collette, R., & Gerson, L. W. (2000). Sexual Assault Nurse Examiner programs in the United States. *Annals of Emergency Medicine, 35*, 353–357.

Clemans, S. E. (2004). Life changing: The experience of rape crisis work. *Affilia, 19*(2), 146–159.

Colindres, A. (2008, March 1). Strip club tax designed to aid rape-crisis centers. *The State Journal Register.* Retrieved March 10, 2008, from http://www.sj-r.com/News/stories/26200.asp

Collins, P. H. (2000). *Black feminist thought* (2nd ed.). New York: Routledge.

Crandall, C., & Helitzer, D. (2003). *Impact evaluation of a Sexual Assault Nurse Examiner (SANE) program.* (NCJ 203276) Washington, DC: National Institute of Justice.

DeKeseredy, W., & Schwartz, M. (2009). *Dangerous exits: Escaping abuse relationships in rural America.* Newark, NJ: Rutgers University Press.

Donavan, R., & Williams, M. (2002). Living at the intersection: The effect of racism and sexism on black rape survivors. *Women & Therapy, 25*(3/4), 95–105.

Du Mont, J., & Parnis, D. (2003). Forensic nursing in the context of sexual assault: Comparing the opinions and practices of nurse examiners and nurses. *Applied Nursing Research, 16,* 173–183.

Durazo, A. C. R. (2007). "We were never meant to survive." In Incite! Women of Color Against Violence (Eds.), *The revolution will not be funded: Beyond the nonprofit industrial complex* (pp. 113–128). Cambridge, MA: South End Press.

Elman, A. (2005). Confronting the sexual abuse of women with disabilities. *VawNet.* Retrieved October 23, 2009, from http://new.vawnet.org/Assoc_Files_VAWNET/AR_SVDisability

Ericksen, J., Dudley, C., McIntosh, G., Ritch, L., Shumay, S., & Simpson, M. (2002). Clients' experiences with a specialized sexual assault service. *Journal of Emergency Nursing, 28,* 86–90.

Estrich, S. (1987). *Real rape.* Cambridge, MA: Harvard University Press.

Florida Council Against Sexual Violence. (2009). *2009 legislative priorities.* Retrieved February 16, 2009, from http://www.fcasv.org/2005_Web/leg_priorities.htm

Frazier, P. A., & Haney, B. (1996). Sexual assault cases in the legal system: Police, prosecutor, and victim perspectives. *Law and Human Behavior, 20*(6), 607–628.

Gilmore, R. W. (2007). In the shadow of the shadow state. In Incite! Women of Color Against Violence (Eds.), *The revolution will not be funded: Beyond the nonprofit industrial complex* (pp. 41–52). Cambridge, MA: South End Press.

Girardin, B. W. (2005). The sexual assault nurse examiner: A win-win solution. *Topics in Emergency Medicine, 27*(2), 124–131.

Gornick, J., Burt, M. R., & Pittman, K. J. (1985). Structure and activities of rape crisis centers in the early 1980s. *Crime & Delinquency, 31*(2), 247–268.

Gornick, J., & Meyer, D. (1998). Changing political opportunity: The anti-rape movement and public policy. *Journal of Policy History, 10*(4), 367–398.

Greenfeld, L. A., & Smith, S. (1999). *American Indians and crime.* (NCJ 173386) Retrieved October 25, 2009, from http://www.ojp.usdoj.gov/bjs/abstract/aic.htm

Hamby, S. L. (2004). Sexual victimization in Indian country: Barriers and resources for Native women seeking help. *VawNet.* Retrieved October 25, 2009, from http://www.mincava.umn.edu/documents/arsvindiancountry/arsvindiancountry.html

Houmes, B. V., Fagan, M. M., & Quintana, N. M. (2003). Establishing a Sexual Assault Nurse Examiner (SANE) program in the emergency department. *The Journal of Emergency Medicine, 25*(1), 111–121.

Hunter, S., Burns-Smith, G., & Walsh, C. (1996). Equal justice? Not yet for victims of sexual assault. *Connecticut Sexual Assault Crisis Services' Newsletter.* Retrieved October 25, 2009, from http://www.connsacs.org/library/justice.html

Hutcheson, N. (2009, January 18). Proposed budget diverts funds for Florida rape crisis centers. *St. Petersburg Times.* Retrieved February 16, 2009, from http://www.tampabay.com/news/publicsafety/crime/article968496.ece

International Association of Forensic Nursing. (2009). *Clinical forensic program registry.* Retrieved January 2, 2009, from http://www.iafn.org/displaycommon.cfm

Jones, N. (2009). *Between good and ghetto: African American girls and inner city violence.* Piscataway, NJ: Rutgers University Press.

Karjane, H. M., Fisher, B. S., & Culler, F. T. (2005). *Sexual assault on campus: What colleges and universities are doing about it.* U.S. Department of Justice, National Institute of Justice. Retrieved December 9, 2009, from www.ncjrs.org/pdffiles/nij/grants/196676.pdf

Konradi, A., & Burger, T. (2000). Having the last word: An examination of rape survivors' participation in sentencing. *Violence Against Women, 6*(4), 351–395.

Ledray, L. (1995). Sexual assault evidentiary exam and treatment protocol. *Journal of Emergency Nursing, 21,* 355–359.

Ledray, L. (1999). *Sexual Assault Nurse Examiner (SANE) development & operation guide.* Washington, DC: U.S. Department of Justice, Office for Victims of Crime.

Ledray, L. (2001, August). Evidence collection and care of the sexual assault survivor. *Violence Against Women Online Resources.* Retrieved August 15, 2006, from http://mincava.umn.edu

Ledray, L. (2005). Data on SANE programs crucial to refining the specialty, improving care. *Journal of Forensic Nursing, 1*(4), 187–188.

Ledray, L., & Simmelink, K. (1997). Efficacy of SANE evidence collection: A Minnesota study. *Journal of Emergency Nursing, 23,* 75–77.

Lehrner, A., & Allen, N. E. (2009). Still a movement after all these years? Current tensions in the domestic violence movement. *Violence Against Women, 15*(6), 656–677.

Lewis, C. M., DiNitto, D., Nelson, T. S., Just, M. M., & Campbell-Ruggaard, J. (2003). Evaluation of a rape protocol: A five year follow-up with nurse managers. *Journal of the American Academy of Nurse Practitioners, 15*(1), 34–39.

Lewis, S. (2003). Sexual assaults in rural communities. *VawNet.* Retrieved October 23, 2009, from http://www.vawnet.org

Littel, K. (2001). *Sexual Assault Nurse Examiner (SANE) programs: Improving the community response to sexual assault victims.* Washington, DC: U.S. Department of Justice, Office for Victims of Crime.

Lonsway, K. A., & Fitzgerald, L. (1994). Rape myths: In review. *Psychology of Women Quarterly, 18,* 133–164.

Low, G., & Organista, K. (2000). Latinas and sexual assault: Towards culturally sensitive assessment and intervention. *Journal of Multicultural Social Work, 8*(1/2), 131–157.

Macy, R. J., Giattina, M. C., Parish, S., & Crosby, C. (2009). Domestic violence and sexual assault services: Historical concerns and contemporary challenges. *Journal of Interpersonal Violence.* Retrieved October 25, 2009, from http://jiv.sagepub.com

Madigan, L., & Gamble, N. (1991). *The second rape: Society's continued betrayal of the victim.* New York: Lexington Books.

Maier, S. L. (2008). Are rape crisis centers feminist organizations? *Feminist Criminology, 3*(2), 82–100.

Martin, P. Y. (2005). *Rape work: Victims, gender, and emotions in organization and community context.* New York: Routledge.

Martin, P. Y., DiNitto, D., Byington, D., & Maxwell, M. S. (1992). Organizational and community transformation: The case of a rape crisis center. *Administration in Social Work, 16,* 123–145.

Martin, P. Y., & Powell, R. M. (1994). Accounting for the "second assault": Legal organizations' framing of rape victims. *Law & Social Inquiry, 19*(3/4), 853–890.

Martin, S., Ray, N., Sotres-Alvarez, D., Kupper, L., Moracco, K., Dickens, P., et al. (2006). Physical and sexual assault of women with disabilities. *Violence Against Women, 12,* 823–837.

Matthews, N. (1989). Surmounting a legacy: The expansion of racial diversity in a local anti-rape movement. *Gender and Society, 3*(4), 518–532.

Matthews, N. (1994). *Confronting rape: The feminist anti-rape movement and the state.* London: Routledge.

McGregor, M. J., Du Mont, J., & Myhr, T. L. (2002). Sexual assault forensic medical examination: Is evidence related to successful prosecution? *Annals of Emergency Medicine, 39,* 639–647.

Monroe, L. M., Kinney, L. M., Weist, M. D., Spriggs Dafeamekpor, D., Dantzler, J., & Reynolds, M. W. (2005). The experience of sexual assault: Findings from a statewide victim needs assessment. *Journal of Interpersonal Violence, 20*(7), 767–776.

National Institute of Justice. (2005). *Research for practice. Sexual assault on campus: What colleges and universities are doing about it.* Retrieved October 22, 2009, from http://www.ojp.usdoj.gov/nij2005

Neville, H. A., & Pugh, A. O. (1997). General and culture-specific factors influencing African American women's reporting patterns and perceived social support following sexual assault. *Violence Against Women, 5*(4), 361–381.

Nosek, M., & Howland, C. A. (1998). Abuse and women with disabilities. *VawNet.* Retrieved October 11, 2009, from http://new.vawnet.org/Assoc_Files_VAWNET/AR_Disab.

O'Brien, C. (1996). Sexual Assault Nurse Examiner (SANE) program coordinator. *Journal of Emergency Nursing, 22,* 532–533.

Oschwald, M., Renker, P., Hughes, R. B., Arthur, A., Powers, L. E., & Curry, M. A. (2009). Development of an accessible audio computer-assisted self-interview (A-CASI) to screen for abuse and provide safety strategies for women with disabilities. *Journal of Interpersonal Violence, 24*(6), 1014–1035.

O'Sullivan, E., & Carlton, A. (2001). Victim services, community outreach, and contemporary rape crisis centers: A comparison of independent and multiservice centers. *Journal of Interpersonal Violence, 16*(4), 343–360.

Patterson, D. (2009). The effectiveness of sexual assault services in multi-service agencies. *VAWnet.* Retrieved October 21, 2009, from http://new .vawnet.org/Assoc_Files_VAWnet/AR_Dual Programs.pdf

Pennington, E. C., Zwemer, F. L., & Krebs, D. (2010, January). Unique sexual assault examiner program utilizing mid-level providers. *The Journal of Emergency Medicine, 38*(1), 95–98.

Pennsylvania Coalition Against Rape. (2002). *Sexual Assault Response Team (SART) guidelines.* Retrieved October 4, 2009, from http://www.pcar .org/med_adv/guidelines

Plichta, S. B., Clements, P. T., & Houseman, C. (2007). Why SANEs matter: Models of care for sexual violence victims in the emergency department. *Journal of Forensic Nursing, 3*(1), 15–23.

Powers, L. E., Hughes, R. B., & Lund, E. M. (2009). Interpersonal violence and women with disabilities: A research update. *VawNet.* Retrieved December 8, 2009, from http://new.vawnet.org/category/main_ Doc.php

Preston, L. D. (2003). The Sexual Assault Nurse Examiner and the rape crisis advocate: A necessary partnership. *Topics in Emergency Medicine, 25*(3), 242–246.

Resnick, H., Acierno, R., Holmes, M., Dammeyer, M., & Kilpatrick, D. (2000). Emergency evaluation and intervention with female victims of rape and other violence. *Journal of Clinical Psychology, 56*(10), 1317–1333.

Resnick, H., Monnier, J., Seals, B., Holmes, M., Nayak, M., Walsh, J., et al. (2002). Rape-related HIV concerns among recent rape victims. *Journal of Interpersonal Violence, 17*(7), 746–759.

Riger, S. (1994). Challenges of success: Stages of growth in feminist organizations. *Feminist Studies, 20,* 275–300.

Riger, S., Bennett, L., Wasco, S. M., Schewe, P. A., Frohmann, L., Camacho, J. M., et al. (2002). *Evaluating services for survivors of domestic violence and sexual assault.* Thousand Oaks, CA: Sage.

Royse, B. (1999). *Non-stranger sexual assault: Rural realities.* National Non-Stranger Sexual Assault Symposium, Proceedings Report. Denver Sexual Assault Interagency Council.

Ruback, B. R., & Menard, K. S. (2001). Rural-urban differences in sexual victimization and reporting: Analysis using UCR and crisis center data. *Criminal Justice and Behavior, 28*(2), 131–155.

Russell, D. E. H. (1990). *Rape in marriage.* Bloomington: Indiana University Press.

Scalzo, T. (2006). Tips for testifying as an expert witness in a violence against women prosecution. *The Voice.* Retrieved December 29, 2008, from http://www.ndaa.org/publications/newsletters/ the_voice_vol_1_no_6_2006.pdf

Schechter, S. (1982). *Women and male violence: The visions and struggles of the battered women's movement.* Boston: South End.

Schmitt, F. E., & Martin, P. Y. (1999). Unobtrusive mobilization by an institutionalized rape crisis center: "All we do comes from victims." *Gender & Society, 13*(3), 364–384.

Sloan, L. M. (2006, Winter). Two movements, two paths, one goal. *Revolution, 1*(1), 3–6.

Smith, G. (2008, November 29). Rape crisis group needs funding. *The Post and Courier.* Retrieved February 16, 2009, from http://www.charleston.net/ news/2008/nov/29/rape_crisis_group_needs_ funding63428

Speck, P., & Aiken, M. (1995). 20 years of community nursing service. *Tennessee Nurse,* 5–18.

Taylor, L., & Gaskin-Laniyan, N. (2009). *Study reveals unique issues faced by deaf victims of sexual assault.* Retrieved October 22, 2009, from http://www .ojp.usdoj.gov/nij/journals/257/deaf-victims

Thompson Sanders, V. L., & Smith West, S. (1992). Attitudes of African American adults toward treatment in cases of rape. *Community Mental Health Journal, 28*(6), 531–536.

Tjaden, P., & Thoennes, N. (2000). *Full report of the prevalence, incidence and consequences of violence against women.* Washington, DC: U.S. Department of Justice.

Townsend, S. M., & Campbell, R. (2007). Homogeneity in community-based rape prevention programs: Empirical evidence of institutional isomorphism. *Journal of Community Psychology, 35,* 371–386.

Ullman, S. E., & Townsend, S. M. (2007). Barriers to working with sexual assault survivors: A qualitative study of rape crisis center workers. *Violence Against Women, 13,* 412–443.

VawNet. (2009). *Violence in the lives of persons who are deaf or hard of hearing. Special collections.* Retrieved October 23, 2009, from http://www.new.vawnet .org/Assoc_Files_VAWNET/AR.SVDisability

Wahab, S., & Olson, L. (2004). Intimate partner violence and sexual assault in Native American communities. *Trauma, Violence, & Abuse, 5*(4), 353–366.

Wasco, S. M., Campbell, R., Howard, A., Mason, G., Schewe, P., Staggs, S., et al. (2004). A statewide evaluation of services provided to rape survivors. *Journal of Interpersonal Violence, 19*(2), 252–263.

Washington Coalition of Sexual Assault Programs. (2008, Spring/Summer). *Connections, X,* 1.

Washington, P. A. (2001). Disclosure patterns of black female sexual assault survivors. *Violence Against Women, 7*(11), 1254–1283.

Websdale, N. (1998). *Rural woman battering and the justice system: An ethnography.* Thousand Oaks, CA: Sage.

Websdale, N. (2001). *Policing the poor: From slave plantation to public housing.* Boston: Northeastern University Press.

White, A. (2001). "I am because we are": Combined race and gender political consciousness among African American women and men anti-rape activists. *Women's Studies International Forum, 24*(1), 11–24.

Whittier, N. (1995). *Feminist generations: The persistence of the radical women's movement.* Philadelphia: Temple University Press.

Zweig, J. M., & Burt, M. R. (2003). Effects of interactions among community agencies on legal system responses to domestic violence and sexual assault in STOP-funded communities. *Criminal Justice Policy Review, 14,* 249–272.

Chapter Authors

Raquel Kennedy Bergen is a Professor and Chair of the Department of Sociology at Saint Joseph's University in Philadelphia, Pennsylvania. She is the author or coauthor of numerous scholarly publications and five books on violence against women, including *Wife Rape: Understanding the Response of Survivors and Service Providers* (Sage, 1996) and *Issues in Intimate Violence* (Sage, 1998). With Claire Renzetti and Jeff Edleson, she edited *Sourcebook on Violence Against Women* (Sage, 2000) and *Violence Against Women: Classic Statements* (Pearson Education, 2005). She coedited *Violence Against Women: Readings from Social Problems* (Rowman and Littlefield, 2005) with Claire Renzetti. She has served as a member of the Pennsylvania State Ethics Commission since 2004, when she was appointed by Governor Edward G. Rendell. She has volunteered as an advocate for battered women and sexual assault survivors for the past 20 years. Her current research explores women's experiences of sexual and physical violence during pregnancy.

Shana L. Maier, B.S., Criminal Justice (Saint Joseph's University); M.S., Criminal Justice (Saint Joseph's University); Ph.D., Sociology (University of Delaware). Dr. Maier is an Associate Professor in the Department of Criminal Justice at Widener University, Chester, PA. Her research interests include violence against women, the treatment of rape victims by the criminal justice system, the transformation of rape crisis centers, and the experiences and struggles of rape victim advocates and Sexual Assault Nurse Examiners. She is the author of articles appearing in *Violence Against Women, Women & Criminal Justice, Journal of Ethnicity in Criminal Justice,* and *Feminist Criminology,* and the coauthor of articles appearing in *Deviant Behavior, International Review of Victimology,* and *Women's Health and Urban Life.*

Personal Reflection

Pamela Teaster

As a gerontologist and a researcher, I became interested in research on the sexual abuse of older adults because of the confluence of two events. First, when I was a graduate student, my mom called me one spring evening to say that a friend of ours, a wealthy woman in her 90s, had been raped. Our friend lived alone, had a great love for animals, and had never married. Members of our community who knew about it were shocked and saddened. Although the police were summoned, she either did not know or would not say who had raped her, and to my knowledge, she never did say. Because my mom knew that I was studying government and aging, she asked me whether I had ever heard of such a thing happening to an old person. I had not. But I can still remember the next day I remarked on the event to one of my classmates and resolved that someday, somehow, I would do something about that.

Second, at a conference, I met a woman who eventually became (and still is) one of my greatest friends and life guides. At the time, she worked at the state Adult Protective Services in Virginia. She told me that almost no one ever studied elder sexual abuse, and she thought that, as a new professor, I should do it. When a tiny amount of competitive internal seed money ($1,000) for research projects became available, I wrote a proposal to gather sexual abuse data from Adult Protective Services staff members in Virginia. I was funded, and for some amazing reason, we ran that study for five years. Because of that early work as principal investigator, I was awarded a National Institute on Aging grant to research the sexual abuse of vulnerable adults in institutions.

My colleagues and I have learned much about reporting and the investigatory process involving the sexual abuse of older adults, particularly women. There is still much to understand about how to help people report more quickly and how to conduct far better investigations. It is critical to know the best ways to intervene in this form of abuse, as too few cases are ever prosecuted. It is critical to focus education and resources on this problem. We really don't know the long-term effects of sexual abuse on the victims, outcomes for the perpetrators, or how we might prevent such occurrences.

Men are not the only perpetrators of sexual abuse. My colleagues and I have found that abuse of men occurs more often than originally thought. Residents are often the abusers in facilities. Sexual abuse happens not just in community settings and not just in facility settings. Sexual abuse is varied and includes touching and fondling and unwanted viewing of media, as well as rape or sodomy. We have shed greater light the sexual abuse of elders. Still, more efforts are needed to prevent this violence as well as to intervene and resolve these occurrences. Greater and focused resources are essential to appropriately address this violence.

CHAPTER 13

An Overview of Community-Based Services for Battered Women

Nicole E. Allen, Sadie E. Larsen, and Angela L. Walden

In this chapter, we provide an overview of community-based services available for battered women and their children, beginning with a brief history of the earliest services offered. Today there are more than 2,000 domestic violence shelters in the United States offering a wide variety of services, from emergency shelter and counseling to advocacy and preventive community outreach. We discuss a number of issues that shelters must grapple with: how women gain access to services (along with barriers to doing so), what rules to establish and what such rules convey, how to evaluate the effectiveness of shelter services, and how to make sure that shelters are culturally competent and accessible to all. One challenge facing shelters is to adequately serve women with multiple needs and women from traditionally marginalized groups.

Second, we address other community-based programs for battered women and their children and give examples of each. Because certain cultural groups have difficulty accessing resources, many programs have been developed that address the needs of specific cultural populations. Universities have been another source of legal and comprehensive advocacy services for battered women, drawing on student populations as a plentiful source of service providers to address the shortage of available advocacy services. Finally, programs have begun to provide services addressing other needs of survivors (e.g., mental or physical health care, legal services) or to collaborate with other agencies in order to expand services. One overarching challenge across many community-based programs for battered women and their children is availability and accessibility, especially in rural areas.

Finally, we discuss efforts to encourage community-wide coordination across systems. Such efforts often focus on coordinating the response of the criminal justice system, but they may also involve improving the health care, human service, and educational systems. Often, collaboration across systems takes the form of coordinating councils formed in local communities. These councils work to better understand and then improve local policies, protocols, and practices to encourage survivor safety and batterer accountability. Challenges for coordinated community response efforts include identifying conditions under which such efforts are most effective, balancing efficiency and inclusiveness, and including the voices of domestic violence service providers and survivors.

Domestic Violence Shelter Programs

Shelter History

Beginning in the 1960s, the battered women's movement, occurring alongside the women's liberation, anti-rape, and civil rights movements, redefined domestic violence from a private matter to a broadly shared experience of women across social groups. Consciousness-raising groups were a common part of this movement; in these groups, women gathered in solidarity to define the "personal as political." Perhaps as an expression of the desire to move from "thought to action" (Dobash & Dobash, 1992, p. 25), in the early 1970s, women who were survivors, community activists, and feminists opened shelters to offer women with abusive partners a refuge from abuse (Dobash & Dobash, 1992; Schechter, 1982).

Early shelters were often a room in a private home. Shelters for women with abusive partners also provided a space for women to gather, to share their experiences, and to support one another as they navigated decisions about their lives and a temporary escape from abusive relationships. In this process, women were able to identify their shared experiences, moving away from explanations of violence as expressions of individual deviance and toward the social and cultural realities that supported widespread violence against women in their homes. Thus, shelters frequently formed the local epicenter for movement activities

that focused not only on encouraging women's safety and well-being, but on institutional advocacy (e.g., criminal justice reform) and social justice (e.g., gender equality). It is important to note that early shelters were not a monolithic group. Some shelters had religious affiliations and/or were socially conservative, while others reflected the social change agenda of the radical feminist movement (Dobash & Dobash, 1992). In spite of such diversity, all shelters focused substantially on meeting women's needs through service provision.

As is often the case with settings that begin as "alternatives," shelter programs have become institutionalized as social service settings with a specific service mandate. Not surprisingly, shelter programs began to seek funding to expand their capacity to serve women. This desire for expanded capacity is also not surprising given the immense number of women who need a refuge from abuse and the diverse array of services that are required to assist them as they navigate their safety. With increased capacity also comes increased need for organizational structures that support such expansion. As noted by Schechter (1982), expanding service provision and responding to the external mandates of funders create specific challenges for settings that aim to challenge the status quo. Balancing service delivery with time and resources for a broader social change agenda is a perennial challenge for domestic violence shelter programs (Hammons, 2004; Lehrner & Allen, 2009).

In sharp contrast to the historical inadequacy of the social service response to women with abusive partners, today there are myriad programs focused on the unique experiences of women with diverse social locations, including, for example, ethnic and racial identity, sexual orientation, immigration status, age, and physical ability. This evolution of services reflects the growing diversity of women organizing to address domestic violence, the recognition that the first wave of the battered women's movement centered on white, middle-class women's experiences and needs, and the expanded knowledge of the ways that women's experiences vary across social groups. Finally, the current array of community-based services involves partnerships across agencies responding to domestic violence and efforts to create broad, community-wide, coordinated responses.

Shelter Program Services

The variety of services currently offered by domestic violence shelter programs has changed extensively from the early days of the battered women's movement. Shelter programs provide abused women and their children with a safe location away from their abusive partner and generally offer a similar range of services, including emergency shelter, counseling, crisis hotlines, advocacy, and educational and preventive community outreach (e.g., Bennett, Riger, Schewe, Howard, & Wasco, 2004; Lyon, Lane, & Menard, 2008). In contrast to early shelters, in today's shelters, program staff is generally composed of professionals, but "lay" employees and volunteers who have been trained to work with abused women still make up an important part of the shelter work force. Staff who are in direct contact with survivors commonly provide them and their children with referrals to a variety of other agencies that provide legal, mental health, housing, vocational, and educational services (Saathoff & Stoffel, 1999). Some programs also offer group or peer counseling, individual counseling, transitional housing, specialized programs for children (e.g., support and education groups), services for marginalized women, and bilingual services. Finally, a variety of nonresidential services, including access to counseling, support groups, advocacy (e.g., legal advocacy or assistance with protection orders), and other services may be widely available to survivors in the community.

It is worth noting that the information provided in this chapter is drawn almost exclusively from literature pertaining to the United States and North America. Yet, the past few decades have also brought about global changes regarding the recognition of women's rights and issues pertaining to domestic violence. As one can imagine, the range of responses to violence against women around the world vary greatly. Dobash and Dobash (1992) note the long history of providing shelter to victims of domestic violence in Great Britain, beginning with the opening of Chiswick Women's Aid in 1972. The provision of battered women's shelter services quickly spread to other countries around the world, and services for survivors of domestic violence continued to expand over the next few decades. In a recent illustration of a comprehensive approach to domestic violence services, Harwin (2006) provided a description of the current array of services provided and/or coordinated by an organization called Women's Aid in England, of which she is the director. Women's Aid coordinates services for hundreds of domestic violence and refuge services across England. Additionally, this organization produces and distributes informational resources and provides training services and programs, offers consultation to government officials regarding initiatives pertaining to violence against women, and runs a national domestic violence helpline (Harwin, 2006).

In other regions of the world, the power and influence of a religious community may be a strong shaping force for the availability and delivery of domestic violence services. As discussed by Palant (2004), this is the case for Jewish survivors of domestic violence living in Israel. Bat-Melech, one of only 14 shelters in Israel created specifically for Jewish women, provides shelter, counseling, and legal aid services, while at the same time providing an environment in which staff members are religiously observant and diverse; each stream of Judaism is represented by at least one staff member. Additionally, the program places great emphasis on helping women learn to live independently in their communities, which, in some cases, is facilitated by connecting them with a rabbi who "grants legitimacy to the woman in her choice" (p. 25). There are countless other examples of the variety of shelters and services for survivors of domestic violence around the world. It is important to keep in mind that services around the world may share similarities, but they also differ with respect to factors that influence service delivery organizations, including their guiding principles and style of service delivery.

Gaining Access to Services

Traditionally, accessing emergency shelter services begins with a phone call to either a hotline or the shelter program itself. Concerned friends or family members may call with requests for information, women in abusive situations may call for themselves, and law enforcement officers may call on behalf of a survivor. In their efforts to maximize survivors' safety, as well as staff's, it is not uncommon for domestic violence programs to require that the location of their shelter remain confidential, but this is changing as many shelter programs now publish their locations in local telephone books and online to increase their visibility and accessibility. Upon her arrival, the survivor may be asked to fill out additional paperwork and provide copies of any personal documents she might have with her, such as identification or medical cards. She may be provided with a copy of the "house rules," which often includes information about curfews, chores, children's bedtimes, and other program mandates or policies. Depending on the program's requirements, a survivor's stay may also be contingent upon her willingness to participate in case management, group therapy, or other program activities. Following her introduction to the staff members and other residents, the woman and her children are given some time to adjust to their new surroundings. Throughout her stay, the survivor will likely meet with a case manager or advocate who will assess, or help her assess, her and her children's needs and provide appropriate referrals and advocacy.

The length of stay at an emergency shelter can be determined by a combination of factors, including the individual program's resources, the client's compliance with shelter rules, and staff members' general sense of how well the client is working toward obtaining independence from the shelter. Stays generally range from a few weeks to a few months. For example, one study determined the median shelter stay to be 60 days; although several shelters had a 30-day limit, a client's actual length of stay was flexible and could be extended depending on the circumstances (Lyon et al., 2008). If she is accepted into a transitional housing program, the client's average stay is often extended beyond a year.

There are more abused women than are represented by the number of survivors who seek emergency shelter or other related services. Although specific help-seeking behaviors are dependent upon each individual's situation, the decision to seek assistance may be influenced by a number of factors. Findings from Leone, Johnson, and Cohan (2007) indicated that women who experienced severe forms of violence were more likely to seek help from formal community resources, whereas women who experienced less severe abuse were less likely to seek formal services and more likely to engage in informal help seeking (e.g., friends or family). Demographic characteristics, such as the victim's socioeconomic status, race, age, and relationship with her partner, also affect her engagement in help-seeking behaviors.

Consistent with previous literature regarding survivors' use of counseling services, findings from Henning and Klesges (2002) indicated that women of lower socioeconomic status, African American women, younger women, and unmarried abused women were less likely to seek these services than were other women. Additionally, survivors are more likely to leave their abusive partners during the summer or around an academic holiday. It is hypothesized that the presence of children in the abusive relationship may play a role in this pattern (Oths & Robertson, 2007). Clearly, survivors with children must weigh additional factors when considering whether or not to leave their partner. For example, batterers may use children as tools for manipulating their partner into staying in the relationship (e.g., by threatening to kidnap or harm the children if she leaves). They may also try to convince their abused partner that she will lose custody of the children if she leaves, try to sabotage her image as a competent mother during custody mediation or court hearings, or make false or exaggerated reports to child protective services. The batterer may continue using or even escalate intimidation tactics after the victim has attempted to end the relationship (Varcoe & Irwin, 2004).

It is important to note that survivors who seek help are not guaranteed to gain access to needed services. Common barriers that hinder success include unreliable transportation or lack of transportation, lack of housing, unemployment, lack of income independent from the abuser, lack of community services for victims, lack of awareness of the services that do exist, and the experience of being retraumatized by service providers (Zweig, Schlichter, & Burt, 2002). Added barriers may be inherent in community agencies because services tend to focus on one type of issue (e.g., domestic violence, mental health, child and family services, or drug and alcohol services). For example, some women seeking shelter may also suffer from mental health or substance abuse issues. For these women, further barriers to obtaining services might include lack of credibility in the eyes of service providers; the batterer's use of co-occurring problems as a means to further abuse; a lack of service agencies knowledgeable about or willing to assist with more than one of the issues of concern; and, in the case of women with cognitive impairments, there may be an inability to understand what is happening with their case (Zweig et al., 2002). It is clear that women with abusive partners have a wide variety of needs and priorities (Allen, Bybee, & Sullivan, 2004), and shelter programs are often challenged to engage in comprehensive advocacy rather than focus on abuse as the only, or even primary, challenge women face.

Shelter Program Rules and Philosophies

The guiding philosophy of a shelter program often dictates the implementation and enforcement of program rules, how a survivor's goals are conceptualized by staff, and how services are delivered. As in all other aspects of their operation, domestic violence shelter programs vary with regard to the creation and enforcement of rules. Some rules arise for the purpose of maintaining a safe environment for shelter residents and staff, such as mandatory curfews or maintaining the confidentiality of the shelter's location. Others may be created in an effort to maintain the shelter's appearance, such as weekly assigned chores. Some rules are implemented by staff to ensure that residents fully participate in the program's services. These may require residents to attend weekly group or individual therapy and meetings with a case manager or advocate.

Although these mandatory policies are considered a necessary component by shelter program staff, in an essay on the role of rules in shelter programs, Osmundson (n.d.) suggests they may also undermine a survivor's autonomy. She offers an example regarding merit-based systems: Women are written up for rule violations, and after a certain number of write-ups, they are asked to leave as a result of their perceived failure to comply with shelter rules. Osmundson asks important questions about the use of rules and suggests careful scrutiny regarding which rules should be implemented: Does a resident who repeatedly misses mandated group therapy appointments deserve to be asked to leave the shelter? Should these group meetings even be a requirement, or should each resident be allowed to have control over her participation in therapy? These questions highlight the need for staff to examine whose interests are being served by shelter rules and how modifications can be made in order to support the survivors' need for autonomy. At best, rules are simply guidelines for maintaining order and establishing a working and living climate that centralizes safety. At worst, shelter programs that do not strive to maintain an empowering environment that is respectful of an individual's autonomy run the risk of replicating a power dynamic that may be reminiscent, with regard to lack of control and autonomy, of the survivor's relationship with the abuser (Vaughn & Stamp, 2003). Thus, shelter programs must work continuously to balance maintaining order with encouraging women's empowerment, autonomy, and dignity.

Indeed, shelters often espouse an empowerment philosophy. This approach emphasizes supporting women to gain greater control over needed resources and opportunities. Yet, there can sometimes be distance between programs' stated service aims and their actual practices (Watkins & Allen, 2008). Sullivan (2006) emphasizes empowerment management in a detailed guide to infusing empowerment practice throughout shelter programs, including direct service to survivors as well as management and board practices.

Evaluating the Effectiveness of Shelter Services

Evaluation research is necessary to ensure that shelter services are adequately meeting the needs of clients. Typically, service evaluations are conducted in response to requests from funding agencies or a governing board. Inquiries into a shelter program's activities aim to uncover the degree to which the program provides its stated services, the effects the services have on the target population, and the way finances are being allocated (Riger et al., 2002). At times, shelters may define a successful shelter resident as one who permanently leaves her abuser, but there is evidence that this may be an unrealistic expectation and a misguided outcome. For example, a follow-up survey of former shelter residents by Snyder and Scheer (1981) found that 55% of the participants interviewed had returned to their abusive partner. Additionally, this narrow definition of

success may be counter to the values of women from collectivist or family-oriented backgrounds. An alternative definition of success can be conceptualized in terms of a program's ability to help the survivor find ways to increase her safety, regardless of her relationship with her abuser (Yoshioka & Choi, 2005). This reframing of "success" broadens the definition and frees the survivor to explore a wider array of options.

Evaluation research findings indicate that domestic violence services are generally effective in producing positive outcomes for survivors. Results from a multi-state evaluation of services provided in 215 shelter program sites indicated that the majority of participants (74%) rated their experience with shelter programs as "very helpful" (Lyon et al., 2008). Only 1% of participants reported that these services had been "not at all helpful." In addition, the majority of women surveyed at both intake and departure from the shelter reported that they had received at least some or all of the help they wanted in their effort to meet the needs they had when they entered the program. Further, a statewide evaluation of four domestic violence program components—hotline services, advocacy, counseling, and emergency shelter—found that participation in any of the four components resulted in an increase in participants' knowledge and perceived support, and that receiving emergency shelter services resulted in increased feelings of safety (Bennett et al., 2004). Participation in advocacy or counseling services also resulted in increased feelings of "improved decision making," and women who had received counseling were found to have an increased sense of self-efficacy and coping skills (Bennett et al., 2004). Emphasizing the importance of empowerment practice, survivors perceived services to be most helpful when clients were given control in decision making, had positive interactions with staff, and perceived that multiple agencies were acting together on their behalf (Zweig & Burt, 2007).

While there is evidence that shelter programs may play a critical role in enhancing women's well-being, it is also the case that such services may not be equally accessible to all women. As the repertoire of shelter services has increased, the range of clients served by shelter programs has also increased. In recent decades, it has become apparent that women who seek shelter are likely to come from a variety of situations and have a multitude of needs (e.g., Goodman & Epstein, 2007; Riger et al., 2002; Zweig et al., 2002). Shelter programs are often challenged to provide adequate services to domestic violence survivors from traditionally marginalized groups, as well as those with co-occurring mental health or substance abuse needs. Given the previous discussions of barriers to obtaining services, the characteristics of women who typically engage in help-seeking behavior, and the unique issues related to serving clients with multiple needs, it is especially important that evaluation research assess not only a program's ability to help current clients, but also ways in which services could be made more accessible and responsive to underserved women.

Diversity and Cultural Competency

There is evidence to suggest that women from certain ethnic minority groups (i.e., African American, American Indian, Alaskan Native) experience higher rates of domestic violence than do whites (Tjaden & Thoennes, 2000). However, women of color and other marginalized women (e.g., immigrants, refugees, lesbians, disabled, and the elderly) may face unique barriers to obtaining domestic violence services (Balsam, 2001; Bhuyan, 2008; Chang, Martin, Moracco, Dulli, Scandlin, & Loucks-Sorrel, 2003; Vinton, 1992; West, Kantor, & Jasinski, 1998). Attending to gaps in shelter service delivery to survivors belonging to marginalized groups requires understanding the unique layers of context affecting these women's lives.

Although the battered women's movement was successful in increasing the response to domestic violence issues, it has been criticized as less inclusive of women of color and other traditionally marginalized groups (Riger et al., 2002). Thus, marginalized women may not seek services, partially because they perceive that services in their area will not be responsive to their particular needs. For example, immigrant women may be less likely to seek shelter services, particularly if they do not speak English. Additionally, many may not report violence because of a fear that they or their partners will be deported (Pan, Daley, Rivera, Williams, Lingle, & Reznik, 2006). Specific cultural beliefs may contribute to the acceptance of violence (e.g., the importance of the family), and women may be particularly likely to adhere to these beliefs because of a desire to retain their own culture in the face of acculturation and discrimination (Espin, 1999). Domestic violence may be experienced as a problem only secondary to other problems (e.g., divorce, immigration, housing), and immigrant women may be reluctant to contact service providers who will not take such contextual factors into consideration (Preisser, 1999). Further, although abused immigrant women are offered certain protections under VAWA, women must meet different eligibility requirements for each of the four protective categories in the Act and must be able to produce evidence of abuse in order to use these protections. The application process is often lengthy, confusing, and intimidating, and immigrant women who are successful in acquiring legal immigration status must wait several years before they are eligible to obtain government benefits (Bhuyan, 2008).

Women of color, like other marginalized groups, may be less likely to obtain formal domestic violence services (e.g., Preisser, 1999; Sorenson, 1996; West et al., 1998). One possible reason is that mainstream shelters may sometimes fail to provide culturally competent services for women of color. For example, Gillum (2008a) found that many African American women were generally dissatisfied with shelters due to, for example, their lack of appropriate hygiene products (e.g., for hair care) and few African American staff members, particularly in shelters in which the majority of clients are African American. In contrast, recent findings have suggested that the majority of racial minority shelter clients (95%) agree or strongly agree that staff had been respectful of their racial background (Lyon et al., 2008). Taken together, these findings suggest that shelter programs may vary in the degree to which they have achieved culturally responsive service delivery. In any case, attending to the diverse ethnic and racial populations likely to be served in a given community—both with regard to diverse representation among staff and the nature of services and resources offered—is critical to increasing the accessibility and appropriateness of shelter-based programs.

Similarly, studies have shown that, overall, relatively few lesbians seek shelter services, and the programs do not target the needs of this population (Balsam, 2001). Findings from an early study of lesbian experiences suggested that those who had sought services from hotlines and women's shelters found them to be unhelpful or only minimally helpful. It is interesting that 64% of participants indicated that they decided to stay in their abusive relationship because they "did not know where, or how, to seek help" (Renzetti, 1988). On a positive note, recent findings have indicated that 97% of surveyed lesbian and gay shelter clients felt that their sexual orientation had been respected by staff. However, given the relatively small number of lesbian and gay individuals residing in shelters (93% of total participants self-identified as heterosexual), these findings should be interpreted with caution (Lyon et al., 2008).

Finally, due to their physical or mental health needs, elderly women and women with disabilities are also likely to encounter obstacles in finding and obtaining services from programs designed to be inclusive of their experiences and attentive to their needs. Both groups may be dependent on their abusers for financial support or physical care. Physical limitations may hinder a survivor's ability to engage independently in help-seeking behaviors or even physically escape from her abuser. Depending upon the nature of their mental, hearing, or communication skills, some survivors with disabilities may not be able to easily convey their needs to others (Nosek & Howland, 1998). Despite these barriers, there is evidence to suggest that many mainstream shelter programs are able to accommodate clients of a variety of ages and with a variety of physical and mental abilities. Ninety-one percent of sampled shelter clients over the age of 50, drawn from 215 programs across 8 states, agreed or strongly agreed that needs related to their age had been addressed by staff (Lyon et al., 2008). In addition, the majority of participating shelter programs (95%) indicated that they would be able to accommodate at least one of the following types of disabilities: physical or mobility, deaf or hard of hearing, visual impairment, cognitive, and other health needs. Thirty-five percent of surveyed programs had the ability to assist clients with any of these disabilities (Lyon et al., 2008).

Lyon et al. (2008) reported largely positive findings regarding the responsiveness of shelters to women with diverse needs, which may reflect success in shelters' ongoing efforts to address the unique needs of women from an array of diverse groups. Indeed, in response to issues related to diversity and cultural competency, many mainstream shelters have expanded their services. For example, the Rockland Family Shelter in New City, New York offers a variety of services that are specifically inclusive for lesbian, gay, bisexual, transgender, and questioning clients and community services for African American, Asian, Haitian, Latino/a, and Orthodox Jewish victims of domestic violence. Further, they have received local, state, and national recognition for their programs and efforts to end intimate partner violence. In 2003, the organization's efforts were recognized by the Asian Women's Alliance for Kinship and Equality (The Rockland Family Shelter, n.d.).

Challenges for Shelter Programs

From the beginning of the battered women's movement, shelter programs have been the backbone of service provision to domestic violence survivors and continue to play a critical role in offering women refuge and resources as they navigate abusive relationships via residential (shelter) and nonresidential programs (e.g., counseling, legal advocacy). In response to the continual challenge to provide services to women with multiple needs and women from traditionally marginalized groups, many mainstream shelter programs have expanded their services. Fortunately, while shelters provide one critical resource for women with abusive partners, the service array is expanding (see Culturally Specific Programs, below). Women with multiple needs challenge traditional methods of community service delivery in which agencies work mostly independent from one another, typically offering services for only a specified need or related set of needs. In response to this, shelter programs have made some successful attempts to create partnerships between other service agencies and coordinated services (see Service-Specific Community-Based Programs and Collaborations, below).

Shelter programs are charged with an intense tripartite task: (a) to engage in effective direct service provision, (b) to engage in institutionalized advocacy to ensure a just and effective response in the many systems positioned to enhance women's safety, and (c) to remain oriented to a broader social change agenda that addresses the multiple intersecting oppressions affecting the lives of women and children (Hammons, 2004; Lehrner & Allen, 2009). Although the extent to which all three of these mandates can be achieved by a single setting is beyond the scope of this chapter, it is worth noting that some shelter programs have refocused their energies to address economic justice issues. For example, the Iowa and Illinois Coalitions

Against Domestic Violence have promoted economic justice initiatives and are providing support to their programs to implement these efforts (e.g., Ciorba VonDeLinde & Correia, 2005; Correia & Ciorba VonDeLinde, 2002; Sanders & Schnabel, 2006). These programs focus on increasing women's economic literacy and, ideally, economic stability through access to greater resources (e.g., employment, education, loans). Such economic justice may provide another critical pathway to safety for survivors.

Community-Based Programs

Culturally Specific Programs

In addition to shelter-based programs, many programs provide services to battered women and their children through other means. Here we present only a few examples of the types of community-based programs available, though a brief search for culturally specific programs suggests the number and types of programs are rapidly increasing.[1] First, some community-based programs have been created in communities of color (and other underserved populations), responding to the need for culturally specific assistance. Many pioneers in the early violence against women movement were white, middle-class women, so many services developed to address violence were shaped by their cultural values (Pan et al., 2006). However, women of color have often highlighted the ways in which their experiences of violence may take different forms or require different responses (e.g., Das Dasgupta, 2000; Gillum, 2008b). Various studies have found that women of color face unique barriers in addition to those

[1]There is a wide variety of policy agencies and initiatives addressing the response to domestic violence across diverse populations. For more information, see, for example, Asian and Pacific Islander Institute on Domestic Violence, Women of Color Network, Alianza National Latino Alliance for the Prevention of Domestic Violence, Institute on Domestic Violence in the African American Community, Battered Women's Justice Project, Chicago Mayor's Office on Domestic Violence, and the National Council of Juvenile and Family Court Judges Greenbook. For information clearinghouses, see National Resource Center on Domestic Violence (http://www.ncadv.org), Family Violence Prevention Fund (http://endabuse.org), and National Online Resource Center on Violence Against Women (http://www.vawnet.org).

faced by all battered women, and that some of these barriers are culture specific. For instance, in focus groups with African Americans, Gillum (2008b) found that women desired services that emphasized the importance of family and religion, something they felt was missing in many existing programs. Similarly, a national study of violence in Hispanic families found that many did not access resources because of a lack of knowledge about or access to culturally competent services (Maciak, Guzman, Santiago, Villalobos, & Israel, 1999).

In response to such concerns, some programs have been created by and for specific cultural groups. Asha Family Services provides a prominent example as the first and only culturally specific domestic violence program in Wisconsin (Asha Family Services, Inc., 2005; Vann, 2003). This program includes a number of components designed with African Americans in mind. First, based on victim-identified priorities, the services provided at Asha are holistic and comprehensive, covering not only violence-related issues, but also mental health, substance abuse intervention and prevention, HIV/AIDS education and counseling, and poverty and welfare system changes. These are in place in part because women will sometimes seek help with domestic violence only through the "back door" of other needs, and also because violence is often not the only issue important to women at a given time. Moreover, as part of a promotion of the "preservation and strengthening of the African American family," services are also provided to men and children who are victims of battering. Thus, an African American-specific "alternative to aggression" group is provided for men and boys, advocacy and support are available for children who witness violence, and case management is available for individuals as well as families. Finally, Asha explicitly incorporates spirituality and encourages men and women to connect or reconnect with their spirituality as an important component of recovery (Vann, 2003).

In New Jersey, Manavi provides culturally specific services to South Asian women experiencing violence, ensuring that "women of South Asian descent in the U.S. can exercise their fundamental right to live a life of dignity that is safe and free from violence" (Manavi, 2007). Formed in the mid-1980s, this organization was the first in the U.S. to focus on violence against South Asian immigrant women. They provide a range of services, including counseling and advocacy, support groups, legal clinics and referrals, transitional housing, and interpretation services. There are several ways that these services are culturally specific. First, services can be provided in the client's language of choice (or interpretation is provided). Second, there is explicit recognition across all services that survivors may be in the process of becoming permanent residents or citizens, unfamiliar with the service and legal systems in the U.S., or unaware of their rights in such systems. The transitional housing provides a place to reduce social isolation among women with similar language, religion, or cultural practices. An example of a practice rooted in the traditions of a particular culture is a no-interest loan program implemented by the organization. Many South Asian women worked but did not feel they had access to the money they earned because traditionally men would take care of the money. Whereas many agencies would simply tell women to ask men for permission to use the money, Manavi created loans for them so that they could obtain needed resources without asking for money from their partners. Das Dasgupta notes that culturally specific services for South Asian women have grown dramatically since the formation of Manavi, with more than 30 programs in the United States today (Das Dasgupta, 2000).

Culturally specific programs have also been created for Native American women. For example, The White Buffalo Calf Women's Society, the first reservation-based shelter for Native Women, was established in 1977 (Jones, 2008). In a more recent effort, key stakeholders among seven Native American tribes living in southern California identified specific needs of Native Women living in their isolated, rural community. These included training those who work with Native Women in Native American culture, efforts to raise community awareness, and inclusion of drug and alcohol treatment services (Jones, 2008). Notably, the Duluth Domestic Abuse Intervention Program's initiative, Mending the Sacred Hoop (MSH), is a social change effort focused on Native communities that works to reform the criminal justice response and service delivery to Native American people "by confronting and challenging the myths still inherent in dominant culture society that are a significant factor in the response of systems to violence against American Indian and Alaska Native Women" (Domestic Abuse Intervention Programs, 2008). MSH provides technical support and assistance locally and internationally (in the U.S. and Canada) to encourage institutional change, grassroots organizing, and culturally responsive service delivery.

In sum, many programs have been developed across the country by and for specific communities of various types. In general, these programs espouse the same principles as the exemplar programs presented above: (1) They centralize the experience and culture of the clientele of the programs. For instance, a program by and for deaf and deaf-blind survivors operates with a TTY phone only, rather than accepting incoming voice calls. They do so for practical reasons but also for political reasons:

> It sends out a message to Deaf and Deaf-Blind people that they come FIRST . . . [and that] hearing people . . . need to accept the fact that real diversity comes only when they do things our way sometimes and it also gives them a chance to practice using the relay so they can later communicate more effectively when victims begin to advocate for themselves. (Merkin & Smith, 1995, pp. 100–101)

(2) Culturally specific programs recognize the ways in which the unique experiences of the cultural group may make it difficult for them to seek help, especially from mainstream organizations. (3) They also celebrate aspects of that culture that can contribute to healthy, violence-free living. For instance, the Two Feathers Native American Family Services program incorporates traditional practices, such as basket making and drumming, into groups for women and children. These groups provide a way to learn skills, support each other, and develop friendships (Tribal Law and Policy Institute, 2004). Culturally specific programs are an important resource for women not comfortable with mainstream domestic violence services.

University-Based Advocacy Programs

Some universities have created advocacy programs to provide services to battered women. These programs represent an important response to the shortage of advocacy services for survivors. Because students are plentiful and relatively inexpensive as advocates, this may present an important opportunity for more intensive advocacy for survivors not connected with other programs. For instance, Bell and Goodman (2001) describe two university-based legal advocacy programs, of which there are more than 40 around the country. At Georgetown University and Catholic University of America, law student volunteers are trained to provide legal advocacy as part of a semester-long course. They then work with a small number of clients through the semester to help them obtain an order of protection. They are thus able to focus intensively on each woman's case. The authors found that after working together for six weeks, women who worked with an advocate reported lower levels of abuse and marginally significant increases in emotional support (Bell & Goodman, 2001).

Although these programs provide an important service to battered women, they focus primarily on one need: legal advocacy. Often women's needs are much broader, which makes comprehensive advocacy an appealing option (Allen et al., 2004). The first such program to be implemented in a university was the Community Advocacy Project, which was established at Michigan State University in the

1980s, as a result of collaboration with battered women (Sullivan, 2000). The program was later implemented at the University of Illinois at Urbana-Champaign in 2004, where it is still running today. Undergraduates are trained to work with survivors. They are then assigned to work intensively with a survivor, one-on-one for 10 weeks. The program is based on a survivor-centered model of advocacy in which battered women are encouraged to define their own needs, from housing to legal assistance to social support. After survivors define their needs, advocates help them generate and access community resources to meet those needs. Such programs respond to the recent call for services to be survivor centered rather than "service defined" (Goodman & Epstein, 2007; Goodman, Glenn, Bohlig, Banyard, & Borges, 2009). These programs result in positive outcomes for survivors with regard to both well-being and safety. Indeed, women in the Michigan State Community Advocacy program were part of a controlled true field experiment, with a two-year follow-up period. During the two-year period, women who participated in the program experienced less violence over time (both emotional and physical), reported higher quality of life and social support, and had greater access to community resources (Sullivan & Bybee, 1999).

Taking a qualitative approach, research into the University of Illinois program aims to illuminate how and why Community Advocacy results in positive outcomes in women's lives from survivors' unique standpoint. Study findings suggest that women appreciate the degree to which the program views them as whole people (as opposed to services that can only "see" and respond to one type of need), has an orientation to information provision and action, and also unconditionally accepts them and recognizes their unique strengths (rather than seeing them as flawed or weak) (Allen, Larsen, Trotter, & Sullivan, in press). Where paraprofessional helpers are available (e.g., in communities with a large volunteer base, including those with colleges and universities), community-based advocacy programs may serve to expand the existing

service infrastructure to support women as they navigate abusive relationships. These programs are particularly well-positioned to respond to the call to return to survivor-centered advocacy approaches echoed by Goodman and Epstein (2007) and others (see Allen et al., 2004; Lehrner & Allen, 2008; Sullivan, 2000).

Service-Specific Collaborations

Many community-based programs are housed in or focus primarily on one main area, such as health care or criminal justice. However, given that domestic violence survivors have an array of needs, many programs have begun to acknowledge the important links between battering and mental and physical health care. In addition to Asha (described above), the Elizabeth Stone House in Jamaica Plains, MA provides an innovative blend of mental health and domestic violence services (Elizabeth Stone House, n.d.; Warshaw & Moroney, 2002). This feminist mental health program was founded in 1974 by a group of women who were former patients in the mental health system. The original alternative mental health program continues in the form of a five-month residential mental health program called The Therapeutic Community. One notable element is that women are permitted to bring their children with them and maintain custody while in treatment (the only such program in the country). In addition to the Therapeutic Community, there is a Battered Women's Program, an eight-week residential program offering services that are similar to many other shelters (e.g., counseling, legal advocacy). One unique element of the Elizabeth Stone House is the decision to house these two programs in the same facility. Residents of each program are allowed and encouraged to participate in the other program as one way to recognize that the issues of battering and mental health are often intertwined. Finally, Elizabeth Stone House also offers a Transitional Living Program that provides an extended opportunity to take advantage of the programs while moving toward independent living. Thus, Elizabeth Stone House offers an integrated curriculum that enables women to receive help for issues concerning both battering and mental health within a single program.

More often, services for battered women involve a collaboration between at least two agencies or organizations, in order to provide a comprehensive response to one need (e.g., health care or legal assistance). For instance, Ulbrich and Stockdale (2002) describe a collaboration between the Family Health Council, Inc. (FHC)—a network of family planning clinics in Western Pennsylvania—and the Women's Center and Shelter of Greater Pittsburgh (along with other domestic violence agencies in other counties). Family planning clinics, especially in rural counties, can play an important role in detecting and responding to domestic violence among patients who may have little other contact with any formalized helping system. Thus, the FHC implemented a project to promote routine screening for domestic violence in four of the rural family planning clinics, including an initial training conducted by the Women's Center and Shelter and ongoing training and support from the FHC. Clinics developed partnerships with local domestic violence agencies so that advocates from the domestic violence agencies could provide counseling services to victims at the health care clinics as well as ongoing support to staff. In one setting, an advocate worked at the clinic one day a week and could take immediate referrals. They reported that this partnership resulted in increased screening and more referrals to domestic violence advocates.

Several other health care agencies have worked to provide a domestic violence advocate to patients onsite (Nudelman, 1999). They may provide many types of services, including advocacy, crisis counseling, and case management. In some cases, these programs are staffed by trained health care personnel. In other cases, battered women's advocates are on call to respond to patients as needed. For instance, A Woman's

Place in Champaign County, Illinois coordinated with local health care agencies to have a domestic violence advocate on call for any identified victims of battering who came through the local emergency room. Similar to the model for rape crisis advocates, members of the health care response team were dispatched to the local hospital when a domestic violence survivor was identified and interested in meeting with an advocate for additional information. Such partnerships have the potential to enhance coordination and continuity between settings for victims with more than one need, as well as to increase awareness of domestic violence and how it can affect women in a variety of ways.

An increasingly common type of collaboration involves community efforts to respond effectively to domestic violence via police services (Sullivan & Keefe, 1999). One example is The Domestic Violence Home Visit Intervention in New Haven, Connecticut (Stover, Rainey, Berkman, & Marans, 2008). This program is based on a collaboration between police supervisors, mental health clinicians, and advocates. Rather than only responding to crisis calls, which police officers are mandated to investigate and which usually result in an arrest, a police-advocate team follows up with families afterward to try to monitor and address ongoing safety concerns. These teams visit families within 72 hours of a reported incident. They go to families' homes during evening hours, when they are likely to be home, and introduce their visit as part of the police department's commitment to the safety and well-being of battered women and their children. Because of the collaboration of police, domestic violence advocates, and social workers, the teams are able to provide information about court orders, victim safety, community resources, psychological care and support, and access to treatment. Other similar programs have additional components, such as having volunteers visit perpetrators in jail to encourage them to take responsibility for their actions and inform them of available batterer intervention programs (Sullivan & Keefe, 1999).

Challenges for Community-Based Programs

One overarching challenge for many community-based programs for battered women and their children is availability and accessibility. Many outstanding programs now exist for women with a variety of needs from a variety of backgrounds. However, these are unlikely to be widely available, especially outside large urban settings. Indeed, several authors have written about the particular difficulties faced by women in rural areas, including fewer resources, longer distances to travel to reach them (without public transportation), and lack of confidentiality (e.g., Sudderth, 2006; Ulbrich & Stockdale, 2002). Likewise, women who live in towns not affiliated with a university or served by a culturally specific program may have no access to programs that would be most helpful to them. Moreover, funding difficulties can contribute to a lack of programs or a difficulty in sustaining them, especially if they are innovative or intensive programs (e.g., Goodman et al., 2007). Finn (2000) describes the Internet as a tool for both direct services and outreach. This is one way that organizations could reach beyond their physical and geographical boundaries to be more inclusive. However, technology comes with its own challenges, as its use may be restricted among rural, poor, and minority populations, precisely the groups such technology should be targeting. Despite such challenges, there are exemplar efforts found across the United States and around the world to encourage accessibility and to effectively respond to domestic violence across disciplinary boundaries.

Coordinated Community Response Efforts

In addition to partnerships between specific responders (e.g., law enforcement and domestic violence providers) there are also efforts to create a "coordinated *community* response" to domestic violence (Shepard & Pence, 1999). Community-wide initiatives are important given that women's needs often span multiple systems, and community-wide partnerships involving an array of relevant responders may enhance the quality of the response to domestic violence by encouraging survivor safety and batterer accountability. Efforts to encourage community-wide coordination across systems take a variety of forms. Three prominent approaches to encouraging coordination are freestanding advocacy agencies, often referred to as Community Intervention Projects (CIP), such as the Domestic Assault Intervention Project (DAIP) in Minnesota; dedicated positions within existing agencies charged with coordination (e.g., integrated case management within the criminal justice system; Shepard, 1999); and coordinating councils or task forces that include representatives from a variety of member agencies (Allen, 2006; Gamache & Asmus, 1999; Shepard, 1999). These collaborative efforts attempt to form connected and communicating networks among the critical responders to domestic violence.

Criminal Justice Coordination

A national leader in and advocate for coordination, the Duluth Domestic Abuse Intervention Programs (DAIP) coordinates multiple agencies within the criminal justice system response. DAIP efforts are driven by clearly articulated goals, including survivor safety and batterer accountability. Most important, the Duluth Model aims to "eliminate domestic violence through written procedures, policies, and protocols governing intervention and prosecution of criminal domestic assault cases" (DAIP, 2008). Coordinated efforts focused on the criminal justice response involve the formation of partnerships among the component parts of the criminal justice system and reformed policies, protocols, and practices to encourage batterer accountability. For example, this often includes successful implementation of mandatory or pro-arrest policies; prosecutors who engage in evidence-based prosecution and assertively pursue domestic violence cases (e.g., have no-drop policies); judges who employ judicial sanctions and sentence with mandated provisions for batterer intervention; and probation officers who take seriously victim safety (e.g., attending to threats of harm, communicating with victims as appropriate) and batterer accountability (e.g., encouraging follow-through with conditions of probation or parole).

Coordinated Responses Beyond the Criminal Justice System

Coordinated responses often focus on the criminal justice response, but can also involve improving the health care, human service, and educational systems (Allen, 2006). For example, the Illinois Health Cares coalitions specifically target systems change in health care settings (i.e., increased screening for domestic violence and appropriate intervention following identification of survivors) and aim to increase awareness of domestic violence as a health care issue (Illinois Violence Prevention Authority, n.d.). In addition, coordinated efforts are beginning to reach beyond formal helping systems to engage stakeholders such as faith-based and business communities (Allen, 2006). For example, Cut It Out is an initiative of the Salons Against Domestic Abuse Fund that works to encourage partnership between salons and local domestic violence programs and to educate salon professionals to recognize warning signs, make safe referrals, and respond to a client who may be a victim of abuse (http://www.cutitout.org). By working across formal and informal networks, communities can create broad preparation to respond to domestic violence when it occurs and create a community narrative that conveys that violence is not accepted. Ideally, human service providers, health care providers (e.g., nurses, midwives, doctors, dentists), teachers, employers, faith leaders, salon professionals, law

enforcement, family, friends, neighbors, and concerned citizens would all be positioned to recognize abuse and respond in a fashion that enhances survivor safety, well-being, and access to resources and holds batterers accountable.

Coordinating Council Efforts

A common vehicle for encouraging collaboration across multiple systems is coordinating councils formed in local communities. Councils may be commonplace because they are the most readily formed venues for bringing stakeholders together to begin a conversation about how to improve the local response to domestic violence (Allen, 2006). These councils include stakeholders from a wide variety of community sectors—all of whom may play a role in responding more effectively to domestic violence survivors (e.g., domestic violence advocates, criminal justice officials, educators, health care providers, concerned citizens, civic groups, local business leaders, faith-based leaders). Council organizers typically convene monthly meetings in which issues related to the local response to domestic violence are discussed, ideally, from a wide variety of stakeholders' perspectives. By bringing together diverse stakeholders, councils foster new relationships among critical responders and create opportunities for enhanced knowledge about the realities of the local system's response and subsequent local action to create change (Allen, Watt, & Hess, 2008). For example, there is some preliminary evidence that the formation and development of councils increases accessibility to protection orders over time (Allen, Todd, Anderson, & Davis, 2009). Yet, councils do not confine their efforts to the criminal justice system (Allen, 2009). Some work on implementing school-based prevention education efforts, while others work to enhance the degree to which local health care settings engage in routine screening for domestic violence or develop protocols to support local faith leaders to respond to domestic violence in their congregations. This diverse approach may be well-positioned to foster a comprehensive *community* response to domestic violence.

Challenges for Coordinated Efforts

Although collaborative approaches to change are abundant, they are not without significant challenges. In fact, there is evidence that many collaborative approaches to community health issues fail to achieve desired outcomes (Roussos & Fawcett, 2000). Thus, it is important to attend to processes as well as outcomes, in order to understand the conditions under which collaborative efforts are poised to facilitate desired outcomes (see Foster-Fishman, Berkowitz, Lounsbury, Jacobson, & Allen, 2001, for a thorough review of facilitators and barriers to collaboration). For example, councils often bring together stakeholders with disparate power bases (e.g., judges, state attorneys, advocates; Allen, 2006; Malik, Ward, & Janczewski, 2008). In the absence of the right conditions, the "stakes" may be particularly high for relatively less powerful stakeholders (e.g., domestic violence survivors and advocates) if councils have not achieved an inclusive climate in which all voices are encouraged and all input is valued (Allen, 2005, 2009; Chavis, 2001; Foster-Fishman et al., 2001; Himmelman, 2001). Creating the right conditions for inclusive communication may be the key to addressing real and important differences in stakeholders' unique and valuable standpoints. For instance, Sudderth (2006) wrote about tensions in a police-advocacy collaboration, brought about in part by differing philosophies and goals between agencies (e.g., feminist advocates' focus on women's safety vs. police focus on enforcing the law and investigating criminal behavior).

Collaborative efforts require effective leaders who are positioned to balance an efficient process (i.e., one where things get done) with an inclusive process (i.e., one where all input is valued; Allen, 2005). Yet, while these (and other) facilitators of collaboration (e.g., broad and representative participation, defined organizational structure)

are important, they are not sufficient to produce desired systems changes alone. For example, the ability of councils to produce change may be limited if the environment in which they operate (e.g., key agency leaders) does not support their efforts or if their members are not empowered to facilitate local action (Allen, Javdani, Lehrner, & Walden, 2009).

Domestic violence service providers (e.g., program directors, advocates) have a critical role to play in representing survivors' voices and assessing the impact of coordinated efforts on survivors' lives. Although leaders in coordinated response have called for the development of survivor advisory groups to coordinate efforts (e.g., Gamache & Asmus, 1999), such advisory bodies appear to be the exception to the rule. Domestic violence providers' proximity to survivors' lives, their current needs, and their current navigations of the system's response positions them uniquely to keep collaborative efforts broadly focused on survivor safety.

Conclusion

The last five decades have seen a transformation in the development and array of services positioned to respond to domestic violence. Shelter programs began as settings that formed the epicenter of social change efforts to respond to domestic violence and continue to provide a vital resource to women with abusive partners and evolve in ways that make them more responsive and accessible. Shelter programs now form only one component of community-based services to respond to domestic violence. Programs serving women from particular social groups (e.g., women with disabilities, women of color, immigrant women, lesbians) have become more common and provide a critical resource not only to women from particular social groups but also to the vitality of the domestic violence movement. Finally, community partnerships and coordinated community responses hold the potential for the broad transformation of systems—both formal and informal—to be poised to respond to domestic violence as it is encountered, to foster survivor safety, and to hold batterers accountable.

References

Allen, N. E. (2005). A multi-level analysis of community coordinating councils. *American Journal of Community Psychology, 35,* 49–63.

Allen, N. E. (2006). An examination of the effectiveness of domestic violence coordinating councils. *Violence Against Women, 12,* 46–47.

Allen, N. E. (2009). *Coordinating the criminal justice response to intimate partner violence: The role of coordinating councils in systems change. A technical report prepared for the National Institute of Justice.* Urbana Champaign: University of Illinois, Department of Psychology.

Allen, N. E., Bybee, D. I., & Sullivan, C. M. (2004). Battered women's multitude of needs: Evidence supporting the need for comprehensive advocacy. *Violence Against Women, 10,* 1015–1035.

Allen, N. E., Javdani, S., Lehrner, A., & Walden, A. (2009). *Putting it all together: Individual empowerment, council features, social capital and community context as correlates of effectiveness in council-based approaches to change.* Manuscript submitted for publication.

Allen, N. E., Larsen, S., Trotter, J. L., & Sullivan, C. M. (in press). *Exploring the core components of an evidence-based community advocacy program for women with abusive partners.* University of Illinois Urbana Champaign.

Allen, N. E., Todd, N., Anderson, C., & Davis, S. (2009). *Council-based approaches to intimate partner violence: Evidence of distal change in the systems response.* Manuscript submitted for publication.

Allen, N. E., Watt, K. A., & Hess, J. Z. (2008). A qualitative study of the activities and outcomes of domestic violence coordinating councils. *American Journal of Community Psychology, 41,* 63–73.

Asha Family Services, Inc. (2005). Retrieved March 30, 2009, from http://www.ashafamilyservices.com

Balsam, K. (2001). Nowhere to hide: Lesbian battering, homophobia, and minority stress. *Women and Therapy, 23,* 25–37.

Bell, M. E., & Goodman, L. A. (2001). Supporting battered women involved with the court system: An evaluation of a law school-based advocacy intervention. *Violence Against Women, 7,* 1377–1404.

Bennett, L., Riger, S., Schewe, P., Howard, A., & Wasco, S. (2004). Effectiveness of hotline, advocacy, counseling, and shelter services for victims: A statewide evaluation. *Journal of Interpersonal Violence, 19,* 815–829.

Bhuyan, R. (2008). The production of the "battered immigrant" in public policy and domestic violence advocacy. *The Journal of Interpersonal Violence, 23,* 153–170.

Chang, J. C., Martin, S. L., Moracco, K. E., Dulli, L., Scandlin, D., & Loucks-Sorrel, M. B. (2003). Helping women with disabilities and domestic violence: Strategies, limitations, and challenges of domestic violence programs and services. *Journal of Women's Health, 12,* 699–708.

Chavis, D. M. (2001). The paradoxes and promise of community coalitions. *American Journal of Community Psychology, 29,* 309–320.

Ciorba VonDeLinde, K., & Correia, A. (2005). *Economic education programs for battered women: Lessons learned from two settings* (Publication #18). Harrisburg, PA: National Resource Center on Domestic Violence.

Correia, A., & Ciorba VonDeLinde, K. (2002). *Integrating anti-poverty work into domestic violence advocacy: Iowa's experience* (Publication #17). Harrisburg, PA: National Resource Center on Domestic Violence.

Das Dasgupta, S. (2000). Charting the course: An overview of domestic violence in the South Asian community. *Journal of Social Distress and the Homeless, 9,* 173–185.

Dobash, R. E., & Dobash, R. P. (1992). *Women, violence, and social change.* London: Routledge.

Domestic Abuse Intervention Programs. (2008). *Mending the sacred hoop.* Retrieved from http://www.theduluthmodel.org/mendingsacredhoop.php

Elizabeth Stone House. (n.d.). Retrieved March 30, 2009, from http://www.elizabethstonehouse.org

Espin, O. M. (1999). *Women crossing boundaries: A psychology of immigration and transformations of sexuality.* New York: Routledge.

Finn, J. (2000). Domestic violence organizations on the web: A new arena for domestic violence services. *Violence Against Women, 6,* 80–102.

Foster-Fishman, P. G., Berkowitz, S. L., Lounsbury, D. W., Jacobson, S., & Allen, N. E. (2001). Building collaborative capacity in community coalitions: A review and integrative framework. *American Journal of Community Psychology, 29,* 241–261.

Gamache, D., & Asmus, M. (1999). Enhancing networking among service providers. In M. F. Shepard & E. Pence (Eds.), *Coordinating community responses to domestic violence: Lessons from Duluth and beyond* (pp. 65–88). Thousand Oaks, CA: Sage.

Gillum, T. (2008a). The benefits of a culturally specific intimate partner violence intervention for African American survivors. *Violence Against Women, 14,* 917–943.

Gillum, T. (2008b). Community response and needs of African American female survivors of domestic violence. *Journal of Interpersonal Violence, 23,* 39–57.

Goodman, L. A., & Epstein, D. (2007). *Listening to battered women: A survivor-centered approach to advocacy, mental health, and justice.* Washington, DC: American Psychological Association.

Goodman, L. A., Glenn, C., Bohlig, A., Banyard, V., & Borges, A. (2009). Feminist relational advocacy: Processes and outcomes from the perspective of low-income women with depression. *The Counseling Psychologist, 37,* 848–876.

Goodman, L. A., Litwin, A., Bohlig, A. Weintraub, S. R., Green, A., Walker, J., et al. (2007). Applying feminist theory to community practice: A multilevel empowerment intervention for low-income women with depression. In E. Aldarondo (Ed.), *Advancing social justice through clinical practice* (pp. 265–290). Philadelphia, PA: Lawrence Erlbaum.

Hammons, S. A. (2004). "Family violence": The language of legitimacy. *Affilia, 19,* 273–288.

Harwin, N. (2006). Putting a stop to domestic violence in the United Kingdom. *Violence Against Women, 12,* 556–567.

Henning, K. R., & Klesges, R. M. (2002). Utilization of counseling and supportive services by female victims of domestic violence. *Violence and Victims, 17,* 623–636.

Himmelman, A. T. (2001). On coalition and the transformations of power relations: Collaborative betterment and collaborative empowerment. *American Journal of Community Psychology, 29,* 277–284.

Illinois Violence Prevention Authority. (n.d.). Retrieved from http://ivpa.org/funded-programs/illinois-health-cares.

Jones, L. (2008). The distinctive characteristics and needs of domestic violence victims in a Native American community. *Journal of Family Violence, 23,* 113–118.

Lehrner, A., & Allen, N. E. (2008). Social change movements and the struggle over meaning-making: A case study of domestic violence narratives. *American Journal of Community Psychology, 42,* 220–234.

Lehrner, A., & Allen, N. E. (2009). Still a movement after all these years? Current tensions in the domestic violence movement. *Violence Against Women, 15,* 656–677.

Leone, J. M., Johnson, M. P., & Cohan, C. L. (2007). Victim help seeking: Differences between intimate terrorism and situational couple violence. *Family Relations, 56,* 427–439.

Lyon, E., Lane, S., & Menard, A., (2008). *Meeting survivors' needs: A multi-state study of domestic violence shelter experiences.* National Institute of Justice. Retrieved March 30, 2009, from http://www.ncjrs.gov/pdffiles1/nij/grants/225025.pdf

Maciak, B. J., Guzman, R., Santiago, A., Villalobos, G., & Israel, B. A. (1999). Establishing LA VIDA: A community-based partnership to prevent intimate violence against Latina women. *Health Education and Behavior, 26,* 821–840.

Malik, N. M, Ward, K., & Janczewski, C. (2008). Coordinated community response to family violence: The role of domestic violence service organizations. *Journal of Interpersonal Violence, 23,* 933–955.

Manavi. (2007). Retrieved March 30, 2009, from http://www.manavi.org/direct.php

Merkin, L., & Smith, M. J. (1995). A community-based model providing services for deaf and deaf-blind victims of sexual assault and domestic violence. *Sexuality and Disability, 13,* 97–106.

Nosek, M. A., & Howland, C. A. (1998). *Abuse and women with disabilities.* Retrieved April 28, 2009, from http://new.vawnet.org/Assoc_Files_VAWnet/AR_disab.pdf

Nudelman, J. (1999). *Building bridges between domestic violence advocates and health care providers.* Retrieved March 30, 2009, from http://vawnet.org

Osmundson, L. A. (n.d.) *Shelter rules: Who needs them?* Retrieved March 29, 2009, from http://www.casa-tpete.org/Documents/lao_shelter_rules.pdf

Oths, K. S., & Robertson, T. (2007). Give me shelter: temporal patterns of women fleeing domestic abuse. *Human Organization, 66,* 249–260.

Palant, E. (2004). A shelter for Orthodox Jewish women in Israel: The experience of helping religious women escape domestic abuse. *Journal of Religion and Abuse, 6,* 19–29.

Pan, A., Daley, S., Rivera, L. M., Williams, K., Lingle, D., & Reznik, V. (2006). Understanding the role of culture in domestic violence: The Ahimsa Project for Safe Families. *Journal of Immigrant and Minority Health, 8,* 35–43.

Preisser, A. B. (1999). Domestic violence in South Asian communities in America: Advocacy and intervention. *Violence Against Women, 5,* 684–699.

Renzetti, C. M. (1988). Violence in lesbian relationships: A preliminary analysis of causal factors. *Journal of Interpersonal Violence, 3,* 381–399.

Riger, S., Bennett, L., Wasco, S. M., Schewe, P. A., Frohmann, L., Camancho, J. M., et al. (2002). *Evaluating services for survivors of domestic violence and sexual assault.* Thousand Oaks, CA: Sage.

The Rockland Family Shelter. (n.d.) Retrieved April 24, 2009, from http://www.rocklandfamilyshelter.org

Roussos, S. T., & Fawcett, S. B. (2000). A review of collaborative partnerships as a strategy for improving community health. *Annual Review Public Health, 21,* 369–402.

Saathoff, A. J., & Stoffel, E. A. (1999). Community-based domestic violence services. *The Future of Children, 9,* 97–110.

Sanders, C. K., & Schnabel, M. (2006). Organizing for economic empowerment of battered women: Women's savings accounts. *Journal of Community Practice, 14,* 47–68.

Schechter, S. (1982). *Women and male violence: The visions and struggles of the battered women's movement.* Boston: South End Press.

Shepard, M. F. (1999). Advocacy for battered women: Implications for a coordinated community response. In M. F. Shepard & E. L. Pence (Eds.), *Coordinating community responses to domestic violence: Lessons from Duluth and beyond* (pp. 115–125). Thousand Oaks, CA: Sage.

Shepard, M. F., & Pence, E. L. (Eds.). (1999). *Coordinating community responses to domestic violence: Lessons from Duluth and beyond.* Thousand Oaks, CA: Sage.

Snyder, D. K., & Scheer, N. S. (1981). Predicting disposition following brief residence at a shelter for battered women. *American Journal of Community Psychology, 9,* 559–566.

Sorenson, S. B. (1996). Violence against women: Examining ethnic differences and commonalities. *Evaluation Review, 20,* 123–145.

Stover, C. S., Rainey, A. M., Berkman, M., & Marans, S. (2008). Factors associated with engagement in a police-advocacy home-visit intervention to prevent domestic violence. *Violence Against Women, 14,* 1430–1450.

Sudderth, L. K. (2006). An uneasy alliance: Law enforcement and domestic violence victim advocates in a rural area. *Feminist Criminology, 1,* 329–353.

Sullivan, C. M. (2000). A model for effectively advocating for women with abusive partners. In J. P. Vincent & E. N. Jouriles (Eds.), *Domestic violence: Guidelines for research-informed practice* (pp. 126–143). London: Jessica Kingsley.

Sullivan, C. M. (2006). *Mission-focused management and empowerment practice: A handbook for executive directors of domestic violence programs.* Harrisburg: Pennsylvania Coalition Against Domestic Violence.

Sullivan, C. M., & Bybee, D. I. (1999). Reducing violence using community-based advocacy for women with abusive partners. *Journal of Consulting and Clinical Psychology, 67,* 43–53.

Sullivan, C., & Keefe, M. (1999). *Evaluations of advocacy efforts to end intimate male violence against women.* Retrieved March 30, 2009, from http://vawnet.org

Tjaden, P., & Thoennes, N. (2000). *Full report of the prevalence, incidence, and consequences of violence against women: Findings from the National Violence Against Women Survey.* (NCJ Publication No. 183781) Washington, DC: U.S. Department of Justice.

Tribal Law and Policy Institute. (2004). *Victim services: Promising practices in Indian country.* (NCJ Publication No. 207019) Rockville, MD: Office for Victims of Crime Resource Center.

Ulbrich, P., & Stockdale, J. (2002). Making family planning clinics an empowerment zone. *Women and Health, 35,* 83–100.

Vann, A. A. (2003). *Developing culturally-relevant responses to domestic abuse: Asha Family Services, Inc.* Retrieved March 30, 2009, from http://vawnet.org

Varcoe, C., & Irwin, L. G. (2004). "If I killed you, I'd get the kids": Women's survival and protection work with child custody and access in the context of woman abuse. *Qualitative Sociology, 27,* 77–99.

Vaughn, M., & Stamp, G. H. (2003). The empowerment dilemma: The dialectic of emancipation and control in staff/client interaction at shelters for battered women. *Communication Studies, 54,* 154–168.

Vinton, L. (1992). Battered women's shelters and older women: The Florida experience. *Journal of Family Violence, 7,* 63–72.

Warshaw, C., & Moroney, G. (2002). *Mental health and domestic violence: Collaborative initiatives, service models, and curricula.* Retrieved April 20, 2009, from http://www.dvmhpi.org/Publications.htm

Watkins, N., & Allen, N. E. (2008). *Evaluation of shelter care services: Final feedback report* (Technical Report). Urbana Champaign: University of Illinois, Department of Psychology.

West, C. M., Kantor, G. K., & Jasinski, J. L. (1998). Sociodemographic predictors and cultural barriers to help-seeking behavior by Latina and Anglo American battered women. *Violence and Victims, 13,* 361–375.

Yoshioka, M. R., & Choi, D. Y. (2005). Culture and interpersonal violence research: Paradigm shift to create a full continuum of domestic violence services. *Journal of Interpersonal Violence, 20,* 513–519.

Zweig, J. M., & Burt, M. R. (2007). Predicting women's perceptions of domestic violence and sexual assault agency helpfulness: What matters to program clients? *Violence Against Women, 13,* 1149–1178.

Zweig, J. M., Schlichter, K. A., & Burt, M. R. (2002). Assisting women victims of violence who experience multiple barriers to services. *Violence Against Women, 8,* 162–180.

Chapter Authors

Nicole E. Allen, Ph.D., is Associate Professor of Community Psychology at the University of Illinois at Urbana-Champaign. Her research examines community collaboration and systems change processes with a focus on the community response to intimate partner violence. To engage these community phenomena at multiple levels of analysis, Dr. Allen consistently employs mixed method designs, including quantitative and qualitative approaches, and has contributed to the scholarly literature via numerous papers and presentations. She is committed to bridging scholarship and action and building community capacity to respond to complex social issues by working closely with community partners in her research and action.

Sadie E. Larsen is a doctoral candidate in clinical/community psychology at the University of Illinois at Urbana-Champaign. She has a long-standing interest in gendered violence and recovery from trauma, and she has worked with victims of such violence in various capacities, from crisis hotline work to therapy and research. She is currently working on her dissertation, conducting a mixed-method analysis of women's recovery from a broad range of stressful or traumatic events.

Angela L. Walden is a doctoral student in clinical/community psychology at the University of Illinois at Urbana-Champaign. She has experience as a domestic violence shelter volunteer and employee, where she performed many duties including survivor advocacy and crisis hotline response. She has also conducted research in the community for the purpose of improving outreach efforts. Her research interests center on issues related to intimate partner violence, including youth-driven efforts for prevention and partner violence in Native American communities. She is currently working on an evaluation of a statewide youth-driven violence prevention program.

Personal Reflection

Valli Kalei Kanuha

 I still recall as if it were yesterday how I first got involved in the battered women's movement. It was March, 1975, and I had just graduated with my MSW and started working at my first "real" job as a social worker in a community health clinic in Minneapolis. One of my assignments was to coordinate our center's child abuse and neglect review committee, in which a multi-disciplinary team of providers at our clinic would review possible cases of "battered child syndrome."

One cold winter morning, I noticed a flyer posted at our staff sign-in board with the heading "Community Meeting on Battered Wives." The flyer described a "growing problem" in our community where women were being abused by their husbands in a manner similar to children who were battered by their parents. Given my understanding of child abuse and neglect, I literally could not comprehend how wives could be "battered" by their husbands. Moreover, it seemed unbelievable that this could possibly be such a significant problem. I went to that meeting, joined by a group of social workers, community organizers, housing advocates, psychologists, and legal aid attorneys, many of whom now comprise some of the most notable foremothers in the movement: Ellen Pence, Sharon Rice Vaughan, Anne Marshall, and Monica Erler. I mark that first meeting of community activists almost 35 years ago as the beginning of my life's work to end violence against women.

I consider it an honor and privilege to have "grown up" as a young feminist in the battered women's movement in Minnesota. I was one of the few women of color and the only Asian (and, of course, Native Hawaiian) doing the work for much of those early years in the Twin Cities. Like so many others, I wrote grants; designed and Xeroxed our first resource booklet (five pages!); facilitated battered women's support groups; and put up sheetrock in −30°F weather, to help build the Harriet Tubman Shelter, the first shelter in Minneapolis. Throughout most of the first decade of our work, from the mid-1970s to 1980s, well-chronicled in Susan Schechter's *Women and Male Violence,* everyone did everything. That is, we lacked—or perhaps did not ideologically value—specialization of tasks and functions in our movement building. It did not matter how much education you had nor how well you could articulate the dynamics of battering, there was a certain leveling among advocates such that all of us were valued for anything and everything we contributed. I cannot recall anyone who did not work directly with women and children, but we also organized rallies, testified before city councils, trained medical personnel, and attended countless and endless meetings to strategize, build programs, and write policy

Today, I think we've lost some of the dynamism, creativity, and sense of promise and possibilities that characterized our early organizing. I refer to our work now as an industry, a byproduct of our enormous success in bringing violence against women into the mainstream of American consciousness. We now have shelters that are corporations, advocate positions that require licensed degree holders, specialist vs. general practitioners, and no funding for community organizing. There are clearly unintended consequences of our best work: battered women are being presumptively arrested for assaulting intimate partners who have held them for years as domestic hostages, children are being lost to the custody of abusive fathers who claim parental alienation syndrome, and too many men and women of color are swept up in the courts and jails of our country, with both perpetrators and survivors alike falling victim to our well-established efforts at criminalizing domestic violence.

Many of us still believe in the early principles and practices that guided our work in the 1970s. We believe in women and we believe that justice can be served if we listen to what women want, rather than telling them what we want them to know and be. We understand that women are the experts of their lives, no matter how many degrees we have or trainings we've attended. And we know that all things are possible if you love and work for freedom each and every day, for those who came before us and for the generations ahead.

CHAPTER 14

Violence Against Women and the Criminal Justice Response

Susan L. Miller, LeeAnn Iovanni, and Kathleen D. Kelley

Violence against women is a global social problem and is manifested in many ways, such as physical, sexual, and psychological abuse in the home; rape of women in interethnic conflicts (e.g., Sudan, Congo); sex trafficking; genital mutilation; and so forth. These acts are not random; male perpetrators are overrepresented, and girls and women are disproportionately the victims. Although particular incidents are headline grabbing, the reality is that violent acts against women and girls are committed every day. Further, these types of violence are situated in institutional arrangements of power and authority as well as individual factors, the link being *gender* as an organizing instrument of social control. Although violence against women takes many forms, this chapter covers criminal justice issues related to intimate partner violence and sexual assault. The need for research and policy attention to violence against women has become important internationally; however, our focus is on the successes and failures of the U.S. criminal justice system (see Chapter 10 for international legal issues about sexual assault).

Intimate Partner Violence: Pro-Arrest Policies

Mandatory and preferred arrest statutes are now the hallmark of the police response to intimate partner violence; officers *have to* or *should* arrest offenders if probable cause exists, even if the violence does not occur in the officer's presence and even if the victim does not desire an arrest. These statutes represent a sea change in criminal justice policy that historically treated intimate partner violence as a private matter in which police officers acted as mediators separating the couple or offering crisis intervention at the scene. But during the 1970s and early 1980s, the battered women's shelter movement elucidated the widespread occurrence of intimate partner violence; the victims' rights movement and the women's movement took a stand against the criminal justice system's inaction, particularly on the part of the police; and civil liability suits brought against police departments successfully argued that officers failed to protect victims. In this atmosphere ripe for change, the pioneering and widely publicized Minneapolis Domestic Violence Experiment provided some evidence that arrest was a better deterrent of repeat domestic violence than were traditional methods of separation and/or mediation (Sherman & Berk, 1984). Many jurisdictions have since modified their law enforcement practices, replacing them with what are known as mandatory and preferred arrest policies.[1]

Following up the Minneapolis experiment in six other cities with improved research methods, the Spouse Assault Replication Program (SARP) yielded mixed findings but suggested that the effect of arrest on subsequent intimate partner violence varies for different groups, depending on the perceived cost of arrest. Arrest may be more likely to deter offenders with high stakes in conformity (married and/or employed) and may even increase the chance of future violence for offenders with low stakes in conformity (unmarried and unemployed; Sherman et al., 1992). Based on SARP data, Maxwell, Garner, and Fagan (2002) concluded that arrest is, on average, a better deterrent than informal police responses, but the effect is modest in comparison to other factors, such as the offender's prior criminal record. Despite formal police intervention, some suspects will continue to victimize their female partners, and thus "arrest is not a panacea for all victims of intimate partner violence" (p. 72). In

research on partner assaults reported in the National Crime Victimization Survey, the effect of arrest on reoffending was small and not statistically significant; however, reporting to the police (regardless of arrest) showed a strong deterrent effect, suggesting that police involvement could alter offenders' attitudes about their violence and perceptions of the cost of future violence (Felson, Ackerman, & Gallagher, 2005).

The wisdom of pro-arrest policies has been disputed. They are meant to deter the individual batterer as well as communicate to the general public a message of social condemnation. They also aim to empower victims by providing a serious response and by unburdening them from decision making. Critics have noted, however, that victims understand their situation and the likely effect of arrest—such as offender retaliation or the economic burden of the loss of his income—better than police officers (Buzawa & Buzawa, 2003). An arrest against their wishes deprives battered women of the choice, albeit a difficult one, to participate in the criminal justice process. Some women may simply want the violence to stop in the immediate situation, and true victim empowerment is best achieved by victim preference over the outcome of police intervention (Buzawa & Buzawa, 2003).

Dual Arrests in Cases of Intimate Partner Violence

Mandatory and preferred arrest policies have, indeed, increased the use of arrest. Earlier studies based on data collected in the 1970s and 1980s revealed arrest rates in the range of 7% to 15%; more recent research, however, finds arrest rates for intimate partner violence incidents ranging

---

[1]As of 2000, all states authorize warrantless arrest of domestic violence suspects based solely on probable cause that an offense occurred (N. Miller, 2004, p. 27). In 22 states plus the District of Columbia, arrest is *required* if the officer determines that probable cause exists; six states have preferred arrest statutes that *encourage* arrest; the remaining 22 states have discretionary statutes that *allow* arrest (Hirschel, Buzawa, Pattavina, Faggiani, & Reuland, 2007). Arrest is mandated for violation of a protection order in 33 states (Hirschel et al., 2007).

from 30% to as high as 75% (Hirschel et al., 2007, p. 7). An unforeseen consequence of mandatory arrest laws has been the increase in the number of women arrested for intimate partner violence, either as sole perpetrators or in the context of a dual arrest, where the woman is arrested along with her male partner (Hirschel et al., 2007; see also DeLeon-Granados, Wells, & Binsbacher, 2006; Feder & Henning, 2005; Muftic, Bouffard, & Bouffard, 2007a; S. L. Miller, 2005; Simpson, Bouffard, Garner, & Hickman, 2006).

Recognizing the problem of dual arrest, many jurisdictions have implemented primary aggressor laws[2] that "seek to ensure that police officers receive guidance in assessing who is the 'real' offender, both in the relationship and in a particular situation, and encourage them to use information about the history of abuse to assist in distinguishing between defensive and offensive injuries" (Hirschel & Buzawa, 2002, p. 1460). Still, there is clearly cause for concern when laws meant to protect battered women instead label and process many victims as offenders. In the context of intimate partner violence, it is important to distinguish between "a *hit* [italics added] absent coercive, controlling tactics and *battering* [italics added]—a systematic use of violence, the threat of violence, and other coercive behaviors to exert power, induce fear, and control another" (Osthoff, 2002, p. 1522). This context renders untenable any claim of gender symmetry—the notion that men and women are equally violent in intimate relationships. Rather, it is usually the male (in a heterosexual relationship) who uses coercive controlling tactics, systematic threats, and violence. Most women who use violence against their partner are using defensive violence in response to ongoing, systematic abuse (Dasgupta, 1999, 2002;

Hamberger, 2005; Kimmel, 2002; Osthoff, 2002; Swan, Gambone, Caldwell, Sullivan, & Snow, 2008).

Although some women may commit acts of intimate partner violence that are not defensive (Moffitt, Caspi, Rutter & Silva, 2001), other factors play a larger role in accounting for arrests of women. In the incident-driven criminal justice system, a woman's single act of violence is not examined in the context of ongoing abuse (S. L. Miller, 2005). Mandatory arrest statutes further limit the influence of situational or contextual factors; the result can be a more legalistic response (Hirschel et al., 2007). Additionally, officers may be attempting to avoid accusations of gender bias, believing that holding parties equally accountable for their actions and demonstrating that the law is being applied fairly provides equity (Renzetti, 1999). Depending on the state statute or local policy, officers may prefer to arrest both parties and leave the issue of the primary aggressor to prosecutors (S. L. Miller, 2005). Moreover, the increased use of arrest due to police desire to avoid civil liability lawsuits may also extend to the arrest of women (Buzawa & Buzawa, 2003; S. L. Miller, 2005) or create an unwillingness to attempt to identify the primary aggressor, resulting in the arrest of both parties (Hirschel et al., 2007).

Women also tend to act in ways that facilitate police action. Women in battering situations more readily admit their use of force vis-à-vis abusive men (Dobash, Dobash, Cavanaugh, & Lewis, 1998), and women are not socialized to use violence, so they vividly remember every incident (Dasgupta, 1999; Kimmel, 2002). When police arrive on the scene, women may still be experiencing emotional trauma and may seem less credible and more combative, thus increasing the chances that they might be

---

[2]As of 2000, a total of 24 states had primary aggressor statutes and most have guidelines to help officers make that determination, such as the comparative extent of injuries, prior domestic violence history, self-defensive actions, and the likelihood of future injury (Hirschel et al., 2007, p. 29). Some states require officers to explain why a dual arrest was made, thereby encouraging officers to exercise judgment (N. Miller, 2004, p. 29). Many states limit the court's authority to issue mutual orders of protection, in order to lessen the chance of a dual arrest (N. Miller, 2004, p. 29).

arrested, in comparison to men who may appear calm (after releasing their anger through violence) and are better able to describe the situation to their advantage (S. L. Miller, 2005). Moreover, men, more savvy about the operation of the system, have been known to manipulate the system by self-inflicting wounds so that police view the woman as assaultive and dangerous, or by initiating a 911 call to proactively define the situation (S. L. Miller, 2005). Women who use violence also risk harsh responses from authorities because their behavior contradicts gender role assumptions of submissiveness (Dasgupta, 1999).

Studies comparing men and women arrested for intimate partner violence suggest the need for vigilance in determining the primary aggressor. Men are more likely to have an arrest history for intimate partner violence (Busch & Rosenberg, 2004; Melton & Belknap, 2003) as well as other types of crimes (Feder & Henning, 2005; Henning & Feder, 2004). Women are more likely to use a weapon (Busch & Rosenberg, 2004; Melton & Belknap, 2003) and are more likely to use available objects, suggesting that women may be "leveling the playing field once abuse has been perpetrated against them" (Melton & Belknap, 2003, p. 344). Women are more likely to show signs of abuse at the time of arrest for the current incident (Busch & Rosenberg, 2004). Police reports are more likely to mention self-defense on the part of women (Melton & Belknap, 2003) or note evidence of mutual combat, suggesting that women are not necessarily "pure perpetrators" (Busch & Rosenberg, 2004, p. 55). Findings from studies examining dual arrests indicate police officers often fail to adequately consider contextual factors. Dual arrests occur despite the woman's initiation of the police contact, her injuries and need for medical attention, the man's provocation of the incident, and a woman's fear or self-defensive behavior (Muftic et al., 2007a). Various factors can also confuse the situation, such as visible injuries to both parties (Muftic et al., 2007a, 2007b), a woman's use of a weapon, or being under the influence of alcohol

(Houry, Reddy, & Parramore, 2006). Police officers can also view criminal justice intervention as a means for the couple to obtain services (Finn & Bettis, 2006).

Criminalizing women for actions they may have taken in self-defense or to otherwise fight back can have serious, negative consequences (Hirschel & Buzawa, 2002). Such overenforcement of the law effectively serves to deny women their rights and privileges as victims, such as transportation to a safe location, temporary housing in a shelter, issuance of a restraining order, or participation in victim assistance and empowerment programs; they may also lose employment or custody of children and incur economic hardship. In addition, women may be reluctant to contact the police to report subsequent abuse, "despite a possible increase in danger from the abuser" (Hirschel & Buzawa, 2002, p. 1459).

Intimate Partner Violence: Pro-Prosecution Policies

Mandatory and preferred arrest policies have resulted in higher caseloads for prosecutors, as well as more cases with victims who do not necessarily desire prosecution. In response, the adoption of *no-drop* prosecution policies aims to ensure further action following arrest, the ultimate goal being to protect victims. No-drop prosecution takes various forms and is implemented to varying degrees. At its extreme, a "hard" or strong no-drop policy removes the responsibility for the charges from the victim, and prosecutors can go so far as to arrest and jail a reluctant victim if she fails to respond to a subpoena to testify (Ford, 2003). A "soft" or flexible no-drop policy respects a victim's request to drop charges, perhaps after counseling or after the suspect makes his first court appearance (Ford, 2003). Support for aggressive prosecution is generally based on the idea that legal considerations, such as crime seriousness, the defendant's prior record, and strength of the evidence, should guide prosecution rather than the wishes of victims. It also sends the message that intimate partner violence is a serious crime that will be prosecuted. Moreover, victim-based prosecution burdens the victim with decision making and can effectively nullify mandatory arrest policies (Peterson & Dixon, 2005).

Victims may oppose prosecution for many reasons: They may simply forgive the abuse and hold on to the hope that a partner will change; they blame themselves for the abuse; or they experience guilt over making the abuse public in court. In some cases, the victim may have left the relationship and negotiated a financial or custody settlement; consequently, she may fear that prosecution will further anger her partner and jeopardize the agreement. One of the leading reasons for victim opposition to prosecution is fear. A study of coordinated responses to intimate partner violence in three states found, across all sites, that fear of defendant retaliation was the most common barrier to prosecution (Harrell, Castro, Newmark, & Visher, 2007).

Aggressive or coerced prosecution in intimate partner violence cases has raised concerns about whose interests are really being served. Zealous prosecutors representing the state may elevate protecting the interests of the general public and sending the message that such violence will not be tolerated over protecting the individual victim (Ford, 2003). Although prosecution may deter some individual, rational offenders, it may also put individual victims in more danger from retaliation by the offender (Ford, 2003), given that most reoffending occurs between arrest and adjudication (Buzawa & Buzawa, 2003). Coercion also deprives a victim of control over her life, transferring control from her abuser to the prosecutor (Ford, 2003). Although this is meant to keep the batterer

from forcing her to drop prosecution, coerced prosecution nonetheless serves state interests in helping to maximize favorable case outcomes (Ford, 2003). Similar to mandatory arrest, ignoring victim preference thus amounts to victim disempowerment, which may lead to distrust of the criminal justice system, decreased crime reporting, and decreased victim satisfaction should charges be dropped later (Buzawa & Buzawa, 2003).

The implementation of no-drop prosecution can vary, depending on the point in the process at which it is applied. It is often paired with an initial screening or filing stage (O'Sullivan, Davis, Farole, & Rempel, 2007; Peterson & Dixon, 2005), in which case it can be viewed as a philosophy rather than a strict policy (Smith, Davis, Nickles, & Davies, 2001). In different New York City jurisdictions, for example, mandatory prosecution varies by nonmandatory (the Bronx) or mandatory (Brooklyn) filing of charges (O'Sullivan et al., 2007; Peterson & Dixon, 2005). With nonmandatory filing, cases are screened out at the filing stage based on victim participation or strength of the evidence; cases are not dropped at prosecution regardless of victim preference. With mandatory filing, prosecutors file charges in nearly all cases, regardless of the victim's participation or strength of the evidence. Thus, they often proceed by relying on "hearsay exceptions" (such as excited utterances, 911 calls), photographs, police testimony, medical reports, or physical evidence, but many cases are dismissed at later stages for insufficient evidence (Peterson & Dixon, 2005).[3] Brooklyn's mandatory filing policy also means the issuance of a temporary order of protection for up to 90 days; assumes victims will be more likely to access safety-related

---

[3]Recent Supreme Court decisions may restrict the ability of prosecutors to use this sort of evidence. In *Crawford v. Washington* (2004), the Supreme Court held that a defendant's Sixth Amendment right to confront witnesses renders inadmissible out-of-court statements that are testimonial, unless the witness is unavailable and the defendant had a prior opportunity to cross-examine the witness. However, in cases of intimate partner violence, a defendant's conduct may play a role in the availability of the complaining witness, and the rule of forfeiture by wrongdoing may override a defendant's confrontation claim (Leventhal & Aldrich, 2006). Further, in *Davis v. Washington* (2006), the Supreme Court held that courts must review out-of-court statements to determine whether their "primary purpose" is testimonial, that is, intended to provide support for an investigation, and thus inadmissible.

services such as counseling, civil legal assistance, or relocation assistance; and entails creation of a court record for consideration in the event of rearrest. Evaluation of the two policies revealed no difference in recidivism (six-month rearrest rates), but this could have been due to their differing more strongly at the initial screening phase; in both jurisdictions, cases that lacked active victim participation would end up being dismissed (O'Sullivan et al., 2007), consistent with the notion that a mandatory policy is not necessarily strictly practiced. Victims supported mandatory filing to a degree (O'Sullivan et al., 2007, p. 58–60): Bronx victims were satisfied with the handling of their individual cases (based on victim preference), but in the abstract preferred the Brooklyn mandatory policy. Although a few Brooklyn victims felt disempowered, most felt the prosecution decision should be made for them because they are torn by attachment to the offender, emotionally vulnerable, and not experts. Brooklyn victims also felt safer with prosecution plus an order of protection, but did not necessarily receive the intended services. Prosecutors thus face a delicate balance of protecting and satisfying victims and holding offenders accountable (see also Davis, Smith, & Taylor, 2003; Smith et al., 2001).

Research on case processing and disposition and recidivism suggests that compared to not filing charges, "doing something" with offenders is perhaps consistent with a "specific deterrent effect of formal intervention beyond arrest" (Wooldredge & Thistlethwaite, 2002, p. 60). In an Ohio study, rearrest rates (two-year follow-up) were higher for persons whose cases were ignored (i.e., no charges filed, 24%) compared to dropping charges (14%), acquittal at trial (13%), attending a counseling program (11%), and probation and/or jail term (17%; Wooldredge & Thistlethwaite, 2002; see also O'Sullivan et al., 2007; Ventura & Davis, 2005; for alternative findings, see Kingsnorth, 2006).

Racial and ethnic minority status complicates involvement with the criminal justice system. Although racial and ethnic minority intimate partner violence victims lacking other alternatives may have to rely more on police assistance, at the same time, African American women may be hesitant to seek relief from a system they perceive deals more harshly with nonwhite men; Asian and Latino women may view expressing a preference for arrest as a betrayal of cultural norms that dictate privacy and deference to family authority (Rasche, 1995). Kingsnorth and Macintosh (2004) found that Asian American victims were less likely to desire arrest but were similar to whites in their desire for prosecution. African American victims were similar to whites in supporting arrest, but significantly less likely to support prosecution. On the other hand, Bui (2001) found race was not important to overall behavior, including submitting a victim statement and obtaining a protection order, but Hispanic women were significantly more likely to support prosecution than were white or African American women. Weisz (2002) found that nearly 65% of a sample of African American women expressed general support for pursuing charges against their abusers, but they were not asked about their actual participation in prosecution, and women who experienced severe violence (according to police reports) were underrepresented in the interviews (Weisz, 2002, p. 31). Problems are amplified for immigrant women, who are often dependent economically and otherwise on husbands or in-laws who themselves may be economically insecure. Their lives are further complicated by fears of deportation if they are illegal immigrants or in arranged marriages (Raj & Silverman, 2002).

Pro-arrest statutes and no-drop prosecution are policy successes that reverse the system's historical trivialization of intimate partner violence. And although the mandatory execution of these policies varies, the overriding philosophy is one of "doing something," which indeed may help many battered women. However, their coercive nature is paternalistic, and a criminal justice response may not be in the best interests of all women; the system's emphasis on offender accountability can jeopardize victim safety. Moreover, mandatory arrest statutes intended to target male batterers have resulted in the gendered injustice of arresting and processing women victims, denying them the services they need. Although primary aggressor statutes aim to guard against dual arrest, officers need more encouragement to apply them, better training on how to distinguish defensive injury, and more clear instructions on what kind information to gather and how to weigh it, and officers' decision making needs to be carefully reviewed (Finn & Bettis, 2006).

Domestic Violence Courts

The courtroom experience has been fraught with problems for intimate partner violence victims, with judges routinely admonishing victims to keep their private business out of court or telling offenders to "kiss and make up" (Epstein, 1999). The past few years, however, have challenged this antiquated thinking, ushering in a variety of "problem-solving courts," such as drug, community, domestic violence, and mental health courts, designed to address the roots of individual and social problems that contribute to crime. These specialized courts use a therapeutic, collaborative, and multidisciplinary approach to case processing (Tsai, 2000); there are now more than 300 such courts (Keilitz, 2000). For intimate partner violence in particular, the courts represent an enormous change, with specific recognition of the unique dynamics of interpersonal crimes and how they differ from stranger crimes (see Mazur & Aldrich, 2003). Judges are better able to address underlying causes and issues, as well as consolidate all domestic violence cases into one courtroom. Common goals are to ensure greater offender accountability and provide appropriate therapy for offenders while better addressing victims' needs.

In a study of a specialized domestic violence court in South Carolina, Gover and her colleagues found that recidivism was reduced and enforcement efforts were enhanced compared to a sample of intimate partner violence offenders

processed in traditional criminal courts (Gover, Brank, & MacDonald, 2007; Gover, MacDonald, & Alpert, 2003). Part of the success was attributed to the court's emphasis on procedural justice principles that highlight processes rather than a focus solely on outcomes; both victims and offenders indicated satisfaction with their court experiences in addition to a highly cooperative courtroom workgroup. Court dockets proceeded efficiently and effectively, and victims and defendants reported positive feelings about their experiences. The overriding goal for the specialized domestic violence court was to identify and address the underlying causes of abuse through treatment and rehabilitation, especially for first-time offenders. With a focus on both process and outcome, this court was successful in its endeavor to provide a more procedurally fair system for victims and offenders that also reduced the reoccurrence of intimate partner violence.

In a Salt Lake City domestic violence court, Mirchandani (2006) found that judges who delivered formal admonishments to offenders, challenged offenders' patriarchal sense of entitlement, and reinforced offender responsibility by stressing interpersonal communication and connections achieved greater success than those who engaged in traditional, adversarial practice. Support for victims is another important aspect of handling intimate partner violence. In a study of a municipal domestic violence court in Kansas City, MO, Camacho and Alarid (2008) found that the inclusion of a victim advocate (from a local domestic violence shelter, acting as a liaison between the victim and the prosecutor) and the actions of the victim assistance program were the most significant factors predicting whether or not a victim attended the disposition hearing and final case outcome (see also Gover et al., 2007).

A staple feature of many specialized courts is judicial monitoring of convicted offenders, in which judges use their unique position as an authority figure to motivate offenders' compliance. In an examination of the effect of judicial monitoring on recidivism (rearrest rates, one-year follow-up) in the Bronx misdemeanor domestic violence court, Rempel, Labriola, and Davis (2008) found no difference between monitored intimate partner violence offenders and those whose sentences did not include monitoring. However, of those rearrested at least once, the monitored offenders averaged fewer total rearrests for any crime and for intimate partner violence specifically. The researchers suggest that rather than surveillance (i.e., superficial court check-ins), more intensive supervision has the potential to result in more positive effects, given its "repeatedly conveying information about behavioral expectations and the consequences of noncompliance; real, individualized interaction between offender and monitoring agent; and application of incentives and sanctions designed to reinforce the linkages between good and bad behavior and resulting consequences" (Rempel et al., 2008, p. 203).

Empirical findings that demonstrate success in meeting the goals of reducing victim blaming, strengthening offender accountability, significantly reducing rearrests for defendants processed in domestic violence courts versus traditional criminal courts, and improving victim safety suggest that these courts contribute greatly to the mission of enabling the criminal justice system to respond more effectively to violence in intimate relationships (Gover et al., 2003).

Civil Options for Intimate Partner Violence

Civil restraining orders or protection orders (POs) emerged as an important legal remedy in response to the reluctance of the criminal justice system to arrest, prosecute, and sentence intimate partner violence offenders. Civil court remedies permitted victims to circumvent an often inadequate criminal process, yet still obtain some relief or have an additional remedy at their disposal. Civil protection orders, which now exist in all 50 states, carry criminal penalties for violations; they are valuable for conveying the message that battering is a public crime deserving of remedy and for the role they play in empowering victims. Victims report that

POs are valuable tools in documenting abuse (Harrell & Smith, 1996) and making them feel safer (Logan & Walker, 2009), despite the fact that less than half the victims thought the offenders would actually believe they had to comply with the order (Logan & Walker, 2009).

Initially, POs were difficult to obtain. Prior to the 1970s, women had to begin divorce proceedings to be eligible (Chaudhuri & Daly, 1992). The early POs were limited to prohibiting contact and/or further violence, but today, judges have wide discretion to craft remedies and stronger sanctions for violations (Eigenberg, McGuffee, Berry, & Hall, 2003). POs not only establish limits to abusers' access to victims but may also include financial arrangements and restrictions on custody; they may limit access to residence, place of employment, children, and children's schools. POs also serve as an alternative form of victim protection if the evidence does not meet the standard of a criminal proceeding or if the victim would be a weak prosecution witness due to drug or alcohol abuse, for example (Finn & Colson, 1990). The federal Violence Against Women Act (VAWA) prohibits the purchase and possession of firearms by defendants who have a PO issued against them. VAWA also requires states to honor protective orders issued by other states, tribes, or nations and to encourage or mandate arrests for violations of POs. Broader definitions regarding eligibility include cohabiting, dating, and former dating partners as well as same-sex partners, although they vary by state (DeJong & Burgess-Proctor, 2006).

Despite the potential effectiveness of civil orders, early research that reviewed state statutory and case law, interviewed judges and victim advocates, and examined program documentation from several jurisdictions (Finn & Colson, 1990, 1998) identified many common weaknesses, such as the narrow eligibility categories for obtaining orders, the decrease in relief remedies if victims are not represented by attorneys, and few options for victims who cannot afford filing fees or cannot obtain orders when courts are not in session (Finn & Colson, 1998, p. 44).

More recent research by Eigenberg and colleagues (2003) found that states have improved access to POs by no longer requiring filing fees (federal VAWA regulations prohibit states from receiving funds if they charge fees), providing ways to keep victims' addresses confidential, and giving victims free copies of their orders, although there has been little change with respect to burden of proof issues (i.e., requiring that victims demonstrate that the preponderance of the evidence supports their claims). About half the states provide enhanced penalties for repeat offenders, and most states seem more willing to embrace mandatory arrest for violators (although this is not necessarily carried out; Eigenberg et al., 2003). In a review of all states' legislation, DeJong and Burgess-Proctor (2006) found that statutes conform to VAWA standards, but states differ dramatically in accessibility of orders.

Violations of POs

The effectiveness of POs often depends on what is contained in the original order and how the police and courts respond to violations (Buzawa & Buzawa, 2003; Sorenson & Shen, 2005); law enforcement's response can be enhanced by serious prosecutorial and judicial actions and meaningful punishment for violators (Logan & Walker, 2009). Findings on violations vary, ranging from a study using police reports that reveals 23% of women experienced physical violence after filing (Carlson, Harris, & Holden, 1999) to the findings in the National Violence Against Women survey, in which 69.7% of those stalked, 67.6% of those sexually assaulted, and 50.6% of those physically assaulted by a partner reported a PO violation (Tjaden & Thoennes, 2000). A meta-analysis of 32 studies revealed that 40% of POs are violated, accompanied by victims' perceptions that worse incidents followed the violations almost 21% of the time (Spitzberg, 2002).

In other research, Diviney, Parekh, and Olson (2009) compared final sentencing decisions ordered by judges to federal and state sentencing guidelines for PO violations in Utah, uncovering substantial deviations from state guidelines. For instance, they found wide deviation from federal guidelines—only 4.5% (six defendants) were ordered to surrender firearms. The shortsightedness of this is not trivial, given that firearms are the leading cause of intimate partner homicides (Gwinn, 2006) and that the removal of firearms is associated with reducing such homicides (Vigdor & Mercy, 2006). The message to batterers is that they can abuse with impunity. Although batterers could be appearing in court for the first time (given the dynamics of battering), they may, in fact, be repeat violent offenders. Diviney et al. (2009) identify the failure to order defendants to treatment as a crucial misstep in helping courts monitor compliance.

Logan and Walker's (2009) research on factors associated with PO violations revealed that almost 60% of women from one state experienced a PO violation, but nonetheless, at least 75% of them reported that the orders were extremely or fairly effective overall. The women who did not see POs as effective were those most likely to have experienced severe physical violence. Stalking emerged as a significant predictor of PO violations for about half the sample and often had been part of the women's lives before obtaining POs. Women who remained in relationships with their abuser after the orders were issued were also at greater risk for continued violence. What also became clear was that official records reveal a lower rate of re-abuse than victim self-report data (see also Hotaling & Buzawa, 2003). Related research in Utah found that the most significant predictors of abuser recidivism were having two or more court reports of noncompliance with treatment, two or more warrants issued by the court for noncompliance, and two or more reports to police about new crimes involving the defendant (Kindness, Kim, Alder, Edwards, Parekh, & Olson, 2009). These findings demonstrate the importance of monitoring defendant behavior to ensure compliance with treatment for intimate partner violence and other court orders.

Overall, the research demonstrates the equivocal nature of civil options. Although POs can be an important legal tool to increase victim safety and victims, overall, seem satisfied with them, the fact remains that few victims obtain POs (Tjaden & Thoennes, 2000) and that their ultimate effectiveness rests on a concerted effort by police to arrest and by courts to enforce these orders and impose meaningful sanctions when the orders are violated.

Sexual Assault

Sexual assault is a pervasive social problem; estimates from the National Violence Against Women Survey (NVAWS) reveal that 18% of women will be sexually victimized at some point in their adult life (Tjaden & Thoennes, 2006). Victims of sexual violence endure many harmful consequences, including mental and physical health complications, increased vulnerability to subsequent incidents of sexual assault, and difficulty adjusting to and functioning in everyday life (Koss, Bailey, Yuan, Herrera, & Lichter, 2003). Victims often seek help from friends, family, rape crisis centers, or the police, but overall, most victims of sexual assault do not report to law enforcement (Campbell, Wasco, Ahrens, Sefl, & Barnes, 2001; Koss, 1985).

Reporting Practices

According to the NVAWS, approximately 80% of victims of sexual assault do not report to police (Kilpatrick, Resnick, Ruggiero, Conoscenti, & McCauley, 2007; Tjaden & Thoennes, 2006). However, reporting rates as low as 5% have also been recorded, indicating that it continues to be one of the most underreported crimes (Fisher, Cullen, & Turner, 2000; Tjaden & Thoennes, 2006). The National Crime Victimization Survey (NCVS) documents numerous reasons victims may choose not to report to police, including not wanting others to find out, not defining their experience as

rape, self-blame, fearing they will not be believed, wanting to protect the perpetrator (if he is a boyfriend, husband, or friend), believing that the criminal justice system will do nothing, and wanting to forget and move on with their life (Vito, Maahs, & Holmes, 2007). These issues contribute to low reporting rates in general, especially in comparison to other crimes (Sable, Danis, Mauzy, & Gallagher, 2006; Tjaden & Thoennes, 2006).

Given that some women experience forced, unwanted sex consistent with the legal definition of rape but may not identify that they have experienced "rape," researchers ask questions that tap experiences consistent with behavioral descriptions of rape (Gavey, 1999). Thus, estimates of the prevalence of rape can vary depending on the source. The Uniform Crime Reports (UCR) uses a legal definition of rape that does not necessarily capture definitions that victims use when they feel they have been sexually assaulted. For example, it does not include forcible sodomy or penetration with an object. In contrast, the NCVS and NVAWS use more inclusive definitions of sexual assault and rape, thus providing a more accurate description of sexual assault derived from victims' perceptions. As Peterson and Muehlenhard (2004) observe, there is no absolute category of "rape victim" merely because an experience fits certain conditions. Personal agency in defining an experience can be just as important to an individual as the experience itself; in the instance of rape victims, control has been taken away from them, and deciding how to label the experience is one of the first steps to taking back control of their life (Amar & Burgess, 2008).

Case Processing

A woman who classifies her experience as sexual assault and decides to report to the criminal justice system faces two broad possibilities: the case will either be dropped (at some point in the process) or it will end with a plea bargain or verdict. After a case is reported, the police investigate and decide whether to forward it to the prosecutor. Police and prosecutors exercise immense discretion in the way they handle cases; there is no criminal recourse for victims if law enforcement drops or refuses to take their case. Decisions to move forward rest on various reasons, such as insufficient evidence to prove an assault happened or pure implausibility that the case will result in a guilty plea or verdict (Caringella, 2009; Martin, 2005). In the NVAWS, only 37% of reported cases were accepted by prosecutors (Tjaden & Thoennes, 2006). Additionally, Tjaden and Thoennes (2006) found that 46% of those who were prosecuted were convicted of a crime; all in all, only 3% of reported cases ended in conviction. Victims may prefer case resolution by plea bargain, despite a lighter sentence, given that trials are public and victims may endure excessive scrutiny and humiliation if subject to cross-examination (Caringella, 2009; Martin, 2005; Taslitz, 1999). Holleran, Beichner, and Spohn (2008) point out that police departments and prosecutors often establish working norms that determine "going rates" for plea bargains, although prosecutors utilize tactics that give them the upper hand in negotiations. Overall, prosecutors were more likely to file charges in cases of "real rape," but predicted likelihood of conviction also played a prominent role (Holleran et al., 2008).

Criminal justice system officials are often most concerned with securing evidence and extracting information, even though methods used to acquire information can be detrimental to victims and result in secondary victimization (Holleran et al., 2008; Martin, 2005). Police may actively deter victims from following through with their cases by discouraging victims from reporting, refusing to take a report altogether (because a case was "not serious enough") or threatening to file felony charges if they believe a victim is lying (Campbell, 2005; Caringella, 2009; Jordan, 2004). Instead of focusing on holding offenders accountable and imposing meaningful sanctions, the system often puts victims at risk of bearing the brunt of the burden when seeking legal recourse.

Differential Treatment by Police

Law enforcement has been criticized for differential case treatment based on victim and assault characteristics that distinguish "simple rape" and "real rape" (Estrich, 1987). "Real rape" reflects the stereotypical situation involving one or several factors: a victim and an offender who are unknown to one another, an interracial combination such as a white victim and a black stranger perpetrator(s), visible physical injury, and the use of force or a weapon (Estrich, 1987). On the other hand, "simple rapes" have characteristics that make them appear less serious, for example, they are typically perpetrated by someone the victim knows, do not result in injuries or employ weapons, and there may be no witnesses or accomplices (Estrich, 1987). "Real rapes" are more clear cut in terms of lack of consent and are viewed as more serious and easier to prosecute. As a result, "real rapes" unify police and prosecutors in their decisions to prioritize them, while "simple rapes" are less likely to proceed through the criminal justice system, even though they account for the majority of rapes and sexual assaults (Estrich, 1987; Taslitz, 1999; Tjaden & Thoennes, 2006). The widespread acceptance of rape myths and how these myths affect victim credibility often means that "simple rape" is taken less seriously (Estrich, 1987; Tjaden & Thoennes, 2006).

Credibility of the victim and her story influence whether a case progresses through the system (Caringella, 2009; Frohmann, 1998; Konradi, 2007; Martin, 2005; Taslitz, 1999). There are several ways that law enforcement officers can challenge the veracity of a complaint and make case progression difficult, ranging from asking the victim to repeat her story in different ways and scrutinizing inconsistencies to expressing doubt in the truth of her story (Caringella, 2009; Holleran et al., 2008; Martin, 2005). Remarkably, Patterson (2008) found that police treat victims whose cases were ultimately prosecuted (i.e., determined credible witnesses) with more compassion than victims whose cases were not prosecuted. To improve the system's response to sexual assault victims, many police departments are now part of a jurisdictional or regional Sexual Assault Response Team, or SART (see Chapter 5), that brings together police, prosecutors, rape crisis advocates, and specially trained Sexual Assault Nurse Examiners (SANEs) to collect forensic evidence from victims and suspects within 72 to 96 hours of the assault (Ledray, 1998). The hope is that with improved communication between justice professionals and the reliability of evidence collected by SANEs, higher conviction rates will result (Littel, 2001; Martin, 2005; Nugent-Borakove, Fanflik, Troutman, Johnson, Burgess, & O'Connor, 2008).

Prosecutorial Practices

Prosecutors also wield a great deal of discretion in deciding which cases to pursue following formal charges. Prosecutorial case decisions have been linked to rape myth beliefs (e.g., the case represents a "real rape") and a reliance on archaic standards of evidence (e.g., documentation of injury, resistance, witnesses; Caringella, 2009; Konradi, 2007). Because of high case loads and the need for favorable conviction rates to ensure re-election, prosecutors often only take cases that they are reasonably sure they can win (Caringella, 2009; Konradi, 2007; Martin, 2005).

When cases are charged by prosecutors but no plea agreement is reached, the next step is a trial. Trials are always a possibility when taking on a case, so prosecutors must be positive that their witness(es) will appear credible in front of a jury (Frohmann, 1998; Holleran et al., 2008; Konradi, 2007; Martin, 2005; Taslitz, 1999); the technique of intimidating a rape victim with the prospect of testifying at trial early in her case processing (presumably to further determine the veracity of the complaint) is called "downstreaming" (Frohmann, 1998). Similar to Patterson's (2008) research on police arrest decisions, Frohmann

(1998) found that prosecutors treated victims more compassionately if they projected the cases would go forward, in comparison to cases in which victims seemed less credible and/or unwilling to continue with prosecution efforts. Some jurisdictions encourage the submission of victim impact statements at the time of sentencing, to give victims an opportunity to publicly state the reasons they want their attacker punished (Konradi & Burger, 2000). Not all victims choose to participate; their cooperation is often determined by how they were treated during their case progression and how much personal support they have (Konradi & Burger, 2000).

During her ethnography of a prosecutor's office, Frohmann (1997, 1998) observed that prosecutors used multiple strategies to systematically reject cases of sexual assault. Frohmann spent eight months collecting data through participant observation in a sexual assault unit of a prosecutor's office in a West Coast major metropolitan area. Specifically examining race, class, and gender, Frohmann (1997) noted how prosecutors reacted to cases with victims of different backgrounds and argued that, although not overtly, prosecutors reproduced dominant stereotypes of race, class, and gender in their decision-making process, consistent with the acceptance of rape myths and the notion of "real rape" (Estrich, 1987). Recent studies have indicated no support for the stereotypical white victim/black suspect scenario because perpetrators often target a victim of the same race (Bouffard, 2000; Wheeler & George, 2005). However, when a man of color sexually assaults a white woman, entrenched stereotypes play a role in case processing (Wheeler & George, 2005), which indicates that a black suspect and white victim scenario continues to play a role in victim credibility (even if indirectly) in the eyes of criminal justice system officials (Konradi, 2007). Given that each case is individually evaluated by police and prosecutors, rape myths and stereotypes could influence case outcome if criminal justice system officials deem them salient.

Effect of Rape Law Reform on Sexual Assault Cases

Legal reforms of the 1970s aimed to improve the system's treatment of victims and simultaneously increase the conviction of offenders by updating rape definitions and removing unnecessary barriers to victim credibility from the legal requirements of rape (Spohn & Horney, 1992). Spohn and Horney (1992) identify four significant changes: replacing "rape" with multiple degrees or offenses of "sexual assault," elimination of resistance requirements, elimination of corroboration requirements, and restrictions on the type of evidence regarding the victim's sexual history that is acceptable in court.

However, Caringella's (2009) recent review of rape law reform highlights a dismal lack of improvement in the treatment of sexual assault cases by the criminal justice system. For example, Caringella reports that overall reporting, arrest, and conviction rates have not noticeably improved for all types of sexual assault. Similarly, expectations have not diminished for proof of resistance, corroboration of stories, and sexual history of the victim. In fact, resistance, corroboration, and sexual history—which are outdated concepts that have no bearing on whether an assault actually occurred—have still not been completely prohibited from case files and courtroom testimony (Caringella, 2009). The fact that corroboration and resistance still play an informal role in distinguishing "simple" from "real" rapes in case processing demonstrates that rape law reform has not come as far in practice as it has in the wording of the law (Caringella, 2009). The continued use of these outdated tactics (albeit in more subtle ways) reinforces the practice that "simple" sexual assaults, such as statutory, acquaintance, and marital rape, are less likely to progress through the system (Caringella, 2009; Estrich, 1987; Holleran et al., 2008). Any successes that rape law reforms facilitate are dwarfed by their failures. The same barriers to reporting that victims encountered prior to the reforms of the 1970s—which included shame, guilt, embarrassment, breach of confidentiality, and the fear of not being believed—remain prevalent today (Caringella, 2009).

Help-Seeking Outside the Criminal Justice System

Because of the high attrition rate of sexual assault cases (Tjaden & Thoennes, 2006), victims' reluctance to report assaults, as well as their experiences with secondary victimization, it is not entirely surprising that many victims choose to seek help elsewhere in the community, such as in counseling, rape crisis centers, and informal social support networks (Ahrens & Campbell, 2000; Campbell, 2005; Martin, 2005). If victims want their attacker to face punishment but do not want to prosecute criminally, civil suits are an alternative (Caringella, 2009). Civil suits have a lesser standard of proof, requiring only a "preponderance of the evidence" to succeed, as opposed to the criminal standard of guilt "beyond a reasonable doubt" for a conviction. In civil cases, however, rape shield laws do not protect against the admissibility of victims' sexual history (which is not allowed in criminal cases) and defendants can countersue for slander, libel, or defamation of character (Caringella, 2009). As a result, after weighing possible gains versus losses, victims of simple rapes may choose to bypass legal options altogether.

Drawing on lessons learned from rape law reforms (Caringella, 2009), rather than simply altering laws and expecting change to happen, educational programs could help to inform the public about sexual assault (Fisher, Daigle, & Cullen, 2008; Morrison, Hardison, Mathew, & O'Neil, 2004). In a review of 59 studies that test the effectiveness of sexual assault prevention interventions, Morrison and colleagues (2004) highlight common challenges (such as population age, lack of access to at-risk populations, eliciting participation in schools, culturally specific and appropriate program content, and a need for program evaluations), but they are also hopeful that effective programs are being developed to combat sexual assault and violence against women nationally and globally.

Fisher et al. (2008) reviewed programs aimed to prevent sexual assault and reduce risk for women. Although risk reduction campaigns can help women and children decrease their risk of being sexually victimized by modifying behaviors and activities, they concentrate on *victims* rather than *perpetrators* (Fisher et al., 2008). Sexual assault prevention programs target both males and females, using the community and culture at large to focus on ending the abusive treatment of women—not just the most serious instances of rape and sexual assault (Fisher et al., 2008; Lonsway et al., 2009; Morrison et al., 2004). Risk reduction programs are a short-term fix in the grander scheme to reduce rape and sexual assault incidence, while the more long-term prevention programs target both potential victims *and* offenders.

Gendered Violence and Restorative Justice

Stemming from the rallying cry of the 1970s victims' rights movement to view victims as the "experts" of their situation who can offer vital case input, restorative justice programs offer victims the opportunity to address violence committed against women in a more informal context. Restorative justice was designed to parallel the formal justice system, and it operates under various models, with most focusing on minor offenses committed by juveniles. The typical process entails a face-to-face meeting between the victim and offender, where each side can be heard and a case outcome is crafted outside the formal courtroom. Given that many feminist scholars believe that some restorative justice programs are inappropriate to use with crimes of sexual assault/rape, child abuse, and

battering (see Busch, 2002; Stubbs, 2002), care is taken to ensure victim safety and offender accountability. A number of restorative justice proponents believe that there may be a place for restorative justice in handling violence against women, with post-conviction therapeutic models that allow victims to tell their stories of the violence they experienced. Post-conviction programs differ from diversionary programs in that no sentence leniency is offered to offenders. Because punishment has already been imposed and the program's goal is to empower victims, there is often less opportunity for offenders to control victims through intimidation and fear. In addition, because the therapeutic restorative justice process includes other people, it provides an opportunity for increased public condemnation.

Three examples of restorative justice programs that address violence against women are (1) the work of Mary Koss and her colleagues in Arizona, who designed and implemented a diversionary restorative justice program that responds to victims and first-time offenders of acquaintance rape, indecent exposure, and peeping (Hopkins & Koss, 2005); (2) Umbreit, Vos, Coates, and Brown's (2003) research and work with victims of violent crimes; and (3) Susan L. Miller's (in press) analysis of a program that uses a post-conviction therapeutic model for victims of rape, intimate partner violence, and incest. Although there are no results yet on long-term effectiveness, the goals of greater victim input, satisfaction, and empowerment are met in these restorative justice programs. The hope is that victim-centered responses reduce victim trauma and honor victims' expressed preferences— all of which could ultimately increase reporting of sexual violence and other forms of violence committed against women. However, it is clear that any restorative justice program to address violence against women must ensure that agreements are based on victims' consent and on equity, and that they are handled by facilitators knowledgeable about the power and control dynamics implicit in sexual and physical violence committed against women.

Conclusion

Given the complex dynamics of intimate partner violence and sexual violence, their roots in society's structured gender inequality, and the unique problems of racial and ethnic minorities, the criminal justice system alone will not solve the problem, and overreliance on the system will preclude pursuing other remedies. For intimate partner violence, punitive responses must be combined with policies and services that address employment, housing, and child care, especially for socially marginal groups whose lives are increasingly regulated by expanding criminal justice monitoring (Dixon, 2008). There are encouraging developments targeting intimate partner violence at the front end. The CDC is promoting prevention efforts, including Choose Respect, which reinforces positive relationship attitudes in adolescents, and the Domestic Violence Prevention Enhancement and Leadership Through Alliances (DELTA), which focuses on preventing initial acts of violence and recognizes the complexity of intimate partner violence in terms of individual, relationship, community, and societal factors. Although practitioners and researchers should continue efforts to improve the criminal justice response, "it is time to correct the imbalance between the criminal justice response and other responses to intimate partner violence" (Peterson, 2008, p. 542). Efforts to address sexual assault and rape must also move beyond risk reduction strategies to devise prevention efforts, in addition to realizing the goals of victim empowerment and more efficacious criminal justice responses, as we continue to challenge cultural tolerance of sexual violence against women.

References

Ahrens, C., & Campbell, R. (2000). Assisting rape victims as they recover from rape: The impact on friends. *Journal of Interpersonal Violence, 15*(9), 959–986.

Amar, A., & Burgess, A. (2008). Rape and its impact on the victim. In R. Hazelwood & A. W. Burgess (Eds.), *Practical aspects of rape investigation: A multidisciplinary approach* (4th ed., pp. 25–39). Washington, DC: CRC Press.

Bouffard, J. (2000). Predicting type of sexual assault case closure from victim, suspect, and case characteristics. *Journal of Criminal Justice, 28,* 527–542.

Bui, H. N. (2001). Domestic violence victims' behavior in favor of prosecution: Effects of gender relations. *Women & Criminal Justice, 12*(4), 51–75.

Busch, A. L., & Rosenberg, M. S. (2004). Comparing women and men arrested for domestic violence: A preliminary report. *Journal of Family Violence, 19*(1), 49–57.

Busch, R. (2002). Domestic violence and restorative justice initiatives: Who pays if we get it wrong? In H. Strang & J. Braithwaite (Eds.), *Restorative justice and family violence* (pp. 223–248). Cambridge, UK: Cambridge University Press.

Buzawa, E. S., & Buzawa, C. G. (2003). *Domestic violence: The criminal justice response.* Thousand Oaks, CA: Sage.

Camacho, C. M., & Alarid, L. F. (2008). The significance of the victim advocate for domestic violence victims in municipal court. *Violence and Victims, 23*(3), 288–300.

Campbell, R. (2005). What really happened? A validation study of rape survivors' help-seeking experiences with the legal and medical systems. *Violence and Victims, 20*(1), 55–68.

Campbell, R., Wasco, S. Ahrens, C., Sefl, T., & Barnes, H. (2001). Preventing the second rape: Rape survivors' experiences with community service providers. *Journal of Interpersonal Violence, 16*(12), 1239–1259.

Caringella, S. (2009). *Addressing rape reform in law and practice.* New York: Columbia University Press.

Carlson, M. J., Harris, S. D., & Holden, G. W. (1999). Protective order and domestic abuse: Risk factors for re-abuse. *Journal of Family Violence, 14*(2), 205–226.

Chaudhuri, M., & Daly, K. (1992). Do restraining orders help? Battered women's experience with male violence and the legal process. In E. S. Buzawa & C. G. Buzawa (Eds.), *Domestic violence: The changing criminal justice response* (pp. 227–252). Westwood, CT: Auburn House.

Crawford v. Washington, 541 U.S. 36 (2004).

Dasgupta, S. D. (1999). Just like men? A critical review of violence by women. In M. F. Shepard & E. L. Pence

(Eds.), *Coordinating community response to domestic violence: Lessons from Duluth and beyond* (pp. 195–222). Thousand Oaks, CA: Sage.

Dasgupta, S. D. (2002). A framework for understanding women's use of nonlethal violence in intimate heterosexual relationships. *Violence Against Women, 8*(11), 1364–1389.

Davis, R. C., Smith, B. E., & Taylor, B. (2003). Increasing the proportion of domestic violence arrests that are prosecuted: A natural experiment in Milwaukee. *Criminology & Public Policy, 2*(2), 263–281.

Davis v. Washington, 126 S. Ct. 2266 (2006).

DeJong, C., & Burgess-Proctor, A. (2006). A summary of personal protection order statutes in the United States. *Violence Against Women, 12*(1), 68–88.

DeLeon-Granados, W., Wells, W., & Binsbacher, R. (2006). Arresting developments trends in female arrests for domestic violence and proposed explanations. *Violence Against Women, 12*(4), 355–371.

Diviney, C., Parekh, A., & Olson, L. (2009). Outcomes of civil protective orders: Results from one state. *Journal of Interpersonal Violence, 24*(7), 1209–1221.

Dixon, J. (2008). Mandatory domestic violence arrest and prosecution policies: Recidivism and social governance. *Criminology & Public Policy, 7*(4), 663–670.

Dobash, R. E., Dobash, R. P., Cavanaugh, K., & Lewis, R. (1998). Separate and intersecting realities: A comparison of men's and women's accounts of violence against women. *Violence Against Women, 4*(4), 382–414.

Eigenberg, H., McGuffee, K., Berry, P., & Hall, W. H. (2003). Protective order legislation: Trends in state statutes. *Journal of Criminal Justice, 31*(5), 411–422.

Epstein, D. (1999). Effective intervention in domestic violence cases: Rethinking the roles of prosecutors, judges, and the court system. *Yale Journal of Law and Feminism, 11*, 3–50.

Estrich, S. (1987). *Real rape: How the legal system victimizes women who say no.* Cambridge, MA: Harvard University Press.

Feder, L., & Henning, K. (2005). A comparison of male and female dually arrested domestic violence offenders. *Violence and Victims, 20*(2), 153–171.

Felson, R. B., Ackerman, J. M., & Gallagher, C. (2005). *Police intervention and the repeat of domestic assault.* (NCJ 210310) Washington, DC: U.S. Department of Justice. Retrieved June 10, 2009, from http://www .ncjrs.gov/pdffiles1/nij/grants/210301.pdf

Finn, M. A., & Bettis, P. (2006). Punitive action or gentle persuasion: Exploring police officers' justifications for using dual arrest in domestic violence cases. *Violence Against Women, 12*(3), 268–287.

Finn, P., & Colson, S. (1990). *Civil protection orders: Legislation, current court practice, and enforcement.* Washington, DC: National Institute of Justice.

Finn, P., & Colson, S. (1998). Civil protection orders. In J. Travis (Ed.), *Legal interventions in family violence: Research findings and policy implications* (pp. 43–47). Washington, DC: National Institute of Justice.

Fisher, B. F., Cullen, F., & Turner, M. (2000). *The sexual victimization of college women* (NCJ 182369). Washington, DC: U.S. Department of Justice. Retrieved September 4, 2009, from http://www .ncjrs.gov/pdffiles1/nij/182369.pdf

Fisher, B., Daigle, L., & Cullen, F. (2008). Rape against women: What can research offer to guide the development of prevention programs and risk reduction interventions? *Journal of Contemporary Criminal Justice, 24*(2), 163–177.

Ford, D. A. (2003). Coercing victim participation in domestic violence prosecutions. *Journal of Interpersonal Violence, 18*(6), 669–684.

Frohmann, L. (1997). Convictability and discordant locales: Reproducing race, class, and gender ideologies in prosecutorial decision making. *Law & Society Review, 31*(3), 531–556.

Frohmann, L. (1998). Constituting power in sexual assault cases: Prosecutorial strategies for victim management. *Social Problems, 45*(3), 393–407.

Gavey, N. (1999). "I wasn't raped, but. . . .": Revisiting definitional problems in sexual victimization. In S. Lamb (Ed.), *New versions of victims: Feminists struggle with the concept* (pp. 57–81). New York: New York University Press.

Gover, A. R., Brank, E. M., & MacDonald, J. M. (2007). A specialized domestic violence court in South Carolina: An example of procedural justice for victims and defendants. *Violence Against Women, 13*(6), 603–626.

Gover, A. R., MacDonald, J. M., & Alpert, G. (2003). Combating domestic violence in rural America: Findings from an evaluation of a local domestic violence court. *Criminology and Public Policy, 3*, 109–132.

Gwinn, C. (2006). Domestic violence and firearms: Reflections of a prosecutor. *Evaluation Review, 30*(3), 237–244.

Hamberger, L. K. (2005). Men's and women's use of intimate partner violence in clinical samples: Toward a gender sensitive analysis. *Violence and Victims, 20*(2), 131–151.

Harrell, A., Castro, J., Newmark, L., & Visher, C. (2007). *Final report on the evaluation of the judicial oversight demonstration: Executive summary.* (NCJ 219386) Washington, DC: U.S. Department of Justice. Retrieved June 23, 2009, from http://www.urban.org/publications/411498.html

Harrell, A., & Smith, B. (1996). Effects of restraining orders on domestic violence victims. In E. Buzawa & C. Buzawa (Eds.), *The role of restraining and protective orders: Do arrest and restraining orders work?* (pp. 214–242). Thousand Oaks, CA: Sage.

Henning, K., & Feder, L. (2004). A comparison of men and women arrested for domestic violence: Who presents the greater threat? *Journal of Family Violence, 19*(2), 69–80.

Hirschel, D., & Buzawa, E. (2002). Understanding the context of dual arrest with directions for future research. *Violence Against Women, 8*(12), 1449–1473.

Hirschel, D., Buzawa, E., Pattavina, A., Faggiani, D., & Reuland, M. (2007). *Explaining the prevalence, context, and consequences of dual arrest in intimate partner cases.* (NCJ 218355) Washington, DC: U.S. Department of Justice. Retrieved May 16, 2009, from http://www.ncjrs.gov/pdffiles1/nij/grants/218355.pdf

Holleran, D., Beichner, D., & Spohn, C. (2008). Examining charging agreement between police and prosecutors in rape cases. *Crime & Delinquency Online.* Retrieved May 27, 2009, from http://cad.sagepub.com/cgi/rapidpdf/0011128707308977v1.pdf

Hopkins, C. Q., & Koss, M. P. (2005). Incorporating feminist theory and insights into a restorative justice response to sex offenses. *Violence Against Women, 11*(5), 693–723.

Hotaling, G. T., & Buzawa, E. S. (2003). *Foregoing criminal processing and the effects of restraining orders for domestic violence victims.* Washington, DC: The Urban Institute.

Houry, D., Reddy, S., & Parramore, C. (2006). Characteristics of victims coarrested for intimate partner violence. *Journal of Interpersonal Violence, 21*(11), 1483–1492.

Jordan, J. (2004). Beyond belief: Police, rape and women's credibility. *Criminal Justice, 4*(1), 29–59.

Keilitz, S. (2000). *Specialization of domestic violence case management in the courts: A national survey.* Williamsburg, VA: National Center for State Courts.

Kilpatrick, D., Resnick, H., Ruggiero, K., Conoscenti, L., & McCauley, J. (2007). *Drug-facilitated, incapacitated, and forcible rape: A national study.* (NCJ 219181) Washington, DC: U.S. Department of Justice. Retrieved September 4, 2009, from http://www.ncjrs.gov/pdffiles1/nij/grants/219181.pdf

Kimmel, M. S. (2002). Gender symmetry in domestic violence: A substantive and methodological research review. *Violence Against Women, 8*(11), 1336–1367.

Kindness, A., Kim, H., Alder, S., Edwards, A., Parekh, A., & Olson, L. M. (2009). Court compliance as a predictor of postadjudication recidivism for domestic violence offenders. *Journal of Interpersonal Violence, 24*(7), 1222–1238.

Kingsnorth, R. F. (2006). Intimate partner violence: Predictors of recidivism in a sample of arrestees. *Violence Against Women, 12*(10), 917–935.

Kingsnorth, R. F., & MacIntosh, R. C. (2004). Domestic violence: Predictors of victim support for official action. *Violence and Victims, 21*(2), 301–328.

Konradi, A. (2007). *Taking the stand: Rape survivors and the prosecution of rapists.* Westport, CT: Greenwood Publishing Group.

Konradi, A., & Burger, T. (2000). Having the last word: An examination of rape survivors' participation in sentencing. *Violence Against Women, 6*(4), 351–395.

Koss, M. (1985). The hidden rape victim: Personality, attitudinal, and situational characteristics. *Psychology of Women Quarterly, 9*(2), 193–212.

Koss, M., Bailey, J., Yuan, N., Herrera, V., & Lichter, E. (2003). Depression and PTSD in survivors of male violence: Research and training initiatives to facilitate recovery. *Psychology of Women Quarterly, 27*(2), 130–142.

Ledray, L. (1998). Sexual assault: Clinical issues SANE development and operation guide. *Journal of Emergency Nursing, 24,* 197–198.

Leventhal, J. M., & Aldrich, L. (2006). The admission of evidence in domestic violence cases after Crawford v. Washington: A national survey. *Berkeley Journal of Criminal Law, 11,* 77. Retrieved August 31, 2009, from http://www.ncdsv.org/publications_crawfordvwashington.html

Littel, K. (2001). Sexual Assault Nurse Examiner programs: Improving the community response to sexual assault victims. *Office for Victims of Crime Bulletin, 4,* 1–19.

Logan, T. K., & Walker, R. (2009). Civil protective order outcomes: Violations and perceptions of effectiveness. *Journal of Interpersonal Violence, 24*(4), 675–692.

Lonsway, K., Banyard, V., Berkowitz, A., Gidycz, C., Katz, J., Koss, M., et al. (2009). *Rape prevention and risk reduction: Review of the research literature for practitioners.* Harrisburg, PA: VAWnet. Retrieved May 17, 2009, from http://www.vawnet.org

Martin, P. Y. (2005). *Rape work: Victims, gender, and emotions in organization and community context.* New York: Routledge.

Maxwell, C. D., Garner, J. H., & Fagan, J. A. (2002). The preventive effects of arrest on intimate partner violence: Research, policy and theory. *Criminology & Public Policy, 2*(1), 51–79.

Mazur, R., & Aldrich, L. (2003). What makes a domestic violence court work? Lessons from New York. *Judges' Journal, 42,* 5–11.

Melton, H. C., & Belknap, J. (2003). He hits, she hits: Assessing gender differences and similarities in officially reported intimate partner violence. *Criminal Justice and Behavior, 3*(3), 328–348.

Miller, N. (2004). *Domestic violence: A review of state legislation defining police and prosecution duties and powers.* Alexandria, VA: Institute for Law and Justice. Retrieved May 13, 2009, from http://www.ilj.org/publications/DV_Legislation-3.pdf

Miller, S. L. (2005). *Victims as offenders: The paradox of women's violence in relationships.* New Brunswick, NJ: Rutgers University Press.

Miller, S. L. (in press). *After the crime: The power of restorative justice dialogues between victims and violent offenders.* New York: New York University Press.

Mirchandani, R. (2006). "Hitting is not manly": Domestic violence court and the re-imagination of the patriarchal state. *Gender & Society, 20*(6), 781–804.

Moffitt, T. E., Caspi, A., Rutter, M., & Silva, P. A. (2001). *Sex differences in antisocial behavior: Conduct disorder, delinquency, and violence in the Dunedin Longitudinal Study.* Cambridge, UK: Cambridge University Press.

Morrison, S., Hardison, J., Mathew, A., & O'Neil, J. (2004). *An evidence-based review of sexual assault preventive intervention programs.* (NCJ 207762) Washington, DC: U.S. Department of Justice. Retrieved November 5, 2005, from http://www.ncjrs.gov/pdffiles1/nij/grants/207262.pdf

Muftic, L. R., Bouffard, J. A., & Bouffard, L. A. (2007a). An exploratory study of women arrested for intimate partner violence: Violent women or violent resistance? *Journal of Interpersonal Violence, 22*(6), 753–774.

Muftic, L. R., Bouffard, L. A., & Bouffard, J. A. (2007b). An exploratory analysis of victim precipitation among men and women arrested for intimate partner violence. *Feminist Criminology, 2*(4), 327–346.

Nugent-Borakove, M., Fanflik, P., Troutman, D., Johnson, N., Burgess, A., & O'Connor, A. (2008). *Testing the efficacy of SANE/SART programs: Do they make a difference in sexual assault arrest and prosecution outcomes?* (NCJ 214252) Washington, DC: U.S. Department of Justice. Retrieved April 16, 2009, from http://www.ncjrs.gov/pdffiles1/nij/grants/214252.pdf

Osthoff, S. (2002). But, Gertrude, I beg to differ, a hit is not a hit is not a hit: When battered women are arrested for assaulting their partners. *Violence Against Women, 8*(12), 1521–1544.

O'Sullivan, C. S., Davis, R. C., Farole, D. J., Jr., & Rempel, M. (2007). *A comparison of two prosecution policies in cases of intimate partner violence mandatory case filing vs. following the victim's lead.* Washington, DC: National Institute of Justice. Retrieved February 3, 2009, from http://www.courtinnovation.org/index.cfm

Patterson, D. (2008). *Constructing justice: How the interactions between victims and detectives affect the quality of rape investigations.* East Lansing: Michigan State University Press.

Peterson, R. R. (2008). Reducing intimate partner violence: Moving beyond criminal justice interventions. *Criminology & Public Policy, 7*(4), 537–545.

Peterson, R. R., & Dixon, J. (2005). Court oversight and conviction under mandatory and nonmandatory domestic violence case filing policies. *Criminology & Public Policy, 4*(3), 535–558.

Peterson, Z., & Muehlenhard, C. (2004). Was it rape? The function of women's rape myth acceptance and definitions of sex in labeling their own experiences. *Sex Roles, 51*(3/4), 129–144.

Raj, A., & Silverman, J. (2002). Violence against immigrant women: The roles of culture, context, and legal immigrant status on partner violence. *Violence Against Women, 8*(3), 367–398.

Rasche, C. E. (1995). Minority women and domestic violence: The unique dilemmas of battered women of color. In B. R. Price & N. J. Sokoloff (Eds.), *The criminal justice system and women: Offenders, victims and workers* (2nd ed., pp. 246–261). New York: McGraw Hill.

Rempel, M., Labriola, M., & Davis, R. C. (2008). Does judicial monitoring deter domestic violence recidivism? Results of a quasi-experimental comparison in the Bronx. *Violence Against Women, 14*(2), 185–207.

Renzetti, C. M. (1999). The challenges to feminism posed by women's use of violence in intimate relationships. In S. Lamb (Ed.), *New versions of victims* (pp. 42–56). New York: New York University Press.

Sable, M., Danis, F., Mauzy, D., & Gallagher, G. (2006). Barriers to reporting sexual assault for women and men: Perspectives of college students. *Journal of American College Health, 55*(3), 157–162.

Sherman, L. W., & Berk, R. A. (1984). The specific deterrent effects of arrest for domestic violence. *American Sociological Review, 49*(2), 261–272.

Sherman, L. W., Schmidt, J. D., Rogan, D. P., Smith, D. A., Gartin, P. R., Cohn, E. G., et al. (1992). The variable effects of arrest in criminal careers: The Milwaukee domestic violence experiment. *Journal of Criminal Law & Criminology, 83*(1), 137–169.

Simpson, S. S., Bouffard L. A., Garner, J., & Hickman, L. (2006).The influence of legal reform on the probability of arrest in domestic violence cases. *Justice Quarterly, 23*(3), 297–316.

Smith, B., Davis, R., Nickles, L., & Davies, H. (2001). *Evaluation of efforts to implement no-drop policies: Two central values in conflict* (NCJ 187772). Washington, DC: U.S. Department of Justice. Retrieved June 10, 2009, from http://www .ncjrs.gov/App/Publications/abstract.aspx?ID= 187772

Sorenson, S. B., & Shen, H. (2005). Restraining orders in California: A look at statewide data. *Violence Against Women, 11*(7), 912–933.

Spitzberg, B. (2002). The tactical topography of stalking victimization and management. *Trauma, Violence, & Abuse, 3*(4), 261–288.

Spohn, C., & Horney, J. (1992). *Rape law reform: A grassroots revolution and its impact.* New York: Plenum Press.

Stubbs, J. (2002). Domestic violence and women's safety: Feminist challenges to restorative justice. In H. Strang & J. Braithwaite (Eds.), *Restorative justice and family violence* (pp. 42–61). Cambridge, UK: Cambridge University Press.

Swan, S. C., Gambone, L. J., Caldwell, J. E., Sullivan, T. P., & Snow, D. L. (2008). A review of research on women's use of violence with male intimate partners. *Violence and Victims, 23*(3), 301–314.

Taslitz, A. (1999). *Rape and the culture of the courtroom.* New York: New York University Press.

Tjaden, P., & Thoennes, N. (2000). *Extent, nature and consequences of intimate partner violence: Findings from the National Violence Against Women Survey.* (NCJ 183781) Washington, DC: U.S. Department of Justice.

Tjaden, P., & Thoennes, N. (2006). *Extent, nature and consequences of rape victimization: Findings from the National Violence Against Women Survey.* (NCJ 210346) Washington, DC: U.S. Department of Justice.

Tsai, B. (2000). The trend toward specialized domestic violence courts: Improvements on an effective innovation. *Fordham Law Review, 68,* 1285–1327.

Umbreit, M. S., Vos, B., Coates, R. B., & Brown, K. A. (2003). *Facing violence: The path of restorative justice and dialogue.* Monsey, NY: Criminal Justice Press.

Ventura, L. A., & Davis, G. (2005). Domestic violence: Court case conviction and recidivism. *Violence Against Women, 11*(2), 255–277.

Vigdor, E. R., & Mercy, J. A. (2006). Do laws restricting access to firearms by domestic violence offenders prevent intimate partner homicide? *Evaluation Review, 30*(3), 313–346.

Vito, G., Maahs, J., & Holmes, R. (2007). *Criminology: Theory, research, and policy* (2nd ed.). Boston: Jones and Bartlett.

Weisz, A. N. (2002). Prosecution of batterers: Views of African American battered women. *Violence and Victims, 17*(1), 19–34.

Wheeler, J., & George, W. (2005). Race and sexual offending: An overview. In K. Barrett & W. George (Eds.), *Race, culture, psychology & law* (pp. 391–402). Thousand Oaks, CA: Sage.

Wooldredge, J., & Thistlethwaite, A. (2002). Reconsidering domestic violence recidivism: Conditioned effects of legal controls by individual and aggregate levels of stake in conformity. *Journal of Quantitative Criminology, 18*(1), 45–70.

Chapter Authors

Susan L. Miller is a Professor in the Department of Sociology and Criminal Justice at the University of Delaware. Her research interests include gender and crime and criminal justice policy issues related to violence against women. Her recent books include *Victims as Offenders: The Paradox of Women's Violence in Relationships* (Rutgers University Press, 2005) and *Criminal Justice Research and Practice: Diverse Voices from the Field* (Northeastern University Press, 2007). Her forthcoming book, *After the Crime: The Power of Restorative Justice Dialogues Between Victims and Violent Offenders* (NYU Press), explores gendered violence and restorative justice issues.

LeeAnn Iovanni holds a Ph.D. in criminology from the University of Maryland and is a Lecturer in the Department of Sociology, Social Work, and Organization at Aalborg University in Denmark. She has published in the areas of labeling theory; deterrence-social control theory as it relates to juvenile delinquency and to dating violence; gender and crime; U.S. criminal justice responses to violence against women; and gendered violence in the Nordic context within a larger European effort to unify research, policy, and practice on interpersonal violence.

Kathleen D. Kelley is a doctoral graduate student in the Department of Sociology and Criminal Justice at the University of Delaware. She received her master's degree in criminal justice from Michigan State University, where she worked on research evaluating the effectiveness of Sexual Assault Nurse Examiners. Her current research interests include violence against women, intersectionality, qualitative methods, and evaluation research.

Personal Reflection

Kathleen Ferraro

I became interested in the criminal justice response to intimate partner violence and sexual assault in the mid-1970s through a confluence of personal, political, and intellectual influences. In 1974 and 1975, while I was a graduate student in sociology at Arizona State University, my first husband subjected me to what later became known as "domestic violence." When I left him and went to stay with friends, he promised "they'll find you in a bloody pool in your office," and he came to my friends' home to drag me back. They called the police, who arrived promptly and told him to leave. While I cowered in the closet, he told the officers, "I'll leave now, but I'll be back and do something through the window and you'll never be able to stop me." An officer put a fatherly arm around his shoulder and said, "Ah, you don't wanna do that now. She's not worth it. Go on home." I was grateful to the officer for getting him to leave. But it was the relatively privileged social status I enjoyed, and the support I received from my circle of family and friends, that enabled my successful escape from that relationship. I never saw him again.

It is hard to imagine, but in 1975 the global battered women's movement was just beginning. The concepts "battered woman" and "domestic violence" had not yet been developed. One of my professors, Erdwin H. Pfuhl, encouraged me to think sociologically about my own abuse, and another, David L. Altheide, gave me the opportunity to begin my first ethnographic project on domestic violence. In 1975, I interviewed the directors of two of the first shelters in the country, Betty Ryan at Faith House and Joanne Rhoades at Rainbow Retreat, both in Phoenix, Arizona. I began working as a volunteer at Rainbow Retreat and gathered data for my first publication, "Hard Love: Letting Go of an Abusive Husband," based on the Al-Anon philosophy of these early shelters. I was awed by these two survivors' passion and commitment to help other women, but I also knew that alcoholism was not the primary cause of abuse. I joined with a group of people to start a shelter, Friends of the Family, that was not oriented toward alcoholism, and that shelter became the site of my dissertation research. I have been studying and working in the movement to end violence against women ever since.

The scholars and activists I have worked with and admired never viewed the criminalization of intimate partner violence as the primary or most significant strategy for addressing violence. We supported enhancing police power to arrest, encouraging arrest where appropriate, and providing support to survivors through the criminal justice process. But our goals were much more expansive, and we were cognizant of the limitations of the criminal justice system for solving deeply embedded social and structural phenomena. We wanted to transform unequal sexual relationships and provide women with the practical and emotional resources for living safe and joyful lives. The conservative political agendas of the 1980s and 1990s pushed these more expansive goals aside as the United States decreased expenditures on social welfare and increased spending on incarceration. I find it ironic when students tell me that the early battered women's movement was a middle-class white women's movement. This notion obscures the crucial contributions of heterosexual and lesbian women from all socioeconomic and racial and ethnic groups and validates the state's cooptation of the movement as the legitimate history of the battered women's movement.

Today, in activism and scholarship, I see a more sophisticated and nuanced understanding of the phenomenon we now call intimate partner violence, as well as of the role of the state in addressing it. There is awareness of the diversity of women's experiences and needs and the negative ramifications of mandating a uniform response to intimate partner violence. I still hear more discussion of "holding batterers accountable" than of holding the community accountable for the well-being of all its members. It is important that all individuals take responsibility for their actions. It is equally important that communities at the local, state, national, and global levels take responsibility for ensuring a just and peaceful world. A society that extracts individual accountability in the absence of social accountability is inherently unjust and inevitably violent.

CHAPTER 15

Health Care for Survivors of Partner and Sexual Violence

Rebecca J. Macy, Dania M. Ermentrout, and Natalie B. Johns

Introduction

Although the health care field has shown a growing awareness of the problem of violence against women, the misperception persists that partner and sexual violence are not issues of concern for health care providers. The problem of violence against women is often thought of as a social problem, one which requires only social interventions. In fact, violence survivors are helped by services that provide legal advocacy in addition to social, economic, and housing support services (R. Campbell, 2006; Roberts & Roberts, 2002). Nevertheless, clear empirical evidence shows the profoundly negative effects of violence on women's physical and mental health. Thus, partner and sexual violence are issues deserving of health care providers' attention and concern. However, the assessment and care of violence survivors in the health care context is not always considered a best or necessary practice (Plichta, 2007). This viewpoint is perpetuated by the unfortunate, long-standing disconnect between the field of domestic violence/sexual assault services and the fields of physical and behavioral/mental health care (Gondolf, 1998; Logan, Walker, Cole, & Leukefeld, 2002; O'Campo, Ahmad, & Cyriac, 2008).

This disconnect is further exacerbated by communication barriers, both real and perceived, between health care providers and violence survivors (Plichta & Falik, 2001; Robinson & Spilsbury, 2008). A recent review of partner violence survivors' experiences of health care found that survivors' lack of privacy in health care settings, providers' inappropriate responses to disclosures, and providers' lack of understanding regarding the emotional consequences of abuse are reasons for survivors' hesitancy to disclose their experiences of violent victimization (Robinson & Spilsbury, 2008). Moreover, the Commonwealth Fund's Survey of Women's Health showed that survivors' reticence to speak with health care providers is not entirely responsible for the communication gap. Of the approximately 30% of women who had discussed their experiences of violence with their providers, 74% had initiated the conversation (Plichta & Falik, 2001). As noted in several chart reviews reported by Hamberger and Phelan (2004), documentation of sexual and partner violence screening and assessment also suffers; only 1% to 4% of charts of patients identified as victims of abuse contained the appropriate documentation. Even when health care practices are put in place to help violence survivors, such services are not universally available or always offered to violence survivors. For example, a recent review of research on emergency services for sexual assault survivors showed that options such as routine screening for sexually transmitted infections, HIV postexposure prophylaxis, and emergency contraception were not routinely provided to all women who sought emergency department services after rape (Martin, Young, Billings, & Bross, 2007).

Health care services are a critical area for violence intervention because survivors not only often seek health care following an assault but will almost certainly seek health care at some point in their lives. If they are well-prepared to address violence, health care providers could play a critical role in connecting survivors with safety services and helping survivors to recover from the trauma and health problems associated with violent victimization (J. Campbell, 2002; Plichta, 2007). Moreover, early identification and response to violent victimization can mitigate health problems (Coker et al., 2002; O'Campo et al., 2008). Nonetheless, many physical and behavioral health care providers are not trained to (a) assess for violence among their patients, (b) work sensitively with violence survivors, or (c) treat violence survivors in ways informed by trauma research (Hamberger & Phelan, 2004; Martin, Young et al., 2007). Health providers have described feeling unprepared to work with violence survivors (O'Reilly, 2007). This lack of training can cause serious problems for survivors who seek health care services from poorly prepared providers. Specifically, survivors report *secondary victimization* by health care providers, a term that

describes survivors being discounted, stigmatized, or marginalized (R. Campbell, 2006).

The aim of this chapter is to help bridge these disconnects by informing readers about six crucial aspects of health care for violence survivors: (1) the physical and mental health consequences of partner and sexual violence, (2) the ways in which violence survivors typically access and use health care services, (3) the current best practices for the assessment of violence with health care patients, (4) the current best practices of crisis-focused health care responses to violence, (5) the issue of violence and health care during pregnancy and the postpartum period, and (6) the concept of trauma-informed health care practices. We based this chapter on the best available empirical evidence. However, the research presented is neither a comprehensive nor a critical review of the literature. Rather, this chapter is based on an overview of the existing research. Table 15.1 illustrates the health care issues we discuss by providing readers with a case scenario of a violence survivor and the corresponding health care strategies.

Physical and Mental Health: The Connections to Partner and Sexual Violence

Physical Health

Partner and sexual violence often lead to physical injuries (J. Campbell, 2002). Medical records of violence survivors have documented various injuries including scratches, bruises, welts, broken bones, head trauma, and spinal cord injuries. Research also shows 50% to 90% of rape survivors have genital injuries (Sommers, 2007). In addition, most partner violence survivors have numerous injuries in multiple locations, with the head, neck, and face the most common locations (Sheridan & Nash, 2007). Injuries are inflicted with various mechanisms, the most frequent of which are blows from a

Table 15.1	Violence Survivor Case Scenario and Health Care Strategies and Interventions

Case Scenario	Health Care Strategies and Interventions
Gloria is a 48-year-old woman who balances weekend work as a licensed practical nurse at a nursing home with her duties as the president of her church women's guild. During the week, she is also a part-time caregiver for her infant granddaughter. Gloria's schedule leaves little time to address her health concerns, which include uncontrolled diabetes and hypertension. Calvin, Gloria's husband of 30 years, has been on the police force in their community for more than two decades, and he plans to retire within five years. Recently, before a shift at the nursing home, Gloria tearfully admitted to her supervisor, Alma, that she would be unable to complete her duties that day due to a recent injury to her right arm. Concerned, Alma asked her about the injuries, and Gloria admitted to a fall at home. Actually, Gloria was injured in an assault perpetrated by Calvin that included sexual violence. Alma offered to take Gloria to the emergency department of the community hospital. Gloria reluctantly agreed to go with Alma but was extremely concerned that reporting her husband's violence might cause him to lose his job, pension, and the health insurance she needs.	**Assessment Strategies:** • After treating Gloria's injury and explaining the confidential nature of their discussion, health care provider assesses Gloria for partner violence in a private room • Provider responds to Gloria's disclosure with support and validation • Provider offers Gloria the services of a Sexual Assault Nurse Examiner (SANE) • Provider offers Gloria a meeting with a social worker and/or violence advocate • Provider documents abuse, treatment, and referrals • If Gloria declines meetings with a social worker, advocate, or SANE, the provider offers Gloria a wallet-sized information card about safety (but only if it is safe for her to take the card) **Crisis Interventions:** • SANE assesses and addresses Gloria's health needs resulting from sexual assault • SANE documents evidence of sexual assault • Social worker and/or violence advocate conduct(s) psychosocial and lethality assessment with Gloria • Social worker and/or advocate develop(s) safety plan with Gloria • Advocate offers shelter, counseling, and/or support group services to Gloria • Social worker connects Gloria with a primary care provider (PCP) in a medical home for treatment of chronic health problems **Ongoing Interventions:** • Gloria remains in the relationship with Calvin, but she agrees to attend individual counseling at a domestic violence agency to learn more about partner violence and safety • Gloria sees a PCP for treatment of her diabetes and hypertension; the PCP regularly assesses and documents any violence Gloria experiences • With Gloria's permission, her domestic violence counselor and PCP communicate regularly and collaborate to facilitate Gloria's health care treatment and promote her safety

hand or strangulation (Sheridan & Nash, 2007). Other research has shown that 11% to 30% of women presenting in U.S. emergency departments with injuries were there because of partner violence (J. Campbell, 2002).

Evidence shows that, as compared with women who have not experienced violent victimization, survivors are more likely to develop persistent and/or recurring physical health problems (Caldwell & Redeker, 2005; J. Campbell, 2002; Coker, 2007; Macy, Ferron, & Crosby, 2009; Martin, Macy, & Young, in press). Further, this research shows that survivors frequently suffer from co-occurring physical health problems and that the severity of physical health problems survivors experience may be so profound they result in functional disability. Health problems likely experienced by violence survivors include sleep disorders as well as chronic pain disorders such as back and neck pain, migraines and headaches, pelvic pain, and arthritis. Violence survivors are also more likely than women who have not experienced violent victimization to have reproductive health problems, such as dysmenorrhea, menorrhagia, sexual dysfunction, and sexually transmitted diseases. Increased rates of gastrointestinal disorders, including stomach ulcers, spastic colon, gastric reflux, indigestion, and diarrhea, are also found among violence survivors. This research also shows that violence is associated with conditions such as hearing loss and heart disease.

Evidence indicates that violence has direct and indirect effects on women's health (J. Campbell, 2002; Coker, Smith, Bethea, King, & McKeown, 2000; Coker et al., 2002). The direct physical health effects, both acute and chronic, result from the injuries sustained during one or more violent assaults. For example, a woman who presents to a health care provider with unexplained chronic pain may be a partner violence survivor with repeated injuries that were previously untreated. The indirect effects of violence on women's health tend to be more insidious, but current—albeit preliminary—research helps illuminate the connections between violence

and disease. One explanation of the mechanism behind the indirect health effects of violence is that survivors have increased levels of chronic inflammation (i.e., increased levels of proinflammatory cytokines; Kendall-Tackett, 2007). This chronic inflammation occurs in response to the psychological consequences of victimization, including depression, hostility, and sleep disturbances. In turn, chronic inflammation impairs survivors' health and leads to conditions such as chronic pain, cardiovascular disease, diabetes, and metabolic syndrome (i.e., the precursor to diabetes).

Mental Health

Relative to women who have not been violently victimized, survivors are more likely to have mental health problems such as depression, anxiety, Posttraumatic Stress Disorder (PTSD), substance abuse, suicidal ideations (e.g., thoughts about wanting to die or that life is not worth living; forming suicide plans), and suicide attempts (J. Campbell, 2002; Logan et al., 2002; Macy et al., 2009; Martin et al., in press). For some survivors, these mental health problems are severe and disabling. Survivors are also likely to have multiple mental health problems, such as the co-occurrence of depression and PTSD.

Many survivors also struggle with substance-related disorders (i.e., substance abuse or substance dependence). Mounting evidence shows that, for some survivors, their misuse or abuse of substances is an effort to manage the psychological effects, trauma symptoms, and mental health problems stemming from violence (Kilpatrick, Acierno, Resnick, Saunders, & Best, 1997; Logan et al., 2002). Further, survivors misuse or abuse a range of substances, including alcohol, illegal drugs, prescription medicines, and tobacco (Logan et al., 2002; Macy et al., 2009; Martin et al., in press). Survivors' use of tobacco may be the mechanism related to some of the chronic physical health problems noted above (e.g., heart disease).

Variation in Health Consequences of Violence

Although the relationship between violence and health has been clearly established, not all violence survivors will experience physical or mental health problems. Further, among survivors who develop health problems, research has shown that the health effects of violence may diminish over time (Macy et al., 2009; Martin et al., in press). That is, as women are able to secure their safety and recover from violence, their health improves. However, because of the severity of the violence experienced, some women may be at greater life-long risk for health problems even after violence has ended. Severe forms of partner and sexual violence have the most serious impact on women's health (J. Campbell, 2002; Martin et al., in press). Some violence researchers have described this phenomenon using the phrase *dose-dependent effect of violence* (J. Campbell, 2002; Coker et al., 2002), which means that as the severity of violence increases, women report increasingly severe health consequences in predictable ways. Moreover, as compared with women who reported a single incident of violent victimization, women who experience repeated victimizations (from the same or different perpetrators) are more likely to report greater incidence and severity of physical and mental health problems (J. Campbell, 2002; Macy et al., 2009; Martin et al., in press).

Differences Between Physical, Sexual, and Psychological Violence

Physical, sexual, and psychological violence have different consequences for survivors' physical and mental health (Coker et al., 2002; Hamberger & Phelan, 2004; Plichta, 2007). Research has shown that sexual violence has an especially harmful effect on women's physical and mental health. As compared with women who experienced physical violence only, women who experienced sexual violence (alone or combined with physical violence) were more likely to develop serious health consequences (Macy et al., 2009; Martin et al., in press; McFarlane, 2007). Nonetheless, the consequences of physical and psychological violence can also be profound. It is noteworthy that psychological partner violence has negative health consequences and is as strongly associated with health problems as is physical partner violence (Coker et al., 2000; Coker et al., 2002).

Survivors Use of Health Care Services

Violence survivors use physical health services and behavioral health care (i.e., services for mental health and substance abuse) at least as often as women who are not violence survivors (Plichta, 2007). In fact, some research has shown that violence survivors use health care services such as prescriptions and hospital admissions more often than women who have not experienced violence (Coker et al., 2000; Tolman & Rosen, 2001). Consistent with the dose-dependent effect of violence described earlier, violence survivors tend to use more health care services as the severity of the violence increases (J. Campbell, 2002). Although partner violence survivors typically seek health care for symptom-based problems, some research shows that survivors are less likely to seek preventive health care such as annual gynecological exams and routine mammograms (Hamberger & Phelan, 2004).

Violence survivors may also experience difficulties in their efforts to treat their chronic physical and mental health problems. For example, HIV-positive women who are also struggling with partner violence may have problems complying with treatment regimens (Gielen, Ghandour, Burke, Mahoney, McDonnell, & O'Campo, 2007). These compliance difficulties, such as adhering to medication schedules and attending appointments, may stem from living with controlling, abusive partners who prevent survivors from addressing their health needs. Alternatively, violence survivors may not be able to fully engage in treatment because of co-occurring health disorders. For instance, the avoidance symptoms associated with PTSD may impede a woman from attending health care appointments. Thus, providers must be able to adapt treatment strategies to help survivors fully engage as partners in their health care. Later in this chapter (and in Table 15.2), we present information about how providers can adapt their intervention strategies to engage and retain survivors in health care.

Assessing Violence in the Health Care Context

History and Controversy

A universal routine screening for partner violence, which encouraged primary care providers to ask all adult female patients about recent experiences of violence, was recommended by the American Medical Association in 1992. Similar recommendations were adopted by other professional associations (e.g., American Nursing Association, American College of Obstetricians and Gynecologists). As a result of these recommendations and the growing evidence base regarding the connections between violence and women's health, health care providers implemented violence screenings in various settings (e.g., emergency departments, primary care, maternity care; Spangaro, Zwi, & Poulos, 2009). However, violence screenings were not universally adopted, and, even where they are implemented, some health care providers "do a poor job of screening" for violence (Hamberger & Phelan, 2004, p. 159). In recent years, the practice of universal screening for violence has become a controversial topic. The U.S. Preventative Task Force concluded that, given the current dearth of randomized controlled trials that have investigated the effectiveness of violence screening and interventions that promote safety for violence survivors, there is insufficient evidence to warrant routine violence screening in primary care (Plichta, 2007; Spangaro et al., 2009). Further, a recent randomized controlled trial investigating partner violence screening in various health care settings showed insufficient evidence to support universal screening, though the findings also showed no harm from screening (MacMillan et al., 2009).

In the face of this ongoing debate, a chorus of violence researchers continues to call for universal screening and assessment for several reasons: (a) the pervasiveness of violence against women; (b) the health implications of violence; (c) the fact that violence against women frequently goes undetected without screening and assessment by health care providers; (d) the fact that most women, whether they have experienced violence or not, welcome health care providers' inquiry about their safety; (e) the clinical importance of accounting for violence when treating women's health problems; and (f) the preliminary evidence showing that assessment leads to increases in safety behaviors and decreases in violence (O'Campo et al., 2008; Plichta, 2007; Robinson & Spilsbury, 2008; Spangaro et al., 2009).

Best Practices in Assessment

Preliminary research shows that violence assessments may have a therapeutic effect as an intervention (Robinson & Spilsbury, 2008; Spangaro et al., 2009). Thus, asking women about violent victimization is best practiced as an assessment intervention rather than a straightforward screening technique. Therefore, when providers raise the issues of abuse and violence, they should be prepared to engage in a conversation with patients. In addition, establishing a trusting and supportive relationship with patients, even during brief clinical encounters, is likely to facilitate women's disclosure of violence, which will allow providers to obtain accurate information about violence (Plichta, 2007; Robinson & Spilsbury, 2008).

Privacy and Confidentiality. Providers should carefully consider the physical setting where they conduct violence assessments. Privacy and confidentiality are paramount concerns for survivors because they are often worried about the repercussions of their disclosure of violence, including the violent partner learning about the disclosure, involvement with child protective services and possible subsequent removal of children, stigmatization, and responses suggestive of victim blaming (Hamberger & Phelan, 2004). Health care researchers have strongly recommended conducting assessments in private offices and rooms, outside the hearing of family members and intimate partners (Robinson & Spilsbury, 2008). These researchers have also reported that some health care providers have given well-intentioned but harmful responses to survivors' disclosures of violence. Harmful responses include actions such as confronting the violent partner or asking the survivor about the cause of injuries while a violent partner is present (Robinson & Spilsbury, 2008). These types of reactions and providers' breaches of confidentiality may only serve to place a woman in greater danger. Thus, providers should emphasize physical privacy as well as be mindful of the confidentiality of any information the woman gives about violence and abuse (Plichta, 2007).

Environmental Considerations. The assessment intervention begins in the waiting room and extends into the offices where medical exams and procedures occur. Women have reported that they appreciate waiting room displays of informative posters and pamphlets about violence that provide details about how they can access help for violent victimization (e.g., contact information for community-based domestic violence and sexual assault agencies; Robinson & Spilsbury, 2008). Information in areas such as waiting rooms, private examination rooms, and patients' restrooms (McNutt, Carlson, Rose, & Robinson, 2002) may signal to women that the providers who work there can offer help for violence survivors. In addition, the strategic placement of pamphlets

and flyers may provide women who are not ready to disclose to a provider with enough information to access help on their own.

Assessment Strategies. The assessment intervention for violence includes asking female patients about abuse and validating women's positive responses (i.e., providing a clear message that the violence was not her fault and that the perpetrator was wrong; showing concern for her well-being). We encourage providers to use valid, standardized instruments to facilitate these assessments. A compendium of partner and sexual violence assessment instruments for use in health care settings is available from the Centers for Disease Control and Prevention (CDC); we recommend that readers obtain a copy of these assessment tools for use in their own practices (Basile, Hertz, & Back, 2007). In addition, Table 15.1 is available as a discussion tool for the review of relevant assessment strategies in a violence survivor case scenario.

While receiving and responding to information about abuse, health care providers should be prepared to show their compassion by using nonjudgmental and active listening approaches in their discussions of violence with survivors (Plichta, 2007; Robinson & Spilsbury, 2008). In addition, providers should be prepared to explain how violence is likely to affect the patient's health but should never pressure a survivor into a specific course of action (Plichta, 2007).

Providers should be certain to refer survivors to safety and violence services. To facilitate these referrals, health care providers should be ready with current information about how and where survivors can access help in their communities (O'Campo et al., 2008; Plichta, 2007; Robinson & Spilsbury, 2008). Referrals can be offered in efficient and practical ways. For example, one study found a reduction in violence and an increase in safety actions among survivors who received a wallet-sized referral card with safety planning information and contact information for safety services (i.e., shelter, legal aid, counseling, and police) as part of an assessment for abuse (McFarlane, Groff, O'Brien, & Watson, 2006). Last, providers should document the abuse and any related interventions and referrals to alert other providers in the treatment facility to the survivors' needs, to facilitate the continuity of care (O'Campo et al., 2008).

Crisis-Focused Health Care for Violence Survivors

Crisis-Focused Health Care Responses for Partner Violence

The emergency department presents a unique opportunity for health care providers to intervene in the problem of partner violence. Of all the areas of health care practice, providers are especially likely to encounter survivors of partner violence in the emergency department (J. Campbell, 2002). In addition, survivors may be especially receptive to engaging in safety services if a crisis event triggered their decision to actively seek emergency health care (Hamberger & Phelan, 2004). Thus, health care providers in the emergency department play a key role in the secondary prevention of partner violence.

A team approach (as illustrated in Table 15.1) is considered a best practice crisis-focused health care response in the emergency department. Using this approach, the emergency medicine providers collaborate with clinic-based social workers or community-based domestic violence advocates to provide both health care and safety services to the survivor (Hamberger & Phelan, 2004; Harris & Weber, 2002; Roberts & Roberts, 2002). The physician leads the team's efforts to assess the patient for violence victimization, obtain a trauma history, and diagnose and treat urgent medical needs. The social worker, in collaboration with the domestic violence advocate (if one is available), leads the team's efforts to assess the survivor's psychosocial needs and resources, conduct a lethality assessment, and develop a comprehensive safety plan for the survivor and her children. (Detailed information about comprehensive safety planning strategies is available through these resources: Gondolf, 1998; Roberts & Roberts, 2002.) In addition, the treatment team should document the effects of the violent assault; such documentation will be needed as supporting evidence, if the survivor decides to pursue criminal charges against the perpetrator (Roberts & Roberts, 2002). If the survivor gives her consent, this documentation should include photographs of the injuries.

The team should also be mindful that sexual violence commonly occurs in the context of partner violence (McFarlane et al., 2005). Therefore, the team needs to be prepared to provide sexual violence crisis-focused health care to the survivor, and a Sexual Assault Nurse Examiner (SANE) should be included as a member of the treatment team. As described below, the documentation of sexual violence requires additional training and expertise.

Crisis-Focused Health Care Responses for Sexual Violence

Over the last 25 years, the health care community has made considerable strides in its response to sexual assault, such as the development of forensic examination protocols that are sensitive to traumatized sexual assault survivors (Green & Panacek, 2005; Sommers, 2007). Nationally, standardized guidelines for examination, documentation, evidence collection, and evidence handling procedures have been developed as a result of collaborative efforts of the Federal Department of Justice and the Office on Violence Against Women (Green & Panacek, 2005). Nevertheless, most health care providers are unfamiliar with evidentiary procedures and crisis intervention techniques for sexual violence survivors who may present for health care services in the aftermath of an assault (Acosta, 2002; Martin, Young et al., 2007). Unfortunately, misguided kindnesses toward survivors, a lack of clarity with respect to instructions for survivors, the absence of formal role assignments regarding who attends to sexual violence survivors, or the lack of formal procedures for handling evidence often results in the destruction of key evidence (Acosta, 2002).

SANE Programs. Developed in 1976, SANE programs train forensic nurses with specific skills in conducting an array of services needed by sexual assault survivors. Key services provided by SANEs include assessment, physical examination, medical diagnosis and treatment under the supervision of a physician, referral to outside resources, evidence collection, documentation, and crisis intervention (Houmes, Fagan, & Quintana, 2003). SANE programs often function within a larger, multidisciplinary service delivery system known as a Sexual Assault Response Team (SART; Houmes et al., 2003). SARTs offer a coordinated community response to sexual assault that links survivors to representatives from the hospital, district attorney's office, law enforcement, crime laboratory, and victim advocacy organizations (Green & Panacek, 2005; Osterman, Barbiaz, & Johnson, 2001). SANE providers are able to provide immediate, skilled response to victims of sexual assault in an emergency health care setting that includes medical management of health care needs, objective forensic examination that complies with medical and legal protocols, and referral to other SART members and community resources (Houmes et al., 2003).

SANE Goals. SANEs have a two-fold goal (Sommers, 2007). First, the SANE addresses the needs of the survivor by attending to the emotional consequences of the assault and to the survivor's health care needs (Green & Panacek, 2005). Second, the SANE seeks to address the crime that has occurred. In the case of sexual assault, the SANE provider's aim is to collect forensic evidence for use in criminal investigation or prosecution. Initial contact with survivors (e.g., through crisis hotlines, in the emergency department) should include counseling the survivor to preserve evidence. The survivor should be guided sensitively to avoid garment changes or cleaning that could potentially destroy evidence. A medical history

should include survivor disclosure of any sexual encounters in addition to the assault that may affect the examination and interpretation of any forensic findings. The provider should also take a detailed, comprehensive, and jargon-free account of the survivor's assault history. In addition, the provider should collect, document, and provide interpretation of forensic evidentiary materials obtained from the physical examination (e.g., semen, saliva, blood, hair, fiber, or skin samples) within the time limit afforded by the state's legal standards (R. Campbell, 1998; Green & Panacek, 2005; Osterman et al., 2001; Sommers, 2007).

It is important to emphasize that the SANE's goal is to collect potential evidence. Ultimately, legal authorities will determine the usefulness of this evidence, if the survivor decides to press charges. Thus, medical records need to be meticulous accounts of the examination and interpretation of findings. Moreover, these records should be objective (i.e., should not include judgments related to either the survivor or the perpetrator or conclusions about the criminal nature of the incident) and should be legible (Acosta, 2002). The SANE should also provide screening for alcohol, amnesic drugs associated with rape, and other drugs that may have left the survivor with impaired memory of the incident (Osterman et al., 2001).

The process of evidence collection may retraumatize the survivor, and considerable care is required when working with vulnerable patients post assault. As such, it is necessary to inform survivors about the purpose of the exam, the protocols that will be used, and their rights regarding consent, which should be obtained before any evidence is collected. Specific consent should be obtained for each step of evidence collection, including the examination, treatment for injuries, collection of photo evidence, and information release to law enforcement (Acosta, 2002). In addition to the formal consent process, discussion with the survivor in advance of each procedure assists the survivor to emotionally prepare for the examination and familiarizes her with the activities involved in evidence collection and medical care (Acosta, 2002). Survivors who are adequately prepared for procedures report experiencing less stress than those who do not receive such preparation. For example, survivors who viewed an informational video before the examination reported less stress related to the postassault examination than did survivors who did not view the video (Martin, Young et al., 2007). The SANE should also elicit the survivor's involvement in making medical decisions, facilitate the survivor's access to crisis intervention services, and arrange for the survivor's psychological assessment. Furthermore, referrals to long-term community-based sexual assault advocacy, counseling, and group support services need to be made available because survivors often prefer a combination of counseling and medical treatments (Martin, Young et al., 2007).

Benefits of SANE. SANE programs are beneficial to both sexual violence survivors and health care organizations for several reasons. The presence of SANEs in emergency health care settings ensures the ready availability of providers who are trained to work with survivors and conduct forensic examinations. In addition, SANE services are cost-effective ways to manage sexual assault because survivors' medical and forensic needs can be addressed by one provider in a single examination (Green & Panacek, 2005). Moreover, the specialized training received by SANEs ensures that proper, objective, and thorough forensic evidence collection and documentation will be provided (Osterman et al., 2001). Finally, SANEs are extensively trained to advocate on behalf of the victim as part of their clinical duties (Osterman et al., 2001). As a result, sexual assault victims are given comprehensive, sensitive care and appropriate referral during the post-assault crisis period.

Sexually Transmitted Infection Screening and Treatment. Another key aspect of health care providers' responses to sexual assault is screening and treatment for sexually transmitted infections (STIs). Though few rigorous studies have been

conducted to determine how many survivors contract an STI following sexual assault (Martin et al., in press), preliminary research shows that nearly a third of violence survivors are infected with STIs (Acosta, 2002; R. Campbell, 1998). Considering this rate, as well as high rates of underreporting for STIs, these figures indicate a need for crisis-focused health care to incorporate STI screening as an integral component of sexual assault response. Health care providers working with violence survivors should offer information and testing for all STIs because a high percentage of women may not be informed about the risks of contracting STIs (R. Campbell, 1998). Administration of a preventative dose of antibiotics to treat STIs potentially contracted during a sexual assault is also an important service that violence survivors have often requested from providers (R. Campbell, 1998).

HIV Postexposure Prophylaxis. HIV postexposure prophylaxis (PEP) is a medication treatment regimen offered to sexual assault victims within 72 hours of an assault, to reduce the risk of contracting HIV (CDC, 2007; Fong, 2001; Myles, Hirozawa, Katz, Kimmerling, & Bamberger, 2000). Survivors of sexual assault are usually concerned about contracting HIV (R. Campbell, 1998). However, definitive evidence that HIV PEP prevents HIV infection (or seroconversion) after sexual assault is lacking (CDC, 2007; Fong, 2001; Myles et al., 2000). In the absence of clear guidelines, some survivors of sexual assault agree to undergo the HIV PEP treatment; however, many survivors who accept PEP cannot complete the regimen because of the medication's side effects. The length, cost, and availability of HIV PEP treatment may result in additional barriers to its full and effective use (Fong, 2001; Martin, Young et al., 2007). To determine a best practice health care policy for HIV PEP, additional research is needed to investigate the potential for psychological harm from the HIV PEP treatment, the effectiveness of HIV PEP following sexual abuse, and the rates of HIV seroprevalence among sexual violence victims and perpetrators (Fong, 2001;

Myles et al., 2000). Recommendations for HIV PEP assessments for adult and adolescent survivors of sexual assault are available from the CDC (2007), and should be used to evaluate each potential exposure on a case-by-case basis when the HIV status of the source of the exposure is unknown or when factors of the assault are associated with significant risk (e.g., number of assailants or type of penetration; CDC, 2007; Fong, 2001).

Emergency Contraception. Health care providers working with victims of sexual assault should provide pregnancy prophylaxis following determination of current pregnancy status (Osterman et al., 2001). Although administration of the morning-after pill (i.e., ethinyl estradiol and norgestrel) can be offered as pregnancy prophylaxis, this treatment is not offered universally. Findings from one study showed that providers offered the morning-after pill only 38% of the time. In a national survey of female survivors of sexual assault, 60% of survivors were not informed about available services for pregnancy testing and prevention (R. Campbell, 1998). Information regarding effectiveness of prophylaxis (75% effective) should be provided as well as instructions to repeat the pregnancy screening if menstruation does not occur within 21 days (Osterman et al., 2001).

Medical Advocacy by Domestic Violence or Sexual Assault Personnel

Staff or volunteers from community-based domestic violence and sexual assault agencies frequently offer advocacy services for survivors who access health care services. The goal of medical advocacy is to support the survivor in the aftermath of violent assault by providing a combination of individual support and collaboration with outside organizations and service providers to ensure adequate, appropriate, and comprehensive service delivery (Harris & Weber, 2002;

Osterman et al., 2001). Providing advocacy for sexual violence survivors in the emergency department involves accompanying the victims during forensic medical examinations and psychological assessments, providing information on the specific roles of individuals involved in the survivor's care, and providing details of the expected medical and forensic examination procedures. Advocacy services also include addressing the survivor's concerns regarding future adverse health effects such as pregnancy and STIs, including HIV (Acosta, 2002; R. Campbell, 1998, 2006; Osterman et al., 2001). Likewise, domestic violence advocates may carry out similar tasks as well as assist survivors with safety planning (Harris & Weber, 2002). Both domestic violence and sexual assault advocates can also link survivors with counseling, support group, and shelter services.

Although the research on the efficacy of domestic violence and sexual assault medical advocacy is limited (Harris & Weber, 2002), preliminary findings show that advocacy is a promising practice. In a recent naturalistic quasi-experimental study, experiences of rape survivors who worked with advocates were compared to those of women who did not have advocacy services. Survivors assisted by advocates reported increased receipt of medical services, emergency contraception, and HIV PEP and significantly fewer negative interactions with health care providers (R. Campbell, 2006).

Health care providers can serve as essential conduits through which women can connect with medical advocates because many women are unaware that such advocates exist (R. Campbell, 2006). One way in which health care providers coordinate with these community-based advocacy services is to enroll in the training programs for volunteers that are offered by local domestic violence or sexual assault organizations. For health care providers, this training may instill confidence in the advocacy process and an appreciation for advocates' roles in a multidisciplinary system. Advocacy training can also increase a provider's familiarity with a range of issues, including the physical and psychological impact of assault, evidence collection, victims' legal rights, and the criminal justice process (R. Campbell, 2006).

Pregnancy and Postnatal Health Care for Violence Survivors

Partner and sexual violence occur during women's pregnancies and in the postpartum period (Jasinski, 2004; McFarlane, 2007). Research has shown that partner violence occurs in as many as 19% of all pregnancies (Sharps, Laughon, & Giangrande, 2007) and that partner violence "may be more common for women than preeclampsia or gestational diabetes" (Gazmararian, Petersen, Spitz, Goodwin, Saltzman, & Marks, 2000, p. 80).

Further, pregnancy sometimes begins with an act of violence (Martin et al., in press; McFarlane, 2007). One national study determined a pregnancy rate of 5% for every rape; this study also determined that half of these sexual assaults resulting in pregnancies were perpetrated by the women's husbands or partners (Holmes, Resnick, Kilpatrick, & Best, 1996). Similarly, another study found that 26% of women in the sample ($n = 77$) reported pregnancies following sexual assault by an intimate partner (McFarlane et al., 2005). Additional research with this same sample showed that women who became pregnant as a result of partner rape had lower rates of live births, higher rates of elective abortions, and higher PTSD scores relative to partner violence survivors who did not conceive through rape (McFarlane, 2007).

The insidious power and control dynamics that often characterize an abusive intimate relationship may also lead to pregnancy, with several researchers finding an association between partner violence and unintended pregnancy (Gazmararian et al., 2000; Pallitto, Campbell, & O'Campo, 2005). In abusive intimate relationships, women may not be able to control their sexual experiences, sexual lives, or reproductive choices (McFarlane, 2007). For example, a violent partner may prevent or limit women's access to and use of birth control. Unintended pregnancies occurring in the context of such partner violence are associated with induced abortions (Coker, 2007).

Violence, Pregnancy, and Health

Partner violence during pregnancy leads to health problems for both women and infants (Jasinski, 2004; O'Reilly, 2007; Sharps et al., 2007). Partner violence experienced during pregnancy increases the likelihood of health problems such as preterm delivery risk, premature rupture of membranes (i.e., "water breaking"), low birth weight infants, fetal trauma, and neonatal death. Women abused during pregnancy have been found to struggle with mental health problems, including postpartum depression (Jasinski, 2004). Furthermore, breastfeeding difficulties have been associated with partner violence (Jasinski, 2004).

Preliminary research has begun to explore the mechanisms by which partner violence during pregnancy results in health problems for women and infants. Research suggests that partner violence may result in maternal biologic changes, including higher cardiac response rates and increased levels of hormones such as cortisol and beta endorphins (Sharps et al., 2007). Such findings suggest that the woman's body responds to the stress associated with partner violence during pregnancy through physical changes that, in turn, lead to later health problems for the woman and her infant. In addition, research shows that violence increases the risk of unhealthy maternal behaviors, such as delayed prenatal care; poor nutrition; and increased rates of smoking and alcohol and drug use (Jasinski, 2004; O'Reilly, 2007). Thus, to the extent that women who are abused may be more likely to engage in unhealthy maternal behaviors (perhaps in an effort to cope with the violence) relative to women who are not abused, partner violence can have an indirect effect on maternal and infant health.

Window of Opportunity

Researchers have described the pregnancy and postpartum periods as a "window of opportunity" for helping women who are abused. Given that women develop relationships with health care professionals during their pregnancies, and many of those relationships are maintained into the postpartum period, researchers posit that these periods offer opportunities for providers to promote safety (Gazmararian et al., 2000; Jasinski, 2004; O'Reilly, 2007; Sharps et al., 2007). Such ongoing relationships may facilitate the trust women need to disclose abuse and seek help.

One of the few studies that investigated intervention effects among pregnant abused women ($n = 329$) used random assignment of participants to compare three types of interventions: a brief intervention, a counseling intervention, and an outreach intervention (McFarlane, Soeken, & Wiist, 2000). McFarlane and colleagues found that threats of violence and physical violence scores decreased among all study participants regardless of the intervention condition. This finding underscores the importance of conducting universal abuse assessments for all women—especially those who are pregnant—in health care settings. Recommendations for universal abuse assessments of pregnant and postpartum women are supported by findings from a research review of pregnancy-associated female homicides that estimated that 16% to 66% of these deaths were perpetrated by intimate partners (Martin, Macy, Sullivan, & Magee, 2007). This study also found that many of these victims had used health care services before their death; however, their health care providers did not know about the violence in their lives, and these victims were never referred to safety services.

Trauma-Informed Health Care for Violence Survivors

Trauma-informed services are a relatively new but promising development in the area of health care for violence survivors (Elliott, Bjelajac, Fallot, Markoff, & Reed, 2005; Fallot & Harris, 2002; Gondolf, 1998; Harris & Fallot, 2001; Markoff, Reed, Fallot, Elliott, & Bjelajac, 2005). Trauma-informed services are based on the assumptions that health care systems and practices can be adapted to account for patients' experiences of violent victimization and that those adaptations will facilitate survivors' engagement in health care services. Trauma-informed services are a treatment framework or service philosophy in which many interventions could potentially be used (Fallott & Harris, 2002). Table 15.2 provides a list of recommended strategies for trauma-informed services and their associated interventions. Strategies for trauma-informed services were developed in the context of mental health and substance abuse treatment; however, the recommendations presented in Table 15.2 also have implications for physical health care. Although presenting detailed information on all aspects of trauma-informed health care services is beyond the scope of this discussion, we provide an overview of this treatment approach and encourage readers to refer to the literature cited for additional details.

Recommended Service Strategies for Trauma-Informed Care of Survivors

Trauma-informed services build from what is empirically known about survivors' lives, their health problems, and the ways that survivors most frequently seek health care services. For example, successful health care interventions for survivors address the complex nature of women's lives, including their roles as mothers (Elliott et al., 2005; Logan et al., 2002). To deliver services in ways that are consistent with a trauma-informed philosophy, providers should anticipate helping women with child care, child custody, and other related issues by offering service referrals and care coordination. Another example of a strategy for trauma-informed service delivery is one in which providers address survivors' co-occurring problems and disorders with concurrent, comprehensive treatment

Table 15.2   Summary of Trauma-Informed Service Strategies

Service Strategy	Associated Interventions	Citations
Recognize impact of violence on human development and survivors' coping, including how survivors' social context affects the impact of violence (e.g., how survivors' lack of resources makes it difficult to achieve safety)	• Help survivors understand how their current behaviors (presenting problems) developed in response to violence and helped survivors cope with violence • Help survivors understand how the social context facilitates or impedes their safety and recovery from violent trauma	• Elliott et al., 2005 • Gondolf, 1998 • Harris & Fallot, 2001 • Markoff et al., 2005
Address co-occurring problems concurrently and comprehensively	• Make recovery from violence and trauma a focus of health care service • Implement services for various health problems simultaneously and in coordination with one another	• Elliott et al., 2005 • Gondolf, 1998 • Logan et al., 2002 • Markoff et al., 2005
Use empowerment philosophy and framework to inform and guide service delivery	• Help survivors gain skills, build internal strengths and resources, and develop interpersonal networks to become less reliant on formal services	• Elliott et al., 2005 • Gondolf, 1998 • Harris & Fallot, 2001
Maximize survivors' choice and control of treatment	• Offer survivors information to enable informed choices about service decisions	• Elliott et al., 2005 • Harris & Fallot, 2001
Establish collaborative relationship with survivors	• Engage survivors in a partnership to maximize survivors' control of treatment as much as possible • Acknowledge power differences in provider and patient relationship	• Elliott et al., 2005 • Harris & Fallot, 2001 • Markoff et al., 2005
Emphasize survivors' resilience	• Stress survivors' adaptive capacities and coping strategies • Deemphasize pathology and symptoms as much as possible	• Elliott et al., 2005 • Gondolf, 1998 • Harris & Fallot, 2001
Minimize the possibility of retraumatization	• Recognize potential of retraumatization from treatments • Minimize use of services and treatments that may have traumatizing effects	• Elliott et al., 2005 • Markoff et al., 2005
Emphasize culturally competent and culturally relevant service delivery practices	• Make treatment relevant for survivors' cultural heritage and context • Collaborate with community workers and advocates from nonmajority community groups for consultation and referral	• Bent-Goodley, 2005 • Elliott et al., 2005 • Gondolf, 1998

Service Strategy	Associated Interventions	Citations
Garner survivors' input into development, delivery, and evaluation of services	• Invite recovered survivors (i.e., survivors who no longer need services) to serve on advisory boards • Invite survivors to participate in service evaluations • Integrate peer-led services into treatment programs (e.g., recovered survivors serve as co-facilitators of groups, outreach workers, or resource specialists)	• Elliott et al., 2005 • Markoff et al., 2005
Provide services in a safe manner	• Deliver services in facilities that ensure survivors' safety, confidentiality, and privacy • Work collaboratively with community domestic violence/sexual assault services to facilitate survivors' safety; offer referrals and care coordination	• Elliott et al., 2005 • Logan et al., 2002
Make services accessible and readily available to survivors	• Offer comprehensive services in one location • Offer services in flexible ways to accommodate survivors' schedules and life responsibilities (e.g., work, parenting)	• Elliott et al., 2005 • Gondolf, 1998 • Logan et al., 2002 • Markoff et al., 2005
Encourage trauma-informed service delivery in the health care organization	• Organizational policies reflect trauma-informed service strategies listed above • All personnel in the health care organization are trained in trauma-informed practices	• Elliott et al., 2005 • Gondolf, 1998 • Harris & Fallot, 2001 • Markoff et al., 2005

strategies. As Logan and colleagues (2002) stated, "providers should avoid the idea that treating one [health problem] is more important or will resolve the other" (p. 355). Moreover, providers should offer comprehensive services in one location, to make the full array of health care services accessible. Further, the interventions should be offered with as much flexibility in scheduling as possible, to accommodate patients' schedules and life responsibilities (e.g., work, parenting).

Considerations of Cultural Relevance

Another critical aspect of trauma-informed service delivery is the consideration of cultural relevance. With a diverse patient population comes the need for culturally relevant services.

Unfortunately, only limited empirical evaluations of the cultural relevance of health care practices for violence survivors have been conducted among women who are not from majority populations or cultural groups (e.g., women of color; recent immigrants; women whose first language is not English; women with disabilities; and lesbian, bisexual, and transgendered women; Lee, Thompson, & Mechanic, 2002). Violence services have been largely developed and evaluated in "culturally neutral" ways (Bent-Goodley, 2005, p. 196). Culturally neutral service development often means that survivors who are not a part of the majority culture are less likely to seek formal services because these services will be—at best—unresponsive to their needs and—at worst—harmful to the women and their families (Bent-Goodley, 2005; Lee et al., 2002).

Even with the dearth of evidence-based interventions to guide their efforts, providers and health care organizations can implement strategies to ensure the cultural relevance of their practices. For example, providers should develop collaborative relationships with community workers and advocates in nonmajority cultural community groups (Gondolf, 1998). These community-based personnel can be invaluable resources for patient referral as well as clinician consultation. In addition, health care organizations should seek to be involved and to build relationships with community groups through engagement activities such as mutual board representation, interagency training, and collaborative community events. Such organizational-group relationships and collaboration with community-based personnel can facilitate interagency patient referrals and care coordination, as well as help to ensure the cultural relevance of the health care organization's policies and practices (Gondolf, 1998).

Limited Research on Trauma-Informed Services

When readers are considering the implementation of trauma-informed services in their practice, we encourage them to be mindful that only preliminary research is available on the efficacy of these service strategies, and more work is needed to clearly establish the efficacy of this framework. However, Morrissey, Jackson, Ellis, Amaro, Brown, and Najavits' (2005) initial findings from a large, multisite, quasi-experimental study showed implementation of trauma-informed strategies had positive benefits for women's trauma and mental health symptoms. On the other hand, similar effects for substance abuse were not found (Morrissey et al., 2005). Given the promise of these initial findings, we urge additional research efforts to extend this work and further investigate the effectiveness of trauma-informed services in diverse health care settings.

Conclusion

Violence against women is a health issue deserving of health care providers' concern and attention. Violence has negative consequences for women's health throughout the life span, including pregnancy. Moreover, the range of health problems discussed in this chapter shows that violence against women is both an acute and a chronic problem, requiring both short- and long-term health care interventions (O'Campo et al., 2008; Plichta, 2007; Spangaro et al., 2009). This chapter also highlights the critical gaps in the health care service system and challenges facing violence survivors who seek health care. To address these system gaps and challenges, health care providers, advocates, researchers, and survivors must collaborate to find creative solutions and innovative approaches. Although myriad health care issues could benefit from such collective efforts, we recommend two areas as especially deserving of attention.

First, much of the research we have cited recommends changes at the policy, organizational, and systems level to improve physical and behavioral health care for violence survivors (R. Campbell, 1998; Hamberger & Phelan, 2004; O'Campo et al., 2008; Plichta, 2007; Robinson & Spilsbury, 2008). This body of research shows that although efforts by individual health care providers to assess for violence and to treat violence survivors in trauma-informed ways are important, gains from such individual-level efforts are likely to have random, haphazard benefits for survivors and are unlikely to be sustained. Thus, organizational, community, and systemic changes are needed to improve health care for violence survivors. Unfortunately, such changes are hampered by the dearth of innovative policies or organizational/systems models to inform such change strategies. Moreover, little research exists to support the efficacy of interventions at the policy, organizational, and systems levels (Plichta, 2007). We strongly urge health care providers, health researchers, violence advocates, and violence researchers to collaborate with violence survivors in the development and rigorous investigation of policy, organizational, and system change strategies.

Second, the lack of evidence-based health care practices and safety services for violence survivors is a tremendous concern. These serious intervention knowledge gaps prohibit the advancement of health care services for survivors (MacMillan et al., 2009). Considerable work is needed to develop an array of evidence-based health care interventions, as well as evidence-based safety services for violence survivors. Many areas of health care practice have little or no evidence to guide providers in addressing health and violence. As before, we urge health care providers, health researchers, violence advocates, and violence researchers to collaborate with violence survivors to develop and rigorously investigate physical and behavioral health care practices for violence survivors.

References

Acosta, M. L. (2002). Collecting evidence for domestic and sexual assault: Highlighting violence against women in health care system interventions. *International Federation of Gynecology and Obstetrics, 78,* 99–104.

Basile, K. C., Hertz, M. F., & Back, S. E. (2007). *Intimate partner violence and sexual violence victimization assessment instruments for use in health care settings: Version 1.* Atlanta, GA: Centers for Disease Control and Prevention, National Center for Injury Prevention and Control.

Bent-Goodley, T. B. (2005). Culture and domestic violence: Transforming knowledge development. *Journal of Interpersonal Violence, 20*(2), 195–203.

Caldwell, B. A., & Redeker, N. (2005). Sleep and trauma: An overview. *Issues in Mental Health Nursing, 26,* 721–738.

Campbell, J. (2002). Health consequences of intimate partner violence. *Lancet, 359,* 1331–1336.

Campbell, R. (1998). The community response to rape: Victims' experiences with the legal, medical, and mental health systems. *American Journal of Community Psychology, 26,* 355–379.

Campbell, R. (2006). Rape survivors' experiences with the legal and medical systems: Do rape victim advocates make a difference? *Violence Against Women, 12,* 30–45.

Centers for Disease Control and Prevention. (2007). *2006 Sexually transmitted diseases treatment guidelines.* Retrieved July 23, 2009, from http://www.cdc.gov/std/treatment/2006/sexual-assault.htm.

Coker, A. L. (2007). Does physical intimate partner violence affect sexual health? A systematic review. *Trauma, Violence & Abuse, 8*(2), 149–177.

Coker, A. L., Davis, K., Arias, I., Desai, S., Sanderson, M., Brandt, H., et al. (2002). Physical and mental health effects of intimate partner violence for men and women. *American Journal of Preventive Medicine, 23*(4), 260–268.

Coker, A. L., Smith, P. H., Bethea, L., King, M., & McKeown, R. (2000). Physical health consequences of physical and psychological intimate partner violence. *Archives of Family Medicine, 9,* 451–457.

Elliott, D., Bjelajac, P., Fallot, R., Markoff, L., & Reed, B. (2005). Trauma-informed or trauma-denied: Principles and implementation of trauma-informed services for women. *Journal of Community Psychology, 33,* 461–477.

Fallot, R. D., & Harris, M. (2002). The trauma recovery and empowerment model (TREM): Conceptual and practical issues in a group intervention for women. *Community Mental Health Journal, 38,* 475–485.

Fong, C. (2001). Post-exposure prophylaxis for HIV infection after sexual assault: When is it indicated? *Emergency Medicine Journal, 18,* 242–245.

Gazmararian, J. A., Petersen, R., Spitz, A. M., Goodwin, M. M., Saltzman, L. E., & Marks, J. S. (2000). Violence and reproductive health: Current knowledge and future research directions. *Maternal and Child Health, 4*(2), 79–84.

Gielen, A. C., Ghandour, R. M., Burke, J. G., Mahoney, P., McDonnell, K. A., & O'Campo, P. (2007). HIV/AIDS and intimate partner violence. *Trauma, Violence & Abuse, 8*(2), 178–198.

Gondolf, E. W. (1998). *Assessing woman battering in mental health services.* Thousand Oaks, CA: Sage.

Green, W. M., & Panacek, E. A. (2005). Sexual assault forensic examination. *Journal of Emergency Medicine, 25,* 97–99.

Hamberger, K. L., & Phelan, M. B. (2004). *Domestic violence screening and intervention in medical and mental health care settings.* New York: Springer.

Harris, M., & Fallot, R. D. (2001). Envisioning a trauma-informed service system: A vital paradigm shift. In M. Harris & R. D. Fallot (Eds.),

Using trauma theory to design service systems (pp. 3–22). San Francisco: Jossey-Bass.

Harris, M. H., & Weber, M. (2002). Providing crisis counselors on-site to victims of domestic violence in the emergency department: A report of a local pilot project. *South Dakota Journal of Medicine, 55,* 147–149.

Holmes, M., Resnick, H. S., Kilpatrick, D. G., & Best, C. L. (1996). Rape-related pregnancy: Estimates and descriptive characteristics from a national sample of women. *American Journal of Obstetrics and Gynecology, 175,* 320–325.

Houmes, B. V., Fagan, M. M., & Quintana, N. M. (2003). Establishing a Sexual Assault Nurse Examiner (SANE) program in the emergency department. *Journal of Emergency Medicine, 25*(1), 111–121.

Jasinski, J. L. (2004). Pregnancy and domestic violence: A review of the literature. *Trauma, Violence & Abuse, 5*(1), 47–64.

Kendall-Tackett, K. A. (2007). Inflammation, cardiovascular disease, and metabolic syndrome as sequelae of violence against women: The role of depression, hostility and sleep disturbance. *Trauma, Violence & Abuse, 8*(2), 117–126.

Kilpatrick, D. G., Acierno, R., Resnick, H. S., Saunders, B. E., & Best, C. L. (1997). A 2-year longitudinal analysis of the relationship between violent assault and substance use in women. *Journal of Consulting and Clinical Psychology, 65,* 834–846.

Lee, R. K., Thompson, V. L. S., & Mechanic, M. B. (2002). Intimate partner violence and women of color: A call for innovations. *American Journal of Public Health, 92,* 530–534.

Logan, T. K., Walker, R., Cole, J., & Leukefeld, C. (2002). Victimization and substance abuse among women: Contributing factors, interventions, and implications. *Review of General Psychology, 6*(4), 325–397.

MacMillan, H. L., Wathen, C. N., Jamieson, E., Boyle, M. H., Shannon, H. S., Ford-Gilboe, M., et al. (2009). Screening for intimate partner violence in health care settings: A randomized trial. *Journal of the American Medical Association, 302*(5), 493–501.

Macy, R. J., Ferron, J., & Crosby, C. (2009). Partner violence and survivors' chronic health problems: Informing social work practice. *Social Work, 54*(1), 29–43.

Markoff, L., Reed, B., Fallot, R., Elliott, D., & Bjelajac, P. (2005). Implementing trauma-informed alcohol and other drug and mental health services for women: Lessons learned in a multisite demonstration project. *American Journal of Orthopsychiatry, 75,* 525–539.

Martin, S. L., Macy, R. J., Sullivan, K., & Magee, M. (2007). Pregnancy-associated violent deaths: The role of intimate partner violence. *Trauma, Violence & Abuse, 8,* 135–148.

Martin, S. L., Macy, R. J., & Young, S. (in press). The impact of sexual violence against women: Health and economic consequences. In J. White & M. Koss (Eds.), *Violence against women and children: Consensus, critical analyses, and emergent priorities, Volume 1: Mapping the terrain.* Washington, DC: American Psychological Association.

Martin, S. L., Young, S. K., Billings, D. L., & Bross, C. C. (2007). Health care-based interventions for women who have experienced sexual violence: A review of the literature. *Trauma, Violence & Abuse, 8,* 3–18.

McFarlane, J. (2007). Pregnancy following partner rape: What we know and what we need to know. *Trauma, Violence & Abuse, 8,* 127–134.

McFarlane, J. M., Groff, J. Y., O'Brien, J. A., & Watson, K. (2006). Secondary prevention of intimate partner violence: A randomized controlled trial. *Nursing Research, 55*(1), 52–61.

McFarlane, J., Malecha, A., Watson, K., Gist, J., Batten, E., Hall, I., et al. (2005). Intimate partner sexual assault against women: Frequency, health consequences, and treatment outcomes. *Obstetrics and Gynecology, 105*(1), 99–108.

McFarlane, J., Soeken, K., & Wiist, W. (2000). An evaluation of interventions to decrease intimate partner violence to pregnant women. *Public Health Nursing, 17*(6), 443–451.

McNutt, L-A., Carlson, B. E., Rose, I. M., & Robinson, D. A. (2002). Partner violence intervention in the busy primary care environment. *American Journal of Preventive Medicine, 22*(2), 84–91.

Morrissey, J. P., Jackson. E. W., Ellis, E. R., Amaro, H., Brown, V. B., & Najavits, L. M. (2005). Twelve-month outcomes of trauma-informed interventions for women with co-occurring disorders. *Psychiatric Services, 56,* 1213–1222.

Myles, J. E., Hirozawa A., Katz, M. H., Kimmerling, R., & Bamberger, J. D. (2000). Postexposure prophylaxis for HIV after sexual assault. *Journal of the American Medical Association, 284,* 1516–1518.

O'Campo, P., Ahmad, F., & Cyriac, A. (2008). The role of health care professionals in intervening with intimate partner violence. In J. Keeling & T. Mason (Eds.), *Domestic violence: A multi-professional approach for health care practitioners* (pp. 107–116). Berkshire, England: Open University Press.

O'Reilly, R. (2007). Domestic violence against women in their childbearing years: A review of the literature. *Contemporary Nurse, 25*, 13–21.

Osterman, J. E., Barbiaz, J., & Johnson, P. (2001). Emergency interventions for rape victims. *Psychiatric Services, 52*, 733–740.

Pallitto, C. C., Campbell, J. C., & O'Campo, P. (2005). Is intimate partner violence associated with unintended pregnancy? *Trauma, Violence & Abuse, 6*, 217–235.

Plichta, S. B. (2007). Interactions between victims of intimate partner violence against women and the health care system: Policy and practice implications. *Trauma, Violence & Abuse, 8*, 226–239.

Plichta, S. B., & Falik, M. (2001). Prevalence of violence and its implications for women's health. *Women's Health Issues, 11*, 244–258.

Roberts, A. R., & Roberts, B. S. (2002). A comprehensive model for crisis intervention with battered women and their children. In A. R. Roberts (Ed.), *Handbook of domestic violence intervention strategies* (pp. 365–395). New York: Oxford University Press.

Robinson, L., & Spilsbury, K. (2008). Systematic review of the perceptions and experiences of accessing health services by adult victims of domestic violence. *Health and Social Care in the Community, 16*(1), 16–30.

Sharps, P. W., Laughon, K., & Giangrande, S. K. (2007). Intimate partner violence and the childbearing years: Maternal and infant health consequences. *Trauma, Violence & Abuse, 8*, 105–116.

Sheridan, D. J., & Nash, K. R. (2007). Acute injury patterns of intimate partner violence victims. *Trauma, Violence & Abuse, 8*, 281–289.

Sommers, M. S. (2007). Defining patterns of genital injury from sexual assault: A review. *Trauma, Violence & Abuse, 8*, 270–280.

Spangaro, J., Zwi, A. B., & Poulos, R. (2009). The elusive search for definitive evidence on routine screening for intimate partner violence. *Trauma, Violence & Abuse, 10*, 55–68.

Tolman, R. M., & Rosen, D. (2001). Domestic violence in the lives of women receiving welfare. *Violence Against Women, 7*(2), 141–158.

Chapter Authors

Rebecca J. Macy, Ph.D., ACSW, LCSW, is an Associate Professor at the School of Social Work at the University of North Carolina at Chapel Hill. She joined the faculty in 2002, after receiving her doctoral degree from the University of Washington in Seattle. In 1993, she received her MSW from Tulane University in New Orleans. She is a licensed social worker with practice experience in community mental health. Her research focuses on physical and mental health consequences of violent victimization, repeated victimizations, processes for coping with traumatic events, and the development of violence prevention and interventions for violence survivors.

Dania M. Ermentrout, MSW, MPH, is a Clinical Instructor at the School of Social Work at the University of North Carolina at Chapel Hill. She received her master's degrees in social work and public health from the University of North Carolina at Chapel Hill. Her research interests include injury and violence prevention and intervention, community-engaged research, and program development and evaluation. She currently manages the evaluation of a psychoeducational therapeutic intervention for women with dual status as survivors and perpetrators of partner violence and their children.

Natalie B. Johns, MSW, MPH, completed her master's degree in social work and her master's degree in public health at the University of North Carolina at Chapel Hill. Her research interests include violence against women, injury prevention and treatment, and community-based research. She currently coordinates a community outreach program for brain injury survivors in North Carolina.

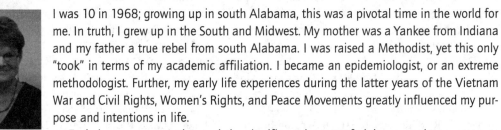

Personal Reflection

Ann Coker

I was 10 in 1968; growing up in south Alabama, this was a pivotal time in the world for me. In truth, I grew up in the South and Midwest. My mother was a Yankee from Indiana and my father a true rebel from south Alabama. I was raised a Methodist, yet this only "took" in terms of my academic affiliation. I became an epidemiologist, or an extreme methodologist. Further, my early life experiences during the latter years of the Vietnam War and Civil Rights, Women's Rights, and Peace Movements greatly influenced my purpose and intentions in life.

Early in my career, I observed the significant impact of violence against women as both a domestic violence advocate in an established shelter and an abortion clinic educator. Although I considered this work essential, it was not fulfilling for me personally because I could not help prevent the violence nor reduce the suffering. I wanted to move toward positive outcomes. Today, I plan and conduct research on understanding violence against women and developing and evaluating prevention interventions in health clinics, colleges, and high schools.

I was fortunate to have been recruited as an endowed professor to research the health effects of violence against women in the first-ever Center for Research on Violence Against Women at the University of Kentucky. The establishment of such centers across the nation is vital to violence prevention because they highlight the significance of violence as a health threat to women and legitimate the study of violence against women as an academic field of inquiry to improve the health and well-being of women and men. Violence against women affects both men's and women's health, yet we continue to focus on women as victims. We need to better understand the trajectory of men's victimization and perpetration as well as the complicated context in which aggression is expressed in intimate relationships. The primary question is, How do we define violence? We need new methodologies to better describe women's and men's experiences with partner violence and, most important, the impact of such experiences on mental and physical health.

Second, we need research that provides data to prove the cost-effectiveness of violence prevention efforts. I envision a world without violence against women or men. Finding effective primary prevention has become my life's work.

CHAPTER 16

Faith-Based Programs and Interventions

Tameka L. Gillum and Shondrah Tarrezz Nash

Introduction

The trauma of intimate partner and sexual violence transcends the physical self. Battering, sexual assault, and emotional abuse by an intimate partner injure the fundamental trust and safety to which we aspire in any meaningful relationship. Violated women, including those deficient of social, legal, and material resources, may consult religion or spirituality to help manage their confusion and renegotiate a sense of solace and control. Considering the hope and survival many accord to religion and spirituality, how might that hope be strengthened through faith communities, institutional leaders, and spiritual principles? Equally important, what roles do these forces play in prolonging and, in some cases, promoting abused women's suffering?

In this chapter, we explore spirituality in abused women's lives and address how faith families and religious establishments can more effectively position themselves as sites of intervention and empowerment. At the same time, we offer a critical analysis of institutional, ideological, and social obstructions, often by these same entities, which can constrain women's efforts toward lives

free of intimate partner violence. Conceptually, in this work, religion relates to an *organized* or formal system of worldviews, practices, and behaviors intended to assist one's connection to a higher power. Spirituality, in contrast, reflects a more *individualistic* investigation of meaning and personal connection to the sacred (see Koenig, McCollough, & Larson, 2001).

An Overview of Intimate Partner Violence in Communities of Faith

Though there is limited research that assesses prevalence rates of intimate partner violence in specific denominations or communities of faith, the literature that does exist highlights the reality that these communities are not immune to such violence (Alsdurf & Alsdurf, 1989; Annis & Rice, 2001; Drumm, Popescu, & Riggs, 2009; Hassouneh-Phillips, 2001b; Horton & Williamson, 1988; Nason-Clark, 2004; Stirling, Cameron, Nason-Clark, & Miedema, 2004; Straus, Gelles, & Steinmetz, 1980). Early research by Straus et al. (1980) indicated that women and men without religious affiliation had the highest rate of violence between partners. Of those religiously affiliated, wife abuse was found to be lowest among Jewish husbands and highest among those of "minority" religious affiliation (religions other than Catholic, Protestant, or Jewish).

One denominational survey of abuse was conducted in the Christian Reformed Church. Registered adult members were randomly selected for participation, with a resulting sample of 688 individuals. Of these, 28% indicated that they had experienced one or a combination of physical, sexual, and emotional abuse (Annis & Rice, 2001). A recent study investigating partner abuse among a conservative Christian denomination found lifetime prevalence rates both consistent with and exceeding national rates (33.8% and 20.1% for the sample vs. 22.1%–37.6% and 7.4%–18.2% nationally for women and men respectively; Drumm et al., 2009).

The Response of Faith Communities to Intimate Partner Violence

Ignorance, Minimization, and Denial

If faced with abuse or psychological maltreatment by an intimate partner, what might an abused woman experience when seeking support from her faith community? Some may find their religious institutions and authorities ill-equipped or resistant to understanding or attending to their needs. The religious press, particularly that of the conservative Protestant rank and file, has been vigilant about what family life is and should be. Prominent religious leaders and populist writers argue that modernity has undermined the strength and stability of families, citing divorce rates, gay/lesbian rights, and rebellious children as evidence that society has abandoned God's plan for men and women. But despite copious media on such controversies, their social impact, and church families' asserted demise, there is a *paucity*

of data on violence in religious families. What is more, there has been reluctance from the pulpit to *unequivocally* condemn family violence (Nason-Clark 1997, 1999).

Part of the institutional hush surrounding intimate partner violence may involve religious authorities' perceptions about the prevalence of abuse in families. Thirty years ago, when educating church leaders about the topic, Adams and Fortune (1995) found that the most common response was, "But no one ever comes to me with these problems" (p. 9). Invariably, they argue, this attitude fed into the belief that battering, rape, and other forms of violation happen to those in other denominations, racial/ethnic groups, and socioeconomic classes and not in their congregation. Studies that are more recent suggest a similar pattern of disbelief or denial. The Jewish, Christian, and Islamic leaders of Ware, Levitt, and Bayer's (2003) study rarely discussed intimate partner violence in their lectures and presumed a low occurrence of such violence in their congregations.

Institutional hush around family violence also may be linked to the church's focus on ideological preservation. Indeed, in many places of worship, "intact," husband-headed congregational families are viewed as an asset to the strength and endurance of religious institutions. Maltreatment or neglect in religious households, however, injures the rhetoric of family values and complicates the core message of agreeable faith-family life (see Nason-Clark, 1997, 1999, 2001). As one religion and domestic violence researcher concludes, "The reality and pervasiveness of violence and abuse is all but ignored so that the message of 'happy Christian families' can live on" (Nason-Clark, 1999, p. 42).

Also problematic, victims may encounter clergy with little or no training in how to identify intimate partner violence, intervene, or sufficiently recognize the scope of the problem (Alsdurf & Alsdurf, 1988, 1989; Nason-Clark, 1997; Rotunda, Williamson, & Penfold, 2004; Shannon-Lewy & Dull, 2005). Although versed in social science explanations of abuse in non-church families, a Canadian sample of evangelical ministers and pastors typified abuse in their own congregations as a spiritual infraction due to confusion about God's design for marital satisfaction. Male-on-female violent behavior was framed as spiritual immaturity or an otherwise religious man's struggle with sin (Nason-Clark, 1999).

Fifty-seven percent of the 41 clergy surveyed in Rotunda et al.'s (2004) exploratory study felt they lacked enough training to enable them to effectively counsel individuals about intimate partner violence. Sixty-five percent stated a domestic violence workshop would be helpful, and 41% endorsed periodic training and continuing education. Only 25% received training related to domestic violence. Similarly, clergy in Nason-Clark's (1997) study lamented their narrow exposure—one or two courses—to counseling issues during their ministerial training. Admittedly, the preparation received was valuable in shaping their personal counseling orientation. However, many recalled that course content was adapted to the expertise or interest of a few seminary professors (e.g., prison ministry or psychiatric inpatient counseling) rather than the breadth of pastoral demands expected in the field.

Limited to No Support for Survivors

If obtained, clergy response to intimate partner violence may be more dissatisfactory for some women than others. In fact, several respondents in Potter's (2007) study, who did *not* seek ministerial assistance while victimized, (1) had presumed their pastors would disbelieve their reports of abuse, (2) witnessed hypocrisy or aberrance in the faith practices of church members and clergy, or (3) observed failure within the clergy to help other abused women.

Both survivors and religious leaders in Ringel and Bina's (2007) study agreed that Orthodox rabbis have or should have a major role in prevention

and intervention. Their perceptions diverged, however, on the efficacy and impact of rabbis in these areas. Of the eight survivors interviewed, only one reported her rabbi had helped by providing her and her spouse with emotional support and assistance in obtaining counseling and financial services. Otherwise, the general response from survivors was that, despite rabbis' best intentions, many lack sufficient training to adequately deal with intimate partner violence. Survivors also criticized rabbis who preferred to focus on "religious dogma that 'they could control'" (Ringel & Bina, 2007, p. 282).

In addition to their lack of training, some clerics may offer ineffective advice (see Shannon-Lewy & Dull, 2005). Seventy-two percent of Pagelow's (1981) sample of 138 victims expressed a range of religious convictions, from moderate to deep, but only 28% sought help from a clergy member. Of these, 80% were (1) advised to go home, consider their wifely duty, and forgive their spouses; (2) advised to see a marriage counselor; or (3) given unhelpful or only religious counsel. Horton, Wilkins, and Wright's (1988) content analysis reported "dissatisfactory" (29) and "very unsatisfactory" (42) responses among 101 victims who contacted a pastor, minister, bishop, priest, or rabbi for assistance. According to the authors, respondents reported at length how pastors focused on the victims' behaviors and, in essence, *their* part ownership of spousal change. Suggestions such as "don't talk" and "cook more appetizing meals" were not well-received. Respondents were most critical of clergy who denied the problem existed, accused them of exaggerating or lying, or considered the victim the cause of the problem and, therefore, were unwilling to listen. In Bowker's (1988) national study of 1,000 battered women, only 34% of the one third who received clergy assistance rated clergy as "very effective" or "somewhat effective" (p. 232). Women in Horton et al.'s study (1988) were advised to "stay and work things out" as God expected and "forgive and forget." Religious authorities warned that divorce was not an option, barring adultery, but assured that "God will change him" through prayer (p. 242). Of further concern, clergy yielded lower effectiveness rates than formal help sources, including district attorneys (38%), social service or counseling agencies (47%), and battered women's shelters (56%) and women's groups (60%). In fact, only physicians and nurses (31%) ranked below clergy in effectiveness.

Women in violent same-sex relationships may experience even less support from religious communities and leaders. A national survey of 1,515 adults found homosexuality a major topic in houses of worship and a frequent focus among evangelical clergy. Of particular concern here is the poll's finding that those who hear clergy discuss homosexuality are more likely to have highly unfavorable views of gays and lesbians. This is especially the case in evangelical churches, where clergy address homosexuality far more negatively than do ministers and priests in other denominations ("Religious Beliefs Underpin Opposition," 2003). As such, sexual minority victims may expect those identified with certain religious groups or belief systems to disregard their relationships and their pain. Some, conceivably, will be reluctant to disclose mistreatment or any incident, for that matter, that could provoke secondary victimization. Experts suggest that sexual minorities may find support via a more personal spirituality, given the negative reception they receive in some ideological establishments (Tan, 2005).

Faith Community and Beliefs Facilitating Suffering of Victims

A woman's faith community can inadvertently amplify her suffering and obstruct escape. Pressure to immediately forgive her perpetrator and continue the relationship is one example. For many, forgiveness is an act of religious duty and, thus, an important obligation for those victimized by another's actions. However, Fortune (1995) argues that quick or premature forgiveness

of an abuser undercuts authentic restoration of well-being for both victim and offender. Reconciliation too soon may also encourage repetition of the cycle of abuse or allow the abuser to avoid accountability for his actions.

Gender role expectations promoted in many faiths may contribute to violence in marital relationships as well as prevent survivors from leaving abusive relationships (Alsdurf & Alsdurf, 1989; Giesbrecht & Sevcik, 2000; Gillum, 2008b; Hassouneh-Phillips, 2001b; Levitt, Swanger, & Butler, 2008; Potter, 2007). Qualitative studies have revealed that religious leaders may endorse traditional gender roles, fault women for marital difficulties, encourage them to remain in abusive relationships, and condemn them for leaving abusive situations (Giesbrecht & Sevcik, 2000; Gillum, 2008b; Hassouneh-Phillips, 2001a; Potter, 2007; Schneider & Feltey, 2009; Yick, 2008). Some may actually endorse the use of physical violence (Potter, 2007). A qualitative study of male perpetrators of intimate partner violence revealed that half the sample of perpetrators endorsed conservative religious teachings that dictate that men should be the decision makers and leaders in relationships. They believed that societal promotion of female-male equality was in conflict with such teaching and led to relationship conflict (Levitt et al., 2008). Research supports that women's ascription to such conservative notions of wifely submission may also contribute to their remaining in abusive relationships for extended periods of time (Alsdurf & Alsdurf, 1989; Horton et al., 1988; Knickmeyer, Levitt, Horne, & Bayer, 2003; Nason-Clark, 2004).

The duties or expectations often attributed to wives—including infinite sexual access—can leave some confused about the nature of sexual violation. Consequently, forced sex in marriage may not be perceived as rape. Interpretations of certain religious texts and discourses might feed this misconception. Cultural traditions, including certain religious teachings, describe wives as "becoming one" with their husband in personal identity (as symbolized by name change) and, what is relevant here, assert their "permanent consent" to intercourse (Yllo & LeClerc, 1988, p. 51). For example, an Old Testament account reads, "Unto the woman he said, I will greatly multiply thy sorrow and thy conception; in sorrow thou shalt bring forth children; and *thy desire shall be to thy husband, and he shall rule over thee* [italics added]" (Gen. 3:16 King James Version). The Apostle Paul records,

> But I would have you know, that the head of every man is Christ; and the head of the woman is the man; and the head of Christ is God. . . . For the man is not of the woman: but the woman of the man. *Neither was the man created for the woman; but the woman for the man* [italics added]. (1 Cor. 11: 3, 8, 9)

Indeed, it has been argued that other passages in the Bible demonstrate a more equitable social arrangement between husbands and wives (Bohn, 1989). However, Bohn (1989) views as more pervasive a "theology of ownership" that proposes that by God's design women are subject to men (p. 105).

The role of patriarchy and sexism is a fixture in many discussions about rape in marriage, including discussions involving women of faith or spirituality (see Dobash & Dobash, 1979; Frieze, 2005; Yllo & LeClerc, 1988). Sheldon and Parent (2002), for example, concluded that the more fundamentalist and sexist the clergy were, the more negative their attitudes toward rape victims. Jeffords' (1984) often-cited study found that individuals with traditional sex-role attitudes are much less likely to believe that forced marital intercourse is undesirable than are persons with modern sex-role attitudes. Regardless of etiology, the experience of marital rape is enduring and deep seated. A religious wife violated by marital rape has to disentangle what rights she has to her body and whether her sacred duties as a wife require that she submit to unwanted sexual acts (Nason-Clark, 1997). Adding insult, she must live with her rapist,

risking repeated sexual assault by her husband (Yllo & LeClerc, 1988).

Faith communities that find doctrinal salience in wifely submission may frustrate an abused woman's efforts at agency. Research has disclosed misuses of religion and imbalanced gender role assignment by both abusers and religious authorities intended to assist the situation (Alsdurf & Alsdurf, 1988, 1989). Alsdurf and Alsdurf's (1988) survey yielded pastors who believed that a wife should submit to her husband and trust that God would honor that submission by stopping abuse or giving her strength to endure it. One quarter of the sample specifically endorsed attitudes affirming the belief that nonsubmission provokes violence.

Meanwhile, trying to make sense of violation can forge an added liability. Conceptualizing suffering as a precursor to growth, spiritual renewal, or a divine punishment may dissuade disclosure or the escape from victimization. For some that do escape, separation or divorce may involve separation or stigmatization from their faith communities (Nason-Clark, 1997; Ringel & Bina, 2007).

As we explore this issue, we should address the reality that culturally specific factors are present as well in the discussion of the intersection of religion/spirituality and intimate partner violence. The fact that some racial and ethnic groups have a history of strong reliance on faith traditions is important to recognize (Abraham, 2000; Perilla, 1999; Potter, 2007). In fact, many authors have argued the need to address religion and faith when intervening in such populations (Arnette, Mascaro, Santana, Davis, & Kaslow, 2007; Bent-Goodley & Fowler, 2006; Gillum, 2008a; Gillum, Sullivan, & Bybee, 2006; Potter, 2007).

For example, in the African American community, the church has always had a strong presence, and African Americans have a long history of strong faith tradition. Consequently, several researchers have documented the importance of addressing spirituality and faith when working with African American survivors

(Arnette et al., 2007; Bent-Goodley & Fowler, 2006; Gillum, 2008a; Gillum et al., 2006). A number of qualitative studies of African American survivors have documented these women's accounts of the importance of spirituality and religious involvement to their ability to cope with and heal from abusive relationships (Gillum, 2008a; Gillum et al., 2006; Potter, 2007; Taylor, 2004; Yick, 2008). Quantitative studies have also documented links between faith-based practices and coping among African American survivors (El-Khoury, Dutton, Goodman, Engel, Belamaric, & Murphy, 2004; Watlington & Murphy, 2006).

Research has also documented the importance of spirituality for Muslim American women as they cope with experiences of abuse. Hassouneh-Phillips (2003) documented that for many Muslim American survivors, their relationship with Allah was an important mechanism for coping with the ongoing violence in their lives. Many participants also experienced changes in their spiritual paths after their abuse experiences as they re-evaluated their faith beliefs. This research has also revealed that factors associated with such a strong faith tradition can also be a barrier to women's safety and accessing help. These include the belief that what occurs in this world doesn't matter, manipulation of religious text by abusers in an effort to maintain power and control, and teachings that stress the importance of marriage and strongly discourage divorce (Hassouneh-Phillips, 2001a, 2001b, 2003).

For those of Jewish faith, the literature supports the notion that faith beliefs, especially among the ultra-Orthodox, contribute to the suppression of the reality of intimate partner violence in this community and interfere with women's help seeking. The insularity of the Jewish community, shame, traditional gender roles, and the Jewish concept of *shalom bayit* (which concerns the maintenance of peace in the home) all impact survivors' decisions to speak out about abuse in their home or seek help, while simultaneously interfering with the community and clergy's provision of support and assistance. In addition, the belief that coming from an abusive or broken home reduces children's chances of having a good marriage often results in women remaining in abusive relationships (Kaufman, 2003; Ringel & Bina, 2007).

It has also been documented that religious institutions in Southeast Asian immigrant communities contribute to women's silence and hinder their help-seeking efforts. Strong sentiments against divorce, promotion of traditional gender roles, devaluing and oppression of women, and the notion of the self-sacrificing wife are promoted by religious institutions in Southeast Asian immigrant communities (Abraham, 2000). Religious leaders consistently reinforce the concept of the woman as the "glue that holds the family together," encouraging her to remain in a relationship despite experiences of abuse (p. 120). Women who are being abused often remain silent for fear of being ostracized by their religious communities, which are the center of the Southeast Asian community in the United States (Abraham, 2000).

Perilla (1999) has discussed the role of the church as a contributing factor in the perpetuation of intimate partner violence among Latino immigrant communities. The primacy of the role of the church, which is usually Catholic or fundamentalist in these communities, in the socialization of Latinas is significant. The clergy often use biblical passages and the image of the Virgin Mary to support their assertions that intimate violence is the fault of the woman and she must modify her behavior to preserve the family. Traditional gender roles and the need to preserve marriage are strenuously promoted, often leading to the silencing of women in these communities (Perilla, 1999).

The Importance of Religion and Spirituality for Intimate Partner Violence Survivors

Women of faith who experience violence in the context of their intimate relationships often experience a degree of spiritual distress surrounding that experience (Bent-Goodley & Fowler, 2006; Boehm, Golec, Krahn, & Smyth, 1999; Dunbar & Jeannechild, 1996; Kriedler, 1995; Mattis, 2002; Spiegel, 1996). Kriedler (1995) argues that the experience of being hurt by someone who should love, cherish, and protect one causes a great deal of spiritual distress. She identifies that such distress can manifest in various ways, including feelings of despair, belief that life is meaningless, or perceptions of oneself as powerless. Other researchers have concurred that because of the importance of spirituality in the lives of many victims of family violence and the spiritual distress that can be caused by victimization, spiritual healing is necessary in order to restore one's sense of meaningfulness of and power over one's life (Dunbar & Jeannechild, 1996; Mattis, 2002; Spiegel, 1996). Boehm and colleagues (1999) also identify that in their talks with women who have experienced intimate partner violence, women have expressed feelings of spiritual anguish in the midst of their abuse.

A violated woman may experience a convergence of suffering—fear of injury and death, loss of material and social support, feelings of betrayal—any of which can derail her sense of self, control, and fairness. Even so, a search for significance in time of stress—coping—can emerge. Much of coping can be characterized as an effort to conserve meaning and efficacy in life given the onset of events that disturb our sense of normalcy. Researchers, for example, find that we bring frames of reference to negative, even life-threatening, events that orient how we view difficulties and organize strategies suited to the demands and challenges of the situation. Other mechanisms of coping seek to transform that meaning and significance by establishing a new orientation system in which a new focus is discovered or re-created (Pargament, 1997; Pargament & Park, 1997) and poised to manage inconsistencies.

Not all religion facilitates coping, and not all ways of coping are linked to the sacred. Nonetheless, those in distress can experience coping and religion as interrelated phenomena. Facilitated by ritual practices, social relationships,

personal beliefs, cultural ideologies, extraordinary accounts, and emotions, religion can be an accessible means by which we organize how critical events are appraised, (re)structured, anticipated, and confronted (see Pargament, 1997; Pargament & Park, 1995). Moreover, for those mired by limitations or the search for meaning, religion offers a compelling set of alternatives with which to interpret human events (Pargament, 1997). Mattis's (2002) examination of the coping repertoires of 23 African American women suggests a recuperative effect among some spiritual and religious practices and involvement. Among the findings, religion and spirituality were integral to questioning and accepting reality, confronting and transcending limitations, growth, and recognizing purpose.

Often overlooked is the storied nature of some religious discourse and how it can bridge distress and healing. When disordered by conflict, the self and its link to the social world may be reframed by narrative scripts (Hunt, 2000) that inspire courses of action in which actors recast their difficulties and help preserve what they care about most deeply. A result may be that needs, desires, and discontents can subjectively sustain some spiritual or religious significance and prediction. For example, women in Nash and Hesterberg's (2009) study reassessed their abuse experiences and renegotiated states of power/powerlessness by co-opting the lifeworlds of biblical figures. Abuse continued; however, each respondent discerned from biblical narrative what she perceived and professed as religion-based strategies to end intimate partner violence.

Although exceptions exist, research on faith and intimate partner violence suggests religion and spirituality are key resources in the lived experiences of many abuse survivors. An evolving, personal spirituality, for example, may provide for some a contextual frame of reference for challenging mistreatment. Abused women in Knickmeyer et al.'s (2003) study demonstrated a spiritual belief system that permitted a flexible and, in some cases, rebellious stance against "legalistic" religious mandates and interpretations that could have trapped them in dangerous relationships. Watlington and Murphy (2006) found that African American survivors who experienced higher levels of spirituality and greater religious involvement reported fewer depressive symptoms (e.g., sadness, pessimism, and worthlessness). The spirituality-depression association remained significant even when accounting for severity of violence exposure, psychological aggression, time since the last abusive episode, and personal income. Religious involvement also was found to be negatively associated with posttraumatic stress symptoms. In Gillum et al.'s (2006) research of 151 female survivors of intimate partner violence, an overwhelming 97% reported spirituality or God as a source of strength or consolation. Moreover, greater involvement in religious institutions (e.g., churches, synagogues, and mosques) viewed as a source of strength or comfort predicted decreased depression and increased quality of life.

Interviews with women who have survived intimate partner violence may help illuminate how religious or spiritual resilience is understood and experienced by the group. In Yick's (2008) metasynthesis of qualitative studies on the role of spirituality and religiosity among survivors, participants conveyed the concept of strength as having dual dimensions, both of which aided in coping. The more concrete aspect of strength came in the form of organizational resources and social support (e.g., faith community and church attendance). Harder to articulate but equally important was how participants discerned strength through God, Allah, or another higher power. Focusing on the concept's more intangible dimension, Yick (2008) writes that strength also was described as "a force . . . a hope . . . an internal knowing or certainty that the help of God would somehow get them through anything" (Yick, 2008, pp. 1297–1298). Other strength-seeking practices included private prayer, meditation, and recitations, which served to beseech God or a higher power for strength, trust, and sometimes change in the abuser.

In light of the above, it is not surprising that a survivor's search for strength, solace, and meaning may lead her to her faith community. Clerics can represent a unique and valuable resource for victims of intimate partner violence. A pastor or minister may have an ongoing relationship with a victim/survivor and an explicit privilege to convey acceptable and nonacceptable family behavior. He or she may play some role in contouring how the victim/survivor understands the world. Given trust and familiarity, a religious authority may have entrée into the victim/survivor's life and experiences in ways different from other helping professionals (see Shannon-Lewy & Dull, 2005).

Also empowering, women of faith may function as an extended family system for abused women within and outside their faith communities. More than 55%, the majority of Nason-Clark's (1997) sample of 250 evangelical women, said they had been involved in supporting an abused woman. The most common form of engagement was emotional support, through which respondents offered friendship, listened, or shared their own stories of abuse. Another form of engagement was physical support. More than 25% of the respondents provided child care, food, material resources, or transportation to a shelter or an appointment with counselors or social services. Other assistance reported by evangelical women in the sample involved spiritual support (e.g., praying with or reading scriptures to a victim), referral suggestions, and informal counseling (e.g., offering advice).

The Need for Faith Communities to Play a Role in Addressing Intimate Partner Violence

Taken together, the above information supports a need for faith communities to play a (better) role in addressing intimate partner violence. Indeed, clergy themselves have acknowledged such a need (United States Conference of Catholic Bishops, 2002). Considering the significance of the church, especially in certain communities, and the respect with which clergy are viewed, faith communities' acknowledgment of and response to this issue has the potential to make a significant statement that intimate partner violence will not be tolerated. Faith communities' diligent efforts to address this issue could help to hold perpetrators accountable, decrease silence surrounding the epidemic, and decrease violence in their congregations and communities. Additionally, for survivors in particular, such measures could give them a voice, provide validation and acknowledgment of their experiences, provide much-needed assistance and support, and facilitate spiritual healing. The literature also supports the positive effects of validation and support from clergy and faith communities (Giesbrecht & Sevcik, 2000; Neergaard, Lee, Anderson, & Gengler, 2007; Pyles, 2007; Rotunda et al., 2004).

Examples of Faith-Based Programs and Interventions

A number of faith-based initiatives and resources have been developed to address the issues of intimate partner violence and sexual assault.

The Black Church and Domestic Violence Institute. The Black Church and Domestic Violence Institute is a nonprofit agency that focuses on leadership development and empowerment of religious leaders in the black church to effectively respond to and prevent domestic violence through clergy training and advocacy. The agency also seeks to develop relationships between domestic violence agencies and congregations with the goal of fostering partnerships to effectively address domestic violence (see http://www.bcdvi.org).

Faith Trust Institute. The Faith Trust Institute is an international organization that works with multiple faith communities to end domestic and sexual violence. Founded in 1977, the organization provides consultation; training; and video, print, and Internet educational resources. The

organization also aims to foster connections between secular domestic and sexual violence organizations and religious organizations (see http://www.faithtrustinstitute.org).

Shalom Bayit. Shalom Bayit, located in the Bay Area of California, is an agency committed to ending domestic violence in the Jewish community. Its mission is "to foster the social change and community response necessary to eradicate domestic violence in the Jewish community." To this end, the agency provides technical assistance and education to community organizations as well as education, peer support, advocacy, healing rituals, and counseling to abused women. The agency also offers a Jewish youth-led dating violence prevention program titled Love Shouldn't Hurt (see http://www.shalom-bayit.org).

Jewish Women International. Jewish Women International has developed resources for teens and young adults. *Strong Girls, Healthy Relationships: A Conversation on Dating, Friendship, and Self-Esteem* is a 12-hour, 6-session healthy relationships curriculum designed for young teenage girls. *When Push Comes to Shove . . . It's No Longer Love* is a 1½-hour program for teens, young adults, and college students designed to educate them about unhealthy and abusive relationships. The organization also publishes a monthly newsletter titled *Domestic Abuse in the Jewish Community* (see http://www.jwi.org).

Mending the Soul Ministries, Inc. This is a nonprofit organization that seeks to empower communities and equip churches to effectively minister to individuals impacted by abuse through the provision of education, technical support, training, and support groups. Their declared vision is to "provide research-based curriculum and resources to equip and train the faith-based community at large on the nature and effects of abuse, sexual brokenness, and healthy intimacy and to serve and partner with community agencies to prevent and respond to abuse" (see http://www.mendingthesoul.org).

Peace and Safety in the Christian Home (PASCH). This coalition of academics, professionals, clergy, and laypersons seeks to "increase peace and safety in the Christian home and in the world it serves by addressing and decreasing domestic and sexual abuse in those homes." This nonprofit entity provides numerous educational resources, hosts conferences, keeps communities informed of related events, and publishes a regular newsletter (see http://www.peaceandsafety.com).

RAVE. This initiative seeks to join social action and knowledge in order to assist families of faith impacted by abuse. It provides resources to clergy, survivors, and the community as well as online training. Part of its mission statement indicates that "RAVE seeks to equip religious leaders to respond to domestic violence in ways that are compassionate, practical, and informed by the latest research and the best practices for professionals . . . walk alongside victims and survivors on their journey toward healing and wholeness . . . hold abusers accountable for their actions, while offering hope for a transformed life" (see http://www.theraveproject.com).

The Soul Sanctuary. The mission of this agency is to "promote healthy relationships and violence-free families." To this end, they provide training for clergy and lay leaders, in-person support groups, and e-support for domestic abuse survivors (see http://www.thesoulsanctuary.org).

Safe Place Ministries. This nonprofit entity's purpose is to "provide education, resources, support, and services to individuals, care providers, and churches, whose lives and ministries have been touched by domestic abuse, childhood sexual abuse, and/or sexual assault." They provide training, direct services to women and children, and a number of resources for victim service providers, church leaders, survivors of abuse, and their affected family and friends (see http://www.safeplaceministries.com).

Family Wellness Warriors Initiative. The purpose of this initiative is to equip organizations and individuals to effectively address the spiritual, emotional, mental, and physical effects of domestic violence, abuse, and neglect in the Alaska Native and American Indian community. To this end, they bring together leaders of the Alaska Native community, the faith community, regional corporations and agencies, health care providers, and other community members. They conduct faith-based conferences and training, disseminate print resources, and generate public awareness campaigns (see http://www.fwwi.org).

Print and Video Resources Developed by Faith Communities. In response to the problem of intimate partner violence, some religious communities have developed resource materials for clergy and congregation members. The Baha'i faith has developed a manual titled *Guidelines for Spiritual Assemblies on Domestic Violence.* The Episcopal Church developed a handbook titled *Breaking the Silence: The Church Responds to Domestic Violence.* The United States Conference of Catholic Bishops has drafted a document titled *When I Call for Help: A Pastoral Response to Domestic Violence Against Women.* The Islamic faith has developed a video resource titled *Garments for One Another: Ending Domestic Violence in Muslim Families.* And the Faith Alive Christian Resource has developed a booklet titled *The Facts About Dating Violence: Love Shouldn't Hurt.*

Websites. Some faith communities have developed Web resources to provide information on intimate partner violence and teen dating violence. These include the Evangelical Lutheran Church in America (http://elca.org/Our-Faith-In-Action/Life-Transitions/Family-Relations/Domestic-Violence.aspx), the Presbyterian Church (http://www.pcusa.org/phewa/padvn) and the Evangelical Covenant Church (http://www.covchurch.org/women/ava/transgenerational-violence).

Coalition and Secular Entity Initiatives. Recognizing the intersection between intimate partner violence and faith, a number of domestic violence coalitions and other secular entities have implemented initiatives to address this issue. Examples include the Montana Coalition Against Domestic and Sexual Violence's faith-based liaison (http://www.mcadsv .com/Faith-Based-1.html); the Washtenaw County Faith-Based Coalition Against Violence (http://css washtenaw.org/cav/index.html); and Fairfax County Virginia's Faith Communities in Action Domestic Violence Prevention Task Force (http:// www.fairfaxcounty.gov/dsm/dviolence/fcia_dvt askforce.htm).

Services Faith Communities Could Offer

There are a number of ways in which religious institutions and faith communities could facilitate spiritual healing and lives free of intimate partner violence for survivors. Indeed, survivors have spoken of the need for faith communities to offer such services (Gillum, 2008b), and many have indicated they turned to clergy and faith communities for assistance when experiencing an abusive relationship (Bent-Goodley & Fowler, 2006; El-Khoury et al., 2004; Potter, 2007; Rotunda et al., 2004). Authors have also cited the need for faith communities to play an active role in addressing this issue (Bent-Goodley & Fowler, 2006; Gillum, 2008b; Gillum et al., 2006; Rotunda et al., 2004). In addition, for many survivors, involvement in a faith community and assistance received from clergy and fellow worshippers has given them the strength to cope with or leave abusive situations, provided much-needed assistance and support for doing so, and facilitated their spiritual healing (Gillum, 2008b; Knickmeyer et al., 2003; Rotunda et al., 2004; Senter & Caldwell, 2002).

So, what can clergy, religious institutions, and faith communities do for survivors? First, having clergy and lay leaders receive education and

training on the issue of intimate partner violence is crucial to raising awareness and facilitating helpful and effective responses. Research indicates that only a relatively small percentage of these individuals have received such training, and most indicate that it would be helpful to them (Rotunda et al., 2004). As indicated in the discussion of the faith-based initiatives above, a number of education and training resources are available. Training would enable these individuals to better understand this issue, assuming they are open to do so, and respond appropriately, providing the emotional and spiritual support that survivors of faith need.

Second, religious institutions and faith communities could offer the much-needed instrumental support to survivors who desire to leave abusive situations. Provision of shelter, housing, food, clothing, transportation, employment connections, child care, and financial assistance are all crucial, in addition to emotional and spiritual support, for women taking this major step in their lives. This is especially true for women who have children and/or have been dependent on their abusers. In addition, providing referrals to community resources for survivors could be especially helpful. This process is often hindered by an apparent distrust between secular and religious intervention milieus. Some ministers fear secular help entities will motivate women to leave their abusers and church communities. Conversely, mainstream professionals are concerned that clergy will advise women to return to their abusers (Nason-Clark, 1999, 2001). However, Nason-Clark (2004) has urgently expressed the need for a partnership between the "[church] steeple and "[abuse] shelter."

Education is a key piece as well. Educating survivors about the existence of intimate partner violence in faith communities and condemning such behavior can raise awareness and provide validation for individuals who may be experiencing violence in their homes. Nason-Clark (2004) suggests that domestic violence, particularly for religious victims/survivors, should be approached and "condemned" through language bearing both religious (e.g., violence is not acceptable to the higher power—and scripture confirms this) and practical significance (e.g., educating her with safety plans, shelter information). As indicated above, silence around the issue and lack of recognition has served to perpetuate violence in many communities.

Support groups led by trained clergy or lay leaders have the potential to be especially helpful to survivors. Groups could also be led by trained domestic violence counselors or advocates from domestic violence services. Not only does a support group validate women's experiences, it facilitates survivors' connections with other women of faith who have had experiences similar to theirs. It also shows women that their faith community cares about their experience and their healing.

Clergy, religious institutions, and faith communities could also offer services to perpetrators in their congregations. There is, indeed, research that indicates that perpetrators sometimes seek counseling from clergy (Rotunda et al., 2004). Education should be paramount. Educating perpetrators on the unacceptability of such violence in faith communities would put perpetrators on notice that clergy are aware of the issue and see it as important to address in their communities. Coupled with that, clergy and lay leaders should hold perpetrators accountable when they come to them seeking counsel or are identified by women who are being abused. Religious leaders could condemn such behavior while simultaneously referring these individuals to appropriate community resources and facilitating healing from their spiritual brokenness. If religious institutions have the appropriate financial and community resources, they may choose to hold classes for perpetrators as well, to lead them on a path to nonviolence and teach them new ways to resolve conflict and value the significant others in their lives.

Faith communities and religious institutions could also offer services to couples prior to their entering into a committed union such as marriage. In light of the reality that many religious institutions offer such programs as premarital classes, inclusion of intimate partner violence education in such classes could also serve to raise awareness and possibly prevent some women from continuing a relationship that may not be physically, mentally, emotionally, or spiritually healthy for them and not a proper representation of a Godly union.

Faith communities and religious institutions could offer many programs and services to their congregations at large to address this issue as well. For example, messages from the pulpit that address intimate partner and sexual violence can take multiple forms and serve multiple purposes. Educating one's congregation about the reality of such violence in communities of faith could serve to raise awareness. Condemning violence from the pulpit can help survivors to understand that such behavior is not appropriate and that they are not deserving of such circumstances. This may encourage survivors to seek assistance if they are experiencing abuse. It may also advise perpetrators that violent behavior is inappropriate and will not be tolerated. It can decrease the silence surrounding intimate partner violence and encourage fellow worshipers to be supportive of women who are experiencing violence and hold accountable men who are perpetrating abuse. Delivering messages that indicate the proper way to interpret scripture, the proper way to treat one's significant other, and the equality of women in relationships could facilitate different and better ways of interacting within these unions.

Including segments or articles on intimate partner violence in newsletters and bulletins as well as hosting church events that educate and raise awareness can be particularly powerful. Partnering with community domestic violence and sexual assault agencies to host community events and fundraisers can have similar effects.

Another avenue for ending the silence and facilitating healing is inclusion of this issue in women's and men's ministries in religious institutions. Many institutions offer programs and services that are specifically geared toward women or men. Women's ministries could educate women about intimate partner violence (including prevalence, warning signs, and available resources), provide a safe place to discuss their experiences, and provide confirmation that they deserve to live a life free from violence in the place that should be their refuge, their home. Men's ministries can also incorporate education on this issue, including prevalence, resources for batterers, information that battering is not appropriate behavior, and proper ways to treat and value a partner.

Though faith communities can and should play a significant role in addressing the issue of intimate partner violence in communities of faith, domestic violence programs can also facilitate activities that recognize the intersection of intimate partner violence and faith for many survivors. For example, programs could offer spiritual or prayer groups on site, especially in domestic violence shelters. Such agencies often offer an array of groups for survivors, including support groups for domestic and sexual violence, parenting groups, groups for those overcoming addiction, and so on. Though these programs recognize the magnitude of such circumstances and the need to address them, they often neglect survivors' spiritual needs as they cope with their experiences. Providing regular interfaith or non-denominational spiritual healing or prayer groups on a volunteer basis could be especially powerful and helpful to a number of survivors. Qualified individuals from the faith community could be brought in to facilitate such groups. Also, providing transportation for resident survivors to attend religious services could facilitate much-needed healing, and simply providing a space in a shelter for meditation or prayer could be very helpful. Initiatives like these could lessen the impact of an already traumatic experience for survivors and potentially increase their social support networks. There are many resources, identified above, that could assist faith communities in implementing the recommendations that have been presented here.

Conclusion

Surviving physical, emotional, and sexual maltreatment by an intimate partner is a terrifying and uncertain venture. Spiritual worldviews and religious communities, for many survivors, are important, if not preferred, resources when managing adversity, including intimate violence. Clergy and laypeople are capable of being important intervention resources. However, there is much for faith communities to learn and do in order to effectively accomplish this.

Intimate partner violence intervention involves a contextual set of skills and help strategies that, at any time, must be readapted to the sometimes erratic life conditions of survivors and the threat of more violence. Faith counselors and clergy who invoke codes of submission and marital permanence or send victims home solely with assurances of divine intervention may indeed satisfy certain religious ideals. However, mandates such as these limit a woman's self-assertion against violation and, in essence, obscure its cumulative harm to her health, self-esteem, and safety. There are other costs as well. A victim could interpret concern for safety and sacred principles as mutually exclusive options if she is imbued with codes or contexts that rigorously restrict agency or confrontation of mistreatment.

We believe that faith institutions must prepare to demonstrate the care, trust, and full consideration needed by many survivors. This involves more than simply training clergy and laypeople to recognize intimate partner violence. It also requires employing that knowledge to identify violation both outside and within their congregations and actively address it. What is more, faith communities and their leaders must create an accepting, communicative space for survivors who seek belief, hope, and action from their faith bodies.

In-church domestic violence programs led by those who comprehensively address the phenomenon—its causes, prevalence, toll, and elimination—are a meaningful beginning to proactive institutional involvement. Openness to partnerships with and referrals to secular help entities will broaden institutional effectiveness as well as increase women's options. But perhaps the greatest challenge for some faith communities will be to understand and own religion's culpability in the toleration and, in some cases, perpetration of abuse.

Indeed, plotting a course between abuse, oppression, restrictive religious teachings, inequality, faith community inaction, and women's responses requires focus and honesty. Even so, such an exercise could help disclose how belief systems might influence manipulation and control. Also paramount, it lays the conceptual groundwork to openly and unambiguously condemn violence, (re)frame maltreatment as contrary to moral ideals, and make accountable those who victimize.

References

Abraham, M. (2000). *Speaking the unspeakable: Marital violence among South Asian immigrants in the United States.* New Brunswick, NJ: Rutgers University Press.

Adams, C. J., & Fortune, M. M. (1995). Preface. In C. J. Adams & M. M. Fortune (Eds.), *Violence against women and children: A Christian theological sourcebook* (pp. 9–13). New York: Continuum.

Alsdurf, J., & Alsdurf, P. (1988). A pastoral response. In A. L. Horton & J. A. Williamson (Eds.), *Abuse and religion: When praying isn't enough* (pp. 165–171). Lexington, MA: D.C. Heath and Company.

Alsdurf, J., & Alsdurf, P. (1989). *Battered into submission: The tragedy of wife abuse in the Christian home.* Downers Grove, IL: Intervarsity Press.

Annis, A. W., & Rice, R. R. (2001). A survey of abuse prevalence in the Christian Reformed Church. *Journal of Religion and Abuse, 3*(3/4), 7–40.

Arnette, N. C., Mascaro, N., Santana, M. C., Davis, S., & Kaslow, N. J. (2007). Enhancing spiritual well-being among suicidal African American female survivors of intimate partner violence. *Journal of Clinical Psychology, 63*(10), 909–924.

Bent-Goodley, T. B., & Fowler, D. N. (2006). Spiritual and religious abuse: Expanding what is known about domestic violence. *Affilia: Journal of Women and Social Work, 21*(3), 282–295.

Boehm, R., Golec, J., Krahn, R., & Smyth, D. (1999). *Lifelines: Culture, spirituality, and family violence.* Edmonton: The University of Alberta Press.

Bohn, C. R. (1989). Domination to rule: The root and consequences of a theology of ownership. In A. L. Horton & J. A. Williamson (Eds.), *Abuse and religion: When praying isn't enough* (pp. 105–116). Lexington, MA: Lexington Books.

Bowker, L. H. (1988). Religious victims and their religious leaders: Services delivered to one thousand battered women by the clergy. In A. L. Horton & J. A. Williamson (Eds.), *Abuse and religion: When praying isn't enough* (pp. 229–234). Lexington, MA: D.C. Heath and Company.

Dobash, R. E., & Dobash, R. P. (1979). *Violence against wives: A case against the patriarchy.* New York: Free Press.

Drumm, R. D., Popescu, M., & Riggs, M. L. (2009). Gender variations in partner abuse: Findings from a conservative Christian denomination. *Affilia: Journal of Women and Social Work, 24*(1), 56–68.

Dunbar, D., & Jeannechild, N. (1996). The stories and strength of women who leave battering relationships. *Journal of Couples Therapy, 6*(1/2), 149–173.

El-Khoury, M. Y., Dutton, M. A., Goodman, L. A., Engel, L., Belamaric, R. J., & Murphy, M. (2004). Ethnic differences in battered women's formal help-seeking strategies: A focus on health, mental health, and spirituality. *Cultural Diversity and Ethnic Minority Psychology, 10*(4), 283–293.

Fortune, M. M. (1995). Forgiveness: The last step. In C. J. Adams & M. M. Fortune (Eds.), *Violence against women and children: A Christian theological resource book* (pp. 201–206). New York: Continuum.

Frieze, I. H. (2005). *Hurting the one you love: Violence in relationships.* Belmont, CA: Thomson Wadsworth.

Giesbrecht, N., & Sevcik, I. (2000). The process of recovery and rebuilding among abused women in the conservative evangelic subculture. *Journal of Family Violence, 15*(3), 229–248.

Gillum, T. L. (2008a). The benefits of a culturally specific intimate partner violence intervention for African American survivors. *Violence Against Women, 14*(8), 917–943.

Gillum, T. L. (2008b). Community response and needs of African American female survivors of domestic violence. *Journal of Interpersonal Violence, 23*(1), 39–57.

Gillum, T. L., Sullivan, C. M., & Bybee, D. I. (2006). The importance of spirituality in the lives of domestic violence survivors. *Violence Against Women, 12*(3), 240–250.

Hassouneh-Phillips, D. (2001a). American Muslim women's experiences of leaving abusive relationships. *Health Care for Women International, 22,* 415–432.

Hassouneh-Phillips, D. S. (2001b). "Marriage is half of faith and the rest is fear Allah": Marriage and spousal abuse among American Muslims. *Violence Against Women, 7*(8), 927–946.

Hassouneh-Phillips, D. (2003). Strength and vulnerability: Spirituality in abused American Muslim women's lives. *Issues in Mental Health Nursing, 24,* 681–694.

Horton, A. L., Wilkins, M. M., & Wright, W. (1988). Women who ended abuse: What religious leaders and religion did for these victims. In A. L. Horton & J. A. Williamson (Eds.), *Abuse and religion: When praying isn't enough* (pp. 235–246). Lexington, MA: Lexington Books.

Horton, A. L., & Williamson, J. A. (1988). *Abuse and religion: When praying isn't enough*. Lexington, MA: Lexington Books.

Hunt, L. (2000). Strategic suffering: Illness narratives as social empowerment among Mexican cancer patients. In C. Mattingly & L. C. Garro (Eds.), *Narrative and the cultural construction of illness and healing* (pp. 88–107). Berkeley: University of California Press.

Jeffords, C. R. (1984). The impact of sex-role and religious attitudes upon forced marital intercourse norms. *Sex Roles, 11,* 543–552.

Kaufman, C. G. (2003). *Sins of omission: The Jewish community's reaction to domestic violence.* Boulder, CO: Westview Press.

Knickmeyer, N., Levitt, H. M., Horne, S. G., & Bayer, G. (2003). Responding to mixed messages and double binds: Religious-oriented coping strategies of Christian battered women. *Journal of Religion and Abuse, 5*(2), 29–53.

Koenig, H. G., McCollough, M. E., & Larson, D. B. (2001). *Handbook of religion and health.* New York: Oxford University Press.

Kriedler, M. C. (1995). Victims of family violence: The need for spiritual healing. *Journal of Holistic Nursing, 13*(1), 30–36.

Levitt, H. M., Swanger, R. T., & Butler, J. B. (2008). Male perpetrators' perspectives on intimate partner violence, religion and masculinity. *Sex Roles, 58,* 435–448.

Mattis, J. S. (2002). Religion and spirituality in the meaning-making and coping experiences of African American women: A qualitative analysis. *Psychology of Women Quarterly, 26,* 309–321.

Nash, S. T., & Hesterberg, L. (2009). Biblical framings of and responses to spousal violence in the narratives of abused Christian women. *Violence Against Women, 15,* 340–361.

Nason-Clark, N. (1997). *The battered wife: How Christians confront family violence.* Louisville, KY: Westminster John Knox Press.

Nason-Clark, N. (1999). Shattered silence or holy hush? Emerging definitions of violence against women in sacred and secular contexts. *Journal of Family Ministry, 3,* 39–55.

Nason-Clark, N. (2001). Woman abuse and faith communities: Religion, violence, and social welfare. In P. D. Nesbitt (Ed.), *Religion and social policy* (pp. 128–145). Walnut Creek, CA: Alta Mira Press.

Nason-Clark, N. (2004). When terror strikes at home: The interface between religion and domestic violence. *Journal for the Scientific Study of Religion, 43*(3), 303–310.

Neergaard, J. A., Lee, J. W., Anderson, B., & Gengler, S. W. (2007). Women experiencing intimate partner violence: Effects of confiding in religious leaders. *Pastoral Psychology, 55,* 773–787.

Pagelow, M. D. (1981). Secondary battering and alternatives of female victims to spouse abuse. In L. H. Bowker (Ed.), *Woman and crime in America* (pp. 277–300). New York: MacMillan.

Pargament, K. I. (1997). *The psychology of religion and coping: Theory, research, practice.* New York: Guilford Press.

Pargament, K. I., & Park, C. L. (1995). Merely a defense? The variety of religious means and ends. *Journal of Social Issues, 51,* 13–32.

Pargament, K. I., & Park, C. L. (1997). In times of stress: The religion-coping connection. In B. Spilka & D. McIntosh (Eds.), *The psychology of religion* (pp. 43–53). Boulder, CO: Westview Press.

Perilla, J. L. (1999). Domestic violence as a human rights issue: The case of immigrant Latinos. *Hispanic Journal of Behavioral Sciences, 21*(2), 107–133.

Potter, H. (2007). Battered black women's use of religious services and spirituality for assistance in leaving abusive relationships. *Violence Against Women, 13*(3), 262–284.

Pyles, L. (2007). The complexities of the religious response to domestic violence: Implications for faith-based initiatives. *Affilia: Journal of Women and Social Work, 22*(3), 281–291.

Religious beliefs underpin opposition to homosexuality. (2003). *The Pew Forum on Religion & Public Life.* Retrieved April 4, 2009, from http://pewforum.org/docs/?DocID=37.

Ringel, S., & Bina, R. (2007). Understanding causes of and responses to intimate partner violence in a Jewish Orthodox community: Survivors' and leaders' perspectives. *Research on Social Work Practice, 17*(2), 277–286.

Rotunda, R. J., Williamson, G., & Penfold, M. (2004). Clergy response to domestic violence: A preliminary survey of clergy members, victims, and batterers. *Pastoral Psychology, 52*(4), 353–365.

Schneider, R. Z., & Feltey, K. M. (2009). "No matter what has been done wrong can always be redone right": Spirituality in the lives of imprisoned battered women. *Violence Against Women, 15*(4), 443–459.

Senter, K. E., & Caldwell, K. (2002). Spirituality and the maintenance of change: A phenomenological study of women who leave abusive relationships. *Contemporary Family Therapy, 24*(4), 543–564.

Shannon-Lewy, C., & Dull, V. T. (2005). The response of Christian clergy to domestic violence: Help or hindrance? *Aggression & Violent Behavior, 10,* 647–659.

Sheldon, J. P., & Parent, S. L. (2002). Clergy's attitudes and attributions of blame toward female rape victims. *Violence Against Women, 8,* 233–256.

Spiegel, M. C. (1996). Spirituality for survival: Jewish women healing themselves. *Journal of Feminist Studies in Religion, 12,* 121–137.

Stirling, M. L., Cameron, C. A., Nason-Clark, N., & Miedema, B. (Eds.). (2004). *Understanding abuse: Partnering for change.* Toronto: University of Toronto Press.

Straus, M. A., Gelles, R. J., & Steinmetz, S. K. (1980). *Behind closed doors: Violence in the American family.* Garden City, NY: Anchor Press/Doubleday.

Tan, P. P. (2005). The importance of spirituality among gay and lesbian individuals. *Journal of Homosexuality, 49,* 135–144.

Taylor, J. Y. (2004). Moving from surviving to thriving: African American women recovering from intimate partner violence. *Research and Theory for Nursing Practice: An International Journal, 18*(1), 35–50.

United States Conference of Catholic Bishops. (2002). *When I call for help: A pastoral response to domestic violence against women.* Retrieved April 9, 2009, from http://www.usccb.org/laity/help.shtml.

Ware, K. N., Levitt, H. M., & Bayer, G. (2003). May god help you: Faith leaders' perspectives of intimate partner violence within their communities. *Journal of Religion and Abuse, 5*(2), 55–81.

Watlington, C. G., & Murphy, C. M. (2006). The role of religion and spirituality among African American survivors of domestic violence. *Journal of Clinical Psychology, 62*(7), 837–857.

Yick, A. G. (2008). A metasynthesis of qualitative findings on the role of spirituality and religiosity among culturally diverse domestic violence survivors. *Qualitative Health Research, 18*(9), 1289–1306.

Yllo, K., & LeClerc, K. (1988). Marital rape. In A. L. Horton & J. A. Williamson (Eds.), *Abuse and religion: When praying isn't enough* (pp. 49–57). Lexington, MA: Lexington Books.

Chapter Authors

**Tameka L. Gillum** is an Assistant Professor in the Public Health department, Community Health Studies division at the University of Massachusetts Amherst. Her research explores and addresses intimate partner violence (IPV) in racial/ethnic minority and sexual minority populations, the development and evaluation of culturally specific prevention and intervention efforts, health clinic-based IPV interventions, and the mental and physical health effects of IPV victimization. She has authored a number of publications in these areas. She is a community psychologist who conducts community-based research and utilizes both qualitative and quantitative methods in her research endeavors.

Shondrah Tarrezz Nash received a doctorate in sociology from the University of Kentucky and conducted postdoctoral research in the Department of African American Studies at the University of Illinois at Chicago. She is also an active board member of a domestic violence shelter and antiviolence organization serving areas of Appalachian Kentucky. An associate professor of sociology at Morehead State University, Dr. Nash examines the coping strategies and experiences of abused Christian and black women victim/survivors.

Personal Reflection

Rev. Dr. Marie Fortune

My interest in addressing faith issues for battered women came from hearing their stories of despair at having gone to a faith leader and being given a response that was not only not helpful, but sometimes was harmful. I had to assume that this was due to ignorance on the part of the faith leader, so my hope was that education and awareness could change this and help faith leaders be resources rather than roadblocks for ending the violence and abuse.

Since 1977, there has been a major shift in the general awareness in faith communities that intimate partner violence and domestic terror are present in our synagogues, mosques, and churches. This is largely due to the courageous witness of many victims and survivors who have come forward and shared their stories. The challenge remains to actively engage faith communities in response and prevention. Intimate partner violence and domestic terror are common experiences inside and outside faith communities. As faith leaders, we have a particular responsibility to name it and claim it as part of our agenda. From an informed position, we have enormous resources to offer to the effort to address and prevent this violence and abuse.

Since I founded FaithTrust Institute in 1977, it has been a national resource for faith communities and secular advocates who want to work more closely with their faith communities. We have laid the foundation for multifaith and faith-specific responses to intimate partner violence and domestic terror. We have produced multicultural resources now in use in the U.S. and around the world. We have collaborated with local, regional, and national organizations to support their work on the ground. We have confronted the cultures of apathy, acceptance, and tacit or not so tacit support of disrespect and exploitation of women and children that have been justified by the misuse of religious teachings. We should never ask a battered woman to choose between safety and her faith community. In fact, her faith community should be her ally in seeking safety and in holding her abuser accountable.

While we have witnessed remarkable change in the past 30 years, much remains to be done. So we continue to develop leadership for this task and collaborate with many colleagues to move this work forward. We can equip faith communities and leaders to be part of the solution, not part of the problem.

CHAPTER 17

School-Based Dating Violence Prevention

From Single Events to Evaluated, Integrated Programming

Claire V. Crooks, Peter G. Jaffe,
David A. Wolfe, Ray Hughes, and Debbie Chiodo

Researchers and policy makers often end their publications on intimate partner violence with a plea to invest in primary prevention programs to help children and adolescents learn healthy relationship skills as a critical part of development. There has been an increasing focus on universal programs for adolescents because in their early dating patterns, adolescents are beginning to develop the first intimate relationships outside their family. Schools are seen as an ideal venue for these programs, and adolescent dating violence prevention programs are becoming quite popular. Despite this increased popularity, there is still relatively little empirical research in the area, and the majority of programs currently implemented have not been rigorously evaluated.

The purpose of this chapter is to provide an overview of the problem of adolescent dating violence and the emergence of programs designed to address this problem. The first section of this chapter will provide an overview of adolescent dating violence. Because the age range of adolescents is approximately 12 to 19 years, there are some significant differences in experiences of dating relationships and violence. We then outline the reasons for the increased interest in dating violence prevention. Initially, most dating violence prevention initiatives were conducted by community partners (such as women's shelters) in schools, and these programs tended to be of short duration and applied an adult-centric model of power and control. There are problems with this approach, which will be outlined briefly. Recently, program developers have worked to create developmentally appropriate dating violence prevention programs. These have drawn from the literature on bullying prevention and apply many of the same general principles. These principles will be identified and described. A number of barriers to developing and implementing effective programs are identified and discussed: (1) lack of developmental awareness, (2) failure to understand the complexity of the school system, and (3) challenges in evaluation research. In contrast to the numerous bullying prevention randomized controlled trials[1] (RCTs) published, there are still only three published RCTs of dating violence prevention programs that have shown significant positive effects.[2] Two of these were delivered as universal prevention programs in the schools (*Safe Dates* and *The Fourth R*) and the other was a targeted prevention program for high-risk youth (the *Youth Relationships Program*). Each of these programs is described, along with research findings. The final section of the chapter will identify and address some of the ongoing challenges and controversies in the field.

Understanding Adolescent Dating Violence

Adolescent dating violence among heterosexual couples is a common and troubling occurrence. As with adult intimate partner violence, there is a wide range of abusive behaviors that adolescents perpetrate. Behaviors include physical violence such as scratching, as well as more severe behaviors such as hitting, punching, choking, and assault with a weapon. Emotional, psychological, and

sexual violence are also evident in adolescent dating violence. Although there is little research on violence among same-sex adolescent couples, existing research suggests that violence is experienced in similar forms in these relationships (Freedner, Freed, Yang, & Austin, 2002; Halpern, Young, Waller, Martin, & Kupper, 2004). In same-sex relationships, there is an additional form of emotional abuse with respect to threatening to "out" someone (Freedner et al., 2002).

Historically, adolescent dating violence was not considered to be an area of much concern, perhaps in part because adolescent dating relationships were not taken very seriously. We now know that adolescent dating violence can have significant negative impacts. Dating violence victimization has been associated with a range of negative psychological and behavioral consequences, including post-traumatic stress disorder and depression (Wolitzky-Taylor et al., 2008), peer violence and suicidal behaviors (Swahn et al., 2008), and health compromising outcomes such as substance use, unhealthy dieting practices, and pregnancy (Silverman, Raj, Mucci, & Hathaway, 2001). It may also predict continued use of violence in intimate partner relationships throughout the lifespan.

Numerous risk factors for dating violence have been identified.[3] These include demographic factors such as low SES and African American ethnicity, although results in this

---

[1]Randomized controlled trials are large evaluation studies in which individuals (or families or schools) are randomly assigned to an intervention or control condition. They are considered to be the gold standard of evaluation research and do not have the same problems associated with other common evaluation designs. For example, comparison group research (whereby the assignment to intervention or control is not random) can be biased if intervention groups are self-selected and potentially more motivated to change. Pre- and post-designs make it impossible to know whether changes are related to an intervention or are simply a function of development. For example, if dating violence rates increase following an intervention, it might be that the intervention had a negative impact, or it might be that rates went up because the participants were older (and more had begun dating), and the intervention may have resulted in a smaller rate increase than would have been observed otherwise. An RCT design ensures that observed changes are the result of the intervention and not pre-existing group differences or a function of development.

[2]All of the published RCT evaluations to date have been of North American programs; consequently, programs from other countries are not discussed in this chapter due to the lack of evidence about their effectiveness.

[3]There have been many studies examining risk factors, often with contradictory results. Readers are referred to O'Keefe (2005) for a thorough and succinct review of this literature.

regard have been inconsistent (see O'Keefe, 2005). Prior experience with or exposure to violence is another risk factor, with some studies showing increased rates of dating violence among youth who have been exposed to parental domestic violence or experienced child maltreatment (Wolfe, Scott, Wekerle, & Pittman, 2001). The acceptance of the use of violence is a strong risk factor for dating violence (Foshee, Bauman, & Linder, 1999). Peer influence has been found to be a significant risk factor and potentially a stronger predictor than family violence (Arriaga & Foshee, 2004). Finally, engagement in other problem behaviors is associated with higher rates of dating violence (e.g., Silverman et al., 2001). In a recent longitudinal analysis of trajectories of intimate partner violence from adolescence to young adulthood, early sexual debut and number of sexual partners were the most robust predictors of violence and whether dating violence persisted over time, underscoring the importance of looking at different problem behaviors together (Halpern, Spriggs, Martin, & Kupper, 2009).

The role of ethnicity in predicting adolescent dating violence is complex. The majority of studies have been cross-sectional. On one hand, some researchers have found higher rates among African Americans and lower rates among Asians and Latinos, with Caucasians falling somewhere in the middle (O'Keefe, 2005). On the other hand, other researchers have found no ethnicity differences once other variables are controlled (Malik, Sorenson, & Aneshensel, 1997). In the previously mentioned study of developmental trajectories with a nationally representative sample, ethnic minority status (non-Hispanic black or Hispanic) was associated with the persistence of dating violence from adolescence to adulthood, even though rates of adolescent dating violence did not differ between non-Hispanic whites and Hispanics (Halpern et al., 2009). Non-Hispanic black youth reported higher rates of dating violence than their non-Hispanic white counterparts as adolescents and young adults, as well as higher rates of persistence between the two developmental stages.

Although these results seem to suggest significant ethnicity differences, the effects may be explained by structural factors such as unemployment and unbalanced gender ratios, rather than ethnicity per se (Wilson, 1996). Qualitative research with youth from a distressed urban community has been highly informative in understanding these patterns (Miller & White, 2003). In one such study, Miller interviewed youth from neighborhoods characterized by intense racial segregation, social isolation, limited resources, concentrated poverty, and high rates of violent crime (Miller, 2001). These interviews identified higher than average rates of dating violence but also strong gender scripts that supported this violence, such as the intense pressure on boys to be "playa"s and to use girls for sex without any emotional attachment. In this subculture, there was significant gender asymmetry in terms of the causes, impacts, and experience of dating violence (Miller & White, 2003). Her work shows that more than ethnicity, it is the intersection of ethnicity and disadvantage that is critical, and that within this group, race- and class-based structural inequalities result in exaggerated notions of masculinity that are linked to dating violence.

Dating Violence Prevalence Estimates

Dating violence behaviors such as insults, threats, and intimidation (i.e., abuse that is not physically violent) are commonly reported among a sizeable minority of youth (25%–35%; Malik, et al., 1997; Cascardi, Avery-Leaf, O'Leary, & Smith Slep, 1999). However, even the more severe forms of dating violence, such as physical and sexual assaults, are relatively prevalent: Ten to twenty percent of youth (boys as well as girls) report being hit, slapped, or forced to have sex by a dating partner (Coker, McKeown, Sanderson, Davis, Valois, & Huebner, 2000; Grunbaum et al., 2002; Silverman et al., 2001). When asked to report on specific behaviors such as hitting, slapping, and punching, 11% of high school students reported perpetrating physical abuse and 28% reported having been a victim of such behavior on at least one occasion, with no significant reporting differences between girls and boys (Wolfe et al., 2001). Data from the National Survey of Adolescence, which surveyed more than 3,500 adolescents, found that the most serious forms of dating violence, including physical assault with serious injury or a weapon, sexual assault, and drug- or alcohol-facilitated rape, were experienced by 1.6% of 12- to 17-year-olds (Wolitzky-Taylor et al., 2008). The only nationally representative survey of partner violence in adolescent same-sex romantic and sexual relationships to date found that 24% of youth had experienced some form of violence and 11% had experienced physical violence (Halpern et al., 2004). Although both of these studies were nationally representative, the rates of violence between heterosexual and same-sex couples cannot be compared, due to different criteria and definitions being employed.

Recently, researchers have begun to examine dating violence among younger adolescents to explore further the use of aggression as youth transition into opposite-sex dating relationships. Data from four diverse U.S. sites show that even among sixth-grade students, reports of physical aggression toward dating partners are common. Among those reporting that they had a recent boyfriend or girlfriend, nearly 31.5% of girls and 26.4% of boys reported being physically aggressive to this person (Simon, Miller, Gorman-Smith, Orpinas, & Sullivan, 2009). This investigation of prevalence rates in youth as young as sixth grade is an important advance in our understanding of dating violence, but these numbers should be interpreted cautiously in light of the high-risk nature of the sample (i.e., all four communities had significantly higher rates of poverty and youth crime than the national averages).

Why is there such a range in prevalence estimates (i.e., from 1.6% to 35%+)? There are numerous reasons for this variability. Adolescent dating violence is extremely difficult to measure. All the same challenges in measuring adult interpersonal violence exist with adolescents, such as privacy concerns and denial and defensiveness, along with added challenges related to developmental changes. Youth tend to date in groups of peers during early adolescence and progress to more adult-like dyadic dating by the end of adolescence, making dating violence measurement difficult. In early group-based dating, it may be very difficult to distinguish dating violence from peer-to-peer harassment and bullying, as these may all be different points along a developmental trajectory. In addition, there may be a fine line between harmful harassing or violent behaviors and developmentally appropriate playful ways of showing interest in others. As youth are only beginning to learn to relate to each other in romantic relationships, there is a transition process where these boundaries are explored. For example, teasing or taking possessions from a peer are two of the ways that pre-adolescents and early adolescents show interest in others, but those same behaviors can be abusive in some contexts. Furthermore, displays of jealousy and controlling behavior may be perceived as signs of love (Levy, 1990).

Determining which behaviors constitute abuse is a complicated issue in conducting adolescent dating violence research. Early research typically depended on adult-derived definitions of which behaviors are considered abusive. Some important qualitative work has challenged the notion that adolescents and adults necessarily agree on the characteristics of healthy and unhealthy or abusive relationships. Furthermore, these descriptions of healthy and unhealthy relationships may differ by gender, either in terms of expectations for boys versus girls or in terms of description by boys versus girls. For example, focus groups with middle school youth found that participants described a healthy relationship as one where the boyfriend and girlfriend are nice to each other, monogamous, and treat each other well (Noonan & Charles, 2009). However, clear differences arose in terms of expectations for boys versus girls. Good girlfriends were described as being supportive, not hanging around other boys, and attending their boyfriends' sporting events. Conversely, good boyfriends were described in terms of traditional gender roles such as pampering and protecting their girlfriends. Gender differences related to definitions of dating violence arise in terms of how girls and boys define abuse. Focus groups with students in grades 9 and 11 found that although boys and girls agree that it is the context that determines whether a behavior is abusive, they differ in terms of their criteria for determining context (Sears, Byers, Whelan, & Saint-Pierre, 2006). Specifically, boys described behaviors as abusive if the *intent* was negative (i.e., if there was anger or an intent to hurt behind it), whereas girls described behaviors as abusive based on *impact* (i.e., if they caused uneasiness, physical or emotional hurt, or fear). Clearly, these differing definitions and descriptions of healthy and abusive relationship behaviors are added challenges in designing and interpreting adolescent dating violence research. These qualitative studies represent an important attempt to better understand adolescents' lived experience, rather than impose adult definitions of abuse.

The other developmental backdrop to consider in estimating prevalence is that youth begin to date at different ages. Thus, prevalence rates will differ among youth in general versus among those who are dating. In the National Survey of Adolescence analysis mentioned previously, the low rates are attributable to both the strict criteria for serious dating violence used by the researchers and to the number of youth included in the sample that were not yet dating. The authors note that their rates would be much higher if they had not included 12- and 13-year-olds in their sample.

Understanding Gender Differences in Dating Violence

Gender differences further complicate the measurement issues of adolescent dating violence. In general, research based on self-report data finds that adolescent girls and boys report similar levels of perpetration (Moretti, Catchpole, & Odgers, 2005), and in some cases, girls report more violence toward dating partners than boys (Foshee et al., 2008; Wolfe et al., 2009). Despite similar rates of self-reported violence for boys and girls, intimate partner violence is not a gender-neutral phenomenon among adolescents. Even when rates of perpetration appear similar for male and female adolescents, these numbers mask important sex differences. An obvious difference is in calculating rates of serious dating violence versus indiscriminately counting any acts of aggression. The National Survey on Adolescence is informative in this regard. When serious forms of dating violence were examined, the experience of victimization for females was nearly five times the victimization rate for males (2.7% versus 0.6%; Wolitzky-Taylor et al., 2008). Gender differences in expression, form, intent, and consequences of aggression between adolescent dating partners, as well as the relational context in which it occurs, underscore the importance of a gender analysis in understanding this phenomenon.

Emerging Directions in Dating Violence Research

Early research on adolescent dating violence was primarily focused on describing the problem, establishing prevalence rates, and identifying associated risk factors and consequences. Recently, researchers began to look more closely at newly identified forms of violence, as well as links between dating violence and other forms of violence. For example, relational aggression— also known as indirect aggression—in dating relationships has been recognized as a separate category of violence with distinct associated impacts (Ellis, Crooks, & Wolfe, 2009). Other researchers have begun to look at constellations of violence together, both violence that is directed toward others in the forms of peer and dating violence and self-directed violence and suicidality (Swahn et al., 2008). Similarly, dating violence has historically been researched separately from sexual harassment, although the two patterns share common features. Our recent study investigating the relationship between the two found that sexual harassment was both associated with and predictive of experiences of dating violence (Chiodo, Wolfe, Crooks, Hughes, & Jaffe, 2009).

Considerations for Prevention Programming

The significant rates of and consequences associated with adolescent dating violence warrant a public health approach focusing on promotion of healthy relationships and prevention of dating violence, rather than relying solely on identification and intervention with youth already perpetrating or experiencing dating violence. The need to be proactive is underscored by the low rates of help seeking among adolescents involved in dating violence. One study found that 60% of victims and 79% of perpetrators did not seek help for dating violence (Ashley & Foshee, 2005). Furthermore, those who did seek help were much more likely to turn to friends and family than professional services. Clearly, a system that relies on intervention alone will not meet the needs of the majority of adolescents involved in dating violence. In building the argument for school-based violence prevention with adolescents, one can consider reasons for a prevention focus in general, particularly the benefits afforded by the school setting, and developmental considerations that make adolescence an appropriate age for prevention efforts.

Interpersonal violence is one of the most difficult behaviors to change, yet it remains an urgent concern of most communities. Youth violence requires complex, intensive, multi-pronged interventions, and even then some individuals continue to be violent well into adulthood. Although there is considerable variability in individual outcomes, dating violence during adolescence raises the likelihood of intimate partner violence during adulthood. Among adults, entrenched patterns of relationship-based violence are extremely difficult to alter. For example,

interventions for men who abuse their intimate partners have modest success, and only when they are integrated into a responsive legal system (Gondolf, 2002). Due to the intransigence of violent behavior once it is entrenched, prevention is the only viable solution if we want to have a meaningful impact on the prevalence and consequences of intimate partner violence (O'Leary, Woodin, & Fritz, 2006). Furthermore, prevention is the best hope of avoiding the harmful consequences of dating violence, whereas a crisis-driven intervention response to youth already involved in dating violence is only instigated after someone has been victimized.

School-based programs are important because school is where much relationship aggression occurs. In addition, violence in schools has a profound negative impact on youths' ability to learn. Conversely, school-based programs also provide an excellent opportunity for youth to learn positive relationship skills. There are several advantages that schools have over other settings. There is access to most children and the structured environment facilitates the implementation of integrated and cohesive programming. Because youth attend school throughout their development, programming can be geared to match their developmental stages. There is some evidence that children who are aggressive in their relationships progress from bullying to harassment to dating violence as they age, parallel to the changing focus on relationships (Connolly, Pepler, Craig, & Taradash, 2000). School-based programming provides the opportunity to match this developmental trajectory and address the most salient forms of interpersonal violence at the appropriate developmental stage. Most important, programs can be delivered in a universal manner, which prevents the stigma of youth being selected to attend a special program.

In addition to being a suitable location for intervention, schools may also play a role as a potential contributor to violence. In a study we conducted examining the relationship between the experience of multiple forms of child maltreatment and violent delinquency among adolescents, our data indicated that school characteristics played a role in two ways (Crooks, Scott, Wolfe, Chiodo, & Killip, 2007). First, overall feelings of school safety across the whole student body contributed to lower rates of violent delinquency. Second, we found evidence of a buffer effect in schools that had implemented a comprehensive program to prevent dating violence and other risk behaviors. Notably, the impact of cumulative forms of childhood maltreatment on risk for engaging in violent delinquency was greater in schools that had not participated in the program, suggesting a school-wide buffering effect for the most vulnerable students. That is, students in schools with a comprehensive prevention program were less likely to engage in violent delinquency than students in schools without these programs, all other risk factors being equal. Although these findings have not been replicated with dating violence per se, they serve as an important reminder that not all school environments are equal and that interventions implemented at the school level have the opportunity to change the environment as well as individual behavior.

Finally, adolescence itself has several attributes that promote it as a time for successful prevention. As the transition from childhood to adulthood, adolescence presents a period of instability and change (American Psychological Association, 1993). Transition periods are often more amenable to change, as a system is already in flux; it is more difficult to introduce change to a system that has achieved homeostasis and thus has considerable inertia. During adolescence, individuals often try on different characteristics and roles and are more open to experimenting with new ways of relating to others. Developing more intimate peer and dating relationships and experimenting with romantic relationships are key developmental tasks. Youth are naturally interested in relationships and are willing to explore the topic, yet they have not become entrenched in patterns of relating to romantic partners. This natural inclination to try new patterns can be used to strengthen their interpersonal capacities by providing adolescents with

growth opportunities that emphasize a more positive mode of relating to others. Conversely, if adolescents are not provided with strong messages about ways to develop healthy dating and peer relationships, they will be more vulnerable to the bombardment of other, less healthy messages conveyed by media and peers.

Schools offer many opportunities for intervention, but they are not without limitation. They do not reach all youth, particularly those at highest risk for poor outcomes, and not all youth find school-based activities engaging (Whitaker et al., 2006). Furthermore, given the complex multiply-determined nature of interpersonal violence, it is conceivable that programs extending beyond school could derive an additional benefit by interacting with more of the environments and structures within which youth function. Finally, the increasing pressure on educators to deliver results in terms of literacy and numeracy has created a situation in which educators and administrators may be reluctant to undertake anything seen as an extra. Solutions to this last concern are addressed later in this chapter.

Given the relative infancy of the empirical literature on dating violence prevention, it is useful to examine the best practice principles that have emerged from other types of violence prevention, such as bullying and peer violence, while remaining cognizant of how dating violence prevention programs may need to differ from other types of violence prevention. There have been numerous large-scale initiatives to identify effective practices in violence prevention. Two of the best-known initiatives are the Surgeon General's Report (U.S. Public Health Service & Office of the Surgeon General, 2000) and the Blueprints Violence Prevention Initiative (Mihalic, Fagan, Irwin, Ballard, & Elliott, 2004). These initiatives identify programs that have been found efficacious under the most rigorous of research conditions, typically numerous RCTs. While these initiatives represent the best-researched programs, many effective programs are not included for the simple reason that conducting research of the scope and complexity required to be identified as a Blueprints Model

Program is an extremely expensive and specialized undertaking. These reports suggest that successful programs (a) are comprehensive in nature; (b) focus on skills; (c) pick appropriate targets for change; (d) use peers; (e) include parents; and (f) attempt to change the larger environment.

Programs that the Surgeon General's report and Blueprints identified as model or promising are comprehensive. Comprehensive programs recognize that risk behaviors occur in many contexts, so successful interventions similarly need to be applicable to individual, family, peer, school, and community circumstances, as much as possible. Programs may also be comprehensive by targeting more than one outcome, such as violence and substance use, since these problems often co-occur. Effective programs do not compartmentalize youth with respect to their environments or their behaviors. Rather, they take a more holistic approach that recognizes the complexity and interrelatedness of different settings for youth and offer knowledge and assistance that is appropriately matched.

Providing youth with opportunities to develop interpersonal skills is the most common feature of effective prevention programs. Social skills training may take numerous forms, which usually involve specific training in conflict management and problem-solving skills. This training typically incorporates a role-play component to give students opportunities to increase their ability and comfort level with their newly developed skills. For example, students may role-play strategies to deal with or confront instances of bullying. In other interventions, students meet in small groups to discuss and role-play positive alternatives to problem behaviors. Skills training is most effective if combined with accurate information about risks and consequences. Similarly, a skills approach is action oriented, not merely a passive discussion of behavioral options (Durlak & Wells, 1997). Some promising prevention programs aimed at relationship-based violence also provide training in help-seeking behavior, such as learning about and navigating social service agencies in the community (Wolfe, Wekerle, Scott, Straatman, Grasley, & Reitzel-Jaffe, 2003).

In addition to promoting social skills, effective violence prevention programs target antisocial attitudes and beliefs associated with aggression and violence. Activities to change attitudes can include awareness raising, such as learning information about violence, and empathy-building exercises. For example, students in the Bullying Prevention Program participate in classroom activities like role-playing, writing, and small-group discussions geared toward helping them gain a better appreciation of the harm caused by bullying (Olweus, Limber, & Mahalic, 1999). In contrast to these successful strategies, programs that target issues only distally related to violence do not have much of an impact. For example, contrary to popular belief, children who engage in bullying seldom suffer from low self-esteem; therefore, targeting poor self-esteem does not change their behavior. Conversely, empathy for victims *is* linked to bullying and is a viable target for reducing such behavior.

Given the significant influence that peers have on adolescent behavior, it is not surprising that effective programs commonly address the peer group factor. The Bullying Prevention Program includes regular classroom meetings about peer relations and encourages students to not condone bullying by peers. Overcoming bystander apathy is a particularly important peer-level target. Children and adolescents are encouraged to think of themselves as having a responsibility to stop others from being victimized, and inclusion of others is promoted as a means for preventing bullying. Other prevention programs use peers as facilitators or mediators to increase the salience of the program.

Although parents are not as actively included in school-based prevention as in some other types of family-based programs, they are nonetheless important. Several of the model school-based prevention programs attempt to increase communication between home and school, which is effective in increasing parent-child connection and parental interest. For example, Project PATHE enlists staff, students, and parents to work collaboratively to design and implement each school's particular program. Engaging these various stakeholders increases their sense of ownership of the program, which translates to investment in the success of the program.

Effective programs recognize that beyond intervening with individual youth, there is a need to address the school climate. Different programs address school climate by restructuring certain aspects of the school or by incorporating additional activities and services. The School Transitional Environmental Program (STEP) is an example of a program that restructures aspects of the school in an attempt to modify school climate. The primary goals of STEP are to increase the level of social support available to students and reduce the amount of flux and complexity as students transfer to high school (Felner & Adan, 1988). To achieve these goals, STEP restructures the role of the homeroom teacher; in their expanded roles, homeroom teachers act as administrators and guidance counselors, including monitoring attendance, helping with course selection, counseling regarding school and personal problems, and communicating with parents. STEP also reduces school disorganization by having all STEP participants in the school enrolled in the same core classes, so that students spend much of their time with the same group of students as opposed to having new people in every class, and all of these core classes are located in the same wing of the school. These structural changes are intended to increase the cohesion or school connectedness of students at risk for academic and behavioral problems, which in turn raises the likelihood of school success. The Bullying Prevention Program also modifies the school climate through restructuring. This program introduces supervision of bullying "hot spots," as well as highly coordinated supervision during break periods and other times when bullying is most likely to occur.

All of the preceding principles can be applied to dating violence prevention. However, there are significant and critical differences between bullying and dating violence that need to be addressed. The most salient of these are the role that gender plays in dating violence and how to effectively incorporate our understanding of dating violence as a gendered phenomenon into programming that will engage youth. This challenge is discussed further in the following section.

Common Problems Faced in Program Development and Implementation

Some areas of violence among children, most notably bullying, have been areas of concern for educators and parents for 30 years. Today, there is widespread acceptance of the idea that addressing and preventing bullying is a fundamental role for schools and communities. There is not the same consensus about the importance and relevance of adolescent dating violence as a legitimate area for prevention efforts. The significance of adolescent dating violence may be underestimated because often adolescent dating relationships are not taken seriously. Dating violence also presents a more complex challenge in terms of responsibility for prevention because these relationships are considered private and take place outside the school environment. Further complicating the issue is the very nature of adolescents and their reticence to disclose personal matters to adults in authority. Because this area is in relative infancy compared to bullying prevention, we outline three barriers that can impede the development and implementation of effective dating violence prevention programs: (1) lack of developmental awareness, (2) failure to understand the complexity of the school system, and (3) challenges in evaluation research.

Lack of Developmental Awareness

One of the ways that dating violence prevention programs must differ from general violence prevention best practice principles is in addressing gender. Some of the initial dating violence prevention programs simply imposed a power and control model of male-to-female adult domestic violence on teenagers. However, the issues and the required analyses are much different for adolescents at their stage of development. Adolescents may be at different stages of awareness in understanding the role that gender plays in their world. Most girls and boys reject a gendered analysis, with girls being protective of the boys and boys often reacting defensively. In fact, in one early study of dating violence education, boys were found to endorse *more* negative attitudes following a presentation on dating violence, and this negativity was further entrenched at follow-up (Jaffe, Sudermann, Reitzel, & Killip, 1992). Both girls and boys feel that there is a double standard whereby boys are condemned for violence but girls' violence is ignored or minimized (Sears et al., 2006). Girls also do not want to hear that they are or will become victims. Girls perceive themselves to have more freedoms than their stereotypical views of abused women trapped by child care responsibilities and poverty. Girls often report as much or more violence than the boys and see themselves able to defend against violence and abuse in relationships (Foshee, Bauman, Ennett, Suchindran, Benefield, & Linder, 2005; Foshee et al., 2008).

It is also important to be more gender strategic in addressing dating violence with boys, to engage them in this issue. Elsewhere (Crooks, Wolfe, & Jaffe, 2007), we have discussed the critical need to engage boys with the "invite, don't indict" stance endorsed by the Family Violence Prevention Fund (http://www.endabuse.org). We have found that boys can be involved in violence prevention and social justice clubs and activities in schools as part of their commitment for social change. Boys need to be approached as part of the solution rather than the problem and given appropriate leadership roles where warranted, with the necessary supports. Specifically, they need access to role models, positive reinforcement for such efforts, and the skills to intervene and lead effectively as young men (Crooks, Goodall, Hughes, Baker, & Jaffe, 2007).

Failure to Understand the Complexity of the School System

The advantages afforded by implementing programs in the school setting were enumerated at the beginning of this chapter. However, there may be many bumps in the road on the way to the successful design, implementation, evaluation, and sustainability of a school-based violence prevention program. We are often asked how to access the school system or how to get a particular program into use in the school system. There are numerous factors that influence successful implementation and sustainability of programs in schools. For example, it is important to recognize the different levels of decision makers (i.e., a district official's endorsement may be needed, but individual classroom teachers maintain freedom over what they teach) and address these in your plan to engage the education system (Crooks, Wolfe, Hughes, Jaffe, & Chiodo, 2008). There are many prevention programs that offer innovative programming but have not been accepted for widespread use in schools, and in many cases, sit gathering dust on a shelf in the principal's or guidance counselor's office. Programs need to be designed with attention to details that increase their likelihood of implementation and sustainability from the outset.

There are a number of areas to consider in designing a program or approaching a school district to consider implementing a program. There are areas of potential alignment that increase acceptability and potential sustainability of a program, such as aligning with curriculum expectations or state policies. There are also potential barriers that need to be identified and addressed prior to presenting a case for adoption of a program by a school, such as costs of specialized training and school policies prohibiting non-teachers from presenting programs during school time. In many cases, these barriers are surmountable, and an awareness of them and identification of possible solutions prior to meeting with educational partners can go a long way. Finally, there may be champions that can be identified within the school system, which may facilitate the adoption of a program. A number of these considerations and opportunities are outlined in a checklist in Table 17.1, which we have adapted from our toolkit on working with Aboriginal youth (Crooks, Chiodo, & Thomas, 2009).

Table 17.1	Checklist for Identifying Areas of Alignment With School Board Policies and Initiatives

Policies	☑ Have you checked the Provincial Ministry or State Education Department policies on violence prevention and aligned your objectives to match their policy statement?
	☑ Are you familiar with any school board policies or initiatives underway with which you could align?
	☑ If you are working with a particular school, are you aware of the school's policies or initiatives?
	☑ Are there teacher federation mandates or requirements that align with your work?
Partnerships	☑ Is there a local school board committee responsible for violence prevention initiatives? If so, can you present your ideas to this committee early in the process to assess interest and feasibility and potentially identify appropriate partners?
	☑ Is there a particular superintendent/consultant with a portfolio for violence prevention? Can you get in touch with this person early on in your planning?
	☑ Are there other community organizations already successfully partnering with the school board that you could use as a resource or mentor? Ask them about their failures in school-based programming as well as their successes.
	☑ Can you recruit an educator to be on your advisory committee or project development team? This individual will be able to assist you with the alignment process throughout all phases of development and delivery.
	☑ Is there someone at the school or board level who is known to be a "champion" of this type of initiative?
Links to Curriculum	☑ Have you decided which grade levels and areas you will be targeting with your initiative? Can you identify particular Ministry/Department curriculum expectations that your initiative matches?
	☑ If your initiative involves community-based individuals doing presentations or facilitating activities, can you develop follow-up activities that teachers can deliver that match specific curriculum expectations?
	☑ Can you utilize recognized literacy strategies in your materials or the follow-up activities?
Role of School Personnel	☑ Have you met with school administrators to determine the school's current programming?
	☑ Are administrators on board with your programming, and will they support their teachers and staff in these initiatives?
	☑ Do teachers have a role in the delivery of the program? As supervisors? Co-facilitators?
	☑ Will teachers require specialized training and/or resources? If so, who will pay for these costs?

Source: Adapted from Crooks et al. (2009).

Above all else, the educational system has a very specific mandate that currently emphasizes numeracy and literacy. This mandate becomes even more reinforced during times of economic uncertainty and budget reductions. To work effectively with this system, it is important to learn its language and find ways to demonstrate how the goals and activities of your program support the system's larger goals and mandate. For example, our team coordinated a multidisciplinary team to develop media literacy lessons that matched specific curriculum expectations for every grade (K-12) and used cutting-edge literacy strategies (http://www.crvawc.ca/CritMedLitCD/index.html). By supporting the goals of teaching to the curriculum expectations and increasing literacy, an issue of critical social importance was embedded into the school system in a way that increased the likelihood of the resource being widely accepted and becoming sustainable.

Although training teachers to implement a program can decrease the cost and increase the likelihood of sustainability compared to programs requiring external facilitation, there may be challenges in this regard, too. Compared to most social service professionals, teachers may not see violence prevention as their mandate or even an area of interest. Furthermore, some teachers will be perpetrators or victims of intimate partner violence in their own relationships, which may decrease their willingness or ability to engage students effectively. Good orientation and training can help with these challenges, but the reality remains that some teachers will not implement these programs effectively regardless of additional training.

Thus, while the education system offers the potential for incredible integration of violence prevention into the daily lives of children, sustainability of these efforts is not automatic. In a recent book, we addressed planning for sustainable change as critical to violence prevention programs (Jaffe, Crooks, & Watson, 2009). We adapted the Transtheoretical Model of Change (Prochaska & DiClemente, 1982) by simplifying it to a three-stage change model to describe the progression of schools with relation to achieving integrated and sustainable safe schools initiatives. We refer to this model as the Safe Schools Continuum, and it includes stages called Developing Awareness, Planning and Responding, and Educating and Leading. The model was revised throughout our research project, based on our work with 23 schools and other educational partners, to ensure that it is a model that makes sense and confers benefit to administrators and their teams. The utility of the Safe Schools Continuum is that awareness of a school's current place on the continuum helps principals and school staff to identify concrete actions that are likely to be successful in moving a school to the next stage. Developing and implementing a safe school plan requires an investment of time and talent from a wide range of school partners. A school that is not yet ready to take on an extensive violence prevention program may be better served by developing smaller interventions and prevention initiatives that will assist the school to build the momentum needed to address the larger issues. Based on a school's readiness for change as described in the Safe Schools Continuum, different strategies and programs may be appropriate (see Jaffe et al., 2009 for a fuller discussion).

Challenges in Evaluation Research

Similar to the fields of child abuse and domestic violence research, the field of adolescent dating violence struggles with ways to apply the best evaluation designs and measurement tools to capture the nature of this behavior and change due to intervention. The first challenge involves ways of measuring the diverse nature of dating abuse/violence and agreeing on what constitutes significant change following an intervention. Due to the hidden and socially unacceptable nature of dating violence, researchers must assess such behavior indirectly using various forms of self-report, observation, and attitudes or knowledge. Any assessment of dating violence perpetration involves somewhat contrived or abstract circumstances rather than direct observation, and thus the results are estimates only. In particular, self-reported acts of dating violence perpetration cannot convey the intensity, frequency, or context of such behavior and thus may not provide a complete and accurate assessment of change. Self-reports of particular abusive acts or behaviors do not capture motivations or circumstances surrounding such acts or distinguish between acts of offense or defense, which may account for the higher rates of dating violence reported by girls than boys noted previously. Despite this challenge, more empirically derived and developmentally appropriate measures have emerged in recent years that standardize the context and may permit subsequent interview or follow-up for further detail.

A second major evaluation challenge concerns the inclusion of control groups, random assignment, and adequate follow-up to intervention. Such design features are critical in drawing evidence-based conclusions about an intervention, yet investigators may compromise on design consideration due to concerns about school buy-in, cost, and lack of programming for students in the control condition. Unfortunately, the use of a weak experimental design has led to programs drawing conclusions on the basis of pre-post differences in attitudes, knowledge, or behavior, which may be related to developmental changes and not sustained intervention effects. To determine effectiveness of a new or expanded program, researchers need to control for changes due to maturity (a particularly critical issue for this age group) and any other interventions received by students. Similarly, because dating violence programs are largely involved in *prevention,* it is of particular value to follow students for a sufficient time period (e.g., one to three years) to determine whether meaningful changes are maintained. Future research on the prevention of dating violence and related problems will require

careful exploration of these and many similar issues pertaining to possible differences in the context, nature, and reporting of violence by boys and girls, along with cooperative partnerships with schools and communities.

Empirically Validated Programs

Given the relatively short history of dating violence prevention programs and the challenges of implementation and evaluation, it is not surprising that very few have been carefully evaluated with an appropriate randomized controlled design and sufficient measurement and follow-up. Short-term changes in attitudes and beliefs have been documented following classroom discussions or assemblies, but few have had sufficient follow-up with the participants or evaluated actual behavioral change. A critical review conducted in 2006 found only two programs that had been rigorously evaluated in an RCT and found to be effective (Whitaker et al., 2006). One of these, the Youth Relationships Project, is a selected prevention program for youth considered to be at risk of dating violence due to histories of child maltreatment or exposure to domestic violence. The other, Safe Dates, is a program that was developed for universal implementation in schools. Since that review, one other RCT has been published on the Fourth R, which is also a universal school-based program. Each of these effective programs is described below, and a comparison of program characteristics is shown in Table 17.2. Research findings for each program are also discussed.

The Youth Relationships Program

The Youth Relationships Program (YRP) is an 18-session group-based intervention designed to reduce all forms of harassment, abuse, and violence by and against dating partners. It was designed to address the needs of teens who had

Table 17.2 Program Characteristics of Effective Adolescent Dating Violence Prevention Programs

Program	Type of Prevention	Ages of Youth	Setting	Duration	Facilitators	Country of Origin	Key Components
Fourth R	Universal	Grades 7 to 12 (different developmentally targeted lessons for each grade)	School; delivered primarily in health and physical education and English classes	Core program; 21 lessons (75 min. each) delivered in Grades 9/10	Teachers with additional training	Canada	• Classroom delivered lessons including skills practice • Youth Action Committee to plan school-wide events • Information for parents
Safe Dates	Universal	Grades 7 to 10 (one set of lessons that can be used with any grade level)	School; attempts are made to integrate into existing courses during class time	9 lessons (50 min. each)	Teachers with additional training; can be delivered by older students or community professionals	U.S.A.	• Classroom delivered • Interactive lessons • School-wide poster competition and play • Information for parents
Youth Relationships Project	Selected	14 to 17	Community	18 sessions	Community service providers (e.g., social workers, counselors)	Canada	• Manualized group therapy intervention • Planning and execution of a social action project in the community

grown up with abuse and trauma experiences in their families of origin and who were thereby at greater risk for violence in their own relationships (Wolfe et al., 1996). This community-based group intervention is manual-based and instructs facilitators to help teens develop positive roles in dating by providing information-building skills, and enabling the participants to be involved in a community service component.

There are three principal sections in the manual: education and awareness, skills building, and social action learning opportunities. Education and awareness sessions focus on helping teens recognize and identify abusive behavior across various domains including woman abuse, child abuse, sexual harassment, homophobia, and racism, with a particular focus on power dynamics in male-female relationships. Information on gender-based abuse and violence, sexual assault, and date rape is presented through guest speakers such as a survivor of woman abuse or a former batterer, videos, and didactic materials regarding power and control. The skill development aspect of the program builds on this knowledge base by exploring available choices and options to solve conflict more amicably and avoid abusive situations. Communication skills include listening, empathy, emotional expressiveness, and assertive problem solving. Students practice and apply these skills to familiar situations, such as consent and personal safety in sexual relations. Finally, social action activities provide participants with information about resources in their community that can help them manage unfamiliar, stressful issues affecting their relationships. These activities involve youth in the community in a positive way to help them overcome their prejudices or fear of community agencies such as police, welfare, and counseling. Social action projects engage youths to be actively involved in opposing attitudes and behaviors that foster gender-based violence and similar issues raised in their group. Social action projects undertaken by the groups include a carwash to raise money for a shelter and the organization of a walk to raise awareness about violence against women.

The YRP was evaluated in a randomized trial with 158 high-risk 14- to 16-year-olds with histories of maltreatment (Wolfe et al., 2003). The control group was an existing care condition, which typically included bimonthly visits from a social worker and the provision of basic shelter and care. The teens in the study completed measures of abuse and victimization with dating partners, emotional distress, and healthy relationship skills at bimonthly intervals, when dating someone. Youth were followed on average for 16 months post-intervention. Self-report and partner-report data showed the intervention to be effective in reducing incidents of physical and emotional abuse over time, relative to controls. An interesting adjunct finding was that symptoms of emotional distress and trauma were also lower over time compared to the control group, even though these symptoms were not directly targeted with the intervention. It is important to remember that these results were observed with older adolescents considered to be high risk and that the YRP was not designed for universal implementation in schools.

The Safe Dates Program

Safe Dates is a school-based program based on the premise that changes in norms regarding partner violence and gender roles and improvement in prosocial skills lead to primary prevention of dating violence. At the secondary prevention level, there is a focus on changing beliefs about the need for help and increasing youths' awareness of available services. The stated goals of the program are to raise awareness of what constitutes healthy and abusive dating relationships, raise awareness of dating abuse and its causes and consequences, equip students with the skills and resources to help themselves or friends in abusive dating relationships, and teach students skills to develop healthy dating relationships. The skills component focuses on positive communication, anger management, and conflict resolution. Safe Dates is structured around nine 45-minute sessions in school, with additional community components. School strategies include curriculum, a theatre production, and a poster contest. Community components include services for adolescents in violent dating relationships and training for service providers. There are also materials available for parents. Teachers who implement the curriculum component receive between one and two days of training, depending on the implementation plan, and community service providers typically receive three hours of training. In 2006, Safe Dates was selected for SAMHSA's National Registry of Evidence-Based Programs and Practices (NREPP) after receiving high ratings on all criteria for strength of evidence and ease of replication.

The Safe Dates Project was evaluated using a randomized trial that involved five waves of data, to examine the effects of the program over time. The evaluation examined the impact of the program on adolescents who had not been involved in dating violence and those who were already showing signs of these difficulties (Foshee et al., 2005). Safe Dates was found to be effective at all four follow-up periods in reducing psychological, moderate physical, and sexual dating violence perpetration and moderate physical dating violence victimization. The program seemed the most effective with adolescents who were already involved in dating violence. The program was equally effective for males and females and for whites and non-whites. The evaluation also examined mediators in the change process. Program effects were mediated by changes in dating violence norms, gender-role norms, and awareness of community services, consistent with the program's stated goals.

The Fourth R

The Fourth R is a school-based universal prevention program that targets dating violence and related risk behaviors. The cornerstone of the core Grade 9 version of the Fourth R is a 21-lesson skill-based curriculum that promotes healthy relationships and targets violence, high-risk sexual behavior, and substance use among adolescents. It is delivered by teachers who receive specialized training. The contention is that relationship skills can be taught in much the same way as the other "three Rs" (reading, 'riting, and 'rithmetic), and establishing these skills as a fundamental part of the high school curriculum is equally essential. The Fourth R is composed of three units to address violence, substance use, and healthy sexuality/sexual behavior. Together, these three units address the triad of adolescent risk behaviors that are connected in terms of co-occurrence, but are also jointly rooted in peer and dating relationships experienced by youth. Adolescents receive ample practice role-playing ways to resolve conflict, both as participants and in the role of bystander. Furthermore, they learn to apply the skills in each of the three areas. For example, instead of learning assertive communication in general, they learn to practice assertive communication during realistic situations, such as dating and peer conflict, pressure to use drugs or alcohol, and pressure to engage in sexual behavior.

Other program components focus on the wider school community and parents. School interventions include staff and teacher awareness education, information about the program, and supplementary activities by the student-led Youth Action Committees (YACs) to increase links between community partners. A YAC is developed with guidance from a teacher, based on a manual that provides guidance in recruitment, training, planning and conducting activities, and evaluating success. Parents are provided with developmental information and parenting strategies relevant to raising adolescents. In addition to the core program for Grade 9 students, there are numerous extensions for other grade levels, curriculum areas, and special populations. For example, we have developed an Aboriginal perspectives version of the Fourth R to respect cultural differences and the historical context of Aboriginal people in Canada, including the impact of residential schools (see http://youthrelationships.org/curriculum_resources/ aboriginal_perspectives.html).[4,5] Beyond looking at the roots of problems in an appropriate historical context, our Aboriginal Perspectives Fourth R includes culturally relevant models of healthy relationships from a holistic perspective and ways to engage the support of the extended family and community in making healthy choices, both of which are important in Aboriginal cultures.

The Fourth R was evaluated in a cluster randomized trial of 1,722 Grade 9 students in Health classes nested in 20 schools (Wolfe et al., 2009). The results indicated that control students used more acts of physical violence toward a dating partner by the end of Grade 11, compared to those receiving intervention. The effect of the intervention was greater among boys than girls. The program was also found to be effective for increasing condom use, especially among sexually active boys. Overall, the study indicated that teaching youth healthy relationship awareness and skills as part of their required health curriculum reduced physical dating violence and increased condom use 2.5 years later. In addition to these findings, using a subsample of 200 students (100 per condition), our research team found significant gains in skill acquisition among students from intervention schools (Crooks et al., 2008). During a 5-minute videotaped role-play interaction, Fourth R students were 2.2 times more likely than controls to show at least one negotiation skill ($p = .013$); 4.8 times more likely to show at least one delay skill ($p = .05$; girls only); and were 50% less likely to yield to the coercive pressures being perpetrated against them. The groups did not differ in terms of complying behaviors. In addition, half the tapes were coded separately by teachers on more face-valid concepts, such as application of skills and communication, as well as a global rating of the likelihood that the student in the video would make a healthy decision in real life. For all of the dimensions coded by teachers, a significant main effect emerged favoring the students who had participated in the Fourth R.

Facing the Challenges in Preventing Dating Violence: The Road Ahead

Although we are encouraged by the progress in the field of dating violence prevention, we recognize that there is a long road ahead. Maura O'Keefe (2005) describes the challenge well and the need for a well-resourced and comprehensive approach:

> It is naïve to think a change in attitudes or behavior can occur unless a long-term, integrated, and multi-dimensional approach is launched at all system levels. Prevention of dating violence will require a clear commitment (both financial and otherwise) with the goal of establishing a consistent, coordinated, and integrated approach in every school and community. Dating violence prevention programs need to be incorporated into systems and institutions serving youth including schools, recreational programs, juvenile justice programs, the foster care system, etc. (p. 9)

---

[4]The term Aboriginal in this context refers to the indigenous peoples of Canada, namely those of First Nations, Métis, or Inuit heritage.

[5]Residential schools were part of an aggressive federal government assimilation policy that resulted in Aboriginal children being removed from their families and communities and sent to school, where they were forbidden to speak their language or maintain any connection to their culture. The conditions of these schools were appalling and many children died there. There were also high rates of physical and sexual abuse. Residential schools existed in some form in Canada for approximately 150 years.

It is somewhat daunting to hold up the progress in the field against the most promising practices according to the Surgeon General's Report (U.S. Public Health Service & Office of the Surgeon General, 2000) and the Blueprints for Violence Prevention Initiative (http://www.colorado.edu/cspv/blueprints/). Securing the funding and collaboration for sustainable violence prevention efforts is a dream for most programs. In our travels around North America, we see the reality in the field is that most programs struggle to be implemented in a consistent manner, and they are rarely comprehensive and integrated into schools or other community institutions.

Apart from programs that emphasize skill development and attitude change among individual youth, there are some encouraging attempts to change the larger environment through social marketing and broad-based awareness programs such as the White Ribbon Campaign in Canada and internationally (http://www.whiteribbon.ca), Jackson Katz's MVP program (http://www.jacksonkatz.com), and the Family Violence Prevention Fund's prevention efforts in the U.S. (http://endabuse.org). The Choose Respect campaign launched in 2006 by the Centers for Disease Control is an excellent example of a comprehensive media campaign of this type (http://www.chooserespect.org). The Web site has a variety of interactive resources for youth and parents. There are fact sheets and guidelines for how to get involved in the issue. A number of video, TV, and radio ads are available, as well as a wide range of print materials.

These organizations and programs try to confront social norms that promote violence in intimate relationships. Some of them specifically call out to men to be mindful of their role in mentoring boys on healthy relationships. They are exciting and innovative campaigns that may provide an important public venue for challenging and changing widespread attitudes and beliefs and promoting healthier alternatives. However, we need to be cautious because there is little research to date that indicates that these messages are penetrating public attitudes and behavior.

One significant challenge where we have barely scratched the surface is examining cultural differences in regard to the nature of dating violence and how programs may need to be significantly revamped to address different populations. All too often, research articles report on ethnicity differences in perpetration and victimization but provide no cultural context to help understand these differences. Beyond looking at a deficit-based model that identifies certain racial or ethnic groups as being at higher risk for dating violence, we need to look at ways that cultural strengths can be accessed as protective factors in interventions. In the U.S., there has been significant work on the Aban Aya violence prevention program for African American youth. Although it does not address dating violence specifically, it has shown promise in reducing violence and related factors among African American males (but not females; Ngwe, Liu, Flay, & Segawa, 2004). There is a dire need for more of these programs that address cultural identity and pride as potential protective factors for marginalized minority youth.

As we reflect on the challenges researchers face in understanding the complexity of dating violence and the difficulty of evaluating the outcomes with the best quantitative and qualitative approaches, we feel cautious about describing the progress in the field. We are reminded to not let our enthusiasm for our steps forward disguise the clear limitations of what our findings are (or are not) telling us and our responsibility in representing these findings to media and policy groups. At the same time, we know that as we write this, there are many exciting randomized controlled trials underway, some of which will provide additional effective programs for combating dating violence. It is the nature of complex longitudinal research that it takes time for effective programs to demonstrate their success sufficiently.

Conclusion

In this chapter, we have outlined the progress in the field of dating violence prevention by examining the state of knowledge and some encouraging developments reflected in programs like the Fourth R, the Youth Relationships Project, and Safe Dates. We reviewed the challenges in trying to implement best practices in school-based and community programs. The complex problems of instituting and completing controlled studies that evaluate these programs were examined. The increasing demand for a better understanding of gender differences in violence prevention and respecting cultural diversity was highlighted.

Bullying, sexual harassment, sexual assault, and dating violence have emerged as diverse subjects that have been examined by researchers and practitioners in schools, communities, and the workplace. Too often there is a silo effect, which limits the ability of program developers and researchers in these different areas to learn from each other. Sometimes researchers are studying the same problems but have different language and definitions, which can impede collaboration and cross-fertilization of ideas. In reflecting on the state of dating violence prevention, we see the need for enhanced collaboration, in order for research and program development to move beyond piecemeal solutions for narrow interests. We envision the development of a more comprehensive prevention framework for abusive behaviors in a range of settings that requires a clearer analysis of gender, sexual orientation, and culture. For example, to what extent is the bullying seen on the playground in Grade 3 connected to the sexual harassment beginning in Grade 6 and dating violence in Grade 9? We need to look at integrative theories that identify common risk and protective factors across the different areas, while still retaining the uniqueness of the different areas, too. National and international groups of prevention scientists and program developers will need to take a leadership role in promoting think tanks and cross-disciplinary conferences to guide us down the road ahead with a more unified approach.

References

American Psychological Association. (1993). *Commission on youth and violence summary report: Vol. I. Violence and youth: Psychology's report.* Washington, DC: Author.

Arriaga, X. B., & Foshee, V. A. (2004). Adolescent dating violence: Do adolescents follow in their friends', or their parents', footsteps? *Journal of Interpersonal Violence, 19,* 162–184.

Ashley, O., & Foshee, V. (2005). Adolescent help-seeking for dating violence: Prevalence, sociodemographic correlates, and sources of help. *Journal of Adolescent Health, 36,* 25–31.

Cascardi, M., Avery-Leaf, S., O'Leary, D., & Smith Slep, A. M. (1999). Factor structure and convergent validity of the Conflict Tactics Scale in high school students. *Psychological Assessment, 11,* 546–555.

Chiodo, D., Wolfe, D. A., Crooks, C. V., Hughes, R., & Jaffe, P. G. (2009). The impact of sexual harassment victimization by peers on subsequent adolescent victimization and adjustment: A longitudinal study. *Journal of Adolescent Health, 45,* 246–252.

Coker, A. L., McKeown, R. E., Sanderson, M., Davis, K. E., Valois, R. F., & Huebner, E. S. (2000). Severe dating violence and quality of life among South Carolina high school students. *American Journal of Preventive Medicine, 19,* 220–226.

Connolly, J. Pepler, D., Craig, W., & Taradash, A. (2000). Dating experiences of bullies in early adolescence. *Child Maltreatment, 5,* 299–310.

Crooks, C. V., Chiodo, D., & Thomas, D. (2009). *Engaging and empowering Aboriginal youth: A toolkit for service providers.* Victoria, BC: Trafford.

Crooks, C. V., Goodall, G. R., Hughes, R., Baker. L. L., & Jaffe, P. G. (2007). Engaging men and boys in preventing violence against women: Application of a cognitive-behavioral model. *Violence Against Women, 13,* 217–239.

Crooks, C. V., Scott, K. L., Wolfe, D. A., Chiodo, D., & Killip, S. (2007). Understanding the link between childhood maltreatment and violent delinquency: What do schools have to add? *Child Maltreatment, 12,* 269–280.

Crooks, C. V., Wolfe, D. A., Hughes, R., Jaffe, P. G., & Chiodo, D. (2008). Development, evaluation and national implementation of a school-based program to reduce violence and related risk behaviors. *Institute for the Prevention of Crime Review, 2,* 109–135.

Crooks, C. V., Wolfe, D. A., & Jaffe, P. G. (2007). School-based adolescent dating violence prevention: Enhancing effective practice with a gender strategic approach. In K. Kendall-Tackett & S. Giacomoni (Eds.), *Intimate partner violence* (pp. 16.1–16.18). Kingston, NJ: Civic Research Institute.

Durlak, J. A., & Wells, A. M. (1997). Primary prevention mental health programs for children and adolescents: A meta-analytic review. *American Journal of Community Psychology, 25*(2), 115–152.

Ellis, W. E., Crooks, C. V., & Wolfe, D. A. (2009). Relational aggression in peer and dating relationships: Links to psychological and behavioral adjustment. *Social Development, 18,* 253–269.

Felner, R. D., & Adan, A. M. (1988). The school transitional project: An ecological intervention and evaluation. In R. H. Price, E. L. Cowen, R. P. Lorion, & J. Ramos-McKay (Eds.), *14 ounces of prevention: A casebook for practitioners* (pp. 111–122). Washington, DC: American Psychological Association.

Foshee, V. A., Bauman, K. E., Ennett, S. T., Suchindran, C., Benefield, T., & Linder G. F. (2005). Assessing the effects of the dating violence prevention program "Safe Dates" using random coefficient regression modeling. *Prevention Science, 6,* 245–258.

Foshee, V. A., Bauman, K. E., & Linder, G. F. (1999). Family violence and the preparation of adolescent dating violence: Examining social learning and social control processes. *Journal of Marriage and the Family, 61,* 331–342.

Foshee, V. A., Karriker-Jaffe, K., Reyes, H., Ennett, S., Suchindran, C., Bauman, K., et al. (2008). What accounts for demographic differences in trajectories of adolescent dating violence? An examination of intrapersonal and contextual mediators. *Journal of Adolescent Health, 42,* 596–604.

Freedner, N., Freed, L. H., Yang, W., & Austin, S. B. (2002). Dating violence among gay, lesbian, and bisexual adolescents: Results from a community survey. *Journal of Adolescent Health, 31,* 469–474.

Gondolf, E. W. (2002). *Batterer intervention systems: Issues, outcomes, and recommendations.* Thousand Oaks, CA: Sage.

Grunbaum, J. A., Kann, L., Kinchen, S. A., Williams, B., Ross, J. G., Lowry, R., et al. (2002). Youth Risk Behavior Surveillance–United States, 2001. *Surveillance Summaries, 51*(SS-4), 1–21.

Halpern, C. T., Spriggs, A. L., Martin, S. L., & Kupper, L. L. (2009). Patterns of intimate partner violence victimization from adolescence to young adulthood in a nationally representative sample. *Journal of Adolescent Health, 45,* 508–516.

Halpern, C. T., Young, M. L., Waller, M. W., Martin, S. L., & Kupper, K. L. (2004). Prevalence of partner violence in same-sex romantic and sexual relationships in a national sample of adolescents. *Journal of Adolescent Health, 35,* 124–131.

Jaffe, P. G., Crooks, C. V., & Watson, C. L. (2009). *Creating safe school environments: From small steps to sustainable change.* London, ON: Althouse Press.

Jaffe, P. G., Sudermann, M., Reitzel, D., & Killip, S. (1992). An evaluation of a secondary school primary prevention program on violence in intimate relationships. *Violence and Victims, 7,* 129–146.

Levy, B. (1990). Abusive teen dating relationships: An emerging issue for the 90s. *Response to the Victimization of Women and Children, 13,* 59.

Malik, S., Sorenson, S. B., & Aneshensel, C. A. (1997). Community and dating violence among adolescents: Perpetration and victimization. *Journal of Adolescent Health, 21,* 291–302.

Mihalic, S. F., Fagan, A., Irwin, K., Ballard, D., & Elliott, D. (2004). *Blueprints for violence prevention.* Washington, DC: U.S. Department of Justice, Office of Justice Programs, Office of Juvenile Justice and Delinquency Prevention.

Miller, J. (2001). *One of the guys.* New York: Oxford University Press.

Miller, J., & White, N. A. (2003). Gender and adolescent relationship violence: A contextual examination. *Criminology, 41,* 1207–1248.

Moretti, M. M., Catchpole, R. E. H., & Odgers, C. (2005). The dark side of girlhood: Recent trends, risk factors and trajectories to aggression and violence. *Canadian Child and Adolescent Psychiatry Review, 14,* 21–25.

Ngwe, J. E., Liu, L. C., Flay, B. R., & Segawa, E. (2004). Violence prevention among African American adolescent males. *American Journal of Health Behavior, 28,* S24–S37.

Noonan, R. K., & Charles, D. (2009). Developing teen dating violence prevention strategies: Formative research with middle school youth. *Violence Against Women, 15,* 1087–1105.

O'Keefe, M. (2005). Teen dating violence: A review of risk factors and prevention efforts. *VAWNet Applied Research Forum.* Retrieved May 15, 2009, from http://new.vawnet.org/Assoc_Files_VAWnet/AR_TeenDatingViolence.pdf

O'Leary, K. D., Woodin, E. M., & Fritz, P. A. T. (2006). Can we prevent hitting? Recommendations for preventing intimate partner violence between young adults. *Journal of Aggression, Maltreatment and Trauma, 13,* 121–178.

Olweus, D., Limber, S., & Mahalic, S. F. (1999). *Bullying prevention program.* Boulder, CO: University of Colorado at Boulder, Center for the Study and Prevention of Violence, Institute of Behavioral Science.

Prochaska, J. O., & DiClemente, C. C. (1982). Transtheoretical therapy: Toward a more integrative model of change. *Psychotherapy: Theory, Research & Practice, 19,* 276–288.

Sears, H. A., Byers, E. S., Whelan, J. J., & Saint-Pierre, M. (2006). "If it hurts you, then it is not a joke": Adolescents' ideas about girls' and boys' use and experience of abusive behavior in dating relationships. *Journal of Interpersonal Violence, 21,* 1191–1207.

Silverman, J. G., Raj, A., Mucci, L. A., & Hathaway, J. E. (2001). Dating violence against girls and associated substance use, unhealthy weight control, sexual risk behavior, pregnancy, and suicidality. *Journal of American Medical Association, 286,* 572–579.

Simon, T. R., Miller, S., Gorman-Smith, D., Orpinas, P., & Sullivan, T. (2009). Physical dating violence norms and behavior among 6th-grade students from four U.S. sites. *Journal of Early Adolescence,* doi: 10.1177/0272431609333301.

Swahn, M. H., Simon, T. R., Hertz, M. F., Arias, I., Bossarte, R. M., Ross, J. G., et al. (2008). Linking dating violence, peer violence, and suicidal behaviors among high-risk youth. *American Journal of Preventive Medicine, 34,* 30–38.

U.S. Public Health Service & Office of the Surgeon General. (2000). *Youth violence: A report of the Surgeon General.* Washington, DC: Department of Health and Human Services.

Whitaker, D. J., Morrison, S., Lindquist, C., Hawkins, S. R., O'Neil, J. A., Nesius, A. M., et al. (2006). A critical review of interventions for the primary prevention of perpetration of partner violence. *Aggression and Violent Behavior, 11,* 151–166.

Wilson, W. J. (1996). *When work disappears.* New York: Alfred A. Knopf.

Wolfe, D. A., Crooks, C. V., Jaffe, P. G., Chiodo, D., Hughes, R., Ellis, W., et al. (2009). A universal school-based program to prevent adolescent dating violence: A cluster randomized trial. *Archives of Pediatric and Adolescent Medicine, 163,* 692–699.

Wolfe, D. A., Scott, K. L., Wekerle, C., & Pittman, A. L. (2001). Child maltreatment: Risk of adjustment problems and dating violence in adolescence. *Journal of the American Academy of Child and Adolescent Psychiatry, 40,* 282–289.

Wolfe, D. A., Wekerle, C., Gough, R., Reitzel-Jaffe, D., Grasley, C., Pittman, A., et al. (1996). *The Youth Relationships Manual: A group approach with adolescents for the prevention of woman abuse and the promotion of healthy relationships.* Thousand Oaks, CA: Sage.

Wolfe, D. A., Wekerle, C., Scott, K., Straatman, A., Grasley, C., & Reitzel-Jaffe, D. (2003). Dating violence prevention with at-risk youth: A controlled outcome evaluation. *Journal of Consulting and Clinical Psychology, 71,* 279–291.

Wolitzky-Taylor, K. B., Ruggiero, K. J., Danielson, C. K., Resnick, H. S., Hanson, R. F., Smith, D. W., et al. (2008). Prevalence and correlates of dating violence in a national sample of adolescents. *Journal of the American Academy of Child and Adolescent Psychiatry, 47,* 755–762.

Chapter Authors

Claire V. Crooks, Ph.D., C.Psych., is a registered clinical psychologist and the Associate Director of the CAMH Centre for Prevention Science in London, Ontario. She is an Adjunct Professor at the University of Western Ontario, in the faculties of Health Sciences, Education, and Psychology. She is the author of more than 40 articles, chapters, and books on adolescent dating violence and risk behaviors, child maltreatment, domestic violence and child custody, and fathers who perpetrate child abuse. She conducts program development and evaluation in the area of adolescent dating violence, with a particular interest in strengths-based programming for Aboriginal youth. She is on the editorial board of Violence Against Women.

Peter G. Jaffe, Ph.D., C.Psych., OC, is at the University of Western Ontario as a Professor in the Faculty of Education and Academic Director for the Centre for Research and Education on Violence Against Women. He is the Director Emeritus for the Centre for Children and Families in the Justice System. For more than 30 years, most of his research and clinical work has involved women and children who have been victims of abuse and involved with the criminal, family, and civil court systems. He has coauthored nine books, 25 chapters, and more than 75 articles related to children, families, and the justice system. He has received many honors for his work, including being named an Officer of the Order of Canada in 2009.

David A. Wolfe, Ph.D., ABPP, is a psychologist and author specializing in issues affecting children and youth, including how to form healthy relationships and prevention of bullying, dating violence, unsafe sex, substance abuse, and other consequences of unhealthy relationships. He holds the inaugural RBC Chair in Children's Mental Health at CAMH and heads the CAMH Centre for Prevention Science in London, Ontario. He is also Professor of Psychiatry and Psychology at the University of Toronto. Since 2007, he has served as Editor-in-Chief of *Child Abuse & Neglect: The International Journal.*

Ray Hughes, M.Ed., has 31 years of experience in education as a teacher, department head, consultant, and university lecturer. He is currently the National Education Coordinator of the Fourth R Project with the CAMH Centre for Prevention Science in London, Ontario and a faculty member at the University of Western Ontario's Faculty of Education. Previously, he was the Learning Coordinator for Safe Schools with the Thames Valley District School Board, where he coordinated the implementation of violence prevention programs for 190 schools and 80,000 students. In 2004, he was appointed to the Ontario provincial government's Safe Schools Action Team.

Debbie Chiodo, M.A., M.Ed. (Counseling), is the Centre Manager and a research associate at the CAMH Centre for Prevention Science in London, Ontario. She is an Adjunct Professor at King's College, University of Western Ontario. Her research includes program evaluation and meta-analytic reviews, with a particular interest in child protection systems. She is currently completing her doctorate at the Faculty of Education, University of Western Ontario, focusing on gendered violence and sexual harassment among adolescents.

Personal Reflection

Jackson Katz

I was a young philosophy student and emerging social justice activist in my sophomore year of college in the late 1970s when I first became aware of the extent of the problem of men's violence against women. I realized quickly that rape and domestic violence were not isolated problems, but rather were intimately connected to larger systems of social, economic, and political inequality (e.g., sexism, heterosexism, racism). I knew that as a man (who was also white and heterosexual) I was in a position to do something about this.

In the early 1990s, I took an education course in graduate school that was called Preventing Violence in America. My professor was Ron Slaby, who had recently developed a K-12 violence prevention curriculum that looked at perpetrators, victims, and bystanders. In the decade since I had graduated from college, much of my organizing and activist effort had been devoted to finding ways to help people see that violence against women was a men's issue. Most people didn't see it that way. The typical response from men was, "I'm a good guy. This isn't my problem."

It occurred to me that thinking about men as "bystanders" was a way to bring many more of them into the work of domestic and sexual violence prevention. This was social justice 101; men who are in a position to prevent or interrupt abusive behavior by other men and yet remain silent are, in a sense, consenting to the abuse. In order to achieve dramatic reductions in gender violence, more men—across the racial, ethnic, and sexual orientation spectrum—would need to challenge each other's sexist attitudes and behaviors, and thus help to change the belief systems and social norms in male culture that perpetuate abuse. At the same time, focusing on girls and women as bystanders—not as potential victims—was a way to bring many more of them into the work of supporting and challenging their peers and others.

In schools, the next stage of gender violence prevention education is institutionalization. We have a good idea of what works in the classroom, the locker room, and the teachers' lounge. But we are woefully short on resources. For example, in schools across the country, the need is so much greater than the available supply of prevention educators. Of course, battered women's programs and rape crisis centers have led prevention education efforts; most educators who have managed to gain access to schools are women who are employed by those institutions. In recent years, momentum has been building for an increase in men's engagement with this work.

It is important to note that the key challenge in school-based efforts is not pedagogical but political, namely, how do we get school systems to prioritize these issues? How do we get school superintendents and principals—many of them men—to take a proactive, leadership role? How do we make gender violence education part of the standard K-12 curriculum, at age-appropriate levels? How do we create the expectation that athletic directors will require all student athletes and coaches to participate? How do we infuse gender violence prevention approaches, such as Mentors in Violence Prevention (MVP), into the curriculum of colleges and graduate schools of education, including programs in educational administration?

I think one of my most significant contributions in this area is my early and ongoing work on the development of the bystander approach, both theoretically and in its application with MVP. I've also helped to foster a growing recognition among educational leaders and policy makers that the participation of boys and men—students, faculty, and administrators—has to be seen as a fundamental and indispensable component of any serious gender violence prevention initiative in the coming years.

CHAPTER 18

Intervening With Men for Violence Prevention

Richard M. Tolman and Jeffrey L. Edleson

This chapter focuses on intervening with men in a variety of contexts to prevent violence against women and children. We first present a brief historical account of intervention programs with men who batter their intimate partners. We then present prevention and ecological frameworks as lenses through which we consider current and possible strategies for intervening with men.

Men, Violence, and Intervention

Earlier chapters in this book have focused on intimate partner violence in heterosexual and same-sex relationships, sexual assault, and a variety of other forms of violence against women. As pointed out in earlier chapters, although women can be violent to their partners, the overwhelming evidence is that intimate partner violence is most often committed by men. In fact, as Hamby (2009) has outlined, men commit more than 90% of sexual violence, create higher levels of fear in their partners, and injure and murder their partners at

much higher rates than do women. This is not to say that women do not commit violent acts against their partners; they commit violence, however, at a much lower rate than men, and it appears to be less severe. Stanko (2006) identifies gender as vitally relevant to how domestic violence is conceptualized, spoken of, and challenged, noting that, "To lose sight and insight by ignoring how gender matters impoverishes any analyses of violence" (p. 549). We also acknowledge that intimate partner violence occurs in same-sex relationships, as was also pointed out earlier in this book. Our focus here, however, is on men's violence directed at their intimate female partners.

Although we sometimes tend to think of intimate partner violence as an issue only recently addressed by society, violence by intimate partners has long been recognized as a problem (Davidson, 1977; Dobash & Dobash, 1978), was discussed in the popular press more than a century ago (Killoran, 1984), and has historically been the subject of social intervention efforts (Edleson, 1991; Gordon, 1988; Pleck, 1987).

The current wave of interventions focused on violence against women began in the mid-1970s as small groups of women formed to aid other women fleeing violence by their intimate partners. These efforts evolved into "safe homes" and temporary shelters and have now expanded to include several thousand battered women's shelters and related service programs. With this expansion came efforts to coordinate these services with other necessary community programs to best provide safety to battered women and their children. Activists working on behalf of battered women in North America began pressuring local governments to intervene in personal relationships to stop violence against women. These efforts, in turn, led to the development of coordinated interventions with violent men.

Social service intervention with men who batter is a more recent development; the first group treatment programs for men who batter were founded in the late 1970s. Early innovators in group treatment programs included EMERGE in Boston, RAVEN in St. Louis, and AMEND in Denver. Interventions with men who batter have dramatically increased over the past three decades. With this increase came efforts to coordinate these services with other necessary community programs to best provide safety to victims and accountability for perpetrators. Early efforts to coordinate interventions were created in Colorado (Domestic Violence Task Force, 1988), California (Soler & Martin, 1983), and elsewhere (see Brygger & Edleson, 1987; Goolkasian, 1986). One of the earliest and best-known coordinated responses was established in 1980 in the small city of Duluth in northern Minnesota. Ellen Pence and other activists in Duluth developed the Domestic Abuse Intervention Project (DAIP; see Pence & Shepard, 1999), which sought to coordinate the efforts of various system responses to violent men and their victims in what is now commonly called "the Duluth Model." Chapter 14 in this book, by Susan Miller and her colleagues, describes in greater detail coordinated community response models.

These new coordinated responses emerged in a context of changes in policies and practices

regarding violence against women (Pence & Shepard, 1999). Throughout the 1970s and into the early 1980s, police responses to intimate partner violence incidents were guided primarily by a crisis intervention orientation to family conflict. In the early 1980s, new pressures on police departments began to build. Pressure from women's organizations and victim rights groups grew, and their agendas converged to bring about a major shift in police and judicial responses to men who batter. These activists' influence was reinforced by successful law suits against police inaction brought by several battered women around the country (e.g., *Thurman v. City of Torrington*, 1984). Victim rights advocates pushed for more severe punishment of offenders by courts, while women's groups advocated for a consistent police and judicial response to crime regardless of where it occurred. Police who arrested perpetrators of violence on the street but did not arrest them for violence in the home were seen by women's groups as perpetuating violence against women and the unequal treatment of women. At the same time, new research showing the greater effectiveness of deterrence (arrest) when intervening with violent men was also being widely disseminated (e.g., Sherman & Berk, 1984).

Increased public pressures, landmark cases, and research showing the effectiveness of arrest combined to dramatically increase the arrests by police of men who batter. Sherman and Cohn (1990) found in a survey of 146 police departments in the United States that over a period of three years (1984 to 1986), police pro-arrest policies increased from 10% to 46%. As a result of these increased arrests, the number of offenders entering the court system from arraignment to trial and sentencing increased dramatically. For the first time, many prosecutors and judges were forced to deal directly with large numbers of intimate partner violence cases (again, see Chapter 14 for more detail on criminal justice responses).

The interests of victim rights advocates and women's groups converged again in the courts. The push for victim rights reinforced pressure from women's groups to make battered women's wishes more influential on court decisions. Many courts, wishing to avoid overcrowded jails, favored a rehabilitation approach that diverted or mandated men who batter into social service treatment programs. It is interesting that arrest by police and mandated rehabilitation sentences were exactly what many coordinated community responses were designed to achieve (see Brygger & Edleson, 1987; Pence, 1983). While seemingly inconsistent, this approach offered men who batter clear and immediate sanctions through arrest (deterrence) as well as motivation to enter treatment to avoid serving a jail sentence (rehabilitation).

In short, changing public attitudes, the outcomes of several landmark cases, pressure from women activists, and new research results led to a greater readiness among police, prosecutors, judges, and social service professionals to work more closely in a multifaceted coordinated community response to men who batter.

Prevention and Ecological Frameworks

This short history of coordinated response demonstrates the need to use a multiple systems perspective to think about ending men's violence against their female partners. However, these criminal justice-based responses primarily deal with violent and abusive behavior after it has occurred. A comprehensive approach to ending violence requires a prevention perspective as well as a multisystem focus. We draw upon both prevention and ecological frameworks in our work with men to end their abuse, but we organize the remaining sections of this chapter around prevention strategies while making reference, where appropriate, to the ecological levels that a particular strategy addresses.

Prevention efforts, as described earlier in Chapter 11, are often classified into three major strategies. For example, in attempting to stop men's intimate partner violence, we can classify various efforts as *indicated* (strategies focused on boys or men who have already acted abusively or aggressively), *selective* (strategies targeting men or boys at greater risk of developing the problem), and *universal* (strategies targeting all boys and men regardless of risk status; Chamberlain, 2008).

Alternatively, an ecological framework provides a way to describe current efforts to end men's violence and also highlights existing gaps. In our earlier description of this model (Edleson & Tolman, 1992), we described how Bronfenbrenner's (1977, 1979, 1986) conceptualization of the human ecology could be applied to intervention efforts with men who batter. Other authors (Carlson, 1984; Douglas, Bathrick, & Perry, 2008; Dutton, 1985, 1988; Heise, 1998) have also suggested ecological frameworks as a way to more broadly understand intimate partner violence.

The ecological framework views human social environments as organized in a series of interacting systems. The *microsystem* is an individual's immediate environment and those directly interacting with him or her. The *mesosystem* is the linkages between systems that directly interact with an individual, for example, overlapping interaction between a man's family, peer group, and his faith community (because members from each of those microsystems may interact with one another). Coordination may also be viewed in terms of the consistency of values and practices within each microsystem (e.g., if messages about the unacceptability of aggression are similar in each microsystem, then the mesosystem exerts more influence than when these values vary among microsystems). The *exosystem* is the set of systems whose interaction may indirectly affect a man's behavior, for example, coordination between police, prosecutors, and the courts. The *macrosystem* is the set of broader social values underlying the way our social institutions are organized. Bronfenbrenner (1986) also added a fifth system, the *chronosystem*, which represents the time dimension over which all other systems are dynamically changing.

Combining the prevention and ecological frameworks, we might consider existing batterer intervention programs and criminal justice responses as *indicated* prevention at the microsystem and mesosystem levels. We will address these types of interventions first. Following this, we focus on *selected* and then *universal* prevention efforts that may be at any level and sometimes at multiple levels. Most of the selected and universal prevention efforts described later in this chapter have not yet been rigorously evaluated, but we will highlight some promising practices as well as consider some other possible preventive efforts where major gaps occur.

Indicated Prevention Strategies

Batterer Intervention Programs

There is great controversy surrounding current interventions with men who batter. First, some object to the extensive use of a "power and control"-based system like law enforcement and the courts to mandate men into rehabilitation services. Use of systems like these model coercive behavior we hope men will turn away from using with their partners. Perhaps even more controversial is the degree to which group psychoeducational programs, to which men are often court mandated, are seen as effective. Several authors argue that current approaches do not work (Dutton & Corvo, 2006); there is an overreliance on both the criminal justice system (Mills, 2003) and psychoeducational groups for men that do not recognize alternative forms of treatment (Dutton & Corvo, 2006). Although efficacy has not been strongly established, the research literature on group intervention approaches provides a basis for continuing these efforts. Clearly, there is need for more rigorous studies (see Gondolf, 2002, 2004) as well as continued development, refinement, and innovation in approaches.

Group programs for men who batter, often called "batterer intervention programs" or "BIPs,"

are generally offered by 1 or 2 professionally trained facilitators working with a group of about 8 to 10 men. These programs vary in length from an intensive weekend retreat to 52 weekly meetings lasting from 1½ to 2 hours. For example, both Washington State and California require court-mandated men to be engaged with programs for 52 weeks.

The predominant model for most BIPs across North America is some combination of didactic teaching and psychosocial or therapeutic processing among group members. Many programs draw heavily on cognitive-behavioral and social learning models of intervention and on a gendered lens for analyzing power relationships in violence between intimates (see Edleson & Tolman, 1992; Gondolf, 2002; Pence & Paymar, 1993).

BIPs have been studied intensively over the past several decades, but the results have been interpreted in vastly differing ways. An article in one popular magazine summarized the findings as follows: "Batterer programs simply aren't working. They are failing. . . . Domestic violence is the only field in which you can fail for 25 years and wind up being considered an expert" (*Esquire Magazine*, cited in Gondolf, 2002, p. 28). Others have, however, drawn much more positive conclusions: "Arrest and treatment of batterers are not a complete solution to the problem of wife assault, but they are probably the best solution we currently have" (cited in Gondolf, 2002, p. 27).

With more than 70 evaluations now published, we do have some ideas about how BIPs work to end violence and threats, but these evaluations have left many questions unanswered. Two reviews of the empirical literature (Bennett & Williams, 2001; Gondolf, 2004) and three additional meta-analyses of selected studies (Babcock, Green, & Robie, 2004; Feder & Wilson, 2005; Saunders, 2008; Smedslund, Dalsbø, Steiro, Winsvold, & Clench-Aas, 2009) have all drawn positive but circumspect conclusions about the success of these programs. In short, there are six key findings about BIPs that can be drawn from the extensive research literature:

1. BIPs have a modest but positive impact on ending violence, with some studies showing them to have a much larger impact on participants when compared to men not participating.

Major reviews of BIPs over this decade have often concluded that these programs have a positive impact on ending and reducing violence by men who participate in them. Meta-analyses, a statistical technique to summarize and average the effect of programs across numerous studies, show small to moderate decreases in recidivism among men who participate in programs, when compared to either program drop outs or those randomly placed in a control group. The strongest results are found in studies using official records of subsequent police arrests and comparing program completers to those who drop out of the program (see Babcock et al., 2004; Feder & Wilson, 2005). In program evaluations where victim reports of the man's behavior were monitored and the program completers were compared to men who were randomly assigned to a no-treatment condition, the results were still positive but less powerful. One caution when interpreting these studies is that men who either dropped out or were assigned to a no-treatment condition may have sought and received help elsewhere, thus shrinking the differences found between BIPs and these groups of men.

2. BIPs help the majority of men end their violence over a period of time.

Perhaps the most comprehensive study of BIPs was funded by the U.S. Centers for Disease Control & Prevention and directed by Dr. Edward Gondolf. This four-city study tracked 840 men participating in group programs and their partners over a 4-year period (Gondolf, 2002, 2004). Gondolf found that the great majority of men who reassault their partners will do so within the first 15 months after their intake into a program. After 30 months from program intake, Gondolf

(2004) found that only 20% of the men who participated in these programs had reassaulted a partner in the past 12 months, and at 48 months after program intake, only 10% of the men had reassaulted their partners in the past 12 months. Thus, by 4 years after intake, approximately 90% of the men had *not* reassaulted their partner in the past year. Gondolf suggests that this increasingly low recidivism rate points to the success of BIPs.

3. It is not yet clear what BIP-specific components help create these changes.

Despite the modestly positive evidence for BIPs, the research does not provide a clear answer to what makes a difference. Studies to date have not provided much insight into what component parts of batterer programs, or which program lengths, lead to change among participants (see Babcock et al., 2004; Bennett & Williams, 2001; Gondolf, 2004). Most programs include some type of cognitive-behavioral therapeutic and educational process, and many address attitudes among men about their relationships with women. It is not clear, however, whether it is these program components, simply the regular monitoring that occurs by participation in a group process, or something else such as enhanced motivation to change that is causing these better outcomes among participants. The studies that have compared components and found no differences further complicate conclusions in this area (see, e.g., Dunford, 2000; Labriola, Rempel, & Davis, 2005).

4. It appears that BIPs incorporating motivational enhancement components help more men change.

One finding that is supported by a few studies indicates that when programs include methods designed to enhance men's motivation to change, the retention and outcomes of men in these programs are improved (see Babcock et al., 2004).

Many of these procedures are based on the widely disseminated motivational interviewing procedures of Miller and Rollnick (2002). These procedures have been found to be successful with substance abusers (see Miller & Wilbourne, 2002) and are only recently being utilized with men who batter (see, e.g., Easton, Swan, & Sinha, 2000; Roffman, Edleson, Neighbors, Mbilinyi, & Walker, 2008).

5. *Typologies of men based on personality traits and variation among men based on racial/ethnic group membership do not appear to predict different outcomes.*

One approach that has received a lot of attention is differentiating types of men who batter so that treatment may be better matched to specific men. Typologies vary, but often categorize men into generally violent, partner violent, and pathological groups (see Cavanaugh & Gelles, 2005 and Holtzworth-Munroe & Meehan, 2004 for reviews). Although researchers have been able to distinguish different types of men, the utility of these typologies to predict differential success in batterer intervention programs has been questioned. White and Gondolf (2000) have found that men of differing personality types appear to behave similarly in terms of program completion and outcome. This led them to conclude that "one size appears to fit most" (White & Gondolf, 2000, p. 486). On the other hand, Saunders (1996) found that participants with antisocial personalities had lower recidivism rates in structured cognitive-behavioral groups, while men with dependent personalities showed reduced recidivism in psychodynamic groups with less structure.

Despite White and Gondolf's (2000) findings, the promise of typologies has not yet been thoroughly tested. Most BIPs do not, at present, differentiate among the types of men who are admitted to their programs or offer differential programming tracks. Many communities have such limited resources that, at most, they offer very limited services to men in their community.

Many BIP facilitators would claim, however, that intervention is already differentiated or individualized, to the extent that group facilitators provide differential attention to men during and between BIP sessions.

Rough grouping of men by typologies may not be the preferred direction, in any case. Holtzworth-Munroe and Meehan (2004) have argued that we shouldn't be categorizing men into one type or another, but perhaps we should see these men as multidimensional, with variation among several factors. Eckhardt, Babcock, and Homack (2004) suggest that perhaps matching treatment to the level of motivation for change that a man expresses may better achieve the original goals of developing typologies.

Much less information is available on the differential impact of BIPs on men of color. There is a small but growing literature that focuses on different types of groups for men of color, particularly African American men. Williams (1994; Gondolf & Williams, 2001) has described three types of treatment for African American men who batter: (1) "color blind," where differences in race or ethnicity don't seem to matter; (2) "culturally specific," where there is a critical mass of men of one race or ethnicity and attention to their community's unique history is implicitly given; and (3) "culturally centered," where the focus of the program design is on a particular racial or ethnic group that makes up most of the men in the group. In tests comparing these programs, it does not appear that any one type of program format is better able to achieve positive outcomes than another (see Buttell & Carney, 2005; Gondolf, 2007).

6. *Men who participate in BIPs that are part of coordinated responses with the criminal justice system achieve better outcomes.*

Last, an important finding of these studies is that BIPs that are embedded in a coordinated community intervention to identify, treat, and hold men accountable appear to provide the most positive outcomes in terms of reassault prevention.

This is a good example of how mesosystem interventions can play a major role in helping other, more direct interventions succeed. Specifically, Gondolf (2004) found that,

> Under the pretrial referral, the men entered the program in an average of 2½ weeks after arrest, as opposed to several months at the post-conviction systems, and they had to reappear in court periodically to confirm their program attendance. This system dramatically reduced no-shows (from 30% to 5%) and sustained a high completion rate of 70% despite the coerced attendance. (p. 619)

In short, men dropped out the least and achieved the best outcomes in systems in which (1) men were moved quickly into treatment, within 2 to 2½ weeks of arrest; (2) there was ongoing monitoring of men's compliance with mandates to treatment by the courts; and (3) the courts responded swiftly, with consequences for men who violated their mandates.

These findings argue strongly for mesosystem efforts involving close coordination between BIPs and court officers, particularly probation officers. In some locales, specific domestic violence probation units have been established to create this close liaison with BIPs.

Although close coordination is desirable, such efforts raise concerns about the type of information that BIP providers should supply to court officers or others, such as custody evaluators, guardians ad litem, and court-appointed special advocates. A man's behavior in a weekly BIP meeting may mask much more severe and dangerous behavior outside the walls of the social service agency. As a result, many BIP providers only feel comfortable providing basic information such as (a) attendance, (b) compliance with program rules, (c) new reports of violence, and (d) occasionally information on the man's past abusive behavior. Providing an estimate of the level of change men have achieved based on their in-group behavior is potentially dangerous and often inaccurate. It is only through long-term

follow-up with current and past partners that men's behavior can be assessed over time.

State Standards for Batterer Intervention

As discussed above, there has been concern about the effectiveness of BIPs. Concern about the rapid proliferation of programs has led to attempts to establish standards for their operation. The creation of these standards is most often initiated at the state level and is another example of a mesosystem strategy. A recent review determined that only six states—Arkansas, Connecticut, Mississippi, New York, South Dakota, and Wyoming—remain without some form of standards or regulations (Maiuro & Eberle, 2008). Standards have generally placed primacy on the safety of victims and attempted to set conditions for program accountability and coordination (Tolman, 2002). State standards vary a great deal. Some are mandatory and require the individual provider and/or the agency batterer intervention program to be certified by a state body that minimum standards have been met. Other states publish guidelines that are suggestive of best practices and voluntary (Maiuro & Eberle, 2008). Most include a mandate or suggestion for assessment procedures and program content, length, and format. To date, only one study has examined whether standards accomplish their intended goals. Bennett and Vincent (2002) examined the implementation of standards in Illinois. They used a variety of methods, including interviews with victim service staff, batterer program staff, judges, and other criminal justice staff; survey data from staff of victim services programs, batterer programs, and intervention programs; and surveys from participants of batterer intervention programs. According to reports by the batterer intervention programs, the standards influenced them to link to other community-based violence prevention efforts, particularly battered women's agencies. Reports from battered women's advocates, on the other hand, also revealed that they believed the standards created a means to interact with batterer programs and hold them accountable for their actions. This system coordination and accountability were among the primary goals of the standards in Illinois.

Standards have been controversial in themselves, with critiques noting it is premature to prescribe or proscribe intervention modalities that have not been supported empirically. Although some states have been quite restrictive in this regard, Maiuro and Eberle (2008) note a trend toward an acceptance of multicomponent interventions. As a result, several states (e.g., Michigan, Oregon, and Texas) have adopted standards that explicitly allow innovation that might be otherwise deterred by overly restrictive standards.

Law Enforcement and Criminal Justice Interventions

Batterer interventions programs, as mentioned earlier in this chapter, have often been conceived as part of a larger coordinated community response to violence. As such, other relevant systems, such as law enforcement, prosecution, and probation, have been engaged as part of a multipronged effort to end or reduce intimate partner violence. These coordinated interventions are also a good example of how coordination in the exosystem can exert a powerful impact on an individual. The role of law enforcement and criminal justice systems is covered more completely in Chapter 14 of this book.

Fathering After Intimate Partner Violence

One new development in batterer intervention is a focus on men as fathers (Bancroft & Silverman, 2002; Edleson & Williams, 2007). These efforts can be considered indicated prevention because they identify fathers after violence has occurred, but also as selective prevention because they attempt to ameliorate the negative impact of

exposure to intimate partner violence on children before they may develop their own aggressive behavior. The focus on fatherhood might also be important in motivating men to end their abuse of their partners (Arean & Davis, 2007; Donovan & Vlais, 2005). Perel and Peled (2008) note that models of intervention with men who batter as fathers can be distinguished by the extent to which they see the issue of fathering as an end in itself or as an entry point into other potential areas of change, such as violent behavior. However, these needn't be mutually exclusive.

There are several examples of emerging programs specifically designed for training men who batter to parent without violence, yet most of these have been established only the in last decade or so. These programs can be classified into two types: (1) parenting programs that are supplementary sessions within existing batterer intervention programs, and (2) separate curricula that are offered to men once they have completed a traditional batterer intervention group curriculum.

One of the best-documented programs is the *Caring Dads* program (Scott, Francis, Crooks, & Kelly, 2006). *Caring Dads* uses a range of approaches, including motivational interviewing, psycho-education, cognitive-behavioral techniques, confrontation, and "shame work." The program seeks to address four goals: (1) engaging men to examine their fathering by developing trust and motivation; (2) increasing awareness and application of child-centered fathering; (3) increasing awareness of, and responsibility for, abusive and neglectful fathering and intimate partner violence; and (4) rebuilding children's trust in the men's fathering and planning for the future.

A preliminary evaluation of the *Caring Dads* program compared pre- to post-intervention measures for 23 participants (Scott & Crooks, 2007). Using self-reports on the Parenting Stress Index, fathers' hostility, denigration, and rejection of the child all decreased significantly, as did angry arousal to child and family situations (Abidin, 1995). There was a low attrition rate for participants (34 of 42 completed). Self-reported partner abuse decreased, but not significantly, leaving in question the program's contribution to violence prevention.

Another well-described and widely disseminated program is the *Fathering After Violence* program, developed by the Family Violence Prevention Fund (Arean & Davis, 2007). This curriculum is designed to be incorporated into existing batterer intervention programs and is based on exercises that (1) create empathy for children's experience of intimate partner violence; (2) identify behaviors that constitute positive modeling by fathers for their children and support the mother's parenting; and (3) increase understanding of fathers' roles in the process of repairing a damaged relationship with their children (see http://www.endabuse.org).

Fleck-Henderson (2004) conducted an initial evaluation of the *Fathering After Violence* curriculum. Data were gathered from approximately 60 participants in three programs in the Boston area. Staff and participants' self-reports provided some support that the curriculum was engaging and readily integrated into the batterer intervention program. The exercises appeared to result in improvements in the three goals noted above. Although attempts to contact partners were not very successful, the majority of those reached (about half) did report positively on the participants' behavior toward their children and were positive about the program. The limitations of this evaluation suggest caution in drawing conclusions about the impact of this curriculum.

Selective Prevention Strategies

Strategies receiving the most attention are those indicated efforts covered above that focus on men who have already committed violence. A number of other efforts have, however, been developed to engage men whose circumstances may put them in a group that shows higher risks

of committing intimate partner violence, for example, men who have experienced or witnessed abuse in their families of origin, unemployed men, and those with a criminal history. Others who may be at greater risk are adolescent fathers and expectant or new fathers. In this section, we focus on selective prevention strategies targeted to at-risk individuals, primarily fathers.

One of the best-known programs for at-risk fathers is the Baltimore-based *Responsible Fatherhood Program* (BRFP; Center for Urban Families, 2009). Participants in this program are primarily noncustodial fathers. Most are unemployed, have not graduated high school, and may have been involved in the criminal justice system and/or used illegal drugs. The program assists these low-income fathers with seeking employment, providing child support, taking steps to reduce recidivism, developing skills for effective parenting, and maintaining healthy relationships. Although these fathers clearly are experiencing multiple stressors and show a number of factors that might predict a high possibility of intimate partner violence, they do not specifically participate in the Baltimore program because of current intimate partner violence or child abuse. However, BRFP actively works to identify violence if it has occurred and motivate men to seek help for their abusive behavior when identified. They have established a cooperative relationship with a batterer intervention program at House of Ruth to provide cross-training and service referrals.

Another program that targets at-risk fathers is the *Con Los Padres* program affiliated with the National Latino Fatherhood and Family Institute (NLFFI) of Bienvenidos Family Services (Carillo & Tello, 2007; NLFFI, 2003). Through 20 weekly classes, the program helps young and expectant fathers aged 16 to 25 to develop positive relationships with their children. Case management services are available for young fathers who need additional support to develop appropriate interaction with their children. The program screens for intimate partner violence and other forms of family and community violence and runs a more structured program that attempts to address existing aggression. This culturally specific program is based on the principles of *un hombre noble*—a noble man. Un hombre noble is a man who keeps his word as the foundation of respectful relationships with his children and others in his life. As the NLFFI curriculum describes,

> Through the process of sitting in a circle with other men who collectively reflect on the reality of their gifts and their baggage, men begin to acknowledge and accept that aggression and violence are not acceptable and realize they cause irreparable damage to themselves and others. (NLFFI, 2003, p. 43)

These programs in Maryland and California highlight the need for prevention efforts to be culturally specific. This specificity may increase the probability of successfully engaging men. Cultural specificity may also increase the effectiveness of intervention by delivering messages that are more readily received by participants, but comparative studies are needed to confirm whether these hypotheses are correct.

A number of selective prevention strategies have also been implemented in youth settings, primarily schools. The *Youth Relationship Program* is a selective prevention program aimed at high school students with a history of child maltreatment, witnessing abuse, or other trauma in their families of origin (Wolfe et al., 1996). The program is described at length in Chapter 17. Another school-based example of selective prevention is the *Mentor Training Program* conducted by the Men Stopping Violence program in Atlanta (Douglas et al., 2008). This program trains college students to mentor high school boys at risk of dropping out of high school and who are having disciplinary problems. Mentors work to promote healthy definitions of masculinity among youth and to promote the prevention of intimate partner violence.

Given the strength of childhood exposure to violence as a predictor for future perpetration (Ehrensaft, Cohen, Brown, Smailes, Chen, & Johnson, 2003; Whitefield, Anda, Dube, & Felitti, 2003), selective prevention efforts might be effectively targeted for this group in settings besides schools. For example, prevention efforts aimed at men with such histories might be particularly relevant when their partners are pregnant. This is a time when men might come into contact with the health system (e.g., at ultrasound or during labor and delivery) and when their concern for their ability to parent and partner might be particularly salient. Given this intersection of access and openness to prevention efforts, screening for traumatic childhood experiences might be effective in identifying men who could benefit from education and support to prevent them abusing partners or children. Of course, this transition time might also be an ideal time for universal prevention efforts, a topic to which we now turn our focus.

Universal Prevention Efforts

Universal prevention strategies move beyond intervention with men who have committed violence (indicated) or those at risk of committing it (selective) to address all men and boys. A key advantage to this strategy is the large number of individuals who can be reached. Applied across a population, even an intervention that generates modest effects can have a widespread impact. Universal prevention programs often involve changing social norms, behaviors, and policies that directly and indirectly contribute to intimate partner violence, and, as such, universal prevention is intrinsically part of a broad-based, long-term agenda. From the ecological framework, one would be focusing on macrosystem interventions when addressing the underlying norms of a society.

Universal prevention programs can include, education, mobilization, and media programs. Universal programs aimed at shifting beliefs and attitudes about violence and building communication and conflict resolution skills are one approach to preventing the onset of intimate partner violence.

Several studies demonstrate the efficacy of school-based programs to prevent dating violence (e.g., Jaffe, Sudermann, Reitzel, & Killip, 1992; Weisz & Black, 2001; Wolfe, Crooks, Lee, McIntyre-Smith, & Jaffe, 2003). Several longitudinal studies found that early conduct disorder and the use of generalized violence predict dating violence perpetration, suggesting that prevention and intervention in the area of conduct problems can also prevent dating violence (Brendgen, Vitaro, Tremblay, & Lavoie, 2001; Capaldi & Owen, 2001; Ehrensaft et. al., 2003; Lavoie, Hebert, Tremblay, Vitaro, Vezina, & McDuff, 2002; Magdol, Moffitt, Caspi, & Silva, 1998).

There is little research on programs to prevent intimate partner violence outside of school settings. One study of a community-based communication and conflict management skills program offered to couples planning to marry found that up to four years after program completion, participants reported better communication and less physical violence in their relationships when compared to a control group, but by the five-year follow-up, the only lasting effect was in the area of men's use of communication skills (Markman, Renick, Floyd, Stanley, & Clements, 1993).

Encouraging Positive Messages

A number of promising community-based efforts in the United States to prevent intimate partner violence have been discussed in the literature (see, e.g., Bowen, Gwiasda, & Brown, 2004; Graffunder, Noonan, Cox, & Wheaton, 2004; Mitchell-Clarke & Autry, 2004). For example, the Institute for Community Peace has worked closely with local communities in the U.S. to develop multipronged violence prevention efforts that are locally defined and designed. Each community with which they worked developed a broad coalition of community stakeholders to address violence in their communities, conducted a needs and an assets assessment, and then implemented a plan that included continuous evaluation. In Australia, the state government of Victoria supports a state-wide

media awards program aimed at influencing community attitudes to intimate partner violence by encouraging journalistic quality in the reporting and characterization of family violence (Donovan & Vlais, 2005).

Another approach is to engage key people in boys' microsystems to educate them in respectful, nonviolent ways of relating to women and girls. For example, *Coaching Boys Into Men* is a national prevention campaign developed by the Family Violence Prevention Fund. It uses public service announcements and other ads to promote the idea that men should communicate to boys that intimate partner violence is unacceptable. A related program is the *Coaching Boys Into Men* leadership program for sports coaches, which attempts to encourage athletic coaches (many of whom are fathers themselves) to have conversations with their team members to promote respect for women and girls and erode support for violence as a defining characteristic of masculinity. The program distributes a "play-book" that provides a curriculum for presenting this information and finding teachable moments to promote these ideas. There is also a more structured weekly curriculum available and a newly developed *Coaches' Training Kit.* Coaches are encouraged to be involved in community outreach and other change efforts as well. Via a Web site, coaches have access to program materials and tips from fellow coaches on how to implement the program. These efforts have not yet been evaluated.

Involving Men as Allies

Globally, institutions and organizations working on intimate partner violence have begun to involve men as key allies in this effort. This marks a shift from focusing on men primarily as perpetrators and embodies a hope that men can be effective partners in prevention efforts. This recognition is exemplified by the U.N. Secretary-General's (2006) in-depth study on ending violence against women, which states, "There is also a need to engage men more effectively in the work on preventing and eliminating such violence, and to tackle stereotypes and attitudes that perpetuate male violence against women" (p. 2).

Efforts to engage men as allies can presumably help to reduce the risk of abuse by men who participate; it can also change the culture that might support other men's behavior. A number of authors have argued that male involvement in campaigns to end intimate partner violence can help to undermine beliefs, attitudes, and power relationships that support violence and transform the culture to support constructions of masculinity that lead to respectful and nonviolent relationships with women (Crooks, Goodall, Baker & Hughes, 2006; Flood, 2005). Berkowitz (2004) has categorized the goals of efforts to engage men into three categories: (1) prevention of men's violence; (2) men's intervention to prevent the violence of other men; and (3) addressing root causes of violence, such as gender socialization. Below we give some examples of strategies to achieve each of these goals. In practice, efforts often address more than one goal.

Numerous factors may have previously deterred men's involvement as allies. Garin (2000) reported a poll of over 1,000 men on barriers to engagement in antiviolence work. Among the reasons endorsed by more than 10% of the men were that no one had asked them to get involved; they did not have time; they did not know how to help; they perceived that they had been vilified and were seen as part of the problem, rather than approached as an important part of the solution; and that intimate partner violence is a private matter and they were uncomfortable getting involved.

Despite these barriers, a recent national telephone survey of 1,020 men, commissioned by the Family Violence Prevention Fund (Hart Research Associates, Inc., 2007), found that men may be more ready to take action than the earlier Garin (2000) poll indicated. Many of the men surveyed (73%) reported that they believed they could personally make a difference in ending sexual and domestic violence, and a majority of

those with children said they were already talking to their sons about the importance of healthy, violence-free relationships. A majority of the men surveyed also said they would make the time for and would be willing to do the following: Donate an old wireless phone to programs that assist victims/prevent violence, sign a pledge to promote respect for women and girls and end violence, sign a petition or contact elected officials to urge strengthening laws, and purchase an item or product that raises awareness and funds or make donations. These survey findings point to the promise of universal prevention efforts to build upon men's current beliefs and increase the number of men who believe that violence is a problem and that they can do something about it.

Most relevant in this list for active involvement is the willingness to sign a pledge. Pledge-based campaigns have been one of the most prominent and successfully disseminated strategies for involving men as allies. Most notable in this regard is the White Ribbon Campaign (WRC). WRC began in Canada in 1991, two years after the Montréal massacre in which a gunman who said he was angry at women killed 14 students and wounded 13 others. Men across Canada were urged to wear white ribbons to commemorate this event.

Using the Berkowitz (2004) framework described above, WRC efforts seek not only to decrease men's willingness to engage in abusive behavior, but also to increase their willingness to challenge other men whose behavior is abusive (e.g., telling a friend who has committed abuse that his behavior is unacceptable and helping him get assistance) or whose behavior contributes to or condones violence against women (e.g., confronting a sexist joke). Currently, the WRC is a worldwide campaign in 47 countries (Carolo, 2009). In the UN report mentioned above, the WRC was named as an example of a successful strategy for involving men.

Like WRC, The Family Violence Prevention Fund's Founding Fathers campaign is aimed at recruiting men who explicitly denounce violence against women and children and promote a culture that respects women. Its activities include publishing an annual full-page ad on Father's Day in the *New York Times* demonstrating men's concern about the issue of partner violence and soliciting additional participation by other men. An international registry of men who have supported the campaign is maintained. Participants are encouraged to take the campaign into their workplaces, with brochures, cards, and other materials that can be distributed to raise awareness and engage others in joining the campaign.

As part of these new efforts, there appears to be an endorsement of the need for and advisability of broader coalitions. Two keys areas for coalition building are other violence prevention fields (e.g., child abuse, community violence) and related social and health issues (e.g., HIV, poverty; Prevention Institute, 2007).

Globally, there has been a strong overlap between efforts to address the spread of HIV and campaigns to involve men in reducing gender violence. Most notably, a recent international meeting was held by MenEngage, a Swedish-funded global alliance of UN agencies and non-governmental organizations from around the world, including sub-Saharan Africa, Latin America, the Caribbean, North America, Asia, and Europe. Established in 2004, the goal of MenEngage is to connect men and boys in work to achieve gender equality—including challenging the structural barriers to that goal—to promote health and reduce violence at the global level. The alliance is an attempt to "scale up" local efforts to achieve progress in transforming gender inequality.

These efforts to organize men to end gender violence are quite broad. As noted in the declaration from MenEngage's recent global symposium, gender equality concerns include intimate partner violence and numerous other domains, for example, violence against children, violence amongst men, the global political economy, sexual diversities and sexual rights, men's and boys' gender-related vulnerabilities, sexual exploitation, sexual and reproductive health and rights,

HIV and AIDS, and environmental concerns (MenEngage, 2009). As these efforts continue, it is clear that the work focused on men who batter is an important, but a relatively small, part of the developing global effort to address men's violence toward women. This broader focus—envisioned perhaps in the early days of the battered women's movement and consistent with the pro-feminist principles of many of the male allies who began work with batterers—is only now becoming a robust and identifiable global movement. There is not yet much data on these efforts, but we look forward to future contributions to inform the opportunities and challenges of this compelling work.

Finally, we want to draw attention to an intersection of indicated and universal prevention taking place in programs for men who batter. One good example is the Men Stopping Violence program in Atlanta (Douglas et al., 2008). Men involved in the Men Stopping Violence's batterer intervention program are required to bring men from their own microsystems (e.g., workplace, peer group, or family) to witness some of the work they are doing in the program. These community witnesses may then promote sustained change of men participating in the program, as they become aware of the participants' commitment to change and can be sources of accountability and support in their microsystems. The inclusion of these men from the community, however, also provides the witnesses with opportunities to examine their own behavior and to potentially engage in further actions to end intimate partner violence.

The Men Stopping Violence program also provides an example of a program that works on many ecological and prevention levels simultaneously. In addition to their BIP work and the Mentors in Training Program described above in the selective prevention section, Men Stopping Violence engages in a number of other programs (Douglas et al., 2008). For example, their Community Restoration Program began as a follow-up program for men who had completed Men Stopping Violence's 24-week BIP, but evolved into a way for those men to participate in community projects, outreach, and advocacy as a form of restorative justice (see Chapter 14 for more on restorative justice). Given their focus on both supporting men in maintaining nonabusive behavior and in community change, the program can be considered both indicated prevention and universal prevention and helps to create exosystem change. Another form of indicated prevention is Men Stopping Violence's parenting classes for fathers, to help correct the damage their battering has caused in their families and to teach them skills for positive parenting without abuse. Men Stopping Violence's focus on fathers also extends to a universal prevention program, Because We Have Daughters. This program provides fathers and their daughters with an opportunity to engage in fun activities and discussions that help fathers be a positive influence in their daughters' lives, heighten awareness of the culture of violence their daughters are growing up in, and engage men in helping to create change in their own lives and in the community.

Conclusion

As the discussion of the work of Men Stopping Violence exemplifies, the work of ending men's violence against women is a task that must be completed at multiple levels of the human ecology and across a continuum of prevention efforts. Although we have attempted in this chapter to classify such strategies as primarily at one level or another, in practice, such efforts are likely to span multiple categories. We have found ourselves inspired and energized by the proliferation of efforts to involve men in greatly varying efforts to end men's violence, both as targets of change and allies of change. At this point in our development as a field, we can find hope in the promise of the innovative practices being developed around the world. We look forward to more of these efforts, as well as additional research that reveals where our future efforts will be most effective and our resources best spent.

References

Abidin, R. R. (1995). *Parenting Stress Index: Professional manual* (3rd ed.). Odessa, FL: Psychological Assessment Resources, Inc.

Arean, J. D., & Davis, L. (2007). Working with fathers in batterer intervention programs: Lessons from the Fathering After Violence Initiative. In J. L. Edleson & O. J. Williams (Eds.), *Parenting by men who batter* (pp. 118–130). New York: Oxford University Press.

Babcock, J. C., Green, C. E. & Robie, C. (2004). Does batterers' treatment work? A meta-analytic review of domestic violence treatment. *Clinical Psychology Review, 23,* 1023–1053.

Bancroft, L., & Silverman, J. G. (2002). *The batterer as parent: Addressing the impact of domestic violence on family dynamics.* Thousand Oaks, CA: Sage.

Bennett, L. W., & Vincent, N. (2002). Standards for batterer programs: A formative evaluation of the Illinois protocol. In R. A. Geffner & A. Rosenbaum (Eds.), *Domestic violence offenders: Current interventions, research, and implications for policies and standards* (pp. 181–197). New York: Hayworth.

Bennett, L., & Williams, O. (2001). *Controversies and recent studies of batterer intervention program effectiveness.* Harrisburg, PA: VAWnet. Retrieved March 18, 2010, from http://www.vawnet.org

Berkowitz, A. D. (2004, October). Working with men to prevent violence against women: An overview (Part 1). *National Resource Center on Domestic Violence, VAWNet Applied Research Forum,* 1–7.

Bowen, L. K, Gwiasda, V., & Brown, M. (2004). Engaging community residents to prevent violence. *Journal of Interpersonal Violence, 19*(3), 356–366.

Brendgen, M., Vitaro, R., Tremblay, R. E., & Lavoie, F. (2001). Reactive and proactive aggression: Predictions to physical violence in different contexts and moderating effects of parental monitoring and caregiving behavior. *Journal of Abnormal Child Psychology, 29*(4), 293–304.

Bronfenbrenner, U. (1977). Toward an experimental ecology of human development. *American Psychologist, 32,* 523–531.

Bronfenbrenner, U. (1979). *The ecology of human development: Experiments by nature and design.* Cambridge, MA: Harvard University Press.

Bronfenbrenner, U. (1986). Ecology of the family as a context for human development: Research perspectives. *Developmental Psychology, 22,* 723–742.

Brygger, M. P., & Edleson, J. L. (1987). The Domestic Abuse Project: A multi-systems intervention in woman battering. *Journal of Interpersonal Violence, 2,* 324–336.

Buttell, F. P., & Carney, M. M. (2005). Do batterer intervention programs serve African American and Caucasian batterers equally well? An investigation of a 26-week program. *Research on Social Work Practice, 15,* 19–28.

Capaldi, D. M., & Owen, L. D. (2001). Physical aggression in a community sample of at-risk young couples: Gender comparisons for high frequency, injury, and fear. *Journal of Family Psychology, 15*(3), 425–440.

Carillo, R., & Tello, J. (2007). Fathers in recovery. In J. L. Edleson & O. J. Williams (Eds.), *Parenting by men who batter: New directions for assessment and intervention* (pp. 131–136). New York: Oxford University Press.

Carlson, B. E. (1984). Causes and maintenance of domestic violence: An ecological analysis. *Social Service Review, 58,* 569–587.

Carolo, H. (2009). *Taking stock of 18 years of activism: White ribbon around the world.* Retrieved March 18, 2010, from http://www.menengage.org/symposium2009_present.asp#1

Cavanaugh, M. M., & Gelles, R. J. (2005). The utility of male domestic violence offender typologies: New directions for research, policy and practice. *Journal of Interpersonal Violence, 20,* 155–166.

Center for Urban Families. (2009). *Baltimore Responsible Father Project.* Retrieved December 9, 2009, from http://www.cfuf.org/BRFP

Chamberlain, L. (2008, March). *A prevention primer for domestic violence: Terminology, tools, and the public health approach.* Harrisburg, PA: VAWnet. Retrieved March 18, 2010, from http://www.vawnet.org

Crooks, C. V., Goodall, G. R., Baker, L. B., & Hughes, R. (2006). Preventing violence against women: Engaging the fathers of today and tomorrow. *Cognitive and Behavioral Practice, 13,* 82–93.

Davidson, T. (1977). Wifebeating: A recurring phenomenon throughout history. In M. Roy (Ed.), *Battered women* (pp. 2–23). New York: Van Nostrand Reinhold.

Dobash, R. E., & Dobash, R. (1978). Wives: The appropriate victims of marital violence. *Victimology: An International Journal, 2,* 426–442.

Domestic Violence Task Force. (1988). *The Denver domestic violence manual.* Denver, CO: City of Denver.

Donovan, R., & Vlais, R. (2005). *VicHealth review of communication components of social marketing. Public education campaigns focusing on violence against women.* Melbourne: Victorian Health Promotion Foundation.

Douglas, U., Bathrick, D., & Perry, P. A. (2008). Deconstructing male violence against women: The Men Stopping Violence community accountability model. *Violence Against Women, 14,* 247–261.

Dunford, F. W. (2000). The San Diego Navy Experiment: An assessment of interventions for men who assault their wives. *Journal of Consulting and Clinical Psychology, 68,* 468–476.

Dutton, D. G. (1985). An ecologically nested theory of male violence toward intimates. *International Journal of Women's Studies, 8,* 404–413.

Dutton, D. G. (1988). *The domestic assault of women.* Boston: Allyn & Bacon.

Dutton, D. G., & Corvo, K. (2006). Transforming a flawed policy: A call to revive psychology and science in domestic violence research and practice. *Aggression and Violent Behavior, 11,* 457–483.

Easton, C., Swan, S., & Sinha, R. (2000). Motivation to change substance use among offenders of domestic violence. *Journal of Substance Abuse Treatment, 19,* 1–5.

Eckhardt, C. I., Babcock, J., & Homack, S. (2004). Partner assaultive men and the stages and processes of change. *Journal of Family Violence, 19,* 81–93.

Edleson, J. L. (1991). Social workers' intervention in woman abuse: 1907–1945. *Social Service Review, 65,* 304–313.

Edleson, J. L., & Tolman, R. M. (1992). *Intervention for men who batter: An ecological approach.* Thousand Oaks, CA: Sage.

Edleson, J. L., & Williams, O. J. (2007). Introduction: Involving men who batter in their children's lives. In J. L. Edleson & O. J. Williams (Eds.), *Parenting by men who batter* (pp. 3–18). New York: Oxford University Press.

Ehrensaft, M. K., Cohen, P., Brown, J., Smailes, E., Chen, H., & Johnson, J. G. (2003). Intergenerational transmission of partner violence: A 20-year prospective study. *Journal of Consulting and Clinical Psychology, 71,* 741–753.

Feder, L., & Wilson, D. B. (2005). A meta-analytic review of court-mandated batterer intervention programs: Can courts affect abusers' behavior? *Journal of Experimental Criminology, 1,* 239–262.

Fleck-Henderson, A. (2004). Application of theoretical frameworks for domestic violence. In F. Danis & L. Lockhart (Eds.), *Breaking the silence in social work education: Domestic violence modules for foundation courses* (pp. 9–13). Washington, DC: CSWE.

Flood, M. (2005). Men's collective struggles for gender justice: The case of anti-violence activism. In M. Kimmel, J. Hearn, & R. W. Connell (Eds.), *The handbook of studies on men and masculinities* (pp. 458–466). Thousand Oaks, CA: Sage.

Garin, G. D. (2000). *Report #5702c.* Washington, DC: Peter D. Hart Research Associates, Inc.

Gondolf, E. W. (2002). *Batterer intervention systems: Issues, outcomes, and recommendations.* Thousand Oaks, CA: Sage.

Gondolf, E. W. (2004). Evaluating batterer counseling programs. *Aggression and Violent Behavior, 9,* 605–631.

Gondolf, E. W. (2007). Culturally focused batterer counseling for African American men. *Criminology & Public Policy, 6,* 341–366.

Gondolf, E. W., & Williams, O. J. (2001). Culturally focused batterer counseling for African American men. *Trauma, Violence, & Abuse, 2*(4), 283–295.

Goolkasian, G. A. (1986). *Confronting domestic violence: A guide for criminal justice agencies.* Washington, DC: National Institute of Justice.

Gordon, L. (1988). *Heroes of their own lives—the politics and history of family violence.* New York: Viking Penguin.

Graffunder, C. M., Noonan, R. K., Cox, P., & Wheaton, J. (2004). Through a public health lens. Preventing violence against women: An Update from the U.S. Centers for Disease Control and Prevention. *Journal of Women's Health, 13*(1), 5–14.

Hamby, S. (2009). The gender debate about intimate partner violence: Solutions and dead ends. *Psychological Trauma, 1,* 24–34.

Hart Research Associates, Inc. (2007). *Father's day poll.* Retrieved December 11, 2009, from http://www.endabuse.org

Heise, L. L. (1998). Violence against women: An integrated, ecological framework. *Violence Against Women, 4,* 262–290.

Holtzworth-Munroe, A., & Meehan, J. C. (2004). Typologies of men who are maritally violent: Scientific and clinical implications. *Journal of Interpersonal Violence, 19,* 1369–1389.

Jaffe, P., Sudermann, M., Reitzel, D., & Killip, S. M. (1992). An evaluation of a secondary school primary prevention program on violence in relationships. *Violence and Victims, 7,* 129–146.

Killoran, M. M. (1984). The management of tension: A case study of Chatelaine Magazine, 1939–1980. *Journal of Comparative Family Studies, 15,* 407–426.

Labriola, M., Rempel, M., & Davis, R. C. (2005). *Testing the effectiveness of batterer programs and judicial monitoring. Final report to the National Institute of Justice.* Retrieved December 7, 2009, from http://www.courtinnovation.org/

Lavoie, F., Hebert, M., Tremblay, R., Vitaro, F., Vezina, L., & McDuff, P. (2002). History of family dysfunction and perpetration of dating violence by adolescent boys: A longitudinal study. *Journal of Adolescent Health, 30*(5), 365–383.

Magdol, L., Moffitt, T. E., Caspi, A., & Silva, P. A. (1998). Developmental antecedents of partner abuse: A prospective-longitudinal study. *Journal of Abnormal Psychology, 107,* 375–389.

Maiuro, R. D., & Eberle, J. A. (2008). State standards for domestic violence perpetrator treatment: Current status, trends, and recommendations. *Violence and Victims, 23*(2), 133–155.

Markman, H. J., Renick, M. J., Floyd, F. J., Stanley, S. M., & Clements, M. (1993). Preventing marital distress through communication and conflict management training: A four and five year follow-up. *Journal of Consulting and Clinical Psychology, 62*(1), 70–77.

MenEngage. (2009). *The Rio de Janeiro MenEngage declaration: Global symposium on engaging men and boys on achieving gender equality.* Retrieved December 9, 2009, from http://menengage.org/symposium2009_rio.asp

Miller, W. R., & Rollnick, S. (2002). *Motivational interviewing* (2nd ed.). New York: Guilford.

Miller, W. R. & Wilbourne, P. L. (2002). Mesa Grande: A methodological analysis of clinical trials of treatments for alcohol use disorders. *Addiction, 97,* 265–277.

Mills, L. G. (2003). *Insult to injury: Rethinking our response to intimate abuse.* Princeton, NJ: Princeton University Press.

Mitchell-Clark, K., & Autry, A. (2004). *Preventing family violence: Lessons from the community engagement initiative.* San Francisco: Family Violence Prevention Fund.

National Latino Fatherhood and Family Institute. (2003). *Fatherhood lessons.* Retrieved December 9, 2009, from http://www.nlffi.org

Pence, E. L. (1983). The Duluth Domestic Abuse Intervention Project. *Hamline Law Review, 6,* 247–275.

Pence, E., & Paymar, M. (1993). *Education groups for men who batter: The Duluth model.* New York: Springer.

Pence, E. L., & Shepard, M. F. (1999). An introduction: Developing a coordinated community response. In M. F. Shepard & E. L. Pence (Eds.), *Coordinating community responses to domestic violence: Lessons from Duluth and beyond* (pp. 3–23). Thousand Oaks, CA: Sage.

Perel, G., & Peled, E. (2008). The fathering of violent men: Constriction and yearning. *Violence Against Women, 14*(4), 457–482.

Pleck, E. H. (1987). *Domestic tyranny: The making of social policy against family violence from colonial times to present.* New York: Oxford University Press.

Prevention Institute. (2007). *Poised for prevention. Advancing promising approaches to primary prevention of intimate partner violence.* Retrieved December 9, 2009, from http://www.prevention institute.org

Roffman, R. A., Edleson, J. L., Neighbors, C., Mbilinyi, L. & Walker, D. D. (2008). The men's domestic abuse check-up: A protocol for reaching the non-adjudicated and untreated man who batters and abuses substances. *Violence Against Women, 14,* 589–605.

Saunders, D. G. (1996). Feminist-cognitive-behavioral and process-psychodynamic treatments for men who batter: Interaction of abuser traits and treatment models. *Violence and Victims, 11,* 393–414.

Saunders, D. G. (2008). Group interventions for men who batter: A summary of program descriptions and research. *Violence & Victims, 23,* 156–172.

Scott, K. L., & Crooks, C. V. (2007). Preliminary evaluation of an intervention program for maltreating fathers. *Brief Treatment and Crisis Intervention, 7,* 224–238.

Scott, K., Francis, K., Crooks, C., & Kelly, T. (2006). *Caring dads: Helping fathers value their children.* Victoria, BC: Trafford.

Sherman, L. W., & Berk, R. A. (1984). The specific deterrent effects of arrest for domestic assault. *American Sociological Review, 49,* 261–272.

Sherman, L. W., & Cohn, E. G. (1990). The effects of research on legal policy in the Minneapolis Domestic Violence Experiment. In D. J. Besharov (Ed.), *Family violence: Research and public policy issues* (pp. 205–227). Washington, DC: American Enterprise Institute.

Smedslund, G., Dalsbø, T. K., Steiro, A., Winsvold, A., & Clench-Aas, J. (2009). Cognitive behavioural therapy for men who abuse their female partner (Review). *The Cochrane Library, 3,* 1–36.

Soler, E., & Martin, S. (1983). *Domestic violence is a crime.* San Francisco: Family Violence Project.

Stanko, E. A. (2006). Theorizing about violence: Observations from the Economic and Social Research Council's Violence Research Program. *Violence Against Women, 12,* 543–555.

Thurman v. City of Torrington, 595 F. Supp. 1521 (D. Conn. 1984).

Tolman, R. M. (2002). An ecological analysis of batterer intervention program standards. In R. A. Geffner & A. Rosenbaum (Eds.), *Domestic violence offenders: Current interventions, research, and implications for policies and standards* (pp. 221–234). Binghamton, NY: The Haworth Press.

U.N. Secretary-General. (2006). *From words to action: In-depth study on all forms of violence against women: Study of the Secretary-General.* Retrieved December 9, 2009, from http://www.un.org/women watch/daw/vaw/v-sg-study.htm

Weisz, A., & Black, B. (2001). Sexual assault and dating violence prevention with urban youth: Assessing effectiveness. *Social Work Research, 25*(2), 89–102.

White, R. J., & Gondolf, E. W. (2000). Implications of personality profiles for batterer treatment. *Journal of Interpersonal Violence, 15,* 467–488.

Whitefield, C. L., Anda, R. F., Dube, S. R., & Felitti, V. J. (2003). Violent childhood experiences and the risk of intimate partner violence in adults: Assessment in a large health maintenance organization. *Journal of Interpersonal Violence, 18*(2), 166–185.

Williams, O. J. (1994). Group work with African American men who batter: Toward more ethnically sensitive practice. *Journal of Comparative Family Studies, 25,* 91–103.

Wolfe, D. A., Crooks, C. V., Lee, V., McIntyre-Smith, A., & Jaffe, P. G. (2003). A meta-analysis of the effects of children's exposure to domestic violence: The need for a developmental framework. *Clinical Child and Family Psychology Review, 6,* 171–187.

Wolfe, D. A., Wekerle, C., Gough, R., Reitzel-Jaffe, D., Crasley, C., Pittman, A. L., et al. (1996). *The youth relationships manual: A group approach with adolescents for the prevention of woman abuse and the promotion of healthy relationships.* Thousand Oaks, CA: Sage.

Chapter Authors

Richard M. Tolman, LMSW, Ph.D., is a Professor at the University of Michigan School of Social Work. He began his work in batterer intervention programs in 1980 at the Male Awareness Project in Anchorage, Alaska. His research focuses on interventions designed to change violent and abusive behavior and the impact of violence on the physical, psychological, and economic well-being of victims. His current projects include research on the impact of and prevention of abuse during pregnancy and involvement of men as allies to end violence against women. He is currently co-Director of the Global Research Program on Mobilizing Men for Violence Prevention, a collaborative project between the University of Michigan and the University of Minnesota.

Jeffrey L. Edleson is a Professor in the University of Minnesota School of Social Work and Director of the Minnesota Center Against Violence and Abuse (http://www.mincava.umn.edu). He is one of the world's leading authorities on children exposed to domestic violence and has published more than 100 articles and 10 books on domestic violence, group work, and program evaluation. He has recently coedited (with Oliver J. Williams) the book *Parenting by Men Who Batter: New Directions in Assessment and Intervention* (Oxford University Press, 2007) and (with Claire Renzetti) the multi-volume *Encyclopedia of Interpersonal Violence* (Sage, 2008).

Personal Reflection

Edward Gondolf

My partner at the time had just come home from a meeting on women's issues. She was noticeably disturbed by the violence against women exposed there and by the recall it prompted of abuse she had experienced in her past. What she introduced to me at that moment opened a door in my mind and soul and eventually a new path in my academic and research work. I ended up supervising social work students at a women's center my partner helped start and volunteering at a recently formed program for men who abused their partners. I vividly remember one particular training session at the men's program. A panel of women told their experiences of being abused, raped, and beaten by men. They then departed the room, and the circle of remaining men were left to sort out our reactions, feelings, and defensiveness to what we had heard. It quickly became clear that we were all complicit in some way, all echoing conflicting views of women, all exposing how far reaching were the issues. We left motivated to do something about it—that included my helping to facilitate what were initially "voluntary" groups for abusive men.

I was soon to shift my research focus as a community psychologist from social impact assessments and community conflict to so-called "batterer programs." We were faced with hard questions about whether our efforts were effective in reducing men's violence against women—or causing more problems. What might we do to make the groups more effective? The questions launched me on a series of visits to other early programs across the country and later to start a few follow-up studies of men in our own groups. Programs rapidly expanded in response to the emerging arrest policies for domestic violence calls, and so did questions about the effectiveness and utility of such programs with court-referred men. Currently, amidst the movement toward "evidence-based practice," program evaluation is even more essential for the justification and funding of programs and interventions of all sorts. There is also an increasing emphasis on the psychological impetus for men's violence that has brought confusion to the field (as well as some fresh insights) and some diversion from the initial attention to the sociological and gendered roots of violence against women.

For more than 20 years, I've been working full time on research, mostly about batterer intervention. Probably our biggest contribution has been an eight-year study of batterer intervention in four large cities. It not only demonstrated the contribution of batterer programs in improving women's safety and well-being; it also reinforced the importance of approaching intervention from a systems perspective. A program's links to the courts, women's services, and other community treatments make a difference. These findings have been particularly important amidst a handful of narrowly focused experimental evaluations that suggest batterer programs are not particularly effective. Our subsequent studies have also exposed the need for risk management of a subgroup of unresponsive and particularly dangerous men and the importance of a coordinated community response to achieving this. Stopping violence goes well beyond the boundaries of a weekly group for a select group of men.

At times, doing research in this area is like being a policy "lawyer." I'm working, like many others, to bring forth compelling and acceptable evidence to the court of academic and policy decision makers. It seems an increasingly important role, given the increase in different perspectives, pet theories, and competing agendas. I also continue to be challenged by the basic questions about human nature implicit in this work: Are we, especially men, inherently violent? Can we change for the better? How are peace, love, and justice achieved in our personal and collective lives? More than one academic discipline, or handful of research studies, is needed to answer these questions. Certainly, we need to be thinking about these sorts of questions more deeply, broadly, and persistently. I'd like to think that the research in the field is helping us do that.

Author Index

Subject Index

Supporting researchers for more than 40 years

Research methods have always been at the core of SAGE's publishing program. Founder Sara Miller McCune published SAGE's first methods book, *Public Policy Evaluation*, in 1970. Soon after, she launched the *Quantitative Applications in the Social Sciences* series—affectionately known as the "little green books."

Always at the forefront of developing and supporting new approaches in methods, SAGE published early groundbreaking texts and journals in the fields of qualitative methods and evaluation.

Today, more than 40 years and two million little green books later, SAGE continues to push the boundaries with a growing list of more than 1,200 research methods books, journals, and reference works across the social, behavioral, and health sciences. Its imprints—Pine Forge Press, home of innovative textbooks in sociology, and Corwin, publisher of PreK–12 resources for teachers and administrators—broaden SAGE's range of offerings in methods. SAGE further extended its impact in 2008 when it acquired CQ Press and its best-selling and highly respected political science research methods list.

From qualitative, quantitative, and mixed methods to evaluation, SAGE is the essential resource for academics and practitioners looking for the latest methods by leading scholars.

For more information, visit **www.sagepub.com**.

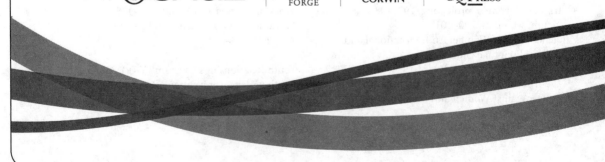